FUNDAMENTALS OF OPERATIONS MANAGEMENT

FUNDAMENTALS OF OPERATIONS MANAGEMENT

Second Edition

Nicholas J. Aquilano
The University of Arizona

Richard B. Chase
University of Southern California

Mark M. Davis
Bentley College

IRWIN

Chicago • Bogota • Boston • Buenos Aires • Caracas
London • Madrid • Mexico City • Sydney • Toronto

Senior sponsoring editor:	Richard T. Hercher, Jr.
Associate editor:	Colleen Tuscher
Marketing manager:	Brian Kibby
Project editor:	Karen M. Smith
Production manager:	Bob Lange
Designer:	Jeanne Rivera/Larry Cope
Cover designer:	Katherine Farmer
Cover photographer:	Carlos Alejandro
Chapter photographer:	Carlos Alejandro
Art coordinator:	Mark Malloy
Compositor:	J. M. Post Graphics, a division of Cardinal Communications Group, Inc.
Typeface:	10/12 Bembo
Printer:	R. R. Donnelley & Sons Co.

Library of Congress Cataloging-in-Publication Data

Aquilano, Nicholas J.
Fundamentals of operations management : instructor's ed. / Nicholas J. Aquilano, Richard B. Chase, Mark M. Davis.—2nd ed.
p. cm.
Includes index.
ISBN 0-256-15972-6 (instructor's ed.).—ISBN 0-256-13219-4 (student's ed.)
1. Production management. I. Chase, Richard B. II. Davis, Mark M. III. Title
TS155.A638 1995
658.5—dc20 94–14029

Printed in the United States of America
3 4 5 6 7 8 9 0 DO 1 0 9 8 7 6

To our wives
Nina, Harriet, and Cookie

And to our children
Don, Kara, and Mark
Laurie, Andy, Glenn and Rob
Andy and Alex

PREFACE

Operations management has undergone a remarkable transformation in recent years. First, there has been an increasing trend away from sophisticated and often highly theoretical mathematical models toward the more pragmatic managerial issues that confront today's operations managers. In addition, where it once primarily addressed manufacturing, operations management has now been expanded to also include services.

In addition, the importance of operations management as an integral part of every organization has been recognized in the public sector as well as the private sector, as manifested by current efforts to reengineer many of the processes within the federal government. Increased competition from both domestic and foreign companies has also brought operations management to the forefront, and with NAFTA becoming a reality and new GATT regulations on the horizon, international competition will only intensify in the foreseeable future. The importance of producing high quality goods and services has been recognized through the Baldrige Awards. Within such an intensely competitive environment, only those companies and organizations that recognize the critical role of the operations management function will be able to survive into the next century.

It was our intent in writing this book to continue to make new inroads in these directions by placing additional emphasis on both the pragmatic perspectives of operations management as well as on service operations. To accomplish this, we introduced two new topic areas: Performance Measurement (Chapter 3) and Waiting Line Management (Chapter 10). In addition, to reflect the many changes that have taken place, we updated Chapter 6, Quality Management, to show how the role of quality is now perceived within organizations. We also placed more emphasis on the topic of process analysis in Chapters 4 and 5 and introduced reengineering in Chapter 11.

Applying the concept of continuous improvement, we have attempted to incorporate many of the suggestions made by reviewers for improving this edition. In so doing we have also attempted to make this book interesting reading to the student. As Benjamin Disraeli once said, "The way to become rich is to be an expert on a dull subject." We hope that this book helps accomplish the former without suffering from the latter.

ACKNOWLEDGMENTS

Although only three names appear on the cover of this book, a project of this magnitude could not be successfully completed without the assistance and cooperation of many individuals. Specifically, we would like to thank the reviewers for their evaluation of the text and for their suggestions and comments. These include Timothy Bergquist, University of Oregon; Dave Carhart, Bentley College (problem checker); Gayla Delong, Northwestern Oklahoma State University; Lissa Galbraith, Florida State University; John Haehl, Lewis-Clark State College; Marilyn Jones, Winthrop College; Birsen Karpak, Youngstown State University; Dennis Krumwiede, Kansas State University; Rich Luebbe, Miami University (Ohio); Mary Jo Maffei, Miami University (Ohio); Robert Mefford, University of San Francisco; and Rao Tatikonda, University of Wisconsin-Oshkosh.

Additionally, we would like to thank Susan Engelkemeyer of Babson College for her assistance and input in preparing Chapter 6 on Quality Management and Janelle Heineke of Boston University for her suggestions and comments with respect to Chapter 10 on Waiting Line Management.

Finally, we would also like to thank Dick Hercher, Karen Smith, Colleen Tuscher, and the rest of the Richard D. Irwin staff for their usual high level of assistance.

Nicholas J. Aquilano
Richard D. Chase
Mark M. Davis

Contents in Brief

CONTENTS

FUNDAMENTALS OF OPERATIONS MANAGEMENT

Chapter 1

Introduction and Overview

EPIGRAPH

The Operations Challenge:
Now corporate offices are focusing on determining what customers really value. This is a good step, but not good enough. Customers do not pay corporations for discovering what they value, but for delivering that value better than the competition.

Arun N. Maira, Director of the Operations Management Consulting Practice for Arthur D. Little, *Los Angeles Times,* May 1, 1991, p. D3.

CHAPTER OUTLINE

KEY TERMS

Global Village
Value Chain
Virtual Enterprise
Transformation Process
Life Cycle Approach
Scientific Management

At the end of World War II, the United States was the obvious world leader in manufacturing. U.S. dominance in this area was the result of both the domestic effort to build facilities in support of the war effort and the destruction of most of the production capabilities in the other industrialized nations of the world. To paraphrase Tom Peters, "Between 1946 and 1973, you couldn't screw up a Fortune 500 company if you tried."[1]

The lack of international competition in the postwar years encouraged U.S. managers to believe that the manufacturing problem in this country was solved, and they consequently shifted their focus to the finance and marketing functions. The operations function, on the other hand, was perceived to be noncritical to the success of the firm. As a result, operations personnel were often treated as second-class corporate citizens, not participating in the firm's top-level policy decisions. In this business environment, the role of operations was perceived to be primarily passive and reactive, with its sole objective to minimize costs.

Courtesy Ford Motor Company

Companies like Ford emphasize the importance of quality.

[1] Tom Peters and KQED Golden Gate Productions, *The Power of Excellence: The Forgotten Customer,* Jack Hilton Productions, Video Publishing House, Inc., 1987.

[2] S. C. Gwynne, "The Long Haul," *Time,* September 25, 1992, pp. 34–38.

Fortunately, there has been a renaissance in operations management (OM) in recent years. Businesses now recognize the importance of operations and the need for highly skilled operations managers. This growing interest in OM has occurred for several reasons, including:

1. *Increased international competition.* With the world rapidly transforming itself into a single **global village,** companies and their markets are no longer immune to those firms that are considered to be world class competitors. While only 7 percent of the firms in the United States were exposed to foreign competition in the 1960s, the number of U.S. firms encountering foreign competition exceeded 70 percent by the late 1980s, and that figure continues to grow.[2]

2. *The role of OM in service operations.* It is now recognized that operations management is critical to the success of both service companies as well as manufacturing firms. The vast majority of those Fortune 500 firms in the service sector achieved their success by having well-run operations. As with manufacturing companies, no service firm today can be called excellent without having superior operations management.

3. *A new paradigm for OM.* As stated earlier, the historical role of operations within most organizations was passive and reactive. This is no longer true. Instead of only trying to minimize costs, the new paradigm for OM, in successful companies, is for it to be proactive in the decision-making process and to maximize the value added to the goods and services produced.

4. *OM exists in all functions.* Today, it is recognized that many of the tools and concepts that are widely used within the operations management function are also applicable to other functional areas. For example, every manager is concerned with such issues as quality and productivity—topics that are presented in this book.

1.1 SPECIFIC OBJECTIVES OF THE BOOK

The specific objectives of this book are to:

1. Present the various elements that comprise the field of operations management.
2. Introduce some OM tools and concepts that can be applied to a wide variety of situations, including non-OM related areas.
3. Develop an appreciation of the need for interaction between operations management and the other management functions within an organization.
4. Introduce some new and evolving concepts within the field of OM.
5. Provide an integrated framework for understanding the field of OM as a whole and its role in an organization.

With respect to the last objective, our goal is to demonstrate that operations management is not just a loosely knit aggregation of tools but rather a *synthesis* of concepts and techniques that relate directly to operating systems and enhance their management. This point is important because OM is frequently confused with operations research (OR),

The Christian Science Monitor, November 24, 1987. Danziger © 1987. Reprinted with permission.

management science (MS), and industrial engineering (IE). The critical difference between OM and these fields is this: OM is a field of management, whereas OR and MS are branches of applied mathematics and IE is an engineering discipline. Thus, while operations managers use the tools of OR and MS in decision making, and are concerned with many of the same issues as IE, OM has a distinct business management role that differentiates it from OR, MS, and IE.

1.2 OPERATIONS MANAGEMENT DEFINED

Operations management may be defined as the management of the direct resources required to produce the goods and services provided by an organization. Exhibit 1.1 illustrates how OM fits within a broad business context.

The marketplace—the firm's customers for its products or services—shapes the corporate strategy of the firm. This strategy is based on the corporate mission, and in essence reflects how the firm plans to use all its resources and functions (marketing, finance, and operations) to gain a competitive advantage. The operations strategy specifies how the firm will employ its production capabilities to support its corporate strategy. (Similarly, the

EXHIBIT 1.1

Summary Model of the Field

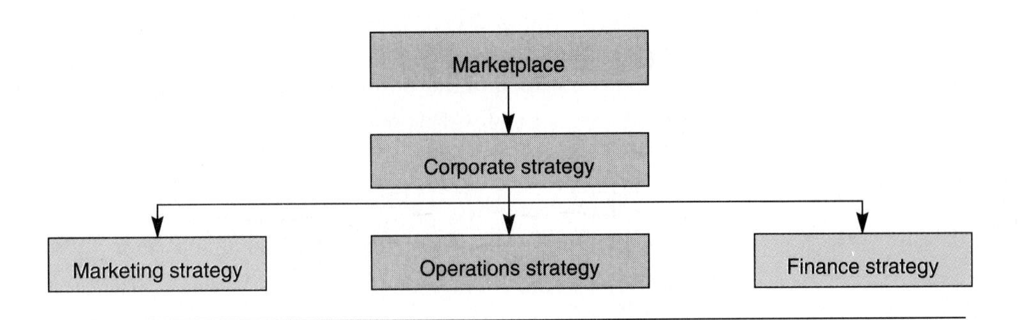

marketing strategy addresses how the firm will sell and distribute its goods and services, and the finance strategy identifies how best to utilize the financial resources of the firm.)

Within the operations function, management decisions can be divided into three broad areas:

- Strategic (long-range) decisions.
- Tactical (medium-range) decisions.
- Operational planning and control (short-range) decisions.

The hierarchical relationship between these three planning functions is shown in Exhibit 1.2.

The strategic issues are usually very broad in nature, addressing such questions as:

- How will we make the product?
- Where do we locate the facility or facilities?
- How much capacity do we need?
- When should we add more capacity?

EXHIBIT 1.2

Hierarchy of Operations Planning

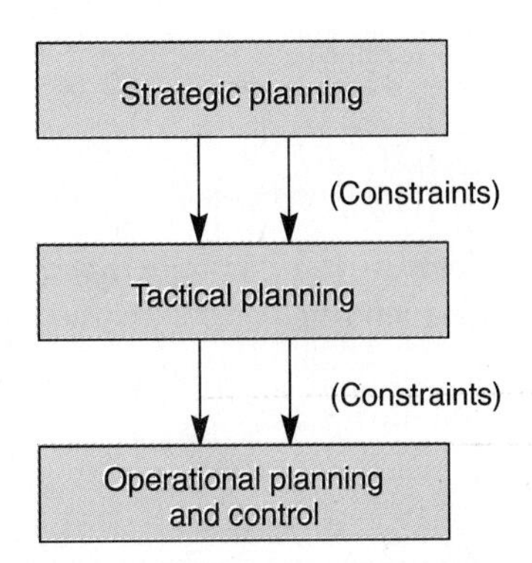

Consequently, by necessity, the time frame for strategic decisions is typically very long, usually several years or more, depending on the specific industry.

Operations management decisions at the strategic level impact the long-range effectiveness of the company in terms of how well it can address the needs of its customers. Thus, for the firm to succeed, these decisions must be in alignment with the corporate strategy. Decisions made at the strategic level become the fixed conditions or operating constraints under which the firm must operate in both the intermediate and short term.

At the next level in the decision-making process, tactical planning primarily addresses the issue of how to efficiently schedule material and labor within the constraints of the strategic decisions that were previously made. Thus, the issues on which OM concentrates at this level are:

- How many workers do we need?
- When do we need them?
- Should we work overtime or put on a second shift?
- When should we have material delivered?
- Should we have a finished goods inventory?

These tactical decisions, in turn, subsequently become the operating constraints under which the operational planning and control decisions are made.

The management decisions with respect to operational planning and control are very narrow and short term, by comparison. For example, the issues at this level are:

- What jobs do we work on today or this week?
- To whom do we assign what tasks?
- What jobs have priority?

1.3 THE OPERATIONS FUNCTION AND ITS ENVIRONMENT

In most manufacturing organizations, operations is viewed as an internal function that is buffered from the external environment by other organizational functions. Orders are generated by the marketing function; supplies and raw materials are obtained through the purchasing function; capital for equipment purchases comes from the finance function; the labor force is obtained through the personnel functions; and the product is delivered by the distribution function.

Buffering the production function (or, as it is sometimes called, the *transformation process*) from direct environmental influence has been traditionally desirable for several reasons:

- Interaction with environmental elements (e.g., customers and salespeople on the production floor) can be a disturbing influence on the transformation process.
- The transformation process is often more efficient than the processes required for obtaining inputs and disposing of finished goods.
- With certain processes (e.g., auto assembly lines and continuous flow processes such as petroleum refining), maximum productivity can be achieved only by operating at a continuous rate which assumes that the market can absorb all of the product being

manufactured. This means that the production process must shift at least some of the input and output activities to other parts of the firm.

- The managerial skills required for successful operation of the production process are often different from those required for successful operation of the boundary systems of marketing and personnel, for example.

However, there are some inherent disadvantages when the transformation process is so totally isolated as an internal function. One is that information lags between the process and the so-called boundary functions; this inevitably leads to inflexibility. Another is that for high-tech products in particular, communications between the shop floor and the customer can be extremely valuable in solving technical problems during production. Finally, some companies, such as Tektronix (as noted in the box below), have found that interaction between the person using the product and the person producing it helps to establish a strong relationship between them and, hence, between their respective organizations as well.

More and more firms are recognizing the competitive advantage achieved when customers are invited to view firsthand their operating facilities. For example, Green Giant believes that the tours of their production facilities that they gave to Japanese distributors was a major factor in their ability to penetrate that market with their Green Giant food products.[3] Similarly, National R_x Services, which offers a mail-order prescription service, encourages insurance companies and HMOs to visit their facilities to assure themselves of the high quality of its prescription-filling process.

In a like manner, companies are working more closely with suppliers. Firms like Toyota, for example, have suppliers deliver product directly to the factory floor, eliminating any need for a stockroom. General Scanning of Watertown, Massachusetts, encourages its vendors to automatically replenish product on the factory floor without purchase orders or incoming reports.

This trend toward having the transformation process work more closely with both suppliers and customers alike is often referred to as a product's **value chain.** We can define a value chain as consisting of all those steps that actually add value to the product without distinguishing where they are added. This concept attempts to eliminate all nonvalue added steps (such as inspections and inventory). This results in a higher degree of dependence among the value-added functions that are linked in the chain. The relationship between the transformation process, its support functions, and the other value-added functions is shown in Exhibit 1.3.

This integration of both suppliers and customers into the transformation process begins to blur the boundaries between what were previously totally independent organizations. What appears to be emerging now is a concept known as the **virtual enterprise,** which is a fully integrated and interlocked network of *inter*dependent organizations. With this new approach, it is often difficult to determine where one organization leaves off and the next one begins.

[3] Jane Ammeson, "When in Rome," *Northwest Airlines World Traveler,* March 1993.

EXHIBIT 1.3

The Value Chain and Its Support Functions

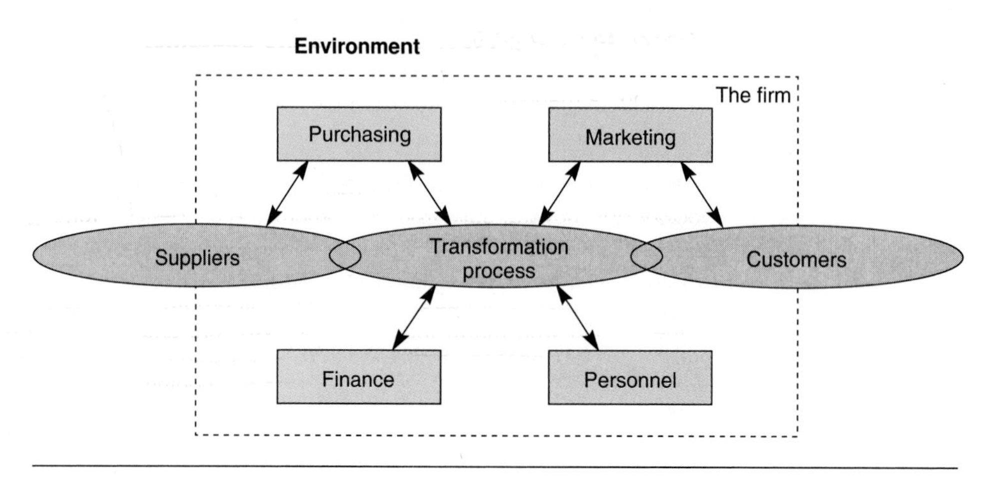

Jobs Related to the Operations Function

Exhibit 1.4 lists some line and staff jobs that are frequently viewed as relating to the operations function. There are more staff specializations in manufacturing than in services because of the focus on materials management and control.

EXHIBIT 1.4

Line and Staff Jobs in Operations Management

Organizational Level	Manufacturing Industries	Service Industries
Upper	Vice president of manufacturing	Vice president of operations (airline)
	Regional manager of manufacturing	Chief administrator (hospital)
Middle	Plant manager	Store manager (department store)
	Program manager	Facilities manager (wholesale distributor)
Lower	Department supervisor	Branch manager (bank)
	Foreman	Department supervisor (insurance company)
	Crew chief	Assistant manager (hotel)
Staff	Production controller	Systems and procedures analyst
	Materials manager	Purchasing agent
	Quality manager	Inspector
	Purchasing agent	Dietician (hospital)
	Work methods analyst	Customer service manager
	Process engineer	

OPERATIONS MANAGEMENT IN ACTION
Linking the Shop-Floor Worker to the Customer

Tektronix, a manufacturer of electronic equipment, has pioneered direct communication between customers and shop-floor employees. Into the shipping carton of every oscilloscope it sells, the company inserts a postcard listing the names of the workers who built the scope along with an "800" number to a phone on the shop floor. Every day the factory gets several calls from customers; the six people working in the repair area who answer them have all received telephone training.

Customers call for various reasons: questions about the use of their oscilloscopes, requests for information about other Tektronix products, and to see if "they can really talk to the person who made their product." Workers and managers meet daily to discuss these calls; if necessary, further conversations with the customer follow up the meetings. In some cases, workers will call customers six months after delivery to find out how well their products are performing.

Source: R. B. Chase and D. A. Garvin, "The Service Factory," *Harvard Business Review,* July–August 1989, pp. 65–66.

1.4 THE TRANSFORMATION PROCESS

Operations management can be viewed as a set of components whose function is concerned with converting a set of inputs into some desired output through what we call a **transformation process.** A component may be a machine, a person, a tool, or a management system. An input may be a raw material, a person, or a finished product from another system. Some transformations that take place are:

- Physical, as in manufacturing.
- Locational, as in transportation.
- Exchange, as in retailing.
- Storage, as in warehousing.
- Physiological, as in health care.
- Informational, as in telecommunications.

These transformations, of course, are not mutually exclusive. For example, a department store can (1) allow shoppers to compare prices and quality (informational), (2) hold items in inventory until needed (storage), and (3) sell goods (exchange). Exhibit 1.5 presents sample input–transformation–output relationships for a wide variety of systems. Note that only the direct components are listed; a more complete system description would, of course, also include managerial and support functions.

1.5 THE LIFE CYCLE APPROACH

The Operations Management Association has defined the OM subject areas listed in Exhibit 1.6. Although it is useful as a topical checklist, an organizing structure for teaching purposes is needed to (1) allow us to view the field of OM as more than just a collection of

EXHIBIT 1.5 Input–Transformation–Output Relationships for Typical Systems

System	Primary Inputs	Components	Primary Transformation Function(s)	Typical Desired Output
Hospital	Patients	MDs, nurses, medical supplies, equipment	Health care (physiological)	Healthy individuals
Restaurant	Hungry customers	Food, chef, waitress, environment	Well-prepared food, well served; agreeable environment (physical and exchange)	Satisfied customers
Automobile factory	Sheet steel, engine parts	Tools, equipment, workers	Fabrication and assembly of cars (physical)	High-quality cars
College or university	High school graduates	Teachers, books, classrooms	Imparting knowledge and skills (informational)	Educated individuals
Department store	Shoppers	Displays, stock of goods, sales clerks	Attract shoppers, promote products, fill orders (exchange)	Sales to satisfied customers
Distribution center	Stockkeeping units (SKUs)	Storage bins, stockpickers	Storage and redistribution	Fast delivery, availability of SKUs

loosely related topics and (2) reflect the management decision-making hierarchy and sequence of events that are actually used in the practice of OM. The structure we have adopted for this book appears to meet these requirements in a straightforward way. We have termed this structure the **life cycle approach,** which follows the progress of the transformation process from its inception to its termination—a concept that we feel reflects the true breadth of the area, and parallels, to a large degree, the relationship among strategic decisions, tactical decisions, and operations planning and control. The following discussion illustrates how a transformation process evolves through its life cycle.

Let us assume that an idea for a product or service is proposed. Questions of marketability, producibility, capital requirements, and so on are examined. If the decision is made to produce this good or service, the final form of the product, the location of the producing facility, and the floor layout all must be specified. The required equipment must be purchased and the production, inventory, and quality control systems designed. The particular tasks to be done must be defined, the functional groups staffed, and production initiated. Quite likely, there will be problems in this startup phase requiring design

EXHIBIT 1.6

Subject Areas in Operations Management

1. Operations strategy
2. Inventory control
3. Aggregate planning
4. Forecasting
5. Scheduling
6. Capacity planning
7. Purchasing
8. Facility location
9. Facility layout
10. Process design
11. Maintenance and reliability
12. Quality control
13. Work measurement

Source: Modified from Operations Management Association, *The Operations Management Newsletter* 1, no. 1 (May–June 1979), p. 14.

EXHIBIT 1.7 **Key Decisions in the Life of a Productive System**

Stages	Key Decision	Chapter
BIRTH of the system	What are the goals of the firm? What product or service will be offered?	Chapters 1, 2 Chapters 1, 2
PRODUCT DESIGN and PROCESS SELECTION	What is the form and quality of the product? Technologically, how should the product be made?	Chapters 4, 5, 6 Chapters 4, 5
DESIGN of the system	How do you design for just-in-time production? How do you determine demand for the product or service? What capacity do you need? Where should the facility be located? What physical arrangement is best to use? How do you manage waiting time? What job is each worker to perform? How will the job be performed and measured? How will the workers be compensated?	Chapter 16 Chapter 7 Chapter 8 Chapter 8 Chapter 9 Chapter 10, 10S Chapter 11 Chapter 11 Chapter 11
STARTUP of the system	How do you get the system into operation?	Chapter 12
The system in STEADY STATE	How do you manage day-to-day activities? How can you improve the system? How do you measure performance?	Chapter 13–18 Chapter 6 Chapter 3

changes, re-layout, and personnel adjustments. Once the facility is in operation, problems become more of the day-to-day type, requiring decisions on scheduling priorities, minor changes to remove inefficiencies, and maintenance to ensure continued operation. We term this the *steady-state* stage.

This steady-state operating condition may be changed in a number of ways: new products may come into the system or new services may be offered; new developments may cause significant changes in methods; markets may shift or even cease to exist. If these changes are moderate, a slight revision may be all that is necessary to bring the system into alignment. At times, though, the needed revisions are of such magnitude that certain phases of the life cycle must be repeated, probably calling for new designs, more or less extensive restaffing, and restarting the revised system. If the system cannot adjust to the stimulus that has generated the need for revision, then, in the extreme case, the enterprise will die (through liquidation) or cease to exist as a separate entity (through sale or merger).

In reality, most organizations operate within this dynamic life cycle. A system, whether it is a manufacturing firm, service business, or government agency, is born of an idea, passes through a growth stage, and continually changes to meet new demands. (Sometimes, of course, it is deliberately terminated.)

Exhibit 1.7 identifies some of the key decision areas with regards to the various stages in a system's life cycle and the respective chapter(s) where each is emphasized. Remember that this is a dynamic process, and several phases in the life cycle may occur simultaneously. Indeed, many firms allocate a large portion of their resources to foster a continual rebirth or rejuvenation program through research and development staffs. Further, although no interconnections are specifically shown in the exhibit, in actuality such

EXHIBIT 1.8

Rejuvenation with Design and Startup of Revised System Begun during Latter Phases of Original System

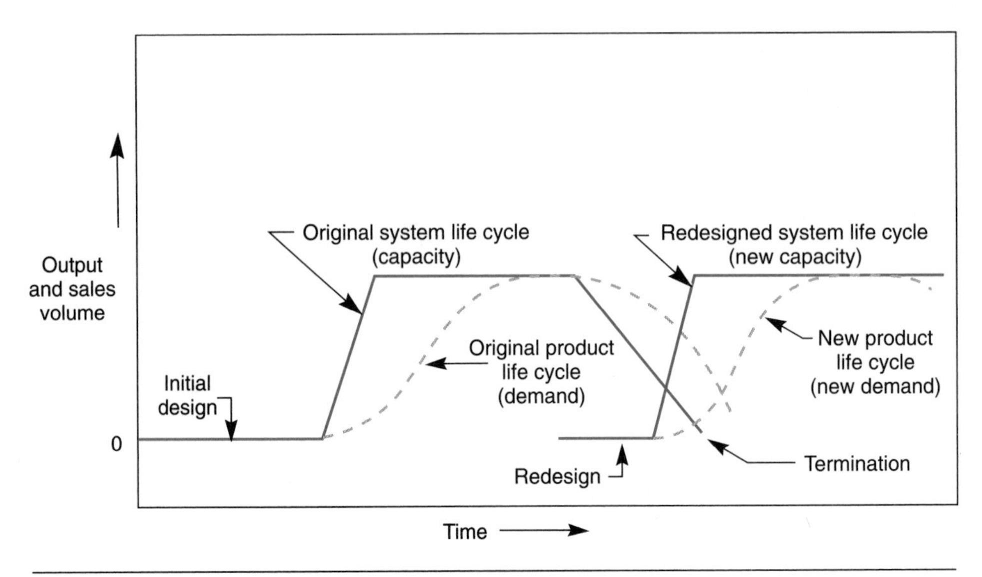

interconnections are common. The introduction of a new product, for example, might cause the system to loop back to basic product design, followed by the activities of process selection, new system design, staffing, and startup.

Exhibit 1.8 shows a graphic example of such rejuvenation. In this illustration we have assumed that a redesign of the system is undertaken during the steady-state and termination phases of the initial system's life cycle. This might be a reasonable strategy in that it permits a startup of the revised system to begin as soon as operations of the initial system are terminated. We have also assumed (for simplicity) that only one new product is to be produced with the redesigned system and that the life cycle curves for both product and system are roughly equivalent to those of their original counterparts. In actuality, of course, these assumptions are highly restrictive since most firms produce several products rather than one, and we would not expect any two system life cycles or any two product life cycles to be identical.

We emphasize that this text is not built around the life cycle of any one system. On the contrary, we have intentionally sought illustrations from a variety of products and services. By doing this, we hope to emphasize the fact that operations management is essential in such diverse systems as hospitals, supermarkets, banks, universities—and, of course, factories.[4]

[4]Roger W. Schmenner, "Every Factory Has a Life Cycle," *Harvard Business Review* 61, no. 2 (March–April 1983), pp. 121–29.

1.6 OPERATIONS MANAGEMENT AND OTHER BUSINESS SPECIALTIES

Operations management is a required course in many business schools, not only because it deals with the basic question of how products and services are created, but also because it affects every other field of business in the real world.

Accountants, be they internal or external to the firm, need to understand the basics of inventory management, capacity utilization, and labor standards to develop accurate cost data, perform audits, and prepare financial reports. Cost accountants in particular must be aware of how just-in-time (JIT) and computer-integrated manufacturing (CIM) work.

Financial managers can use inventory and capacity concepts in judging the need for capital investments and forecasts of cash flow and in the management of current assets. Further, there is a mutual concern between OM and finance in specific decisions such as make-or-buy and plant expansion and/or relocation.

Marketing specialists need to understand what operations can do relative to meeting customer due dates, product customization, and new product introduction. In service industries, marketing and production often take place simultaneously, so a natural mutuality of interest should arise between marketing and OM.

Personnel specialists need to be aware of how jobs are designed, the relationship between standards and incentive plans, and the types of skills required of the direct work force.

MIS specialists often install information systems that they themselves design or that are developed as off-the-shelf software by computer companies. Moreover, a major application of computers in business is in the area of production control.

Where applicable, engineers need to better understand how products are made, so that new product designs can take maximum advantage of the most recent manufacturing technologies.

1.7 HISTORICAL DEVELOPMENT OF OM

Scientific Management

Although we could claim that operations management has existed since the dawn of civilization, the advent of **scientific management** around the turn of the century is probably the major historical landmark for the field. This concept was developed by Frederick W. Taylor, an imaginative engineer and insightful observer of organizational activities.

The essence of Taylor's philosophy was that scientific laws govern how much a worker can produce per day and that it is the function of management to discover and use these laws in the operation of productive systems (and the function of the worker to carry out management's wishes without question). Taylor's philosophy was not greeted with approval by all his contemporaries. On the contrary, some unions resented or feared scientific management—and with some justification. In too many instances, managers of the day were quick to embrace the mechanisms of Taylor's philosophy—time study, incentive plans, and so forth—but ignored their responsibility to organize and standardize the work to be done. For many firms, workers were often viewed as just another asset, like plant and equipment.

Taylor's ideas were widely accepted in contemporary Japan, and a Japanese translation of Taylor's book, *Principles of Scientific Management* (titled *The Secret of Saving Lost Motion*), sold more than two million copies. To this day, there is a strong legacy of Taylorism in Japanese approaches to manufacturing management.[5]

Notable co-workers of Taylor were Frank and Lillian Gilbreth (motion study, industrial psychology) and Henry L. Gantt (scheduling, wage payment plans). Their work is well known to management scholars. However, it is probably not well known that Taylor, a devout Quaker, requested "cussing lessons" from an earthy foreman to help him communicate with workers; that Frank Gilbreth defeated younger champion bricklayers in bricklaying contests by using his own principles of motion economy; or that Gantt won a presidential citation for his application of the Gantt chart to shipbuilding during World War I.

Moving Assembly Line

The year 1913 saw the introduction of one of the machine age's greatest technological innovations—the moving assembly line for the manufacture of Ford automobiles.[6] Before the line was introduced, in August of that year, each auto chassis was assembled by one worker in about 12½ hours. Eight months later, when the line was in its final form, with each worker performing a small unit of work and the chassis being moved mechanically, the average labor time per chassis was 93 minutes. This technological breakthrough, coupled with the concepts of scientific management, represents the classic application of labor specialization and is still common today.

Hawthorne Studies

Mathematical and statistical developments dominated the evolution of operations management from Taylor's time up to around the 1940s. An exception was the Hawthorne studies, conducted during the late 1920s and early 1930s by a research team from the Harvard Graduate School of Business Administration and supervised by the sociologist Elton Mayo. These experiments were designed to study the effects of certain environmental changes on the output of assembly workers at Western Electric's Hawthorne plant in Chicago, Illinois. The unexpected findings, reported in *Management and the Worker* (1939) by F. J. Roethlisberger and W. J. Dickson, intrigued sociologists and students of "traditional" scientific management alike. To the surprise of the researchers, changing the level of illumination, for example, had much less effect on the output than the way in which the changes were introduced to the workers. That is, reductions in illumination in some instances led to increased output because workers felt an obligation to their group to keep output high. Discoveries such as these had tremendous implications for work design and

[5]Charles J. McMillan, "Production Planning in Japan," *Journal of General Management* 8, no. 4, pp. 44–71.

[6]Ford is said to have gotten the idea for an assembly line from observing a Swiss watch manufacturer's use of the technology. Incidentally, all Model-T Fords were painted black. Why? Because black paint dried fastest.

motivation and ultimately led to the establishment of personnel management and human relations departments in most organizations.

Operations Research

World War II, with its complex problems of logistics control and weapons-systems design, provided the impetus for the development of the interdisciplinary, mathematically oriented field of operations research. Operations research (OR) brings together practitioners in such diverse fields as mathematics, psychology, and economics. Specialists in these disciplines customarily form a team to structure and analyze a problem in quantitative terms so that a mathematically optimal solution can be obtained. As mentioned earlier in the chapter, operations research, or its approximate synonym *management science,* now provides many of the quantitative tools used in operations management as well as other business disciplines.

OM Emerges as a Field

In the late 1950s and early 1960s, scholars began to write texts dealing specifically with operations management as opposed to industrial engineering or operations research. Writers such as Edward Bowman and Robert Fetter (*Analysis for Production and Operations Management* [1957]) and Elwood S. Buffa (*Modern Production Management* [1961]) clearly noted the commonality of problems faced by all productive systems and emphasized the importance of viewing production operations as a system.

Today, operations management is acknowledged as a legitimate functional area within every organization, be it for profit or not-for-profit, public or private, manufacturing or service. Those companies that recognize the contributions that the operations management function can make toward achieving their respective corporate goals will lead the way into the next century.

1.8 CONCLUSION

Operations management is recognized today as a critical functional area within every organization. No longer is operations management considered to be subservient to the finance and marketing areas; instead, it is now treated as equal. Firms that fail to recognize the significant contribution that the operations management function can make will lose profits and market share to those firms that do. The once-passive role of operations management, which concentrated solely on minimizing costs, has been replaced by a more proactive position of maximizing value.

Some of the major issues facing operations management executives today in this constantly changing business environment include:

1. Reducing the development and manufacturing time for new products and services.
2. Achieving and sustaining high quality while keeping costs down.
3. Integrating new technologies and control systems into existing production systems.

4. Obtaining and training qualified workers and managers.
5. Working effectively with other functions of the business (marketing, engineering, finance, and personnel) to accomplish the goals of the firm.
6. Controlling production and service activities at multiple sites in decentralized organizations.
7. Working effectively with suppliers and being user-friendly for customers.
8. Working effectively with new partners formed by strategic alliances (for example, IBM and Apple Computers).

All of these issues are interrelated. The key to success is for operations management to do all of these at a level that is competitive primarily with foreign companies in both international and domestic markets.

1.9 REVIEW AND DISCUSSION QUESTIONS

1. What is the difference between OM and OR?
2. What were the underlying reasons for the lack of emphasis on operations management in the post-World War II years?
3. What are the advantages of bringing customers into the technical core?
4. Take a look at the want ads in *The Wall Street Journal* and evaluate the opportunities for an OM major with several years of experience.
5. What are the major factors leading to the resurgence of interest in OM today?
6. Explain the difference, from an operations management perspective, between cost minimization and value maximization.
7. Using Exhibit 1.5 as a model, describe the input–transformation–output relationships found in the following systems?
   a. An airline.
   b. A state penitentiary.
   c. A branch bank.
   d. A bakery.
   e. A clothing manufacturer.
8. What is the life cycle approach to production/operations management? Does it make sense to you? Could it be applied to any other fields you are studying?
9. What are the implications for marketing of Tektronix's "hot-line" to the shop-floor worker?
10. What do we mean by the expression *value chain,* as it applies to the transformation process of a product or service?

1.10 SELECTED BIBLIOGRAPHY

Ammeson, Jane. "When in Rome." *Northwest Airlines World Traveler,* March 1993.

Buffa, Elwood S. *Modern Production Management.* New York: John Wiley & Sons, 1961.

Chase, Richard B., and Eric L. Prentis. "Operations Management: A Field Rediscovered." *Journal of Management* 13, no. 2 (October 1987), pp. 351–66.

Chase, Richard B., and David A. Garvin. "The Service Factory." *Harvard Business Review* 67, no. 4 (July–August 1989), pp. 61–69.

Deming, W. Edwards. *Out of the Crisis.* Cambridge, Mass.: Massachusetts Institute of Technology Center for Advanced Engineering Study, 1986.

Gwynne, S. C. "The Long Haul." *Time,* September 25, 1992, pp. 34–38.

Goldratt, Eliyahu M., and Jeff Cox. *The Goal.* Croton-on-Hudson, N.Y.: North River Press, 1986.

Hayes, Robert H.; Steven C. Wheelwright; and Kim B. Clark. *Dynamic Manufacturing.* New York: Free Press, 1988.

Hammonds, K. H., and M. Roman. "Itching to Get onto The Factory Floor." *Business Week,* October 14, 1991.

McMillan, Charles J. "Production Planning in Japan." *Journal of General Management* 8, no. 4, pp. 44–71.

Peters, Tom, and KQED Golden Gate Productions. *The Power of Excellence: The Forgotten Customer.* Jack Hilton Productions, Video Publishing House, Inc., 1987.

Schmenner, Roger W. "Every Factory Has a Life Cycle." *Harvard Business Review* 61, no. 2 (March–April 1983), pp. 121–29.

Schonberger, Richard J. *World Class Manufacturing: The Lessons of Simplicity Applied.* New York: Free Press, 1986.

Skinner, Wickham, "Manufacturing—Missing Link in Corporate Strategy," *Harvard Business Review,* May–June 1969, pp. 136–45.

________. "The Focused Factory." *Harvard Business Review,* May–June 1974, pp. 113–21.

Chapter 2

Competitiveness and Operations Strategy

EPIGRAPH

The wealth and power of the United States depends upon maintaining mastery and control of production.

Stephen S. Cohen and John Zysman, *Why Manufacturing Matters: The Myth of the Post-Industrial Economy* (New York: Basic Books, 1987).

In the next century, the United States will be our farm and Western Europe our boutique.

Attributed to a Japanese minister of trade in Gore Vidal, "Rebirth of a Nation: Why Italy Works," *Los Angeles Times,* May 1, 1988.

CHAPTER OUTLINE

KEY TERMS

Competitiveness

International Competition

Operations Strategy

Four Basic Operations Strategies
- Cost
- Quality
- Delivery
- Flexibility

Competitive Priorities of Manufacturers

A company that is considered to be world class recognizes that its ability to compete in the marketplace is highly dependent on its developing an operations strategy that is properly aligned with its overall goals and mission. A company's *competitiveness* refers to the relative position of a firm (in comparison to that of other firms) in the marketplace. *Operations strategy* refers to how the operations management function can contribute to a firm's ability to achieve a competitive advantage in that marketplace.

2.1 COMPETITIVENESS DEFINED

Competitiveness is about winning. A boxing match is a good example of competition. The person with the most points or the one left standing at the end of the match wins. The sides and the rules of the game are easily defined. What about business? Defining sides, or competitors, and the rules of the game becomes much more difficult when considering global markets than when talking about a boxing match.

The emphasis in the 1990s is on speed, or short cycle management and increased customization. The ability to rapidly develop and produce custom products depends heavily on the operations function of the firm. Quality, price, dependability, and responsiveness are all indicators of how well a company is converting inputs into outputs.

Firms within a given industry compete with one another for market share. Nations also compete with one another for shares of global markets. In 1985, the President's Council on Industrial Competitiveness offered this definition of **international competition:**

> Competitiveness for a nation is the degree to which it can, under free and fair market conditions, produce goods and services that meet the test of international markets while simultaneously maintaining and expanding the real incomes of its citizens.

2.2 OPERATIONS STRATEGY

Introduction

As stated in Chapter 1, U.S. companies in the post-World War II era experienced tremendous consumer demand. As a result, emphasis in manufacturing in this country was placed on turning out high volumes of products in order to satisfy this demand.

During this period, corporate strategy was usually developed by the marketing and finance functions. The manufacturing or operations function would then be told to produce the required products at minimum cost without having any understanding or input into the overall goals of the company. Within this framework, the production function in an organization concentrated primarily on obtaining low-cost, unskilled labor and constructing highly automated facilities, both with the intent of minimizing production costs.

The Emergence of Operations Strategy

The role of the operations management function (i.e., to minimize production costs), remained virtually unchanged throughout the 1950s and early 1960s. By the late 1960s, C. Wickham Skinner of the Harvard Business School, who is often referred to as the grandfather of operations strategy, recognized this weakness among U.S. manufacturers and suggested the need for an operations strategy to complement the existing marketing and finance strategies. In one of his initial articles on the subject, Skinner referred to manufacturing as the missing link in corporate strategy.[1]

Subsequent work in this area by researchers at the Harvard Business School, including Abernathy, Clark, Hayes, and Wheelwright, continued to emphasize the importance of using the strengths of a firm's manufacturing facilities as a competitive weapon in the marketplace.

What Is Operations Strategy?

Operations strategy is concerned with the development of a long-term plan for determining how to best utilize the major resources of the firm so that there is a high degree of compatibility between these resources and the firm's long-term corporate strategy. Operations strategy addresses very broad questions about how these major resources should be configured in order to achieve the desired corporate objectives. Typical operations strategy issues include:

How big do we make the facilities?
Where do we locate them?
When do we build them?
What type of process(es) do we install to make the products?

Each of these issues is addressed in greater detail in subsequent chapters. In this chapter we want to take a more macroscopic perspective to better understand how these issues are interrelated.

Types of Operations Strategies

From the work of Skinner and others, **four basic operations strategies** were identified. These were **cost, quality, delivery,** and **flexibility.** These four strategies translate directly into characteristics that are used to describe various processes by which a company can manufacture its products or provide its services, and are, again, discussed in greater detail in a subsequent chapter.

Cost Within every industry, there is usually a segment of the market that buys strictly on the basis of low cost. To successfully compete in this niche, a firm must necessarily,

[1] C. Wickham Skinner, "Manufacturing—The Missing Link in Corporate Strategy," *Harvard Business Review* 47, no. 3 (May–June 1969), pp. 136–45.

therefore, be the low-cost producer. But even doing this doesn't always guarantee profitability and success.

Products sold strictly on the basis of cost are typically commodity-like in nature. In other words, customers cannot distinguish the products of one firm from those of another. As a result, customers use cost as the primary determinant for making a purchase.

However, this segment of the market is frequently very large and many companies are lured by the potential for significant profits, which are associated with the large unit volumes of product. As a consequence, the competition in this segment is exceedingly fierce—and so is the failure rate. After all, there can only be one low-cost producer, who usually establishes the selling price in the market.

Quality Quality can be divided into two categories: product quality and process quality. The level of quality in a product's design will vary as to the market segment it is aimed for. Obviously, a child's first two-wheel bicycle is of significantly different quality than the bicycle of a world-class cyclist. The use of thicker sheetmetal and the application of extra coats of paint are some of the product quality characteristics that differentiate a Mercedes-Benz from a Hyundai. One advantage of offering higher-quality products is that they command higher prices in the marketplace.

The goal in establishing the "proper level" of product quality is to focus on the requirements of the customer. Overdesigned products with too much quality will be viewed as being prohibitively expensive. Underdesigned products, on the other hand, will lose customers to products that cost a little more but are perceived by the customers as offering much greater benefits.

Process quality is critical in every market segment. Regardless of whether the product is a child's first two-wheeler or a bicycle for an international cyclist, or whether it is a Mercedes-Benz or a Hyundai, customers want products without defects. Thus, the goal of process quality is to produce error-free products through the concept of continuous improvement.

Speed of Delivery Another market niche considers speed of delivery to be an important determinant in its purchasing decision. Here, the ability of a firm to be able to provide consistent and fast delivery allows it to charge a premium price for its products.

Flexibility Flexibility, from a strategic perspective, refers to the ability of a company to offer a wide variety of products to its customers. Flexibility is also a measure of how fast a company can convert its process(es) from making an old line of products to producing a new product line. Product variety is often perceived by the customer to be a dimension of quality.

Factory Focus and Trade-Offs

Central to the concept of operations strategy, during the late 1960s and early 1970s, was the notion of factory focus and trade-offs. The underlying logic was that a factory could not excel simultaneously on all four performance measures. Consequently, management had to decide which parameters of performance were critical to the firm's success, and then concentrate or focus the resources of the firm on those particular characteristics. For those firms with very large, existing manufacturing facilities, Skinner even suggested the creation of a Plant-within-a-Plant (PWP) concept, in which different locations within the facility would be allocated to different product lines, each with their own operations strategy. Even the workers, under the PWP concept, would be separated in order to minimize the confusion associated with shifting from one type of strategy to another.[2]

For example, if a company wanted to focus on speed of delivery, then it could not be very flexible in terms of its ability to offer a wide range of products. For example, McDonald's provides very fast service but offers a very limited menu. Similarly, a low-cost strategy was not compatible with either speed of delivery or flexibility. High quality was also viewed as a trade-off to low cost.

Establishing Priorities

Beginning in the mid 1960s, competition became more intense as more and more foreign companies began to invade markets that were predominantly controlled by U.S. firms. This trend toward a more global perspective in terms of market competition continues to this day. In the mid 1960s, for example, only 7 percent of the U.S. economy was exposed to international competition. However, by the 1980s this figure exceeded 70 percent, and continues to grow.[3]

With the world becoming a single-world economy (or global village), there has emerged a group of companies that have adopted an international perspective toward both manufacturing and marketing. Within this global arena, competition is significantly more intense, due to both the greater number of "players" and the tremendous profit opportunities that exist.

Those companies that have excelled on the international level have been often referred to as *world-class manufacturers*. Events in the world marketplace during the 1970s and 1980s, in terms of the growing intensity in competition, forced these companies to reexamine the concept of operations strategy, especially in terms of the so-called "necessary" trade-offs. Managers began to recognize that they didn't really have to make trade-offs between different strategies. What emerged instead was a realization for the need to establish priorities among the four strategies, as dictated by the marketplace. Exhibit 2.1 presents the sequence or priorities in which these four strategies were introduced.

In the late 1960s and early 1970s, cost was the primary concern, a hold-over from the philosophy of the 1950s that manufacturing's only objective was to minimize production costs. However, as more and more companies began to produce low-cost products, the need became apparent to develop other ways to differentiate themselves from their competitors. The priority thus shifted to quality. Companies at this time obtained a competitive advantage by producing high-quality products, which allowed them to charge more—although price still was a factor in the consumer's buying decision. However,

---

[2] C. Wickham Skinner, "The Focused Factory," *Harvard Business Review* 52, no. 3 (May–June 1974), pp. 113–22.

[3] S.C. Gwynne, "The Long Haul" *Time*, September 28, 1992, pp. 34–38.

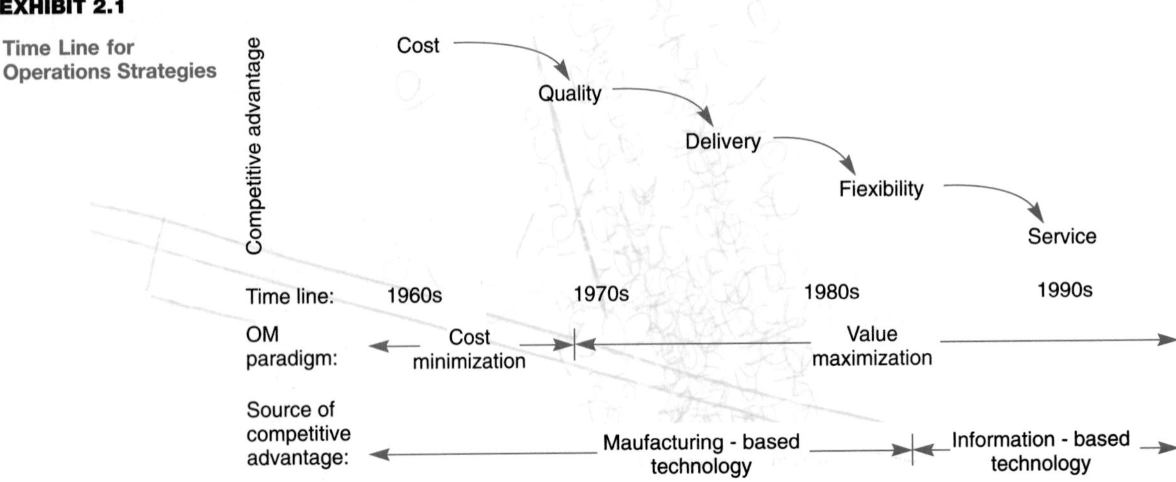

EXHIBIT 2.1

Time Line for Operations Strategies

competition again soon caught up, and everyone was offering high-quality products that were reasonably priced.

Companies, in looking to obtain another competitive advantage in the marketplace, turned to speed of delivery as a means of differentiating themselves from the rest of the pack. Now the ante into the "game" was high-quality products that were reasonably priced and which could be delivered quickly to the customer.

In recent years, George Stalk, Jr., a leading management "guru," has identified speed of delivery as a major factor in determining the success of a company, stating that there is a very high correlation between both profit and growth in market share, and the speed with which a firm can deliver its products.[4] Companies are therefore concentrating their resources on reducing product lead times with very dramatic results. Products that once took weeks or months to deliver are now being shipped within hours or days of the receipt of an order.

Eventually, the competition again caught up and the more aggressive firms looked for still another means to obtain a competitive advantage. This time flexibility was selected, as manifested by the ability of the firm to produce customized products. Now the marketplace dictated that for firms to be successful, they had to produce reasonably priced, customized products of high quality that could be quickly delivered to the customer.

A good example of a firm that has accomplished this is the National Bicycle Company in Japan. A customer places an order for a bicycle at a retail bicycle shop, and is immediately seated on a special bike frame to obtain his or her individual measurements. These specifications, along with other information such as color choice and special silk-screening instructions (e.g., name) are then faxed to the bicycle factory, where an

[4] George Stalk, Jr., "Time—The Next Source of Competitive Advantage," *Harvard Business Review*, July–August 1988, pp. 41–51.

Louis Psihoyos/Matrix International, Inc.

At the National Bicycle Company in Japan, most of the basic assembly work, such as the wiring of this brake cable, is left to humans, not robots. One worker assembles nearly the entire bike, which provides a sense of satisfaction.

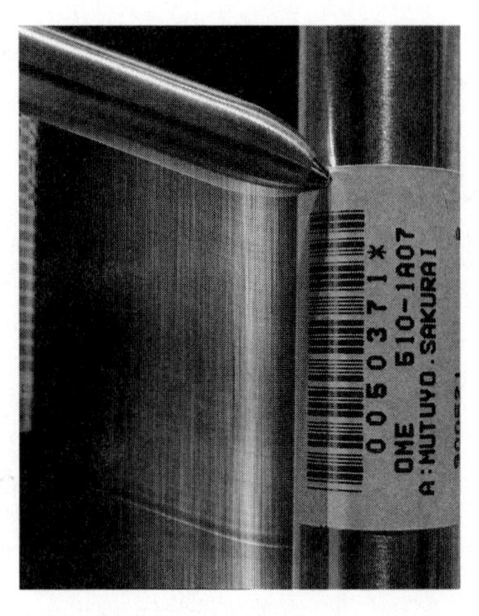

Louis Psihoyos/Matrix International, Inc.

National Bicycle Company demonstrates mass customization by attaching the name of the future owner, along with a bar code that provides specific instructions to the robotic welders, to the bicycle frame as it goes through the various stages of the manufacturing process.

order for that particular bicycle is immediately generated and released to the floor. The total cycle time to produce the bike is three hours, although the actual delivery is about two weeks (market surveys have suggested that this is the "optimum" delivery time, in terms of peaking customer satisfaction).[5]

As the "rules" for operations strategy shifted from that of primarily reducing manufacturing costs to that of including quality, speed of delivery, and flexibility, the paradigm for the operations management function has also shifted. The paradigm of minimizing production costs has been replaced with that of maximizing value.

The Information Age

Today, world-class manufacturing companies are again looking for a breakthrough that will provide them with another competitive advantage in the marketplace. The 1993 annual meeting of the Operations Management Association (OMA) focused on the topic of service breakthroughs, with several presentations suggesting that service (as shown in Exhibit 2.1), in particular post-purchase service, is the method by which companies will differentiate themselves in the near future. Cadillac and Nissan, for example, are already offering extensive warranty packages that include such things as road service, travel planning, and the use of loaner vehicles during the warranty period.

Warranty packages such as these will permit companies to capture all the data pertaining to product defects and malfunctions (at least those that occur during the warranty period).

[5] Susan Moffatt, "Japan's New Personalized Production," *Fortune,* October 22, 1990, pp. 132–35.

Such information can then be fed back into the product design process to further refine the product. These types of product warranties are very similar to the service guarantees advocated by Hart.[6]

With the incorporation of this type of consumer information into the operations process, companies will officially make the transition from the manufacturing age into the information age. Previously, competitive advantages were achieved through the operations processing capability of the company. Now, the competitive advantage is achieved primarily by using information from the marketplace.

In summary, the evolution of operations strategy, from being virtually nonexistent in the post-World War II days to playing a critical role in the success of an organization, is shown in Exhibit 2.1. Also included in this figure is the change in paradigms for the operations management function and the transition from the manufacturing age to the information age.

Operations Strategy in a Manufacturing Company

To achieve success in the current world marketplace, top management in manufacturing firms must fully understand the role of the operations management function and its contribution, in terms of supporting and influencing the corporation's overall strategic goals. In today's highly competitive environment (which will become more competitive in future years), only those firms that properly utilize all of their resources will succeed and prosper. Those that do not will fail. Firms whose managers ignore the contribution that the operations management function can make in the development of corporate goals will fall into this latter category.

2.3 COMPETITIVENESS IN THE UNITED STATES

The United States currently has a serious competitiveness problem. Rationalizations abound. Some claim with a good deal of justification that manufacturing lacks the government support provided to its competitors. Also, a large portion of the blame is frequently put on the relative strength of the dollar against foreign currencies. However, the U.S. trade deficit increased during the 1970s when the dollar depreciated by 15 percent. Thus, although weakness in the dollar stimulates exports, long-term reliance on a cheaper dollar is a risky solution at best.

Some say that our reliance on manufacturing is outdated and, given our shift to services, there *is* no problem. And, indeed, exported services have produced a surplus in the trade-balance equation. However, even here, the trend has been moving toward a deficit. While business services do not constitute all services, they do include the major services traded in international markets, such as travel, transportation (both passenger and cargo), construction, engineering, consulting, banking, communications, and insurance.

Moreover, those who see a shift to the service economy as a salvation miss two crucial

[6] Christopher W. L. Hart, "The Power of Unconditional Service Guarantees," *Harvard Business Review* 66, no. 4 (July–August 1988), pp. 56–62.

points. First, service and manufacturing are closely linked with each other. Many services are purchased by manufacturing firms, for example, advertising, legal, health care, and accounting services. The United States cannot be supported only by a strong service sector. Second, although foreign purchases of U.S. services are high at the present time, it is naive to believe that foreign manufacturers and their developing societies will forever be dependent on these services. Japan is building a strong financial base that is already competing with and even surpassing the United States in both the world and domestic marketplaces.

Another rationalization for the disappointing performance of the United States in the global marketplace is that the poor performers are just isolated industries and that overall performance is what really matters. This might be true; a dollar's worth of exported wheat has the same value as a dollar's worth of electronics. Unfortunately, the poor performance is not isolated to just a few industries. Portfolio theory has taught us the benefits of diversification. The United States needs a more diversified portfolio in exports, and an increasing number of U.S. goods are no longer competitive in the world marketplace.

U.S. business leaders and policymakers have been slow to recognize that the superiority of industry cannot be taken for granted. The global marketplace is a reality, and we are not competitive in a large number of areas. According to the MIT Commission on Industrial Productivity, there are five basic causes for this:

> *1.* American business decisions have been frequently characterized by *short time horizons,* and a related tendency to give excessive weight to financial issues relative to other criteria. This preoccupation with short-term financial results has had among its consequences a lack of staying power on the part of affected firms, reflected in underinvestment in R&D (research and development) and the physical and human capital needed to maintain technological leadership in a field once the first big returns have been captured.
>
> *2.* *Strategic weaknesses* among American companies have arisen particularly as a consequence of parochial attitudes, which have frequently led these firms to pay insufficient attention to the capabilities and intentions of foreign competitors, and to the opportunities presented by foreign markets. Intensifying international competition has forced U.S. companies in a broad range of industries to become less insular, but many firms still seem to be poor imitators even when imitation would be advantageous.
>
> *3.* A lack of cooperation in individual and organizational relationships within and among U.S. firms has been another key barrier to improved productivity performance. Within firms there are often organizational "walls" separating product design, process design, manufacturing, marketing and R&D; and individuals, often highly trained professionals, have frequently been unable to work in teams.
>
> *4.* *Weaknesses in human resource management and organization* have prevented the full benefits of technical change from being realized. Firms have tended to view labor more as a cost factor to be minimized than as a productive, evolving resource. The importance of a well-trained, well-motivated, and adaptable work force to firm performance has frequently been underestimated.
>
> *5.* The commission has also found evidence of *recurring weaknesses in technological practice.* While U.S. companies in many industries have made key technological advances, weaknesses in designing simple, reliable, and manufacturable products, failures to build quality into products at the design stage, weaknesses in the design of manufacturing processes and in

production operations, and a related tendency to overinnovate on product but underinnovate on process have often led to a loss in market position, or in some cases an inability to establish one.

The solutions to the competitiveness problem appear to lie in reversing the attitudes and strategies enumerated in the MIT Commission report. That is,

1. Place less emphasis on short-term financial payoffs and invest more in R&D.
2. Revise corporate strategies to include responses to foreign competition. This, in turn, calls for greater investment in people and equipment to improve manufacturing capability.
3. Knock down communication barriers within organizations and recognize mutuality of interests with other companies and suppliers (the former relative to international competition, in particular).
4. Recognize that the labor force is a resource to be nurtured, not just a cost to be avoided.
5. Get back to basics in managing production operations. Build in quality at the design stage. Place more emphasis on process innovations rather than focusing sole attention on product innovations.

In sum, we must become better at managing our productive capabilities in all dimensions—in strategy and in the five P's of operations: people, plants, parts, processes, and planning and control systems.

2.4 COMPETITIVE PRIORITIES

In the preceding section, we discussed the MIT Commission's priorities for becoming competitive as a nation in manufacturing. In this section, we present **competitive priorities of manufacturers:** what manufacturing executives from around the world themselves see as priorities for their firms.

In a 1992 survey conducted by Boston University, senior manufacturing executives were asked to rate the importance of 15 designated manufacturing capabilities. The ranking of these capabilities by American, European, and Japanese companies is shown in Exhibit 2.2.

Conformance quality tops the list of capabilities important to U.S. manufacturing managers. What is top on the Japanese manager's list? Product reliability. The reason: The Japanese have already achieved consistent conformance quality and are looking at the next level of challenge. Also of interest is the increasing attention being paid to time-based capabilities (as shown by on-time delivery being ranked second in each geographic area). Customers want to be responsively provided with a variety of products and order volumes. In addition, they increasingly expect service along with their products.

EXHIBIT 2.2

Top Five Competitive Capabilities, 1990–1995

Rank	Europe	Japan	United States
1	Conformance quality	Product reliability	Conformance quality
2	On-time delivery	On-time delivery	On-time delivery
3	Product reliability	Fast design change	Product reliability
4	Performance quality	Conformance quality	Performance quality
5	Delivery speed	Product customization	Price

Source: Jay S. Kim and Jeffrey G. Miller, *Building the Value Factory: A Progress Report for U.S. Manufacturing,* Boston University Manufacturing Roundtable, 1992.

2.5 MEETING THE COMPETITIVE CHALLENGE

There are many examples of firms in the United States that have risen to the competitive challenge. Monroe Auto Equipment, for example, has succeeded at producing such high-quality shock absorbers that one of its customers, Toyota of Japan, recently gave an appraisal of "defects—zero" in a shipment of 60,000 shocks. Exhibit 2.3 illustrates how a number of companies are improving the time they take to get their new products to market.

The "OM in Action" on the next page describes how Compaq Computer managers focus on quality through and with their suppliers and even with their competitors to maintain and enhance the timing, quality, and marketability of their products.

EXHIBIT 2.3

Shortening Product Cycle Times

Company/Product	Product Cycle Time Reduction
General Motors New Buick model	60 to 40 months
Hewlett-Packard Computer printer	52 to 24 months
IBM Personal computer	48 to 13 months
Honeywell Thermostat	48 to 12 months
Ingersoll Rand Air grinder	42 to 12 months
Warner Electric Clutch brake	36 to 10 months

Source: Data from *Developing Products in Half the Time* by Donald Reinersen and Preston Smith (New York: Van Nostrand Reinhold, 1990), reported in *Boardroom Reports,* June 15, 1991, p. 7.

OPERATIONS MANAGEMENT IN ACTION
Compaq Computer

Swaying from the ceiling at its Houston factory is a white banner that reads:

WE AT COMPAQ COMPUTER ARE ABSOLUTELY COMMITTED TO PROVIDE DEFECT FREE PRODUCTS AND SERVICES TO OUR CUSTOMERS.

The message jibes with what one sees below: a sparkling assembly line, surrounded by potted ficus trees and ferns, washed with light from vast skylights, that looks more like an expensive health club than a factory. Founded in 1982, the company has its ideal inscribed in its name, an amalgam of the words *computer, compact,* and *quality.*

A maker of IBM-compatible PCs as well as ultrafast computers that manage data on office networks, Compaq has grown into an 11,800-employee business that last year [1990] earned $455 million on $3.6 billion in sales. It commands 20 percent of the world PC market, compared with 25 percent each for IBM and Apple Computer, and has almost no foreign rivals, except in the fast-growing field of laptop PCs. Still, competition is ferocious—fighting for sales, Compaq cut prices on its computers in 1991 as much as 34 percent and warned that second-quarter earnings would drop 80 percent.

Part of Compaq's success derives from its speed at offering the latest processor chips, disk drives, and display screens in its products. Yes, even faster than IBM. A major challenge, says CEO and co-founder Rod Canion, is to keep a breakneck pace of innovation across burgeoning product lines—nine new ones last year alone.

When the company was small, speeding products to market seemed a breeze. Today Compaq tries to maintain its entrepreneurial edge through small product-development teams that include marketers, designers, engineers, and manufacturing experts. Rather than moving a new computer step by step from drawing board to the factory, explains Canion, "The secret is to do all things in parallel."

Compaq's greatest advantage, Canion believes, is that it buys most components rather than making them itself: "Vertical integration is the old way of doing things. The way to succeed in the 1990s is to be open to technology from anywhere in the world." (Japanese competitors, such as Toshiba, continue to make nearly all their components.)

When Compaq needed a hard disk drive for its first laptop in 1986, it considered building one itself. Instead, it helped finance Conner Peripherals, a Silicon Valley startup with a disk drive already under way. "We worked so closely with Conner that they were literally an extension of our design team," says Canion. "We got all the benefits but weren't tied down. If another company had come along with a better drive, we'd have bought from them as well."

In March [1991], Compaq began a nervy foray beyond the realm of PCs into the $7.5-billion-a-year market for powerful desktop workstations used primarily by scientists and engineers. Rather than attacking market leaders Sun Microsystems and Hewlett-Packard head-on, Compaq assembled more than a dozen hardware and software companies, including Microsoft and Digital Equipment Corp., in an alliance. The group aims to win by defining a new technical standard for high-speed desktop computing, much like the IBM standard in PCs. Any workstation designed in accordance with the standard would work with any other. That would free customers to buy the latest, fastest machine without fear of being wedded to a single manufacturer.

Industry experts think rivalry among participants may tear the alliance apart. Observes

Dick Shaffer, editor of *Computer Letter:* "All the participants are entrepreneurial companies with big egos." The group's prospects may not become clear until late next year, when Compaq and other members are due to roll out the new computers and software. If the products all work together, Compaq's workstation would be a winner. If not, says Stewart Alsop, publisher of *PC Letter,* Compaq may have to lower its sights: "As a $3.6 billion company, Compaq can't keep up a high rate of growth anymore just by building PCs."

Source: "The New American Century," *Fortune,* Special Issue, Spring/Summer 1991, p. 27.

2.6 MANUFACTURING OPERATIONS' ROLE IN CORPORATE STRATEGY

Wheelwright and Hayes have identified four stages in the integration of operations strategy into the overall support of corporate goals. Top management and production managers view the decisions and choices that must be made in these stages very differently. A summary of these stages is found in Exhibit 2.4.

Stage 1: Internally neutral. Manufacturing operations capability is viewed as the result of a few simple decisions about capacity, location, technology, and vertical integration. Typically, top management makes these decisions with the aid of consultants. The company's own production staff handles only day-to-day, "get-the-product-out-the-door" decisions. The workers and managers in the operations departments tend to be low-skilled. There is constant performance measurement because top management wants to be aware of any variance quickly to take corrective action. Operations' potential negative impact needs to be minimized. Innovation in process technology is very slow. Management takes few investment risks in the manufacturing area.

Stage 2: Externally neutral. This stage is frequently seen in manufacturing-intensive organizations such as steel. Here operations management is viewed as relatively standardized and unsophisticated. Investment in process technology is reactive, being made only when competitors make changes. Top management is primarily concerned with decisions about resource allocation (capital investments), with emphasis on economy-of-scale criteria. In acquiring new technologies, parity with competitors is sought and new technologies are purchased rather than developed. America's failing smokestack industries (such as steel) and the loss of their markets to foreign competition are evidence of the lack of effectiveness of this stage.

Stage 3: Internally supportive. In this stage—a considerable change from the neutrality of the preceding two stages—all the manufacturing decisions are used to support corporate strategy. The operations staff is given the authority to make decisions, and those decisions are expected to be consistent with overall goals. The corporate strategy is translated into terminology that is meaningful to manufacturing. A longer-term, creative view of the

EXHIBIT 2.4

Stages in Operations Manufacturing Strategic Role

Stage	Role	Characteristics
Stage 1	Minimize manufacturing's negative potential: "internally neutral"	Outside experts are called in to make decisions about strategic manufacturing issues. Internal, detailed management control systems are the primary means for monitoring manufacturing performance. Manufacturing is kept flexible and reactive.
Stage 2	Achieve parity with competitors: "externally neutral"	"Industry practice" is followed. The planning horizon for manufacturing investment decisions is extended to incorporate a single business cycle. Capital investment is the primary means for catching up with competition or achieving a competitive edge.
Stage 3	Provide credible support to the business strategy: "internally supportive"	Manufacturing investments are screened for consistency with the business strategy. A manufacturing strategy is formulated and pursued. Longer-term manufacturing developments and trends are addressed systematically.
Stage 4	Pursue a manufacturing-based competitive advantage: "externally supportive"	Efforts are made to anticipate the potential of new manufacturing practices and technologies. Manufacturing is involved "up front" in major marketing and engineering decisions (and vice versa). Long-range programs are pursued in order to acquire capabilities in advance of needs.

Source: Reprinted by permission of the *Harvard Business Review.* An exhibit from "Competing through Manufacturing" by Steven C. Wheelwright and Robert H. Hayes (January/February 1985).

operations function is taken, but only as long as the creative direction is consistent and in alignment with the already existing strategy.

Stage 4: Externally supportive. In this stage, operations is expected not only to support corporate strategy but also to contribute to its initial development. The operations management function gives the company its competitive advantage, such as low cost or high quality. The scope of decisions is long-term. Investment is made not only in the capital resources but also in work force and systems.

In a true Stage 4 company, the operations management function, like all other business functions, takes a proactive role. The formal and informal communication between finance, marketing, accounting, personnel, and other functions is considerable. There is a horizontal structure, with no one function being more important than another.

2.7 OPERATIONS' ROLE IN SERVICE FIRM COMPETITIVENESS

The competitiveness of a service firm is generally *more* dependent on the strength of its operations capabilities than it is for a manufacturing company. For example, a manufacturing company may be outstanding in its design capabilities but only so-so in its operations,

EXHIBIT 2.5 Stages of Service Firm Competitiveness

Stage	SERVICE DIMENSIONS					
	Service Quality	Back Office	Customer	Introduction of New Technology	Work Force	First-Line Management
I. Available for service	Second to cost: ▪ High variability	Counting room	Satisfy unspecified customer at minimum cost	Only when necessary for survival: ▪ Under duress	Negative constraint	Controls workers
II. Journeyman	Attempts to meet customer expectations: ▪ Consistent on a few key dimensions	Plays important role in total service: ▪ Given attention, but still a separate role	Market segment whose basic needs are understood	When justified by cost savings	Efficient resource; disciplined (follows procedures)	Controls process
III. Distinctive competence achieved	Exceeds customer expectations: ▪ Consistent on multiple dimensions	Equally valued with front office; plays integral role	Collection of individuals whose various needs are understood	When promises to enhance service	Adaptive—permitted to select among alternative procedures	Listens to customers; coaches/facilitates workers
IV. World-class service delivery	Raises customer expectations; seeks challenges: ▪ Continuous improvement	Proactive—develops own capabilities, generates opportunities	Source of stimulation, ideas, and opportunity	Source of firstmover advantages, creates ability to do things competitors can't do	Innovative—creates procedures	Listened to by top management as source of new ideas; mentors workers to enhance career growth.

Source: R. B. Chase and R. H. Hayes, "Beefing-Up Operations in Service Firms," *Sloan Management Review,* Fall 1991, pp. 17–28.

EXHIBIT 2.6

Defining the Four Stages of Service Firm Competitiveness

Stage	Characteristics
I. Available for service	■ Firm survives for reasons other than performance (e.g., a government agency) ■ Operations reactive, at best
II. Journeyman	■ Firm neither sought out nor avoided ■ Operations reliable but uninspired
III. Distinctive competence achieved	■ Firm sought out based on reputation for meeting customer expectations ■ Operations continually excels, reinforced by management and systems supporting intense customer focus
IV. World-class service delivery	■ Firm name synonymous with service excellence; exceeds customers' expectations, delighting rather than satisfying; leaves competitors in the dust ■ Operations is quick learner, fast innovator; masters every step of service delivery process; provides capabilities superior to competitors

Source: R. B. Chase and R. H. Hayes, "Beefing-Up Operations in Service Firms," *Sloan Management Review*, Fall 1991, pp. 17–28.

yet still be a market leader. Such a situation cannot exist in a service operation, where the operations activities constitute all or part of the product. The inseparability of product from process means that a service firm's competitiveness and its operations competitiveness are always closely linked. This linkage between operations strategy and corporate goals is shown in the four-stage model given in Exhibit 2.5.

The first column of the exhibit lists four proposed stages of service firm competitiveness (defined in Exhibit 2.6). Across the top are the major service dimensions that operations executives must address in strategy development. The entries in the table reflect our interpretation of the views held by senior management of companies that fit into each stage.

Some additional comments about the framework: First, the stage attained by any given firm is a composite. Every service delivery system embodies a unique set of choices about service quality, work-force policies, and so forth. A company may be at a different stage for a given dimension, or have service units that are further or less advanced than others. What determines a firm's overall stage is where the balance falls along these different dimensions—where, in a sense, the firm's center of gravity lies. Second, a firm can be very competitive (Stage III or even Stage IV) even if it is not outstanding on all dimensions. This could happen when it is doing an exceptional job on its critical success factors. Third, it is difficult or impossible to skip a stage in moving up the ladder. A company obviously must achieve journeyman performance before distinctive competence, and distinctive competence before becoming world class. (It is, however, possible to move through the stages relatively rapidly. For example, Scandinavian Airlines System [SAS] instituted some 120 service improvements that moved it from Stage I to Stage III within the space of a year and a half.) Finally, it is all too easy to slip back a stage. The Los Angeles Police Department (LAPD), for example, was viewed as being equivalent to a Stage III law enforcement organization before the Rodney King beating was made public.[7]

2.8 CONCLUSION

Competitiveness and the various operations strategies through which it is achieved are the underlying themes throughout the study of operations management. Decisions made at the operations strategy level impact all of the other management decisions within the operations management area. With global competition becoming more intense in the foreseeable future, companies, in order to succeed, must adopt the operations strategy that best meets the needs of its customers. Chapter 4 discusses the product development and process analysis as they relate to strategy in a manufacturing company. Chapter 5 addresses these issues from a service perspective.

2.9 REVIEW AND DISCUSSION QUESTIONS

1. What is meant by competitiveness?
2. What are the four major categories of operations strategy? How has their relationship to each other changed over the years?
3. For each of the different strategies, describe the unique characteristics of the market niche with which it is most compatible.
4. During 1988, the dollar showed relative weakness with respect to foreign currencies, such as the yen, mark, and pound. This stimulated exports. Why would long-term reliance on a lower-valued dollar be at best a short-term solution to the competitiveness problem?
5. The MIT Commission on Industrial Productivity identified "preoccupation with short-term financial results" as one of five recurring weaknesses leading to the decline in competitiveness of U.S. industry. If you assume that every U.S. firm's existence is dependent on its financial survival, would the MIT Commission's conclusion lead to the demise of American industry?
6. You are the president of a computer chip manufacturing firm and your firm's market share is being threatened by overseas manufacturers operating at lower cost with higher-quality products. Your manufacturing plant is operating at Stage 1 as defined by the Wheelwright-Hayes model in Exhibit 2.4. Would you change the stage that manufacturing operates in? If so, which organizational and strategic changes would be needed to support your decision?
7. In your opinion, do business schools have competitive priorities?
8. Contrast the two four-stage models of manufacturing and services. What parallels and differences do you see relative to the role of operations in the two models?
9. Why does the "proper" operations strategy keep changing for companies that are world-class competitors?
10. What is meant by the expression "manufacturing is entering the information age?"

[7] One of the authors of this book had the unique experience of lecturing on service quality to 100 of the LAPD's senior staff, including the chief, during the height of the King controversy.

2.10 SELECTED BIBLIOGRAPHY

Cohen, Stephen S., and John Zysman. *Why Manufacturing Matters: The Myth of the Post-Industrial Society*. New York: Basic Books, 1987.

Giffy, C.; A. V. Roth; and G. M. Seal. *Competing in World-Class Manufacturing*. National Center for Manufacturing Sciences. Homewood, Ill.: Business One Irwin, 1990.

Gwynn, S. C. "The Long Haul." *Time,* September 28, 1992.

Hayes, Robert H.; Steven Wheelwright; and Kim B. Clark. *Dynamic Manufacturing: Creating the Learning Organization*. New York: Free Press, 1988.

Hart, Christopher W. L. "The Power of Unconditional Service Guarantees." *Harvard Business Review* 66, no. 4 (July–August 1988), pp. 56–62.

Kim, Jay S., and Jeffrey G. Miller. *Building the Value Factory: A Progress Report for U.S. Manufacturing*. Boston University Manufacturing Roundtable, 1992.

Moffatt, Susan. "Japan's New Personalized Production." *Fortune,* October 22, 1990.

Skinner, C. Wickham, "Manufacturing—The Missing Link in Corporate Strategy." *Harvard Business Review* 47, no. 3, (May–June 1969), pp. 136–45.

———. "The Focused Factory." *Harvard Business Review* 52, no. 3 (May–June 1974), pp. 113–22.

———. *Manufacturing: The Formidable Competitive Weapon*. New York: John Wiley and Sons, 1985.

Stalk, George, Jr. "Time—The Next Source of Competitive Advantage." *Harvard Business Review,* July–August 1988.

Starr, Martin K. "Global Production and Operations Strategy." *Columbia Journal of World Business* 19, no. 4 (Winter 1984), pp. 17–32.

———. *Global Competitiveness: Getting the U.S. Back on Track*. New York: W. W. Norton and Co., 1988.

Swaim, Jeffery C., and D. Scott Sink. "Current Developments in Firm or Corporate Level Productivity Measurements and Evaluation." *Issues in White Collar Productivity*. Atlanta, Ga.: Institute of Industrial Engineering, 1984, pp. 8–17.

Wheelwright, Steven C., and Robert H. Hayes. "Competing through Manufacturing." *Harvard Business Review,* January–February 1985.

Chapter 3

Measures of Performance and Benchmarking

EPIGRAPH

If you can't measure it, you can't manage it.

Peter Drucker

CHAPTER OUTLINE

KEY TERMS

Productivity

Capacity

Capacity Utilization

Agile Manufacturing

Flexibility

Process Velocity

Benchmarking

Without proper measures of performance, managers would be unable to determine how well their organizations are doing or how they compare with the performance of their competitors. They would be like a ship's captain, adrift on the ocean with no land in sight, and without a compass or other navigational instruments to guide them. With a myriad of performance measures available, managers must be selective in identifying and adopting only those that are most critical to their firms' success.

This chapter presents several commonly accepted measures of performance which are widely used across various industries in both manufacturing and services. However, for specific industries and segments within those industries, there may exist additional, highly specialized measures of performance which are more appropriate.

3.1 THE NEED TO MEASURE PERFORMANCE

A key factor in the success of every organization is the ability to measure its performance. Feedback on performance permits management to determine whether or not the established standards or goals are being met. If they are not, management can then make the necessary adjustments to improve performance.

There are many varieties of performance measures. Depending on the specific industry and market niche within that industry, some measures of performance are more critical than others. For example, in a fast food outlet, a key performance measure is the speed with which food is delivered to the customer. In an upscale restaurant, however, key performance indicators may be the variety of the menu items and the quality of food served.

Today we are in the information age, and management, as is everyone else, is inundated with reams of reports containing data on all aspects of a company's performance. It is, therefore, essential for management to identify those key performance indicators that best reflect the performance of their companies and which can identify where they should focus their efforts.

The increased recognition in measuring key performance factors has been attributed, in part, to the notion of benchmarking, which is discussed later in this chapter.

3.2 TYPES OF PERFORMANCE MEASURES

Productivity

Productivity is a measure of how well we convert the inputs of our transformation process into outputs. In its broadest sense, productivity is therefore defined as:

$$\text{Productivity} = \frac{\text{Outputs}}{\text{Inputs}}$$

To increase productivity, we want to make this ratio of outputs to inputs as large as practical.

EXHIBIT 3.1

Examples of Productivity Measures

Partial measure	$\frac{\text{Output}}{\text{Labor}}$ or $\frac{\text{Output}}{\text{Capital}}$ or $\frac{\text{Output}}{\text{Materials}}$ or $\frac{\text{Output}}{\text{Energy}}$
Multifactor measure	$\frac{\text{Output}}{\text{Labor + Capital + Energy}}$ or $\frac{\text{Output}}{\text{Labor + Capital + Materials}}$
Total measure	$\frac{\text{Output}}{\text{Inputs}}$ or $\frac{\text{Goods and services produced}}{\text{All resources used}}$

Source: David J. Sumanth and Kitty Tang, "A Review of Some Approaches to the Management of Total Productivity in a Company/Organization," *Institute of Industrial Engineering Conference Proceedings,* Fall 1984, p. 305. Copyright Institute of Industrial Engineers, 25 Technology Park/Atlanta, Norcross, Georgia 30092.

As presented in Exhibit 3.1, productivity may be expressed as partial measures, multifactor measures, or total measures. If we are concerned with the ratio of output to a single input, we have a *partial productivity measure.* If we want to look at the ratio of output to a group of inputs, but not all inputs, we have a *multifactor productivity measure.* If we want to express the ratio of all outputs to all inputs, we have a *total measure of productivity* that might be used to describe the productivity of an entire organization, or even a nation.

A numerical example of productivity is presented in Exhibit 3.2. The data reflects quantitative measures of input and output (in dollars) associated with the production of a certain product. Notice that for the multifactor and partial measures it is not necessary to

EXHIBIT 3.2

Numerical Example of Productivity Measures

Input and Output Production Data $	
Output	
1. Finished units	10,000
2. Work in process	2,500
3. Dividends	1,000
4. Bonds	
5. Other income	
Total output	13,500
Input	
1. Human	3,000
2. Material	153
3. Capital	10,000
4. Energy	540
5. Other expense	1,500
Total input	15,193

Productivity Measure Examples

Total measure:

$$\frac{\text{Total output}}{\text{Total input}} = \frac{13{,}500}{15{,}193} = .89$$

Multifactor measures:

$$\frac{\text{Total output}}{\text{Human + Material}} = \frac{13{,}500}{3{,}153} = 4.28$$

$$\frac{\text{Finished units}}{\text{Human + Material}} = \frac{10{,}000}{3{,}153} = 3.17$$

Partial measures:

$$\frac{\text{Total output}}{\text{Energy}} = \frac{13{,}500}{540} = 25$$

$$\frac{\text{Finished units}}{\text{Energy}} = \frac{10{,}000}{540} = 18.52$$

EXHIBIT 3.3

Partial Measures of Productivity

Business	Productivity Measure
Restaurant	Customers (meals)/labor hour
Retail store	Sales/square foot
Chicken farm	lb of meat/lb of feed
Utility plant	Kilowatts/ton of coal
Paper mill	Tons of paper/cord of wood

use total output as the numerator. Often it is desirable to create measures that represent productivity as it relates to some particular output of interest. For example, total units might be the output of interest to a production control manager whereas total output may be of key interest to the plant manager. This process of aggregation and disaggregation of productivity measures provides a means of shifting the level of analysis to suit a variety of productivity measurement and improvement needs.

As noted in Exhibit 3.2, all the figures are in dollars. Often, however, management can better understand how the company is performing when other measures are used. In these cases, only partial measures of productivity can be used, as we cannot combine dissimilar units such as labor hours and pounds of material. Some commonly used partial measures of productivity are presented as examples in Exhibit 3.3. Such partial measures of productivity give the manager information in familiar units, allowing the manager to more easily relate these measures to the actual operations.

Productivity is what we call a *relative measure*. In other words, to be meaningful, it needs to be compared with something else. For example, what can we learn from the fact that we operate a restaurant, and that its productivity last week was 8.4 customers/labor hour? (Nothing!)

Productivity comparisons can be made in two ways. First, a company can compare itself with similar operations within its industry, or can use industry data when it is available (e.g., comparing productivity among the different stores in a franchise).

Another approach is to measure productivity over time within the same operation. Here we would compare our productivity in one time period with that of the next.

As stated above, a primary reason for tracking productivity is to assess relative productivity growth or decline, an indicator of competitive position. Exhibit 3.4A shows the productivity growth rate for the United States, West Germany, and Japan from 1950 through 1989. This disturbing picture is mirrored by Exhibit 3.4B, which displays the share of world exports of these three nations. As national productivity increases, a nation is able to provide higher-quality products at lower prices than those provided by less productive nations.

The decline in export share for the United States has begun to reverse in recent years due in part to quality and productivity efforts and to a weaker dollar. Again, accepting that such factors as currency trade rates are out of the control of operations managers, the focus remains on the improvement of operations.

EXHIBIT 3.4 **National Productivity Growth and World Export Comparisons**

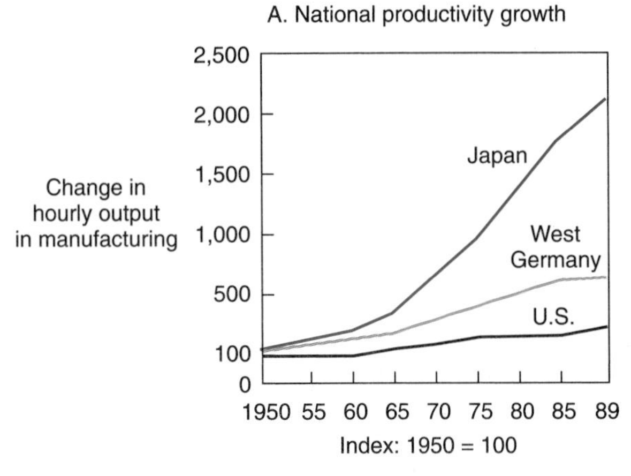

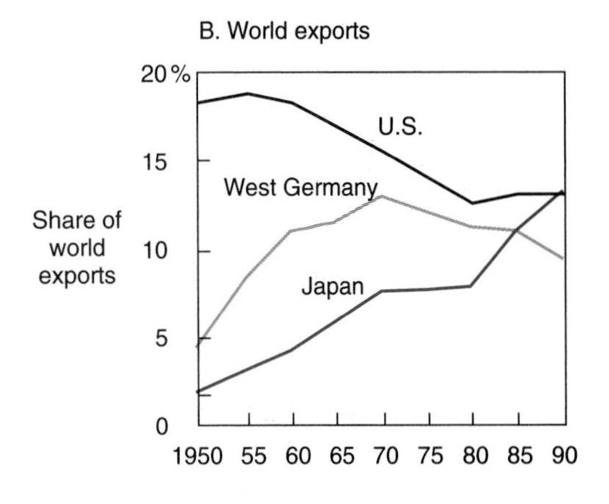

Source: *Fortune* Special Issue, Spring/Summer 1991.

Capacity

Capacity is a measure of the output capability of a process. This performance measure is typically presented in units of output per unit of time, although, as we shall see later in the section, this is not always appropriate. Examples of measures of capacity include:

Operation	Measure of Capacity
Steel plant	Tons of steel per year
Brewery	Barrels of beer per year
Auto plant	Automobiles per week
Restaurant	Customers per hour
Health clinic	Patients per day

As noted by the examples, measures of capacity exist for both manufacturing and services. The major difference between manufacturing and services, in terms of measuring capacity, is that service measures of capacity usually include the customer, since the customer is typically an integral part of the process.

Design capacity is defined as the ideal output rate at which a firm would like to produce under normal circumstances and for which the system was designed. Depending on the product or process and goals of the company, design capacity could even be predicated on a five-day-a-week, single-shift operation. *Maximum capacity* is used to define the maximum output rate that could be achieved when productive resources are used to their maximum. Typically, most firms can operate effectively at maximum capacity for only short periods of time. Operating at maximum capacity, for example, results in higher energy costs, the need for overtime wage premiums, and increased machine breakdowns due to the lack of time to conduct scheduled preventive maintenance.

The degree to which a firm utilizes its productive capacity is referred to as **capacity utilization,** which is defined as follows:

$$\text{Capacity utilization} = \frac{\text{Actual output}}{\text{Design capacity}}$$

For example, if an automobile assembly plant had a design capacity of 3,600 cars per week, and actually produced only 2,700 cars in one week, then its capacity utilization for that week would be:

$$\text{Capacity utilization} = \frac{2{,}700}{3{,}600} = 75\%$$

With this definition of capacity utilization, it is possible to have utilization rates that are in excess of 100 percent, which should be a warning to management that excessive production costs are being incurred.

So far, we have measured capacity in terms of units of output per unit of time, which is appropriate as long as the output is relatively homogeneous (e.g., cars, stereos, etc.). However, when the output units are highly variable, especially in terms of process requirements, a more meaningful measure of capacity is often expressed in terms of one of the inputs. Consider, for example, a flexible machining center that can make parts that take anywhere from five minutes to two hours to produce. The capacity of the center, in terms of units produced per week, could vary significantly, depending on which particular units were being produced. In this case, a better measure of capacity utilization would be:

$$\text{Capacity utilization} = \frac{\text{Actual machine hours used}}{\text{Total machine hours available}}$$

Such measures of capacity utilization will, therefore, become more popular as the flexibility of processes increases to permit wider varieties of products to be made. This approach to measuring capacity utilization is also more applicable to many service operations that have a very high labor content and also require that labor to perform a wide variety of tasks. Examples here include medical doctors, whose tasks can vary from performing surgical operations to having office visits and attending required meetings. College professors provide another good example. In addition to teaching students, they are also required to conduct research and be of service to the college and the community. In both these instances, capacity as measured in terms of available hours per week is clearly the appropriate measure.

Quality

The quality of a process is usually measured by the defect rate of the products produced. Defects include those products that are identified as nonconforming, both internally (prior to shipping the product to the customer) as well as externally (i.e., products whose defects are found by the customer). The topic of process quality measurement and control, in terms of defects, is presented in greater detail in Chapter 6.

Courtesy Brunswick Corporation

In a measurement of performance, a stern-drive boat engine manufactured by the Mercury Marine Division of Brunswick Corporation receives a final in-water quality test.

There are additional measures of a process's overall quality. With increasing awareness and concern for the environment, for example, the amount of toxic waste generated is also a measure of a process's quality. The amount of scrap and waste material produced is another process quality indicator.

Speed of Delivery

Many companies are experiencing increased pressure with respect to speed of delivery. Firms that once took weeks and months to deliver a product are now doing so in hours and days. As George Stalk, Jr., has pointed out, there is high correlation between increased profits and growth in market share and a company's ability to deliver products quickly to the customer.[1]

Speed of delivery has two dimensions to measure. The first is the amount of time between when the product is ordered to when it is shipped to the customer, which is known as a product's *lead time.* Companies that produce standard products eliminate lead times by producing products for finished goods inventory. This is referred to as a *make-to-stock system.* Under this system, orders are immediately filled from existing inventories,

[1] George Stalk, Jr., "Time—The Next Source of Competitive Advantage," *Harvard Business Review,* July–August 1988.

thereby eliminating any lead times. Companies that produce customized products, however, do not have the luxury of a finished goods inventory. These firms have what we call a *make-to-order system,* requiring a lead time before the finished product can be shipped.

The other dimension in measuring speed of delivery is the variability in the delivery time. In many cases, this dimension is more critical than the estimated lead time itself. In other words, customers, be they other companies or end users, do not like uncertainty. Uncertainty affects work scheduling, capacity utilization, etc., which negatively affects the overall efficiency of the process. Thus, the less variability in delivery times, the better.

Flexibility

Currently, the competitive advantage for many companies lies in their ability to produce customized products to meet individual customer needs. The capability of a company to provide such customized products in a timely manner is often referred to as **agile manufacturing. Flexibility** is the measure of how well the company's transformation process meets these performance requirements.

There are three dimensions of flexibility. The first type of flexibility indicates how quickly a process can convert from producing one product or family of product(s) to another. For example, many U.S. automobile assembly plants still require a minimum of several weeks shutdown annually in order to convert from one model year to the next, indicating a degree of inflexibility in this area.

Another measure of a process's flexibility is its ability to react to changes in volume. Those processes that can accommodate large fluctuations in volume are said to be more flexible than those that cannot. Most service operations are very flexible on this dimension, because of their inability to inventory demand. (For example, customers wanting to eat at a restaurant on Saturday night will not wait until Monday morning.) Thus, service operations such as retail stores, restaurants, and health clinics can adjust to meet the demand from only a few customers per hour to several hundred customers per hour. The typical assembly line operation in a manufacturing facility similarly cannot adjust. The volume of output from an assembly line is fixed, and consequently companies with this type of process must resort to other means of balancing supply and demand. For example, appliance makers and automobile companies offer discounts and low-cost financing to encourage consumer buying during low periods of demand, due in part to their inability to adjust the outputs of their manufacturing facilities without shutting them down entirely.

The third dimension of flexibility is the ability of the process to produce more than one product simultaneously. Thus, the more products that a process can produce at a time, the more flexible it is said to be.

Process Velocity

Process velocity is a relatively new measure of performance. Also known as *manufacturing velocity,* process velocity is the ratio of actual throughput time that it takes for a product to go through the process divided by the value-added time required to complete the product or service.

For example, if the throughput time for a product is six weeks, and the actual value-added time to complete the product is four hours, then the process velocity of this product is:

$$\text{Process velocity} = \frac{\text{Total throughput time}}{\text{Value-added time}}$$

$$\text{Process velocity} = \frac{6 \text{ weeks} \times 5 \text{ days per week} \times 8 \text{ hours per day}}{4 \text{ hours}} = 60$$

A process velocity of 60, in this case, means that it takes 60 times as long to complete the product as it does to do the actual work on the product itself.

Process velocities in excess of 100 are not uncommon. For example, University Microfilms, Inc. (UMI), the largest publisher of dissertations in the United States, took 150 days to process a manuscript, although only two hours were actually spent on the manuscript itself, adding value. For UMI, the process velocity for a manuscript was therefore:

$$\text{Process velocity} = \frac{150 \text{ days per manuscript} \times 8 \text{ hours per day}}{2 \text{ hours}} = 600$$

UMI was able to reduce the throughput time to 60 days, thereby lowering its process velocity to 240.

As noted by the example above, the concept of process velocity is equally applicable to manufacturing and services. Process velocity can also be applied to any particular segment of the process, or to the overall process. For example, a firm may want to focus only on its manufacturing velocity, in which case it would look at the throughput time from when the product is first begun to when it is completed and ready to ship. A broader perspective may measure process velocity from the time when the customer first places the order for the product to when payment is finally received and the check has cleared.

In the past, especially in the United States, companies have focused solely on increasing the efficiency of the value-added time, which often constitutes only a very small portion of a product's overall time in the process.

3.3 BENCHMARKING[2]

Benchmarking is simply a comparison of a company's performance in certain areas with the performance of other firms in its industry and/or with those firms that are identified to be world-class competitors in specific functions and operations. Benchmarking can cut across traditional industry lines, providing opportunities for new and innovative ways to increase performance. For example, Xerox, in its desire to deliver products quickly,

[2] This section is adapted from Robert C. Camp, *Benchmarking: The Search for Industry Best Practices That Lead to Superior Performance,* Milwaukee, Wisc.: ASQC Quality Press, 1989.

studied how L. L. Bean of Freeport, Maine, a mail order company well-known for fast accurate service, accomplished this.

Firms that want to compete as world-class organizations in the highly competitive global arena must attain "best of breed" status in those performance parameters that are critical for success in their respective industries and market segments. This can be accomplished only through measuring and comparing their performance with that of others, and then instituting the necessary actions for improvement. Companies like AT&T, Du Pont, Ford Motor, IBM, Eastman Kodak, Milliken, Motorola, Xerox, and other industry leaders, in an attempt to increase both quality and productivity now use benchmarking as a standard management tool.

Benchmarking Defined

David T. Kearns, CEO of Xerox Corporation, defines benchmarking as follows:

> Benchmarking is the continuous process of measuring products, services, and practices against the toughest competitors or those companies recognized as industry leaders.[3]

Several key elements in this definition should be emphasized. Continuous measuring implies that benchmarking is an iterative process with no end. With competition constantly "raising the bar," accepted levels of performance yesterday will not be tolerated by the customer tomorrow. Only through constant monitoring of our performance and that of our competitors will we be able to know where we stand at any point in time.

Benchmarking means measurement. This can be accomplished internally within the organization as well as externally with competitors and world-class firms. It is important for management to be cognizant that benchmarking is not limited only to manufacturing, but can also be applied to all of the functional areas in an organization. This means that it can be used for products, services, and processes/practices.

Benchmarking should not be limited only to direct competitors. Rather it should focus on those firms or business functions or operations within firms that have achieved recognition as world-class operations. In other words, "benchmarking is the search for best practices that leads to superior performance."

Key Steps in Benchmarking

Robert Camp, based on his experience with Xerox Corporation, has identified five phases that are necessary for successfully implementing benchmarking within an organization. These phases are planning, analysis, integration, action, and maturity.

---

[3] Robert C. Camp, *Benchmarking: The Search for Industry Best Practices That Lead to Superior Performance,* p. 10.

Planning. This phase of benchmarking identifies the areas that we should benchmark, the specific organizations against which we should be benchmarking, the type of data we should collect, and the ways we should collect that data.

Analysis. The analysis phase focuses on obtaining an in-depth understanding of our firm's existing practices and processes as well as those of the organizations against which we will be benchmarking.

Integration. Here we use the findings from the first two phases to define those target areas that we want to change. As part of this phase, we need to ensure that benchmarking concepts are implemented in the corporate planning process, and that benchmarking is accepted by all levels of management.

Action. The benchmarking findings and associated goals must be translated into action. Those individuals who actually perform the tasks should determine how the findings can best be incorporated into the existing process.

Maturity. An organization reaches maturity when the best business practices that have been identified have been incorporated into all of the relevant business processes, thereby ensuring superior performance for the organization as a whole.

These five phases and the various steps within each phase are summarized in Exhibit 3.5.

Types of Benchmarking

There are two general categories of benchmarking: functional benchmarking and generic benchmarking.

Functional benchmarking addresses performance comparisons with the best functional areas, regardless of the industry in which they are located. The benefits to this are several. First, a firm may have less difficulty in obtaining benchmarking partners in other industries which are not direct competitors. In addition, it is often easy to identify those firms that are considered to be the "best of breed" in performing a specific function. The L. L. Bean example presented at the beginning of this section provides a good example of functional benchmarking. Other examples of leaders in specific functional areas include General Electric (information systems), John Deere (service parts logistics) and Ford (assembly automation).

Generic benchmarking is concerned with specific processes that are virtually the same for all industries that use these processes. Generic benchmarking can easily identify the "best of the best" practices, and since the process is virtually the same, provides targets that can be more readily acceptable by members of the organization. Examples of leaders in generic benchmarking include the Federal Reserve Bank (bill scanning) and Citicorp (document processing).

EXHIBIT 3.5

Benchmarking Process Steps

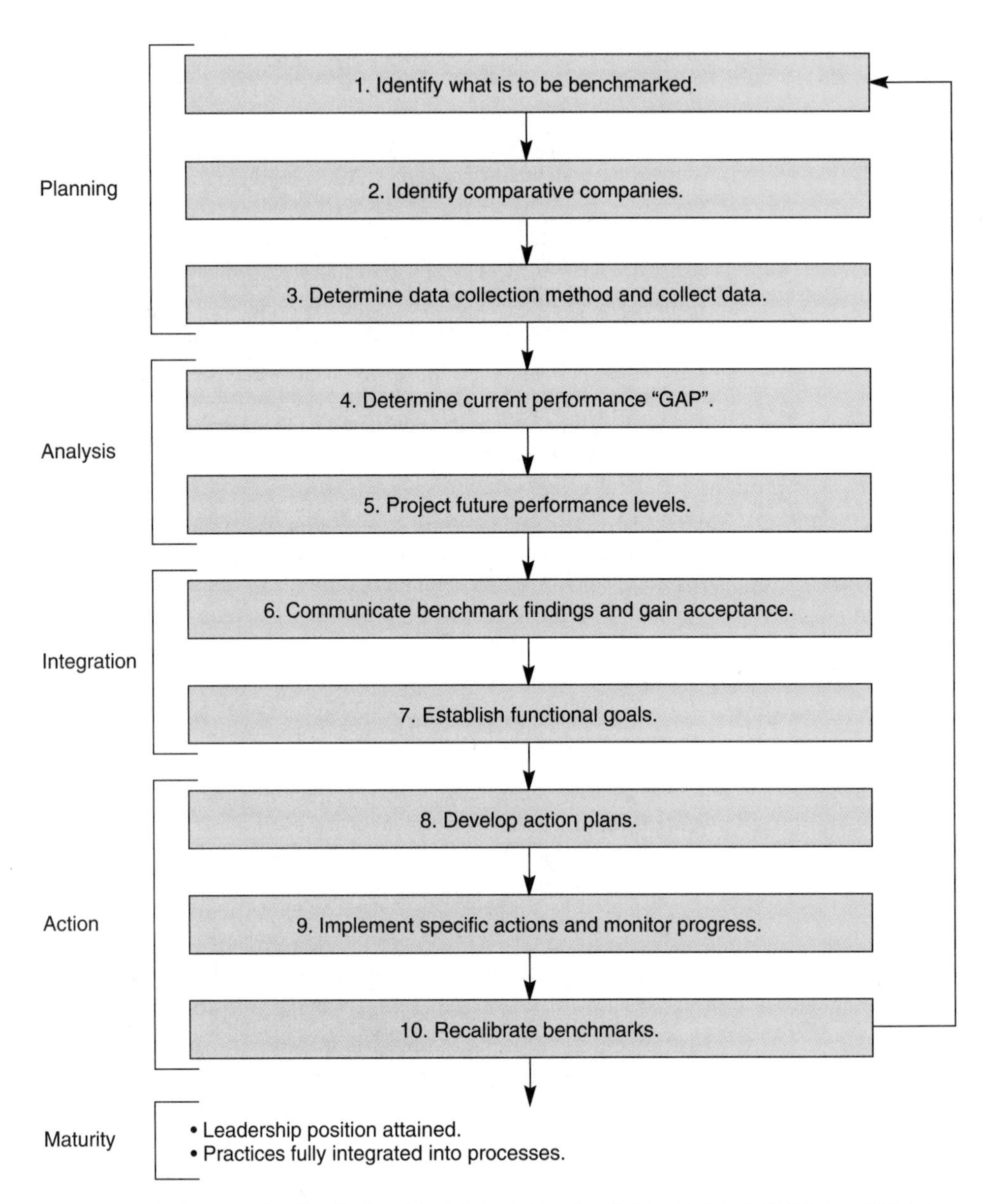

Source: Robert C. Camp, *Benchmarking: The Search for Industry Best Practices That Lead to Superior Performance,* Milwaukee, Wisc.: ASQC Quality Press, 1989.

3.4 CONCLUSION

No matter where we work or what we do, be it in manufacturing or services, we need to measure the performance of our organization in order to know where we are and where we should be in comparison to our competition. Performance measures come in various shapes and sizes. It is therefore essential for the manager to identify those performance measures that best provide him/her with the proper information that will allow intelligent and effective decision making.

To be most meaningful, performance measures should be compared with something. Traditionally these comparisons have been within an organization, looking at trends over a period of time. Other comparisons were done with industry data that was readily available.

More recently, however, companies have begun looking outside their industries in order to find those firms that have the best practices in a particular functional area or in a specific type of process. This policy of seeking out the best of the best is referred to as benchmarking.

Proper performance measurement and benchmarking are critical elements for those firms that want to compete successfully in the global marketplace. In such a fiercely competitive environment, where the rules are constantly changing and the standards are constantly being raised, only those firms that are cognizant of both their capabilities and those of their competitors will survive.

3.5 REVIEW AND DISCUSSION QUESTIONS

1. Why are performance measures important?
2. What are the different types of performance measures? Give examples of each for specific industries.
3. What is productivity? Explain partial, multi-factor, and total factor productivity.
4. What do we mean when we say productivity is a "relative" measure?
5. What are the typical performance measures for quality, speed of delivery, and flexibility?
6. What should the criteria be for management to adopt a particular performance measure?
7. What is benchmarking? Why is it important for firms that want to compete globally to adopt benchmarking?
8. What is the difference between functional benchmarking and generic benchmarking?

3.6 SOLVED PROBLEM

PROBLEM

1. A furniture manufacturing company has provided the following data. Compare the labor, raw materials and supplies, and total productivity of 1990 and 1993.

		1990	1993
Output:	Sales value of production	$22,000	$35,000
Input:	Labor	10,000	15,000
	Raw materials and supplies	8,000	12,500
	Capital equipment depreciation	700	1,200
	Other	2,200	4,800

SOLUTION

	1990	1993
Partial productivities		
Labor	2.20	2.33
Raw materials and supplies	2.75	2.80
Total productivity	1.05	1.04

3.7 PROBLEMS

1. Two types of cars, *X* and *Y*, were produced by a car manufacturer in 1994. Quantities sold, price per unit, and labor hours follow. What is the labor productivity for each car? Explain the problem(s) associated with the labor productivity.

	Quantity	$/Unit
X Car	4,000 units sold	$8,000/car
Y Car	6,000 units sold	$9,500/car
Labor, *X*	20,000 hours	$12/hour
Labor, *Y*	30,000 hours	$14/hour

2. Exhibit 3.2 illustrates various productivity measures. Calculate human and capital partial and multifactor productivity measures for output measured as work in process plus finished unit.
3. A U.S. manufacturing company operating a subsidiary in an LDC (less developed country) shows the following results:

	U.S.	LDC
Sales (units)	100,000	20,000
Labor (hours)	20,000	15,000
Raw materials (currency)	$ 20,000	FC 20,000
Capital equipment (hours)	60,000	5,000

a. Calculate partial labor and capital productivity figures for the parent and subsidiary. Do the results seem misleading?

b. Now compute multi-factor labor and capital productivity figures. Are the results better?

c. Finally, calculate raw material productivity figures (units/$ where $1 = FC 10). Explain why these figures might be greater in the subsidiary.

3.8 SELECTED BIBLIOGRAPHY

Bernstein, A. "Quality is Becoming Job One in the Office, Too." *Business Week,* April 29, 1991.

Camp, Robert C. *Benchmarking: The Search for Industry Best Practices That Lead to Superior Performance.* Milwaukee, Wisc.: American Society for Quality Control, Quality Press, 1989.

Main, Jeremy. "How to Steal the Best Ideas Around." *Fortune* October 19, 1992.

Port, Otis, and Geoffrey Smith. "Beg, Borrow and Benchmark." *Business Week,* November 30, 1992.

Productivity Perspectives. Houston, Tex.: American Productivity Center, January 1985.

Stalk, George, Jr. "Time—The Next Source of Competitive Advantage." *Harvard Business Review,* July–August 1988.

Swaim, Jeffery C., and D. Scott Sink. "Current Developments in Firm or Corporate Level Productivity Measurements and Evaluation." *Issues in White Collar Productivity.* Atlanta, Ga.: Institute of Industrial Engineering, 1984, pp. 8–17.

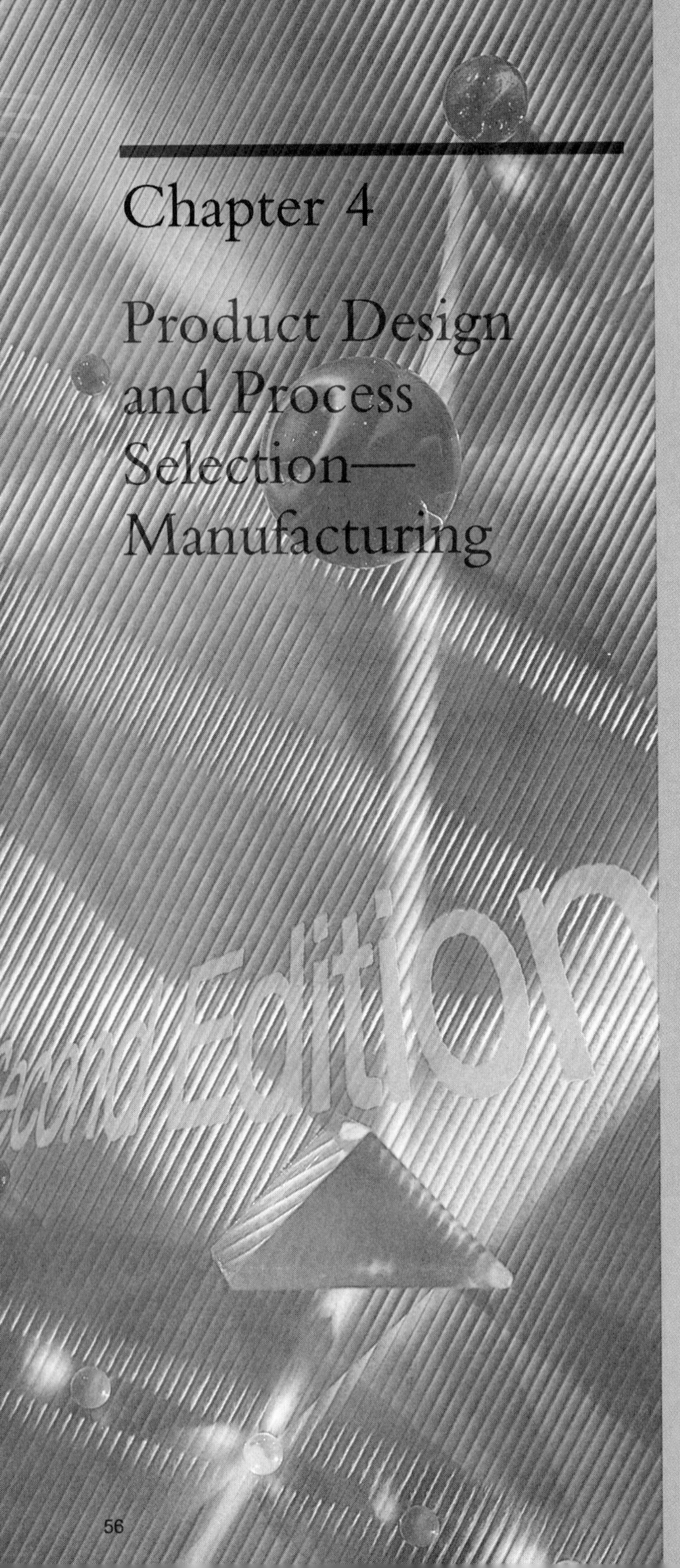

Chapter 4

Product Design and Process Selection—Manufacturing

EPIGRAPH

The following poem is credited to Mr. Kenneth Lane, a design engineer at General Electric Company:

As Some Men See Us

The Designer bent across his board
Wonderful things in his head were stored
And he said as he rubbed his throbbing bean
"How can I make this thing tough to machine?
If this part here were only straight
I'm sure the thing would work first rate,
But 'twould be so easy to turn and bore
It never would make the machinists sore.
I better put in a right angle there
Then watch those babies tear their hair
Now I'll put the holes that hold the cap
Way down in here where they're hard to tap.
Now this piece won't work, I'll bet a buck
For it can't be held in a shoe or chuck
It can't be drilled or it can't be ground
In fact the design is exceedingly sound."
He looked again and cried—"At last—
Success is mine, it can't even be cast."

We rediscovered this gem cited in Elwood S. Buffa, *Modern Production Management* (New York: John Wiley and Sons, 1961), p. 343, originally from J. P. Hahir, "A Case Study in the Relationship between Design Engineering and Production Engineering," *Proceedings, 5th Annual Industrial Engineering Institute,* University of California, Berkeley–Los Angeles, 1953.

CHAPTER OUTLINE

KEY TERMS

Industrial Design
Product Specifications
Project Processes
Intermittent Processes
Line-Flow Processes
Break-Even Analysis
Machining Centers
Numerically Controlled (NC) Machines
Industrial Robots
Computer-Aided Design and Manufacturing (CAD/CAM)
Flexible Manufacturing System (FMS)
Computer-Integrated Manufacturing (CIM)
Islands of Automation
Process Flow Design
Manufacturing Cycles

In today's fiercely competitive environment, no company can rest on the successful introduction of any one new product. Product life cycles are growing increasingly shorter, and the more successful firms are reducing new product development times to a fraction of what they once were. Consequently, competition has the ability to react more quickly to changes in the marketplace, thereby substantially reducing the advantages of any one new product introduction, regardless of how innovative it is. As noted in the previous chapter, George Stalk, Jr., pointed out that the speed with which a company can introduce a new product can, therefore, significantly affect both its profit margins and market share.[1]

With the trend toward shorter product life cycles, the successful manufacturer must consistently be able to: (1) generate new product ideas; (2) convert these ideas into good, functional designs that are user-friendly; (3) ensure that these designs are readily manufacturable; and (4) select the appropriate production process that is most compatible with the market's requirements. In addition, all of this must be accomplished in an increasingly shorter time frame.

This chapter addresses some of the basic issues in product design and manufacturability, and the factors associated in selecting the proper production process. We include here a discussion of the product/process relationship and some of the features associated with automated processes such as computer-aided design and computer-aided manufacturing (CAD/CAM) and flexible manufacturing systems (FMS).

4.1 PRODUCT DESIGN AND DEVELOPMENT SEQUENCE

A recent review of successful product designs, ranging from razors and lap-top computers to power tools and outdoor grills, identified several factors that these products and their manufacturers shared, including:

- *Design from the outside in:* Make the customer's use of the product the focus of all product development.
- *Partner deeply:* Involve all of the relevant functional areas (e.g., marketing, engineering, purchasing, and manufacturing) early in the design process to assist in defining the new product.
- *Partner widely:* With the emergence of the virtual enterprise, organizational boundaries are becoming unclear. Designers must therefore partner with all stakeholders—both internal and external.
- *Design the product upfront:* Match the right product for the right market niche. Upfront design analysis will eliminate faulty concepts early.
- *Get physical fast:* Use prototypes to visualize a concept and to obtain quick feedback from both users and managers.
- *Design for manufacturability:* Always design a product that will meet established quality, cost, and delivery parameters. Manufacturing issues are as important to success as ergonomics, aesthetics, and function.

[1]George Stalk, Jr., "Time—The Next Source of Competitive Advantages," *Harvard Business Review,* July–August 1988.

- *Surprise the user:* Always build something extra into the product that will unexpectedly delight the customer. This creates customer loyalty and increases the chances of having a truly "hot" product.[2]

The three phases to designing a product are the functional (or breadboard) design, industrial (aesthetics and user-oriented design), and design for manufacturability (cost, materials, process choices, etc.).

Functional Design

The use of the term *breadboard* as slang for *functional design* most likely originated in the electronics field when electronic components were assembled and connected to terminals attached to flat boards. These were reminiscent of boards used by grandmothers and great-grandmothers in making bread. The major intent of a functional design is to develop a functional working model of the product, without regard for what it will finally look like.

Industrial Design

Designing for aesthetics and for the end user is generally termed **industrial design.** Industrial design is probably the area most abused by manufacturers. When frustrated with products—setting the VCR, working on the car, or operating a credit card telephone at the airport—most of us have said to ourselves, "The blankety blank person who designed this should be made to work on it!" Often, parts are inaccessible, operation is overly complicated, and/or there is no logic to setting or controlling the unit. Sometimes even worse conditions exist: metal edges are sharp and consumers cut their hands trying to reach in to make adjustments or repairs.

Many products on the market today have too many technological features—far more than necessary. The fact is that most purchasers of electronic products cannot fully operate them and consequently only use a small number of the available features. This proliferation of features has occurred because computer chips are inexpensive and adding more controls adds negligible cost. Including an alarm clock or a calculator on a microwave oven would be little added cost. But, do you, the consumer, really need it? What happens when you lose the operator's manual that explains how to operate these complex devices?

So many features have been added to VCRs and to VCR remote controls, for example, that they have been rendered not only unusable but also unreadable. But in reducing the complexity of design, the pendulum seems to have swung too far to oversimplified controls. On-screen programming has removed much of the confusion with remote controls.

One of the best-rated industrial designers is Harmut Esslinger of frogdesign studios (with a small *f*) in Menlo Park, California. Esslinger's studio has produced designs for General Electric Company, Eastman Kodak Company, 3M Company, Apple Computer, NeXt Computer, and Sony Corporation.

---

[2] B. Nussbaum, "Hot Products: Smart Design Is the Common Thread," *Business Week,* June 7, 1993.

EXHIBIT 4.1 Good and Bad Practice in the Design of Cross Sections to be Extruded

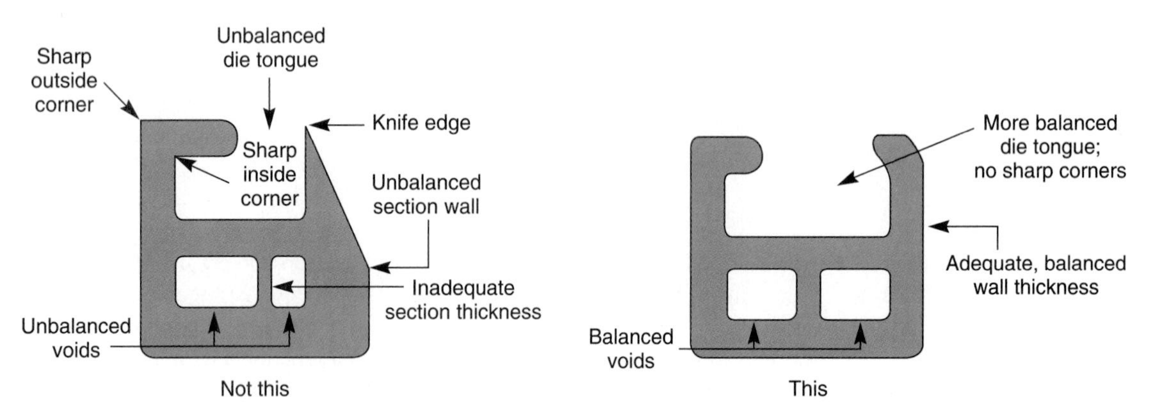

Source: James L. Bralla, ed. *Handbook of Product Design for Manufacturing* (New York: McGraw-Hill, 1986), pp. 3–10.

Design for Manufacturability

In translating the functional product design into a manufacturable product, designers must consider many aspects. They can use a variety of methods and alternative materials to make a product. Material choices can be ferrous (iron and steel), aluminum, copper, brass, magnesium, zinc, tin, nickel, titanium, or several other metals. The nonmetals include polymers (thermoplastics, thermosetting plastics, and elastomers), wood, leather, rubber, carbon, ceramics, glass, gypsum, concrete, as well as several others. Further, all of these materials can be formed, cut, and shaped in many ways. There are extrusions, stampings, rolling, powder-metal, forgings, castings, injection molding, along with a very large selection of machining processes.

In evaluating a product's design for manufacturability, the designers must follow certain rules, depending on the process selected. For example, Exhibit 4.1 shows two designs to be created through an extrusion process. In extrusion, which is similar to squeezing toothpaste from a tube, material is squeezed through a die and comes out of the other side in the desired shape. To make the squeezing easier, metals are usually heated. A good extrusion design avoids sharp points and sharp corners and contains a balance in the pattern. Examples of extrusions are metal screen door mouldings, window frames, and plastic picture frames.

In designing for manufacturability, it is also desirable to keep the number of individual parts to a minimum. In electronics, manufacturers accomplish this by combining circuits that have been in different components into larger and larger integrated circuits. Not only does this increase the speed within the circuits, because electrons don't have to travel as far, but it also reduces the physical size and increases reliability. Reliability is increased by eliminating the many connections necessary when the circuits were in separate parts. Exhibit 4.2 shows how to reduce a simple bracket from five parts to one by focusing on the purpose of the part, the fabrication, and the assembly procedure used for its manufacture.

EXHIBIT 4.2

Design Change to Reduce the Number of Parts in a Bracket

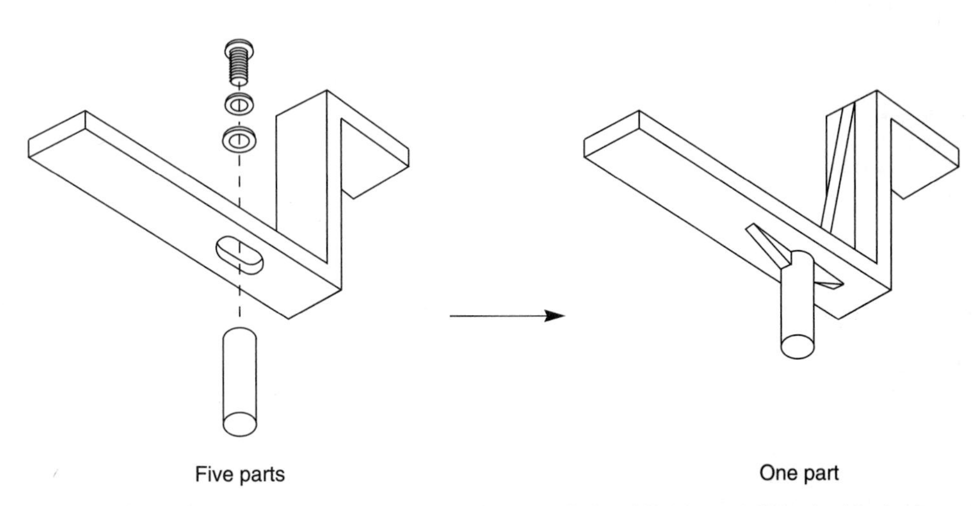

Bart Huthwaite. "Managing at the Starting Line: How to Design Competitive Products," Workshop at the University of Southern California–Los Angeles, January 14, 1991, p. 7.

The output of the product design activity is the **product's specifications.** These specifications provide the basis for production-related decisions such as the purchase of materials, selection of equipment, assignment of workers, and the size and layout of the production facility. Product specifications, while commonly thought of as blueprints or engineering drawings, often take other forms ranging from precise quantitative and qualitative statements to rather fluid guidelines. Physical products tend to have traditional blueprint specifications, while a service firm's design specifications tend to be more general.

While designing for manufacturability, we must still remember to design for the consumer. A basic rule in design is to:

> Be obvious. Design a product so that a user can look at it, understand it, and figure out how to use it—quickly, and without an instruction manual.

4.2 FREQUENCY OF DESIGN CHANGES

Should products be changed every year, twice a year, every two years? How often a firm changes design depends, in large part, on its marketing strategy. An example of very frequent design changes is Sony Corporation and its Walkman cassette player. (See Exhibit 4.3.)

Sony introduced its Walkman to the market in 1979. It was an immediate success. Two years later, Sony brought out a new model to keep ahead of its competitors. Since 1979, the rate of new Walkman products introduced by Sony has accelerated; Sony has brought out more than 160 models of the Walkman.

EXHIBIT 4.3

The Total Number of Different Walkman-Type Cassette Players Produced by Several Manufacturers

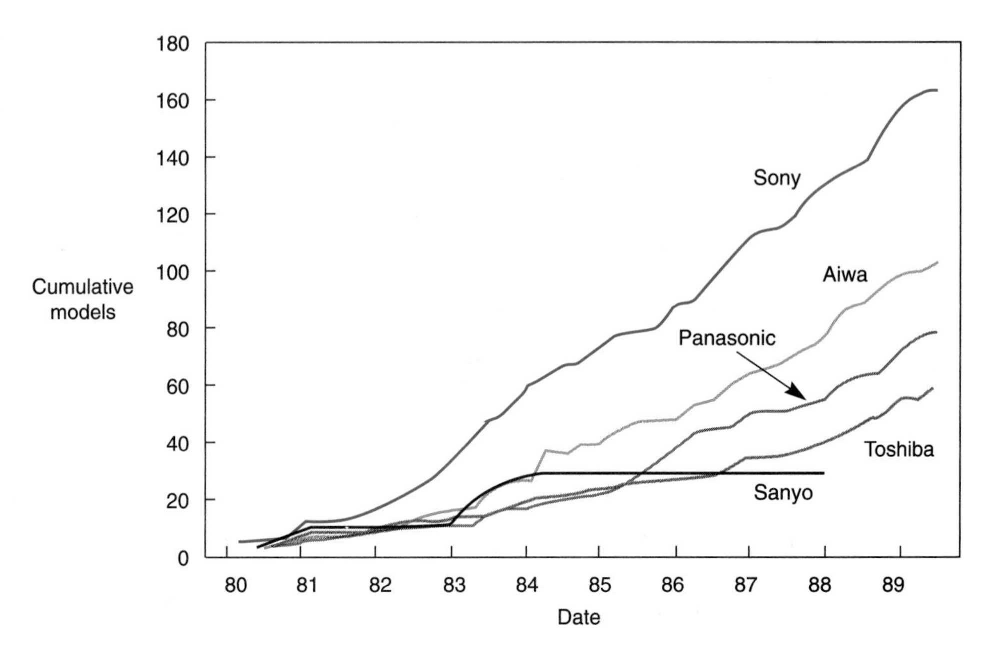

Source: Susan Walsh Sanderson and Vic Uzumeri, "Strategies for New Product Development and Renewal: Design-Based Incrementalism," Center for Science and Technology Policy, School of Management, Rensselaer Polytechnic Institute, Troy, NY 12180.

Sony has relied on "design-based incrementalism." That is, product families are upgraded and enhanced throughout their life cycles. Such changes are small, frequent, and both technological and topological. *Technological innovation* is introducing new technology that enhances the function, adds higher quality, or lower production cost (e.g., developing a new motor). *Topological design* is the rearrangement or remanufacture of well-understood components (e.g., making smaller parts, a more compact unit, easier functioning, more appealing, or creating product distinction, etc.). Due to its policy of incrementalization, Sony could bring out its "My First Sony" line for children in less than one year because it was built on existing products.

One of the main reasons attributed to the success of Japanese companies is their ability to quickly introduce new products to the market. Their speed of introduction is also compatible with their philosophy of "Ready, Fire, Aim." In the same time that a typical U.S. company takes to conduct extensive and time-consuming market analyses, their Japanese counterparts will launch several new products, letting the market itself determine what is good and what is not. The key in successfully implementing this strategy is the flexibility of the manufacturing function to easily convert production capacity from one product to another.

EXHIBIT 4.4

Costs Committed and Costs Expended from Product Concept to Production

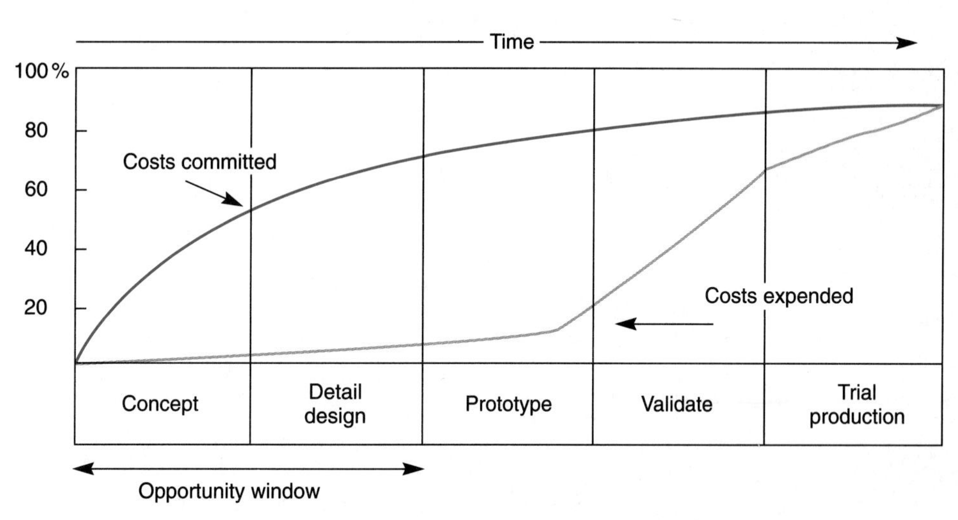

Source: Bart Huthwaite, "Managing at the Starting Line: How to Design Competitive Products," Workshop at the University/Southern California–Los Angeles, January 14, 1991, p. 3.

Opportunity for Product Design Change

Exhibit 4.4 shows the design-to-production phases. This cycle extends from concept through full production. Note that Concept and Design commit about 70 percent of the product's manufacturing costs while expending only about 5 percent of the total costs. (Committed costs are defined as the production costs directly resulting from the design, including materials, labor, processes, and so forth.) Often, manufacturers spend far too little time finding all the flaws during the design stage of a new product. Therefore, a more prudent approach might suggest expending a bit more to ensure a good, sound, user-friendly design and expecting to profit through reduced committed cost.

Concurrent Engineering

A major trend in manufacturing companies is early and continuing involvement with new products by production, materials planning, and engineering support groups to ensure that the products are effectively managed throughout their life cycles. At Hewlett-Packard, this responsibility is seen as carrying through product development, transition to manufacturing, volume production, and obsolescence.

Concurrent engineering can be used interchangeably with the terms *simultaneous engineering* or *concurrent design*. Obviously, as these terms imply, continual interaction and parallel actions are necessary throughout the entire process from initial product design through production. Other areas such as marketing and purchasing need to be involved and interact with the different phases of design and development. Their input is critical concerning production planning, productive capacity, and the availability of parts and materials. The sequence from product design to delivery to the marketplace is not a series of consecutive steps. Continual interaction throughout the process ensures that a well-designed product is released to the market at a good price and on time.

4.3 ORIGIN OF THE PRODUCT IDEA

Every new product starts with an idea. Exhibit 4.5 outlines the "formal" steps leading from the idea stage to actual production. While these steps are not clear-cut increments, nevertheless they do define a flow or a general sequence of phases involved in the process.

Typically, most American firms generate the majority of their product ideas by listening to their customers. In addition, many companies encourage their own employees to generate new product ideas and to contribute to the development of those currently being investigated. At Hewlett-Packard, for example, product design engineers leave whatever they are working on out on their desks so that others may come by and tinker with their projects.

Narrowing Down the Product Alternatives

The idea-gathering process often leads to more ideas than can be translated into producible products, so a screening procedure is instituted to eliminate those ideas that clearly are infeasible. In this screening process, some ideas are rejected because they do not meet the company's overall objectives or its marketing, operations, or financial criteria. Marketing criteria include competition, ability to cross sell, promotional requirements, and distribution considerations. Operational criteria include compatibility with current processes, equipment, facilities and suppliers. Financial criteria combine marketing and operational concerns and focus on risk, investment requirements, cost accounting, anticipated profit margin, and length of life cycle.

If the product passes the screening procedure, a more rigorous analysis of its cost and revenue characteristics is undertaken. Here the tools of financial analysis—break-even charts and rate-of-return calculations—come into play (see Appendix A). The major problem associated with these tools is that their value is limited to short-run evaluation of the product alternatives, because in many cases long-term developments in costs, the competition, and the economy make the numerical inputs inaccurate within a year.

Financial analysis generally yields information on how many units must be sold. Meanwhile, the marketing department runs studies of potential demand to determine how many units are *likely* to be sold, and conducts marketing-mix analyses, which attempt to determine *how* they are to be sold. This process can be quite involved, however. Some recent thinking has raised the point that existing organizations and procedures stifle creativity and new-product development. We need an innovative way of thinking about how new-product development can be done better and faster.

EXHIBIT 4.5 Product Design and Development Sequence

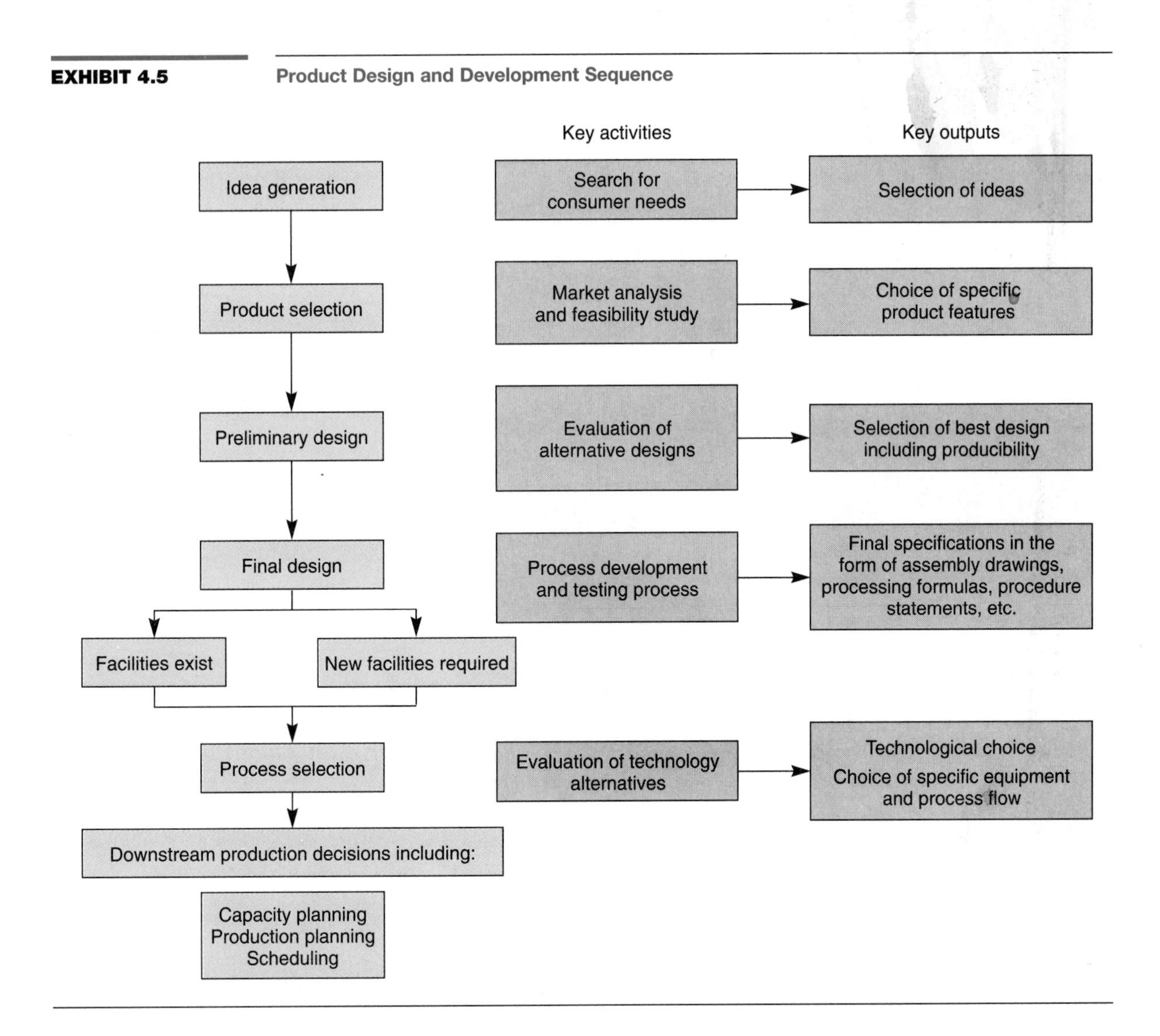

4.4 PROCESS SELECTION

Process Structures

Manufacturing operations are categorized into three broad types of process structures, each category depending to a large extent on the volume of product(s) to be produced. These three categories are often referred to as **project processes, intermittent processes,** and **line-flow processes.** While we identify three discrete categories, we should emphasize that the different types of manufacturing processes that exist should be viewed as a continuum, and that any one company may incorporate a combination of these processes

EXHIBIT 4.6

Types of Processes

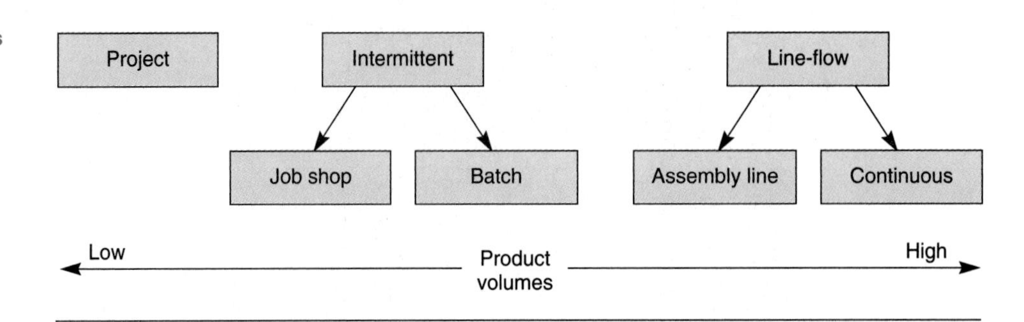

in the manufacture of its products. As seen in Exhibit 4.6, for example, intermittent processes are further divided into job shop and batch processes, and line-flow processes are likewise divided into assembly line and continuous processes.

Project process

A project-oriented process usually involves the manufacture of a single, one-of-a-kind product. Examples here include the production of a movie and the erection of a skyscraper. Building a customized car to compete in the Indianapolis 500 race is another good example. The major strength of a project-type process is that it is totally flexible to meet the individual needs of the customer.

Variable costs in this category are comparatively very high. On the other hand, fixed costs are negligible or even nonexistent. (In the extreme case, when there is truly only one product to build, all costs are expensed and there are no fixed costs at all.)

Skilled personnel are usually required for this type of process, as they must often work independently, with minimal guidance and supervision. In addition, workers here need to be well trained in a variety of tasks.

Intermittent process

As shown in Exhibit 4.6, intermittent type processes can be further divided into job shop and batch processes. We define a job shop as a process where a specific quantity of a product is produced only once. Numbered prints from a painting, programs for concerts, and T-shirts commemorating specific events are good examples of products made in a job shop process.

A batch process produces the same item again and again, usually in specified lot sizes. McDonald's is a good example of a batch process where hamburgers are cooked throughout the day in lot sizes of 12.

Variable costs are still relatively high with intermittent processes, although they are usually lower than those of a project-type process. However, higher fixed costs are incurred with these processes. Similarly, worker skills remain high, though somewhat less than those required for projects.

Mark Davis

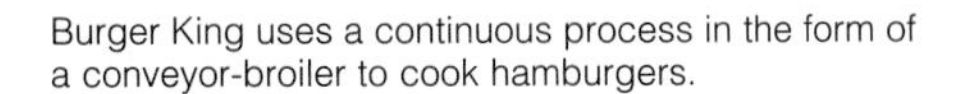

Burger King uses a continuous process in the form of a conveyor-broiler to cook hamburgers.

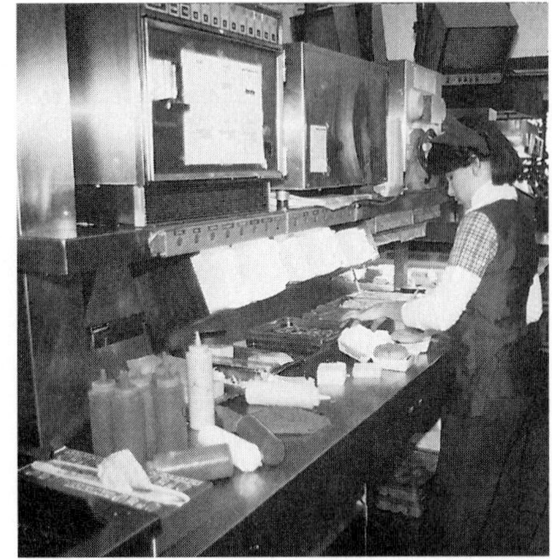

Mark Davis

Burger King employees then individually assemble the hamburgers to customer requirements so customers can "have it their way."

Line-flow process

As with intermittent processes, line-flow processes are frequently divided into two additional types of processes: assembly line and continuous. Assembly line processes manufacture individual, discrete products. Examples here include electronic products such as VCRs and CD players, as well as automobiles and kitchen appliances. Continuous processes are exactly what their name implies—continuous, producing products that are not discrete. Petroleum refineries and chemical plants provide good examples of continuous processes.

Line-flows are characterized by high fixed costs and low variable costs, and are often viewed as the most efficient of the three types of processes. Labor skill, especially in assembly-line operations, is typically very low, as workers are required to learn only a very few simple operations. Line-flows are used for only the highest volumes of products, are very focused, and consequently are the most inflexible of the three processes.

Product-Process Matrix

The relationship between the different types of processes and their respective volume requirements is often depicted on a product-process matrix shown in Exhibit 4.7, which is similar to the widely cited Hayes and Wheelwright product-process matrix. In this matrix, as volume increases and the product line narrows (the horizontal dimension), specialized equipment and standardized material flows (the vertical dimension) become economically feasible. This evolution in process structure is frequently related to the product's life cycle stage (introduction, growth, and maturity).

The industries listed within the matrix are presented as ideal types that have found their

EXHIBIT 4.7

Matching Major Stages of Product and Process Life Cycles

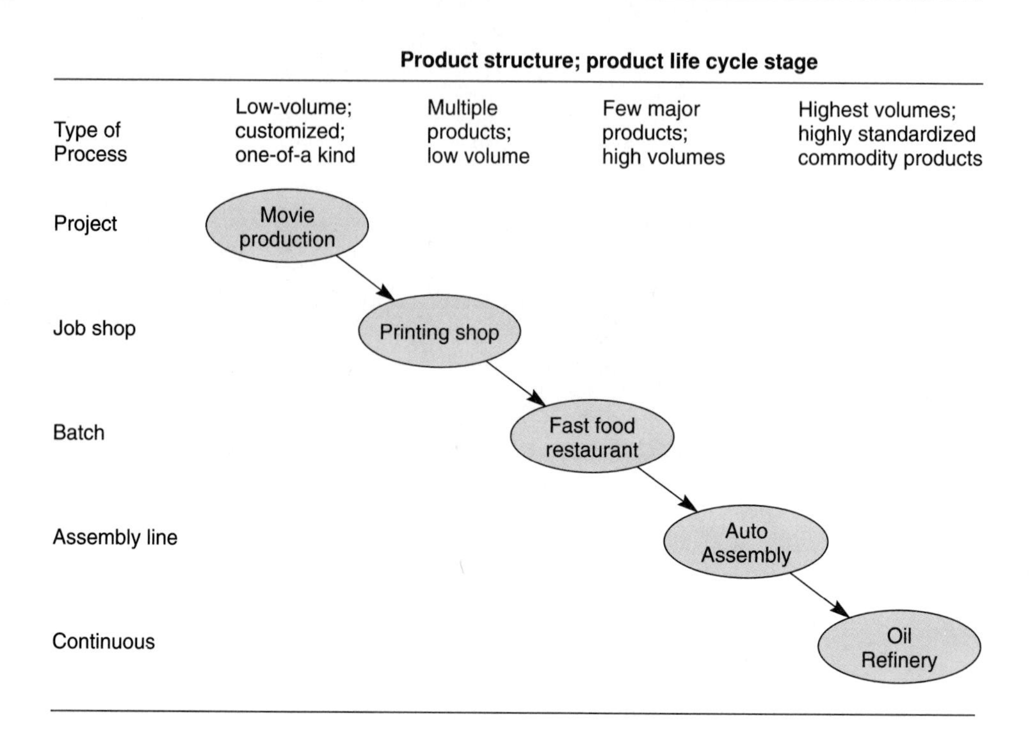

process niche. It certainly is possible for an industry member to choose another position on the matrix, however. For example, Volvo makes cars on movable pallets rather than on an assembly line. Thus, on the matrix it would be at the intersection of process stage II and product stage III. Volvo's production rate is lower than its competitors because it is giving up the speed and efficiency of the line. On the other hand, the Volvo system has more flexibility and better quality control than the classic automobile production line. Similar kinds of analysis can be carried out for other types of process-product options through the matrix.

It may be a little easier to understand the logic of a product-process matrix if we divide it into some component parts and simplify the final result. Part A of Exhibit 4.8 shows a traditional product life cycle from product conception through product termination. Part B relates the frequency of changes made in the product design to the stages of the product life cycle. Logically, most of the product changes occur during the initial stages of the life cycle, before major production starts. The product tends to go through many changes—simplification, adding features, newer materials, and so forth. The motivation here is for more performance and perhaps for a broader market. During the maturity stage of the product and during its decline, very few additional changes are made (unless the product undergoes intentional redesign, which then places it on another new product life cycle).

Changes in the production process, as shown in Part C of Exhibit 4.8, occur most

EXHIBIT 4.8 **Product and Process Life Cycles**

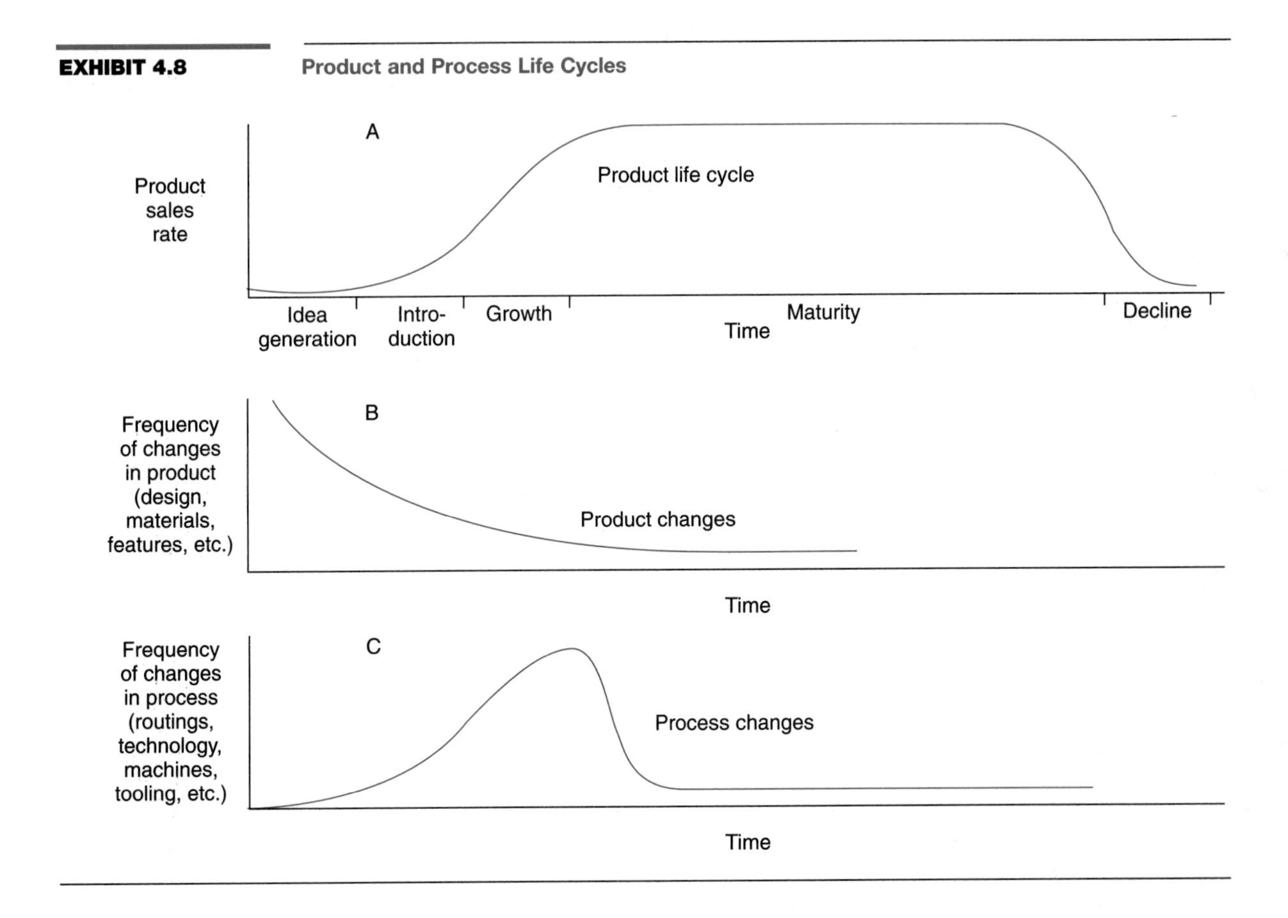

rapidly during the early stages of production design and startup. This is where choices are made in the production layout, equipment choices, tooling, and so on. The intention here is to reduce production costs. Also, both product and process engineers work together to reduce costs and increase product performance through joint efforts in the material changes to facilitate manufacture. When full production occurs, few additional changes are made. During the termination phase of the process, some additional process changes occur; these are due in part to switching the smaller production volumes to different equipment and facilities.

During the early stages in a product's life cycle when production quantities are small (certainly during the product research and development stages), manufacturing likely takes place in a functional type layout, which we usually call a *process-oriented layout.* Here, all similar machines and processes are grouped together in one location and used for many different products. As production volumes increase, machines and processes may be grouped to simplify the product's flow through the factory. This ultimately results in assembly lines, which are considered to be *product-oriented layouts.*

EXHIBIT 4.9

Major Decision Variables in Equipment Selection

Decision Variable	Factors to Consider
Initial investment	Price Manufacturer Availability of used models Space requirements Need for feeder/support equipment
Output rate	Actual versus rated capacity
Output quality	Consistency in meeting specs Scrap rate
Operating requirements	Ease of use Safety Human factors impact
Labor requirements	Direct to indirect ratio Skills and training
Flexibility	General-purpose versus special-purpose equipment Special tooling
Setup requirements	Complexity Changeover speed
Maintenance	Complexity Frequency Availability of parts
Obsolescence	State of the art Modification for use in other situations
In-process inventory	Timing and need for supporting buffer stocks
Systemwide impacts	Tie-in with existing or planned systems Control activities Fit with manufacturing strategy

Specific Equipment Selection

The choice of specific equipment follows the selection of the general type of process structure. Exhibit 4.9 shows some key factors that should be considered in the selection decision. Firms may have both general-purpose equipment and special-purpose equipment. For example, a machine shop could have both lathes and drill presses (general-purpose) as well as transfer machines (special-purpose). An electronics firm may have a single-function test module that performs only one test at a time (general-purpose) and also have a multifunction test unit that performs multiple tests at the same time (special-purpose). As computer-based technology evolves, however, the general-purpose/special-purpose distinction becomes blurred, since the general-purpose machine will increasingly have the capability to produce just as efficiently as many special-purpose ones.

Process Technology Evolution

Soon after the Industrial Revolution started, machines began to substitute for human labor, and mechanized technology replaced many manual tasks. As the volume of standardized products grew, it become more economical to design special-purpose, highly focused machines that were dedicated to the production of a single part or product. Ultimately, in discrete-parts manufacturing, these machines became linked through material-handling devices. Now, both material movement and direct production can be performed with automated equipment.

Before the 1960s, the state of the art in manufacturing was the mechanized assembly line used by automobile manufacturers. Today, although many car companies still use many of the same processes (which may explain why U.S. automotive manufacturers are still losing market share to foreign competition), leading-edge applications of process technology are found in other industries. This is particularly true in metal fabrication and electronic component manufacturing, where the objective is to approach the flexibility and speed of such process industries as chemicals and foods. Process industries are held up as a model because their processes require no hands-on production by workers. All operations are built into the machine and can be changed by turning a dial or altering a computer code.

Choosing among Alternative Processes and Equipment

A standard approach for choosing among alternative processes and/or equipment is with **break-even analysis.** A break-even chart visually presents alternative individual and relative profit and losses as a function of the number of units produced. The choice obviously depends on anticipated demand. For example, suppose a manufacturer has identified the following options for obtaining a machined part: It can buy the part at $200 per unit (including materials), it can make the part on a numerically controlled semiautomatic lathe at $75 per unit (including materials), or it can make the part on a machining center at $15.00 per unit (including materials). There is negligible fixed cost if the item is purchased; a semiautomatic lathe costs $80,000, and a machining center costs $200,000.

Whether we approach this as a cost minimization or as a profit maximization problem really makes no difference, as long as the relationships remain linear; that is, variable costs and revenue are the same for each incremental unit. Exhibit 4.10 shows the break-even points for each of the three alternatives. If demand is expected to be more than 2,000 units (point A), the machine center is the best choice since this would result in the lowest total cost. If demand is between 640 (point B) and 2,000 units, the NC lathe is the cheapest. If demand is less than 640 (between 0 and point B), the most economical alternative is to buy the product.

Consider the effect of revenue, assuming the part sells for $300 each. As Exhibit 4.10 shows, profit (or loss) is the distance between the revenue line and the alternative process cost. At 1,000 units, for example, maximum profit is the difference between the $300,000 revenue (point C) and the semiautomatic lathe cost of $160,000 (point D). For this quantity the semiautomatic lathe is the cheapest of the alternatives available. The optimal choices for both minimizing cost and maximizing profit are the lowest segments of lines: origin to B, to A, and to the right side of the exhibit.

4.5 PROCESS AUTOMATION

The term *automation* is familiar to all, but a commonly agreed-upon definition still eludes us. Some authorities view automation as a totally new set of concepts that relate to the automatic operation of a production process; others view it simply as an evolutionary

EXHIBIT 4.10

Break-Even Chart of Alternative Processes

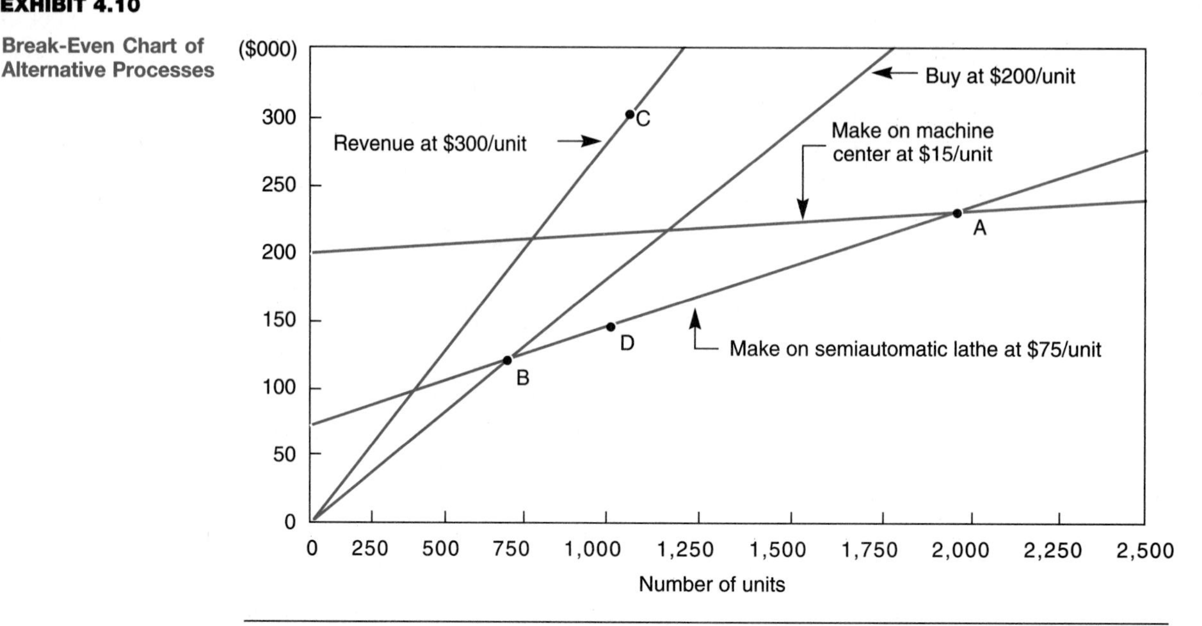

development in technology in which machinery performs some or all of the process-control function. Automation is a set of concepts, but it is also evolutionary in the sense that it is a logical and predictable step in the development of equipment and processes.

Some major developments in manufacturing automation include machining centers, numerically controlled machines, industrial robots, computer-aided design and manufacturing systems, flexible manufacturing systems, computer-integrated manufacturing, and islands of automation.

Machining centers not only provide automatic control of a machine but carry out automatic tooling changes as well. For example, a single machine may be equipped with a shuttle system of two worktables that can be rolled into and out of the machine. While work is being done at one table, the next part is mounted on the second table. When machining on the first table is complete, it is moved out of the way and the second part is moved into position.

Numerically controlled (NC) machines are under the control of a digital computer. Feedback control loops determine the position of the machine tooling during the work, constantly compare the actual location with the programmed location, and correct as needed. This eliminates time lost during setups, and applies to both high-volume, standardized types of products as well as low-volume, customized products.

Industrial robots are substitutes for human manipulation and other highly repetitive functions. A robot is a reprogrammable machine with multiple functions that can move devices through specialized motions to perform any number of tasks. It is essentially a mechanized arm that can be fitted with a variety of handlike fingers or grippers, vacuum

Courtesy H.J. Heinz Co.

A lab technician inspects the canning line at the Heinz Pet Products plant in Bloomsburg (Pennsylvania). Automation, coupled with process flexibility, has allowed Heinz to handle 1,000 different brands of private label pet food in addition to the company's own range.

cups, or a tool such as a wrench. Robots are capable of performing many factory operations ranging from machining processes to simple assembly.

Exhibit 4.11 examines the human motions a robot can reproduce. Advanced capabilities have been designed into robots to allow vision, tactile sensing, and hand-to-hand coordination. In addition, some models can be "taught" a sequence of motions in a three-dimensional pattern. As a worker moves the end of the robot arm through the required motions, the robot records this pattern in its memory and repeats them on command.

One of the major contemporary approaches to the product design process is **computer-aided (or -assisted) design (CAD).** *CAD* may be defined as carrying out all structural or mechanical design processes of a product or component at a specially equipped computer terminal. Engineers design through a combination of console controls and a light pen that draws on the computer screen or electronic pad. Different perspectives of the product can be visualized by rotating the product on the screen, and individual components can be enlarged to examine particular characteristics. Depending on the sophistication in software, on-screen testing may replace the early phases of prototype testing and modification.

CAD has been used to design everything from computer chips to potato chips. Frito-Lay, for example, used CAD to design its O'Grady's double-density, ruffled potato chip. CAD is also now being used to custom design swimsuits. Measurements of the wearer are fed into the CAD program, along with the style of suit desired. Working with

EXHIBIT 4.11

Typical Robot Axes of Motion

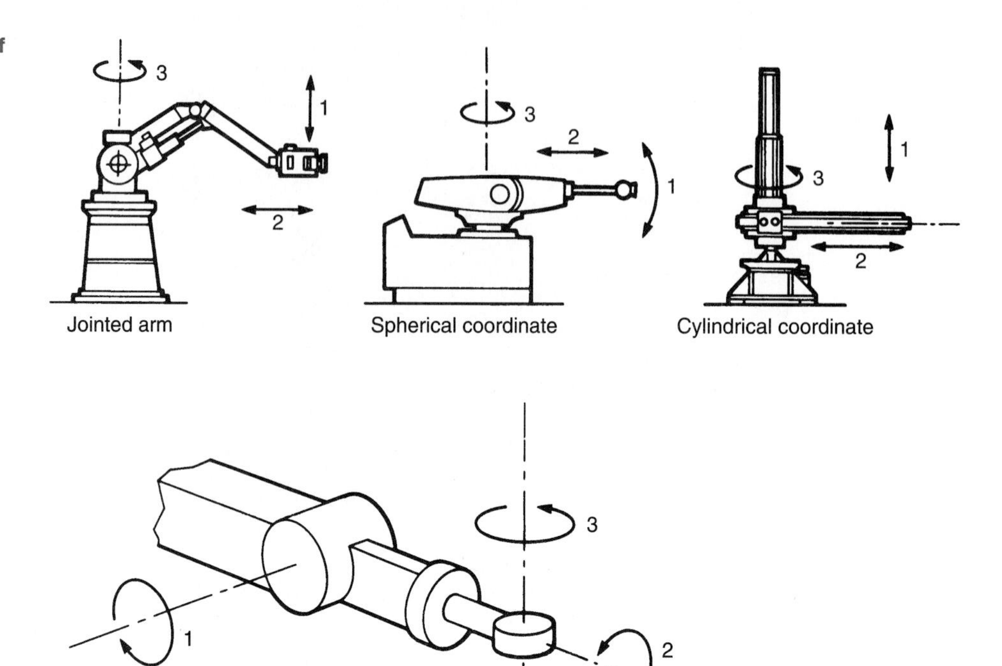

Source: L. V. Ottinger, "Robotics for the IE: Terminology, Types of Robots," *Industrial Engineering,* November 1981, p. 30. Reprinted with permission.

the customer, the designer modifies the suit design as it appears on a humanform drawing on the computer screen. Once the design is decided upon, the computer prints out a pattern, and the suit is cut and sewn on the spot.

Computer-aided design and manufacturing (CAD/CAM) uses a computer to **integrate** component design and processing instructions. In current CAD/CAM systems, when the design is finalized, the link to CAM is made by producing the manufacturing instructions. Because of the efficiency of CAD/CAM systems, design and manufacture of small lots can be both fast and low in cost.

Even though CAD/CAM systems are usually limited to larger companies because of the high initial cost, they do increase productivity and quality dramatically. More alternative designs can be produced, and the specifications can be more exact. Updates can be more readily made, and cost estimates more easily drawn. In addition, computer-aided process planning (CAPP) can shorten and, in some cases, even eliminate traditional process planning.

A **flexible manufacturing system (FMS)** actually refers to a number of systems that

"Seems like only yesterday it was serving drinks and doing little chores around the house."

Business Week, April 29, 1991.

"The Art of Product Design," HBR Photo File, *Harvard Business Review,* November–December 1990, p. 107.

differ in the degree of mechanization, automated transfer, and computer control. Andrew Kusiak has nicely defined and shown five systems and how they are usually related to the annual production and number of different parts used.[3] These systems are the flexible manufacturing module, cell, group, production system, and line (see Exhibit 4.12).

A flexible manufacturing module is a numerically controlled (NC) machine supported with a parts inventory, a tool changer, and a pallet changer. A flexible manufacturing cell consists of several flexible manufacturing modules organized according to the particular product's requirements. A flexible manufacturing group is a combination of flexible manufacturing modules and cells located in the same manufacturing area and joined by a material handling system, such as an automated guided vehicle (AGV).

A flexible production system consists of flexible manufacturing groups that connect different manufacturing areas, such as fabrication, machining, and assembly. A flexible manufacturing line is a series of dedicated machines connected by automated guided vehicles (AGVs), robots, conveyors, or some other type of automated transfer devices.

Computer-integrated manufacturing (CIM) integrates all aspects of production into one automated system. Design, testing, fabrication, assembly, inspection, and materials handling may all have automated functions within the area. However, in most companies, communication between departments still flows by means of paperwork. In CIM, these islands of automation are integrated, thus eliminating the need for the paperwork. A computer links all sectors together, resulting in more efficiency, less paperwork, and less personnel expense.

Islands of automation refers to the transition from conventional manufacturing to the automated factory. Typical islands of automation include numerically controlled machine tools, robots, automated storage/retrieval systems, and machining centers.

[3]Andrew Kusiak, "Flexible Manufacturing Systems: A Structural Approach," *International Journal of Production Research* 23, no. 6 (1985), pp. 1057–73.

EXHIBIT 4.12

Relationships of Different Classes of FMSs, Number of Different Parts, and Annual Production of Parts

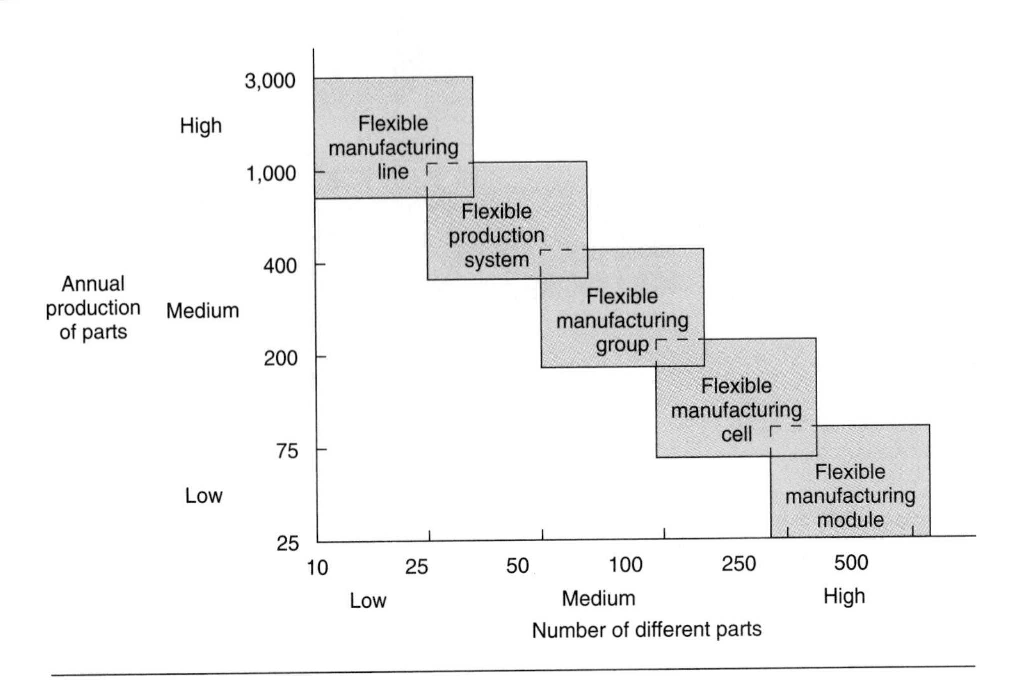

4.6 PROCESS FLOW DESIGN

Process flow design focuses on the specific processes that raw materials, parts, and subassemblies follow as they move through the plant. The most common production management tools used in planning the process flow are assembly drawings, assembly charts, route sheets, and flow process charts. Each of these charts is a useful diagnostic tool that can be used to improve operations during the process's steady state. Indeed, the standard first step in analyzing any production system is to map the flows and operations using one or more of these techniques. These are the "organization charts" of the manufacturing system.

An *assembly drawing* (see Exhibit 4.13) is simply an exploded view of the product showing all of its component parts. An *assembly chart* (Exhibit 4.14) uses the information presented in the assembly drawing to define (among other things) how the parts go together, their order of assembly, and, often, the overall material flow pattern.[4] An *operation and route sheet* (Exhibit 4.15), as its name implies, specifies operations and process routing for a particular part. It conveys such information as the type of equipment, tooling, and operations required to complete the part.

A *flow process chart* such as that shown in Exhibit 4.16, typically uses standard American

[4] Also called a *Gozinto chart,* named, so the legend goes, after the famous Italian mathematician Zepartzat Gozinto.

EXHIBIT 4.13

Plug Assembly Drawing

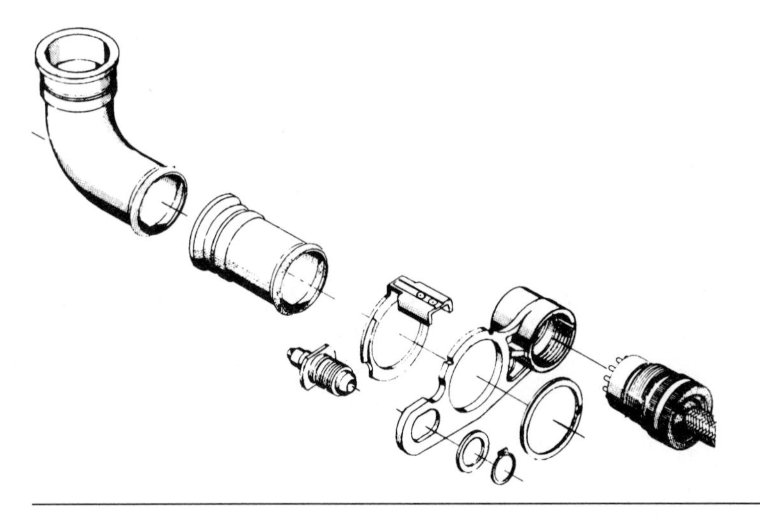

Society of Mechanical Engineers (ASME) symbols to denote what happens to the product as it progresses through the production facility. The symbols for the various processes are explained at the side of the chart. As a rule, the fewer the delays and storages in the process, the better the flow.

The Manufacturing Cycle

As we previously stated, in order to reduce both design time and production time, constant interaction must occur during product design and process selection. During the **manufacturing cycle,** the production function interacts with virtually every other function of the enterprise (see Exhibit 4.17). Because we examine the activities that take place during the cycle throughout this text, we won't explain all of them here. At this point, however, we want to highlight some of the major organizational interrelationships that have an ongoing impact on production.

First, there are two engineering groups—manufacturing engineering and industrial engineering. Manufacturing engineering's major responsibilities typically include (1) advising the product design group on producibility of the product, (2) planning process flow along the lines mentioned earlier, (3) specifying the tooling and equipment required, and (4) updating the bill of materials (BOM, the listing of parts that make up the product). Industrial engineering's major responsibilities typically include (1) determining work methods and time standards, (2) developing the specifics of the plant layout, (3) conducting cost and productivity improvement studies, and (4) implementing operations research projects.

Second, it is common to refer to all functions shown in the exhibit, other than sales and marketing, product design, and production per se, as manufacturing support groups. This

EXHIBIT 4.14

Assembly (or Gozinto) Chart for Plug Assembly

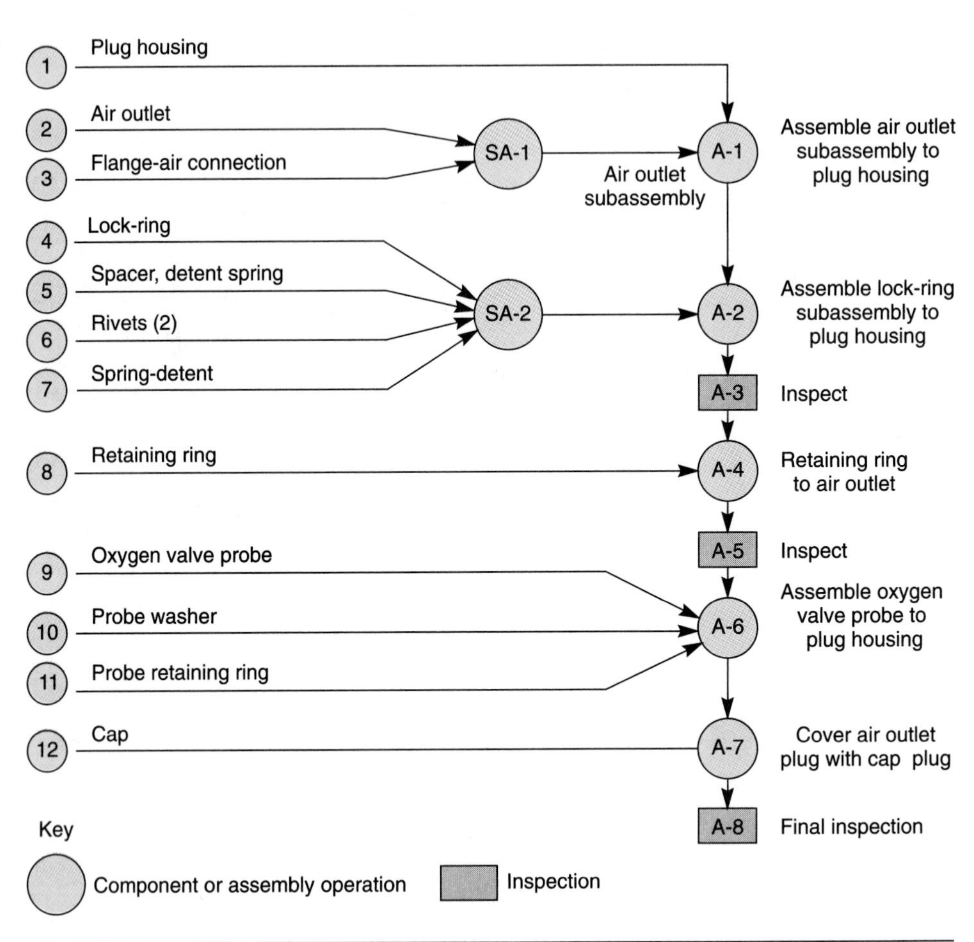

conveys the idea that the role of these activities is, quite simply, to help in the frequently complicated task of manufacturing.

Finally, the plant manager is responsible for coordinating these groups, the production manager is responsible for coordinating the direct production work force, and, in multisite firms, the vice president of manufacturing is responsible for coordinating the manufacturing activities throughout the plant network.

4.7 CONCLUSION

It is becoming more and more apparent that successful manufacturing firms are not simply a collection of vaguely related activities, but rather well-integrated and well-disciplined production organizations. Indeed, just like a physical machine, each part of the manufac-

EXHIBIT 4.15

Operation and Route Sheet for Plug Assembly

Material Specs.		Part Name	Plug Housing	Part No.	TA 1274
Purchased Stock Size		Usage	Plug Assembly	Date Issued	
Pcs. Per Pur. Size		Assy. No.	TA 1279	Date Sup'd.	
Weight		Sub. Assy. No.		Issued By	

Oper. No.	Operation Description	Dept.	Machine	Set Up Hr.	Rate Pc/Hr.	Tools
20	Drill 1 hole .32 +.015 -.005	Drill	Mach 513 Deka 4	1.5	254	Drill Fixture L-76, Jig #10393
30	Deburr .312 +.015 -.005 Dia. Hole	Drill	Mach 510 Drill	.1	424	Multi-Tooth burring Tool
40	Chamfer .900/.875, Bore .828/.875 dia. (2 Passes), Bore .7600/.7625 (1 Pass)	Lathe	Mach D109 Lathe	1.0	44	Ramet-1, TPG 221, Chamfer Tool
50	Tap Holes as designated - 1/4 Min. Full Thread	Tap	Mach 514 Drill Tap	2.0	180	Fixture #CR-353, Tap, 4 Flute Sp.
60	Bore Hole 1.133 to 1.138 Dia.	Lathe	H & H E107	3.0	158	L44 Turrent Fixture, Hartford
						Superspacer, pl. #45, Holder #L46,
						FDTW-100, Inser #21, Chk. Fixture
70	Deburr .005 to .010, Both Sides, Hand Feed To Hard Stop	Lathe	E162 Lathe	.5	176	Collect #CR179, 1327 RPM
80	Broach Keyway To Remove Thread Burrs	Drill	Mach. 507 Drill	.4	91	B87 Fixture, L59 Broach, Tap. .875120 G-H6
90	Hone Thread I.D. 822/.828	Grind	Grinder		120	
95	Hone .7600/.7625	Grind	Grinder		120	

EXHIBIT 4.16

Flow Process Chart of Plug Housing from Plug Assembly

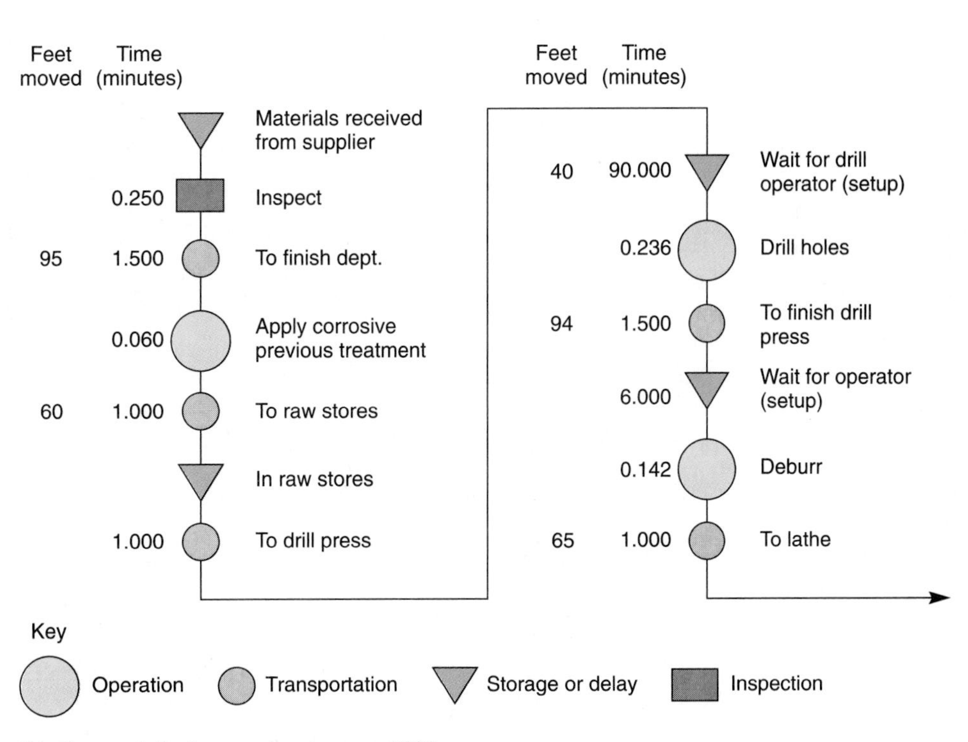

Note: These production times were based on a run of 500 items.
Source: Arizona Gear & Manufacturing Company.

EXHIBIT 4.17 The Manufacturing Cycle

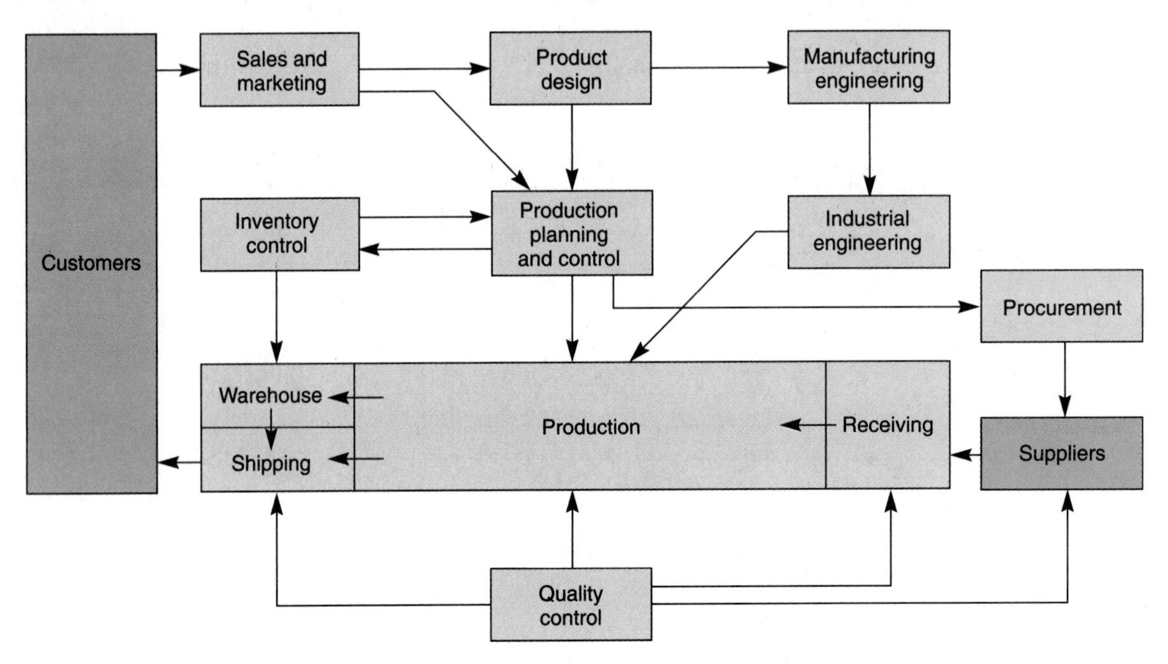

Source: Modified from Mikell P. Groover, *Automation, Production Systems, and Computer-Aided Manufacturing* (Englewood Cliffs, N.J.: Prentice Hall, 1980).

turing system—labor, equipment, and management—has an important role to play in achieving that success. It is also apparent that computer-based technology will be altering the ways products and factories are designed and manufacturing processes are carried out. How much of an impact such innovations will have across all industries is one of the most intriguing questions to be answered in the coming years. We do know, however, that product life cycles will continue to shorten, thereby increasing the pressure for faster and more timely new product introductions.

4.8 REVIEW AND DISCUSSION QUESTIONS

1. What factors have contributed to the increased emphasis on faster product development and introduction?
2. Discuss the product design phases of functional design, industrial design, and design for manufacturability. Which do you think is the most important?
3. Discuss "design-based incrementalism," which is the frequent product redesign throughout the product's life. What are the pros and cons of this idea?

4. Discuss the "ready, fire, aim" philosophy of many Japanese companies with respect to new product introduction. How does it compare with that of the typical U.S. company?
5. Why is daily contact between engineering and production groups so important in making early involvement effective?
6. What are the three major categories of processes, and how do they differ in terms of operational characteristics?
7. What is the product-process matrix telling us? How does automation change its basic premise?
8. Why is manufacturing management more than simple production management?
9. Assume that a firm would like to manufacture a new product. What are the areas of responsibility for each of the functional areas (marketing, finance, accounting, personnel, production)?
10. Why is it important that managers understand the relationship between the various stages of a product's life cycle and the different types of processes that are available for manufacturing that product?
11. Discuss concurrent engineering and how it can benefit a production system.
12. What is a flexible manufacturing system (FMS)?

4.9 SOLVED PROBLEMS

PROBLEM

1. Jana and Marla, two recent business school graduates, have decided to open their own copy-service business on a part-time basis. They estimate that their annual fixed costs are $32,000 and their average variable cost for each copy sold at $.03. They expect their selling price to average $.07 per copy.
   a. Draw the break-even chart for their business, and indicate all of the relevant costs.
   b. What is their break-even point in dollars? In number of copies?
   c. After their first year of operations, in which they generated $84,000 in revenues, Jana and Marla decide to pay themselves each $5,000 per year in salaries. What does their annual sales now have to be if they want to make the same amount of profit as they did in their first year?

SOLUTION

Fixed cost = F = \$32,000

Variable cost per copy = V = \$.03 each

Selling price per copy = P = \$.07 each

a.

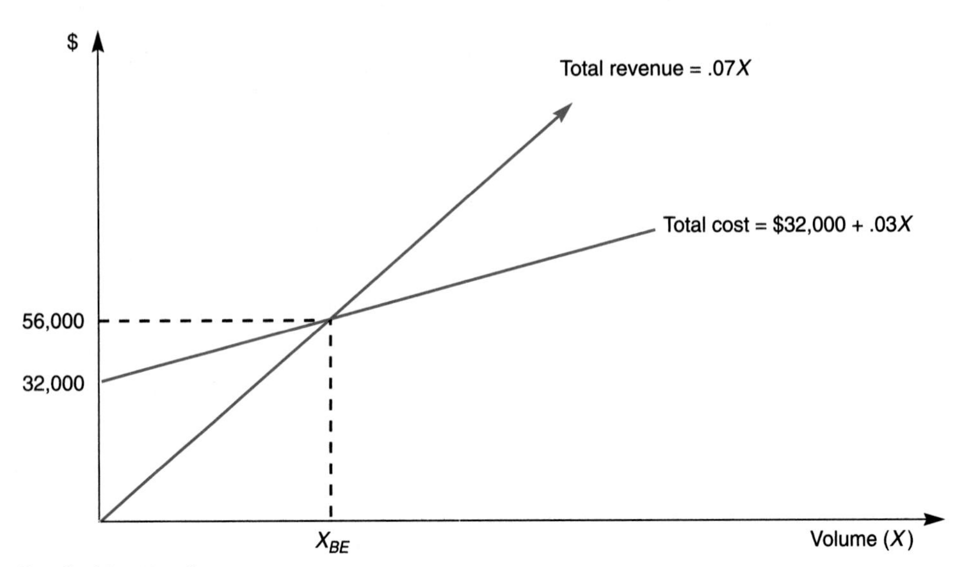

b. Breakeven: Total revenue (TR) = Total cost

$$TR = TC$$
$$.07X = 32{,}000 + .03X$$
$$.07X - .03X = 32{,}000$$
$$.04X = 32{,}000$$
$$X = X_{BE} = \frac{32{,}000}{.04} = 800{,}000 \text{ copies}$$

At this point, $TR > TC$

$TR = .07X$ $\quad$ $TC = 32{,}000 + .03X$

$= .07\ (800{,}000)$ $\quad$ $= 32{,}000 + .03(800{,}000)$

$= \$56{,}000$ $\quad$ $= 56{,}000$

c. $TR = .07 \quad X = \$84{,}000$

$X = 1{,}200{,}000$ copies

$TC = 32{,}000 \quad + .03(1{,}200{,}000)$

$= 32{,}000 \quad + 36{,}000 = 68{,}000$

Profit = $TR - TC$

$84{,}000 - 68{,}000 = \$16{,}000$ for the first year

New for next year: Fixed cost = 32,000 + 2(5,000) = \$42,000

$$\begin{aligned}
\text{Profit} &= TR - TC \\
16{,}000 &= .07X - (42{,}000 + .03X) \\
16{,}000 &= .04X - 42{,}000 \\
.04X &= 58{,}000 \\
X &= 1{,}450{,}000 \text{ copies}
\end{aligned}$$

PROBLEM

2. Peter McWalters is president of Transformonics, a firm that produces power transformers for personal computer manufacturers. Peter's analysis of the various methods by which a new model of transformer can be built has been narrowed down to one of three alternatives. Because of the rapidly changing technology in the industry, Peter estimates the product life of the transformer to be one year. Marketing has estimated that it can sell 5,000 of these new transformers within that time period. The three alternative processes are:

   - Use existing equipment and fixtures, and hire high-skilled machinists and technicians at \$16.00 per hour (including benefits). With this method, each transformer will require two (2) labor-hours to assemble.
   - Use existing equipment, but invest \$30,000 in new fixtures and instruction manuals to simplify some of the more complicated operations. Semi-skilled workers could therefore be employed at \$12.00 per hour (including benefits), with each transformer requiring one (1) labor-hour to complete.
   - Invest \$75,000 in new equipment, fixtures, and instruction manuals. This approach would eliminate all of the complicated procedures, thereby requiring only unskilled labor, which could be hired at \$6.00 per hour (including benefits). With this method, each motor would require only 20 labor-minutes to complete.

   a. Draw a break-even chart using total cost versus volume for the above processes.
   b. Calculate the two break-even volumes (i.e., those volumes at which you shift from one process to another).
   c. Which alternative would you recommend, and why?

SOLUTION

Process 1: Variable cost = (2 hrs/unit)(\$16.00/hr) = \$32/unit

Total cost = $32X$

Process 2: Variable cost = (1 hr/unit)(12.00/hr) = \$12/unit

Fixed cost = \$30,000

Total cost (TC_2) = $30{,}000 + 12X$

Process 3: Variable cost = (⅓ hr/unit)(\$6.00/hr) = \$2/unit

Fixed cost = 75,000

Total cost (TC_3) = $75{,}000 + 2X$

a.

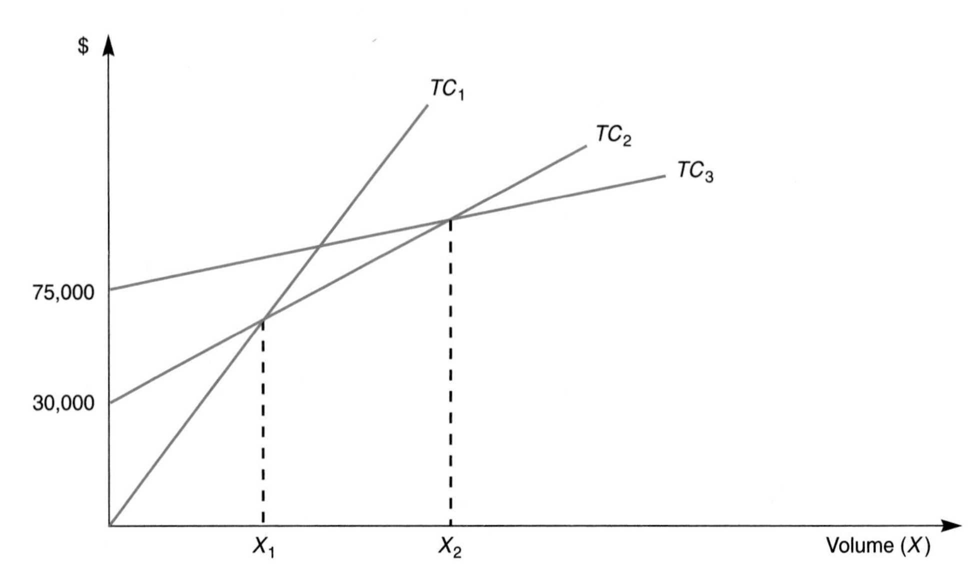

b.

$$TC_1 = TC_2 \qquad TC_2 = TC_3$$
$$32X_1 = 30{,}000 + 12X_1 \qquad 30{,}000 + 12X_2 = 75{,}000 + 2X_2$$
$$20X_1 = 30{,}000 \qquad 10X_2 = 45{,}000$$
$$X_1 = 1{,}500 \text{ units} \qquad X_2 = 4{,}500 \text{ units}$$

Thus, if: $X \leqslant 1{,}500$ units, choose process 1.

$1{,}500 \leqslant X \leqslant 4{,}500$ units, choose process 2.

$4{,}500 \leqslant X$, choose process 3.

c. Since the projected annual unit sales is 5,000 units, process 3 should be selected because it provides the minimum cost at that volume.

4.10 PROBLEMS

1. *a.* List specific products that you especially like. What do you like most about them?
   b. Create a list of products that you dislike or are unhappy with. What don't you like about them?
   c. Are there some common reasons for your lists? For example, is it more important for products that you don't see or see very little to be functional rather than being attractive (e.g., the furnace or air conditioning in the house, the transmission or engine in the car)? Is it more important for things to be well designed that other people see and relate to you such as your car, your clothes, or your apartment or home furnishings?
   Can you formulate some general design guidelines based on your answers?
2. Pick a product and make a list of issues that need to be considered in its design and manufacture. The product can be something like a stereo, a telephone, a desk, a kitchen

appliance, etc. Consider the functional and aesthetic aspects of design as well as the important concerns for manufacturing.

3. Mary Entrepreneur is considering introducing a new novelty item for sale to summer visitors in the Catskill Mountains in upstate New York: a wraparound belt with pockets in which vacationers could carry their suntan lotion, playing cards, and snacks. The belt, which she will market as the "Borscht Belt," was greeted with great enthusiasm by members of a local health club.

   The prototype model consists of six identical naugahyde pockets sewn onto a terrycloth belt, and a metal buckle available in the shape of each of the 12 different astrological signs. Once production begins, Mary will obtain naugahyde and terrycloth in bulk rolls, and buckles will be supplied by a local machine shop. Mary has two heavyduty sewing machines and a stud-riveting machine (left over from her Bruce Springsteen Levi pants production) to attach the belt buckles. Before entering production, she would like to know:
   a. What an assembly chart for the belts would look like.
   b. What a flow process chart for the entire operation, from raw materials receipt to final inspection, would look like.

4. SYSTEM DESIGN EXERCISE
   The purpose of this exercise is to gain experience in setting up a manufacturing process. (We suggest that this be done as a team project.) Assignment:
   a. Get one Ping Pong paddle.
   b. Specify the type of equipment and raw materials you would need to manufacture that paddle, from the receipt of seasoned wood to packaging for shipment.
   c. Assume that one unit of each type of equipment is available to you and is already placed in a rented hangar at your local airport. Further assume that you have a stock of seasoned wood and other materials needed to produce and box 100 paddles. Making reasonable assumptions about times and distances where necessary,
      (1) Develop an assembly drawing for the paddle.
      (2) Prepare an assembly chart for the paddle.
      (3) Develop a flow process chart for the paddle.
      (4) Develop a route sheet for the paddle.

4.11 READING: JAPANESE MANUFACTURING

In the United States, many writers have written books and articles, given lectures, and consulted on the various secrets to Japan's success. An article by Kuniyasu Sakai gives a startling revelation about Japanese manufacturing. We quote only a section of this article as he has stated his point of concern so clearly.

The Feudal World Of Japanese Manufacturing*

In my conversations with Americans and other foreign businesspeople, I am constantly amazed at how little they seem to know about the realities of Japanese industry. At a time when Japan accounts

*Kuniyasu Sakai, "The Feudal World of Japanese Manufacturing," *Harvard Business Review,* November–December 1990, pp. 38–39.

industry, it seems both foolish—and in some ways dangerous—for Western executives to have such a tenuous understanding of their Japanese trading partners.

Over the past four decades, I have built up a group of several dozen small and midsize companies in a wide variety of businesses, most related to electronics manufacturing. I know well the real world of Japanese manufacturing. I also know that foreign executives have no idea how it works.

My businesses produce high-tech products for some of the best-known companies in Japan—all of which are familiar to customers around the world. Yet my companies' names remain unknown, as they should. They exist to support the efforts of the larger companies that can afford to advertise and distribute the products we make. I am happy to leave that business to them. I do not even mind that customers the world over buy products that one of my companies designed and built, all the time praising some famous Japanese company whose logo is on the switch. That is the nature of my business, and I really do not expect consumers to know or even care who built their television or their computer.

I do, however, expect Western executives in important manufacturing industries to know. And what astounds me—and my Japanese colleagues—is that, despite so much "revisionist" thinking about Japan, so many Western businesspeople still know so little about corporate Japan. It seems that the myths of the 1960s are still alive and well. The most prominent and enduring of these myths is the notion that Japanese industry is made up of a handful of powerful giants with factories spanning the nation and workers forming an army of loyal employees who are cared for until retirement by a paternalistic corporation.

This is absolute nonsense.

The Secret Revealed

The giant Japanese manufacturers have become household names worldwide. Companies like Matsushita, Toshiba, NEC, Hitachi, Sony, and Fujitsu have become strong because they produce what the world wants to buy. Their reputations for advanced R&D, innovative products, low-cost and high-quality manufacturing are legendary. Moreover, they seem to have an uncanny ability not just to invent remarkable new products but also to borrow ideas, rework them, tinker with them, and produce something totally "new" from a product concept that originated elsewhere. More often than not, they shrink the new product, add a few gadgets, and find a way to sell it for half what the industry was expecting. A year later, they bring out a newer model and cut prices on the old one before anyone else even has a copy on the market.

How do they do that? What is their secret?

How can the giant Japanese manufacturers, big and resourceful as they are, continue to come up with one idea after another, make a quantum jump from theoretical to applied technology in a single year, and squeeze production costs below what should be economically feasible? And how do they do it year after year, growing more profitable at every step along the way?

The answer is simple: they don't.

Like the Wizard of Oz, Japan's giant industrial combines are not what they appear to be. They do not develop all of their own product line, nor do they manufacture it. In reality, these huge businesses are more like "trading companies." That is, rather than design and manufacture their own goods, they actually coordinate a complex design and manufacturing process that involves thousands of smaller companies. The goods you buy with a famous maker's name inscribed on the case are seldom the product of that company's factory—and often not even the product of its own research. Someone else designed it, someone else put it together, someone stuck it in a box with the famous maker's name on it and then shipped it to its distributors.

Does this operation sound unnecessarily complex? Obviously, these huge corporations have their own factories and workers. So why don't they employ their own resources to produce the goods they sell?

They do, of course—but only partially. For instance, it would make very little sense for an electronics giant like Matsushita to farm out the design, manufacture, and assembly of a refrigerator or microwave oven. These products are ideally suited to mass production in the kind of large, highly automated factories that the giant companies can afford. Their factories produce hundreds of thousands of these units every year.

But what about products that companies must continually redesign to compete for public acceptance—like headphone stereos, small compact disc players, or personal computers? Redesigning means retooling a production line. It means sourcing new parts and lots of other things. For a typical product, a company might expect to sell 30,000 units in a few months, retool, sell another 50,000 units, redesign some basic components, retool again, see what the competition brings out, retool again, and on and on, throughout the life cycle of the entire product line. Although some of the giant makers are now employing the newest flexible manufacturing systems (FMS) to allow them more freedom in production, this retooling process is something many big companies want to eliminate.

Thus they farm out much of this business to subcontractors—smaller companies they can depend on. These companies, in turn, faced with redesigning and producing a product three or four times a year, will subcontract the design or manufacture of a dozen key components to still smaller companies.

How extensive is this subcontracting pyramid? Would you guess a few dozen companies? A few hundred? Think again. One electronics company I know has well over 6,000 subcontractors in its industrial group, most of them tiny shops that exist just to fill a few little orders for the companies above them.

Welcome to the real world of Japanese manufacturing.

QUESTION

Relate the various phases of the entire process from idea generation through design for manufacturability as covered in this chapter to Kuniyasu's comments about current Japanese manufacturing. How do you think American firms should react or respond to this? Or should they?

4.12 READING: THE BEST-ENGINEERED PART IS NO PART AT ALL*

Putting together NCR Corp.'s new 2760 electronic cash register is a snap. In fact, William R. Sprague can do it in less than two minutes—blindfolded. To get that kind of easy assembly, Sprague, a senior manufacturing engineer at NCR, insisted that the point-of-sale terminal be designed so that its parts fit together with no screws or bolts.

The entire terminal consists of just 15 vendor-produced components. That's 85 percent fewer parts, from 65 percent fewer suppliers, than in the company's previous low-end model, the 2160. And the terminal takes only 25 percent as much time to assemble. Installation and maintenance are also a breeze, says Sprague. "The simplicity flows through to all of the downstream activities, including field service."

---

*Otis Port, "The Best-Engineered Part Is No Part at All," *Business Week,* May 8, 1989, p. 150.

The new NCR product is one of the best examples to date of the payoffs possible from a new engineering approach called "design for manufacturability," mercifully shortened to DFM. Other DFM enthusiasts include Ford, General Motors, IBM, Motorola, Perkin-Elmer, and Whirlpool. Since 1981, General Electric Co. has used DFM in more than 100 development programs, from major appliances to gearboxes for jet engines. GE figures that the concept has netted $200 million in benefits, either from cost savings or increased market shares.

Nuts to Screws

One U.S. champion of DFM is Geoffrey Boothroyd, a professor of industrial and manufacturing engineering at the University of Rhode Island and the co-founder of Boothroyd Dewhurst Inc. This tiny Wakefield (R.I.) company has developed several computer programs that analyze designs for ease of manufacturing.

The biggest gains, notes Boothroyd, come from eliminating screws and other fasteners. On a supplier's invoice, screws and bolts may run mere pennies apiece, and collectively they account for only about 5 percent of a typical product's bill of materials. But tack on all of the associated costs, such as the time needed to align components while screws are inserted and tightened, and the price of using those mundane parts can pile up to 75 percent of total assembly costs. "Fasteners should be the first thing to design out of a product," he says.

Had screws been included in the design of NCR's 2760, calculates Sprague, the total cost over the lifetime of the model would have been $12,500—per screw. "The huge impact of little things like screws, primarily on overhead costs, just gets lost," he says. That's understandable, he admits, because for new-product development projects "the overriding factor is hitting the market window. It's better to be on time and over budget than on budget but late."

But NCR got its simplified terminal to market in record time without overlooking the little details. The product was formally introduced last January, just 24 months after development began. Design was a paperless, interdepartmental effort from the very start. The product remained a computer model until all members of the team—from design engineering, manufacturing, purchasing, customer service, and key suppliers—were satisfied.

That way, the printed-circuit boards, the molds for its plastic housing, and other elements could all be developed simultaneously. This eliminated the usual lag after designers throw a new product "over the wall" to manufacturing, which then must figure out how to make it. "Breaking down the walls between design and manufacturing to facilitate simultaneous engineering," Sprague declares, "was the real breakthrough."

The design process began with a mechanical computer-aided engineering program that allowed the team to fashion three-dimensional models of each part on a computer screen. The software also analyzed the overall product and its various elements for performance and durability. Then the simulated components were assembled on a computer workstation's screen to assure that they would fit together properly. As the design evolved, it was checked periodically with Boothroyd Dewhurst's DFM software. This prompted several changes that trimmed the parts count from an initial 28 to the final 15.

No Mock-Up

After everyone on the team gave their thumbs-up, the data for the parts were electronically transferred directly into computer-aided manufacturing systems at the various suppliers. The NCR designers were so confident everything would work as intended that they didn't bother making a mock-up.

DFM can be a powerful weapon against foreign competition. Several years ago, IBM used Boothroyd Dewhurst's software to analyze dot-matrix printers it was sourcing from Japan—and found it could do substantially better. Its Proprinter has 65 percent fewer parts and slashed assembly time by 90 percent. "Almost anything made in Japan," insists Professor Boothroyd, "can be improved upon with DFM—often impressively."

QUESTIONS

1. What tools from this chapter is NCR using?
2. How important is the simplicity of design throughout all aspects of the product use: design, manufacture, use by customer, product service, and maintenance?

4.13 SELECTED BIBLIOGRAPHY

Adler, Paul S.; Henry E. Riggs; and Steven C. Wheelwright. "Product Development Know-How: Trading Tactics for Strategy." *Sloan Management Review,* Fall 1989, pp. 7–17.

Boggs, Robert N. "Rogues' Gallery of 'Aggravating Products,'" *Design News,* October 22, 1990, pp. 130–33.

Bolwijn, P. T., and T. Kumpe. "Manufacturing in the 1990s—Productivity, Flexibility, and Innovation." *Long Range Planning* 23, no. 4 (1990), pp. 44–57.

Dixon, John R., and Michael R. Duffy. "The Neglect of Engineering Design." *California Management Review,* Winter 1990, pp. 9–23.

Drucker, Peter F. "The Emerging Theory of Manufacturing." *Harvard Business Review,* May–June 1990, pp. 94–102.

Edmondson, Harold E., and Steven C. Wheelwright. "Outstanding Manufacturing in the Coming Decade." *California Management Review,* Summer 1989, pp. 70–90.

Gardner, Dana. "Tech Toys for Grownups." *Design News,* December 3, 1990, pp. 63–66.

Hamilton, Joan O'C. "Rebel with a Cause." *Business Week,* December 3, 1990, pp. 130–33.

Hammer, Michael. "Reengineering Work: Don't Automate, Obliterate." *Harvard Business Review,* July–August 1990, pp. 104–12.

Huthwaite, Bart. *Design for Competitiveness: A Concurrent Engineering Handbook,* Institute for Competitive Design, 530 N. Pine, Rochester, Mich.

Jonas, Norman. "Can America Compete?" *Business Week,* April 20, 1987, pp. 45–69.

Kusiak, Andrew. "Flexible Manufacturing Systems: A Structural Approach." *International Journals of Production Research* 23, no. 6 (1985), pp. 1057–73.

Machlis, Sharon. "Three Shortcuts to Better Design," *Design News,* November 19, 1990, pp. 89–91.

Main, Jeremy. "Manufacturing the Right Way." *Fortune,* May 21, 1990, pp. 54–64.

Nussbaum, Bruce. "Hot Products: Smart Design Is the Common Thread." *Business Week,* June 7, 1993.

Nussbaum, Bruce, and Robert Neff. "I Can't Work This Thing!" *Business Week,* April 29, 1991, pp. 58–66.

Pare, Terence P. "Why Some Do It the Wrong Way." *Fortune,* May 21, 1990, pp. 75–76.

Port, Otis. "The Best Engineered Part Is No Part at All." *Business Week,* May 8, 1989, p. 150.

Roehm, Harper A.; Donald Klein; and Joseph F. Castellano. "Springing to World-Class Manufacturing." *Management Accounting,* March 1991, pp. 40–44.

Sakai, Kuniyasu. "The Feudal World of Japanese Manufacturing." *Harvard Business Review,* November–December 1990, pp. 38–49.

Sanderson, Susan Walsh, and Vic Uzumeri. "Strategies for New Product Development and Renewal: Design-Based Incrementalism." Center for Science and Technology Policy, School of Management, Rensselaer Polytechnic Institute, May 1990.

Spenser, William J. "Research to Product: A Major U.S. Change." *California Management Review,* Winter 1990, pp. 45–53.

Stalk, George, Jr. "Time—The Next Source of Competitive Advantage." *Harvard Business Review,* July–August 1988.

Wheelwright, Steven C., and W. Earl Sasser, Jr. "The New Product Development Map," *Harvard Business Review,* May–June 1989, pp. 112–27.

Ziemke, M. Carl, and Mary S. Spann. "Warning: Don't Be Half-Hearted in Your Efforts to Employ Concurrent Engineering." *Industrial Engineering,* February 1991, pp. 45–49.

Chapter 5

Product Design and Process Selection—Services

EPIGRAPH

After paying for dinner at a restaurant, I asked the cashier who took my money in stony silence why she didn't at least say thank you. "Why should I?" she asked, "It says thank you on your check, doesn't it?"

Comedian Jay Leno, on the "Tonight Show"

CHAPTER OUTLINE

KEY TERMS

Service Package

Facilities-Based Services

Field-Based Services

Customer

High Degree of Customer Contact

Low Degree of Customer Contact

Service-System Design Matrix

Service Blueprint

Every day we are exposed to a wide variety of services. Examples include how we travel (taxis, airlines), where we eat (restaurants) and stay (hotels), how we take care of ourselves (HMOs, health clubs), and how we entertain ourselves (movies, concerts). Services, in fact, make up the vast proportion of the economies of the highly developed countries of the world. For example, services represent more than 70 percent of the GNP in the United States.

Services differ from manufacturing operations in many respects. In services, customers typically interact directly with the service delivery process, and production and consumption take place simultaneously. Services are considered to be intangible, that is, they cannot be stored. An empty seat on an airline or a vacant hotel room cannot be saved for a busy period when all of the available seats or rooms are being used.

Because of these differences, specifically the direct interaction of the customer with the process, the analysis of service systems must be broader in approach and also include the marketing and human resource management functions within an organization.

Karl Albrecht and Ron Zemke's *Service America!* gets to the heart of the issue of managing service operations in stating: Every time a customer comes into contact with any aspect of the company it is a "moment of truth," and it can create either a positive or a negative impression about the company.[1] How well these moments of truth are managed depends on a carefully designed service delivery system.

In order to better understand services, we begin this chapter by presenting several approaches to classifying services. Next, we introduce different service strategies and how to design a service delivery system that is compatible with a specific strategy. Finally, we present three distinctly different approaches to designing service delivery systems.

5.1 THE NATURE AND IMPORTANCE OF SERVICES

Our study of services begins with seven generalizations about what must be considered a vast topic.

1. Everyone is an expert on services. We all think we know what we want from a service organization and, by the very process of living, we have a good deal of experience with the service creation process.
2. Services are idiosyncratic and situation dependent. What works well at one time may prove disastrous at another time, even with the same service. For example, an individual staying at a hotel during the week while on business will have a different set of performance criteria than a person on a weekend vacation.
3. Product quality is not service quality. An auto dealership may do good work on your car, but it may take a week to get the job done. Product quality may be viewed

[1] Jan Carlzon, president, Scandinavian Airlines System, quoted in Karl Albrecht and Ron Zemke, *Service America! Doing Business in the New Economy* (Homewood, Ill.: Dow Jones-Irwin, 1985), p. 19.

as "what" is being delivered to the customer; service quality can be defined as "how" it is delivered.

4. Most services contain a mix of tangible and intangible attributes that constitute a **service package,** and this package requires different approaches to design and management than does the production of goods.
5. High-contact services (described later) are *experienced,* whereas goods are *consumed.*
6. Effective management of services requires an understanding of marketing and personnel, as well as operations.
7. Services often take the form of encounters between the customer and the service delivery process, involving face-to-face, phone, electromechanical, and/or mail interactions. (The term *encounter,* by the way, is defined as "in conflict or battle" and hence is often an appropriate definition as we make our way through the service economy.)

"OM in Action" presents some assorted facts about the impact of services on our economy.

OPERATIONS MANAGEMENT IN ACTION
Some Facts about Services

- In 1990, 71 percent of the U.S. GNP resulted from services—a 4 percent increase in 10 years. During the same time the contribution from manufacturing decreased by 2 percent.
- In 1986, the number of persons employed increased by 2.5 million; 87 percent of this increase was in services.
- In 1989, 77 percent of all U.S. workers were employed in service-producing jobs.
- Services have increased their employment share 6 percent between 1975 and 1985.
- More than half of all U.S. service workers are employed in white-collar, often highly skilled, occupations.
- Foreign trade in 1986:
  - The United States reported $133.8 billion of service trade.
  - Services netted a $33.1 billion surplus.
  - The trade surplus in services has grown by 200 percent since 1976.
- Of the total investment in new plants and equipment made in 1985, 73 percent was from the service sector.
- In 1986, the number of service companies rose by 2.4 percent and accounted for every one of the 10 fastest-growing business categories. The top five were health clubs (28 percent increase), beauty shops (16 percent), doctors/health services (15 percent), investment management/other (14 percent), and hotels/lodging (12 percent).
- Mac attack (some statistics on McDonald's):
  - Average number on payroll: 500,000 people.
  - Number of workers employed over past 30 years: 8 million (7 percent of the entire U.S. work force, or 1 out of every 15 American workers).

- Largest job training organization in the United States (the U.S. Army is number two).

Source: From various issues of the *Monthly Labor Review*.

Types of Service Organizations

Service management issues exist in three broad organizational contexts:

1. *Service businesses* are organizations whose primary business requires interaction with the customer to produce the service. Familiar examples of service businesses include banks, airlines, hospitals, law firms, retail stores, restaurants, and so on. Within this category, we can make a further major distinction: **facilities-based services,** where the customer must go to the service facility, and **field-based services,** where production and consumption of the service take place in the customer's environment (e.g., cleaning and home repair services).

Technology has allowed for the transfer of many facility-based services to field-based services. Dental vans bring the dentist to your home. Some auto repair services have repair-mobiles. Telemarketing brings the shopping center to your TV screen.

2. *Customer support services* provide support to external customers who have already purchased the goods and/or services of the company. Included here are 800-numbers for registering complaints and obtaining additional information on the firm's products. (Tektronix provides a good example of this—see Chapter 1.) Product maintenance and repair services also fall into this category.

3. *Internal services* are the services required to support the activities of the larger organization. These services include such functions as data processing, accounting, engineering, and maintenance. Their customers are the various departments within the organization that require such services. Incidentally, it is not uncommon for an internal service to start marketing its services outside the parent organization and become a service business itself.

Our emphasis in this chapter is on service businesses, but the concepts are equally applicable to customer support services and internal services.

A Contemporary View of Service Management

A glance at the management section in your local book store provides ample evidence of the concern for service among practitioners. The way we now view service parallels the way we view quality: The **customer** is (or should be) the focal point of all decisions and actions of the service organization. This philosophy is captured nicely in the service triangle shown in Exhibit 5.1. Here, the customer is the center of everything—the service strategy, the systems, and the people who serve him or her. From this perspective, the organization correctly exists only to serve the customer, and the systems and the people exist to facilitate the process of service. Some suggest that the service organization also exists to serve the work force because they generally determine how the service is perceived by the customers. Relative to the latter point, the customer gets the kind of service that management deserves; in other words, how management treats the worker is

EXHIBIT 5.1

The Service Triangle

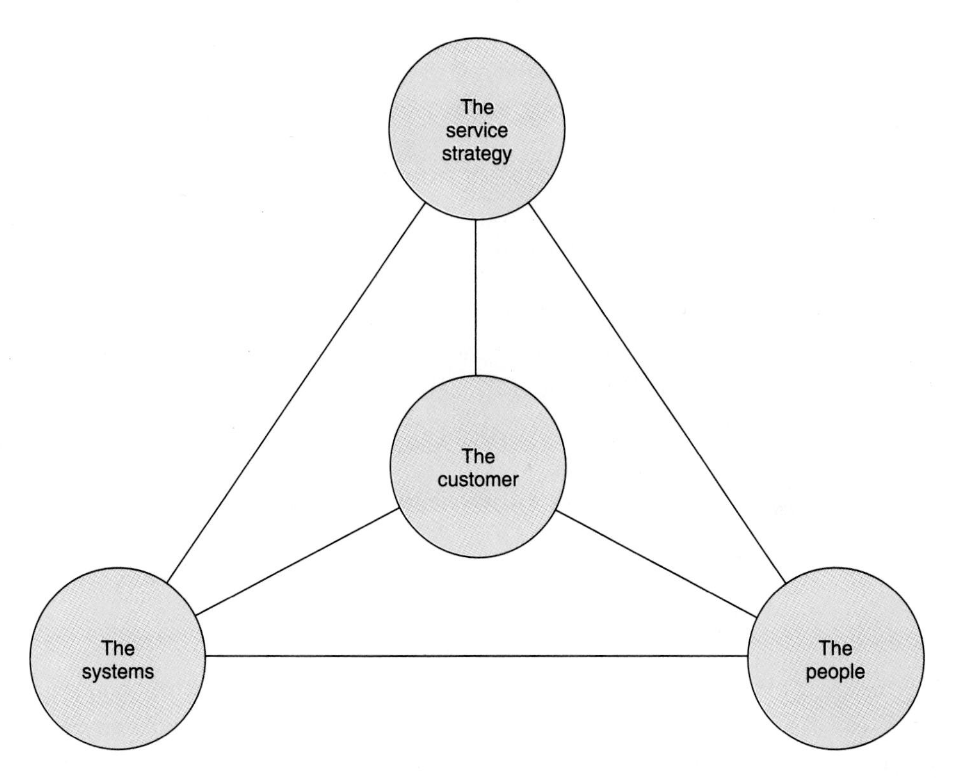

Source: Karl Albrecht and Ron Zemke, *Service America! Doing Business in the New Economy* (Homewood, Ill., Dow Jones-Irwin, 1985), p. 41.

generally how the worker will treat the public—if the work force is well trained and well motivated by management, they will respond by properly treating their customers efficiently and with courtesy.

The role of operations in the triangle is a major one. Operations is responsible both for service systems (procedures, equipment, and facilities) and for managing the service work force who typically comprise the majority of employees in large service organizations. However, before we discuss this role in depth, it is useful to first classify services to show how the customer affects the operations function.

5.2 AN OPERATIONAL CLASSIFICATION OF SERVICES

Services systems are generally classified along industry lines (financial services, health services, transportation services, and so on). These groupings, though useful in presenting aggregate economic data, are not particularly appropriate for OM purposes because they

Mark Davis

Postal workers sorting mail in one of the central post offices in Guangzhou, P.R.C. This post office provides same-day delivery in its immediate vicinity to letters mailed before 9:00 A.M.

tell us little about the process. In manufacturing, by contrast, there are fairly evocative terms to classify production activities that transcend industry lines (such as *intermittent* and *continuous production*); when applied to a manufacturing setting, they readily convey the essence of the process. While it is possible to describe services in these same terms, we need another item of information to reflect the fact that the customer is involved in the production system. That item, which we believe operationally distinguishes one service system from another in its production function, is the extent of customer contact in the creation of service.

Customer contact refers to the presence of the customer in the system, and *creation of the service* refers to the work process that is involved in providing the service itself. *Extent of contact* here may be roughly defined as the percentage of time the customer must be involved in the system relative to the total time it takes to perform the customer service. Generally speaking, the greater the percentage of contact time between the service system and the customer, the greater the degree of interaction between the two during the production process.

From this concept of customer contact, it follows that service systems with a **high degree of customer contact** are more difficult to control and more difficult to rationalize than those with a **low degree of customer contact.** In high-contact systems, the customer can affect the time of demand, the exact nature of the service, and the quality of service since the customer is involved in the process.

Exhibit 5.2 describes the implications of this distinction. Here we see that each design decision is impacted by whether or not the customer is present during service delivery. We

EXHIBIT 5.2

Major Differences between High- and Low-Contact Systems in a Bank

Design Decision	High-Contact System (a branch office)	Low-Contact System (a check processing center)
Facility location	Operations must be near the customer.	Operations may be placed near supply, transport, or labor.
Facility layout	Facility should accommodate the customer's physical and psychological needs and expectations.	Facility should focus on production efficiency.
Product design	Environment as well as the physical product define the nature of the service.	Customer is not in the service environment so the product can be defined by fewer attributes.
Process design	Stages of production process have a direct, immediate effect on the customer.	Customer is not involved in majority of processing steps.
Scheduling	Customer is in the production schedule and must be accommodated.	Customer is concerned mainly with completion dates.
Production planning	Orders cannot be stored, so smoothing production flow will result in loss of business.	Both backlogging and production smoothing are possible.
Worker skills	Direct work force constitutes a major part of the service product and so must be able to interact well with the public.	Direct work force need only have technical skills.
Quality control	Quality standards are often in the eye of the beholder and hence variable.	Quality standards are generally measurable and hence fixed.
Time standards	Service time depends on customer needs, and therefore time standards are inherently loose.	Work is performed on customer surrogates (e.g., forms), thus time standards can be tight.
Wage payment	Variable output requires time-based wage systems.	"Fixable" output permits output-based wage systems.
Capacity planning	To avoid lost sales, capacity must be set to match peak demand.	Storable output permits capacity at some average demand level.

also see that when work is done behind the scenes (in this case a bank's processing center), it is performed on customer surrogates—reports, databases, and invoices. We can, therefore, design it according to the same principles we would use in designing a factory. That is, to maximize the amount of items processed during the production day.

Obviously, there can be tremendous diversity of customer influence and hence system variability within high-contact service systems. For example, a bank branch offers both simple services such as cash withdrawals that take just a minute or so, and complicated services such as loan application preparation which can take in excess of an hour. Moreover, these activities may range from being self-service through an ATM, to coproduction where bank personnel and the customer work together as a team to develop the loan application. We have more to say on the ways to configure service activities in subsequent sections of this chapter.

EXHIBIT 5.3

The Service Process Matrix

		Degree of Interaction and Customization	
		Low	High
Degree of Labor Intensity	Low	Service factory: Airlines Trucking Hotels Resorts and recreation	Service shop: Hospitals Auto repair Other repair services
	High	Mass service: Retailing Wholesaling Schools Retail aspects of commercial banking	Professional service: Doctors Lawyers Accountants Architects

Source: Roger W. Schmenner, "How Can Service Businesses Survive and Prosper?", *Sloan Management Review* 27, no. 3 (Spring 1986), pp. 21–32.

In another attempt to better understand services in general, Roger Schmenner proposes a method for classifying services along two dimensions.[2] The first dimension, degree of customer interaction and customization, closely parallels the degree of customer contact we discuss above. In addition, Schmenner also includes the degree of labor intensity required to deliver the service. From these two factors he develops a service process matrix, as shown in Exhibit 5.3.

Within this matrix, Schmenner defines four broad categories of services:

1. *Service factory,* characterized by a low degree of labor intensity and a low degree of customer interaction and customization.
2. *Service shop* has the same low degree of labor intensity, but has a higher degree of customer interaction and customization.
3. *Mass service* is defined by a high degree of labor intensity, but has a relatively low degree of customer interaction.
4. *Professional service* requires both a high degree of labor intensity as well as a high degree of customer interaction and customization.

This type of classification scheme provides service managers with some insights in developing strategies for their respective organizations. For example, those services that exhibit a low degree of labor intensity are usually capital intense with high fixed costs. These firms cannot easily adjust capacity to meet changes in demand and must, therefore, attempt to smooth out the demand during peak periods by shifting it to off-peak times.

The issues confronting service managers with high labor intensity operations requires a

[2] Roger W. Schmenner, "How Can Service Businesses Survive and Prosper?" *Sloan Management Review* 27, no. 3 (Spring 1986).

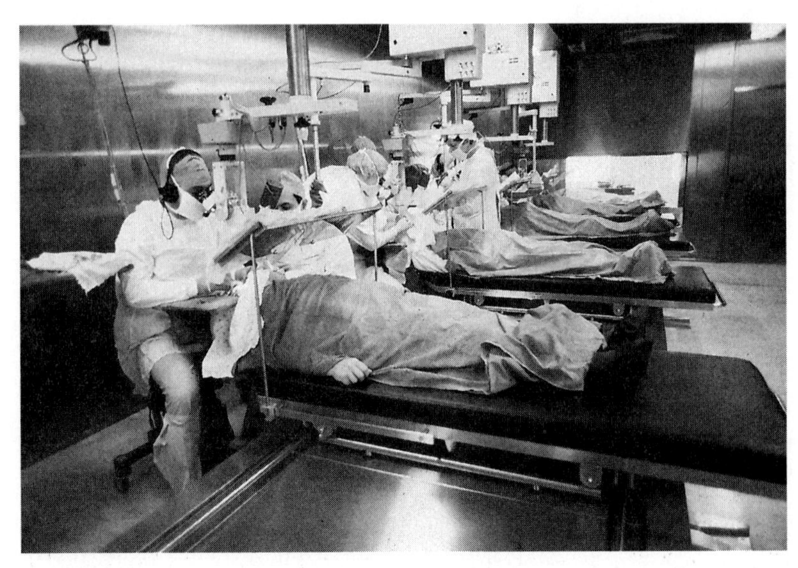

Tass/Sovfoto

Russian cataract surgery is performed in an assembly-line fashion.

different focus. Here, work force management is paramount, with emphasis being placed on hiring, training, and scheduling.

This approach to classifying services cuts across industry lines, providing service managers with a better understanding of the strengths and weaknesses within their own operations. Through this perspective, managers can look at similar operations in other industries to seek ways for improving their respective operations.

5.3 DESIGNING SERVICE ORGANIZATIONS

Designing a service organization entails the execution of four elements of what James Heskett refers to as the "Service Vision."[3] The first element is identification of the target market (Who is our customer?); the second is the service concept (How do we differentiate our service in the market?); the third is the service strategy (What is our service package and the operating focus of our service?); and fourth is the service delivery system (What are the actual processes, staff, and facilities by which the service is created?).

Choosing a target market and developing the service package are top management decisions setting the stage for the direct operating decisions of service strategy and delivery system design.

Several major factors distinguish service design and development from typical manufactured product development. First, the process and the product must be developed

[3] James L. Heskett, "Lessons from the Service Sector," *Harvard Business Review,* March–April 1987, pp. 118–26.

simultaneously; indeed, in services the process is the product. (We make this statement with the general recognition that many manufacturers are using such concepts as concurrent engineering and DFM [design for manufacture] as approaches to more closely link product design and process design.)

Second, although equipment and software that support a service can be protected by patents and copyrights, a service operation itself lacks the legal protection commonly available to goods production. Third, the service package, rather than a definable good, constitutes the major output of the development process. Fourth, many parts of the service package are often defined by the training individuals receive before they become part of the service organization. In particular, in professional service organizations (PSOs) such as law firms and hospitals, prior certification is necessary for hiring. Fifth, many service organizations can change their service offerings virtually overnight. Routine service organizations (RSOs) such as barbershops, retail stores, and restaurants have this flexibility.

Service Strategy: Focus and Advantage

Service strategy begins by selecting the operating focus by which the service firm will compete. These include:

- Speed and convenience of service delivery.
- Price of the service.
- Variety of services (essentially a one-stop shopping philosophy).
- Quality of the tangible goods that are central to or accompany the service. Examples include a "world-class" corned beef sandwich or an easily understood insurance policy.

These strategic choices of focus are not unlike those for a manufacturing company.

Service managers are increasingly recognizing the importance of focusing their operations to satisfy specific market segments. For example, the Shouldice Hospital in Toronto, Canada, only performs certain types of hernia operations; Holiday Inns now has separate divisions to focus on different segments of the lodging industry (Holiday Inns, Embassy Suites, Crowne Plazas, and Hampton Inns), as does Marriott (Marriott, Courtyards, Residence Inns, and Fairfield Inns).

Integrating marketing and operations to achieve competitive advantage

Achieving a competitive advantage in services requires integration of service marketing with service delivery so that the firm can meet or exceed customer expectations. This holds true no matter which competitive dimensions are emphasized. Companies that do extremely well (or extremely poorly) in this process create legends (or nightmares) (Exhibit 5.4).

As we shall see, a key factor in successfully satisfying, or rather delighting, customers is not to overpromise, thereby raising customer expectations beyond a realistic level. For example, Dunkin' Donuts's approach to this is "We promise a lot, but deliver a lot more." An overview of the elements leading to service advantage and service oblivion is shown in Exhibit 5.5. As can be seen in the diagram, marketing typically has responsibility for communicating the service promise to the customer and thereby creating customer

EXHIBIT 5.4

Levels of Satisfaction Achieved Due to Service Performance

Delighted
Satisfied
Customer experience
Legends
Dissatisfied
Irritated
Nightmares
Angry
Service performance

Source: The MAC Group: Building Value through Creating a Service Advantage, 1 Montgomery St., Telesis Tower, Suite 1700, San Francisco, CA 94104.

EXHIBIT 5.5 **Service Measurement Monitoring and Recovery Process**

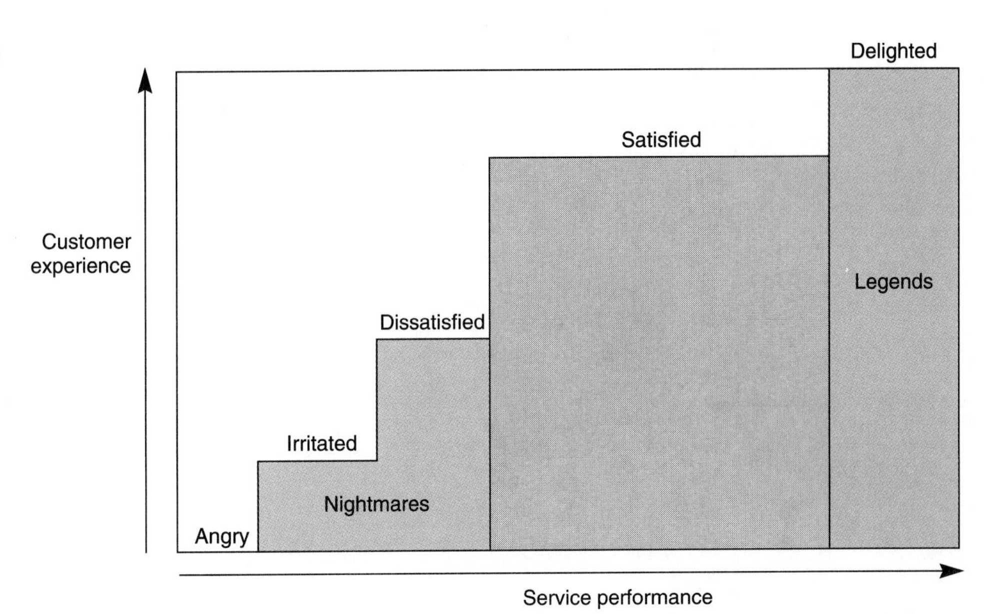

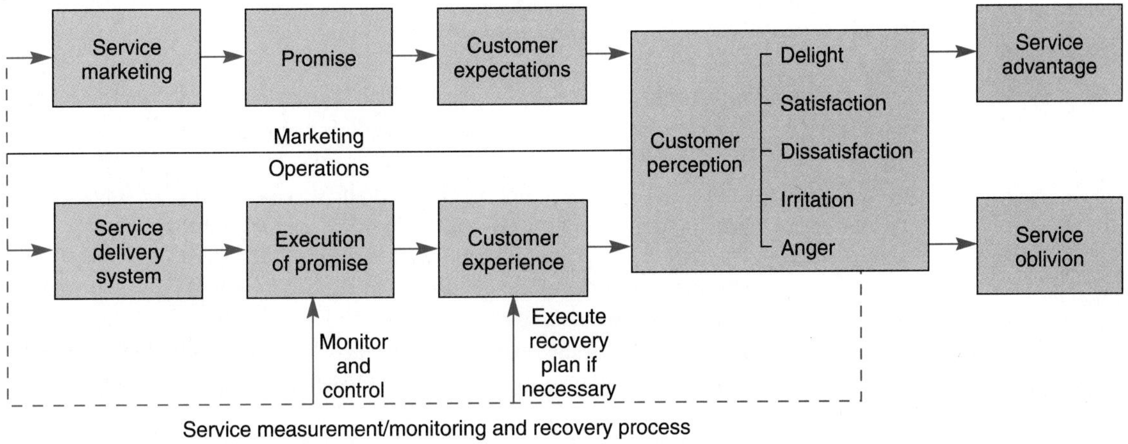

Service marketing
Promise
Customer expectations
Customer perception
Delight
Satisfaction
Dissatisfaction
Irritation
Anger
Service advantage
Marketing
Operations
Service delivery system
Execution of promise
Customer experience
Service oblivion
Monitor and control
Execute recovery plan if necessary
Service measurement/monitoring and recovery process

Source: The MAC Group: Building Value through Creating a Service Advantage, 1 Montgomery St., Telesis Tower, Suite 1700, San Francisco, CA 94104. June 1990.

expectations about service outcomes. Operations is responsible for the actions executing the promise and managing the customer experience. The feedback loop indicates that if outcomes are not satisfactory or do not create service advantage, management may alter either the service marketing strategy or the delivery system. The need to monitor and control the execution phase and have a recovery plan to diffuse negative reactions before the customer leaves the system is also indicated.

Monitoring and controlling involves the standard managerial actions of reassigning workers to deal with short-run demand variations (e.g., Lucky Supermarkets opening up another checkout stand when there are more than three people waiting in line); checking with customers and employees as to how things are going; and for many services, simply being visible to customers.

Recovery planning involves training frontline workers to respond to such situations as overbooking, lost luggage, or a bad meal. It also requires that management empower its workers to be able to resolve customer problems immediately. In general, customer satisfaction is inversely related to the amount of time required to resolve the problem.

5.4 STRUCTURING THE SERVICE ENCOUNTER: THE SERVICE-SYSTEM DESIGN MATRIX

Service encounters can be structured in a number of different ways. The **service-system design matrix** in Exhibit 5.6 identifies six common alternatives.

The top of the matrix shows the degree of customer/server contact: the *buffered core,* which is physically separated from the customer; the *permeable system,* which is penetrable by the customer via phone or face-to-face contact; and the *reactive system,* which is both penetrable and reactive to the customer's requirements. The left side of the matrix shows what we believe to be a logical marketing proposition, namely, that the greater the amount of contact, the greater the opportunity to generate additional sales; the right side shows the impact on production efficiency as the customer exerts more influence on the operation.

The entries within the matrix list the ways in which service can be delivered. At one extreme, service contact is by mail; customers have little interaction with the systems. At the other extreme, customers are treated on an individual basis through face-to-face contact. The remaining four entries in the exhibit contain varying degrees of interaction.

As one would anticipate, production efficiency decreases as the customer contact time increases, thereby giving the customer more influence on the system. To offset this, however, the face-to-face contact provides greater opportunity to sell additional products. Conversely, low contact, such as mail, allows the system to work more efficiently because the customer is unable to significantly affect (or disrupt) the system. However, there is relatively little, if any, sales opportunity for additional product sales at this end of the spectrum.

There can be some shifting in the positioning of each entry. Consider the Exhibit 5.6 entry, "face-to-face tight specs." This refers to those situations where there is little variation in the service process—neither customer nor server has much discretion in creating the service. Fast-food restaurants and Disneyland come to mind. "Face-to-face loose specs" refers to situations where the service process is generally understood but there are options in the way it will be performed or the physical goods that are a part of it. A full-service restaurant or a car sales agency are examples. Face-to-face total customization refers to service encounters whose specifications must be developed through some interaction between the customer and server. Legal and medical services are of this type, and the degree to which the resources of the system are mustered for the service determines whether the system is reactive or merely permeable. Examples would be the mobilization of an advertising firm's resources in preparation for an office visit by a major client, or an operating team scrambling to prepare for emergency surgery.

Exhibit 5.7 is an extension of the design matrix, showing the different worker requirements, operations focus, and types of technical innovations as the degree of customer/service system contact changes. For worker requirements, the relationships between mail contact and clerical skills, on-site technology and helping skills, and phone contact and verbal skills are self-evident. Face-to-face tight specs require procedural skills in particular, because the worker must follow the routine in conducting a generally standardized, high-volume process. Face-to-face loose specs frequently call for trade skills (shoemaker, draftsperson, maitre d', dental hygienist) to finalize the design for the service. Face-to-face total customization tends to call for diagnostic skills of a professional to ascertain the needs or desires of the client.

Strategic Uses of the Matrix

The service-system design matrix has both operational and strategic uses. Its operational uses are reflected in its identification of worker requirements, focus of operations, and innovations previously discussed. Some of its strategic uses are

1. Enabling systematic integration of operations and marketing strategy. Trade-offs become more clear-cut, and, more important, at least some of the major design variables are crystalized for analysis purposes. For example, the matrix indicates that it would make little sense relative to sales for a service firm to invest in high-skilled workers if it plans to operate using tight specs.
2. Clarifying exactly which combination of service delivery the firm is actually providing. As the company incorporates the delivery options listed on the diagonal, it is becoming diversified in its production process.
3. Permitting comparison with other firms in the way specific services are delivered. This helps to pinpoint a firm's competitive advantage.
4. Indicating evolutionary or life cycle changes that might be in order as the firm grows. Unlike the product-process matrix for manufacturing, however, where natural growth moves in one direction (from intermittent to line-flow as a volume increases), the evolution of service delivery can move in either direction along the diagonal as a function of the trade-off between efficiency and the potential to generate additional sales.
5. Providing flexibility. The user of the matrix can go into depth, placing particular

EXHIBIT 5.6 Service-System Design Matrix

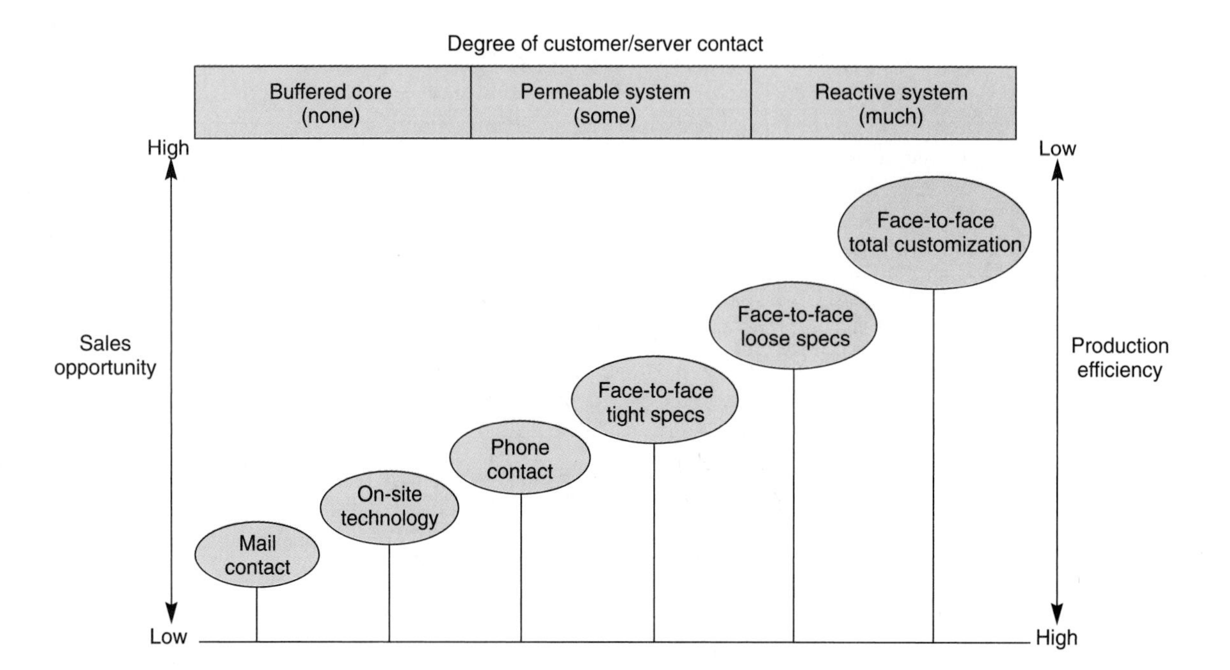

EXHIBIT 5.7 Characteristics of Workers, Operations, and Innovations Relative to the Degree of Customer/Service Contact

Degree of customer/server contact

Low ← → High

Worker requirements	Clerical skills	Helping skills	Verbal skills	Procedural skills	Trade skills	Diagnostic skills
Focus of operations	Paper handling	Demand management	Scripting calls	Flow control	Capacity management	Client mix
Technological innovations	Office automation	Routing methods	Computer databases	Electronic aids	Self-serve	Client/worker teams

service products of a small firm or individual department on it, or cover a large service organization at a more aggregated level.

5.5 SERVICE BLUEPRINTING

Just as is the case with manufacturing process design, the standard tool for service process design is the flowchart. In 1978, Lynn Shostack added the concept of the *line of visibility* and emphasized the identification of potential fail points in her version of the flowchart called a **service blueprint.**[4] She has also made a compelling argument for having blueprints on every aspect of a service, and having the "keeper of the blueprint" as a specific job function in any large service organization. Current practice in some companies is to have blueprints available on computers so when problems arise, senior managers can zero in on any portion of a service process and thereby make more informed decisions about how to resolve them. One example is the service blueprint for a cash account at a discount brokerage, as shown in Exhibit 5.8.

A key element in developing the service blueprint is the *line of visibility.* All activities above the line take place in direct contact with the customer. Those activities below the line are considered to be "backroom" operations, taking place without the customer's presence. Activities above the line of visibility, therefore, need to focus on providing good service; backroom operations, on the other hand, should focus on increasing process efficiency.

As an example, the steps involved in developing a blueprint for a simple shoeshine process, including a profitability analysis, are as follows:

1. *Identify processes.* The first step in creating such a blueprint is mapping the processes that constitute the service. Exhibit 5.9 maps out the various steps in providing a shoeshine. As the service is simple and clear-cut, the map is straightforward. It might be useful to specify how the proprietor will perform the step called *buff.*

2. *Isolate fail points.* Having diagrammed the processes involved, the designer can now see where the system might go awry. For example, the shoeshiner may pick up and apply the wrong color wax, so the designer must build in a subprocess to correct this possible error. The identification of fail points and the design of fail-safe processes are critical. The consequences of service failures can be greatly reduced by analyzing fail points at the design stage.

3. *Establish a time frame.* Since all services depend on time, which is usually the major cost determinant, the designer should establish a standard execution time.

4. *Analyze profitability.* The customer can spend the three minutes between standard and acceptable execution time at the shoeshine parlor waiting in line or during service, if an error occurs or if the shoeshiner does certain things too slowly. Whatever its source, a delay can affect profits dramatically. Exhibit 5.10 quantifies the cost of delay; after four minutes the proprietor loses money. A service designer must establish a time-of-service-execution standard to ensure a profitable business.

---

[4] G. Lynn Shostack, "Designing Services That Deliver," *Harvard Business Review* 62, no. 1 (January–February 1984), p. 135.

EXHIBIT 5.8 Service Blueprint for a Cash Account at a Discount Brokerage

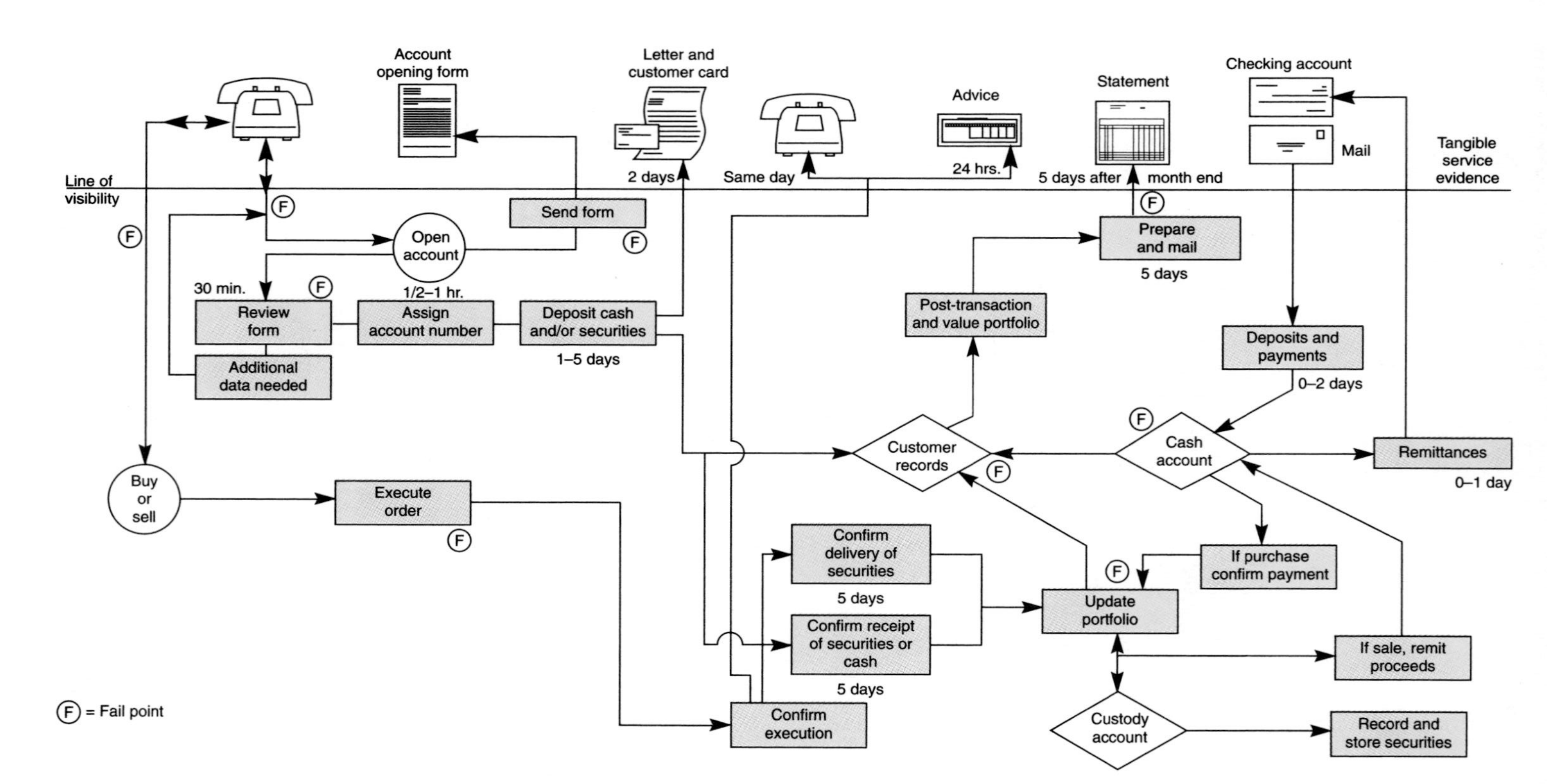

Source: Adapted from G. Lynn Shostack, "Designing Services That Deliver," *Harvard Business Review* 62, no. 1 (January–February 1984), p. 138.

EXHIBIT 5.9 Blueprint for a Corner Shoeshine

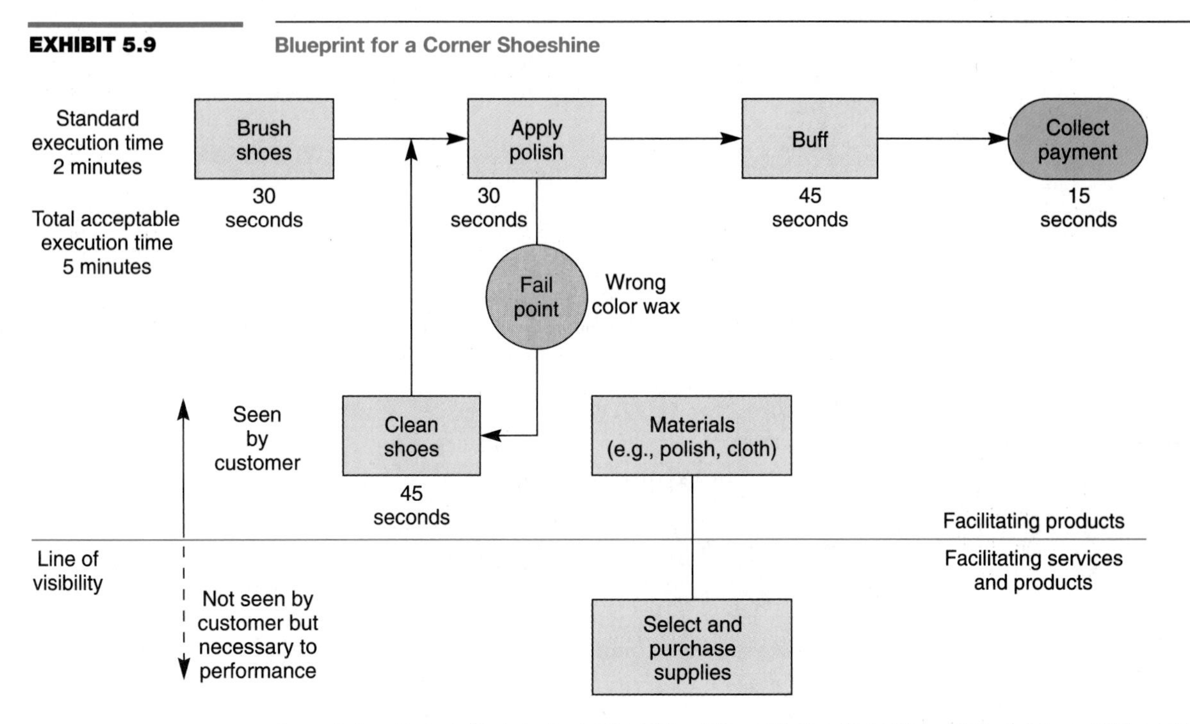

Source: G. Lynn Shostack, "Designing Services That Deliver," *Harvard Business Review* 62, no. 1 (January–February 1984), p. 134.

EXHIBIT 5.10

Shoeshine Profitability Analysis

	EXECUTION TIME		
	2 Minutes	3 Minutes	4 Minutes
Price	$.50	$.50	$.50
Costs			
Time @ $.10 per minute	.20	.30	.40
Wax	.03	.03	.03
Other operating expenses	.09	.09	.09
Total costs	$.32	$.42	$.52
Pretax profit	$.18	$.08	($.02)

Source: G. Lynn Shostack, "Designing Services That Deliver," *Harvard Business Review* 62, no. 1 (January–February 1984), p. 135.

In the shoeshine example, the standard execution time is two minutes. Research showed that the customer would tolerate up to five minutes of performance before lowering his or her assessment of quality. Acceptable executive time for a shoeshine is then five minutes.

5.6 THREE CONTRASTING SERVICE DESIGNS

The three general approaches to delivering on-site services are the production line approach made famous by McDonald's Corporation, the customer involvement approach made famous by ATMs and gas stations, and the personal attention approach made famous by Nordstrom department stores.

The Production Line Approach

The production line approach pioneered by McDonald's refers to more than just the steps required to assemble a Big Mac. Rather, as Theodore Levitt notes, it is treating the delivery of fast food as a manufacturing process rather than a service process.[5] The value of this philosophy is that it overcomes many of the problems inherent in the concept of service itself. That is, service implies subordination or subjugation of the server to the served; manufacturing, on the other hand, avoids this connotation because it focuses on things rather than people. Thus, in manufacturing and at McDonald's, "the orientation is toward the efficient production of results not on the attendance on others." Levitt notes that besides McDonald's marketing and financial skills, the company carefully controls "the execution of each outlet's central function—the rapid delivery of a consistently uniform, high-quality mix of prepared foods in an environment of obvious cleanliness, order, and cheerful courtesy. The systematic substitution of equipment for people, combined with the carefully planned use and positioning of technology, enables McDonald's to attract and hold patronage in proportions no predecessor or imitator has managed to duplicate."

Levitt cites several aspects of McDonald's operations to illustrate the concepts:

- The McDonald's french fryer allows cooking of the optimum number of french fries at one time.
- A wide-mouthed scoop is used to pick up the precise amount of french fries for each order size. (The employee never touches the product.)
- Storage space is expressly designed for a predetermined mix of prepackaged and premeasured products.
- Cleanliness is pursued by providing ample trash cans in and outside each facility (and the larger outlets have motorized sweepers for the parking area).
- Hamburgers are wrapped in color-coded paper.
- Through painstaking attention to total design and facilities planning, everything is built

---

[5] Theodore Levitt, "Production-Line Approach to Service," *Harvard Business Review* 50, no. 5 (September–October 1972), pp. 41–52.

integrally into the (McDonald's) machine itself—into the technology of the system. The only choice available to the attendant is to operate it exactly as the designers intended.

The Customer Involvement Approach

In contrast to the production line approach, C. H. Lovelock and R. F. Young propose that the service process can be enhanced by having the customer take a greater participatory role in the production of the service.[6] Automatic teller machines, self-service gas stations, salad bars, and in-room coffee-making equipment in motels are good examples of where the service burden is shifted to the consumer. Obviously, this philosophy requires some selling on the part of the service organization to convince customers that this is beneficial to them. To this end, Lovelock and Young propose a number of steps, including developing customer trust, promoting the benefits of cost, speed, and convenience, and following up to make sure that the procedures are being effectively used. In essence, this turns customers into "partial employees" who must be trained in what to do and be compensated primarily through low prices charged for the service.

The Personal Attention Approach

The following example by Tom Peters describes how Nordstrom department store operationalizes its personal attention philosophy.[7]

> After several visits to a store's men's clothing department, a customer's suit still did not fit. He wrote the company president, who sent a tailor to the customer's office with a new suit for fitting. When the alterations were completed, the suit was delivered to the customer—free of charge.
>
> This incident involved the $1.3 billion, Seattle-based Nordstrom, a specialty clothing retailer. Its sales per square foot are about five times that of a typical department store. Who received the customer's letter and urged the extreme (by others' standards) response? Co-chairman John Nordstrom.
>
> The frontline providers of this good service are well paid. Nordstrom's salespersons earn a couple of bucks an hour more than competitors, plus a 6.75 percent commission. Its top salesperson moves over $1 million a year in merchandise. Nordstrom lives for its customers and salespeople. Its only official organization chart puts the customer at the top, followed by sales and sales support people. Next come department managers, then store managers, and the board of directors at the very bottom.
>
> Salespersons religiously carry a "personal book," where they record voluminous information about each of their customers; senior, successful salespeople often have three or four bulging books, which they carry everywhere, according to Betsy Sanders, the vice president who orchestrated the firm's wildly successful penetration of the tough southern California market. "My objective is to get one new personal customer a day," says a budding Nordstrom star. The system helps him do just that. He has a virtually unlimited budget to send cards, flowers, and

[6] C. H. Lovelock and R. F. Young, "Look to Customers to Increase Productivity," *Harvard Business Review* 57, no. 2, pp. 168–78.

[7] Tom Peters, *Quality!* Palo Alto, Calif.: TPG Communications, 1986, pp. 10–12.

thank-you notes to customers. He also is encouraged to shepherd his customer to any department in the store to assist in a successful shopping trip.

He also is abetted by what may be the most liberal returns policy in this or any other business: Return *anything,* no questions asked. Sanders says that "trusting customers,"or "our bosses" as she repeatedly calls them, is vital to the Nordstrom philosophy. President Jim Nordstrom told the *Los Angeles Times,* "I don't care if they roll a Goodyear tire into the store. If they say they paid $200, give them $200 (in cash) for it."Sanders acknowledges that a few customers rip the store off—"rent hose from us," to use a common insider's line. But this is more than offset by goodwill from the 99 percent-plus who benefit from the "No Problem at Nordstrom" logo that the company lives up to with unmatched zeal.

No bureaucracy gets in the way of serving the customer. Policy? Sanders explains to a dumbfounded group of Silicon Valley executives, "I know this drives the lawyers nuts, but our whole 'policy manual' is just one sentence, 'Use your own best judgment at all times.'" One store manager offers a translation, "Don't chew gum. Don't steal from us."

No matter what approach is taken, seven common characteristics of well-designed service systems have been identified:

1. *Each element of the service system is consistent with the operating focus of the firm.* For example, when the focus is on speed of delivery, each step in the process should help to foster speed.
2. *It is user-friendly.* This means that the customer can interact with it easily—that is, it has good signage, understandable forms, logical steps in the process, courteous service workers that are available to answer questions, and is easily accessible.
3. *It is robust.* That is, it can cope effectively with variations in demand and resource availability. For example, if the computer goes down, effective backup systems are in place to permit service to continue.
4. *It is structured so that consistent performance by its people and systems is easily maintained.* This means that the tasks required of the workers can be performed repeatedly with a high level of consistency, and the supporting technologies are truly supportive and reliable.
5. *It provides effective links between the back office and the front office so that nothing falls between the cracks.* In other words, the barriers between the different functional areas are reduced or eliminated.
6. *It manages the evidence of service quality in such a way that customers see the value of the service provided.* Many services do a great job behind the scenes but fail to make this visible to the customer. This is particularly true where a service improvement is made. Unless customers are made aware of the improvement through explicit communication about it, the improved performance is unlikely to gain maximum impact.
7. *It is cost-effective.* There is minimum waste of time and resources in delivering the service.

5.7 CONCLUSION

How to manage services better clearly lags behind understanding how to manage manufacturing better. In fact, many of the concepts that have been successfully developed in manufacturing have been adopted by service operations. Nevertheless, services are different from manufacturing, and managers must recognize these differences (the prime difference being the interaction of the customer with the service delivery process). Although service design was once considered an art form, specific logical approaches to better design and management of service systems are slowly emerging.

At the same time, there also appears to be a blurring between what we typically think of as manufacturing firms and what we think of as service firms. For example, companies such as Bally Manufacturing, Turner Construction, and Exxon Pipeline, which started out as manufacturing firms, are now listed among the Fortune 500 service companies. IBM, which is considered to be a manufacturer, derives a major portion of its revenues and profits from various services that it provides. In fact, within manufacturing (as we noted in Chapter 2) we predict that service will be the next source of competitive advantage.

5.8 REVIEW AND DISCUSSION QUESTIONS

1. Who is the "customer" in a jail? A cemetery? A summer camp for children?
2. How has price competition changed McDonald's basic formula for success?
3. Is it possible for a service firm to use either a production line approach or a self-serve design and still keep a high customer focus (personal attention)? Explain and support your answer with examples.
4. Explain why a manager of a bank home office should be evaluated differently than a manager of a bank branch office.
5. Identify the high-contact and low-contact operations in the following services:
   a. A dental office.
   b. An airline.
   c. An accounting office.
   d. An automobile agency.
6. Some suggest that customer expectation is the key to service success. Give an example from your own experience to support or refute this assertion.
7. Where would you place a drive-in church, a campus food vending machine, and a bar's automatic mixed drink machine on the service-system design matrix?
8. What do customer expectations have to do with service quality?
9. Using Schmenner's classification scheme, identify different segments within a broad service industry (e.g., food service, health care, transportation, etc.) that meet the characteristics found in at least two of the four quadrants, and discuss the key managerial issues in each segment.

5.9 PROBLEMS

1. Place the following functions of a department store on the service-system design matrix: Mail order (i.e., catalog), phone order, hardware, stationery, apparel, cosmetics, customer service (i.e., complaints).
2. Do the same as in the previous problem for a hospital with the following activities and relationships: Physician/patient, nurse/patient, billing, medical records, lab tests, admissions, diagnostic tests (e.g., X-rays).
3. The service designer for the shoeshine shop of Exhibits 5.9 and 5.10 has decided to study the following changes:
   - Add a premium two-coat service, which will repeat Steps 2 and 3 (Apply polish and Buff). The price of the premium service will be set at $.70.
   - Provide each customer (both regular and premium) with a receipt and a sample of shoe polish imprinted with the shop's name. This will add $.01 to operating expenses and 0.5 minutes to the execution time but will provide the customer with some tangible evidence of the service.

   Both of these changes are to be made simultaneously. Do the following:

   a. Draw the blueprint for the premium service.
   b. Provide a profitability analysis for the premium service.
   c. Provide an updated profitability analysis for the regular service.
4. SYSTEM DESCRIPTION EXERCISE

   The first step in studying a production system is to develop a description of that system. Once a system is described, we are better able to determine why the system works well or poorly and to recommend production-related improvements. Since we are all familiar with fast-food restaurants, try your hand at describing the production system employed at, say, a McDonald's. In doing so, answer the following questions:

   a. What are the important aspects of the service package?
   b. Which skills and attitudes are needed by the service personnel?
   c. How can customer demand be altered?
   d. Provide a rough-cut blueprint of the delivery system. (It is not necessary to provide execution times—just diagram the basic flow through the system.) Critique the blueprint. Are there any unnecessary steps or can fail points be eliminated?
   e. Can the customer/provider interface be changed to include more technology? More self-serve?
   f. Which measures are being used to evaluate and measure the service? Which could be used?
   g. How does it measure up on the seven characteristics of a well-designed service?

5.10 SELECTED BIBLIOGRAPHY

Albrecht, Karl, and Ron Zemke. *Service America! Doing Business in the New Economy* (Homewood, Ill.: Dow Jones-Irwin, 1985).

Bitran, Gabriel R., and Johannes Hoech. "The Humanization of Service: Respect at the Moment of Truth." *Sloan Management Review,* Winter 1990, pp. 89–96.

Chase, R. B. "The Customer Contact Approach to Services: Theoretical Bases and Practical Extensions." *Operations Research* 21, no. 4 (1981), pp. 698–705.

Cohen, Morris A., and Hau L. Lee. "Out of Touch with Customer Needs?" *Sloan Management Review,* Winter 1990, pp. 55–66.

Collier, D. A. *Service Management: The Automation of Services.* Reston, Va.: Reston Publishing, 1986.

Davidow, William H., and Bro Uttal. "Service Companies: Focus or Falter," *Harvard Business Review* 67, no. 4 (July–August 1989), pp. 77–85.

Farsad, Behshid, and Ahmad K. Elshennawy. "Defining Service Quality Is Difficult for Service and Manufacturing Firms."*Industrial Engineering,* March 1989, pp. 17–20.

Firnstahl, Timothy W. "My Employees Are My Service Guarantee." *Harvard Business Review,* July–August 1989, pp. 28–33.

Fitzsimmons, J. A., and R. S. Sullivan. *Service Operations Management.* New York: McGraw-Hill, 1983.

Flint, Jerry, and William Heuslein. "An Urge to Service." *Forbes,* September 18, 1989, pp. 172–74.

Hackett, Gregory P. "Investment in Technology: The Service Sector Sinkhole?" *Sloan Management Review,* Winter 1990, pp. 97–103.

Heskett, James L. *Managing in the Service Economy.* Cambridge, Mass.: Harvard University Press, 1986.

________. "Lessons from the Service Sector." *Harvard Business Review,* March-April 1987, pp. 118–26.

Levitt, Theodore. "Production-Line Approach to Service." *Harvard Business Review* 50, no. 5 (September-October 1972), pp. 41–52.

Lovelock, C. H., and R. E. Young. "Look to Customers to Increase Productivity." *Harvard Business Review* 57, no. 2, pp. 168–78.

Peavey, Dennis E. "It's Time for a Change." *Management Accounting,* February 1990, pp. 31–35.

Peters, Tom. *Quality!* Palo Alto, Calif.: TPG Communications, 1986.

Schmenner, Roger W. "How Can Service Businesses Survive and Prosper?" *Sloan Management Review* 27, no. 3 (Spring 1986).

Shapiro, Benson P.; V. Kasturi Rangan; Rowland T. Moriarty; and Elliot B. Ross. "Manage Customers for Profits, Not Just Sales." *Harvard Business Review,* September–October 1987, pp. 101–8.

Shostack, G. Lynn. "Designing Services That Deliver." *Harvard Business Review* 62, no. 1 (January-February 1984), p. 135.

Sonnenberg, Frank K. "Service Quality: Forethought, Not Afterthought." *Journal of Business Strategy,* September–October 1989, pp. 54–57.

Chapter 6

Quality Management

EPIGRAPH

Quality management is not just a strategy. It must be a new style of working, even a new style of thinking. A dedication to quality and excellence is more than good business. It is a way of life, giving something back to society, offering your best to others.

George Bush

CHAPTER OUTLINE

KEY TERMS

Total Quality Management (TQM)
Quality Dimensions
Quality at the Source
Continuous Improvement
Design Quality
Conformance Quality
Quality Function Deployment
House of Quality
Quality Gurus
Statistical Process Control (SPC)
Fitness for Use
Cost of Quality
Cost of Prevention
Cost of Detection/Appraisal
Cost of Failure
Internal Failure Costs
External Failure Costs
Seven Management and Planning (MP) Tools
Seven Basic Quality Control (QC) Tools
Taguchi Methods
ISO 9000

The quality movement can trace its roots back to Walter Shewhart's development of the first process control chart in the 1920s, while he was employed as a statistician at Bell Labs. During World War II, the use of statistics to monitor the quality of wartime supplies increased out of necessity, due in part to both the vast quantities of material being produced and the shortage of labor on the home front. Emphasis on quality began to gain momentum in Japan shortly after World War II, with significant contributions being made by W. Edwards Deming and Joseph Juran, both of whom, like Shewhart, were statisticians.

In the United States, however, the importance of quality as a key element in the success of an organization didn't begin to be recognized until the late 1970s. In 1980, NBC presented a documentary entitled "If Japan Can, Why Can't We?" which highlighted Deming's significant contribution to improving the quality of Japanese products. Only after this documentary was aired was Deming asked to assist U.S. companies in improving the quality of their products. The shift in focus of U.S. companies to quality, beginning in the 1980s, has not gone unnoticed. Significant improvements in the quality of U.S. products has been recognized by consumers. The Ford Taurus, for example, is now the best-selling car in the United States, a distinction previously held by the Honda Accord for many years.

In this chapter we introduce some of the basic concepts of **total quality management (TQM)**, which are critical elements in the successful implementation of quality programs not only in Japan, but also in North America and Europe. As part of this discussion, we present some of the traditional as well as emerging technical topics that directly relate to quality, with which all managers should be familiar. While we emphasize the technical aspects that are required for a successful quality effort, we also recognize the importance of the human element, in terms of providing the proper leadership and the need for worker involvement as an integral part of the quality improvement process. To quote Tom Peters, "Most quality programs fail for one of two reasons: They have system without passion, or passion without system."[1] We also introduce the concept of using quality as a strategic, offensive weapon instead of its historically defensive use.

6.1 THE STRATEGIC ROLE OF QUALITY

For many years following World War II, quality was viewed primarily as a defensive function rather than as an offensive weapon for use in developing new markets and increasing market share. In this role, the main purpose of the quality control (QC) function (as it was referred to then) was to reduce the number of customer complaints that were received. As a result, there was a heavy reliance on inspection (i.e., sorting the good from the bad) rather than on prevention. This strategy formed the basis for the belief that higher quality was more expensive, that is, the more one inspects, the better the quality. The quality control manager often reported to the manufacturing manager, and therefore had little or no power in terms of his or her ability to either halt production or hold up the shipment of faulty products.

[1] Tom Peters, *Thriving on Chaos* (New York: Knopf, 1987), p. 74.

Superstock, Inc.

A baseball bat factory employee is shown using quality standards in 1951.

Today, however, more and more companies recognize the value of using quality as an offensive, strategic weapon. In adopting this approach, these firms are able to both identify new market niches and increase their market share in existing ones. However, in taking the offensive with quality, managers must realize that there is more than one facet or dimension on which it can focus, and, in fact, some of these may even be in conflict. David Garvin[2] has identified eight different **quality dimensions** on which a company can compete. These are: (1) performance, (2) features, (3) reliability, (4) conformance, (5) durability, (6) serviceability, (7) aesthetics, and (8) perceived quality.

Performance

Performance is a measure of a product's primary operating characteristics. Since performance can be measured in specific quantitative terms, a product's performance characteristics are often compared and ranked with those of the competition. With an automobile, for example, performance characteristics would include how fast it could accelerate from 0 to 60 mph and its fuel efficiency in terms of miles per gallon. For a commercial airplane, performance might include its cruising speed and the runway distances required for it to take off and land.

[2] David Garvin, "Competing on the Eight Dimensions of Quality," *Harvard Business Review* (November–December 1987), pp. 101–9.

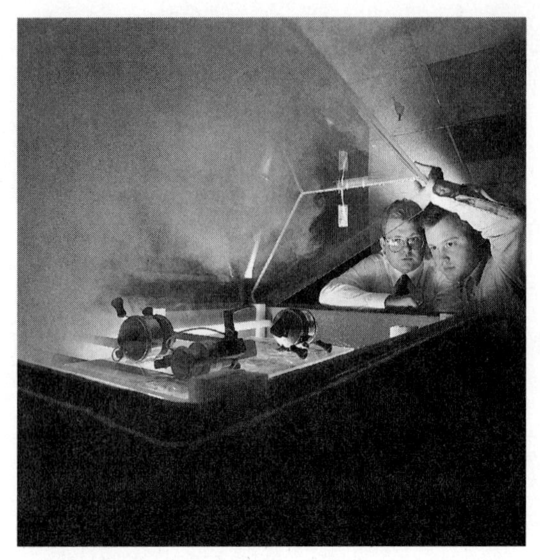

Courtesy Brunswick Corporation

Fishing reels manufactured by the Zebco Division of Brunswick Corporation undergo a special humidity testing procedure to measure durability and ensure quality.

Features

The wider the variety of product models and/or variations a company can offer its customers, the higher the perceived quality of those products, because customers perceive customization as a dimension of quality. New Balance, for example, focused on this dimension when it introduced several choices of width in its line of athletic footwear. Often customization can be accomplished by providing options that can further enhance the product. Modularization (using a combination of standard modules or subassemblies to custom design a product for a customer) provides another approach for accomplishing this.

Reliability

The reliability of a product relates to the probability that the product will fail within a specified time. Reliability is often measured as the mean time between failures (MTBF) or the failure rate per unit of time or other measure of usage. High product reliability is important in such products as airplanes, computers, and copying machines. Stratus Computers, for example, has successfully carved out a niche for itself in the highly competitive computer industry by offering "fault-free" computer systems. The bored Maytag repairman with no service calls offers another good example of product reliability.

designed a car in which one of the spark plugs could not be removed without pulling out the entire engine. The speed of the repair is also important, in that it affects the overall number of products needed in those circumstances where constant coverage is required. Using a city's paramedic service as an example, the frequency and the amount of time a paramedic vehicle requires repair and maintenance impacts directly on the total number of vehicles needed to provide the proper level of coverage.

Aesthetics

Aesthetics is obviously an area where there is a high degree of individual judgment. This dimension is one in which all of the parties involved can never agree as to what constitutes good quality. In fact, in terms of aesthetics, good quality to one group of customers might even be perceived as poor quality to another group. Companies, therefore, have an opportunity with this quality dimension to seek out a very specific market niche.

MEASURES

	Service Example: Checking Account at Bank
tio, power	Time to process customer requests
	Automatic bill paying
failure	Variability of time to process requests
(with repair)	Keeping pace with industry trends
repair	Resolution of errors
tesy of dealer	Courtesy of teller
ak-finished cabinet	Appearance of bank lobby
Consumer Reports ranking	Advice of friends, years in business

ul E. Plsek, "Defining Quality at the Marketing/Development Interface," *Quality Progress* (June 1987),

ceived Quality

According to Garvin, perceived quality is directly related to the reputation of the firm that manufactures the product. Often, total information about the various quality aspects of a product are not available, especially when it is a new product that is being introduced for the first time. Consequently, customers rely heavily on the past performance and reputation of the firm making the product, attaching a perceived value based on the previous performance of the company's other products.

Exhibit 6.1 provides two examples, from Paul Plsek, of the dimensions of quality: a stereo amplifier that meets the signal-to-noise ratio standard, and a checking account transaction in a bank. (Note that Plsek substitutes response for conformance and refers to perceived quality as reputation.)

6.2 THE ELEMENTS OF TQM

There are four primary elements that are integral to every successful TQM program. These elements are (1) leadership, (2) employee involvement, (3) product/process excellence, and (4) customer focus.

Leadership

The leadership provided by an organization's management is a major cornerstone in the development and implementation of a successful TQM program. When properly executed, a TQM program is companywide, transcends traditional functional areas, and involves all of the firm's employees. It therefore requires vision, planning, and communication, all of which are the responsibility of top management. Studies have indicated that although TQM programs often do not receive total commitment from management, this commitment is considered to be a critical element in successfully implementing such programs.

Top management can demonstrate its commitment to a TQM program in several ways. These include incorporating TQM into the firm's overall strategy, and demonstrating by actions as well as by words that quality is the number one operating priority of the organization.

Employee Involvement

Employee involvement is another critical element in successfully implementing a TQM program. By involving all employees in the decision-making process, management is able to receive inputs from those nearest the problems and, thus, in the best position to recommend viable solutions. Employee involvement also takes advantage of the skills and knowledge of all employees, which appears to be prevalent in world-class operations.

A key element in employee involvement is that each worker assumes the responsibility for inspecting the quality of his or her own work. This is referred to as **quality at the source.** This view changes the often adversarial practice of having a QC inspector, typically from the QC department, making decisions about good or bad quality. This philosophy, as currently practiced, extends beyond the worker to include the work group, all departments, and the suppliers of parts and services to the organization.

Product/Process Excellence

Product/process excellence involves the quality of the product's design and analysis of field failures. It also includes statistical process control (SPC) and other analytical tools (which are discussed later in this chapter).

Process control is concerned with monitoring quality *while the product is being produced or the service is being performed.* Typical objectives of process control plans are to provide timely information on whether currently produced items are meeting design specifications and to detect shifts in the process that signal that future products may not meet specifications. The actual control phase of process control occurs when corrective action is taken, such as when a worn part is replaced, a machine is overhauled, or a new supplier is found. Process control concepts, especially statistically based control charts, are being used in services as well as in manufacturing. (The actual application of process control and the use of statistics to support it are presented in greater detail later in this chapter.)

An underlying philosophy in achieving product/process excellence is the concept of **continuous improvement.** This has a general meaning and a specific TQM meaning. Its general meaning is an ongoing effort to simply make improvements in every part of the organization relative to all of its deliverables to its customers. Its more specific meaning focuses on continual improvement in the quality of the processes by which work is accomplished. Thus, the phrase continuous process improvement often defines its purpose in the context of TQM.

Customer Focus

What we mean by customer focus is that "your product isn't reliable unless the customer says it's reliable," and "your service isn't fast unless the customer says it's fast." Thus, the customer's perception of quality must be taken into account in setting acceptable quality levels. Translating customer quality demands into specifications requires marketing (or product development) to accurately determine what the customer wants and product designers to develop a product (or service) that can be produced to consistently achieve that desired level of quality. This, in turn, requires that we have an operational definition of quality, an understanding of its various dimensions, and a process for including the voice of the customer in those specifications. The quality of a product or service may be defined by the quality of its design (i.e., product quality) and the quality of its conformance to that design (i.e., process quality). **Design quality** refers to the inherent value of the product in the marketplace and is thus a strategic decision for the firm, as discussed earlier in this chapter.

Conformance quality refers to the degree to which the product or service design specifications are met. It, too, has strategic implications, but the execution of the activities involved in achieving conformance are of a tactical day-to-day nature. It should be evident that a product or service can have high design quality but low conformance quality, and vice versa.

The operations function and the quality organization within the firm are primarily concerned with quality of conformance. Achieving all the quality specifications is typically the responsibility of manufacturing management, where a product is involved, and branch operations management in a service industry.

Both design quality and conformance quality should provide products that meet the customer's objectives for those products. This is often termed the product's *fitness for use,* and it entails identifying those dimensions of the product (or service) that the customer wants and developing a quality control program to ensure that these dimensions are met.

Quality function deployment. One approach for translating the voice of the customer into the design specifications of a product is **quality function deployment** (QFD).[3] This approach, which uses interfunctional teams from marketing, design engineering, and manufacturing, has been credited by Toyota Motor Corporation for reducing the costs on its cars by more than 60 percent by significantly shortening design times.

The QFD process begins with studying and listening to customers to determine the characteristics of a superior product. Through market research, the consumers' product needs and preferences are defined and broken down into categories called *customer attributes.* For example, an automobile manufacturer would like to improve the design of a car door. Through customer surveys and interviews, it determines that two important customer attributes desired in a car door are that it "stays open on a hill" and is "easy to close from the outside." After the customer attributes are defined, they are weighted based on their relative importance to the customer. Next, the consumer is asked to compare and rate the company's products with the products of competitors. This process helps the company to determine those product characteristics that are important to the consumer

[3] The term *quality* is actually a mistranslation of the Japanese word for *qualities.* Because QFD is widely used in the context of quality management, however, we elected to put it in this chapter rather than in Chapter 3 on product design.

EXHIBIT 6.2

Completed House of Quality Matrix for a Car Door

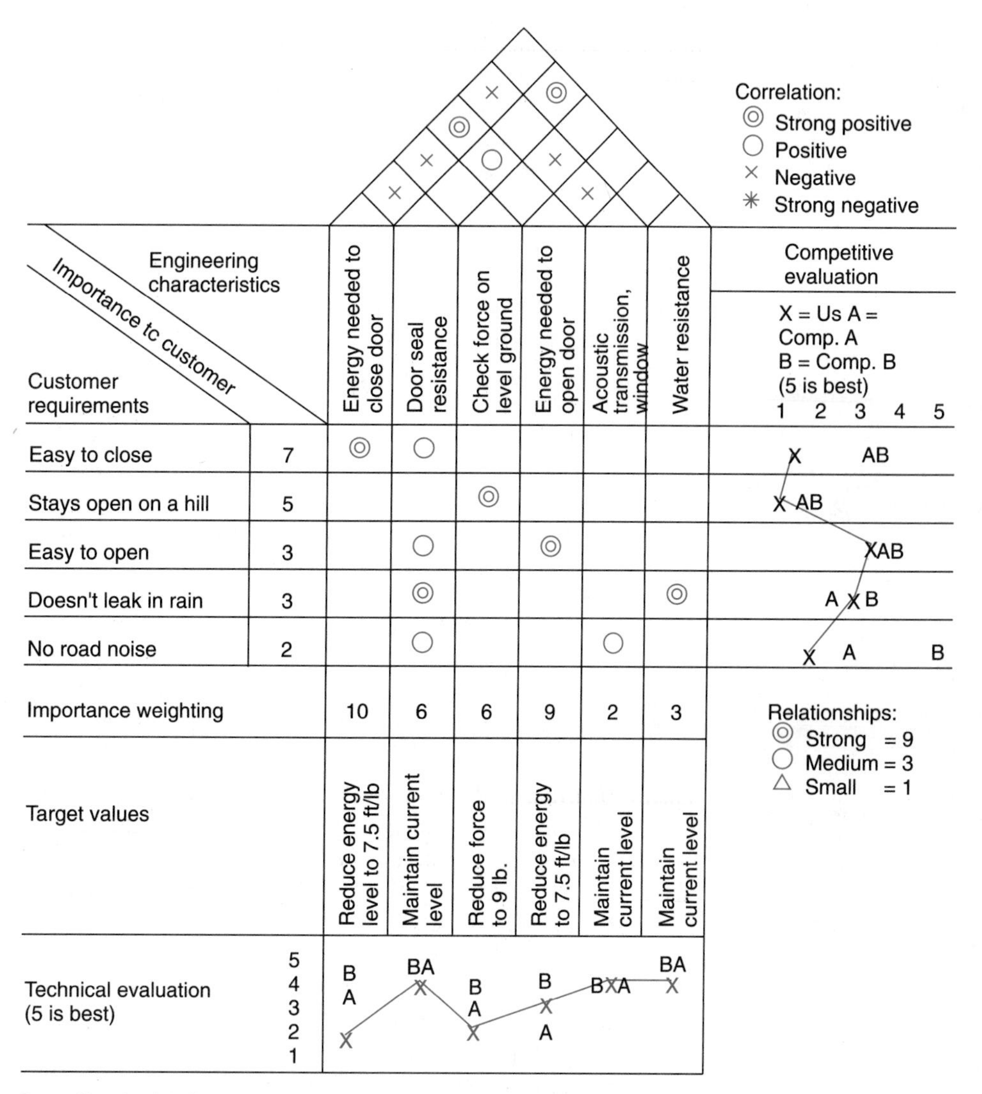

Source: Based on John R. Hauser and Don Clausing, "The House of Quality," *Harvard Business Review* (May–June 1988), pp. 62–73.

and to evaluate its product in relation to others. The end result is a better understanding and focus on the product characteristics that require improvement.

Customer attribute information forms the basis for a matrix called the **house of quality** (see Exhibit 6.2). By building a house of quality matrix, the cross-functional QFD team can use customer feedback to make engineering, marketing, and design decisions. The matrix helps the team to translate customer attribute information into concrete operating or engineering goals. The important product characteristics and goals for improvement are jointly agreed on and detailed in the house. This process encourages the different departments to work closely together and results in a better understanding of one another's goals and issues. However, the most important benefit of the house of quality is that it helps the team to focus on building a product that satisfies customers.

Supplier–customer links. Supplier–customer links refer to the fact that everybody in an organization has a customer. Such customers may be internal (e.g., the next worker or next department in the production process) as well as external (distributors, retailers, or end users). Each of these customers has quality requirements with respect to one or more of the dimensions presented earlier. Some have argued that the only customer that really matters is the person who buys the product or service. We agree with this view up to a point: It is important to keep your eye on the ball with respect to whom the organization serves. On the other hand, an organization is a network of relationships among people each of whom is dependent on his or her co-workers to create the product or service. Thinking of co-workers downstream in the production process as internal customers is simply a way of creating a cooperative and focused network to achieve the results required by the end customer.

6.3 THE GURUS OF QUALITY MANAGEMENT

There have been many individuals involved in the quality revolution over the years. However, three have been recognized as the **quality gurus** for their valuable contributions and forward thinking. They are W. Edwards Deming, Joseph M. Juran, and Philip Crosby. While they share much in common in terms of how they view quality (e.g., all three support the concept of continuous improvement), each has left his own unique stamp on the quality movement. Consequently, their philosophical approaches to quality are significantly different. A comparison of the three quality gurus is presented in Exhibit 6.3.

Deming

A thorough understanding of **statistical process control (SPC)** is the basic cornerstone of Deming's approach to quality. In fact, the Japanese were so impressed with his knowledge of SPC that they invited him back to teach the subject to Japanese managers and workers. The Japanese have recognized Deming's tremendous contribution to the success of their companies by naming their highest award for industrial excellence after him—the Deming Prize. (Another indicator that U.S. companies are making significant progress toward improving quality is that Florida Power & Light, a non-Japanese company, was recently awarded the Deming Prize.)

One of Deming's major contributions focused on disproving the fallacy that it costs more to make better-quality products. He demonstrates that just the opposite is true: a

EXHIBIT 6.3 **The Quality Gurus Compared**

	Crosby	Deming	Juran
Definition of quality	Conformance to requirements	A predictable degree of uniformity and dependability at low cost and suited to the market	Fitness for use
Degree of senior management responsibility	Responsible for quality	Responsible for 85% of quality problems	Less than 20% of quality problems are due to workers
Performance standard/ motivation	Zero defects	Quality has many "scales": use statistics to measure performance in all areas; critical of zero defects	Avoid campaigns to do perfect work
General approach	Prevention, not inspection	Reduce variability by continuous improvement; cease mass inspection	General management approach to quality, especially human elements
Structure	14 steps to quality improvement	14 points for management	10 steps to quality improvement
Statistical process control (SPC)	Rejects statistically acceptable levels of quality	Statistical methods of quality control must be used	Recommends SPC but warns that it can lead to tool-driven approach
Improvement basis	A process, not a program; improvement goals	Continuous to reduce variation; eliminate goals without methods	Project-by-project team approach; set goals
Teamwork	Quality improvement teams; quality councils	Employee participation in decision making; break down barriers between departments	Team and quality circle approach
Costs of quality	Cost of nonconformance; quality is free	No optimum, continuous improvement	Quality is not free, there is an optimum
Purchasing and goods received	State requirements; supplier is extension of business; most faults due to purchasers themselves	Inspection too late; allows defects to enter system through AQLs; statistical evidence and control charts required	Problems are complex; carry out formal surveys
Vendor rating	Yes and buyers; quality audits useless	No, critical of most systems	Yes, but help supplier improve
Single sourcing of supply		Yes	No, can neglect to sharpen competitive edge

Source: Modified from John S. Oakland, *Total Quality Management* (London: Heinemann Professional Publishing Ltd., 1989), pp. 291–92.

high-quality process is, in fact, less costly than a low-quality one. When products are made properly the first time, substantial savings accrue from the elimination of unnecessary labor for rework and repairs and the cost to scrap nonconforming material.

EXHIBIT 6.4

Deming's Plan-Do-Check-Act (PDCA) Cycle

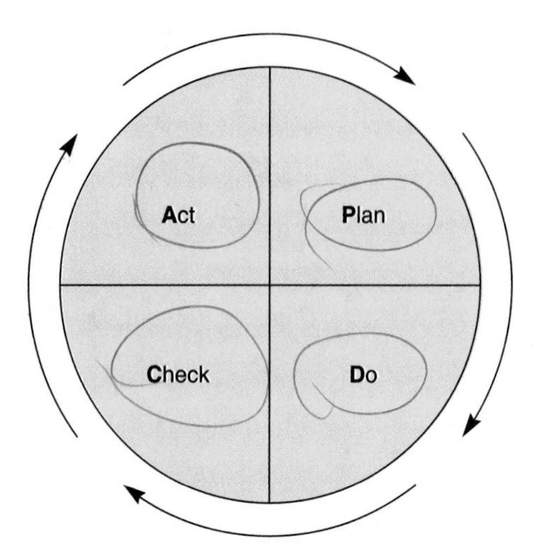

Source: Mary Walton, *Deming Management at Work* (New York: Perigree Books, 1991), p. 22.

Another significant contribution that Deming made is the development of the plan-do-check-act (PDCA) cycle, which he first introduced to the Japanese. Prior to the PDCA cycle, Americans especially were used to seeing projects/activities that have a beginning and an end. However, the PDCA cycle, as shown in Exhibit 6.4, adopts a circular approach, emphasizing the need for continuous improvement.

According to Deming, 85 percent of the quality problems generated by a company can be attributed to management, because they have the power to make the decisions that impact on the current systems and practices. His extensive consulting experiences with such companies as Ford, Nashua Corp., and Florida Power & Light have supported this claim. Over the years, Deming has developed a 14-point program that he offers as a guideline to companies for improving quality within their respective organizations. These 14 points are presented in Exhibit 6.5.

Juran

Like Deming, Juran also visited Japan shortly after the end of World War II to assist in rebuilding its industrial base. Also, like Deming, Juran emphasized the importance of producing quality products, and thus directed his efforts while in Japan toward teaching quality concepts and their application to the factory floor. Based on his experiences with Japanese companies, Juran developed an approach to quality that focuses primarily on three areas: (1) quality planning, (2) quality control, and (3) quality improvement.

According to Juran, the quality of a product is defined as **fitness for use,** as viewed by the

EXHIBIT 6.5

Deming's 14-Point Program for Improving Quality

1. Create constancy of purpose for improvement of product and service.
2. Adopt the new philosophy.
3. Cease dependence on mass inspection.
4. End the practice of awarding business on the price tag alone.
5. Improve constantly and forever the system of production and training.
6. Institute training.
7. Institute leadership.
8. Drive out fear.
9. Break down barriers between staff areas.
10. Eliminate slogans, exhortations, and targets for the work force.
11. Eliminate numerical quotas.
12. Remove barriers to pride in workmanship.
13. Institute a vigorous program of education and retraining.
14. Take action to accomplish the program.

Source: Mary Walton, *Deming Management at Work* (New York: Perigree Books, 1991), pp. 17–18.

customer. Juran further defines fitness for use as consisting of five components: (1) quality of design, (2) quality of conformance, (3) availability, (4) safety, and (5) field use. In evaluating a product's fitness for use, Juran takes into account the total life cycle of the product.

Juran uses the cost of quality as his framework for introducing his approach to quality. In doing so, he divides the cost of quality into three major categories: (1) cost of prevention, (2) cost of detection/appraisal, and (3) cost of failure, all of which are presented in greater detail later in this chapter.

Crosby

Unlike Deming and Juran, both of whom were trained initially as statisticians, Crosby was educated as an engineer and began his career in manufacturing. After working for several large companies, primarily in quality-related positions, he founded his own "Quality College" in Florida in 1979.

Crosby's philosophy, which is similar in some respects to Deming's, states that any organization can reduce its total overall costs by improving the quality of its processes. In one of his first books, Crosby preaches that "quality is free." According to Crosby, the cost of providing poor-quality goods and services is significant. He estimates that the cost of producing poor quality can run as high as 25 percent of revenues for manufacturing companies and 40 percent of operating expenses in service operations. Crosby also claims that companies that have successfully implemented quality programs can expect to reduce their costs of quality to less than 2.5 percent of sales.[4] In China, the cost of poor quality can be extremely high! (See the "OM in Action" that follows.)

[4] Philip B. Crosby, *Quality Is Free* (New York: New America Library, 1979), p. 15.

OPERATIONS MANAGEMENT IN ACTION

Talk about the Cost of Quality!

MANAGERS EXECUTED FOR SHODDY QUALITY

(Beijing)—Eighteen factory managers were executed for poor product quality at Chien Bien Refrigerator Factory on the outskirts of the Chinese capital. The managers—12 men and 6 women—were taken to a rice paddy outside the factory and unceremoniously shot to death as 500 plant workers looked on.

Minister of Economic Reform spokesman, Xi Ten Haun, said the action was required for committing unpardonable crimes against the people of China. He blamed the managers for ignoring quality and forcing shoddy work, saying the factory's output of refrigerators had a reputation for failure. For years, factory workers complained that many component parts did not meet specification and the end product did not function as required. Complaining workers quoted the plant manager as saying, "Ship it." Refrigerators are among the most sought-after consumer items in China. Customers, who waited up to five years for their appliances, were outraged.

"It is understandable our citizens would express shock and outrage when managers are careless in their attitudes toward the welfare of others," Huan says. "Our soldiers are justified in wishing to bring proper justice to these errant managers."

The executed included the plant manager, the quality control manager, the engineering managers, and their top staff.

Source: Excerpted from *The Wall Street Journal* (October 17, 1989).

6.4 THE COST OF QUALITY

Following Juran's model, we divide the **cost of quality** into three major categories: (1) **cost of prevention,** (2) **cost of detection/appraisal,** and (3) **cost of failure.** The third category, the cost of failure, is further subdivided into internal failure costs and external failure costs.

The total cost of quality is the sum of the costs in all three categories. The typical percentages of total quality costs that are estimated for each of the three categories are shown in Exhibit 6.6.

Cost of Prevention

Prevention costs, by definition, are those costs incurred by an organization in its effort to prevent defective goods and services from being produced and/or delivered to the customer. Included in this category are investments in machinery, technology, and education programs that are designed to reduce the number of defects that the process produces. Also included in this category are the costs to administer the firm's quality program, data collection and analysis, and vendor certification. All of the quality gurus strongly support investments in this category because the returns are so high, including the

EXHIBIT 6.6

Typical Quality Cost Ratios

Category	Feigenbaum	Juran and Gryna
Prevention costs	5%–10%	0.5%–5%
Detection/appraisal costs	20%–25%	10%–50%
Failure costs	65%–70%	Internal: 25%–40%
		External: 20%–40%
Total cost of quality	100%	100%

Source: A.V. Feigenbaum, *Total Quality Control*, 3rd ed. (New York: McGraw-Hill, 1983), p. 112; and Joseph M. Juran, and F.M. Gryna. *Quality Planning and Analysis* (New York: McGraw-Hill, 1970), p. 60.

benefits gained from increasing customer satisfaction and reducing scrap losses and rework expenses.

Cost of Detection/Appraisal

Detection or appraisal costs are those costs associated with evaluating the quality of the product. Costs included in this category are: incoming material inspection, tests and inspection throughout the transformation process, test equipment maintenance, and products destroyed during destructive testing.

Cost of Failure

These costs pertain to nonconforming and nonperforming products. Also included in this category are the costs associated with the evaluation, disposition, and consumer affairs aspects of such failures. As stated earlier, we further subdivide failure costs into internal and external failure costs.

Internal failure costs are identified as those costs that are eliminated if no defects were produced within the system. They include only those costs attributed to defects that are found before the products are delivered to the customer. Examples of internal failure costs include: scrap, rework/repair, retesting of reworked/repaired products, downtime, yield losses due to process variability, and the disposition of the defective items.

External failure costs are those costs that are incurred after the product has been delivered to the customer. Included in this category are: the cost of returned material, warranty charges, field survey costs, legal expenses from lawsuits, customer dissatisfaction, loss of revenues due to downgrading products as seconds, and costs of allowances/concessions made to customers.

It is generally now recognized that increased spending on prevention provides significant returns in the form of reductions in detection/appraisal and failure costs—and in the overall cost of quality, as shown in Exhibit 6.7. The old adage, "An ounce of prevention is worth a pound of cure" is thus also most appropriate for quality.

Often, increases in productivity occur as a byproduct of efforts to reduce the cost of quality. A bank, for example, set out to improve quality and reduce the cost of quality and

EXHIBIT 6.7 Increased Prevention Costs Reduce Total Quality Costs

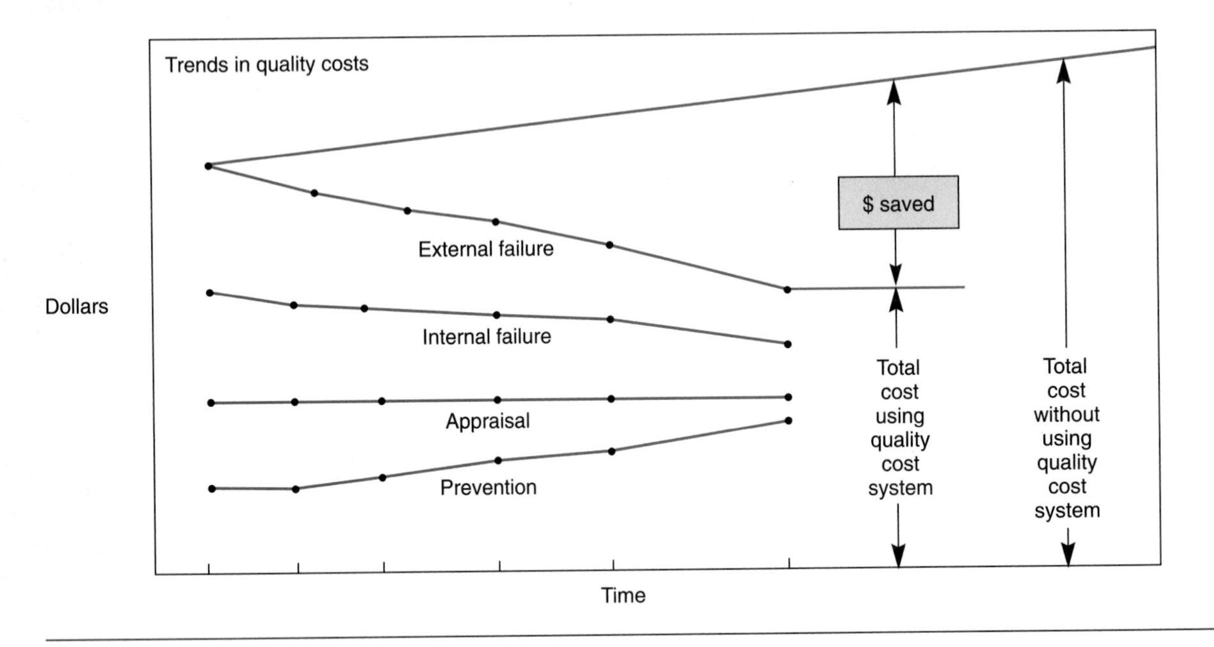

found that it had also boosted productivity. The bank developed this productivity measure for the loan processing area: the number of tickets processed divided by the resources required (labor cost, computer time, ticket forms). Before the quality improvement program, the productivity index was 0.2660 [2,080/($11.23 × 640 hours + $0.05 × 2,600 forms + $500 for systems costs)]. After the quality improvement project was completed, labor time fell to 546 hours and the number of forms to 2,100 for a change in the index to 0.3088, or an increase in productivity of 16 percent.

6.5 THE SEVEN MANAGEMENT AND PLANNING TOOLS[5]

The **seven management and planning (MP) tools** are not really new, as they evolved out of the post-World War II efforts in the field of operations research and the work of total quality control (TQC) leaders in Japan. The Japanese effort was coordinated by a committee of the Society for QC Technique Development. In 1979, after seven years of refining and testing, this committee published *Seven New Quality Tools for Managers and Staff*. In 1983, GOAL/QPC of Methuen, Massachusetts, discovered this book and had it translated into English. The seven MP tools, as illustrated in Exhibit 6.8, are:

[5] This section is adapted from Michael Brassard, *The Memory Jogger Plus+* (Methuen, Mass.: GOAL/QPC, 1989).

EXHIBIT 6.8

The Seven Management and Planning Tools

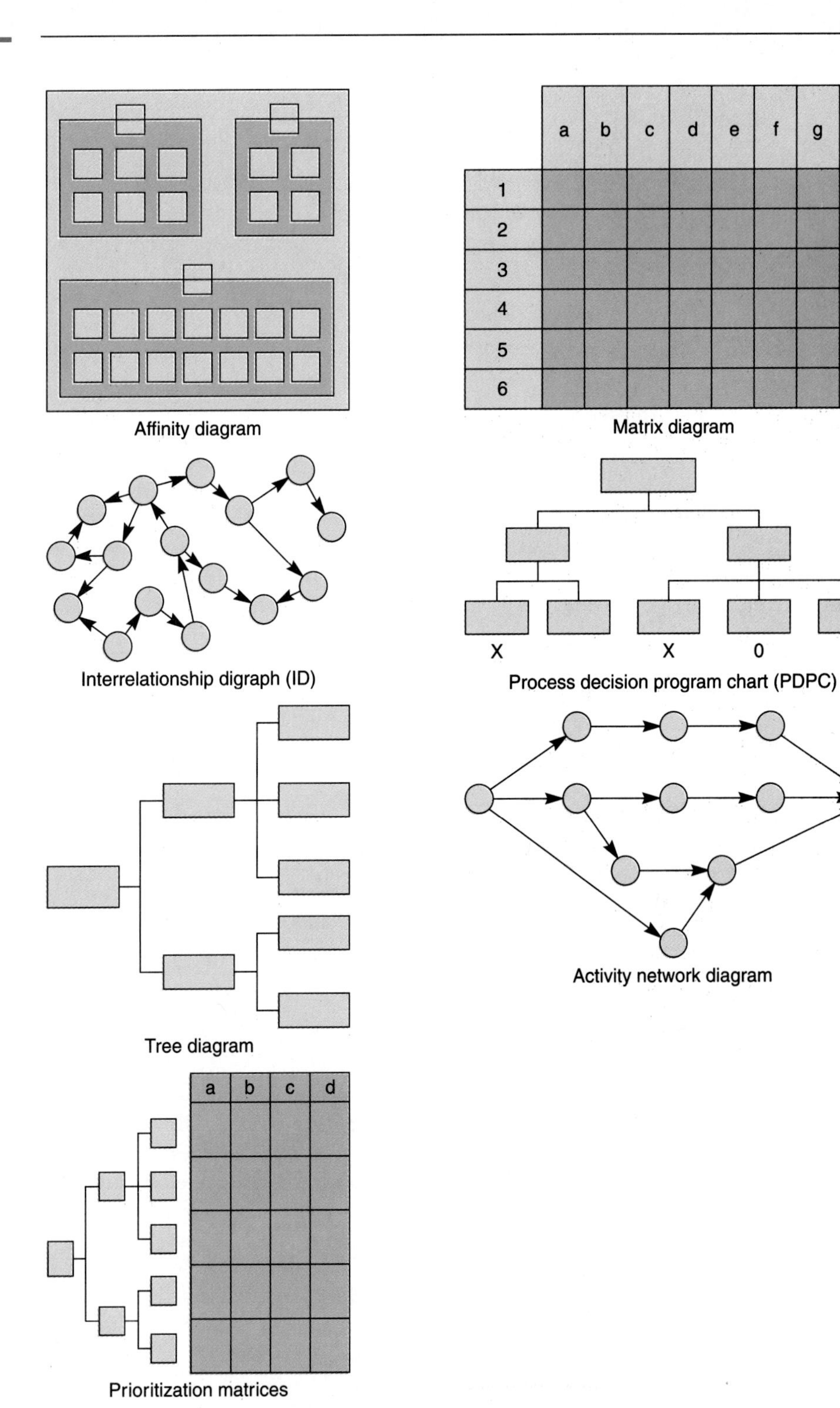

Source: Michael Brassard, *The Memory Jogger Plus+* (Methuen, Mass.: GOAL/QPC, 1989).

- Affinity diagram—KJ Method®[6]
- Interrelationship digraph (ID)
- Tree diagram
- Prioritization matrices
- Matrix diagram
- Process decision program chart (PDPC)
- Activity network diagram

Affinity Diagram—KJ Method

The affinity diagram is used to gather large quantities of language data from a group of individuals. These data are typically nonquantitative in nature, taking the form of ideas, opinions, and issues. Once identified, the affinity diagram organizes the data into groupings based on the relationship that exists among the items in the group. The affinity diagram is primarily a creative process rather than a logical one.

Interrelationship Digraph (ID)

The contribution of the interrelationship digraph is its ability to take complex, multivariable problems or desired outcomes and explore and/or display all of the interrelated factors involved. The ID can graphically show the logical, and often causal, relationships that exist among these factors.

Tree Diagram

The tree diagram is a tool that allows the manager to systematically map out, in increasing detail, all of the paths and related tasks that need to be accomplished in order to achieve a desired goal and its related subgoals. In its presentation, a tree diagram resembles a traditional organization chart or a family tree.

Prioritization Matrices

These tools take tasks, issues, and/or possible actions and allow management to prioritize them based on established weighting criteria. The prioritization matrices incorporate a combination of tree and matrix diagram techniques, which allows management to narrow down the options available to only those that are most desirable and/or effective.

Matrix Diagram

The matrix diagram identifies the connection or correlation between the ideas/issues in one group and those in another group. (The purpose of this matrix is very similar to that of the matrix developed in the QFD process.) At each intersection on the matrix, a

[6] The name KJ Method is a registered trademark of its originator, Jiro Kawakita.

relationship between the pertinent ideas/issues is indicated as either existing or not existing. In its most common application, the matrix diagram takes the necessary tasks, often from the tree diagram, and graphically shows their relationships with people, functions, and other tasks. This particular tool is often used to identify who is responsible for completing the different parts of an implementation plan.

Process Decision Program Chart (PDPC)

The PDPC maps out every conceivable event and contingency plan that can occur in the transition from the problem statement to the obtaining of possible solutions. This tool is also used to identify dependent events and their sequence of occurrence when the problem or goal to be accomplished is unfamiliar.

Activity Network Diagram

The activity network diagram allows management to efficiently plan and schedule a complex project or program and all of its related tasks and subtasks. It forecasts estimated completion times and monitors all of the tasks and subtasks to ensure that required due dates are met. More specific information on how to use this tool and its application to other areas is presented in Chapter 12, on project planning and control.

6.6 THE SEVEN BASIC QUALITY CONTROL TOOLS

Within the quality literature, seven basic tools have been identified that can assist managers in organizing, displaying, and analyzing process-generated data. These **seven basic quality control (QC) tools,** shown in Exhibit 6.9, are: (1) process flow charts, (2) run (trend) charts, (3) scatter diagrams, (4) cause and effect diagrams, (5) Pareto charts, (6) histograms, and (7) statistical process control charts.

Process Flow Charts

Process flow charts or diagrams simply block out each of the different steps and their sequence that are required to produce either a good or a service. In service operations this procedure is often referred to as "blueprinting" the process, as discussed in Chapter 5.

Run Charts

Run charts look similar in appearance to statistical process control charts, only there are no control limits. The data plotted on run charts can include anything that is important to managers, such as productivity performance and sales. An application of a run chart in a service industry is shown in Exhibit 6.10.

EXHIBIT 6.9

The Seven Basic Quality Control (QC) Tools

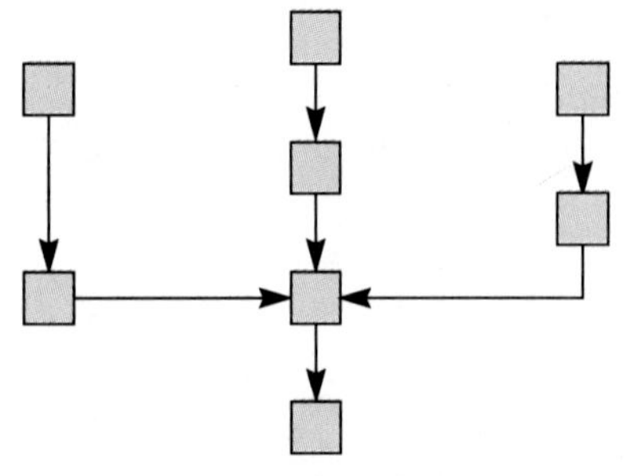

Process flow chart

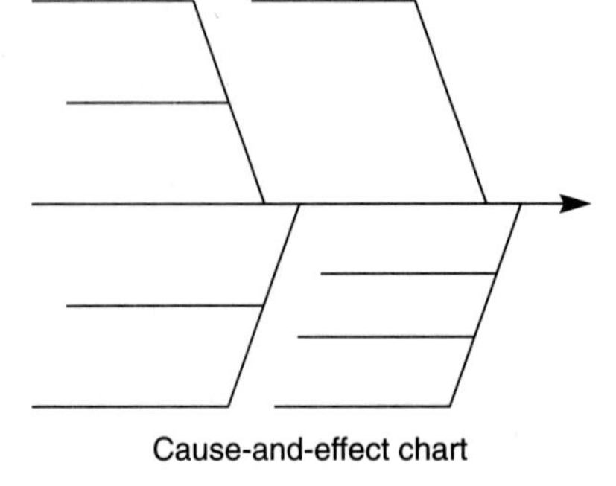

Cause-and-effect chart

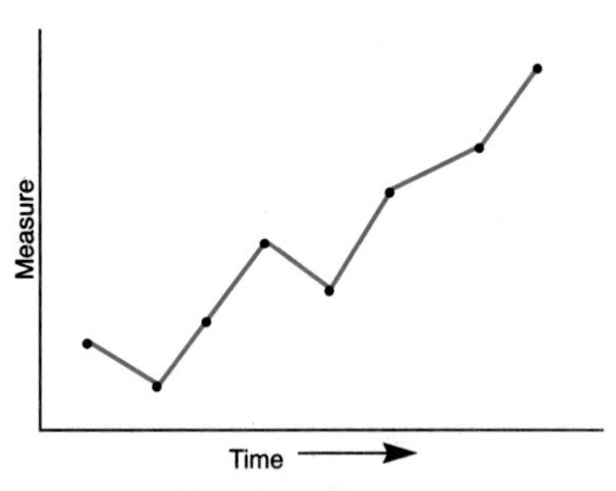

Run (trend) chart

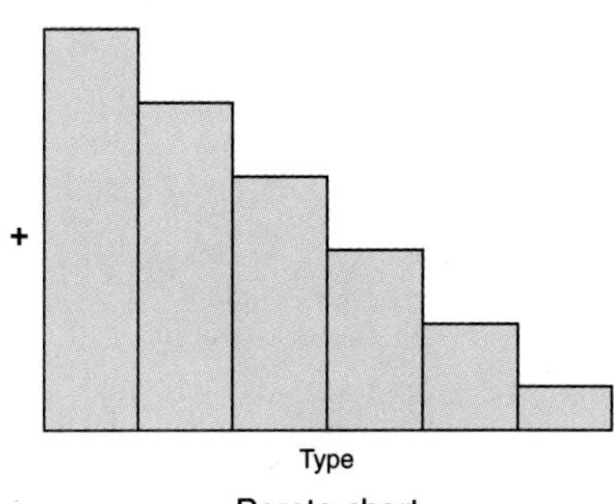

Pareto chart

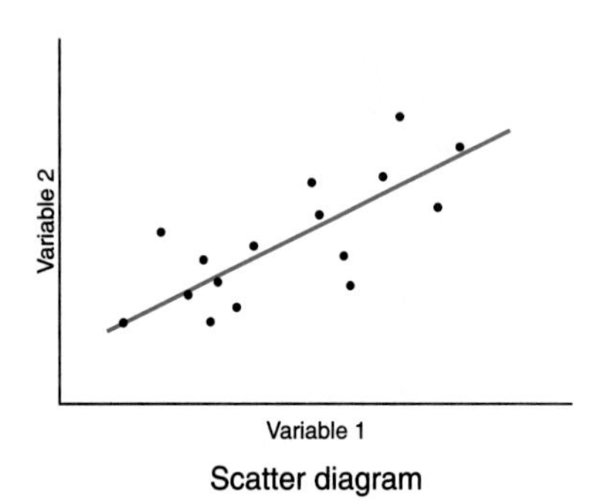

Scatter diagram

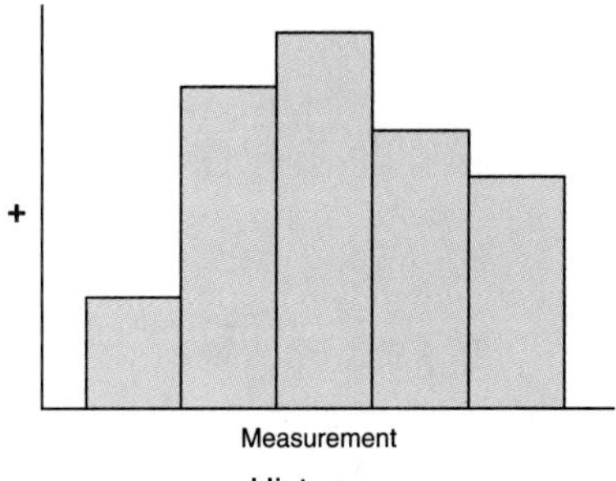

Histogram

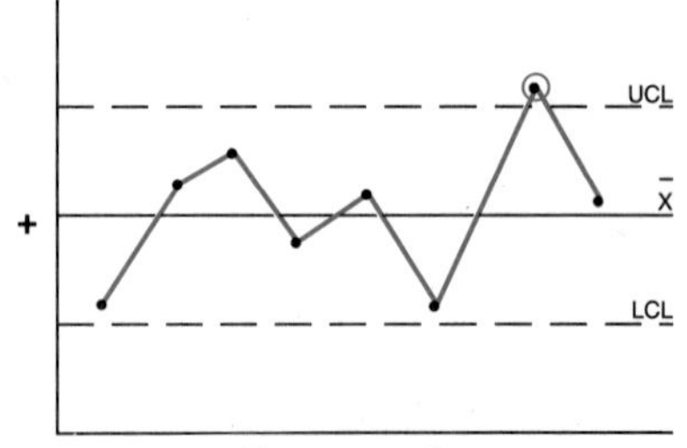

Statistical process control chart

Source: Adapted from GOAL/QPC, Methuen, Mass. Used with permission.

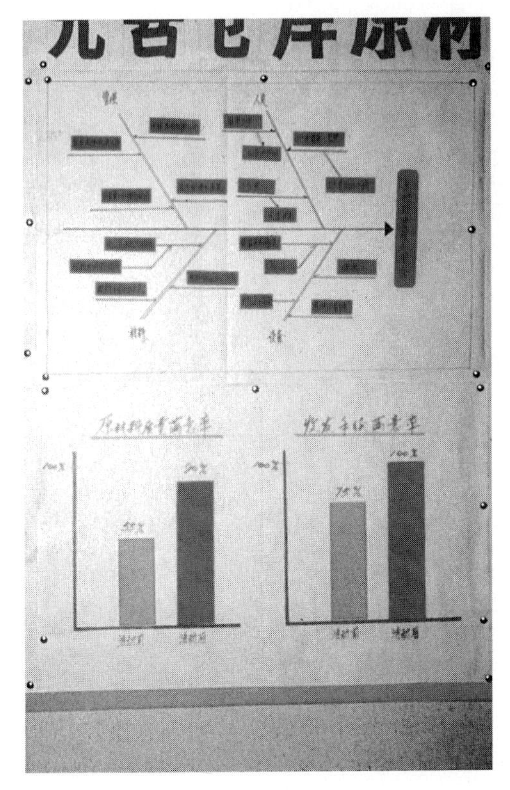

Mark Davis

Examples of a cause-and-effect diagram and a histogram in a hotel in Guangzhou, P.R.C.

Scatter Diagrams

These diagrams are used to demonstrate the existence of a relationship between two variables or product characteristics.

Cause-and-Effect Diagrams

Cause-and-effect diagrams, also referred to as fishbone diagrams (because of their shape) and Ishikawa diagrams, attempt to identify all of the potential causes for a recurring defect or failure. These potential causes are divided into several broad categories: methods, materials, machinery, and labor. Recently, the environment has been added as a fifth category. An example of a cause-and-effect diagram is shown in Exhibit 6.11, where an airline's management is trying to identify the different causes for flight departure delays.

EXHIBIT 6.10

Run Chart of Midway Airlines Departure Delays

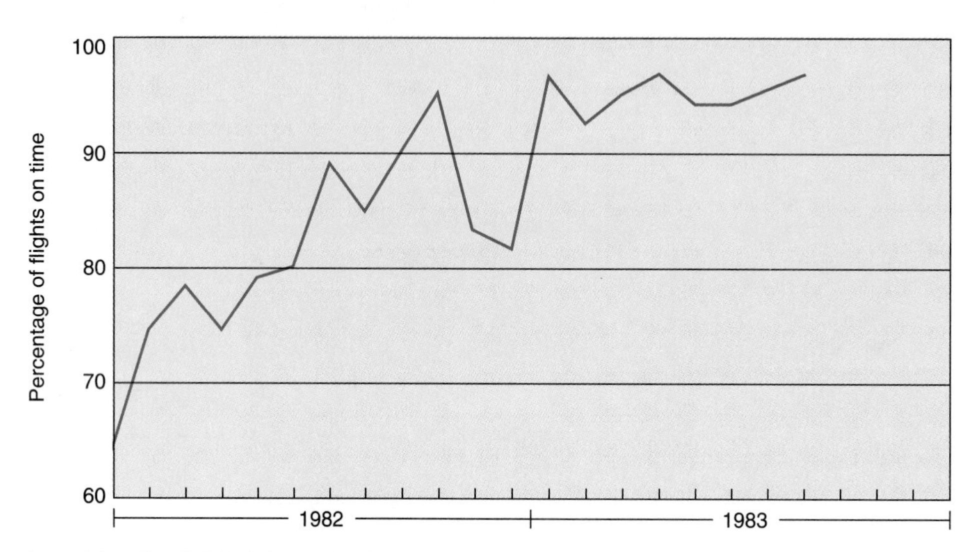

Source: Adapted from D. D. Wychoff, "New Tools for Achieving Service Quality," *Cornell Hotel and Restaurant Administration Quarterly* (November 1984), p. 246.

Pareto Charts

Pareto charts provide an organized approach for ranking data (e.g., types of defects) in descending order by their frequency of occurrence. Using Pareto charts, managers can establish a priority for addressing quality problems, those with the highest frequency being ranked first. Pareto charts allow managers to "control the critical few"; in other words, they allow managers to focus their attention on the relatively few, but critical, factors that impact on their firm. From Pareto charts we have the "80/20" rule that states, for example, that 80 percent of the problems are caused by 20 percent of the types of defects.

Histograms

Histograms use a bar chart approach to display the frequency of occurrence of those factors that are of interest to management. Although they resemble Pareto charts, histograms do not prioritize the data that are displayed.

Statistical Process Control (SPC) Charts

Statistical process control (SPC) charts are the most sophisticated of the seven tools, requiring the user to have a working knowledge of statistics. These charts plot the status of a process over time, and have a central, target value, as well as control limits to indicate

EXHIBIT 6.11 **Portion of Midway Airlines Fishbone Analysis—Causes of Flight Departure Delays**

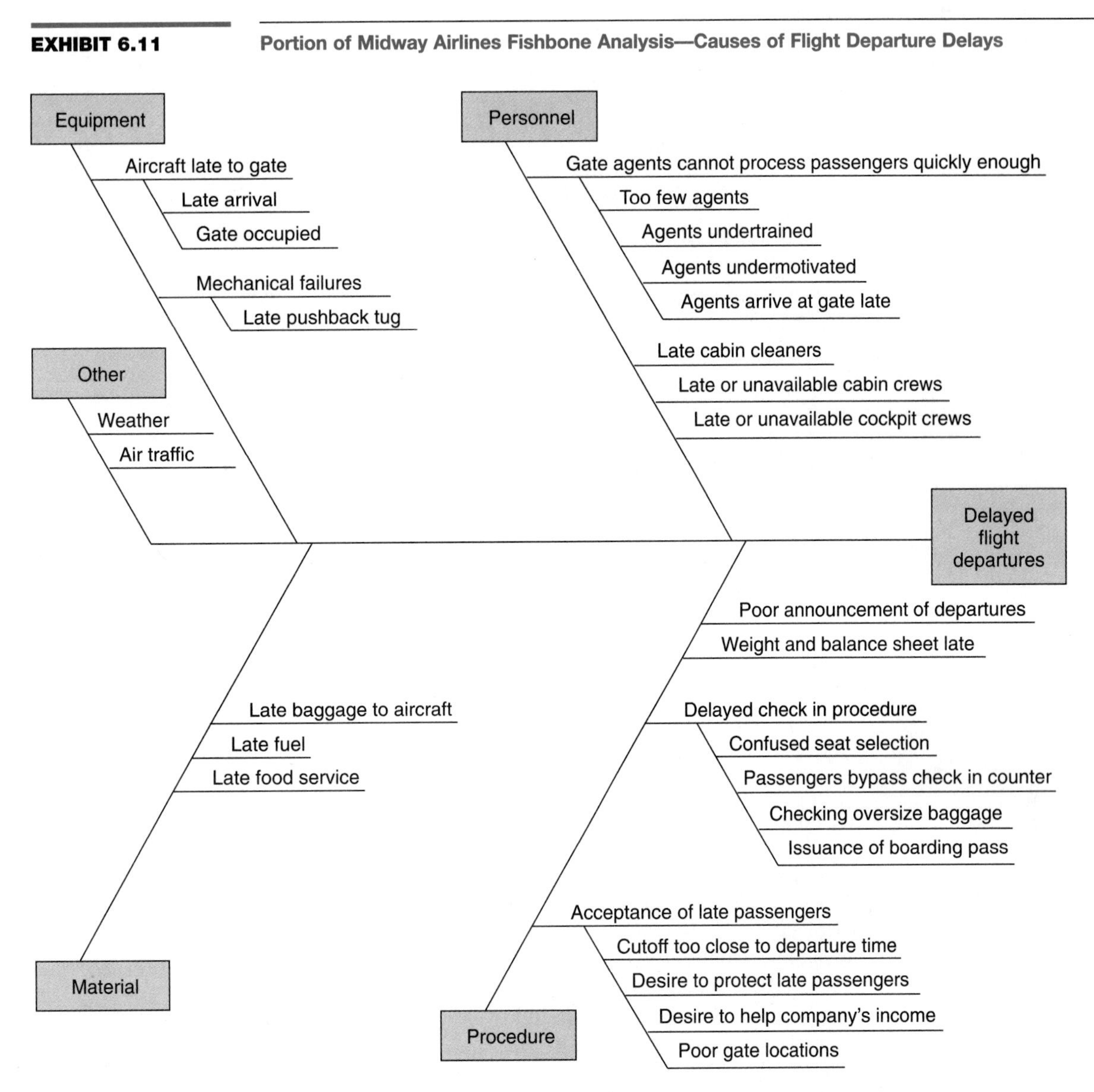

Source: Adapted from D. D. Wychoff, "New Tools for Achieving Service Quality," *Cornell Hotel and Restaurant Administration Quarterly* (November 1984), p. 246.

when the process is out of control. The use and application of SPC charts is discussed in greater detail in the next section.

6.7 STATISTICAL PROCESS CONTROL

Statistical process control (SPC) is a quantitative method for monitoring a process to determine whether the process is operating as it should or if it is out of control. SPC allows management and workers to distinguish between random fluctuations that are inherent in the process and special, unique variations that might indicate that some form of corrective action is required. SPC, in essence, provides a way to distinguish among the different sources of variation that occur in a process.

Process Control Using Attribute Measurements

Measurements by attributes means taking samples and using a single decision—the item is good, or it is bad. Because it is a yes-no decision, we can use simple statistics to create an upper control limit (UCL) and a lower control limit (LCL). We can draw these control limits on a graph and then plot the fraction defective of each individual sample tested. The process is assumed to be working correctly when the samples, which are taken periodically at predetermined time intervals, continue to stay within the control limits.

$$\bar{p} = \frac{\text{Total number of defects from all samples}}{\text{Number of samples} \times \text{Sample size}}$$

$$s_p = \sqrt{\frac{\bar{p}(1 - \bar{p})}{n}}$$

$$\text{UCL} = \bar{p} + zs_p$$

$$\text{LCL} = \bar{p} - zs_p$$

where $\bar{p}$ is the fraction defective, s_p is the standard deviation, and z is the number of standard deviations for a specific confidence. Typically, $z = 3$ (99.7 percent of confidence) and is the most common control limit used.

Exhibit 6.12 shows information that can be gained from control charts. We do not give an example of attribute process control here so that in the next section we can demonstrate $\overline{X}$ and R charts, which tend to have wider application in process control.

Process Control with Variable Measurements Using $\overline{X}$ and R Charts

$\overline{X}$ (mean) and R (range) charts are widely used in statistical process control.

In attribute sampling, we determine whether something is good or bad, fit or didn't fit—it is a go/no-go situation. In variables sampling, we measure the weight, volume, number of inches, or other variable measurements, from which we develop control charts to determine the acceptability or rejection of the process output based on those measurements.

EXHIBIT 6.12 **Control Chart Evidence for Investigation**

Upper control limit

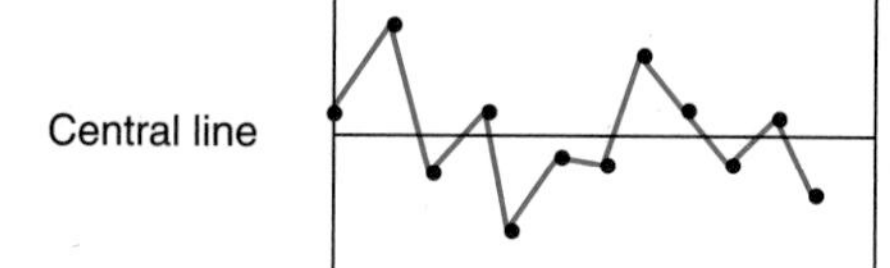

Normal behavior.

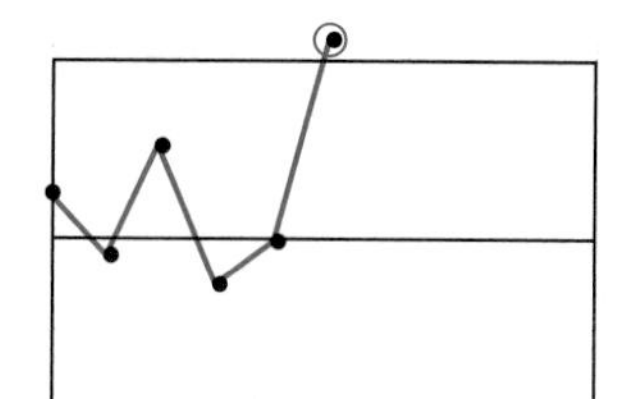

One plot out above. Investigate for cause of abnormal performance.

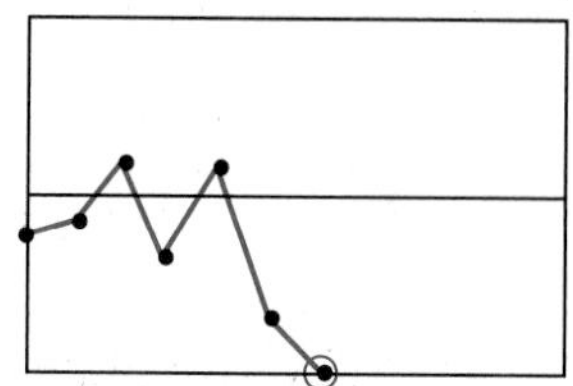

One plot out below. Investigate for cause of abnormal performance.

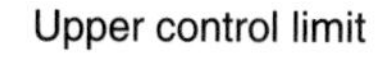

Central line

Lower control limit

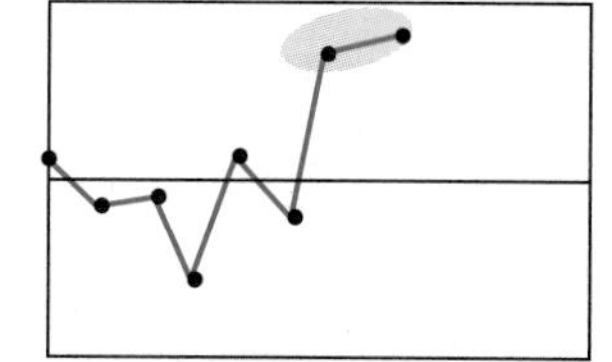

Two plots near upper control. Investigate for cause of abnormal performance.

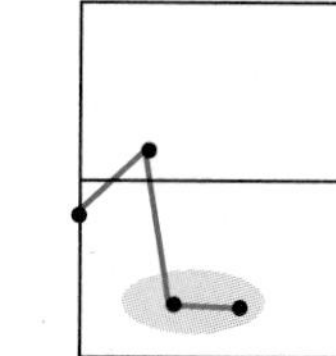

Two plots near lower control. Investigate for cause of abnormal performance.

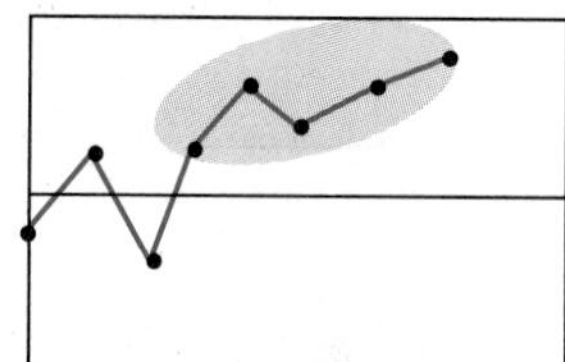

Run of five above central line. Investigate for cause of sustained abnormal performance.

Central line

Lower control limit

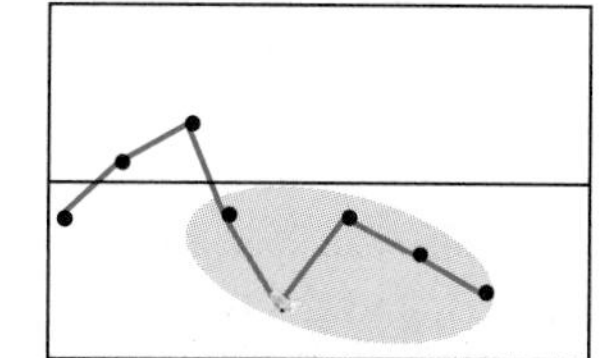

Run of five below central line. Investigate for cause of sustained abnormal performance.

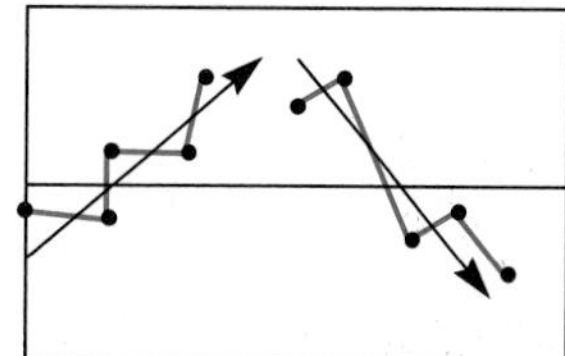

Trend in either direction five plots. Investigate for cause of progressive change.

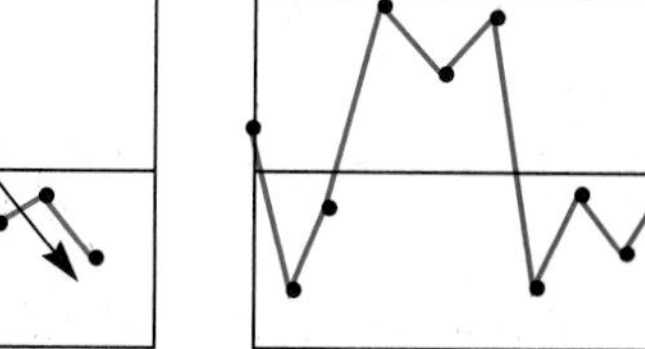

Erratic behavior. Investigate.

Upper control limit

Central line

Lower control limit

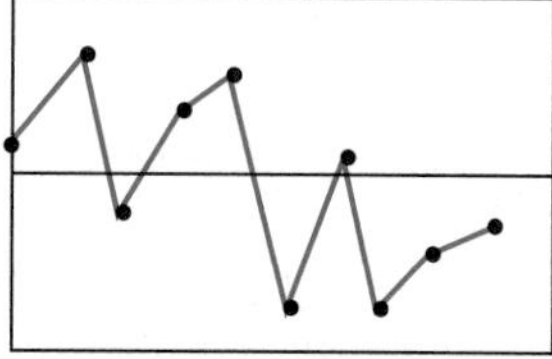

Sudden change in level. Investigate for cause.

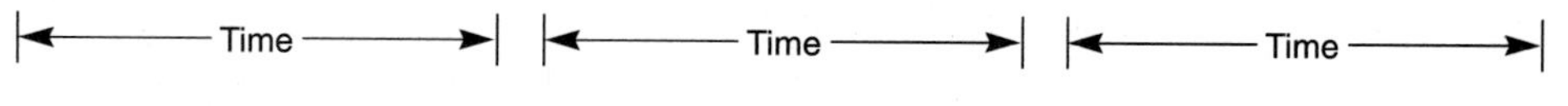

Source: Bertrand L. Hansen, *Quality Control: Theory and Applications,* © 1963, p. 65. Reprinted by permission of Prentice Hall, Inc., Englewood Cliffs, N.J.

There are four main issues to address in creating a control chart: the size of the sample, the number of samples, the frequency of samples, and the control limits.

Size of sample

For industrial applications in process control, it is preferable to keep the sample size small. There are two main reasons: first, the sample needs to be taken within a reasonable length of time, otherwise the process might change while the sample is being taken. Second, the larger the sample, the more it costs to take.

Sample sizes of four or five units seem to be the preferred numbers. The *means* of samples of this size have an approximately normal distribution, no matter what the distribution of the parent population looks like. Sample sizes greater than five give narrower control limits and, thus, are more sensitive. For detecting finer variations of a process it may be necessary, in fact, to use larger sample sizes. However, when sample sizes exceed 15 or so, it would be more appropriate to use the standard deviation (σ) and $\overline{X}$ charts rather than R and $\overline{X}$ charts. One advantage of using the R charts is that the range is easier to calculate than the standard deviation.

Number of samples

Once the chart has been set up, each sample taken can be compared to the chart and a decision made about whether the process is acceptable. To set up the charts, however, prudence (and statistics) suggest that 25 or so samples be taken.

Frequency of samples

How often to take a sample is a trade-off between the cost of sampling (along with the cost of the unit if it is destroyed as part of the test), and the benefit of adjusting the system. Usually, it is best to start off with frequent sampling of a process and taper off as confidence in the process builds. For example, one might start with a sample of five units every half hour and end up feeling that one sample per day is adequate.

Control limits

Standard practice in statistical process control for variables is to set control limits at three standard deviations above the mean and three standard deviations below. This means that 99.7 percent of the sample means are expected to fall within these control limits (i.e., within a 99.7 percent confidence interval). Thus, if one sample mean falls outside this obviously wide band, we have strong evidence that the process is out of control.

How to Construct $\overline{X}$ and R Charts

An $\overline{X}$ chart is simply a plot of the means of the samples that were taken from a process. $\overline{X}$ is the average of the means.

An R chart is a plot of the range within each sample. The range is the difference between the highest and the lowest value in that sample. As stated earlier, R values provide an easily calculated measure of variation used like a standard deviation. $\overline{R}$ is the average of the ranges of each sample. More specifically, these terms are defined:

$$\overline{X} = \frac{\sum_{i=1}^{n} X_i}{n}$$

where

$\overline{X}$ = Mean of the sample
i = Item number
n = Total number of items in the sample

$$\overline{\overline{X}} = \frac{\sum_{j=1}^{m} \overline{X}_j}{m}$$

where

$\overline{\overline{X}}$ = The average of the means of the samples
j = Sample number
m = Total number of samples

$$\overline{R} = \frac{\sum_{j=1}^{m} R_j}{m}$$

where

$\overline{R}$ = Average of the measurement differences R for all samples
R_j = Difference between the highest and lowest values in the sample

E. L. Grant and R. Leavenworth computed a table that allows us to easily compute the upper and lower control limits for both the $\overline{X}$ chart and the R chart.[7] These are defined as:

Upper control limit for $\overline{X} = \overline{\overline{X}} + A_2\overline{R}$
Lower control limit for $\overline{X} = \overline{\overline{X}} - A_2\overline{R}$
Upper control limit for $R = D_4\overline{R}$
Lower control limit for $R = D_3\overline{R}$

Where the values for A_2, D_3 and D_4 are obtained from Exhibit 6.13.

Example

We would like to create an $\overline{X}$ and an R chart for a process. Exhibit 6.14 shows the measurements that were taken of all 25 samples. The last two columns show the average of the sample $\overline{X}$ and the range R.

[7] E. L. Grant and R. Leavenworth, *Statistical Quality Control* (New York: McGraw-Hill, 1964), p. 562. Reprinted by permission.

EXHIBIT 6.13

Factors for Determining from $\overline{R}$ the 3-Sigma Control Limits for $\overline{X}$ and R Charts

Number of Observations in Subgroup n	Factor for $\overline{X}$ Chart A_2	FACTORS FOR R CHART	
		Lower Control Limit D_3	Upper Control Limit D_4
2	1.88	0	3.27
3	1.02	0	2.57
4	0.73	0	2.28
5	0.58	0	2.11
6	0.48	0	2.00
7	0.42	0.08	1.92
8	0.37	0.14	1.86
9	0.34	0.18	1.82
10	0.31	0.22	1.78
11	0.29	0.26	1.74
12	0.27	0.28	1.72
13	0.25	0.31	1.69
14	0.24	0.33	1.67
15	0.22	0.35	1.65
16	0.21	0.36	1.64
17	0.20	0.38	1.62
18	0.19	0.39	1.61
19	0.19	0.40	1.60
20	0.18	0.41	1.59

Upper control limit for $\overline{X} = UCL_{\overline{X}} = \overline{\overline{X}} + A_2\overline{R}$

Lower control limit for $\overline{X} = LCL_{\overline{X}} = \overline{\overline{X}} - A_2\overline{R}$

Upper control limit for $R = UCL_R = D_4\overline{R}$

Lower control limit for $R = LCL_R = D_3\overline{R}$

Note: All factors are based on the normal distribution.

Source: E. L. Grant, *Statistical Quality Control*, 6th ed. (New York: McGraw-Hill, 1988). Reprinted by permission of McGraw-Hill, Inc.

$$\text{Upper control limit for } \overline{X} = \overline{\overline{X}} + A_2\overline{R}$$
$$= 10.21 + .58(.60) = 10.56$$
$$\text{Lower control limit for } \overline{X} = \overline{\overline{X}} - A_2\overline{R}$$
$$= 10.21 - .58(.60) = 9.86$$
$$\text{Upper control limit for } R = D_4\overline{R}$$
$$= 2.11(.60) = 1.26$$
$$\text{Lower control limit for } R = D_3\overline{R}$$
$$= 0(.60) = 0$$

Exhibit 6.15 shows the $\overline{X}$ chart and R chart with a plot of all the sample means and ranges of the samples. All the points are well within the control limits, although sample 23 is close to the $\overline{X}$ lower control limit. The $\overline{X}$ chart shows how well the process is centered about the target mean. The R chart demonstrates the degree of variability in the process.

Process Capability

Process control chart limits can be compared to design specification limits to determine if the process itself is not capable of making products within design specification (or

EXHIBIT 6.14

Measurements in Samples of Five from a Process

Sample Number	Each Unit in Sample					Average $\bar{X}$	Range R
1	10.60	10.40	10.30	9.90	10.20	10.28	.70
2	9.98	10.25	10.05	10.23	10.33	10.17	.35
3	9.85	9.90	10.20	10.25	10.15	10.07	.40
4	10.20	10.10	10.30	9.90	9.95	10.09	.40
5	10.30	10.20	10.24	10.50	10.30	10.31	.30
6	10.10	10.30	10.20	10.30	9.90	10.16	.40
7	9.98	9.90	10.20	10.40	10.10	10.12	.50
8	10.10	10.30	10.40	10.24	10.30	10.27	.30
9	10.30	10.20	10.60	10.50	10.10	10.34	.50
10	10.30	10.40	10.50	10.10	10.20	10.30	.40
11	9.90	9.50	10.20	10.30	10.35	10.05	.85
12	10.10	10.36	10.50	9.80	9.95	10.14	.70
13	10.20	10.50	10.70	10.10	9.90	10.28	.80
14	10.20	10.60	10.50	10.30	10.40	10.40	.40
15	10.54	10.30	10.40	10.55	10.00	10.36	.55
16	10.20	10.60	10.15	10.00	10.50	10.29	.60
17	10.20	10.40	10.60	10.80	10.10	10.42	.70
18	9.90	9.50	9.90	10.50	10.00	9.96	1.00
19	10.60	10.30	10.50	9.90	9.80	10.22	.80
20	10.60	10.40	10.30	10.40	10.20	10.38	.40
21	9.90	9.60	10.50	10.10	10.60	10.14	1.00
22	9.95	10.20	10.50	10.30	10.20	10.23	.55
23	10.20	9.50	9.60	9.80	10.30	9.88	.80
24	10.30	10.60	10.30	9.90	9.80	10.18	.80
25	9.90	10.30	10.60	9.90	10.10	10.16	.70
				$\bar{\bar{X}}$ =		10.21	
				$\bar{R}$ =			.60

tolerance) limits. In section A of Exhibit 6.16, we see a process that on average is producing items within the control limits but its variation is such that it can't meet specifications for all items. Exhibit 6.16B shows reduction in this variability, but the process is still deficient. Finally, in Exhibit 6.16C, we see that the process variability has been brought under control. How is this accomplished? By working to improve the performance of each source of variance: workers, machine, tooling, setup, material, and the environment.

Process capability ratio. In order for a process to be both in control and within tolerance, the part tolerance limits must be equal to or wider than the upper and lower limits of the process control chart. Since these control limits are at plus or minus three standard deviations (3 sigma), the tolerance limits must exceed 6 sigma. A quick way of making this determination is through the use of a process capability ratio. This ratio is calculated by dividing the tolerance width by 6 sigma (the process capability), as shown in the following formula in which s, the sample standard deviation, is substituted for σ, the population standard deviation.

EXHIBIT 6.15

$\overline{X}$ **Chart and** R **Chart**

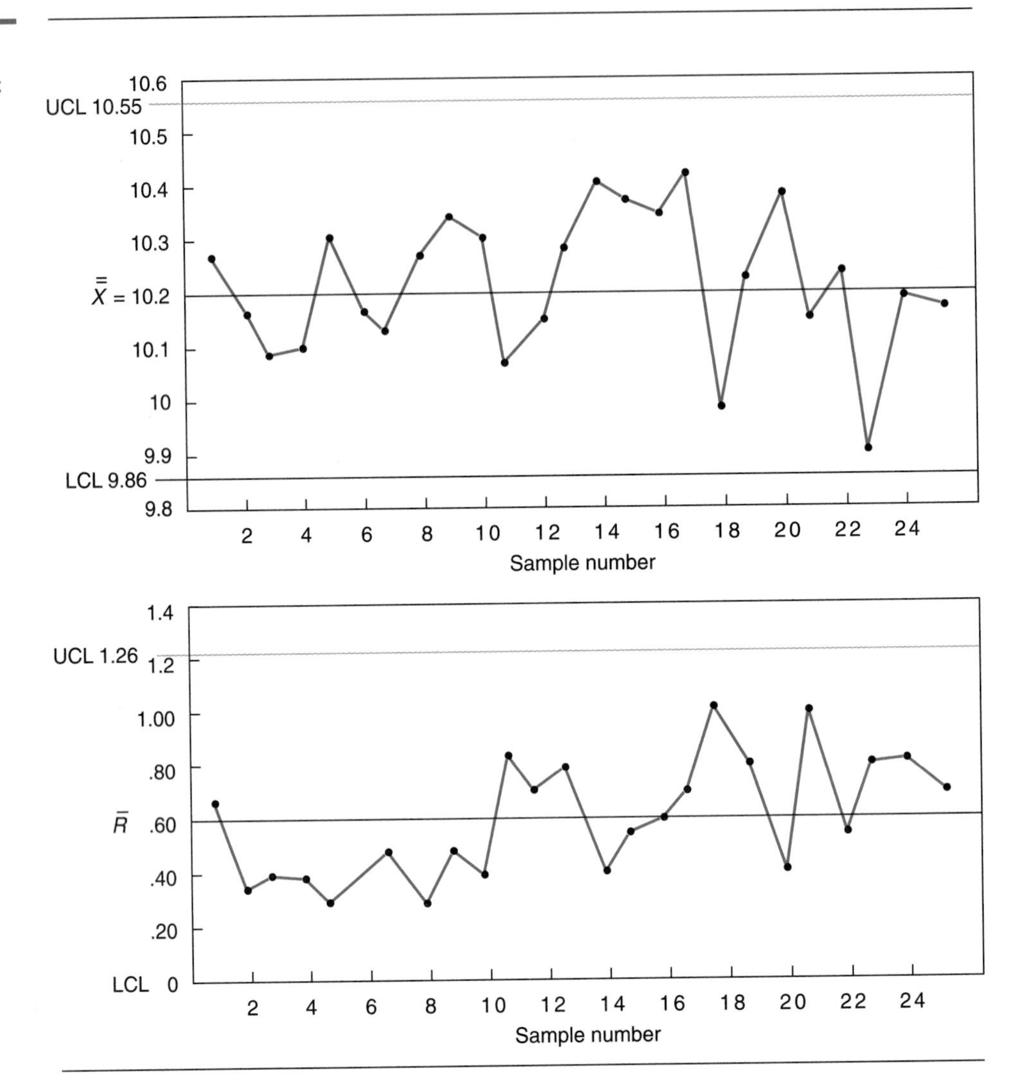

$$\text{Process capability ratio} = \frac{\text{Upper tolerance limit} - \text{Lower tolerance limit}}{6s}$$

The larger the ratio, the greater the potential for producing parts within tolerance from the specified process. A ratio that is greater than 1 indicates that the tolerance limit range is wider than the actual range of measurements. If the ratio is less than 1, then some parts will be out of tolerance. The minimum capability index is frequently established at 1.33. Below this value, design engineers have to seek approval from manufacturing before the product can be released for production.

EXHIBIT 6.16 **Reducing Process Variance So That All parts Are in Within Specification (Tolerance)**

A. Process not capable, but in statistical control

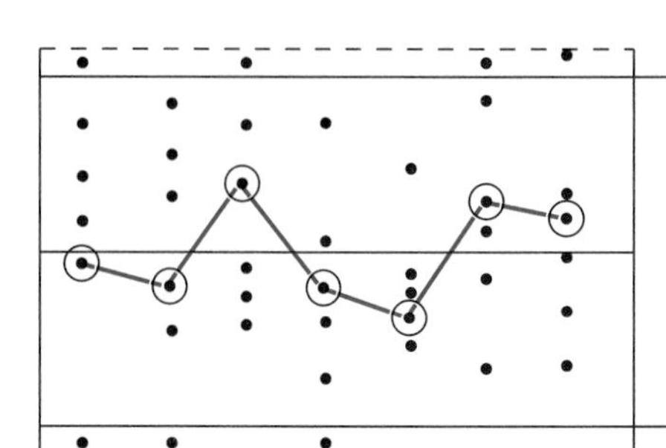

Normal variance pattern, but variance is too great for all individual unit measurements to be within tolerance limits. (Seven of 35 are outside.)

B. Process variance reduced, but still not capable of defect-free production

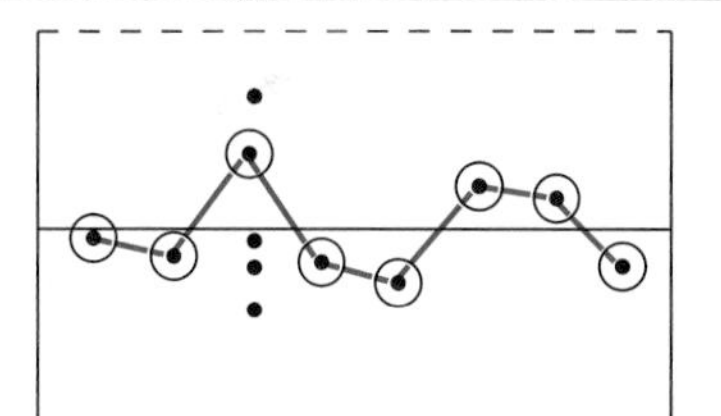

Variance is reduced so that control limits for sample means are inside the tolerance limits, but individual units will still be produced outside the tolerance limits just through normal variation.

C. Process capable of defect-free production

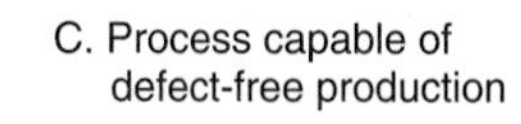

Variance now is so greatly reduced that no individual measurements should fall outside tolerance even if the central tendency of the process is not centered in the tolerance range.

Tolerance: The range within which all individual measurements of units produced is desired to fall.

Source: Robert W. Hall, *Attaining Manufacturing Excellence: Just-in-Time Manufacturing. Total Quality, Total People Involvement* (Homewood: Ill.: Dow Jones–Irwin, 1987), p. 66.

Capability index (C_{pk}). The process capability ratio does not specifically indicate how well the process is performing relative to the target dimension. Thus, a second performance index, called C_{pk}, must be employed to determine whether the process mean is closer to the upper specification limit, USL, or the lower specification limit, LSL.

$$C_{pk} = \min\left[\frac{\overline{X} - \text{LSL}}{3s}, \frac{\text{USL}\ \overline{X}}{3s}\right]$$

When C_{pk} equals the capability ratio, then the process mean is centered between the two specification limits. Otherwise, the process mean is closest to the specification limit corresponding to the minimum of the two C_{pk} ratios. Consider the following example.

Example

A manufacturing process produces a certain part with a mean diameter of 2 inches and a standard deviation of .03 inches. The upper specification limit equals 2.05 inches and the lower specification limit equals 1.9 inches. From this information, a process capability ratio and C_{pk} were calculated.

$$\text{Process capability ratio} = \frac{2.05 - 1.90}{6(.03)} = .833$$

$$C_{pk} \text{ for LSL} = \frac{2 - 1.90}{3(.03)} = 1.11$$

$$C_{pk} \text{ for USL} = \frac{2.05 - 2}{3(.03)} = .56$$

From the process capability ratio, we can conclude that the process is not capable of producing parts within the design's specification. The C_{pk} analysis points out that the process mean is closer to the upper tolerance limit. Given this information, work can be done on the manufacturing process to increase the process capability ratio, and also to center the mean between the two specification limits. This may involve, for example, a simple adjustment of a machine tool setting.

6.8 TAGUCHI METHODS

Throughout this chapter we have discussed quality control from the point of view of process adjustments. In what many have termed a revolution in quality thinking, Genichi Taguchi of Japan has suggested the following: Instead of constantly fiddling with production equipment to ensure consistent quality, design the product to be robust enough to achieve high quality despite fluctuations on the production line. This simple idea has been employed by such companies as Ford Motor Company, ITT, and IBM; as a result, they have saved millions of dollars in manufacturing costs.

Taguchi methods are basically statistical techniques for conducting experiments to determine the best combinations of product and process variables to make a product. *Best* means lowest cost with highest uniformity. This can be a complicated, time-consuming process. For example, in designing the process for a new product, one might find that a single processing step with only eight process variables (machine speed, cutting angle, and so on) could be combined in up to 5,000 different ways. Thus, finding the combination that makes the product with the highest uniformity at the lowest cost can't be done efficiently by trial and error. Taguchi has found a way around this problem by focusing on only a few combinations that represent the overall spectrum of product/process outcomes.

Taguchi is also known for the development of the concept of a quality loss function (QLF) that relates the cost of quality directly to the variation in a process. The following discussion from an article by Joseph Turner develops this concept in detail.

IS AN OUT-OF-SPEC PRODUCT REALLY OUT OF SPEC?

VARIATION AROUND US

It is generally accepted that, as variation is reduced, quality is improved. Sometimes that knowledge is intuitive. If a train is always on time, schedules can be planned more precisely. If clothing sizes are consistent, time can be saved by ordering from a catalog. But rarely are such things thought about in terms of the value of low variability. With engineers, the knowledge is better defined. Pistons must fit cylinders, doors must fit openings, electrical components must be compatible, and boxes of cereal must have the right amount of raisins—otherwise quality will be unacceptable and customers will be dissatisfied.

However, engineers also know that it is impossible to have zero variability. For this reason, designers establish specifications that define not only the target value of something, but also acceptable limits about the target. For example, if the target value of a dimension is 10 in., the design specifications might then be 10.00 in. ± 0.02. This would tell the manufacturing department that, while it should aim for exactly 10 in., anything between 9.98 in. and 10.02 in. is OK.

The traditional way of interpreting such a specification is that any part that falls within the allowed range is equally good, while any part falling outside the range is totally bad. This is illustrated in Exhibit 6.17. (Note that the cost is zero over the entire specification range, and then there is a quantum leap in cost once the limit is violated.)

Taguchi has pointed out that such a view is nonsense for two reasons:

1. From the customer's view, there is often practically no difference between a product just inside specifications and a product just outside. Conversely, there is a far greater difference in the quality of a product that is at the target and the quality of one that is near a limit.
2. As customers get more demanding, there is pressure to reduce variability. The underlying philosophy in Exhibit 6.17 does not recognize this pressure.

Taguchi suggests that a more correct picture of the loss is shown in Exhibit 6.18. Notice that in this graph the cost is represented by a smooth curve. There are dozens of

EXHIBIT 6.17

A Traditional View of the Cost of Variability

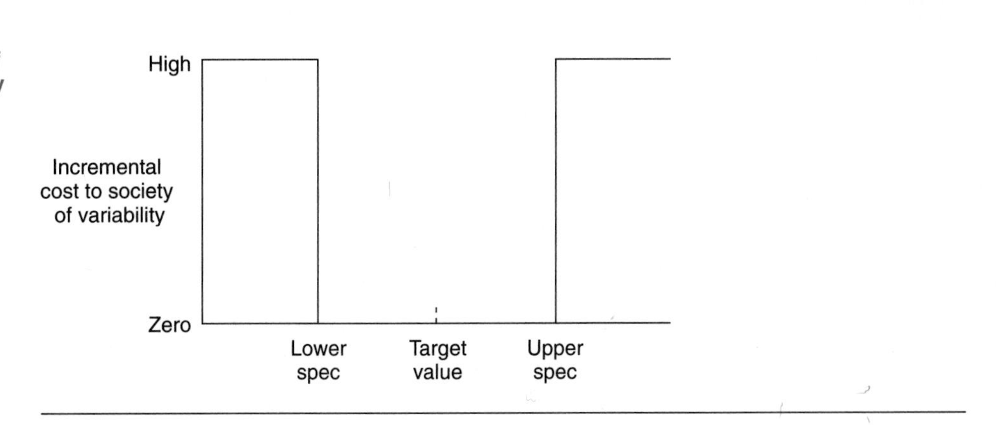

(continued)

illustrations of this notion: the meshing of gears in a transmission, the speed of photographic film, the temperature in a workplace or department store. In nearly anything that can be measured, the customer sees not a sharp line, but a gradation of acceptability. Customers see the loss function as Exhibit 6.18 rather than Exhibit 6.17.

What are the elements of loss to society? While different authorities suggest different things, it seems reasonable to think of both internal and external costs. Internally, the more variable the manufacturing process, the more scrap generated and the more a company will have to spend on testing and inspecting for conformance. Externally, customers will find that the product does not last as long or work as well if it is not close to target. Perhaps, when used in adverse situations, the product will not perform at all, even though it meets specifications that were developed based on normal usage.

While the actual shape of the loss curve might vary considerably, a simple parabolic curve, as shown in Exhibit 6.18, has a lot of intuitive appeal, especially when specification limits are symmetrical about the target value. With a parabola, the loss is relatively small when we are close to the target and grows at an increasing rate the farther we move from the target.

Of course, if products are consistently scrapped when they are outside specifications, the loss curve flattens out in most cases at a value equivalent to scrap cost in the ranges outside specifications. This is because such products, theoretically at least, will never be sold, so there is no external cost to society. However, in many practical situations, either the process is capable of producing a very high percentage of product within specifications and/or 100 percent checking is not done and/or out-of-spec products can be reworked to bring them to within specs. In any of these situations, the parabolic loss function is usually a reasonable assumption.

In such cases, the following formula applies:

(1) $L = K(x - a)^2$

where

L = Loss to society associated with a unit of product produced at a value x

a = Target value for the variable; assume that at a, $L = 0$

K = A constant.

x = The actual measurement of the variable.

EXHIBIT 6.18

Taguchi's View of the Cost of Variability

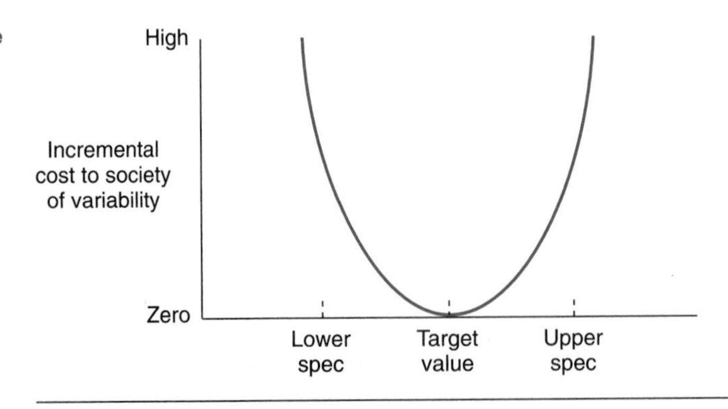

(continued)

Then, substituting the following variables, and solving for K:

c = The loss associated with a unit of product produced at *a* specification limit, assuming that the loss for a unit at target is zero

d = Distance from the target to the spec limit

(2) $K = c/d^2$

With n units of product, the average loss per unit becomes:

(3) $\overline{L} = K[\Sigma(x - a)^2/n]$

While this formula assesses average loss, it is somewhat cumbersome because data are not usually collected in a way that makes the computation of $\Sigma(x - a)^2$ convenient. However, data are often available on the historical mean and standard deviation for the item of interest. When these are known, the average loss is closely approximated by:

(4) $\overline{L} = K[s^2 + (\overline{x} - a)^2]$

where

$\overline{x}$ = Process average

s = Process standard deviation.

The only difficulty in applying the preceding formula to a practical situation is coming up with a valid estimate of *c,* the incremental loss to society associated with a unit of product produced at the limit, compared to the loss associated with a unit produced at target. While this is, at best, a guesstimate, it is possible for knowledgeable people to suggest a value that represents educated thinking. One group of engineers suggested the value should be one tenth of the selling price of a particular item. This means that if a unit were right at the limit, there is a reasonable chance that, because of test variability, the unit might fail final inspection. Furthermore, there is a reasonable chance the customer would encounter greater problems with a unit at the limit than with a unit made at target, and this would result in loss to the customer and possible warranty returns. While

EXHIBIT 6.19

Example of Automotive Part

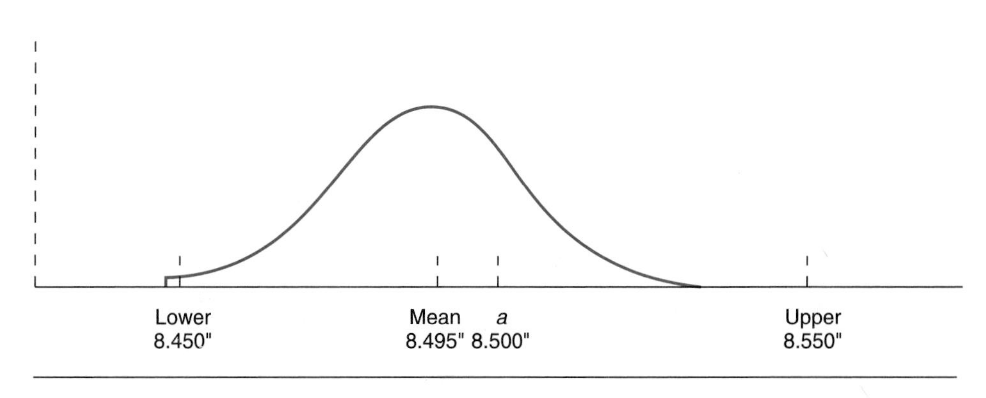

(continued)

this estimate was admittedly a bit arbitrary, it seemed a reasonable starting point as a minimum estimate and resulted in a surprisingly high estimated loss value.

This approach is illustrated in the following example: The specification for a key dimension on an automotive part is 8.5 in. ± 0.05 in. Historical data indicate that over the past several months, the mean value has been 8.492 in. and the standard deviation, 0.016 in. The part sells for $20, and engineers have estimated the loss to society as $2 for a part that is exactly at the upper or lower limit. Production is 250,000 parts per year. The situation is pictured in Exhibit 6.19.

Applying equation (4), the average loss per part is

$$\bar{L} = [2/(.05)^2]\,[.016)^2 + (.008)^2] = 25.6 \text{ cents}$$

Applying this to the volume of 250,000 units produces a total annual loss of $64,000. If engineers want to reduce this loss, they can pursue three avenues:

1. Shift the mean value so it is on target (i.e., 8.5 in.).
2. Reduce the variability (for example, make $s = 0.01$ in.).
3. Accomplish both 1 and 2.

Applying equation (4) to the three situations produces the following results:

1. By moving the mean value to target, $\bar{L} = 20.5$ cents; total annual loss = $51,250.
2. By reducing the variability to $s = 0.01$ in., $\bar{L} = 13.1$ cents; total annual loss = $32,750.
3. By accomplishing both 1 and 2, $\bar{L} = 8$ cents; total annual loss = $20,000.

Note that if higher or lower estimates were used for *c*, the resulting numbers would be affected proportionately. Thus, it is possible to easily perform a sensitivity analysis assuming a range of values for *c*. For example, if *c* were estimated at $4 rather than $2, all of the results would be exactly double those shown.

Source: Adapted from Joseph Turner, "Is an Out-of-Spec Product Really Out of Spec?" *Quality Progress* (December 1990, pp. 57–59.

6.9 ISO 9000

In 1987, the International Organization for Standards (ISO) published the **ISO 9000** series on international standards. There are five standards in the series: ISO 9000 (Quality Management and Quality Assurance Standards—Guidelines for Selection and Use); ISO 9001 (Quality Systems—Model for Quality Assurance in Design/Development, Production, Installation and Servicing); ISO 9002 (Model for Quality Assurance in Production and Installation); ISO 9003 (Quality Systems—Model for Quality Assurance in Final Inspection and Test); and ISO 9004 (Quality Management and Quality System Elements—Guidelines).

These standards have been adopted as national standards in more than 60 countries around the world, including all of the developed countries. Although originally developed with a focus on manufacturing companies, these standards can also be applied, with minor modifications, to service operations.

ISO 9000 was initially designed in Europe, and it is there that it has had the greatest impact. Today, over 40,000 companies are ISO 9000 certified; the vast majority are within the 12 nations that comprise the European Union (EU). In fact, starting in 1992, companies within the EU require their suppliers to be audited and registered under ISO 9000. The purpose of these ISO 9000 standards is to provide a common basis for evaluation so that a purchaser in one country can be assured of the quality system of a supplier in another country without having to complete and individual audit each time.

This requirement has also provided the necessary impetus for U.S. firms to obtain ISO 9000 certification in order that they may do business in the EU. In addition, major organizations within the United States have also adopted ISO 9000, including the U.S. Department of Defense, AT&T, and DuPont. To increase awareness, a wide variety of courses and conferences on ISO 9000 are offered frequently on both a national and international basis.

6.10 CONCLUSION

The production and delivery of high-quality goods and services is a critical element in determining the success of an organization. No longer is quality relegated to a passive, defensive role as once was the case; rather, it can now contribute offensively as a strategic weapon in defining market niches. Total quality management (TQM) consists of four integral components, all of which are necessary for a TQM program to succeed. High quality is not more expensive; in fact, just the reverse is true. High quality is cost effective, especially when emphasis is placed on preventing defects from occurring in the first place.

Thus, quality management as a strategic issue should not be approached with an off-the-shelf program devised by others. Quality must be integrated internally and externally (see Exhibit 6.20). Managers are paid to use new concepts, but more important, to lead customization and integration of these concepts into their organizations. The supplement to this chapter dealing with the Malcolm Baldridge National Quality Award gives numerous examples of how award-winning companies have accomplished this customization and integration.

6.11 REVIEW AND DISCUSSION QUESTIONS

1. Is quality free? Debate!
2. What are the quality dimensions, as defined in Exhibit 6.1, for each of the following:
   a. IBM personal computer.
   b. School registration process.
   c. Steakhouse.
3. An agreement is made between a supplier and a customer such that the supplier must ensure that all parts are within tolerance before shipment to the customer. What is the effect on the cost of quality to the customer?
4. In the situation described in Question 3, what would be the effect on the cost of quality to the supplier?

EXHIBIT 6.20 **Three Schools of Total Quality Management Programs**

	Total Quality Harangue	Total Quality Tools	Total Quality Integration
Noticeable characteristics	Exhortation, lots of talk about quality; generally a marketing campaign intended to create buying signals without incurring the expense of fundamental changes	Introduction of specific tools; viz, statistical process control, employee involvement programs, and/or quality circles	Serious review of all elements of the organization; efforts to involve suppliers and customers
Rationale	Management may believe that quality is better than generally known or may be creating a smoke screen; viz, "everybody's doing it," "it's the thing to do these days"	Valued customers insist on implementation of a team program; or competitors have introduced successful programs creating a "bandwagon" effect	Systematic effort to improve earnings through differentiation based on quality
Responsibility for quality	Unchanged; specific function within organization assigned responsibility for quality	Lower-level members of organization regardless of function	Shared responsibility, senior management accepts responsibility to create an environment encouraging quality
Structural changes	None; the organization remains unchanged	Incremental changes within functional areas or processes	Dramatic changes integrating functions within the organization and involving customers and suppliers in the total production process
Representative employee attitudes and behaviors	Total quality is just a fad, "this too shall pass"; smart employees learn to keep their heads down, they talk about quality when expected to but know that business continues as usual	"It's a nice idea, too bad management isn't really serious about quality"; clever employees participate in seminars and use appropriate tools to fix obvious flaws in their areas of responsibility, but are careful not to rock the boat	"At last, we've got a chance to do it right"; committed employees study the total quality vision, actively search for opportunities to improve performance across the organization, challenge conventional assumptions, and seek to involve customers and suppliers
Role of the quality professional	Police officer, watchdog	Resident expert, advisor	Strategic leaders, change agent

Source: Eric W. Skopec, Strategic Visions Inc. (used by permission).

5. What are the limitations of QFD for designing a service encounter?
6. If line employees are required to assume the quality control function, their productivity will decrease. Discuss this.
7. "You don't inspect quality into a product; you have to build it in." Discuss the implications of this statement.

8. "Before you build quality in, you must think it in." How do the implications of this statement differ from those of Question 7?

6.12 SOLVED PROBLEMS

PROBLEM

1. Completed forms from a particular department of an insurance company were sampled on a daily basis as a check against the quality of performance of that department. In order to establish a tentative norm for the department, one sample of 100 units was collected each day for 15 days, with these results:

Sample	Sample Size	Number of Forms with Errors
1	100	4
2	100	3
3	100	5
4	100	0
5	100	2
6	100	8
7	100	1
8	100	3
9	100	4
10	100	2
11	100	7
12	100	2
13	100	1
14	100	3
15	100	1

a. Develop a *p*-chart using a 95 percent confidence interval (1.95 S_p).
b. Plot the 15 samples collected.
c. What comments can you make about the process?

SOLUTION

Insurance company forms.

a. $\bar{p} = \dfrac{46}{15(100)} = .031$

$S_p = \sqrt{\dfrac{\bar{p}(1-\bar{p})}{n}} = \sqrt{\dfrac{.031(1-.031)}{100}} = \sqrt{.0003} = .017$

$\text{UCL} = \bar{p} + 1.96S_p = .031 + 1.96(.017) = .064$

$\text{LCL} = \bar{p} - 1.96S_p = .031 - 1.96(.017) = -.002 \text{ or zero}$

b. The defectives are plotted here.

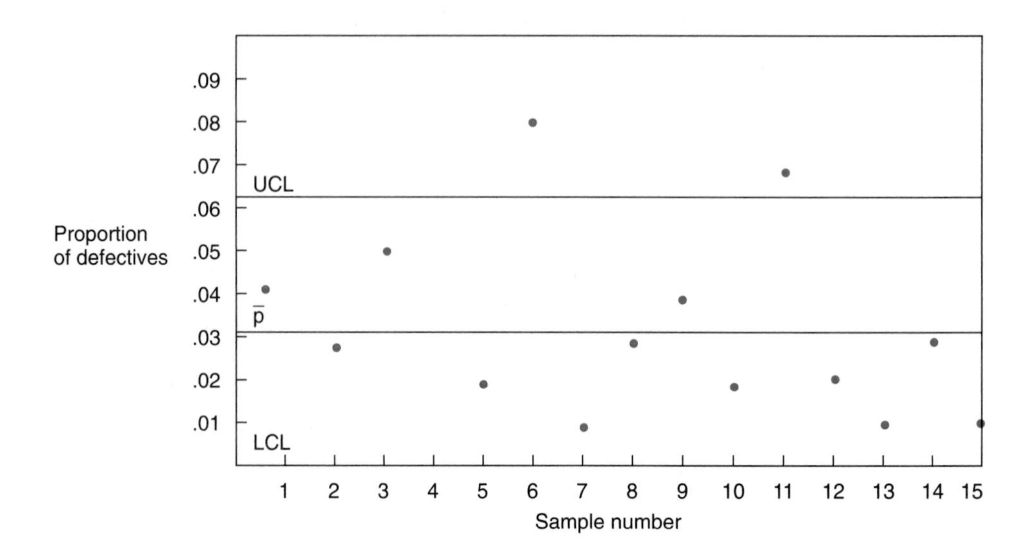

c. Of the 15 samples, 2 were out of the control limits. Since the control limits were established as 95 percent, or 1 out of 20, we would say that the process is out of control. It needs to be examined to find the cause of such widespread variation.

PROBLEM

2. Management is trying to decide whether Part A, which is produced with a consistent 3 percent defective, should be inspected. If it is not inspected, the 3 percent defectives will go through a product assembly phase and have to be replaced later. If all Part A's are inspected, one-third of the defectives will be found, thus raising the quality to 2 percent defectives.
   a. Should the inspection be done if the cost of inspecting is $0.01 per unit and the cost of replacing a defective in the final assembly is $4.00?
   b. Suppose the cost of inspecting is $0.05 per unit rather than $0.01. Would this change your answer in *a*?

SOLUTION

Should Part A be inspected?

.03 defective with no inspection.
.02 defective with inspection.

a. This problem can be solved simply by looking at the opportunity for 1 percent improvement.

Benefit = .01($4.00) = $0.04
Cost of inspection = $0.01

Therefore, inspect and save $0.03 per unit.

b. A cost of $0.05 per unit to inspect would be $0.01 greater than the savings, and therefore, inspection should not be performed.

6.13 PROBLEMS

1. The following is a partial house of quality for a golf club. Provide an importance weighting from your perspective (or that of a golfing friend) in the unshaded areas. If you can, compare it to a club where you or your friend plays using the QFD approach.

WHATs versus HOWs Strong relationship: • Medium relationship: ○ Weak relationship: △	Physical aspects	Course location	Ground maintainance	Landscaping	Pin placement	Course tuning	Tee placement	Service facilites	Customer-trained attendants	Top quality food	Highly rated chefs	Attractive restaurant	Tournament activites	Calloway handicapping	Exciting door prizes	Perception issues	Invitation only	Types of guests	Income level	Celebrity
Physical aspects																				
Manicured grounds																				
Easy access																				
Challenging																				
Service facilites																				
Restaurant facilites																				
Good food																				
Good service																				
Good layout																				
Plush locker room																				
Helpful service attend																				
Tournament facilites																				
Good tournament prize																				
Types of players																				
Fair handicapping sys																				
Perception issues																				
Prestigious																				

2. A company currently using an inspection process in its material receiving department is trying to install an overall cost reduction program. One possible reduction is the elimination of one of the inspection positions. This position tests material that has a defective content on the average of 0.04. By inspecting all items, the inspector is able to remove all defects. The inspector can inspect 50 units per hour. Hourly rate including fringe benefits for this position is $9. If the inspection position is eliminated, defects will go into product assembly and will have to be replaced later at a cost of $10 each when they are detected in final product testing.
   a. Should this inspection position be eliminated?
   b. What is the cost to inspect each unit?
   c. Is there benefit (or loss) from the current inspection process? How much?

3. A metal fabricator produces connecting rods with an outer diameter that has a 1 ± .01 inch specification. A machine operator takes several sample measurements over time and determines the sample mean outer diameter to be 1.002 inches with a standard deviation of .003 inches.
   a. Calculate the process capability ratio for this example.
   b. What does this figure tell you about the process?
4. Ten samples of 15 parts each were taken from an ongoing process to establish a *p*-chart for control. The samples and the number of defectives in each are shown here.

Sample	*n*	Number of Defects in Sample
1	15	3
2	15	1
3	15	0
4	15	0
5	15	0
6	15	2
7	15	0
8	15	3
9	15	1
10	15	0

   a. Develop a *p*-chart for 95 percent confidence (1.96 standard deviations).
   b. Based on the plotted data points, what comments can you make?
5. Output from a process contains 0.02 defective units. Defective units that go undetected into final assemblies cost $25 each to replace. An inspection process, which would detect and remove all defectives, can be established to test these units. However, the inspector, who can test 20 units per hour, is paid a rate of $8 per hour, including fringe benefits. Should an inspection station be established to test all units?
   a. What is the cost to inspect each unit?
   b. What is the benefit (or loss) from the inspection process?
6. There is a 3 percent error rate at a specific point in a production process. If an inspector is placed at this point, all the errors can be detected and eliminated. However, the inspector is paid $8 per hour and can inspect units in the process at the rate of 30 per hour.
   If no inspector is used and defects are allowed to pass this point, there is a cost of $10 per unit to correct the defect later on.
   Should an inspector be hired?
7. Resistors for electronic circuits are being manufactured on a high-speed automated machine. The machine is being set up to produce a large run of resistors of 1,000 ohms each.
   To set up the machine and to create a control chart to be used throughout the run, 15 samples were taken with 4 resistors in each sample. The complete list of samples and their measured values are as follows:

Sample Number	Readings (in ohms)			
1	1010	991	985	986
2	995	996	1009	994
3	990	1003	1015	1008
4	1015	1020	1009	998
5	1013	1019	1005	993

Sample Number	Readings (in ohms)			
6	994	1001	994	1005
7	989	992	982	1020
8	1001	986	996	996
9	1006	989	1005	1007
10	992	1007	1006	979
11	996	1006	997	989
12	1019	996	991	1011
13	981	991	989	1003
14	999	993	988	984
15	1013	1002	1005	992

Develop an $\overline{X}$ chart and an R chart and plot the values. From the charts, what comments can you make about the process? (Use 3-sigma control limits as in Exhibit 6.13, p.144.)

8. You are the newly appointed assistant administrator at a local hospital, and your first project is to investigate the quality of the patient meals put out by the food-service department. You conducted a 10-day survey by submitting a simple questionnaire to the 400 patients with each meal, asking that they simply check off either that the meal was satisfactory or unsatisfactory. For simplicity in this problem, assume that the response was 1,000 returned questionnaires from the 1,200 meals each day. The results ran as follows:

	Number of Unsatisfactory Meals	Sample Size
December 1	74	1,000
December 2	42	1,000
December 3	64	1,000
December 4	80	1,000
December 5	40	1,000
December 6	50	1,000
December 7	65	1,000
December 8	70	1,000
December 9	40	1,000
December 10	75	1,000
	600	10,000

   a. Construct a *p*-chart based on the questionnaire results, using a confidence interval of 95.5 percent, which is two standard deviations.

   b. What comments can you make about the results of the survey?

9. The state and local police departments are trying to analyze crime rate areas so that they can shift their patrols from decreasing-rate areas to areas when rates are increasing. The city and county have been geographically segmented into areas containing 5,000 residences. The police recognize that all crimes and offenses are not reported; people either do not want to become involved, consider the offenses too small to report, are too embarrassed to make a policy report, or do not take the time, among other reasons. Every month, because of this, the police are contacting by phone a random sample of 1,000 of the 5,000 residences for data on crime (the respondents are guaranteed anonymity). The data collected for the past 12 months for one area are as follows.

Month	Crime Incidence	Sample Size	Crime Rate
January	7	1,000	0.007
February	9	1,000	0.009
March	7	1,000	0.007
April	7	1,000	0.007
May	7	1,000	0.007
June	9	1,000	0.009
July	7	1,000	0.007
August	10	1,000	0.010
September	8	1,000	0.008
October	11	1,000	0.011
November	10	1,000	0.010
December	8	1,000	0.008

Construct a $\bar{p}$-chart for 95 percent confidence (1.96) and plot each of the months. If the next three months show the number of crime incidences (out of 1,000 sampled) in this area as:

January = 10 February = 12 March = 11

what comments can you make regarding the crime rate?

10. Some of the citizens complained to city council members that there should be equal protection under the law against the occurrence of crimes. The citizens argued that this equal protection should be interpreted as indicating that high-crime areas should have more police protection than low-crime areas. Therefore, police patrols and other methods for preventing crime (such as street lighting or cleaning up abandoned areas and buildings) should be used proportionately to crime occurrence.

    In a fashion similar to Problem 9, the city has been broken down into 20 geographical areas, each containing 5,000 residences. The 1,000 sampled from each area showed the following incidence of crime during the past month.

Area	Number of Crimes	Sample Size	Crime Rate
1	14	1,000	0.014
2	3	1,000	0.003
3	19	1,000	0.019
4	18	1,000	0.018
5	14	1,000	0.014
6	28	1,000	0.028
7	10	1,000	0.010
8	18	1,000	0.018
9	12	1,000	0.012
10	3	1,000	0.003
11	20	1,000	0.020
12	15	1,000	0.015
13	12	1,000	0.012
14	14	1,000	0.014
15	10	1,000	0.010
16	30	1,000	0.030
17	4	1,000	0.004
18	20	1,000	0.020
19	6	1,000	0.006
20	30	1,000	0.030
	300		

Suggest a reallocation of crime protection effort, if indicated, based on a *p*-chart analysis. In order to be reasonably certain in your recommendation, select a 95 percent confidence level (i.e., $Z = 1.96$).

11. AmalgoTech engineers are trying to improve the design of a gear that has an outer diameter of 13 inches with a tolerance of plus or minus .003 inches. Available inspection data from the past year indicates that the mean value of the diameter has been 13.001 with a standard deviation of .0025 inches. The gear sells for $125. The estimated loss to society is $20 for any gear that has a diameter at the upper or lower tolerance limit. Annual sales of the gear amount to 40,000 units.
    a. Calculate the average loss per unit of production.
    b. What is the expected loss per year?
    c. What happens to the average loss per unit and the expected loss per year if the mean is shifted to the target value of 13 inches?

12. The operations manager of a small metal fabricating company is concerned about the variability of a milling process. Although the average width of a metal connector is identical to the target of .25 inches, the standard deviation of the process is .01 inches. The tolerance limits for the part are plus or minus .008 inches. The expected loss to society for any metal connector that is produced with widths at the limits of tolerance is $1.75 per unit. The specialized connectors sell for $18.00 each.
    a. Calculate the average loss per unit of production.
    b. If the average width shifts from the target value of .25 inches but stays within tolerance, what will happen to value of the average loss per unit of production?
    c. What is the value of the average loss per unit if the standard deviation can be reduced from .01 to .0075?

13. The Eau de Fawcett Beverage Company has developed a line of sophisticated beverages targeted for couples who both work and have no children. This segment of the consumer market is often referred to as "DINKS" (i.e., Double Income, No Kids). This new line of beverages is thus being produced under the label "Drinks for Dinks." The bottles for this product are filled on automatic equipment which has been adjusted so that the average fill per bottle is 11 ounces. Historically, it has been determined that the standard deviation of the filling equipment is .16 ounces. Every hour, a sample of 36 bottles is taken at random from the process, and the average volume is calculated and plotted on an $\overline{X}$ chart.
    a. Draw an $\overline{X}$ process control chart with limits of ±3 standard deviations, correctly labeling the UCL and LCL.
    b. The average sample volumes for Monday morning were as follows:

Hour	7:00 AM	8:00 AM	9:00 AM	10:00 AM	11:00 AM
Average volume	11.09	10.95	10.82	11.06	11.23

    Plot the average volume for each hour on the process control chart. Do you think that the process is in control?

14. Perri and Scott own a small restaurant in Burlington, VT. Because they are also students at the University of Vermont, there are times when neither of them can be at the restaurant. Recently, they have been receiving a large number of customer complaints about the quality of their restaurant's food.
    a. Draw a fishbone diagram for the restaurant's operation and identify potential causes in each of the major categories (e.g., methods, materials, machinery and labor). Be specific.

   b. What other quality control tool(s) would you use to reduce the number of customer complaints as quickly as possible?

15. Allison Jon, the manager of the 800 number reservation service for a nationwide chain of luxury hotels, is concerned about the productivity of her operation. Analysis of past data shows that it should take an average of five minutes to properly process a reservation and that the standard deviation is 30 seconds. Every day, Allison randomly samples how long it takes to make each of 25 reservations.
   a. Set up a process control chart with 95% confidence limits.
   b. If the sample results show that the average reservation time is significantly above the upper control limit, what might be some of the causes for the longer reservation times? How would you correct these problems?
   c. Should Allison have any concern if the average reservation time was significantly below the lower control limit? Why?

6.14 CASE: VAPORTECH PRESSURE TRANSDUCERS

Vaportech is a small company in the business of producing pressure transducers, devices used to sense changes in pressure in jet engines. The production process involves 16 steps of intricate assembly, followed by test and final inspection. Any transducers that fail a test or inspection are sent to a separate rework area. Three types of pressure transducers are built on the same assembly line. The only difference in the transducers is the spring; each model uses a different spring tension. The pressure transducers are pressure-tested in batches of 25 common units for 16 hours. One-hundred-percent final inspection is conducted after the test to check the torque applied to several connecting devices and to look for any material blemishes.

Fully 35 percent of the cost of producing parts is consumed by the rework and final inspection processes. The yield of acceptable products from the test area is 80 percent. Of the units that pass test, 12 percent fail final inspection. The company employs 16 full-time assemblers, 3 full-time technicians, 6 full-time final inspectors, and 5 rework technicians.

Jim Gladstone, the production manager, is frustrated by the failure in promoting the importance of quality. In front of each assembler, signs promoting "Customer Is Number 1" and "Quality Is Everyone's Responsibility" are covered with pictures of spouses and children. Each employee received a full day of training on the importance of quality, yet yield is low and rework costs are on the rise.

The assemblers blame the quality of vendor-supplied parts for the test and inspection failures. The vendors claim that all parts are 100-percent inspected prior to being shipped to Vaportech. The test technicians blame problems on the poor workmanship of the assemblers. Production morale is low and turnover of employees is becoming a pressing problem. One thing is certain. Jim Gladstone desperately needs to do something to improve quality and lower costs. What action should Jim take to achieve this?

6.15 SELECTED BIBLIOGRAPHY

Brassard, Michael. *The Memory Jogger Plus+.* Methuen, Mass.: GOAL/QPC, 1989.

Crosby, Philip B. *Quality Is Free.* New York: McGraw-Hill, 1979.

________. *Quality without Tears.* New York: McGraw-Hill, 1984.

________. *Running Things.* New York: McGraw-Hill, 1986.

Deming, Walter E. *Quality, Productivity, and Competitive Position.* Cambridge, Mass.: MIT Center for Advanced Engineering Study, 1982.

________. *Out of the Crisis.* Cambridge, Mass.: MIT Center for Advanced Engineering Study, 1986.

Durand, San G.; D. W. Marquardt; R. W. Peach; and J. C. Pyle. "Updating the ISO 9000 Quality Standards: Responding to Marketplace Needs." *Quality Progress,* July 1993, pp. 23–28.

Feigenbaum, A. V. *Total Quality Control.* 3rd ed. New York: McGraw-Hill, 1983.

Garvin, David. "Competing on the Eight Dimensions of Quality." *Harvard Business Review,* November–December 1987.

Gitlow, Howard S., and Shelly J. Gitlow. *The Deming Guide to Quality and Competitive Position.* Englewood Cliffs, N.J.: Prentice Hall, 1987.

Ishikawa, Kaoru. (translated by David J. Lu). *What Is Total Quality Control?—The Japanese Way.* Englewood Cliffs, N.J.: Prentice Hall, 1985.

ISO 9000: Handbook of Quality Standards and Compliance. Needham Heights, Mass.: Allyn and Bacon.

Juran, Joseph M. *Quality Control Handbook.* 3rd ed. New York: McGraw-Hill, 1979.

Juran, Joseph M., and F. M. Gryna. *Quality Planning and Analysis.* New York: McGraw-Hill, 1970.

Mann, N. R. *The Keys to Excellence: The Story of the Deming Philosophy.* Los Angeles, Calif.: Prestwick Books, 1985.

March, A. "A Note on Quality: The Views of Deming, Juran and Crosby." Note No. 9-687-011, ICCH, Harvard Business School, Cambridge, MA, 1986.

Oakland, John S. *Total Quality Control.* London: Heinemann, 1989.

Peters, Tom. *Thriving on Chaos.* New York: Knopf, 1987.

________. and Robert H. Waterman, Jr. *In Search of Excellence.* New York: Harper and Row, 1982.

Scherkenbach, W. W. *The Deming Route to Quality and Productivity: Road Maps and Road Blocks.* Rockville, Md.: Mercury Press/Fairchild Publications, 1986.

Shingo, Shigeo. *Zero Quality Control: Source Inspection and the Poka-yoke System.* Stamford, Conn.: Productivity Press, 1986.

Taguchi, G. *Introduction to Off-line Quality Control.* Magaya: Central Japan Quality Control Association, 1979.

________. *On-line Quality Control during Production.* Tokyo: Japanese Standards Association, 1987.

Tenner, A. R., and I. J. DeToro. *Total Quality Management.* Reading, Mass.: Addison-Wesley, 1992.

Townsend, Patrick L., and Joan E. Gebhart. *Commit to Quality.* New York: John Wiley and Sons, 1986.

Walton, Mary. *Deming Management at Work.* New York: Perigree Books, 1991.

Supplement

The Malcolm Baldrige National Quality Award

EPIGRAPH

A decision to apply for the Baldrige is a marketing/public relations issue. A decision to adopt the criteria may be a matter of survival.

SUPPLEMENT OUTLINE

KEY TERMS

Public Law 100–107

Deming Prize

Baldrige Criteria
1. Leadership
2. Information and Analysis
3. Strategic Quality Planning
4. Human Resource Utilization
5. Quality Assurance of Products and Services
6. Quality Results
7. Customer Satisfaction

At the annual awards ceremony for the Malcolm Baldrige National Quality Award, the Commerce Department of the United States displays all the pomp and drama of the Miss America pageant.[1] On a stage bedecked by blue, white, and gold bunting, following fanfare from a military band, the president of the United States presents the government's most prestigious business award to four winners from corporate America. The suspense is a little less riveting than a beauty pageant, as the winners are preannounced. Also, the executives of the winning companies aren't expected to embrace each other and shed tears of joy.

Like beauty queens, many of the contenders have put in grueling months of preparation behind the scenes. Winning the award is considered valuable public relations and is just as eagerly sought by companies as the Miss America crown is by beauty queens.

In 1987, Congress created what has since become the template for quality management for thousands of U.S. companies, the Malcolm Baldrige Award. In this supplement, we provide an updated version of the outstanding Harvard Business School Case Note by W. L. Hart, C. Bogen, and L. Harper, and present portions of the 1991 application guidelines describing the award's philosophies and evaluation system.[2] We also include some material from the Baldrige preparation course taken by Baldrige examiners, an excerpt from Xerox's 1990 winning application, summaries of the quality programs and results of some other Baldrige winners, and some suggestions on what it takes to win the award. At the end of the supplement, we provide a description of the First National Bank of Chicago's quality program, which can be used as a vehicle for readers to consider the broad features of the Baldrige Award.

S6.1 BACKGROUND

On August 20, 1987, President Ronald Reagan affixed his signature to **Public Law 100–107.** This groundbreaking legislation, known commonly as the Malcolm Baldrige National Quality Improvement Act, established the nation's annual award to recognize total quality management in American industry. The Malcolm Baldrige National Quality Award represents the United States government's endorsement of quality as an essential part of successful business strategy in the 1980s and beyond.

By establishing a national quality improvement act, Congress sought to encourage greater U.S. competitiveness through the recognition and commendation of exceptional quality in American business. As an instrument of government, the Baldrige Award seeks to improve quality and productivity by:

1. Helping to stimulate American companies to improve quality and productivity for the pride of recognition while obtaining a competitive advantage through decreased costs and increased profits.

[1] Stephen Kreider Yoder et al., "All That's Lacking Is Bert Parks Singing, Cadillac, Cadillac," *The Wall Street Journal,* December 13, 1990, p. 1.

[2] W. L. Hart, Christopher Bogen, and Lee Harper, "The Malcolm Baldrige National Quality Award," Harvard Business School, 1989.

EXHIBIT S6.1

Baldrige Award Winners, by Category

Manufacturing	Service	Small Business
Motorola Inc. (1988) Westinghouse Commercial Nuclear Fuel Division (1989) Milliken & Co. (1989) Xerox Business Products (1989) Cadillac (1990) IBM Rochester (1990) Solectron (1991) Zytec Corp. (1991) AT&T Network Systems Group (1992) Texas Instruments, Inc. (1992)	Federal Express (1990) AT&T Universal Card Services (1992) The Ritz-Carlton Hotel (1992)	Globe Metallurgical Inc. (1988) Wallace Co. (1990) Marlow Industries (1991) Granite Rock Co. (1992)

2. Establishing guidelines and criteria that can be used by business, industrial, governmental, and other organizations in evaluating their quality improvement efforts.
3. Recognizing the achievements of those companies that improve the quality of their goods and services and thereby provide an example to others.
4. Providing specific guidance for other American organizations that wish to learn how to manage for high quality by making available detailed information on how winning organizations were able to change their cultures and achieve quality eminence.

Without question, the Baldrige Award and its comprehensive criteria for evaluating total quality in an organization have had considerable impact. Some observers have begun referring to the award as the Nobel Prize for business. (See Exhibit S6.1 for past winners.) In the first four months of 1989, the National Institute of Standards and Technology (NIST), which helps administer the award, sent out approximately 25,000 application forms, each containing the 192-point Baldrige criteria for assessing overall organization quality. In 1990, they were deluged with requests for more than 180,000 applications.

Applications are reviewed without funding from the United States government. Review expenses are paid primarily through application fees and partial support for the reviews is provided by the Baldrige Foundation. Through extensive volunteer efforts by members of the Board of Examiners, application review fees are kept to a minimum.

Indeed, quality has become a business imperative for a growing number of American corporations. Market competition, from auto and semiconductor sales to package delivery and financial services, is increasingly taking place in a world arena. Confronted by foreign competitors that often enjoy lower labor costs and their home government's active policy support, American firms are turning to companywide total quality management as a strategy to reduce their costs, improve productivity, and increase customer satisfaction and customer loyalty—all of which tend to translate into increased market share, higher profits, and greater overall competitiveness. "Quality," observes a senior

Photograph courtesy of the National Institute of Standards and Technology, Office of Quality Programs, Gaithersburg Maryland, 20899. Photograph by Steuben.

In 1987, President Ronald Reagan passed the Malcolm Baldrige National Quality Improvement Act. This Act established the prestigious Baldrige Award, presented annually to those companies that have exhibited superior total quality management.

vice president at Federal Express, "is to economic success as the nuclear reaction is to energy production: the output is wildly disproportionate to the input once it builds to a chain reaction."

Though many of the analytical techniques most commonly associated with quality control were developed in the United States, the Japanese transformed quality from arcane statistical analysis used primarily to control variability in manufacturing processes to a system of values that have broad-reaching implications for nearly all business activities. Quality was a linchpin in Japan's post–World War II reconstruction strategy. Doggedly pursuing this strategy, the tiny island nation has risen from economic ruin to what sometimes seems to be near hegemony in many industries.

For nearly 40 years Japan has recognized its corporate quality leaders by bestowing on them the prestigious **Deming Prize** (see Exhibit S6.2), named after the American statistician, Dr. W. Edwards Deming, who championed many of the analytical techniques employed in formal quality control. The Deming Prize has become so esteemed in Japan that each year, much like America's Academy Awards, millions of Japanese watch the Deming Prize ceremony, which is aired live on television.

EXHIBIT S6.2

Comparison of the Deming Prize and Baldrige Award

Japan's highly coveted Deming Prize recognizes successful efforts in instituting companywide quality control (CWQC) principles. The Deming Prize is awarded to all companies that meet a standard based on the evaluation process. For those that do not qualify, the examination process is automatically extended (up to two times over three years). Although both the Deming Prize and the Baldrige Award are designed to recognize outstanding business accomplishments, some notable differences follow:

Topic	Baldrige Award	Deming Prize
Primary focus	Customer satisfaction and quality	Statistical quality control
Grading criteria	Leadership Information and analysis Strategic quality planning Human resource utilization Quality assurance Quality results Customer satisfaction	Policy and objectives Organization and operation Education and extension Data gathering/reporting Analysis Standardization Control Quality assurance Effects Future plans
Winners	Maximum of two per category	All firms meeting standard
Scope	United States firms only	Firms from any country
Grading time	Six months	One year
First award	1987	1951
Sponsor	National Institute of Standards and Technology	Union of Japanese Scientists and Engineers

Source: David Bush and Kevin Dooley, "The Deming Prize and Baldrige Award: How They Compare," *Quality Progress*, January 1989, pp. 28–30.

S6.2 THE BALDRIGE AWARD AND QUALITY CRITERIA

Named after Malcolm Baldrige, who served as United States Secretary of Commerce from 1981 until his death in July of 1987, the Baldrige National Quality Award focuses on an organization's total quality management system and the improvements that system generates. To evaluate and recognize effective quality systems, Baldrige administrators at NIST created a comprehensive process and set of quality criteria based on the comments and observations of experts from throughout the country. The **Baldrige criteria** consequently reflects the combined experience and wisdom of many people. As a set of principles, it is nondenominational in the sense that it does not favor any one system or dogma (see Exhibit S6.3). Instead, the Baldrige criteria are designed to be flexible, evaluating quality on three broad dimensions: (1) the soundness of the approach or systems; (2) the deployment or integration of those systems throughout the entire organization; and (3) the results generated by those systems (see Exhibit S6.4).

The Baldrige quality criteria focuses on seven broad topical areas that are integrally and dynamically related (see Exhibit S6.5). Leadership is the starting point and a key measure of an organization's total quality program. Leadership drives the entire quality system,

EXHIBIT S6.3

Core Values and Concepts in the Award Criteria

The award criteria are built on a set of core values and concepts. Together, these values and concepts represent the underlying basis for integrating the overall customer and the company operational performance requirements. These core values and concepts are:

- Quality is defined by the customer.
- The senior leadership of business must create a customer orientation, clear quality values, and high expectations.
- Quality excellence derives from a well-designed and well-executed approach to continuous improvement.
- Success in meeting quality and performance objectives increasingly depends on work-force quality and involvement.
- Shortening the response time of all operations and processes of the company needs to be part of the quality improvement effort.
- Design quality and defect and error prevention should be major elements of the quality system.
- A company must have a strong future orientation and a willingness to make long-term commitments.
- Operations and decisions of the company need to be based on facts and data.
- Companies should seek to build internal and external partnerships to better accomplish their overall goals.
- A company's quality system objectives should address corporate responsibility and citizenship.

Source: Taken from the 1993 Baldrige Award application.

EXHIBIT S6.4

Baldrige Criteria—Scoring Guidelines

Score	Approach	Deployment	Results
0%	No systems evident	Limited to examples	Anecdotal
10–40%	Beginnings of sound, systematic, prevention-based approach	Major areas Extension plans	Positive trends in major areas with evidence that results are caused by approach
50%	Sound, systematic, effective, approach refined through evaluation/ improvement cycles World-class approach Excellent integration	Full deployment Excellent integration	Excellent (world-class) results in major areas Good to excellent results in support areas Sustained results Results clearly caused by approach

which in the Baldrige vernacular consists of four areas: Information and Analysis, Planning, Human Resource Utilization, and Quality Assurance. Actual quantitative and anecdotal results tracked over time provide a method to measure progress and to judge the effectiveness of the system. Customer satisfaction is the ultimate goal or touchstone of an organization's combined quality programs.

EXHIBIT S6.5 **Examination Categories (Dynamic relationships)**

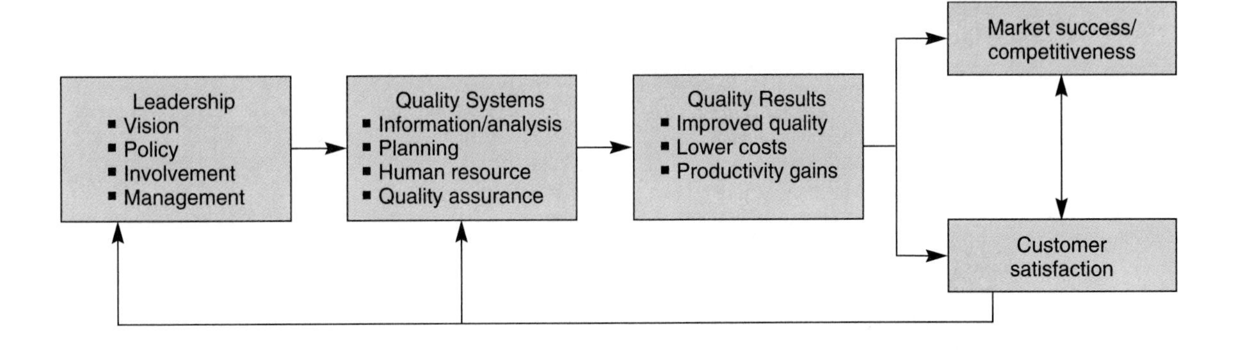

In short, the Baldrige criteria create an integrated set of indicators of excellence and continuity that describes total quality. In the Baldrige view, total quality is a value system. It is a way of life, an approach to doing business that affects every corporate decision and permeates the entire organization.

When a company applies for the Baldrige Award or uses the Baldrige criteria internally to evaluate its quality program, its organization must address 32 subcategories and 99 individual items that fall under the seven broad topical areas. Each topical area and subcategory are weighted according to general importance (see Exhibit S6.6).

For evaluation purposes, a maximum 1,000 points are allocated for the seven Baldrige quality categories. Just as the Japanese stress the importance of both the means and ends when considering quality, the Baldrige criteria tie approximately half their points to the quality process (methods and means) and half to the results (ends and trends). The means or process is a leading indicator of the ends that will be attained. In turn, the results verify that the appropriate process is in place and being used effectively.

Leadership, to which 10 percent of the applicant's total score is assigned, examines how senior executives create and sustain clear and visible quality values in the organization. This section also focuses on top management's involvement in and commitment to creating and championing quality both inside and outside the company.

At the heart of the Baldrige criteria is the belief that quality permeates every nook and cranny, including the executive suite, of preeminent companies. In these organizations, senior management plays a constant, direct, and active role in quality improvement. "I will tell you that today, as an operating general manager, one of the highest priorities I have every day is quality," observes a Motorola executive. "It governs every single decision I make. I never ask a question about how much did we ship; I only ask the question of how much improvement did we get in quality."

From leadership, the Baldrige criteria next focus on **Information and Analysis,** which

EXHIBIT S6.6

Examination Categories and Items

Categories/Items	Maximum Points
1.0 Leadership	**100**
1.1 Senior executive leadership	40
1.2 Quality values	15
1.3 Management for quality	25
1.4 Public responsibility	20
2.0 Information and analysis	**70**
2.1 Scope and management of quality data and information	20
2.2 Competitive comparisons and benchmarks	30
2.3 Analysis of quality data and information	20
3.0 Strategic quality planning	**60**
3.1 Strategic quality planning process	35
3.2 Quality goals and plans	25
4.0 Human resource utilization	**150**
4.1 Human resource management	20
4.2 Employee involvement	40
4.3 Quality education and training	40
4.4 Employee recognition and performance management	25
4.5 Employee well-being and morale	25
5.0 Quality assurance of products and services	**140**
5.1 Design and introduction of quality products and services	35
5.2 Process quality control	20
5.3 Continuous improvement of process	20
5.4 Quality assessment	15
5.5 Documentation	10
5.6 Business process and support service quality	20
5.7 Supplier quality	20
6.0 Quality results	**180**
6.1 Product and service quality results	90
6.2 Business process, operational, and support service quality results	50
6.3 Supplier quality results	40
7.0 Customer satisfaction	**300**
7.1 Determining customer requirements and expectations	30
7.2 Customer relationship management	50
7.3 Customer service standards	20
7.4 Commitment to customers	15
7.5 Complaint resolution for quality improvement	25
7.6 Determining customer satisfaction	20
7.7 Customer satisfaction results	70
7.8 Customer satisfaction comparison	70
Total points	**1,000**

accounts for 7 percent of the overall application score. This section examines the scope, validity, and use of the data underlying a company's total quality system. Next comes **Strategic Quality Planning,** which accounts for 6 percent of the Baldrige application score. This section examines how a company integrates quality planning into its overall business planning and then explores strategies for achieving and retaining short-term and long-term quality leadership. In its efforts to internalize quality, for instance, Globe Metallurgical Inc. has created a five-year quality plan tied directly to its five-year strategic plan. The company's long-term quality plan covers 96 items in 20 pages, including projects, goals, responsibility assignments, and target dates. Moreover, employees throughout the company keep two-year quality calendars on their walls with dates and deadlines for all important quality assignments.

Human Resource Utilization, which represents 15 percent of the overall Baldrige application score, examines an organization's effectiveness in developing and using the full potential of its work force for quality improvement. Worker participation, education and training, recognition of achievements, and workplace environment are a few of the areas covered.

How important is human resource development in quality-driven companies? At an organization such as Westinghouse's CNFD, nearly 90 percent of the work force has received quality-related training in the past three years. Indeed, Motorola spends $45 million annually to support one million hours of training of which at least 40 percent "is devoted to quality improvement processes, principles, technology, and objectives."

The **Quality Assurance of Products and Services,** to which 14 percent of the application's total score is assigned, scrutinizes a company's overall quality control systems. First, it closely examines the ways an organization attempts to design quality into its goods and services, and then it evaluates the manner in which the company integrates quality control with continuous quality improvement. The Baldrige criteria views quality assurance in far-reaching terms, asking companies to demonstrate that their control systems actively involve suppliers, dealers, distributors, and all other external providers of the organization's goods and services.

The Baldrige criteria's sixth area of focus is **Quality Results.** Curt Reimann, director of the Baldrige Award, explains the importance of this category, which accounts for 18 percent of the application's total score, by observing that "if it doesn't get measured, it doesn't get improved." Quantitative results, tracked over time, provide verification that appropriate quality control systems are in place and function well. This sixth category evaluates current quality levels and improvement trends over a three- to five-year time horizon. Both product and process quality trends are examined, comparing an organization's results to industry averages and to the performance of competitors. This concept of benchmarking an organization's performance against its own historical performance and the performance of other companies is central to the Baldrige criteria. By tracking their own and competitors' performances over time, organizations become involved in continuous evaluation to effect continuous improvement and learning. It's not surprising that Baldrige winners excel in collecting, analyzing, and using their results to drive continuous quality improvement. Globe Metallurgical, for example, calculates the daily cost of nonconformance figures for its operations. Motorola states that its organization has saved $250 million from quality improvements over the past two years. Richard Buetow, Motorola's director of quality, estimates his company has received a 20 to 1 return for every dollar invested in its quality improvement programs. This kind of quantification and continual improvement has helped Globe, Motorola, and Westinghouse's CNFD set new world standards for their products.

Customer Satisfaction is the last Baldrige category and the final arbiter of the merit and effectiveness of an organization's quality system. In the Baldrige view, customer satisfaction is the ultimate goal of quality. Appropriately, this section accounts for 30 percent of the application's total score. Companies are asked to examine extensively their knowledge of their customers, their customer service systems, and their ability to meet their customers' requirements.

All Baldrige winners carry to extremes their commitment to customer satisfaction. Motorola managers, for instance, wear pagers so that customers can reach them at any time, any place. Globe responds to all customer queries and complaints—no matter from where the complaint emanates—within 24 hours, and CNFD, which has had 100 percent on-time delivery for the past three years and a product reliability record that approaches perfection, creates quality teams comprised of CNFD employees and customers.

The 7 categories and 28 items that must be addressed in the examination have been selected because of their importance to virtually all businesses. Nevertheless, the importance of the categories and items to address may not be equally applicable to all businesses, even to businesses of comparable size in the same industry. Specific business factors that may bear upon the evaluation are considered at every stage of preparation for evaluations as well as in the evaluations themselves. An outline of the key business factors and how they are considered in the award examination follows:

- Size and resources of the applicant.
- Number and types of employees.
- Nature of the applicant's business: products, services, and technologies; special requirements of customers or markets.
- Scope of the applicant's market: local, regional, national, or international regulatory environment within which the applicant operates.
- Importance of suppliers, dealers, and other external businesses to the applicant and the degree of influence the applicant has over its suppliers.

S6.3 APPLICATIONS OF THE BALDRIGE QUALITY CRITERIA

For companies using them, the Baldrige criteria serve many purposes. Indeed, part of the Baldrige criteria's power lies in the fact that they can be applied in many different ways to organizations whose quality improvement programs are of all different maturities.

As a practical tool for assessing operations, the Baldrige guidelines can be used:

1. To help define and design a total quality system.
2. To evaluate ongoing internal relationships among departments, divisions, and functional units within an organization.
3. To assess and assist outside suppliers of goods and services to a company.
4. To assess customer satisfaction.

Early-stage companies can literally use the Baldrige guidelines as a checklist or blueprint to help them design their overall quality programs. Middle-stage companies can use them as a road map to guide them down the road to continued quality improvement. Finally, advanced-stage companies can use them as an evaluative tool to help fine-tune their quality programs and benchmark them against other industry and world leaders.

The Baldrige guidelines also provide a common language for discussing quality across companies, functional areas, industries, and disciplines. By providing a broad, flexible approach to assessing total quality, the Baldrige system fosters improved information sharing and overall communications. These activities, in turn, lead employees and management to develop a shared meaning of total quality that can be built into the organization's goals and policies. From such shared meaning develops an organizational value system that is customer-focused, quality-driven, and central to the culture of the company. So deeply does Motorola believe in the value of total quality control that the company has ordered all 3,500 of its suppliers to apply for the Baldrige Award, as tangible evidence of their commitment to total quality management, or lose Motorola's business.

The role of the Baldrige Award as an instructor of quality is also rapidly growing. The application process compels management and employees:

1. To recognize the far-reaching importance of quality.
2. To examine the organization's total quality progress and current standing.
3. To exchange information between departments, divisions, and organizational levels.

Assimilating the Baldrige view of total quality can also lead to actions with profound long-term consequences. At Globe, Motorola, and Westinghouse's CNFD, quality planning has been elevated to the same level as strategic planning and integrated with it. Indeed, all these organizations have wrought significant cultural and organizational changes to support companywide total quality.

S6.4 AWARD PROCESS

Thousands of companies have requested the Baldrige guidelines for internal use. (Many firms use the guidelines to improve the quality within their respective organizations.) However, a much smaller number of companies actually submit the 50- to 75-page written applications in May, formally seeking the award. In 1988, the Baldrige Award's first year, 66 companies applied. In 1989, 40 companies applied; in 1990, 97 applied; in 1991, 106 applied; and in 1992, 90 applied. Ultimately, no more than two companies in each of the three categories—manufacturing, service, and small business—are named Baldrige winners.

The Baldrige applications are scored by quality experts from business, consulting, and academia. Of the 1,000 points that can possibly be awarded on the overall application, only 11 of 66 applicants received more than 751 points in 1988. A good company usually falls in the 500 range on the Baldrige scoring.

Only about 10 percent of the applicants become Baldrige finalists and receive site visits from a team of examiners. From this group of finalists, the Baldrige winners are chosen. All companies applying for the award receive from the examiners written feedback reports

EXHIBIT S6.7

Observations of Higher and Lower Scores

Higher Scores	Lower Scores
More quantitative	Passive leadership
Benchmarking	Reactive customer systems
Problem solving	Limited benchmarking
Analysis	"Plateau effects"
External orientation	Weak integration
"Missionary"	Absence of evaluation-change cycles
Knowledge of world quality scene	Partial deployment/involvement
Suppliers, dealers, customers	
Full deployment/integration/involvement	
Proactive customer systems	

summarizing the examiners' findings of the company's organizational strengths and weaknesses.

Many companies speculate about the best way to prepare a winning application. The preparation course taken by the Baldrige examiners discusses general observations about winners and losers (see Exhibit S6.7); however, there is no right approach. Curt W. Reimann, director of the Baldrige Award, lists eight critical factors for which the judges and examiners look:

1. A plan to keep improving all operations continuously.
2. A system for measuring these improvements accurately.
3. A strategic plan based on benchmarks that compare the company's performance with the world's best.
4. A close partnership with suppliers and customers that feeds improvements back into the operation.
5. A deep understanding of the customers so that their wants can be translated into products.
6. A long-lasting relationship with customers, going beyond the delivery of the product to include sales, service, and ease of maintenance.
7. A focus on preventing mistakes rather than merely correcting them.
8. A commitment to improving quality that runs from the top of the organization to the bottom.[3]

One Fortune 500 company acknowledged that over several weeks, it deployed more than 80 people and spent more than $250,000 in its unsuccessful efforts to write, edit, and professionally publish a winning application in 1988. In contrast, one person wrote Globe Metallurgical's application over a three-day weekend.

For those companies that actually win Baldrige Awards, sudden celebrity is assured. The three 1988 winners report receiving between 10 to 15 calls daily from organizations

[3] Jeremy Main, "How to Win the Baldrige Award," *Fortune,* April 23, 1990, pp. 101–16.

wishing to learn about their winning strategies. Even a small company such as Globe, which employs less than 150 people, has seen inquiries come pouring in from throughout the world, including invitations to speak on quality in Moscow, Beijing, and London. (In fact, one of its owners resigned from the company to devote full time to consulting on the Baldrige.)

S6.5 CONCLUSION

Seven years after the establishment of the Malcolm Baldrige National Quality Award, the award's vital signs are strong. In that time, it has grown from a fragile infant into a young adolescent. Will the Baldrige Award incite the broad-based revolution in American productivity and competitiveness that the members of Congress hoped to foment when drafting the Malcolm Baldrige Quality Improvement Act of 1987? That remains to be seen.

The initial response to the Baldrige criteria for evaluating total quality has been overwhelmingly positive. The Baldrige guidelines are proving to be useful and inspirational to scores of companies at all different stages of developing and deploying total quality systems. Moreover, the award itself has brought international attention and prestige to a handful of American companies that have clearly demonstrated their preeminent leadership in total quality management.

The experience of the award's winners suggests that companies throughout the country—indeed, around the world—are deeply interested and concerned about quality.[4] In fact, many of the leading companies in the United States that plan to do business in the European Union (EU) are adopting the Baldrige Award criteria as their vision to be followed beyond the basic requirements of the ISO 9000 standards.

S6.6 REVIEW AND DISCUSSION QUESTIONS

1. What are the commonalities among the Baldrige Award-winning companies profiled in this chapter?
2. How could you apply the Baldrige Award criteria to your university?
3. "Baldrige criteria are more appropriate for evaluating manufacturing firms than service firms." Comment.
4. How is the award process beneficial to companies who do not win?
5. Discuss the implications of Motorola's requirement that its suppliers must apply for the award to continue to supply to Motorola.
6. Discuss the ways that the winning companies discussed in section 6.8 provide superior service to their customers.
7. Although over 60 percent of the Baldrige Award criteria are based on quality and customer

[4]John J. Kendrick, "U.S. Companies Bone Up on EC/ISO 9000 Series Standards," *Quality,* May 1990, p. 13.

satisfaction, universities tend to focus their courses on the other categories. Discuss the reasons for and the implications of this emphasis.

S6.7 READING: EXCERPT FROM 1991 XEROX APPLICATION*

Xerox fulfills many complex requirements to meet all the diverse needs of our customers. The true measure of our product and service quality is the total value we provide our customers—the degree to which we enable them to make their offices more productive and achieve a competitive advantage in their marketplaces.

Xerox customers range from small businesses to major corporations to all aspects of government. Users range from expert operators, who look upon the product as production equipment, to casual users, who may use it only two or three times during the work day. A general purpose copier in an office environment may average 100 users, which means it must withstand rugged treatment.

Our customers tell us that their basic requirements are product quality, copy quality, reliability, operability, and productivity. The value of these product attributes in relation to the total cost of ownership is the final determinant of customer satisfaction with the product. Satisfaction with Xerox as a business partner extends beyond the product to include the competence and professionalism of our sales, service and administrative people.

The results of Xerox quality improvement efforts follow, in the order of importance to our customers.

The primary measure of product quality is defects per machine. Reading Exhibit 1A shows the continuous improvement in manufacturing quality we have achieved despite our increasingly severe criteria over this time span. A defect is defined as any variance from customer requirements. In the early 1980s, manufacturing tracked only those defects attributable to internal operations. However, with the beginning of the total quality approach, defects arising from all causes were given equal focus. Beginning in 1985, Xerox manufacturing quality measurements became a mirror image of customer requirements. This includes not only the specifications for product and packaging, but simulations of field install procedures and customer use. Two further refinements were instituted in 1986 and 1988 as this process reached full TQC maturity: gross defect reporting and initial audit reporting. These changes disallowed waivers for any reason, effectively focusing management action on achieving zero defects. Based on our examination of other copier manufacturers, these are the most stringent requirements in the industry.

After a new machine is installed, quality results for reliability are monitored via customer reports. In order to verify internal results, we use early unscheduled maintenance calls as a key indicator. Reading Exhibit 1B shows the performance of Xerox products during the first 30 days of use. A 40 percent improvement has been achieved in the last four years, coinciding with manufacturing improvements.

Xerox manufacturing people are continuously working to systematically eliminate defect causes in order to fail-safe the process. Using statistical tools and guided by Cost of Quality (COQ) analysis, each product team targets and tracks quality improvement. In the Webster assembly plant, the 1090 product team, working with their suppliers in the Webster components plant, reduced electrical connector defects by 70 percent. The 1025 product team reduced their largest defect problem, photoreceptor damage, by 40 percent using problem-solving tools; and the 1065 team improved

* Source: 1991 Xerox Baldrige Award application.

READING EXHIBIT 1 Xerox Product Quality and Performance

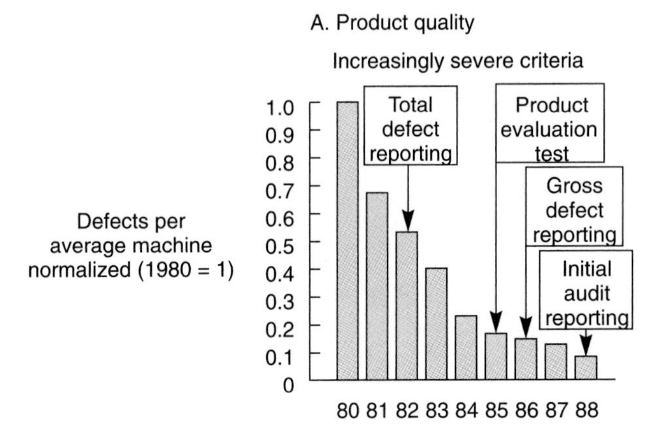

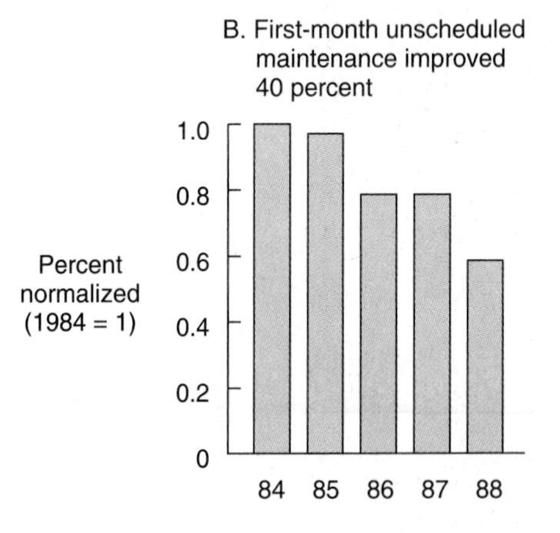

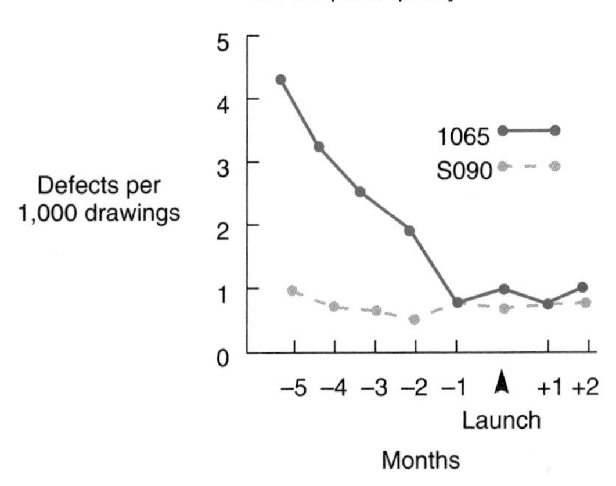

settings on pretransfer transports by 85 percent. Improvements such as these are reviewed daily in the plant manager's quality meeting.

This quality management process begins in advance of manufacturing. In 1985 for instance, a 1065-copier QIT calling themselves "Organizing for Quality" led the way for marked improvement in pilot-plant quality when the 50 Series entered that Phase in 1987. Reading Exhibit 1C shows the improved performance of the 5090, which utilized the process, over the 1065. All products currently under development use this process.

S6.8 READING: 1990 AWARD RECIPIENTS*

Cadillac Motor Car Company

During the 1980s, able foreign and domestic competitors gained market share at Cadillac's expense. By effectively integrating quality into all endeavors—from product planning to personnel practices—Cadillac has reversed its decline in market share, attracting new buyers while boasting the highest percentage of repeat buyers in the car industry. Its partnerships with the United Auto Workers have been a catalyst in this transformation. Cadillac employs about 10,000 people at its Detroit-area headquarters, four Michigan-based manufacturing plants, and 10 sales and service zone offices in the United States.

Cadillac's turnaround began in 1985 with implementation of simultaneous engineering (SE), the first of several major changes designed to ensure that the division's products and services would be first to meet or exceed the expectations of potential buyers. More than 700 employees and supplier representatives now participate on SE teams responsible for defining, engineering, marketing, and continuously improving all Cadillac products. Alongside customers and employees, suppliers and dealers are fully integrated into Cadillac's customer-focused quality improvement efforts. Three-fourths of the division's 55 Product Development and Improvement Teams have suppliers as members. External suppliers must demonstrate continuous improvement in meeting "targets for excellence" in five key areas: quality, cost, delivery, technology, and management. Virtually all measures of performance indicate that continuous quality improvement is paying off for Cadillac.

IBM Rochester

The concept of quality at IBM Rochester is linked directly to the customer. Detailed features are crafted from analysis of needs and expectations of existing and potential owners of computer hardware and software manufactured by IBM Rochester. Customers are directly involved in every aspect of the product from design to delivery. Managers and nonmanagers alike have clearly defined quality improvement goals. Often working in teams that erase departmental boundaries, they have the authority to determine how best to accomplish those goals.

IBM Rochester, which employs more than 8,100 people, recently strengthened its strategic quality initiatives by formulating improvement plans based on six critical success factors: improved product and service requirements definition, enhanced product strategy, six sigma defect elimination strategy, further cycle time reductions, improved education, and increased employee involvement and ownership.

The IBM Rochester quality culture has been transformed from reliance on technology-driven processes to market-driven processes directly involving suppliers, business partners, and customers, delivering solutions. A 30-percent productivity improvement occurred between 1986 and 1989. Product-development time for new mid-range computer systems has been reduced by more than half, while the manufacturing cycle has been trimmed 60 percent since 1983. Customers benefited from a threefold increase in product reliability and a reduced cost. IBM Rochester's share of the world market for intermediate computers increased one full percentage point in both 1988 and 1989, and revenue growth in 1989 was double the industry rate.

---

* Source: 1991 Baldrige Application Guidelines.

Federal Express Corporation

Federal Express's "People-Service-Profit" philosophy guides management policies and actions. Employees are encouraged to innovate and make decisions that advance quality goals. Federal Express provides employees with the information and technology needed to continuously improve their performance. Consistently included in listings of the best U.S. companies to work for, Federal Express has a "no lay-off" philosophy, and its "guaranteed fair treatment procedure" for handling employee grievances is used as a model by firms in many industries.

Seventeen years ago Federal Express launched the air-express industry. The company achieved high levels of customer satisfaction and experienced rapid sales growth. Today, approximately 90,000 Federal Express employees, at over 1,650 sites, process 1.5 million shipments daily. Domestic overnight and second-day deliveries account for nearly three-fourths of the total, with the remainder being international deliveries. The firm's air cargo fleet is now the world's largest. Federal Express revenues totaled $7 billion in fiscal year 1990.

Customer satisfaction is high, but past accomplishments do not ensure future success. Through a quality improvement program focusing on 12 Service Quality Indicators (SQIs) tied to customer expectations, the Memphis-based firm sets higher standards for service and customer satisfaction. The company has set up cross-functional teams for each service component in the SQI. Two of these corporatewide teams have over 1,000 employees working on improvements. Measuring themselves against a 100 percent service standard, managers and employees strive to improve all aspects of Federal Express.

Wallace Co., Inc.

Founded in 1942, Wallace is a family-owned distribution company headquartered in Houston that primarily serves the chemical and petrochemical industries. Its 10 offices, located in Texas, Louisiana, and Alabama, distribute pipe, valves, and fittings, as well as value-added specialty products such as actuated valves and plastic-lined pipe. Wallace distributes directly in the Gulf Coast area but serves international markets as well. In 1989, sales totaled $79 million. The company employs 280 associates, all of whom have been trained in quality improvement concepts and methods.

The Wallace quality initiatives have paid numerous dividends. Since 1987, Wallace's market share has increased from 10.4 percent to 18 percent. In 1985, Wallace adopted a long-term strategy of Continuous Quality Improvement. In only a few years, the company distinguished itself from its competitors by setting new standards for service. Wallace effectively merged business and quality goals, built new partnerships with customers and suppliers, and instilled associates with a commitment to one overriding aim: total customer satisfaction. Nearly everyone at Wallace is a member of a quality team.

Wallace established a Total Customer Response Network that must respond to all inquiries and complaints within 60 minutes. Its customer base has expanded. As a result, since 1987 its sales volume has grown 69 percent and, because of greater efficiency, operating profits through 1989 increased 7.4 times.

S6.9 CASE: THE FIRST NATIONAL BANK OF CHICAGO'S QUALITY PROGRAM*

Skeptics say it is impossible to measure quality in service industries like banking, air travel and insurance. The First National Bank of Chicago believes it has proven the skeptics wrong.

In 1981, the bank set out to increase its market share by positioning itself as the quality provider of corporate cash management services. (Cash management services are non-credit services like checking, funds transfer, and shareholder services.) Management at First Chicago believes that a strategy focused on quality is the best way any company can respond to competition.

First Chicago was pleasantly surprised to find that an emphasis on quality also helps control costs: The quality program has resulted in savings of $7 million to $10 million annually, the bank claims.

Founded in 1863, First Chicago reportedly is the 11th largest bank holding company and the 10th largest bank in the United States. It also is the largest bank in the Midwest. It is the oldest and largest national bank operating under its original name and charter.

The company has 13,000 employees working worldwide. Its common stock is listed on the New York, Midwest, Pacific, London and Tokyo exchanges, and it has about 11,700 shareholders. The 57 offices worldwide are organized into three business areas: global corporate banking, consumer banking, and middle-market banking.

Since 1971, the required return on equity of the banking industry has been on the decline. If a bank wants to stay alive, First Chicago believes, it must change its business mix, its pricing, and/or its costs.

The focus on providing high-quality services stemmed from research indicating that quality is the key controllable buying determination in non-credit services. First Chicago was determined to become the best in the non-credit services business.

"Satisfying customer needs and expectations is the number-one reason for being in any business," says Aleta Holub, vice president for quality assurance at First Chicago. "Customers' standards are constantly rising. A company's failure to respond to raised expectations is like denying the force of the tide. It can leave you high and dry on the beach, while customers sail off to competitors' ports." The bank began the quality process by altering its organizational framework. Separate strategic business units were created—each based on an individual product family.

The strategic business unit manager suddenly became an entrepreneur. The manager was vested with the power to control not only expenses, but also product features, pricing, promotion, and quality. The new structure provides all the essential elements for a manager to meet customer requirements. "The strategic business unit framework brought our managers closer to our customer and made them more directly accountable for the quality of our products," says Holub.

Each business unit has its own customer-service representatives to handle inquiries and problems. They act as conduits, communicating customer concerns to the business unit. Through this decentralized customer-service approach, the customer talks to a service representative trained as a product specialist. Because the customer-service function and production area are in the same location, the representatives can respond more efficiently to problems.

The non-credit services area of First Chicago designed a quality program to insure "that we were doing the right things right the first time," says Holub.

"By asking and listening to our customers, we learned that what they wanted and expected most from us was timeliness, accuracy and responsive service. These are issues not unlike those faced by

---

*Source: This article is adapted from Case Study 61, written by Steve R. Stewart, staff writer at the Houston-based American Productivity and Quality Center.

other service industries . . . surely on-time, accurate, and responsive service are quality elements that customers want and expect from airlines, insurance companies, doctors, and so on," she says.

The next step was to make certain that customer priorities were being met by the bank. An extensive performance measurement system using nearly 700 charts was developed to track on a weekly basis every business unit's performance in relation to its products and the corresponding customer concerns. For example, the accurate processing of money transfers and the turnaround time for letters of credit are measured. By concentrating on the attributes of each major product and service, the bank learns how to fix a quality problem or sustain a quality advantage.

"A customer-based assessment of quality allows a company to recognize if its customers are satisfied with the current attributes of its products," says Holub. The bank's reporting system includes a series of different customer surveys conducted throughout the year.

Using the customer's perspective and industry standards, a management team established minimum acceptable performance (MAP) levels for each indicator, as well as goals for exceptional performance. "These goals are a point of pride and a source of competition among the business unit managers," Holub claims.

The minimum acceptable performance and goal lines for each chart are set by the strategic business unit manager and approved by senior management. To encourage performance improvement, the minimum acceptable and goal lines are continually adjusted upward, "so that the carrot is always just in front of the rabbit," Holub says.

To help increase management's commitment to the performance measurement program, a management bonus system was put in place, with bonuses tied to attainment of minimum acceptable performances and goals for each business unit.

Each unit's performance charts are reviewed weekly with senior department management. All this measuring is not done simply to encourage in-house competition. The measuring provides early warning when something is wrong so that corrective action can be taken.

"For example, when the chart showing the time taken to answer the telephone-initiated money transfers started to reflect a downward trend, the business unit manager analyzed the operation," says Holub. "The manager discovered that calls were backing up during peak periods and slowing down the average. So personnel were shifted around to accommodate peak times. Soon after, performance improved."

Bank customers and suppliers are invited to weekly performance measurement meetings. "A twofold benefit is gained by inviting both customers and suppliers to attend these meetings," says Holub. "First, the bank has an additional forum in which to learn about customers' expectations and concerns involving their products and services. We regularly use that knowledge to refine and improve both. More important, we are sending a loud and clear message that the customer is our central interest.

"The second benefit is that service levels from our vendors also have improved. Vendors are invited to see how well they are doing in relation to the bank's performance objectives," she says.

At the weekly performance meetings, competing vendors sit next to each other. For instance, the IBM Corporation representative may sit beside the competitor from Tandem Computers Inc. Each vendor has the chance to view the other's performance and to prepare ways to do better. The bank believes that it receives its "fair share plus" of vendors' attention and service.

The bank's quality efforts do not stop with the performance measurement system. First Chicago currently has more than 30 active quality circles. These small groups are brought together to identify problems or opportunities and to recommend actions to improve performance.

For example, a quality circle in the money transfer group spotted a potential improvement in the processing of money transfers initiated by telephone. This group discovered that 67 percent of the authorization cards used to verify money transfer requests were being returned by customers with incomplete or inaccurate information. This caused additional checking and confirmation, which resulted in delays in processing time.

The group analyzed the problem and presented the following recommendations:

- Send a sample card with instructions to customers.
- Transfer card-update responsibility to the customer-service unit.
- Develop a method to provide confirmation personnel with more information on the verification screen.

All three recommendations were approved and implemented, and cards are now being returned with more complete and accurate information. The combination of properly completed cards and improved information flow has improved processing time in the unit by more than one-third.

Yet another element of the First Chicago quality process is a program that the bank refers to as its behavioral engineering systems training (BEST) program. This program evaluates individual employee performance. It permits a manager to look at how each staff member is performing, so he or she can identify the source of the problem and work with that person to fix the problem.

To supplement the BEST program, the company's business units have added individual performance programs. The "Walk an Extra Mile" program recognizes customer-service employees who go out of their way to help an external or internal customer. Customer surveys are part of the evaluation process for service employees. Recognition awards vary according to the desires of employees in each business unit but include cash and tickets to sporting events.

Positive strokes such as "most improved," "best sustained superior performance," and "most effective in improving quality in a changing environment" were all given to work "teams" at First Chicago's 1986 non-credit services performance awards banquet. The bank realizes the importance of recognizing the accomplishments of employee groups within the business units. These "teams," however, vary in structure.

Some employees form a team from their normal work group and address problems affecting their department's productivity. Then there are employee teams based on larger issues. These team members might not normally work together.

A team also can be a form of recognition for accurate performance by a number of employees. For instance, an employee who consistently makes no errors over a specified time period is honored by being made part of a team. This type of team is an honor group, not a problem-solving group.

A dozen employee teams—one for each month—receive recognition and attend a banquet each year. Each month's winning team receives a plaque and a paid group outing of its choice. The outing usually is dinner, theater or a sports event. There is a maximum of $100 per person, with a ceiling of $1,000 per group. Each team member also receives a certificate and an entry in a grand-prize drawing held during the annual banquet. The grand prize is round-trip airfare for two in the United States, plus $500 spending money. Several weekend trips also are awarded.

One of the winning teams was the crossed-account project team. This team handled the problem of deposits credited to the wrong account. When deposits are credited incorrectly, one account has too high a balance and the other, too low. This calls for float (uncollected funds) adjustments in both accounts. In this situation, customers may make incorrect cash management choices if they access balance information before adjustment can be made.

"Our customers were not pleased, and the problems caused our customer-service area hours of unnecessary research to rectify the accounts," says Elverage Allen of check collection/production, who nominated the winning team.

The crossed-account project team identified the causes of crossed accounts, established procedures to eliminate them, and reduced these accounts and the corresponding float adjustments from 649 in

May 1985 to 37 during the following March. By the year's end, the team had cut the number of crossed accounts to eight.

First Chicago believes the quality emphasis has had a measurable effect on performance. In 1982, one of the bank's operations experienced an average of one error in every 4,000 transactions. Today, the figure is one in 10,000.

"The success of the quality program within the non-credit services area alone is telling proof that providing excellent products and services, and containing costs, can be mutually compatible efforts," says president Richard L. Thomas. "In fact, we have learned firsthand that an emphasis on quality is one of the most effective ways to control costs."

For example, Thomas says, it generally costs First Chicago just under $10 to perform a money transfer. But that is a transfer done right the first time. If the money goes to the wrong place or does not make it on schedule, the cost of fixing an error can quickly rocket to $400 or more, depending on the amount of money involved, the complexity of the case, and so on. Thus, reduction in the error rate has saved millions of dollars.

First Chicago realized the importance of communicating the quality commitment to its customers. So annually, the bank puts together a comprehensive booklet of key performance measurement charts for customers to see what the bank monitors and how it performs in those areas. The company's advertising theme, "Performance has always been a Chicago tradition," also reflects the quality emphasis.

QUESTION

Evaluate the approach, deployment, and results of First Chicago's Quality Program. Based on your analysis, do they have Baldrige potential?

S6.10 SELECTED BIBLIOGRAPHY

Bush, D., and K. Dooley. "The Deming Prize and Baldrige Award: How They Compare." *Quality Progress,* January 1989, pp. 28–30.

Hart, C. W. L.; Christopher Bogan; and Lee Harper. "The Malcolm Baldrige National Quality Award." Harvard University Case Note, 1989.

Kendrick, John J. "U.S. Companies Bone Up on EC/ISO 9000 Series Standards." *Quality*, May 1990, p. 13.

Main, Jeremy. "How to Win the Baldrige Award." *Fortune,* April 23, 1990, pp. 101–16.

1991 Baldrige Award application instructions.

1991 Xerox Baldrige Award application.

Yoder, Stephen Kreider, et al. "All That's Lacking Is Bert Parks Singing, Cadillac, Cadillac." *The Wall Street Journal,* December 13, 1990, p. 1.

Chapter 7

Forecasting

EPIGRAPH

Forecasting is difficult, especially about the future.

Chinese fortune cookie

CHAPTER OUTLINE

KEY TERMS

Time Series Analysis
Simple Moving Average
Weighted Moving Average
Exponential Smoothing
Smoothing Constant Alpha (α)
Smoothing Constant Delta (δ)
Mean Absolute Deviation (MAD)
Tracking Signal
Linear Regression Forecasting
Causal Relationships

Forecasting plays an important role in all aspects of business. It is the basis of corporate long-run planning. In the functional areas of finance and accounting, forecasts provide the basis for budgetary planning and cost control. Marketing relies on sales forecasting to plan new products, compensate sales personnel, and make other key decisions. Production and operations personnel use forecasts to make periodic decisions involving process selection, capacity planning, facility layout; and for continual decisions about production planning, scheduling, and inventory.

Managers need to recognize that a forecast is never perfect. There are simply too many factors in the business environment that cannot be predicted or controlled with certainty. Therefore, rather than search for the perfect forecast, what is far more important is to establish the practice of continual review of forecasts and to learn to live with inaccurate forecasts. This is not to say that we should not try to improve the forecasting model or methodology, but that we should try to find and use the best forecasting method available, *within reason*.

The goal of this chapter is to present an introduction to several forecasting techniques and models (both qualitative and quantitative) that are commonly used in business, recognizing that additional and more sophisticated forecasting techniques and models are available for people seeking more in-depth knowledge in this area. We address primarily time series techniques and causal relationships, including a discussion of the sources of error and their measurement.

7.1 DEMAND MANAGEMENT

The purpose of demand management is to coordinate and control all of the sources of demand so that the productive system can be used efficiently and the product delivered on time.

Where does the demand for a firm's product or service come from, and what can a firm do about it? There are two basic sources of demand—dependent demand and independent demand. *Dependent demand* is the demand for a product or service that is caused by the demand for other products or services. For example, if a firm sells 1,000 tricycles, there is no question that 1,000 front wheels and 2,000 rear wheels are needed. This type of internal demand does not need a forecast, simply a tabulation. As to how many tricycles the firm might sell, this is called *independent demand* because its demand is independent or does not depend on the demand for other products.[1] We discuss independent and dependent more fully in Chapters 14 and 15.

There isn't too much a firm can do about dependent demand. It must be met (although the product or service can be purchased rather than produced internally). However, there's a lot that a firm can do about independent demand, if it wants to. The firm can:

1. *Take an active role to influence demand.* The firm can apply pressure on its sales force, it can offer incentives both to customers and to its own personnel, it can wage

[1] There are obviously other product relationships such as complimentary products, causal relationships, and so forth.

campaigns to sell products with advertising and promotion programs, and it can cut prices. These actions can increase demand. Conversely, demand can be decreased through price increases or reduced sales efforts.

2. *Take a passive role and simply respond to demand.* There are several reasons a firm may not try to change demand but simply accept what happens. If a firm is running at full capacity it may not want to do anything about demand. Other reasons are a firm may be powerless to change demand because of the expense to advertise, the market may be fixed in size and static, or that demand is beyond their control (e.g., sole supplier). There are other competitive reasons, legal reasons, environmental reasons, and ethical and moral reasons why market demand is passively accepted.

A great deal of coordination is required to manage these dependent and independent demands. These demands originate both internally and externally in the form of new product sales from marketing, repair parts for previously sold products from product service, restocking from the factory warehouses, and supply items for manufacturing. In this chapter, our primary interest is in forecasting for independent items.

7.2 TYPES OF FORECASTING

Forecasting can be classified into three basic types—*qualitative, time series analysis,* and *causal relationships.*

Qualitative techniques are subjective or judgmental in nature, and are based on estimates and opinions. Such techniques are used primarily when there is no data available. **Time series analysis,** the primary focus of this chapter, is based on the idea that data relating to past demand can be used to predict future demand. Causal forecasting assumes that demand is related to some underlying factor or factors in the environment. Time series analysis is typically used in short-range situations, like forecasting worker schedules. Causal forecasting is usually used for longer-term issues, such as selecting a site for a retail operation. Exhibit 7.1 briefly describes some of the different varieties of the three basic types of forecasting models. In this chapter we discuss the three time series analysis methods in the exhibit and the first of the causal techniques.

7.3 COMPONENTS OF DEMAND

In most cases, the demand for products or services can be broken down into five components: average demand for the period, a trend, seasonal influence, cyclical elements, and random variation. Exhibit 7.2 illustrates a demand over a four-year period, showing the trend, cyclical, and seasonal components, and randomness around the smoothed demand curve.

Cyclical factors are more difficult to determine since the time span may be unknown or the cause of the cycle may not be considered. Cyclical influence on demand may come from such occurrences as political elections, war, economic conditions, or sociological pressures.

EXHIBIT 7.1 **Forecasting Techniques and Common Models**

I. Qualitative	*Subjective; judgmental. Based on intuition, estimates and opinions.*
Delphi method	An interactive learning process involving a group of experts who respond to a questionnaire. A moderator compiles results and formulates a new questionnaire which is again submitted to the group.
Market research	Sets out to collect data in a variety of ways (surveys, interviews, etc.) to test hypotheses about the market. These are typically used to forecast long-range and new-product sales.
Historical analogy	Ties what is being forecast to a similar item. Important in planning new products where a forecast may be derived by using the history of a similar product.
II. Time series analysis	*Based on the idea that the history of occurrences over time can be used to predict the future.*
Simple moving average	A time period containing a number of data points is averaged by dividing the sum of the point values by the number of points. Each, therefore, has equal influence. These points may be weighted equally or unequally, as seen fit by experience.
Exponential smoothing	Recent data points are weighted more, with weighting declining exponentially as data become older.
Regression analysis	Fits a straight line to past data generally relating the data value to time. Most common fitting technique is least squares.
Trend projections	Fits a mathematical trend line to the data points and projects it into the future.
III. Causal	*Tries to understand the system underlying and surrounding the item being forecast. For example, sales may be affected by advertising, quality, and competitors.*
Regression analysis	Similar to least squares method in time series but may contain multiple variables. Basis is that forecast is caused by the occurrence of other events.
Input/output models	Focuses on sales of each industry to other firms and governments. Indicates the changes in sales that a producer industry might expect because of purchasing changes by another industry.
Leading indicators	Statistics that move in the same direction as the series being forecast but move before the series, such as an increase in the price of gasoline indicating a future drop in the sale of large cars.

Random variations are caused by chance events. Statistically, when all the known causes for demand (average, trend, seasonal, and cyclical) are subtracted from the total demand, what remains is the unexplained portion of demand. If one is unable to identify the cause of this remainder, it is assumed to be purely random chance.

In addition to these five components there is often autocorrelation, which denotes the persistence of occurrence. More specifically, the value expected at any point is highly correlated with its own past values. For example, if a line is relatively long at one time, then a short period of time later one would expect the line still to be long.

When the demand is random, the demand from one time period to another may vary widely. Where high autocorrelation exists, the demand is not expected to change very much from one time period to the next.

Trend lines are the usual starting point in developing a forecast. These trend lines are then adjusted for seasonal effects, cyclical, and any other expected events that may influence the final forecast. Exhibit 7.3 shows four of the most common types of trends. A linear trend obviously reflects a straight continuous relationship. An S-curve is typical of a product's growth and maturity cycle. The critical points on the S-curve are where the

EXHIBIT 7.2

Historical Product Demand Consisting of a Growth Trend, Cyclical Factor, and Seasonal Demand

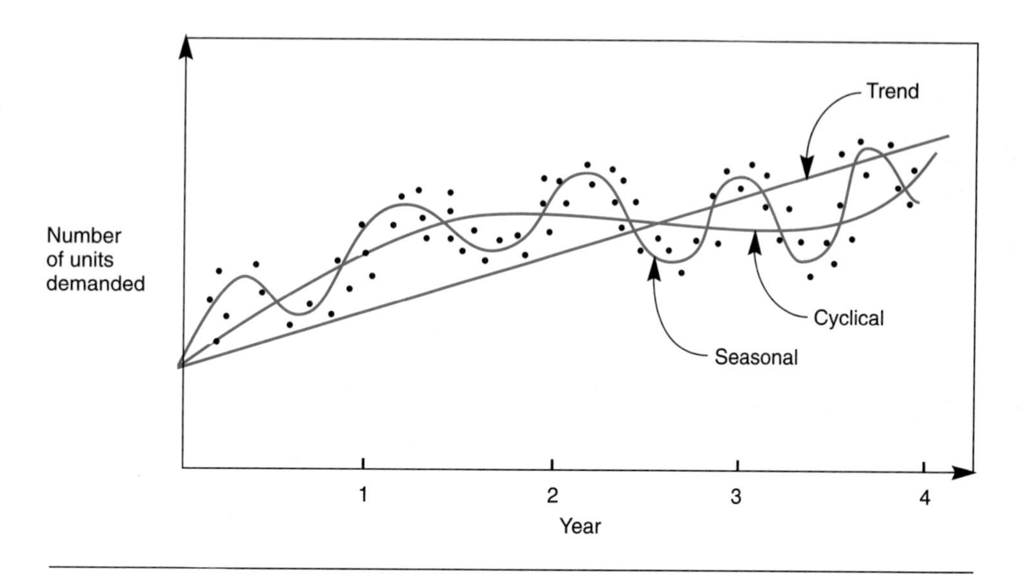

trend makes a transition from slow growth to fast growth and from fast to slow. An asymptotic trend starts with the highest demand growth at the beginning, which then tapers off. Such a curve could happen when a firm enters an existing market with the objective ofsaturating and capturing a large share of the market. An exponential curve is common in products with explosive growth. The exponential trend suggests that sales will continue to increase—an assumption that may not be safe to make.

7.4 TIME SERIES ANALYSIS

Time series forecasting models try to predict the future based on past data. For example, sales figures collected for each of the past six weeks can be used to forecast sales for the seventh week. Quarterly sales figures collected for the past several years can be used to forecast future quarters.

Exhibit 7.4 shows three time series models and some of their characteristics. For comparison we've also included one qualitative and one causal model. Note that the moving average and exponential smoothing are the best and easiest to use for short-term forecasting with little data required, and provide average results. The long-term models are more complex, requiring much more data input, and provide high accuracy. In general, the short-term models compensate for random variation and adjust for short-term changes (such as consumers' responses to a new product). Medium-term forecasts are useful for seasonal effects, and long-term models detect general trends and are especially useful in identifying major turning points. Which forecasting model or models a firm should adopt depends on several factors, including: (1) forecasting time horizon, (2) data availability,

EXHIBIT 7.3 Common Types of Trends

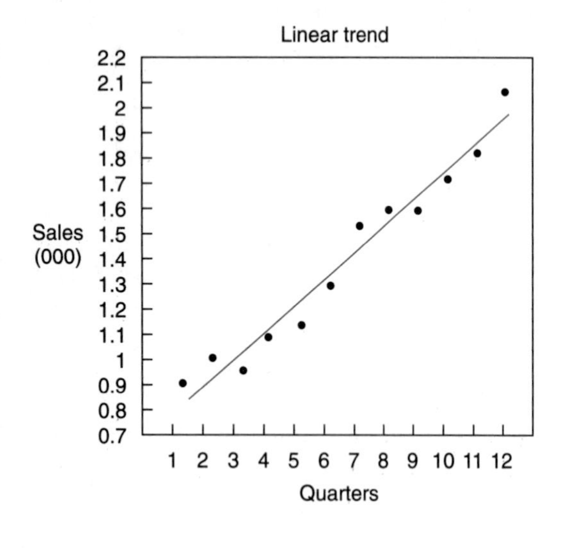

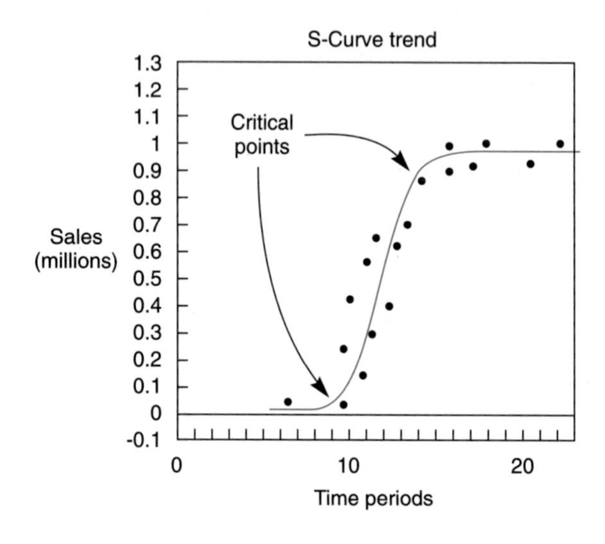

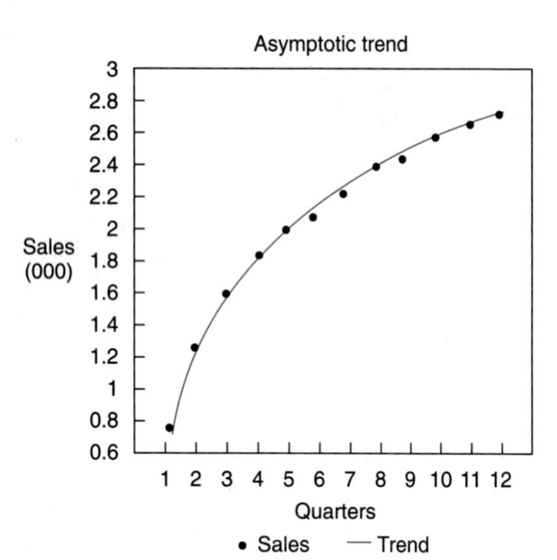

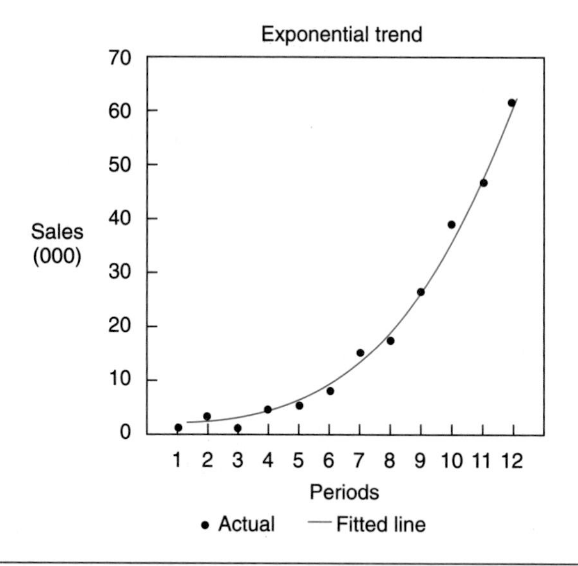

EXHIBIT 7.4

Comparison of Forecasting Techniques

Technique	Time Horizon	Model Complexity	Model Accuracy	Data Requirements
I. Qualitative forecasts	Long	High	Varies	High
II. Time series				
Moving average	Short	Very low	Medium	Low
Exponential smoothing	Short	Low	Fair	Very low
Linear regression	Long	Medium high	Medium high	High
III. Causal				
Regression analysis	Long	Fairly high	High	High

(3) accuracy required, (4) size of the forecasting budget, and (5) availability of qualified personnel.

Simple Moving Average

When demand for a product is neither growing nor declining rapidly, and if it does not have any seasonal characteristics, a **simple moving average** can be useful in identifying a trend within the data fluctuations. Thus, if we want to forecast June with a five-month moving average, we can take the average of January, February, March, April, and May. When June passes, the forecast for July would be the average of February, March, April, May, and June. This is the way Exhibits 7.5 and 7.6 were computed, using both a three-week and a nine-week simple moving average.

Although it is important to select the best period for the moving average, there are several conflicting effects related to period length: the longer the moving-average period, the greater the random elements are smoothed (which may be desirable in many cases). However, if there is a trend in the data—either increasing or decreasing—the moving average has the adverse characteristic of lagging the trend. Therefore, while a shorter time span produces more oscillation, there is a closer following of the trend. Conversely, a longer time span gives a smoother response but lags the trend.

Exhibit 7.6 graphs the data in Exhibit 7.5, illustrating the effects of various lengths of the period of a moving average. We see that the growth trend levels off at about the 23rd week. The three-week moving average responds better in following this change than the nine-week, although overall, the nine-week average is smoother.

The main disadvantage in calculating a moving average is that all individual elements must be carried as data since a new forecast period involves adding the newest data and dropping the oldest data. For a three- or six-period moving average, this is not too severe; however, plotting a 60-day moving average for the usage of each of 20,000 items in inventory would involve a significant amount of data.

EXHIBIT 7.5

Forecast Demand Based on a Three- and a Nine-Week Simple Moving Average

Week	Demand	3-Week	9-Week	Week	Demand	3-Week	9-Week
1	800			16	1,700	2,200	1,811
2	1,400			17	1,800	2,000	1,800
3	1,000			18	2,200	1,833	1,811
4	1,500	1,067		19	1,900	1,900	1,911
5	1,500	1,300		20	2,400	1,967	1,933
6	1,300	1,333		21	2,400	2,167	2,011
7	1,800	1,433		22	2,600	2,233	2,111
8	1,700	1,533		23	2,000	2,467	2,144
9	1,300	1,600		24	2,500	2,333	2,111
10	1,700	1,600	1,367	25	2,600	2,367	2,167
11	1,700	1,567	1,467	26	2,200	2,367	2,267
12	1,500	1,567	1,500	27	2,200	2,433	2,311
13	2,300	1,633	1,556	28	2,500	2,333	2,311
14	2,300	1,833	1,644	29	2,400	2,300	2,378
15	2,000	2,033	1,733	30	2,100	2,367	2,378

EXHIBIT 7.6 Moving Average Forecast of Three- and Nine-Week Periods versus Actual Demand

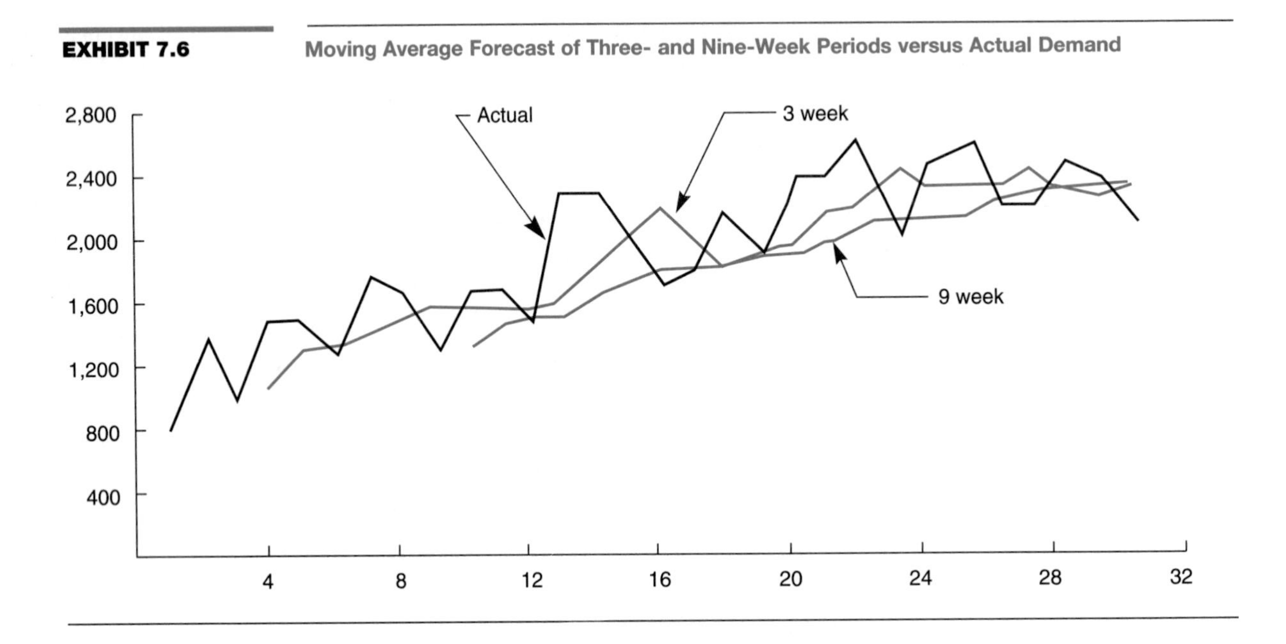

Whereas the simple moving average gives equal weight to each component of the moving-average database, a **weighted moving average** allows each element to be weighted by a factor, where the sum of all weighting factors equals one. For example, a department store may find that in a four-month period the best forecast is derived by using 40 percent of the actual sales for the most recent month, 30 percent of two months ago, 20 percent of three months ago, and 10 percent of four months ago. If actual sales experience was as follows,

Month 1	Month 2	Month 3	Month 4	Month 5
100	90	105	95	?

the forecast for month 5 would be:

$$F_5 = 0.40(95) + 0.30(105) + 0.20(90) + 0.10(100)$$
$$= 38 + 31.5 + 18 + 10$$
$$= 97.5$$

Suppose sales for month 5 actually turned out to be 110; then the forecast for month 6 would be:

$$F_6 = 0.40(110) + 0.30(95) + 0.20(105) + 0.10(90)$$
$$= 44 + 28.5 + 21 + 9$$
$$= 102.5$$

The weighted moving average has a definite advantage over the simple moving average in being able to vary the effects between older data and more recent data. However, it is more inconvenient and thus more costly to use.

Exponential Smoothing

In the previous methods of forecasting (simple and weighted moving average), the major drawback is the need to continually carry a large amount of historical data. As each new piece of data is added in these methods, the oldest observation is dropped, and the new forecast is calculated. In many applications (perhaps in most), the most recent occurrences are more indicative of the future than those in the more distant past. If this premise is valid—that the importance of data diminishes as the past becomes more distant—then **exponential smoothing** may be the most logical and easiest method to use.

The reason this is called "exponential smoothing" is because each increment in the past is decreased by $(1 - \alpha)$, or

	Weighting at $\alpha = 0.05$
Most recent weighting = $\alpha(1 - \alpha)^0$	0.0500
Data 1 time period older = $\alpha(1 - \alpha)^1$	0.0475
Data 2 time periods older = $\alpha(1 - \alpha)^2$	0.0451
Data 3 time periods older = $\alpha(1 - \alpha)^3$	0.0429

Therefore, the exponents 0,1,2,3 . . . , etc. give this method its name.

Exponential smoothing is the most used of all forecasting techniques. It is an integral part of virtually all computerized forecasting programs, and is widely used in ordering inventory in retail firms, wholesale companies, and service agencies.

Exponential smoothing accomplishes virtually everything that can be done with moving average forecasts, but requires significantly less data. The exponential **smoothing constant alpha (α)** is a value between 0 and 1. If the actual demand tends to be relatively stable, we choose a small α to lessen the effects of short-term or random fluctuations, which is similar to having a moving average that involves a large number of periods. If the real demand tends to fluctuate rapidly, we would prefer to use a large value for α to keep up with these changes. This is similar to using a moving average with a small number of periods.

The major reasons that exponential smoothing techniques have become so well accepted are

1. Exponential models are surprisingly accurate.
2. Formulating an exponential model is relatively easy.
3. The user can understand how the model works.
4. There is very little computation required to use the model.
5. Computer storage requirements are small because of the limited use of historical data.
6. Tests for accuracy as to how well the model is performing are easy to compute.

In the exponential smoothing method, only three pieces of data are needed to forecast the future: the most recent forecast, the actual demand that occurred for that forecast period, and a smoothing constant alpha (α). This smoothing constant determines the level of smoothing and the speed of reaction to differences between forecasts and actual occurrences. The value for the constant is arbitrary and is determined both by the nature of the product and the manager's sense of what constitutes a good response rate. For example, if a firm produced a standard item with relatively stable demand, the reaction rate to differences between actual and forecast demand would tend to be small, perhaps just a few percentage points. However, if the firm were experiencing growth, it would be desirable to have a higher reaction rate, to give greater importance to recent growth experience. The more rapid the growth, the higher the reaction rate should be. Sometimes, users of the simple moving average switch to exponential smoothing but like to keep the forecasts about the same as the simple moving average. In this case, α is approximated by $2 \div (n + 1)$ where n was the number of time periods.

The equation for an exponential smoothing forecast is

$$F_t = (1 - \alpha)\ F_{t-1} + \alpha A_{t-1}$$

or rewritten as

$$F_t = F_{t-1} + \alpha(A_{t-1} - F_{t-1})$$

where

F_t = The exponentially smoothed forecast for period t

F_{t-1} = The exponentially smoothed forecast made for the prior period

A_{t-1} = The actual demand in the prior period

α = The desired response rate, or smoothing constant

This equation states that the new forecast is equal to the old forecast plus a portion of the error (the difference between the previous forecast and what actually occurred).[2]

To demonstrate the method, assume that the long-run demand for the product under study is relatively stable and a smoothing constant (α) of 0.05 is considered appropriate. If the exponential method were used as a continuing policy, a forecast would have been made for last month.[3] Assume that last month's forecast (F_{t-1}) was 1,050 units. If 1,000 actually were demanded, rather than 1,050, the forecast for this month would be:

$$\begin{aligned} F_t &= F_{t-1} + \alpha(A_{t-1} - F_{t-1}) \\ &= 1{,}050 + 0.05(1{,}000 - 1{,}050) \\ &= 1{,}050 + 0.05(-50) \\ &= 1{,}047.5 \text{ units} \end{aligned}$$

Because the smoothing coefficient is small, the reaction of the new forecast to an error of 50 units is to decrease the next month's forecast by only 2½ units.

As discussed above, exponential smoothing has the shortcoming of lagging changes in

---

[2]Some writers prefer to call F_t a smoothed average.

[3]When exponential smoothing is first introduced, the initial forecast or starting point may be obtained by using a simple estimate or an average of preceding periods.

EXHIBIT 7.7 **Exponential Forecasts versus Actual Demands for Units of a Product over Time Showing the Forecast Lag**

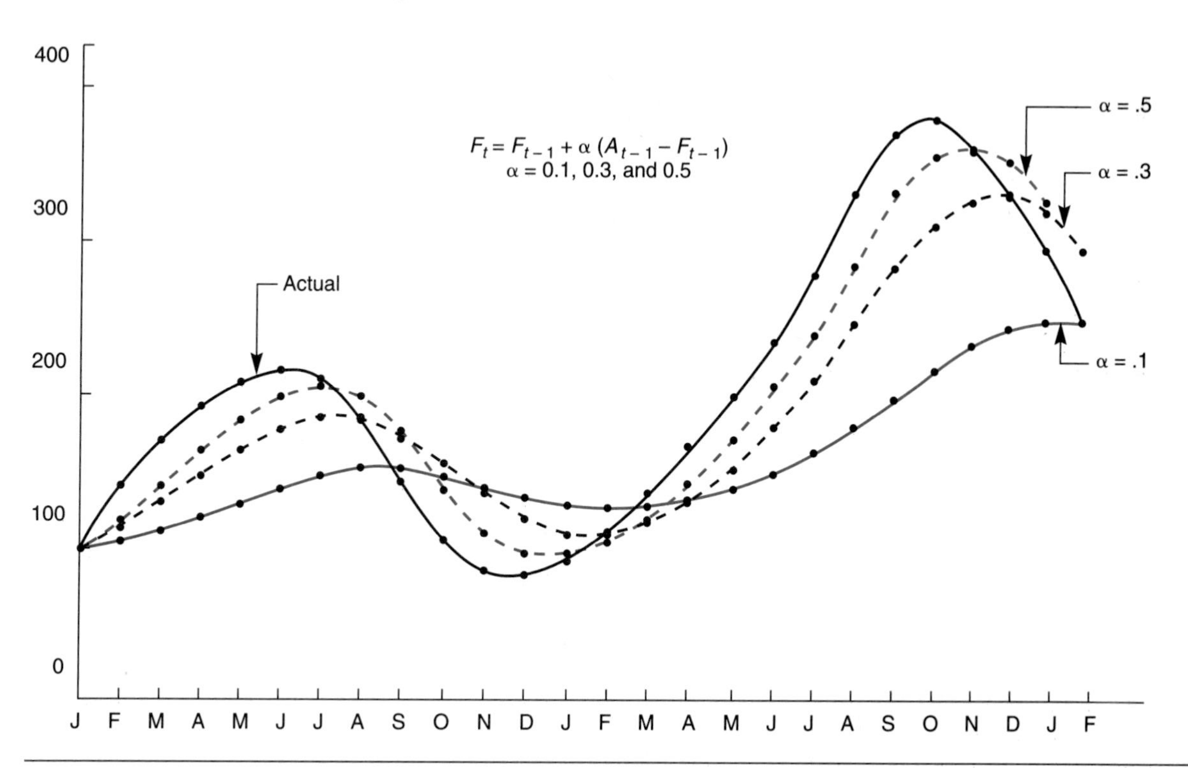

demand. Exhibit 7.7 shows actual data plotted as a smooth curve to show the lagging effects of the exponential forecasts. The forecast lags during an increase or decrease, but overshoots when a change in the direction occurs. Note that the higher the value of alpha, the more closely the forecast follows the actual. To help in closer tracking of actual demand, a trend factor may be added. What also helps is to adjust the value of alpha. This is termed *adaptive forecasting.* Both trend effects and adaptive forecasting are briefly explained in following sections.

The simple exponential smoothing model has many applications in OM in addition to inventory control. William Berry, Vincent Mabert, and Myles Marcus have shown that simple exponential smoothing can be valuable in scheduling services, such as bank tellers.[4]

Trend effects in exponential smoothing

Remember that an upward or downward trend in data collected over a sequence of time periods causes the exponential forecast to always lag behind (i.e., be above or below) the actual occurrence. Exponentially smoothed forecasts can be corrected somewhat by adding

[4]William L. Berry, Vincent A. Mabert, and Myles Marcus, "Forecasting Teller Window Demand with Exponential Smoothing," *Journal of the Academy of Management* 22, no. 1 (March 1979), pp. 129–37.

in a trend adjustment. To correct for the trend, we need two smoothing constants. In addition to the smoothing constant α, the trend equation also uses a **smoothing constant delta** (δ). The delta reduces the impact of the error which occurs between the actual and the forecast. If both alpha and delta are not included, the trend would overreact to errors.

To initiate the trend equation, the trend value must be entered manually. This first trend value can be an educated guess or a computation based on observed past data.

The equation to compute the forecast including trend (FIT) is

$$FIT_t = F_t + T_t$$

where

$$F_t = FIT_{t-1} + \alpha(A_{t-1} - FIT_{t-1})$$
$$T_t = T_{t-1} + \alpha\delta(A_{t-1} - FIT_{t-1})$$

For example, assume an initial starting, F_{t-1} of 100 units, a trend, T_{t-1} of 10 units, an alpha of .20, and a delta of .30. If actual demand turned out to be 115 rather than the forecast 100, calculate the forecast for the next period.

Adding the starting forecast and the trend, we have

$$FIT_{t-1} = F_{t-1} + T_{t-1} = 100 + 10 = 110$$

The actual A_{t-1} is given as 115. Therefore,

$$\begin{aligned} F_t &= FIT_{t-1} + \alpha(A_{t-1} - FIT_{t-1}) \\ &= 110 + .2(115 - 110) = 111.0 \\ T_t &= T_{t-1} + \alpha\delta(A_{t-1} - FIT_{t-1}) \\ &= 10 + (.2)(.3)(115 - 110) = 10.3 \\ FIT_t &= F_t + T_t = 111.0 + 10.3 = 121.3 \end{aligned}$$

If, instead of 121.3, the actual turned out to be 120, the sequence would be repeated and the forecast for the next period would be:

$$\begin{aligned} F_{t+1} &= 121.3 + .2(120 - 121.3) = 121.04 \\ T_{t+1} &= 10.3 + (.2)(.3)(120 - 121.3) = 10.22 \\ FIT_{t+1} &= 121.04 + 10.22 = 131.26 \end{aligned}$$

Adaptive forecasting. There are two approaches for adjusting the value of alpha. One uses various values of alpha and the other uses a tracking signal.

1. *Two or more predetermined values of alpha.* Clay Whybark measures the amount of error between the forecast and the actual demand.[5] Depending on the degree of error, different values of alpha are used. Alpha values are not computed but are discrete values selected by Whybark. For example, if the error is large, alpha is 0.8; if the error is small, alpha is 0.2.

2. *Computed values for alpha.* D. W. Trigg and D. H. Leach use a tracking signal that

[5] D. Clay Whybark "A Comparison of Adaptive Forecasting Techniques," *The Logistics Transportation Review* 9, no. 1 (1973), pp. 13–26.

computes whether the forecast is keeping pace with genuine upward or downward changes in demand (as opposed to random changes).[6] The tracking signal is defined as the exponentially smoothed actual error divided by the exponentially smoothed absolute error. Alpha is set equal to this tracking signal and therefore changes from period to period within the possible range of 0 to 1.

In logic, computing alpha seems simple. In practice, however, it is quite prone to error. There are three exponential equations—one for the single exponentially smoothed forecast as done in the previous section of this chapter, one to compute an exponentially smoothed actual error, and the third to compute the exponentially smoothed absolute error. Thus, the user must keep three equations running in sequence for each period. Further, assumptions must be made during the early periods until the technique has a chance to start computing values. For example, alpha must be given a value for the first two periods until actual data are available. Also, the user must select a smoothing constant in addition to alpha, which is used in the actual and absolute error equations. Clearly, anyone using adaptive forecasting on a regular basis would be wise to use a programmable calculator or a computer.

Forecast Errors

When we use the word *error,* we are referring to the difference between the forecast value and what actually occurred. So long as the forecast value is within the confidence limits, as we discuss below in "Measurement of Error," this is not really an error. However, common usage refers to the difference as an error.

Demand for a product is generated through the interaction of a number of factors too complex to describe accurately in a model. Therefore, all forecasts contain some degree of error. In discussing forecast errors, it is convenient to distinguish between *sources of error* and the *measurement of error.*

Sources of Error

Errors can come from a variety of sources. One common source that many forecasters are unaware of is caused by projecting past trends into the future. For example, when we talk about statistical errors in regression analysis, we are referring to the deviations of observations from our regression line. It is common to attach a confidence band (i.e., statistical control limits, which are described in Chapter 6), to the regression line to reduce the unexplained error. However, when we then use this regression line as a forecasting device by projecting it into the future, the error may not be correctly defined by the projected confidence band. This is because the confidence interval is based on past data; it may or may not hold for projected data points and therefore cannot be used with the same confidence. In fact, experience has shown that the actual errors tend to be greater than those predicted from forecast models.

---

[6] D. W. Trigg and D. H. Leach, "Exponential Smoothing with an Adaptive Response Rate," *Operational Research Quarterly* 18 (1967), pp. 53–59.

Errors can be classified as bias or random. *Bias errors* occur when a consistent mistake is made. Sources of bias are failing to include the right variables; using the wrong relationships among variables; employing the wrong trend line; mistakenly shifting the seasonal demand from where it normally occurs; and the existence of some undetected secular trend. *Random errors* can be defined simply as those that cannot be explained by the forecast model being used. These random errors are often referred to as "noise" in the model.

Measurement of Error

Several of the common terms used to describe the degree of error are *standard error, mean squared error* (or *variance*), and *mean absolute deviation.* In addition, *tracking signals* may be used to indicate the existence of any positive or negative bias in the forecast.

Standard error is discussed in the section on linear regression in this chapter. Since the standard error is the square root of a function, it is often more convenient to use the function itself. This is called the *mean square error,* or variance.

The **mean absolute deviation (MAD)** was in vogue in the past but subsequently was ignored in favor of standard deviation and standard error measures. In recent years, however, MAD has made a comeback because of its simplicity and usefulness in obtaining tracking signals. MAD is the average error in the forecasts, using absolute values. It is valuable because MAD, like the standard deviation, measures the dispersion (or variation) of observed values around some expected value.

MAD is computed using the differences between the actual demand and the forecast demand without regard to sign. It is equal to the sum of the absolute deviations divided by the number of data points, or, stated in equation form,

$$\text{MAD} = \frac{\sum_{t=1}^{n} |A_t - F_t|}{n}$$

where

t = Period number
A = Actual demand for the period
F = Forecast demand for the period
n = Total number of periods
$| \ |$ = A symbol used to indicate the absolute value disregarding positive and negative signs

When the errors that occur in the forecast are normally distributed (which is assumed to be the usual case), the mean absolute deviation relates to the standard deviation as

$$1 \text{ standard deviation} = \sqrt{\frac{\pi}{2}} \times \text{MAD, or approximately } 1.25 \text{ MAD.}$$

Conversely,

$$1 \text{ MAD} = 0.8 \text{ standard deviation}$$

EXHIBIT 7.8

A Normal Distribution with a Mean = 0 and a MAD = 1

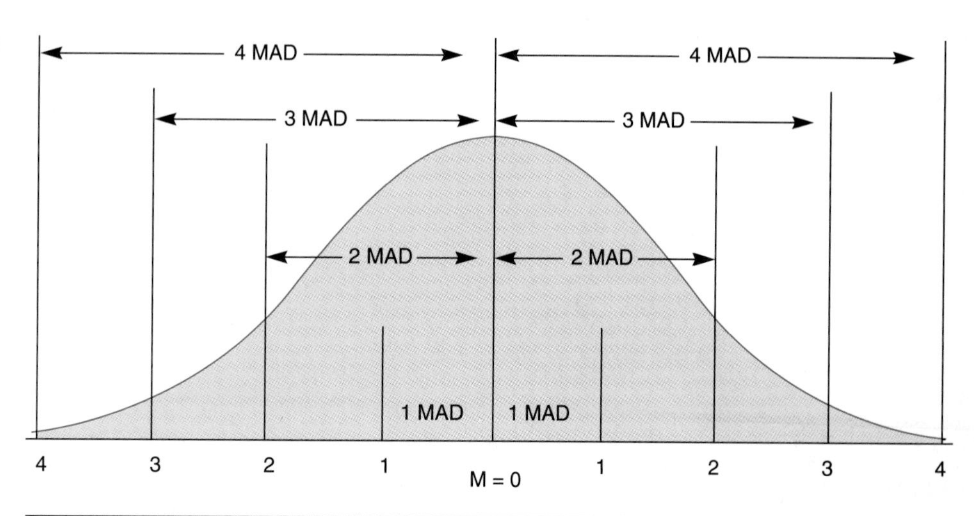

The standard deviation is the larger measure. If the MAD of a set of points was found to be 60 units, then the standard deviation would be 75 units. And, in the usual statistical manner, if control limits were set at plus or minus 3 standard deviations (or ± 3.75 MADs), then 99.7 percent of the points would fall within these limits.

A **tracking signal** is a measurement that indicates whether the forecast average is keeping pace with any genuine upward or downward changes in demand. As used in forecasting, the tracking signal is the *number* of mean absolute deviations that the forecast value is above or below the actual occurrence. Exhibit 7.8 shows a normal distribution with a mean of zero and a MAD equal to one. Thus, if computing the tracking signal and finding it equal to minus 2, we can notice that the forecast model is providing forecasts that are quite a bit above the mean of the actual occurrences.

A tracking signal can be calculated using the arithmetic sum of forecast deviations divided by the mean absolute deviation. Exhibit 7.9 illustrates the procedure for computing MAD and the tracking signal for a six-month period where the forecast had been set at a constant 1,000 and the actual demands that occurred are as shown. In this example, the forecast, on the average, was off by 66.7 units and the tracking signal was equal to 3.3 mean absolute deviations.

We can obtain a better indication of what the MAD and tracking signal mean by plotting the points on a graph. While not completely legitimate from a sample size standpoint, we plotted each month in Exhibit 7.10 to show the drifting of the tracking signal. Note that it drifted from minus 1 MAD to plus 3.3 MADs. This happened because actual demand was greater than the forecast in four of the six periods. If the actual demand doesn't fall below the forecast to offset the continual positive RSFE, the tracking signal would continue to rise and we would conclude that assuming a demand of 1,000 is a bad forecast.

Acceptable limits for the tracking signal depend on the size of the demand being forecast

EXHIBIT 7.9

Computing the Mean Absolute Deviation (MAD), the Running Sum of Forecast Errors (RSFE), and the Tracking Signal from Forecast and Actual Data

Month	Demand Forecast	Actual	Deviation	(RSFE)	Abs Dev	Sum of Abs Dev	MAD*	$TS = \frac{RSFE^{\dagger}}{MAD}$
1	1,000	950	−50	−50	50	50	50	−1.00
2	1,000	1,070	+70	+20	70	120	60	.33
3	1,000	1,100	+100	+120	100	220	73.3	1.64
4	1,000	960	−40	+80	40	260	65	1.23
5	1,000	1,090	+90	+170	90	350	70	2.43
6	1,000	1,050	+50	+220	50	400	66.7	3.31

*Mean absolute deviation (MAD). For Month 6, MAD = 400 ÷ 6 = 66.7.

†Tracking signal = $\frac{RSFE}{MAD}$. For Month 6, $TS = \frac{RSFE}{MAD} = \frac{220}{66.7} = 3.3$ MADs.

EXHIBIT 7.10

A Plot of the Tracking Signals Calculated in Exhibit 7.9

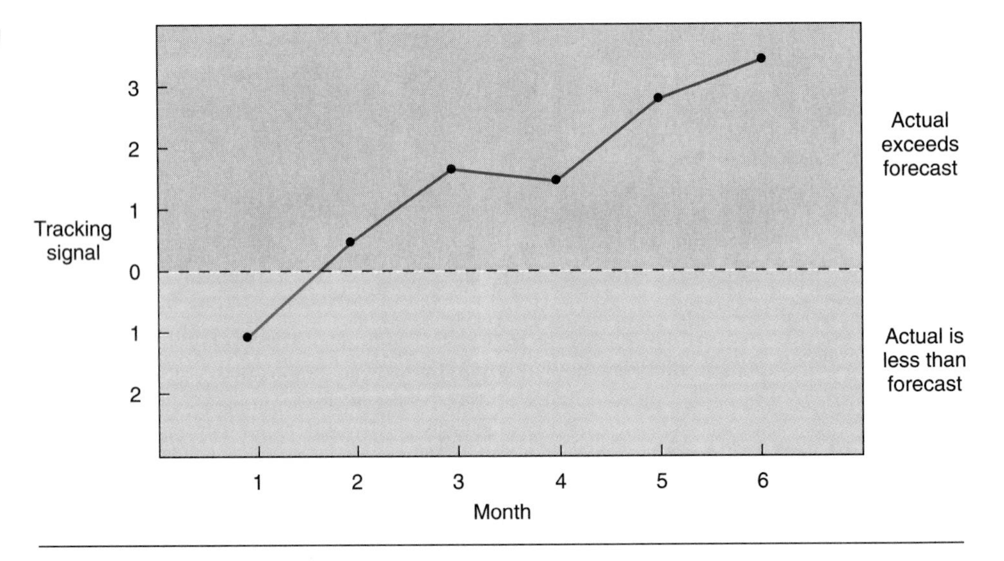

(high-volume or high-revenue items should be monitored frequently) and the amount of personnel time available (narrower acceptable limits cause more forecasts to be out of limits and therefore require more time to investigate). Exhibit 7.11 shows the area within the control limits for a range of zero to four MADs.

In a perfect forecasting model, the sum of the actual forecast errors would be zero; that is, the errors that result in overestimates should be offset by errors that are underestimates. The tracking signal would then also be zero, indicating an unbiased model, neither leading nor lagging the actual demands.

Often, MAD is used to forecast errors. It might then be desirable to make the MAD

EXHIBIT 7.11

The Percentages of Points Included within the Control Limits for a Range of 0 to 4 MADs

CONTROL LIMITS		
Number of MADs	Related Number of Standard Deviations	Percentage of Points Lying within Control Limits
±1	0.798	57.048
±2	1.596	88.946
±3	2.394	98.334
±4	3.192	99.856

more sensitive to recent data. A useful technique to do this is to compute an exponentially smoothed MAD (i.e., MAD_t) as a forecast for the next period's error range. The procedure is similar to single exponential smoothing covered earlier in this chapter. The value of the MAD_t forecast is to provide a range of error; in the case of inventory control, this is useful in setting safety stock levels.

$$MAD_t = \alpha |A_{t-1} - F_{t-1}| + (1 - \alpha)MAD_{t-1}$$

where

MAD_t = Forecast MAD for the tth period

α = Smoothing constant (normally in the range of 0.05 to 0.20)

A_{t-1} = Actual demand in the period t - 1

F_{t-1} = Forecast demand for period t - 1

Linear Regression Analysis

Regression can be defined as a functional relationship between two or more correlated variables and is used to predict one variable given the other. The relationship is usually developed from observed data. Linear regression refers to the special class of regression where the relationship between variables is assumed to be represented by a straight line.

The linear regression equation takes the form $Y = a + bX$, where Y is the value of the dependent variable that we are solving for, a is the Y intercept, b is the slope, and X is the independent variable (in time series analysis, X is units of time).

This approach is useful for long-term forecasting of major occurrences and aggregate planning. For example, linear regression would be very useful to forecast demands for product families. Even though demand for individual products within a family may vary widely during a time period, demand for the total product family is surprisingly smooth.

The major restriction in using **linear regression forecasting** is, as the name implies, that past data and future projections are assumed to fall about a straight line. While this does limit its application, sometimes, if we use a shorter period of time, linear regression analysis can still be used.

Linear regression is used for both time series forecasting and for causal relationship forecasting. When the dependent variable (usually the vertical axis on a graph) changes as a result of time (plotted as the horizontal axis) it is time series analysis. If one variable changes because of the change in another variable, this is a causal relationship (such as the number of deaths from lung cancer increasing with the number of people who smoke).

The following example illustrates the least squares method for obtaining the linear regression equation that forecasts sales for future quarters.

Example

A firm's sales for a product line during the 12 quarters of the past three years were as follows:

Quarter	Sales
1	600
2	1,550
3	1,500
4	1,500
5	2,400
6	3,100
7	2,600
8	2,900
9	3,800
10	4,500
11	4,000
12	4,900

The firm wants to forecast each quarter of the fourth year, that is, quarters 13, 14, 15, and 16. The least squares equation for linear regression is

$$Y = a + bX$$

where

Y = Dependent variable computed by the equation (sales in this example)

y = Dependent variable data point (see below)

a = Y intercept

b = Slope of the line

X = Independent variable (time period in this example)

The least squares method identifies the line *that minimizes the sum of the squares of the vertical distances* between each data point (y) and its corresponding point on the line (Y). If a straight line is drawn through the general area of the points, the difference between the point and the line is $y - Y$. Exhibit 7.12 shows these differences. The sum of the squares of the differences between the plotted data points and the line points is

$$(y_1 - Y_1)^2 + (y_2 - Y_2)^2 + \ldots + (y_{12} - Y_{12})^2$$

The best line to use is the one that minimizes this total.

As stated above, the straight line equation is

$$Y = a + bX$$

EXHIBIT 7.12

Least Squares Regression Line

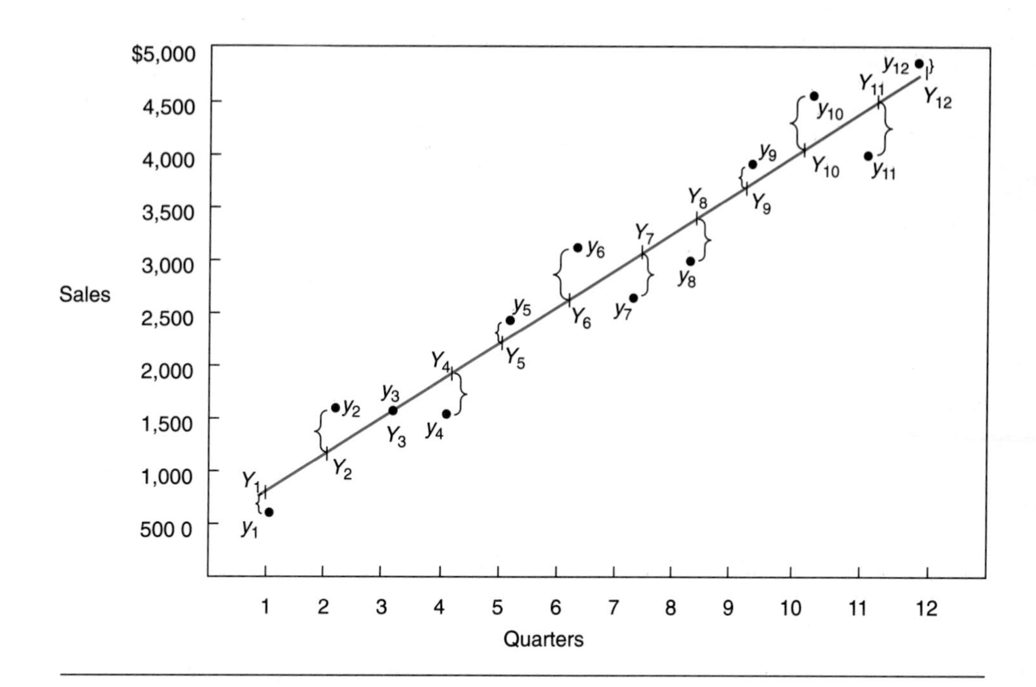

In the least squares method, the equations for a and b are

$$a = \overline{Y} - b\overline{X}$$

$$b = \frac{\Sigma XY - n\overline{X} \cdot \overline{Y}}{\Sigma X^2 - n\overline{X}^2}$$

where

a = Y intercept
b = Slope of the line
$\overline{Y}$ = Average of all Ys
$\overline{X}$ = Average of all Xs
X = X value at each data point
y = Y value at each data point
n = Number of data points
Y = Value of the dependent variable computed with the regression equation

Exhibit 7.13 shows these computations carried out for the 12 data points. Note that the final equation for Y shows an intercept of 441.6 and a slope of 359.6. The slope shows that for every unit change in X, that Y changes by 359.6.

EXHIBIT 7.13

Least Squares Regression Analysis

(1) X	(2) Y	(3) XY	(4) X^2	(5) Y^2	(6) Y New
1	600	600	1	360,000	801.3
2	1,550	3,100	4	2,402,500	1,160.9
3	1,500	4,500	9	2,250,000	1,520.5
4	1,500	6,000	16	2,250,000	1,880.1
5	2,400	12,000	25	5,760,000	2,239.7
6	3,100	18,600	36	9,610,000	2,599.4
7	2,600	18,200	49	6,760,000	2,959.0
8	2,900	23,200	64	8,410,000	3,318.6
9	3,800	34,200	81	14,440,000	3,678.2
10	4,500	45,000	100	20,250,000	4,037.8
11	4,000	44,000	121	16,000,000	4,397.4
12	4,900	58,800	144	24,010,000	4,757.1
78	33,350	268,200	650	112,502,500	

$\overline{X} =$ 6.5
$\overline{Y} =$ 2,779.17
$b =$ 359.6153
$a =$ 441.6666

Therefore: $Y = 441.66 + 359.6\,X$
$S_{YX} = 363.9$

Strictly based on this equation, the forecasts for periods 13 through 16 would be

$Y_{13} = 441.6 + 359.6\,(13) = 5{,}116.4$

$Y_{14} = 441.6 + 359.6\,(14) = 5{,}476.0$

$Y_{15} = 441.6 + 359.6\,(15) = 5{,}835.6$

$Y_{16} = 441.6 + 359.6\,(16) = 6{,}195.2$

The standard error of estimate, or how well the line fits the data, is[7]

$$S_{YX} = \sqrt{\frac{\sum_{i=1}^{n} (y_i - Y_i)^2}{n - 2}}$$

The standard error of estimate is computed from the first and last columns of Exhibit 7.13:

[7] An equation for the standard error that is often easier to compute is

$$S_{YX} = \sqrt{\frac{\Sigma Y\mathrm{d0001}^2 - a\Sigma Y - b\Sigma YX}{n - 2}}$$

$$S_{YX} = \sqrt{\frac{(600 - 801.3)^2 + (1.550 - 1,160.9)^2 + (1,500 - 1,520.5)^2 + \ldots + (4,900 - 4,757.1)^2}{10}}$$

$$S_{YX} = 363.9$$

7.5 CAUSAL RELATIONSHIP FORECASTING

To be of value for the purpose of forecasting, any independent variable must be a leading indicator. For example, if the weather service or the *Farmer's Almanac* predicted that next winter was to have an abnormally large number of snow storms, people would probably go out and buy snow shovels and snow blowers in the fall. Thus, the weather prediction or the *Farmer's Almanac* are said to be leading indicators of the sale of snow shovels and snow blowers. These can be viewed as **causal relationships** where the occurrence of one event causes the occurrence of the other. Running out of gas while driving down a highway, however, does not provide useful data to forecast that the car will stop. The car will stop, of course, but we would like to know enough in advance in order to do something about it. A "low gas level" warning light, for example, is a good forecasting device.

The first step in causal relationship forecasting is to identify those occurrences that are really the causes. Often leading indicators are not causal relationships but in some indirect way may suggest that some other things might happen. Other noncausal relationships just seem to exist as a coincidence. One study some years ago showed that the amount of alcohol sold in Sweden was directly proportional to teachers' salaries. Presumably this was a spurious, or false, relationship.

We show just one example of a forecast using a causal relationship.

Example

The Carpet City Store in Carpenteria has kept records of its sales (in square yards) each year, along with the number of permits for new houses in its area. Carpet City's operations manager believes forecasting sales is possible if housing starts are known for that year. First, the data are plotted on Exhibit 7.14, with

Year	Number of Housing Start Permits	Sales (in sq. yds.)
1983	18	13,000
1984	15	12,000
1985	12	11,000
1986	10	10,000
1987	20	14,000
1988	28	16,000
1989	35	19,000
1990	30	17,000
1991	20	13,000

X = Number of housing start permits

Y = Sales of carpeting

EXHIBIT 7.14

Causal Relationship: Sales to Housing Starts

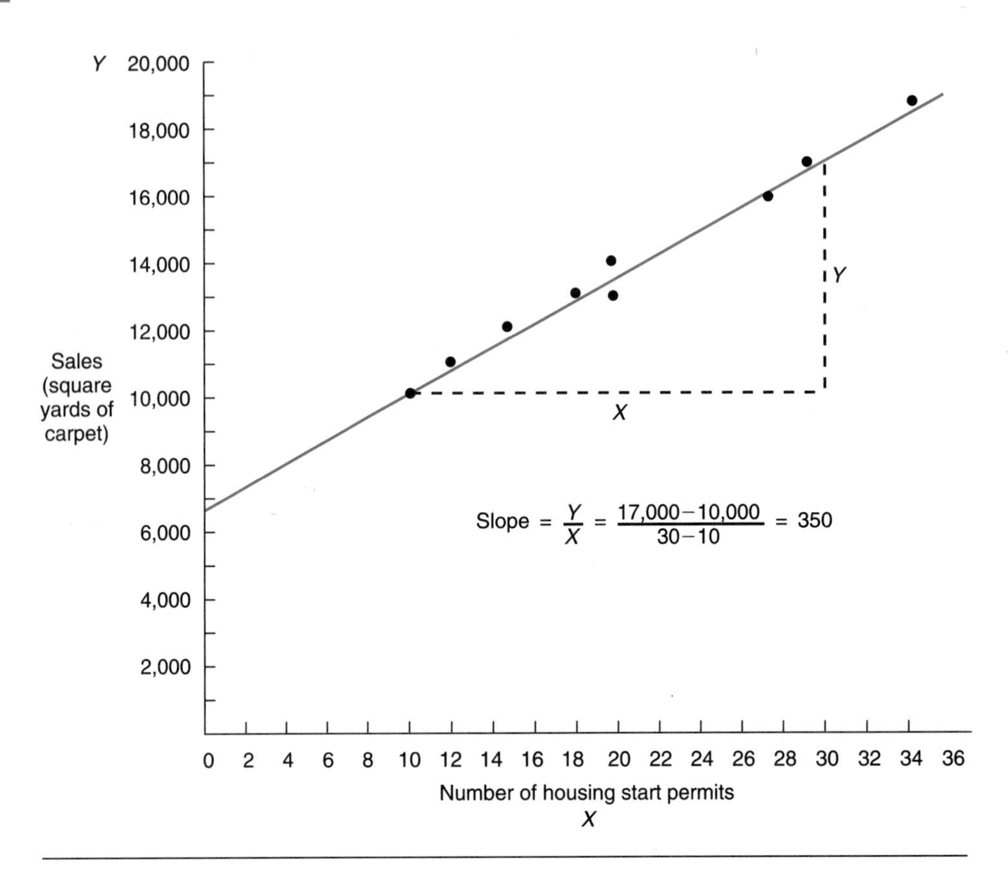

Since the points appear to be in a straight line, the manager decides to use the linear relationship $Y = a + bX$. We solve this problem by using the least squares method. Solving for a and b, using the equations presented earlier in this chapter, we obtain the following forecasting equation:

$$Y = 6{,}698.5 + 344.2X$$

Now, suppose that there are 25 housing permits granted in 1992. The 1992 sales forecast would therefore be:

$$Y = 6{,}698.5 + 344.2(25) = 15{,}303.5 \text{ square yards}$$

In this problem, the lag between filing the permit with the appropriate agency and the new homeowner coming to Carpet City to buy carpet makes a causal relationship feasible for forecasting.

Multiple Regression Analysis

Another forecasting technique is multiple regression analysis, in which a number of variables are considered, together with the effects of each on the item of interest. For example, in the home furnishings field, the effects of the number of marriages, housing starts, disposable income, and the trend can be expressed in a multiple regression equation, as

$$S = B + B_m(M) + B_h(H) + B_i(I) + B_t(T)$$

where

S = Gross sales for year
B = Base sales, a starting point from which other factors have influence
M = Marriages during the year
H = Housing starts during the year
I = Annual disposable personal income
T = Time trend (first year = 1, second = 2, third = 3, and so forth)

and B_m, B_h, B_i, and B_t represent the influence on expected sales of the number of marriages and housing starts, income, and trend, respectively.

Forecasting by multiple regression is very appropriate when a number of factors might influence a variable of interest—in this case, sales. Its difficulty lies with the data gathering, and particularly with the mathematical computation. Fortunately, standard programs for multiple regression analysis are available for most computers, relieving the need for tedious manual calculation.

7.6 COMPUTER PROGRAMS

Many commercial forecasting programs are available. Some exist as library routines within a mainframe computer system, some may be purchased separately from a vendor, and some are part of larger programs. Many programs are available for PCs. Most computer manufacturers either produce their own, team up with a software company, or entice software companies to write programs for their computers.

All but the most sophisticated forecasting formulas are quite easy to understand. Anyone who can use a spreadsheet such as Lotus® 1-2-3®, Quattro Pro®, Symphony®, or Excel®, can create a forecasting program on a PC. Depending on one's knowledge of the spreadsheet, a program can be written in anywhere from a few minutes to a couple of hours. How this forecast is to be used by the firm could be the bigger challenge. If the demand for many items is to be forecast, this becomes a data-handling problem, not a problem in the forecasting logic.

7.7 CONCLUSION

Forecasting is fundamental to any planning effort. In the short run, a forecast is needed to predict the requirements for materials, products, services, or other resources to respond to changes in demand. Forecasts permit adjusting schedules and varying labor and materials. In the long run, forecasting is required as a basis for strategic changes, such as developing new markets, developing new products or services, and expanding or creating new facilities.

For long-term forecasts that lead to heavy financial commitments, great care should be taken to derive the forecast. Several approaches should be used. Causal methods such as regression analysis or multiple regression analysis are beneficial. These provide a basis for discussion. Economic factors, product trends, growth factors, and competition, as well as a myriad of other possible variables, need to be considered and the forecast adjusted to reflect the influence of each.

Short- and intermediate-term forecasting, such as required for inventory control, and staffing and material scheduling, may be satisfied with simpler models, such as exponential smoothing with perhaps an adaptive feature or a seasonal index. In these applications, thousands of items are usually being forecast. The forecasting routine should therefore be simple and run quickly on a computer. The routines should also detect and respond rapidly to definite short-term changes in demand while at the same time ignoring the occasional spurious demands. Exponential smoothing, when monitored by management to adjust the value of alpha, is an effective technique.

As said in the Epigraph at the beginning of the chapter, "Forecasting is difficult, especially about the future." A perfect forecast is like a hole-in-one in golf: great to get but we should be satisfied just to get close to the cup—or, to push the metaphor, just to land on the green. The ideal philosophy is to create the best forecast that you reasonably can and then have sufficient flexibility in the system to adjust for the inevitable forecast error.

7.8 REVIEW AND DISCUSSION QUESTIONS

1. What is the difference between dependent and independent demand?
2. Examine Exhibit 7.4 and suggest which model you might use for: (1) bathing suits; (2) demand for new houses; (3) electrical power usage; (4) new plant expansion plans.
3. What is the logic in the least squares method of linear regression analysis?
4. Give some very simple rules you might use to manage demand for a firm's product. (An example is "limited to stock on hand.")
5. What strategies are used by supermarkets, airlines, hospitals, banks, and cereal manufacturers to influence demand?
6. All forecasting methods using exponential smoothing, adaptive smoothing, and exponential smoothing including trend require starting values to get the equations going. How would you select the starting value for, say, F_{t-1}?
7. From the choice of simple moving average, weighted moving average, exponential smoothing, and single regression analysis, which forecasting technique would you consider the most accurate? Why?
8. Give some examples that you can think of that have a multiplicative seasonal trend relationship.
9. What is the main disadvantage of daily forecasting using regression analysis?
10. What are the main problems with using adaptive exponential smoothing in forecasting?
11. How is a seasonal index computed from a regression line analysis?

12. Discuss the basic differences between the mean absolute deviation (MAD) and the standard deviation.
13. What implications do the existence of forecast errors have for the search for ultrasophisticated statistical forecasting models?
14. Causal relationships are potentially useful for which component of a time series?

7.9 SOLVED PROBLEMS

PROBLEM

1. Sunrise Baking Company markets doughnuts through a chain of food stores and has been experiencing over- and underproduction because of forecasting errors. The following data are their demands in dozens of doughnuts for the past four weeks. The bakery is closed Saturday, so Friday's production must satisfy demand for both Saturday and Sunday.

	4 Weeks Ago	3 Weeks Ago	2 Weeks Ago	Last Week
Monday	2,200	2,400	2,300	2,400
Tuesday	2,000	2,100	2,200	2,200
Wednesday	2,300	2,400	2,300	2,500
Thursday	1,800	1,900	1,800	2,000
Friday	1,900	1,800	2,100	2,000
Saturday } Sunday }	2,800	2,700	3,000	2,900

Make a forecast for this week on the following basis:

a. Daily, using a simple four-week moving average.

b. Daily, using a weighted average of 0.40, 0.30, 0.20, and 0.10 for the past four weeks.

c. Sunrise is also planning its purchases of ingredients for bread production. If bread demand had been forecast for last week at 22,000 loaves and only 21,000 loaves were actually demanded, what would Sunrise's forecast be for this week using exponential smoothing with $\alpha = 0.10$?

d. Supposing, with the forecast made in (*c*), this week's demand actually turns out to be 22,500. What would the new forecast be for the next week?

SOLUTION

a. Simple moving average, 4-week.

Monday $\dfrac{2{,}400 + 2{,}300 + 2{,}400 + 2{,}200}{4} = \dfrac{9{,}300}{4} = 2{,}325$ doz.

Tuesday $= \dfrac{8{,}500}{4} = 2{,}125$ doz.

Wednesday $= \dfrac{9{,}500}{4} = 2{,}375$ doz.

Thursday $= \dfrac{7{,}500}{4} = 1{,}875$ doz.

Friday, Saturday, and Sunday $= \dfrac{19{,}200}{4} = 4{,}800$ doz.

b. Weighted average with weights of .40, .30, .20, and .10.

	(.10)		(.20)		(.30)		(.40)		
Monday	220	+	480	+	690	+	960	=	2,350
Tuesday	200	+	420	+	660	+	880	=	2,160
Wednesday	230	+	480	+	690	+	1,000	=	2,400
Thursday	180	+	380	+	540	+	800	=	1,900
Friday, Saturday, and Sunday	470	+	900	+	1,530	+	1,960	=	4,860
	1,300	+	2,660	+	4,110	+	5,600	=	13,670

c. $F_t = F_{t-1} + \alpha(A_{t-1} - F_{t-1})$

$= 22{,}000 + 0.10(21{,}000 - 22{,}000)$

$= 22{,}000 - 100$

$= 21{,}900$ loaves

d. $F_{t+1} = 21{,}900 + \alpha(22{,}500 - 21{,}900)$

$= 21{,}900 + .10(600)$

$= 21{,}960$ loaves

PROBLEM

2. A specific forecasting model was used to forecast demands for a product. The forecasts and the corresponding demands that subsequently occurred are shown below.

Use the MAD and tracking signal technique to evaluate the accuracy of the forecasting model.

Month	Actual	Forecast
October	700	660
November	760	840
December	780	750
January	790	835
February	850	910
March	950	890

SOLUTION

Evaluate the forecasting model using MAD and tracking signal.

Month	Actual Demand	Forecast Demand	Actual Deviation	Cumulative Deviation (RSFE)	Absolute Deviation
October	700	660	40	40	40
November	760	840	−80	−40	40
December	780	750	30	−10	10
January	790	835	−45	−55	55
February	850	910	−60	−115	115
March	950	890	60	−55	55
				Total dev. =	315

$$\text{MAD} = \frac{315}{6} = 52.5$$

$$\text{Tracking signal} = \frac{-55}{52.5} = -1.05$$

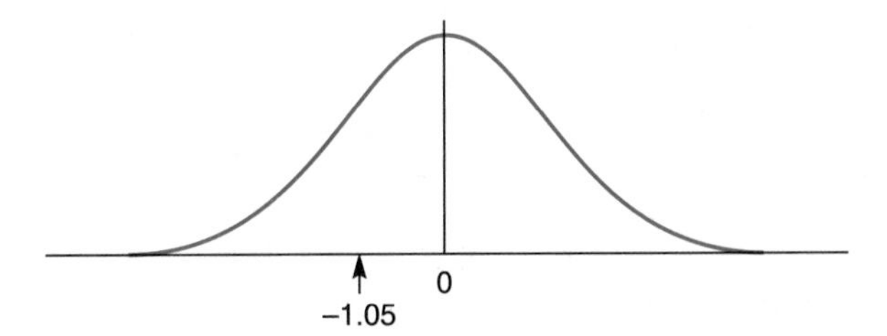

Forecast model is well within the distribution.

PROBLEM

3. Quarterly data for the last two years are given below. From this data prepare a forecast for the upcoming year using decomposition.

Period	Actual
1	300
2	540
3	885
4	580
5	416
6	760
7	1,191
8	760

SOLUTION

(1) X Period	(2) Y Actual	(3) Period Average	(4) Seasonal Factor	(5) Deseasoned Demand
1	300	358	0.527	568.99
2	540	650	0.957	564.09
3	885	1,038	1.529	578.92
4	580	670	0.987	587.79
5	416		0.527	789.01
6	760		0.957	793.91
7	1,191		1.529	779.08
8	760		0.987	770.21
Total	5,432	2,716	8.0	
Average	679	679	1	

Column 3 is seasonal average. For example, the first quarter average is

$$\frac{300 + 416}{2} = 358$$

Column 4 is the quarter average (column 3) divided by the overall average (679). Column 5 is the actual data divided by the seasonal index.

	X Period	Deseasoned Demand	X^2	XY
	1	568.99	1	569.0
	2	564.09	4	1,128.2
	3	578.92	9	1,736.7
	4	587.79	16	2,351.2
	5	789.01	25	3,945.0
	6	793.91	36	4,763.4
	7	779.08	49	5,453.6
	8	770.21	64	6,161.7
Sums	36	5,432	204	26,108.8
Average	4.5	679		

Regression results for deseasonalized data.

$$b = \frac{(26{,}108) - (8)(4.5)(679)}{(204) - (8)(4.5)^2}$$

$$= 39.64$$

$$a = \bar{y} - b\bar{x}$$

$$a = 679 - 39.64(4.5)$$

$$= 500$$

Therefore, the deseasonalized regression results are

$$Y = 500 + 39.64X$$

Period	Trend Forecast	Seasonal Factor	Final Forecast
9	857.4	0.527	452.0
10	897.0	0.957	858.7
11	936.7	1.529	1,431.9
12	976.3	0.987	963.3

7.10 PROBLEMS

1. Demand for stereo headphones and CD players for joggers has caused Nina Industries to experience a growth of almost 50 percent over the past year. The number of joggers is continuing to expand, so Nina expects demand for headsets to also expand, since there have, as yet, been no safety laws passed to prevent joggers from wearing them.

   Demands for the stereo units for last year were as follows:

Month	Demand (units)	Month	Demand (units)
January	4,200	July	5,300
February	4,300	August	4,900
March	4,000	September	5,400
April	4,400	October	5,700
May	5,000	November	6,300
June	4,700	December	6,000

a. Using least squares regression analysis, what would you estimate demand to be for each month next year? Follow the general format in Exhibit 7.13.

b. To be reasonably confident of meeting demand, Nina decides to use three standard errors of estimate for safety. How many additional units should be held to meet this level of confidence?

2. The historical demand for a product is:

Month	Demand
January	12
February	11
March	15
April	12
May	16
June	15

a. Using a weighted moving average with weights of 0.60, 0.30, and 0.10, find the July forecast.

b. Using a simple three-month moving average, find the July forecast.

c. Using single exponential smoothing with $\alpha = 0.2$ and a June forecast = 13, find the July forecast. Make whatever assumptions you wish.

d. Using simple linear regression analysis, calculate the regression equation for the preceding demand data.

e. Using the regression equation in (*d*), calculate the forecast for July.

3. The following tabulations are actual sales of units for six months and a starting forecast in January.

a. Calculate the forecast for the remaining five months using simple exponential smoothing with alpha = 0.2.

b. Calculate the MAD for the forecasts.

	Actual	Forecast
January	100	80
February	94	
March	106	
April	80	
May	68	
June	94	

4. Sales data for two years is given below. The data is aggregated with two months of sales in each "period."

Period	Sales	Period	Sales
January-February	109	January-February	115
March-April	104	March-April	112
May-June	150	May-June	159
July-August	170	July-August	182
September-October	120	September-October	126
November-December	100	November-December	106

a. Plot the data on a graph.
b. Fit a simple linear regression model to the sales data.
c. In addition to the regression model, determine multiplicative seasonal index factors. A full cycle is assumed to be a full year.
d. Use the results from parts (*b*) and (*c*) to prepare a forecast for the next year.

5. The tracking signals that were computed using the past demand history for three different products are shown below. Each product used the same forecasting technique.

	TS 1	TS 2	TS 3
1	−2.70	1.54	0.10
2	−2.32	−0.64	0.43
3	−1.70	2.05	1.08
4	−1.1	2.58	1.74
5	−0.87	−0.95	1.94
6	−0.05	−1.23	2.24
7	0.10	0.75	2.96
8	0.40	−1.59	3.02
9	1.50	0.47	3.54
10	2.20	2.74	3.75

Discuss the tracking signals for each product and what the implications are.

6. Prepare a forecast for each quarter of the next year from the following past two years' quarterly sales information. Assume that there are both trend and seasonal factors and that the season cycle is one year. Use time series decomposition.

Quarter	Sales
1	160
2	195
3	150
4	140
5	215
6	240
7	205
8	190

7. Tucson Machinery, Inc., manufactures numerically controlled machines, which sell for an average price of $0.5 million each. Sales for these NCMs for the past two years were as follows:

Quarter	Quantity (units)
1990	
I	12
II	18
III	26
IV	16
1991	
I	16
II	24
III	28
IV	18

a. Do a simple linear regression analysis.
b. Find the trend and seasonal factors.
c. Forecast sales for 1992.

8. Not all the items in your office supply store are evenly distributed as far as demand is concerned, so you decide to forecast demand to help you plan your stock. Past data for lined tablets for the month of August are as follows:

Week 1	300
Week 2	400
Week 3	600
Week 4	700

a. Using a three-week moving average, what would you forecast the next week to be?
b. Using exponential smoothing with alpha equal to 0.20, if the exponential forecast for week 3 was estimated as the average of the first two weeks [(300 + 400)/2 = 350)], what would you forecast week 5 to be?

9. Following are the actual tabulated demands for an item for a nine-month period, from January through September. Your supervisor wants to test two forecasting methods to see which method was better over this period.

Month	Actual
January	110
February	130
March	150
April	170
May	160
June	180
July	140
August	130
September	140

a. Forecast April through September using a three-month moving average.
b. Using simple exponential smoothing to estimate April through September. (Use $\alpha = .3$ and assume that the forecast for March was 130.)
c. Use MAD to decide which method produced the better forecast over the six-month period.

10. A particular forecasting model was used to forecast a six-month period. The forecasts and the actual demands that resulted are shown:

Month	Forecast	Actual
April	250	200
May	325	250
June	400	325
July	350	300
August	375	325
September	450	400

Find the tracking signal and state whether you think the model being used is giving acceptable answers.

11. Harlen Industries has a very simple forecasting model: take the actual demand for the same month last year and divide that by the number of fractional weeks in that month, producing the average weekly demand for that month. This weekly average is used as the weekly forecast this year.

The following eight weeks shows the forecast (based on last year) and the demand that actually occurred.

Week	Forecast Demand	Actual Demand
1	140	137
2	140	133
3	140	150
4	140	160
5	140	180
6	150	170
7	150	185
8	150	205

a. Compute the MAD of forecast errors.
b. Using the RSFE, compute the tracking signal.
c. Based on your answers to (*a*) and (*b*) what comments can you make about Harlen's method of forecasting?

12. The historical demand for a product is: January, 80; February, 100; March, 60; April, 80; and May, 90.
a. Using a simple four-month moving average, what is the forecast for June? If June experienced a demand of 100, what would your forecast be for July?
b. Using exponential smoothing with $\alpha = 0.20$, if the forecast for January had been 70, compute what the exponentially smoothed forecast would have been for the remaining months through June.
c. Using the least squares method, compute a forecast for June, July, and August.
d. Using a weighted moving average with weights of 0.30, 0.25, 0.20, 0.15, and 0.10, what is June's forecast?

13. In this problem, you are to test the validity of your forecasting model. Following are the forecasts for a model you have been using and the actual demands that occurred.

Week	Forecast	Actual
1	800	900
2	850	1,000
3	950	1,050
4	950	900
5	1,000	900
6	975	1,100

Use the method stated in the text to compute the MAD and the tracking signal and draw a conclusion as to whether the forecasting model you have been using is giving reasonable results.

14. Assume that your stock of sales merchandise is maintained based on the forecast demand. If the distributor's sales personnel call on the first day of each month, compute your forecast sales by each of the three methods requested here.

Month	Actual
June	140
July	180
August	170

a. Using a simple three-month moving average, what is the forecast for September?
b. Using a weighted moving average, what is the forecast for September with weights of .20, .30, and .50 for June, July, and August, respectively?
c. Using single exponential smoothing and assuming that the forecast for June had been 130, calculate the forecasts for September with a smoothing constant alpha of .30.

15. The historical demand for a product is:

Month	Demand
April	60
May	55
June	75
July	60
August	80
September	75

a. Using a simple four-month moving average, calculate a forecast for October.
b. Using single exponential smoothing with $\alpha = 0.2$ and a September forecast = 65, calculate a forecast for October.
c. Using simple linear regression, calculate the trend line for the historical data. To help in your calculations, the following data are given: The X axis is April = 1, May = 2, and so on. The Y axis is demand.

$$n = 6$$
$$\Sigma X = 21$$
$$\Sigma Y = 405$$
$$\Sigma X^2 = 91$$
$$\Sigma Y^2 = 27{,}875$$
$$\Sigma XY = 1{,}485$$

d. Calculate a forecast for October.

16. A forecasting method you have been using to predict product demand is shown in the following table along with the actual demand that occurred.

Forecast	Actual
1,500	1,550
1,400	1,500
1,700	1,600
1,750	1,650
1,800	1,700

a. Compute the tracking signal using the mean absolute deviation and running sum of forecast errors (RSFE).
b. Comment on whether you feel the forecasting method is giving good predictions.

17. Sales during the past six months have been as follows:

January	115
February	123
March	132
April	134
May	140
June	147

a. Using a simple three-month moving average, make forecasts for April through July. What is the main weakness of using a simple moving average with data that is patterned like this?
b. Using single exponential smoothing with alpha = 0.70, if the forecast for January had been 110, compute the exponentially smoothed forecasts for each month through July. Is this method more accurate for this data? Why or why not?
c. Using the least squares method, compute the forecasts for the rest of the year. Does your regression line seem to fit the January through June data well? If so, briefly describe a pattern of data with which linear regression would not work well.
d. Calculate the mean absolute deviation for January through June using the trend equation from (*c*).

18. Actual demand for a product for the past three months was:

Three months ago	400 units
Two months ago	350 units
Last month	325 units

a. Using a simple three-month moving average, what would the forecast be for this month?
b. If 300 units actually occurred this month, what would your forecast be for the next month?
c. Using simple exponential smoothing, what would your forecast be for this month if the exponentially smoothed forecast for three months ago was 450 units and the smoothing constant was 0.20?

19. After using your forecasting model for a period of six months, you decide to test it using MAD and a tracking signal. Following are the forecasted and actual demands for the six-month period:

Period	Forecast	Actual
May	450	500
June	500	550
July	550	400
August	600	500
September	650	675
October	700	600

a. Calculate the tracking signal.
b. Decide whether your forecasting routine is acceptable.

20. Goodyear Tire and Rubber Company is the world's largest rubber manufacturer, with automotive products accounting for 82 percent of sales. Cooper Tire and Rubber Company is the ninth largest tire manufacturer in the world, with tires accounting for about 80 percent of sales.

Shown below are the earnings per share for each company by quarter for the period from the first quarter of 1988 through the second quarter of 1991. Forecast the earnings per share for the remainder of 1991 and 1992. Use exponential smoothing to forecast the third period of 1991, and the time series decomposition method to forecast the last two quarters of 1991 and all four quarters of 1992. (It's much easier to solve this problem on a computer spreadsheet so that you can see what's going on.)

		EARNINGS PER SHARE ($)	
Year	Quarter	Goodyear Tire	Cooper Tire
1988	I	1.67	0.17
	II	2.35	0.24
	III	1.11	0.26
	IV	1.15	0.34
1989	I	1.56	0.25
	I	2.04	0.37
	III	1.14	0.36
	IV	0.38	0.44
1990	I	0.29	0.33
	II	d0.18 (loss)	0.40
	III	d0.97 (loss)	0.41
	IV	0.20	0.47
1991	I	d1.54 (loss)	0.30
	II	0.38	0.47

a. For the exponential smoothing method, choose the first quarter of 1988 as the beginning forecast. Make two forecasts: one with an alpha of 0.10 and one with an alpha of 0.30.

b. Using the MAD method of testing the forecasting model's performance, and the actual data from 1988 through the second quarter of 1991, how well did the model perform?

21. Consolidated Edison Company of New York, Inc., sells electricity, gas, and steam to New York City and Westchester County. Sales revenue for the years 1984 to 1994 are shown below. (1993 and 1994 are estimated.) Forecast the revenues for 1995 through 1998. Use your own judgment, intuition, or common sense concerning which model or method to use, as well as the period of data to include.

Year	Revenue ($ millions)	Year	Revenue ($ millions)
1984	5,728.8	1990	5,738.9
1985	5,497.9	1991	5,873.1
1986	5,197.7	1992	5,932.9
1987	5,094.4	1993	6,020.0
1988	5,108.8	1994	6,260.0
1989	5,550.6		

22. Dana and Kerry own a chain of aerobic and fitness centers for women. They recently hired a consultant to help identify which factors significantly affect the volume of sales at a location. Based on the consultant's analysis, the three most significant factors were: 1) average age of adult females within a three mile radius, 2) number of adult females living or working within a three mile radius, and 3) average household income within a three mile radius. Using

multiple regression analysis, the consultant developed the following equation to forecast sales for a new location:

Sales = 410,411 − 4,417 (average age) + 4.62 (number of females) + 1.55 (average income)

Dana and Kerry are currently evaluating four potential sites. The data for each of these sites follows.

Site	Average Age	Number of Females	Average Income
A	47 yrs	14,000	$77,000
B	22	21,000	49,000
C	32	9,000	54,000
D	37	16,000	83,000

Calculate the forecasted sales for each site. Which one should Dana and Kerry select for their next location if their goal is to maximize their sales?

7.11 SELECTED BIBLIOGRAPHY

Abraham, B., and J. Ledolter. *Statistical Methods for Forecasting*. New York: John Wiley & Sons, 1983.

Armstrong, J. Scott. "Forecasting by Extrapolation: Conclusions from 25 Years of Research." *Interfaces* 14, no. 6 (November 1984), pp. 52–66.

Bails, Dale G., and Larry C. Peppers. *Business Fluctuations: Forecasting Techniques and Applications*. Englewood Cliffs, N.J.: Prentice Hall, 1982.

Bowerman, B. L., and R. T. O'Connell. *Time Series Forecasting*. Boston: Duxbury, 1986.

Box, G. E. P., and G. M. Jenkins. *Time Series Analysis: Forecasting and Control*. 2nd ed. Oakland, Calif.: Holden-Day, 1976.

Brown, Robert G. *Decision Rules for Inventory Management*. New York: Holt, Rinehart & Winston, 1967.

Cryer, J. *Time Series Analysis*. Boston: Duxbury, 1986.

Ekern, S. "Adaptive Exponential Smoothing Revisited." *Journal of the Operations Research Society* 32 (1981), pp. 775–82.

Gardner, Everette S. "Exponential Smoothing: The State of the Art." *Journal of Forecasting* **4,** no. 1 (March 1985).

Hank, J. E., and A. Reitsch. *Business Forecasting*. 2nd ed. Boston: Allyn & Bacon, 1986.

Makridakis, Spyros; Steven C. Wheelwright; and Victor E. McGee. *Forecasting: Methods and Applications*. 2nd ed. New York: John Wiley & Sons, 1983.

________. "The Accuracy of Extrapolation (Time Series) Methods: Results of a Forecasting Competition." *Journal of Forecasting* 1 (1982), pp. 111–15.

Smith, Bernard T. *Focus Forecasting: Computer Techniques for Inventory Control*. Boston: CBI Publishing, 1984.

Sweet, A. L. "Adaptive Smoothing for Forecasting Seasonal Series." *AIIE Transactions* 13 (1981), pp. 243–48.

Taylor, S. G. "Initialization of Exponential Smoothing Forecasts." *AIIE Transactions* 13 (1981), pp. 199–205.

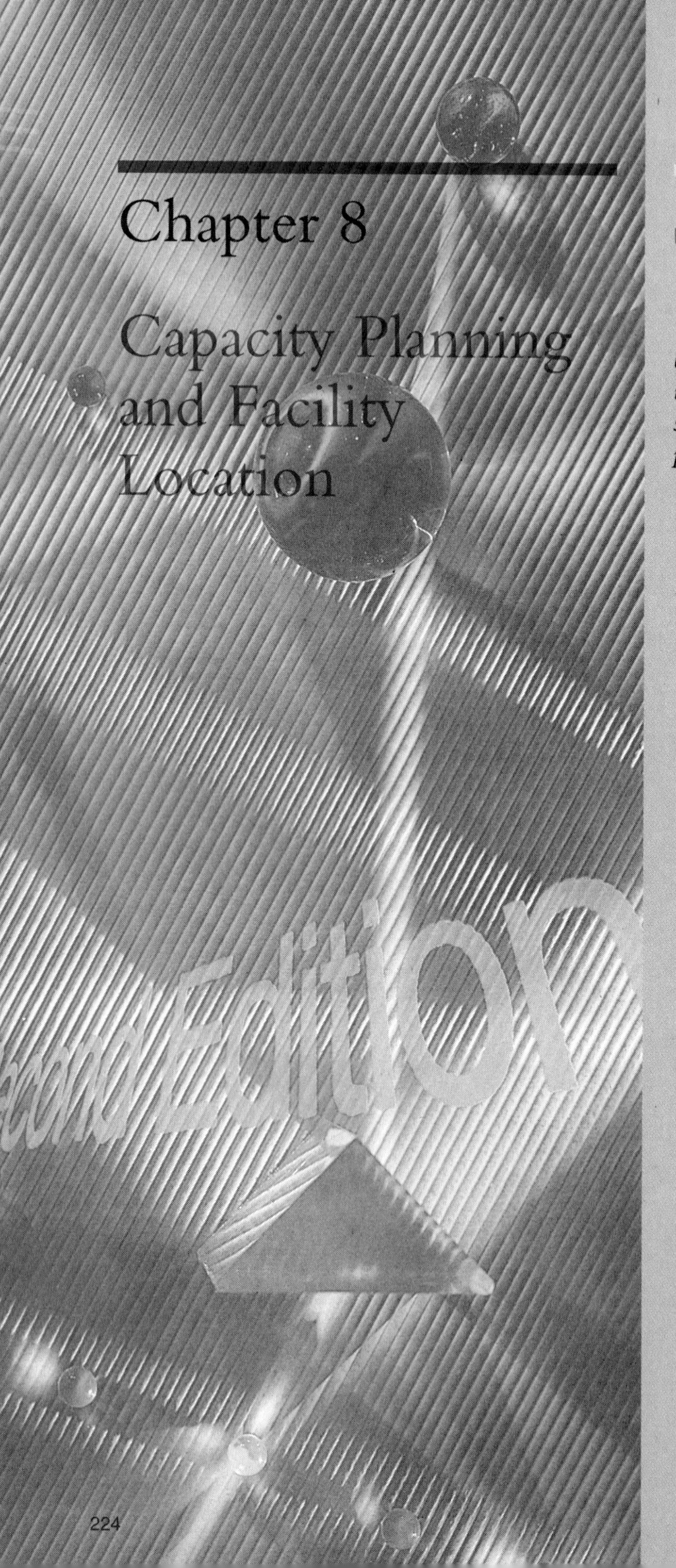

Chapter 8

Capacity Planning and Facility Location

EPIGRAPH

The response to new technologies should not be building large plants with huge bureaucracies that ultimately result in diseconomies of scale. Rather, firms should attempt to have facilities that have a focused product line and no more than 500 employees.

Ulf Hoglund
Chief Executive, GKN Automotive (Germany) Speech at the Designing and Sustaining World-Class Organizations Conference, Carnegie Mellon University, May 31, 1991.

CHAPTER OUTLINE

KEY TERMS

Capacity
Capacity Flexibility
Agile Manufacturing
Complexity
Capacity Planning
Decision Tree
Center Of Gravity Method

The decision to locate and build a manufacturing facility is a long-term commitment that typically requires a substantial investment. As discussed in Chapter 2, the strategic decisions as to where to build a plant, how big to make it, when to build it, and what processes to install in it significantly impact subsequent operating decisions for a long time.

Although the initial investment is usually much smaller for a service operation, the risks associated with selecting a site tend to be much higher, as the success of a location is often determined by both the demographic parameters of the immediate area and the unique characteristics of the site.

In both manufacturing and services, an incorrect site location decision is very expensive, because a substantial portion of the initial investment is frequently not recoverable. Thus, management needs to take a very hard look at these types of decisions. The goal of this chapter is to identify the different factors involved and to provide a rational framework for making these decisions, specifically, how big to make the facility and where to locate it.

Deciding "how much" entails capacity planning, which is the focus of the first part of this chapter; answering the "where" question involves facility location analysis, which is the focus of the second part. In practice, however, the questions are very much linked together as evidenced by two competitive imperatives:

1. The need to produce close to the customer due to time-based competition, trade agreements, and shipping costs.
2. The need to locate near the appropriate labor pool to take advantage of low wage costs and/or high technical skills.

We discuss elements of both imperatives in the next "OM in Action."

OPERATIONS MANAGEMENT IN ACTION
VW's Reasons to Produce in Czechoslovakia

Volkswagen (VW) bought a 31 percent stake in Skoda, an auto plant, when it was turned into a joint-stock company in 1991. The shareholding will increase to a controlling 70 percent by 1995; VW also plans to invest $6.4 billion in Skoda over the next 10 years.

This expansion bolsters VW's position as Europe's biggest car manufacturer, just ahead of Fiat. VW aims to more than double Skoda's annual production to 400,000 cars a year by 1997. VW believes that Skoda will be able to produce vehicles for about 30 percent less than their German factories because of low Czechoslovakian wages. Moreover, owning a company producing less expensive cars under a different brand name will make VW more competitive at the lower end of the market.

The main reason VW is investing heavily in Skoda is to expand its manufacturing capacity to meet an expected boom in car sales with the opening markets of Eastern Europe. The huge pent-up demand for cars in Eastern Europe just as the Western European new-car market turns down is a mouth-watering prospect for VW and other competitors.

Source: "The People's Car Heads East," *The Economist*, December 15, 1990, p. 74.

8.1 IMPORTANCE OF CAPACITY DECISIONS

The **capacity** of the production system defines the firm's competitive boundaries. Specifically, it sets the firm's response rate to the market, its cost structure, its work-force composition, its level of technology, its management and staff support requirements, and its general inventory strategy. If capacity is inadequate, a company may lose customers through slow service or by allowing competitors to enter the market. If capacity is excessive, a company may have to reduce its prices to stimulate demand, underutilize its work force, carry excess inventory, or seek additional, less profitable products to stay in business.

Factors Affecting Capacity

Capacity is affected by both external and internal factors. The external factors include government regulations (working hours, safety, pollution), union agreements, and supplier capabilities. The internal factors include product and service design, personnel and jobs (worker training, motivation, learning, job content, and methods), plant layout and process flow, equipment capabilities and maintenance, materials management, quality control systems, and management capabilities.

8.2 IMPORTANT CAPACITY CONCEPTS

Best Operating Level

The *best operating level* is that of capacity for which the average unit cost is at a minimum. This is depicted in Exhibit 8.1. Note that as we move down the unit cost curve for each plant size, we achieve economies of scale until we reach the best operating level, and then we encounter diseconomies of scale as we exceed this point.

Economies and Diseconomies of Scale

The concept of economies of scale is well known: as product volumes increase, the average cost per unit decreases. This concept can be related to a best operating level for a given plant size. As shown in Exhibit 8.1, economies of scale (as well as diseconomies of scale) are found not just between the cost curves for each plant, but within each one as well.

Exhibit 8.1 also shows the best operating levels, V_A, V_B, V_C, and V_D for plant sizes A, B and C, and D, respectively. Economies of scale occur for several reasons. With larger volumes, fixed costs are spread out over a greater number of units, thereby reducing the amount allocated to each product. With larger volumes, a firm can also take advantage of quantity discounts, thereby reducing material costs. Scale factors, which are associated with larger facilities, are a third source of economies of scale. For example, with processing operations like breweries and refineries, to double the capacity of a facility increases its costs by about 40 percent, which reflects the ratio of the change in volume in a cylinder or

EXHIBIT 8.1

Economies of Scale

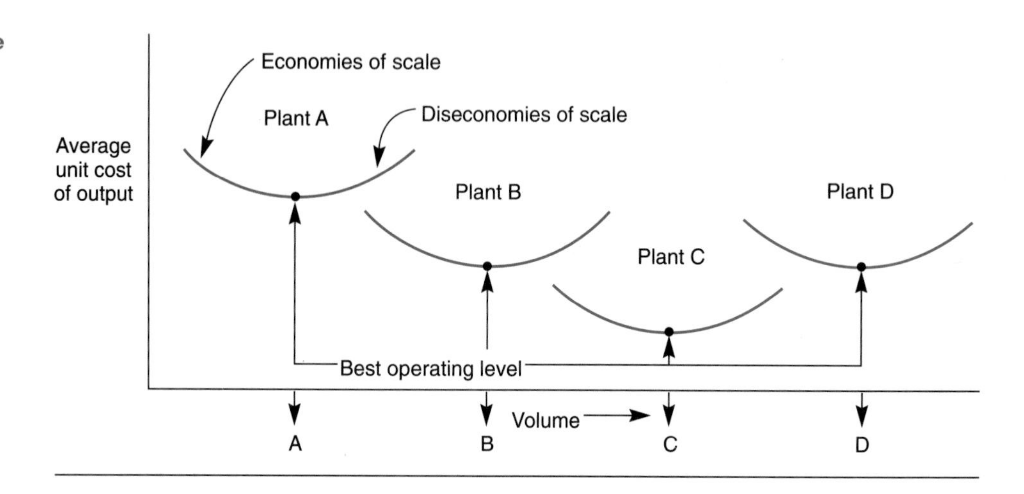

pipe to its outside area (e.g., to double the volume through a pipe requires about 141 percent more material for the larger pipe).

Diseconomies of scale can also occur for several reasons. When the best operating level in a plant is exceeded, additional costs are incurred. These added costs can take the form of overtime, inefficient scheduling, and machine breakdowns resulting from a lack of time to perform preventive maintenance. Diseconomies of scale can also occur with larger plants, as indicated by Plant D in Exhibit 8.1. This could be due to an inability to efficiently coordinate material flows and schedule workers. Organizational factors can also contribute to diseconomies of scale. With larger facilities, the contribution of each individual is diminished. Management and workers become more segregated and communicate less with each other. In operations that have a labor union, for example, grievances per 100 employees tend to increase in relation to the size of the plant.

Although finding the best size and operating level is illusive, managers often set policies regarding the maximum size for any one facility. As a result, the real challenge is predicting how costs will change for different output rates and facility sizes. This assessment requires careful attention to the different causes of economies of scale for each situation.

In the past several years, we have begun to see that diseconomies of scale come much sooner than we previously anticipated. This recognition, along with technological capability to do more in a plant, has resulted in a shift toward small facilities. The steel industry, with its declining number of big, integrated plants and its corresponding shift toward minimills, is a well-known case in point.

Capacity Flexibility

Capacity flexibility essentially means having the capability to deliver what the customer wants within a lead time shorter than competitors'. Such flexibility is achieved through flexible plants, processes, workers, and through strategies that use the capacity of other organizations. **Agile manufacturing** is another term that reflects the ability of a facility to react quickly to changes in the marketplace.

Flexible plants

Perhaps the ultimate in plant flexibility is the *zero-changeover-time* plant. Using movable equipment, knockdown walls, easily accessible and reroutable utilities, such a plant can adapt to change in real time. An analogy to a familiar service business captures the flavor quite well—a plant with equipment "that is easy to install and easy to tear down and move—like the Ringling Bros.–Barnum and Bailey Circus in the old tent-circus days."[1]

Flexible processes

Flexible processes are epitomized by flexible manufacturing systems on the one hand, and simple, easy set-up equipment on the other. Both of these technological approaches permit rapid low-cost switching from one product line to another, enabling what is sometimes referred to as *economies of scope*. (By definition, economies of scope exist when multiple products can be produced at a lower cost in combination than they can separately.)

Flexible workers

Flexible workers have multiple skills and the ability to switch easily from one kind of task to another. They require broader training than specialized workers and need managers and staff support to facilitate quick changes in their work assignments.

Using external capacity

Two common strategies for creating flexibility by using the capacity of other organizations are subcontracting and sharing capacity. An example of subcontracting is Japanese banks in California subcontracting check-clearing operations to the First Interstate Bank of California's check clearinghouse. An example of sharing capacity is two domestic airlines flying different routes with different seasonal demands exchanging aircraft (suitably repainted) when one's routes are heavily used and the other's are not.

Capacity Balance

In a perfectly balanced plant, the output of Stage 1 provides the exact input requirement for Stage 2, Stage 2's output provides the exact input requirement for Stage 3, and so on. In practice, however, achieving such a "perfect" design is usually both impossible and undesirable. One reason is that the best operating levels for each stage generally differ. For instance, Department 1 may operate most efficiently over a range of 90 to 110 units per month while Department 2, the next stage in the process, is most efficient at 75 to 85 units per month, and Department 3, the third stage, works best over a range of 150 to 200 units per month. Another reason is that variability in product demand and the processes themselves generally lead to imbalance except in automated production lines which, in

---

[1] See R. J. Schonberger, "The Rationalization of Production," *Proceedings of the 50th Anniversary of the Academy of Management* (Chicago: Academy of Management, 1986), pp. 64–70.

essence, are just one big machine. There are various ways of dealing with imbalance. One is to add capacity to those stages that are the bottlenecks. This can be done by temporary measures such as scheduling overtime, leasing equipment, or going outside the system and purchasing additional capacity through subcontracting. A second way is through the use of buffer inventories in front of the bottleneck stage to assure that it always has something to work on. A third approach involves duplicating the facilities of that department which is the cause of the bottleneck.

Capacity and Complexity

One of the main factors that must be considered in capacity planning is how much **complexity** is added to the manager's job as a result of how that capacity is deployed. This is especially true in multisite services where the locations of capacity are, by definition, widely disbursed and inherently difficult to coordinate.

Exhibit 8.2 provides a summary of how choices among various capacity and design features affect managerial complexity. Obviously, the higher the complexity of the operations, the more difficult the capacity planning process.

8.3 CAPACITY STRATEGIES

There are three major strategies for adding capacity: proactive, neutral, and reactive. Each has its strengths and weaknesses. Which strategy to adopt is dependent, to a large extent, on the operating characteristics of the facility and the overall strategy of the firm.

Proactive

With a proactive strategy, management anticipates future growth and builds the facility so that it is up and running when the demand is there, as seen in Exhibit 8.3A. With this strategy, opportunity costs resulting from lost sales due to an inability to meet demand are

EXHIBIT 8.2

The Contributors to Managing and Planning Complexity in Multisite Services

Capacity Dependent Choices	MANAGERIAL COMPLEXITY	
	Low	High
Number of facilities	Few	Many
Diversity of facility types	Standardized	Nonstandardized
Dispersion of facilities	Concentrated	Scattered
Breadth of service offering	Narrow	Broad
Number of employees	Few	Many
Degree of backward integration	Little	Much
Volume of transactions	Few	Many

Source: W. E. Sasser, R. Paul Olsen, and D. D. Wyckoff, *Management of Service Operations* (New York: Allyn & Bacon, 1978), p. 562.

EXHIBIT 8.3

Strategies for Adding Capacity

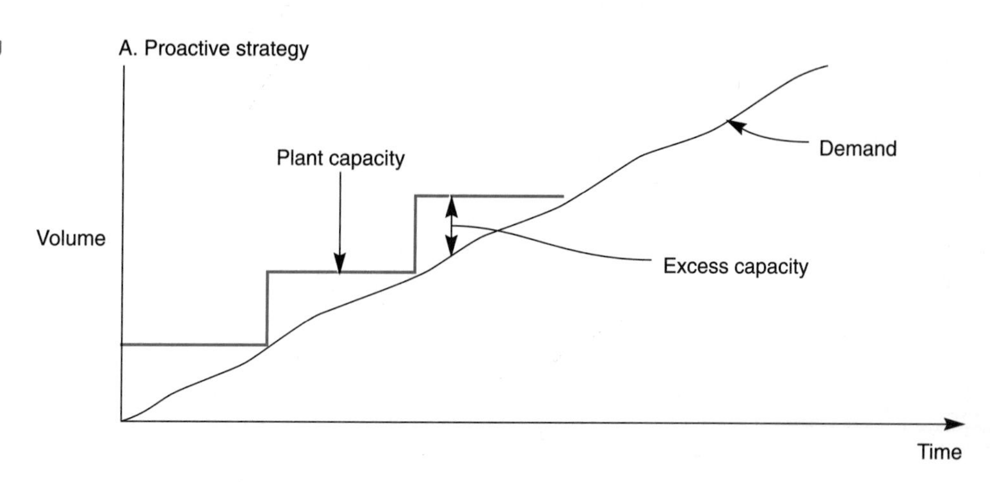

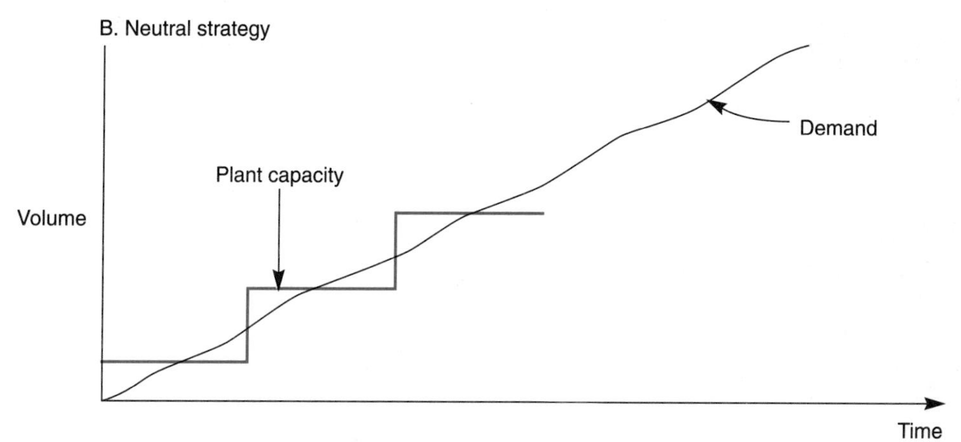

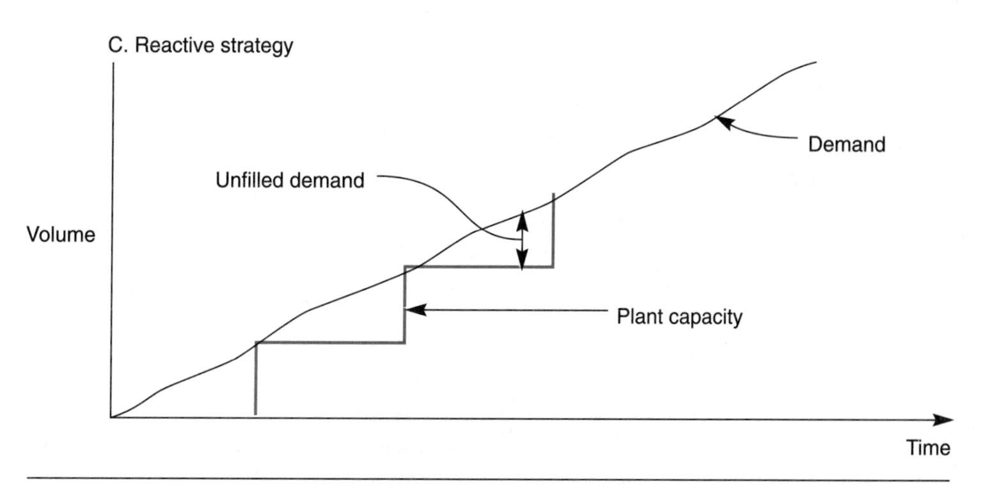

minimized, although the firm does have to allocate fixed costs over a relatively small volume of units during the plant's initial period of operation. This strategy is most compatible for a plant where the labor costs are a significant portion of total manufacturing costs, such as in low-volume assembly operations (e.g., footwear manufacturing).

Neutral

A neutral strategy for adding capacity simply takes a middle-of-the-road approach. As seen in Exhibit 8.3B, capacity is planned to be available when demand is about 50 percent of total capacity. The issue here, as with reactive strategy, is how best to satisfy demand before the plant is up and operating.

Reactive

Plant capacity is not added when a reactive strategy is adopted until all of the planned output from the facility can be sold. Thus, with this strategy, the plant is not brought on line until demand equals 100 percent of its capacity, as shown in Exhibit 8.3C. Operating costs are minimized with this approach, as the plant is producing at its desired optimal output, beginning with its first day of operation. This strategy is most conducive to process-oriented operations that have very high fixed costs, regardless of the volume produced, and low variable costs.

The main problem with this strategy, as with the neutral strategy, is how best to meet the unfilled demand before the plant is in operation. One approach, if the firm has other plants that produce the same product(s), is to manufacture the products temporarily (albeit inefficiently) at these other locations, utilizing additional shifts and overtime as necessary.

8.4 CAPACITY PLANNING

The objective of **capacity planning** is to specify which level of capacity will meet market demands in a cost-efficient way. Capacity planning can be viewed in three time durations: long range (greater than one year), intermediate range (the next 6 to 18 months), and short range (less than six months).

Our focus in this chapter is on long-range capacity planning, where the firm makes its major investment decisions. In addition to planning large chunks of capacity (such as a new factory) typical long-range capacity planning efforts must also address the demands for individual product lines, individual plant capabilities, and allocation of production throughout the plant network. Typically, these are carried out according to the following steps:

1. Forecast sales for each product line.
2. Forecast sales for individual products within each product line.
3. Calculate labor and equipment requirements to meet product line forecasts.
4. Project labor and equipment availabilities over the planning horizon.

Capacity Planning Using Decision Trees

A frequently used approach that addresses the different steps involved in capacity planning is called a **decision tree.** The tree format provides not only an understanding of the problem but also assists us in finding a solution. A decision tree is a schematic model of the sequence of steps in a problem and the conditions and consequences of each step.

Decision trees are composed of decision nodes with branches to and from them. By convention, squares represent decision points and circles represent chance events. Branches from decision points show the choices available to the decision maker; branches from chance events show the probabilities of their occurrence. The primary concern in using decision trees is the ability to obtain accurate probabilities for the chance events.

In solving decision tree problems, we work from the end of the tree backward to the start of the tree. As we work back, we calculate the expected values at each step.

Once the calculations are made, we prune the tree by eliminating from each decision point all branches except for the one with the highest expected payoff. This process continues until the first decision to be made is reached, at which time the decision problem is thereby solved.

The following example demonstrates an application of decision trees solving a capacity planning problem for Hackers Computer Store.

Example

The owner of Hackers Computer Store is considering what to do with his business over the next five years. Sales growth over the last couple of years has been good, but sales could grow substantially if a major electronics firm is built in his area as proposed. Hackers' owner sees three options: the first is to enlarge his current store, the second is to locate at a new site, and the third is to simply wait and do nothing. The decision to expand or move would take little time and, therefore, the store would not lose revenue. If nothing were done the first year and strong growth occurred, then the decision to expand would be reconsidered. Waiting longer than one year would allow competition to move in and make expansion no longer feasible.

The assumptions and conditions are:

1. Strong growth as a result of the increased population of computer fanatics from the electronics firm has a 55 percent probability.
2. Strong growth with a new site would give annual returns of $195,000 per year. Weak growth with a new site would mean annual returns of $115,000.
3. Strong growth with an expansion would give annual returns of $190,000 per year. Weak growth with an expansion would mean annual returns of $100,000.
4. At the existing store with no changes, there would be returns of $170,000 per year if there is strong growth and $105,000 per year if growth is weak.
5. Expansion at the current site would cost $87,000.
6. The move to the new site would cost $210,000.
7. If growth is strong and the existing site is enlarged for the second year, the cost would still be $87,000.

EXHIBIT 8.4

Decision Tree for Hackers Computer Store

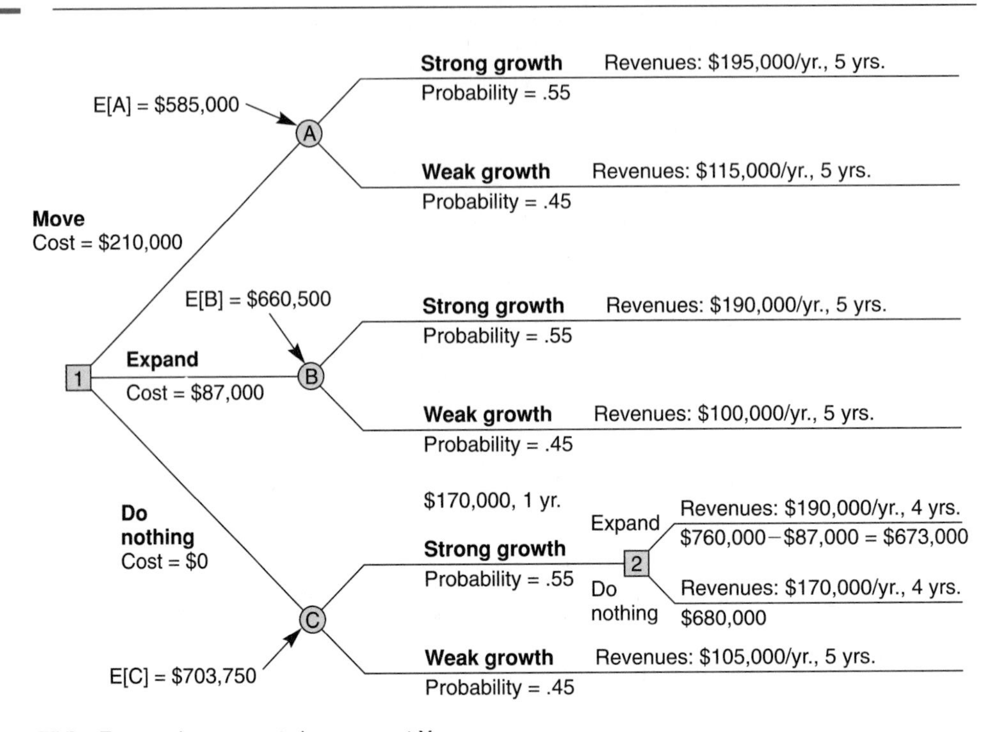

8. Operating costs for all options are equal.
9. Although the time value of money should be taken into consideration in this type of problem, we do not include it in this example in order to provide a clearer understanding of the decision tree analysis methodology.

We construct a decision tree to advise Hackers's owner on the best action.

Exhibit 8.4 shows the decision tree for this problem. There are two decision points (square nodes), and three chance occurrences (round nodes). The value of the nodes and decision points are as follows:

Node A. Move to new location.	
Return with strong growth	$195,000/yr. × 5 yrs. = $975,000
Return with weak growth	$115,000/yr. × 5 yrs. = $575,000
Expected return at A =	($975,000 × .55) + ($575,000 × .45)
=	$795,000
Less new site costs =	−210,000
New site net return	$585,000

Node B. Enlarge the existing store.
Return with strong growth $190,000/yr. + 5 yrs. = $950,000
Return with weak growth $100,000/yr. × 5 yrs. = $500,000
Expected return at B = ($950,000 × .55) + ($500,000 × .45)
= $747,500
Less costs of expansion = −87,000
Expansion net return $660,500

Decision point 2. After one year, reconsider:
Enlarging existing store:
Return with strong growth $190,000/yr. × 4 yrs. = $760,000
Less expansion costs − 87,000
Net return $673,000
Keeping existing store the same:
Return with strong growth $170,000/yr. × 4 yrs. = $680,000

Decision point 2 shows the choice of $673,000 if the existing store is enlarged versus $680,000 if the existing store is kept the same. Therefore, we would prune the expansion branch because it is less.

Node C. Do nothing.
Strong growth in first year = $170,000/yr. × 1 yr. = $170,000
Value of best decision of not to expand = 680,000
$850,000

Weak growth in first year = $105,000
Keep store the same next four years (4 × $105,000) = 420,000
$525,000
Expected return at Node C = (.55 × $850,000) + (.45 × $525,000)
= $703,750

Based upon this analysis, the best choice is to do nothing at this time, which has a value of $703,750 compared to $585,000 for the new site and $660,500 for the expansion.

8.5 FACILITY LOCATION

For manufacturers, the facility location problem is broadly divided into two categories: factory location and warehouse location. Within this categorization, we may be interested in locating the firm's first factory or warehouse, or locating an additional factory or warehouse relative to existing facilities.

The general objective in choosing a location is to select that site or combination of sites that minimizes three groups of costs: regional costs, outbound distribution costs, and inbound distribution costs. Regional costs are those associated with a given locale and include such items as land, construction, labor, local taxes, and energy costs. Outbound distribution costs are those costs incurred in shipping products to retailers, wholesalers, and other plants in the network. Inbound distribution costs refer to the availability and costs of raw materials and supplies, as well as the lead time to acquire these inputs. Because the location of the initial plant is usually determined by the historical context of the firm, economic analysis of facility location has focused on the problem of adding warehouses or factories to the existing production-distribution network.

Plant Location Methods

"If the boss likes Bakersfield, I like Bakersfield." The set of decisions that a company must make in choosing a plant location are summarized in Exhibit 8.5. While the exhibit implies a step-by-step process, virtually all activities listed take place simultaneously. As suggested by the preceding vote for Bakersfield, political decisions may occasionally override systematic analysis.

The evaluation of alternative regions, subregions, and communities is commonly termed *macro analysis,* and the evaluation of specific sites in the selected community is termed *micro analysis.* Some of the techniques used for macro analyses are factor-rating systems, and center of gravity. A detailed cost analysis would accompany each of these methods, of course.

Factor-rating systems

Factor-rating systems are perhaps the most widely used of the general location techniques because they provide a mechanism to combine diverse factors in an easy-to-understand format.

By way of example, a refinery assigned the following range of point values to major factors affecting a set of possible sites.

	Range
Fuels in region	0 to 330
Power availability and reliability	0 to 200
Labor climate	0 to 100
Living conditions	0 to 100
Transportation	0 to 50
Water supply	0 to 10
Climate	0 to 50
Supplies	0 to 60
Tax policies and laws	0 to 20

Each site was then rated against each factor and a point value selected from its assigned range. The sums of assigned points for each site were then compared and the site with the maximum number of points was selected.

One of the major problems with simple point-rating schemes is that they do not account for the wide range of costs that may occur within each factor. For example, there

EXHIBIT 8.5

Plant Search: Company XYZ

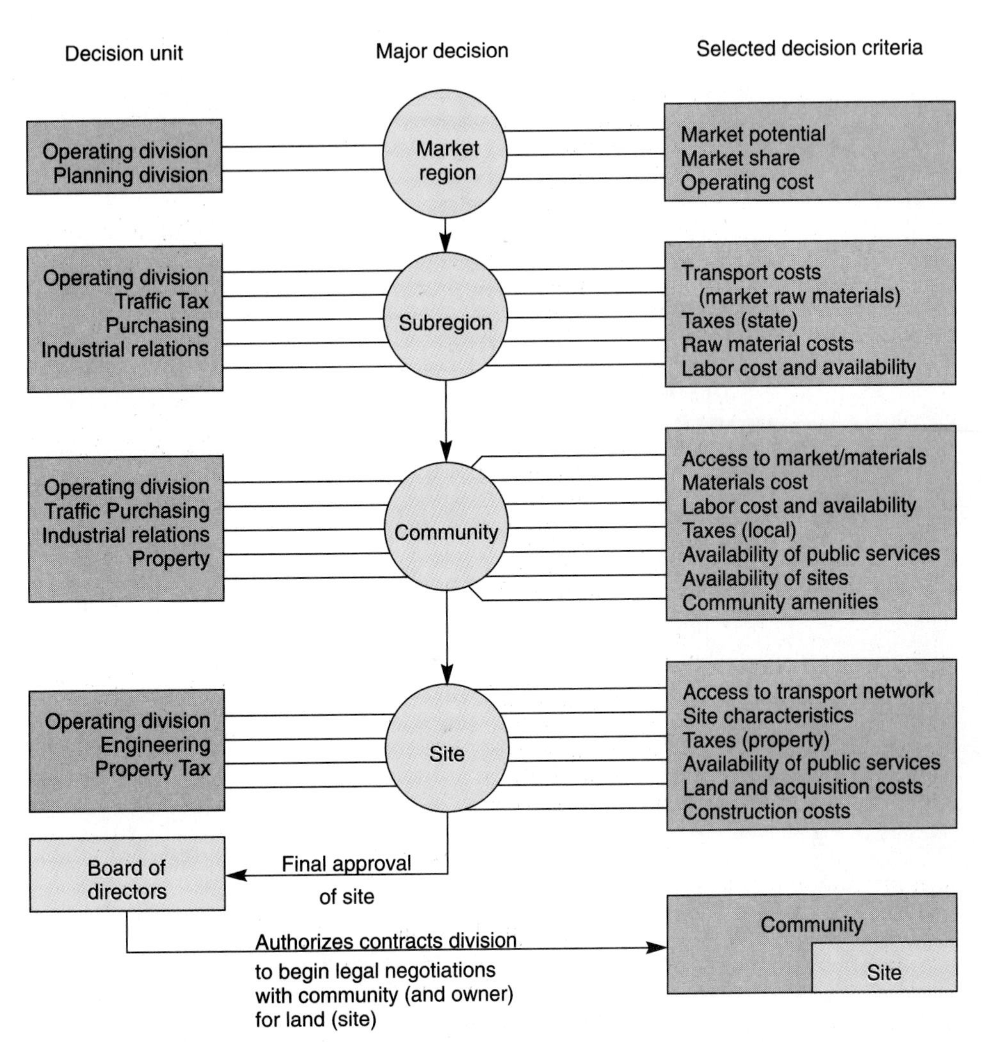

Source: Thomas M. Carroll and Robert D. Dean. "A Bayesian Approach to Plant-Location Decisions," *Decision Sciences* 11, no. 1 (January 1980), p. 87.

may be only a few hundred dollars' difference between the best and worst locations on one factor and several thousands of dollars' difference between the best and the worst on another. The first factor may have the most points available to it but it provides little help in making the location decision; the latter factor may have few points available but potentially shows a real difference in the value of locations. To deal with this problem, Phillip Hicks and Areen Kumtha suggest that the possible points assigned to each factor be derived using a weighting scale based on standard deviations of costs rather than simply total cost amounts.[2] This method is useful and the interested reader should consult the original publication for more details.

Another problem with this approach is that often the values for some of the factors included in the decision analysis are highly subjective, the quality of the public education system and the quality of life in a certain location being good examples.

Center of gravity method

The **center of gravity method** is a technique for locating an additional single facility that considers the existing facilities, the distances between them, and the volumes of goods that need to be shipped. The technique is often used to locate intermediate or distribution warehouses. In its simplest form, this method assumes that inbound and outbound transportation costs are equal, and it does not include special shipping costs for less than full loads.

The center of gravity method begins by placing the existing locations on a coordinate grid system. The choice of coordinate systems is entirely arbitrary. The purpose is to establish relative distances between locations. Using longitude and latitude coordinates might be helpful in international decisions. An example of a grid layout is shown in Exhibit 8.6.

The center of gravity is found by calculating the X and Y coordinates that result in the minimal transportation cost. The following formulas are used:

$$C_x = \frac{\Sigma d_{ix} V_i}{\Sigma V_i}$$

$$C_y = \frac{\Sigma d_{iy} V_i}{\Sigma V_i}$$

where

C_x = X coordinate of the center of gravity
C_y = Y coordinate of the center of gravity
d_{ix} = X coordinate of the ith location
d_{iy} = Y coordinate of the ith location
V_i = Volume of goods moved to or from the ith location

Example

The HiOctane Refining Company needs to locate an intermediate holding facility between its refining plant in Long Beach and its major distributors. The coordinate map is shown in Exhibit 8.6. The amounts of gasoline shipped between its plant and distributors and their respective coordinates are shown in Exhibit 8.7.

[2]Phillip E. Hicks and Areen M. Kumtha, "One Way to Tighten Up Plant Location Decisions," *Industrial Engineering* 9 (April 1971), pp. 19–23.

EXHIBIT 8.6

Grid Map for Center of Gravity Example

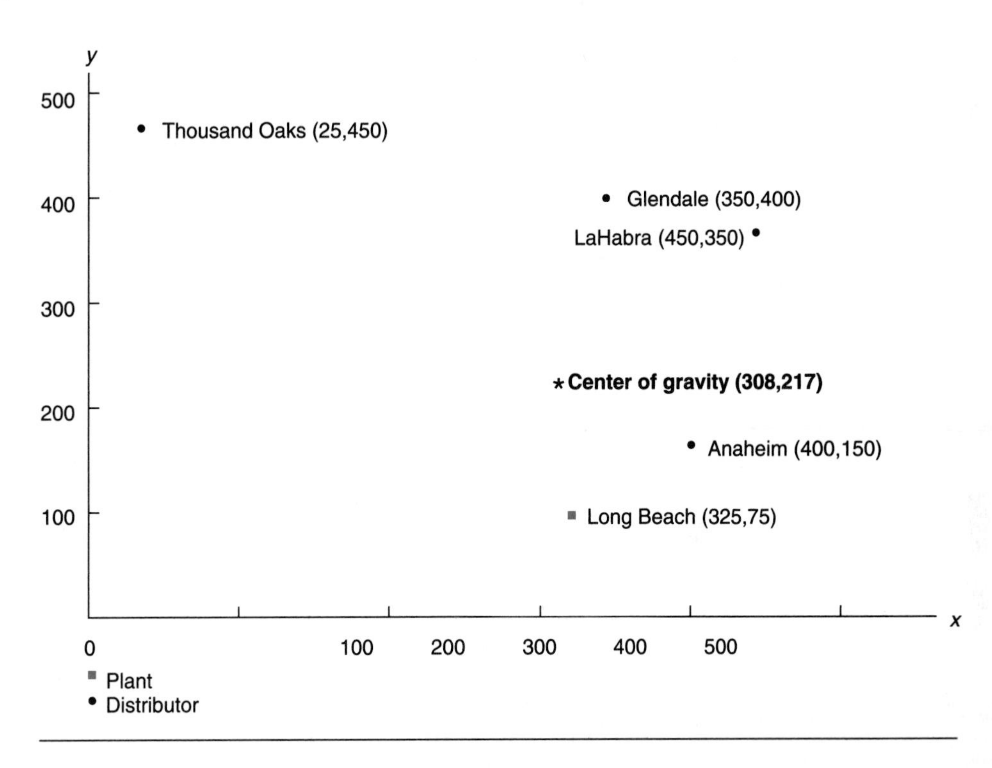

In this example, the data for the Long Beach location (the first location) are

$$d_{1x} = 325$$
$$d_{1y} = 75$$
$$V_1 = 1{,}500$$

Using the information in Exhibits 8.6 and 8.7, we are able to calculate the coordinates of the center of gravity as follows:

EXHIBIT 8.7

Shipping Volumes, Center of Gravity Example

Location	*X*-coordinate	*Y*-coordinate	Gallons of Gasoline per Month (000,000)
Long Beach	325	75	1,500
Anaheim	400	150	250
LaHabra	450	350	450
Glendale	350	400	350
Thousand Oaks	25	450	450

$$C_x = \frac{(325 \times 1{,}500) + (400 \times 250) + (450 \times 450) + (350 \times 350) + (25 \times 450)}{1{,}500 + 450 + 250 + 350 + 450}$$

$$= \frac{923{,}750}{3{,}000}$$

$$= 307.9$$

$$C_y = \frac{(75 \times 1{,}500) + (150 \times 250) + (350 \times 450) + (400 \times 350) + (450 \times 450)}{1{,}500 + 450 + 250 + 350 + 450}$$

$$= \frac{650{,}000}{3{,}000}$$

$$= 216.7$$

This gives management the X and Y coordinates of approximately 308 and 217 respectively, and provides an initial starting point to search for a new site. By examining the location of the calculated center of gravity on the grid map, we can see that it might be more cost efficient to ship directly between the Long Beach plant and the Anaheim distributor than to ship via a warehouse near the center of gravity. Before a location decision is made, management would probably recalculate the center of gravity, changing the data to reflect this (i.e., decrease the gallons shipped from Long Beach by the amount Anaheim needs and remove Anaheim from the formula).

Detailed cost analysis

A detailed cost analysis must be done before a location decision is finalized. Exhibit 8.8, taken from *Factory* magazine, presents an actual cost analysis used by a company contemplating the relocation of its plant. Note that present-value calculations using the time value of money are also commonly used to augment cost calculations shown in this exhibit.

8.6 LOCATING SERVICE FACILITIES

In service organizations, the facility location decision is also major; as a rule, the choice of locale is based on nearness to the customer rather than on resource considerations. Because of the variety of service firms and the relatively low cost of establishing a service facility compared to one for manufacturing, new service facilities are far more common than new factories and warehouses. Indeed, there are few communities in which rapid population growth has not been paralleled by a concurrent rapid growth in retail outlets, restaurants, municipal services, and entertainment facilities.

Services typically have multiple sites to maintain close contact with customers. The location decision is closely tied to the market segmentation decision. If the target market is college-age groups, locations in retirement communities, despite desirability in terms of cost, resource availability, and so forth, are not viable alternatives. The requirements of the target market also affect the number of sites to be built, the size, and the characteristics of

EXHIBIT 8.8 **Cost Analysis Example** (Present location versus recommended communities)

Operating Expenses	Present Location	Community A	Community B	Community C
Transportation				
Inbound	$ 202,942	$ 212,209	$ 207,467	$ 220,009
Outbound	480,605	361,268	393,402	365,198
Labor				
Hourly direct and indirect	1,520,943	1,339,790	1,146,087	1,223,416
Fringe benefits	304,189	187,571	126,070	159,044
Plant overhead				
Rent of carrying costs	271,436	290,000	280,000	295,000
Real estate taxes	43,345	39,000	34,000	39,000
Personal property and other locally assessed taxes	16,899	—	—	8,500
Fuel for heating	19,260	11,000	9,500	13,000
Utilities				
Power	56,580	61,304	41,712	49,007
Gas	18,460	19,812	13,767	16,633
Water	12,474	8,200	4,500	4,500
Treatment of effluent	6,376	—	2,300	—
State factors				
State taxes	67,811	73,400	44,920	71,000
Workers' compensation insurance	30,499	24,000	14,000	17,000
Total	$3,051,819	$ 2,627,554	$ 2,317,725	$ 2,481,337
Savings through construction of new plant				
New plant layout		$(210,000)	$(210,000)	$(210,000)
Reduced materials handling		(38,000)	(38,000)	(38,000)
Elimination of present local interplant movements		(60,000)	(60,000)	(60,000)
Reduced public warehousing		(30,000)	(30,000)	(30,000)
Reduced supervisory personnel		(27,000)	(27,000)	(27,000)
Savings through new construction		$(365,000)	$(365,000)	$(365,000)
Annual operating costs	$3,051,819	$ 2,262,554	$ 1,952,725	$ 2,116,337
Potential annual savings over present location		$ 789,265	$ 1,099,094	$ 935,482
Percentage of savings		25.9%	36.0%	30.7%

Source: "New Plants and Expansions, End of Tunnel May Be in Sight," *Factory* (September 1975), p. 57.

the sites. Whereas manufacturing location decisions are often based on minimizing costs, many of the service location decision techniques attempt to maximize the profit potential of various sites.

Screening Location Sites at La Quinta Motor Inns

Selecting good sites plays a crucial role in the success of a service operation such as a hotel chain. Of the four major marketing considerations—price, product, promotion, and location—location and product have been shown to be the most important for multisite firms. As a result, hotel chain owners who can pick good sites quickly have a distinct competitive advantage.

EXHIBIT 8.9

Summary of the Variables that Correlated with Operating Margin in 1983 and 1986

Variable	1983	1986
ACCESS	.20	
AGE	.29	.49
COLLEGE		.25
DISTCBD		−.22
EMPLYPCT	−.22	−.22
INCOME		−.23
MILTOT		.22
NEAREST	−.51	
OFCCBD	.30	
POPULACE	.30	.35
PRICE	.38	.58
RATE		.27
STATE	−.32	−.33
SIGNVIS	.25	
TRAFFIC	.32	
URBAN	−.22	−.26

Source: Reprinted by permission of Sheryl E. Kimes and James A. Fitzsimmons, "Selecting Profitable Hotel Sites at La Quinta Motor Inns," *Interfaces* 20 (March–April 1990). Copyright 1990 The Institute of Management Sciences, 290 Westminster Street, Providence, Rhode Island 02903 USA.

Thirty-five variables were identified for inclusion in a study to assist La Quinta Motor Inns in screening potential locations for its new hotels.[3] Data were collected on 57 existing La Quinta Inns. A technique known as *exploratory data analysis* identified 16 variables that correlated with operating profit in 1983 and 1986 (see Exhibit 8.9).

A multiple regression model was then constructed and in its final form appears as follows:

$$\begin{aligned}\text{Profitability} = 39.05 &- 5.41 \times \text{State population per inn (1,000)}\\ &+ 5.86 \times \text{Price of the inn}\\ &- 3.91 \times \text{Square root of the median income of the area (1,000)}\\ &+ 1.75 \times \text{College students within four miles.}\end{aligned}$$

The model shows that profitability is negatively affected by market penetration, positively affected by price, negatively affected by higher incomes (the inns do better in lower median income areas), and positively affected by colleges nearby.

La Quinta implemented the model on a Lotus 1-2-3 spreadsheet and routinely uses the spreadsheet to screen potential real estate acquisitions. The founder and president of La Quinta has accepted the model's validity and no longer feels obligated to personally select the sites.

This example shows that a specific model can be obtained from the requirements of service organizations and used to identify those features that are most important in making

[3]Sheryl E. Kimes and James A. Fitzsimmons, "Selecting Profitable Hotel Sites at La Quinta Motor Inns," *Interfaces* 20 (March–April 1990), pp. 12–20.

the right site selection. The next "OM in Action" discusses the expansion criteria and strategies of AM/PM International, a chain of convenience stores.

OPERATIONS MANAGEMENT IN ACTION
How AM/PM International Selects Its Sites

AM/PM convenience stores are a subsidiary of the ARCO Corporation. These stores are usually connected with service stations. The goals of AM/PM International are to leverage the existing AM/PM program through brand licensing agreements in foreign countries and joint-venture participation. Furthermore, ARCO wants to participate aggressively in emerging international markets and leverage its international presence. ARCO also wants to generate additional long-term profits.

To select a new potential country, AM/PM International looks at four main criteria:

1. The population should be over 1 million in a targeted city.
2. Annual per-capita income should be over $2,000.
3. The political system should be fairly stable.
4. The host country should have minimal restrictions on hard currency repatriation.

Once AM/PM has selected a potential country for its business, it evaluates further, the country's:

1. Stage of industrial development.
2. People/car ratio. (This is important because the AM/PM stores are located in service stations.)
3. Population density in rural and urban areas.
4. Availability and cost of labor.
5. Infrastructure (supply and distribution, equipment availability, real estate cost, and reliability of utilities).
6. Tax regulations.
7. Legal issues.

AM/PM International uses franchising as a rapid and convenient way to expand in the Pacific Rim, Europe, and North America. The company's prospective list of candidate countries for the next expansion includes Italy, France, Denmark, Mexico, Brazil, Malysia, and Canada.

AM/PM's international expansion strategy is based on three points:

First, using the existing service station staff to run the convenience store.

Second, for the first year an American-trained manager works closely with the new licensee.

Third, to develop new stores in selected countries as quickly as possible.

Source: ARCO presentation to U.S.C. MBA students, June 5, 1991.

Courtesy The Boeing Company

Location was not the main concern when Boeing built this manufacturing facility in Everett, Washington, because its products can be delivered anywhere!

8.7 CONCLUSION

Like so many topics in operations management, capacity planning and location decisions are becoming heavily affected by the information revolution and globalization of production. The emergence of the network firm (or *hollow corporation* that coordinates production of multiple suppliers rather than manufacturing the products in house) has changed the way management views its available capacity, and the growth of international markets has altered its location strategies. It is already clear that the operations executives in many companies must catch a plane to see the multiple shop floors that constitute the capacity of their organizations.

8.8 REVIEW AND DISCUSSION QUESTIONS

1. List some practical limits to economies of scale; that is, when should a plant stop growing?
2. What are some capacity balance problems faced by the following organizations or facilities?
   a. An airline terminal.
   b. A university computing center.
   c. A clothing manufacturer.
3. What are the primary capacity planning considerations for foreign companies locating their facilities in the United States?
4. What are some major capacity considerations in a hospital? How do they differ from those of a factory?

5. Develop a list of five major reasons why a new electronics firm should move into your city or town.
6. How do facilities planning decisions differ for service facilities and manufacturing plants?
7. Management may choose to build up capacity in anticipation of demand or in response to developing demand. Cite the advantages and disadvantages of both approaches.
8. Which motivations typically cause firms to initiate major capacity/facilities planning projects, such as the one described in Exhibit 8.4?
9. What is capacity balance? Why is this condition difficult to achieve? What methods are used to deal with capacity imbalances?
10. How does the emergence of the network firm (hollow corporation) change the way management plans for capacity?
11. Does it make sense to you that a particular plant is working at 110% of capacity?

8.9 SOLVED PROBLEM

PROBLEM

Sam Malone, owner of Cheers, is moving to Los Angeles and trying to decide whether to lease a bar at a site near the Ventura Freeway in Hollywood or build a new bar near a fork in the Slauson Freeway in Inglewood. The bar will be built on state-leased land that will be part of a new expanded intersection in 10 years. Thus, there is no salvage value at the termination of the 10-year period.

The initial lease will run for a period of two years. If the owner is satisfied at that time, he will extend the lease for an additional eight years. Sam attaches a 50–50 probability to this renewal. If the lease is canceled, Sam knows of another cafe-bar nearby that will be available for leasing, but the lease will be 30 percent more than the present site. Given this information and the information in the table below, develop a decision tree to help Sam choose between these sites. (Use a 10-year planning horizon.) Disregard the cost of capital.

Decision Variables	Hollywood Site	Probability	Inglewood Site	Probability
Cost to lease per year	$250,000			
Cost to build			$1,000,000	
Gross revenue per year				
High sales	700,000	0.5	400,000	0.5
Medium sales	500,000	0.3	300,000	0.3
Low sales	300,000	0.2	200,000	0.2
Operating costs per year	200,000		200,000	

SOLUTION

Lease decision

@D	Revenue for 8 years = 8[.5(700,000) + 0.3(500,000) + 0.2(300,000)]		$4,480,000
	Lease cost for 8 years = 8(250,000)	$2,000,000	
	Operating cost for 8 years = 8(200,000)	1,600,000	3,600,000
	Net income		$ 880,000

@E	Revenue for 8 years = 8[.5(700,000) + 0.3(500,000) + 0.2(300,000)]		$4,480,000
	Lease cost 30 percent greater or 1.30(250,000)	$ 325,000	
	Lease for 8 years = 8(325,000)	2,600,000	
	Operating cost for 8 years = 8(200,000)	$1,600,000	4,200,000
	Net income		$ 280,000

@C Net income = 0.5(880,000) + 0.5(280,000) = 580,000

@B Net income = Revenue for 2 years − Operating cost for 2 years −Lease cost for 2 years + Value of node C
= 2[.5(700,000) + 0.3(500,000) + 0.2(300,000)] −2(250,000) − 2(200,000) + $580,000
= $800,000

Build in Inglewood

@F	Revenue for 10 years = 10[0.5(400,000) + 0.3(300,000) + 0.2(200,000)]	$3,300,000
	Operating costs for 10 years = 10(200,000)	−2,000,000
	Plus salvage value	—0—
		1,300,000
@A	Less cost to build	−1,000,000
	Net income	$ 300,000

The best decision is to lease, with a net income of $800,000; building would produce a net income of only $300,000.

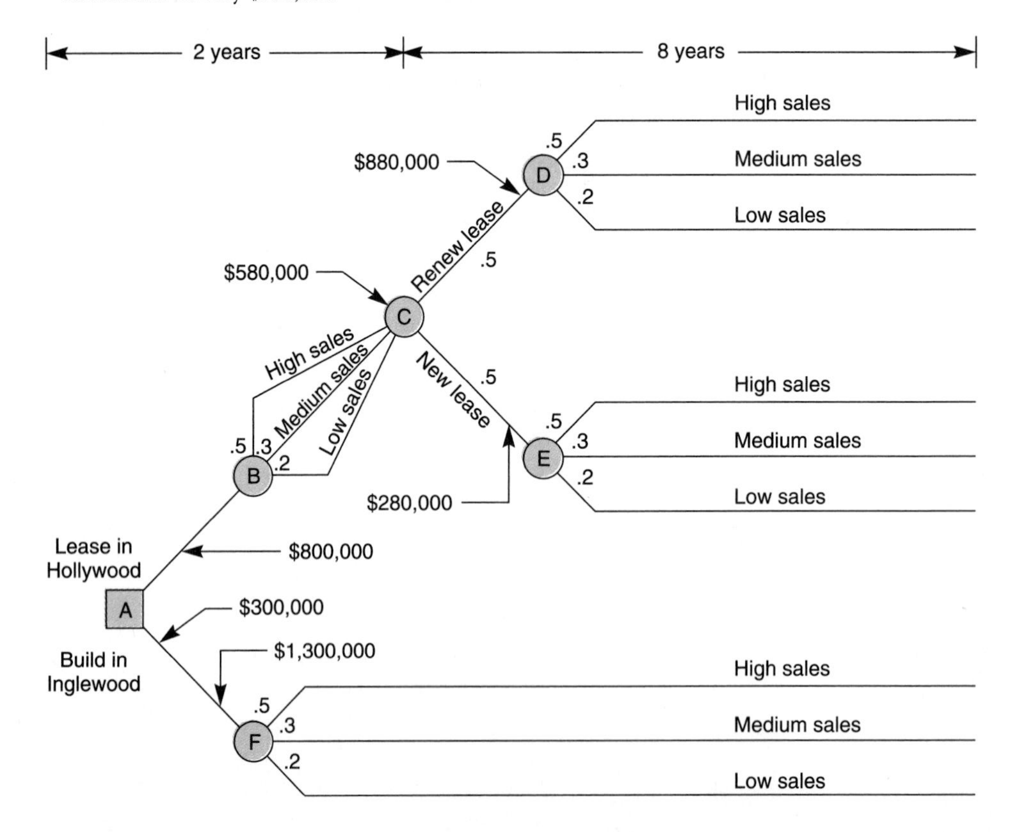

8.10 PROBLEMS

1. Cool Air, a manufacturer of automotive air conditioners, currently produces its XB-300 line at three different locations, Plant A, Plant B, and Plant C. Recently, management decided to build all compressors, a major product component, in a separate dedicated facility, Plant D.
   Using the center of gravity method and the information displayed in Exhibits 8.10 and 8.11, determine the best location for Plant D. Assume a linear relationship between volumes shipped and shipping costs (no premium charges).
2. Refer to the information given in Problem 1. Suppose management decides to shift 2,000 units of production from Plant B to Plant A. Does this change the proposed location of Plant D, the compressor production facility? If so, where should Plant D be located?
3. A builder has located a piece of property that he would like to buy and eventually build on. What he does not yet know is exactly what he will build. The land is currently zoned for four

EXHIBIT 8.10

Plant Location Matrix

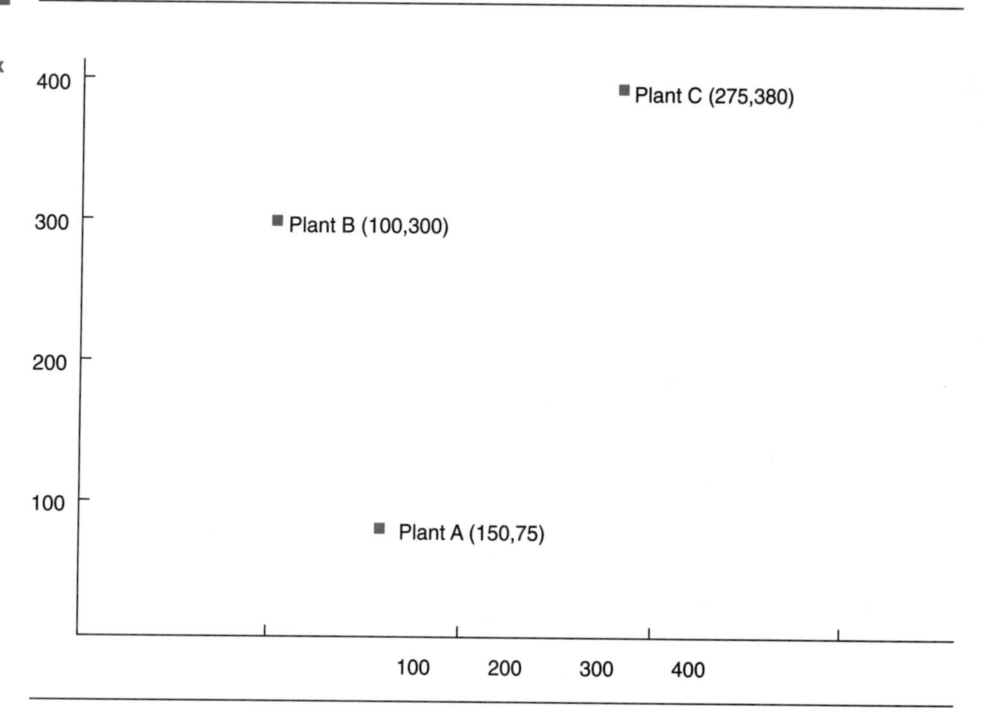

EXHIBIT 8.11

Quantity of Compressors Required by Each Plant

Plant	Compressors Required per Year
A	6,000
B	8,200
C	7,000

homes per acre, but he is planning to request new zoning. What he builds depends on approval of zoning requests and your analysis of this problem to advise him. With his input and your help, the decision process has been reduced to the following costs, alternatives, and probabilities:

Cost of land: $2 million.

Probability of rezoning: .60.

If the land is rezoned, there will be additional costs for new roads, lighting, and so on, of $1 million.

If the land is rezoned, the contractor must decide whether to build a shopping center or 1,500 apartments that the tentative plan shows would be possible. If he builds a shopping center, there is a 70 percent chance that he can sell the shopping center to a large department store chain for $4 million over his construction cost which excludes the land, and there is a 30 percent chance that he may be able to sell it to an insurance company for $5 million over his construction cost (also excluding the land). If, instead of the shopping center, he decides to build the 1,500 apartments, he places probabilities on the profits as follows: There is a 60 percent chance that he can sell the apartments to a real estate investment corporation for $3,000 each over his construction cost and a 40 percent chance that he may be able to get only $2,000 each over his construction cost (both exclude his land cost).

If the land is not rezoned, he will comply with the existing zoning restrictions and simply build 600 homes on which he expects to make $4,000 over his construction cost on each one (excluding his cost of land).

Draw a decision tree of the problem and determine the best solution and the expected net profit.

4. Chubby Chicken, a fast food chain specializing in rotisserie chicken, wants to expand its operations into eastern Europe, specifically Tallinn, Estonia. Unfortunately, because of the lack of supporting vendors (meat purveyors and processors, fruit and vegetable wholesalers, etc.), it has decided to build its own central commissary to do the initial food preparation in support of the fast food outlets. The initial plan calls for the constructiuon of five outlets in Tallinn over the next three years. The x and y coordinates and projected sales of each outlet are shown below.

Store	X Coordinate	Y Coordinate	Annual Sales (Estonian Kroons)
A	15	40	2,000,000 EEK
B	35	20	2,700,000
C	10	75	3,100,000
D	60	50	2,300,000
E	15	25	1,800,000

One of the first tasks, therefore, is to determine where to locate the central commissary in order to minimize distribution costs. Find the coordinates for locating the central commissary where it best minimizes the total distribution costs. (Assume that the quantity of food distributed to each store is directly proportional to its annual sales.)

8.11 CASE: COMMUNITY HOSPITAL*

In 1983, Community Hospital, which had served the downtown area of a large West Coast city for more than 25 years, closed and then built a new hospital in a thinly populated area about 30 miles west of the city. The new hospital, also named Community Hospital, was located on a parcel of land owned by the original hospital for many years.

This new hospital, which opened October 1, 1983, is a four-story structure that includes all the latest innovations in health-care technology. The first floor houses the emergency departments; intensive care unit; operating room; radiology, laboratory, and therapy departments; pharmacy; housekeeping and maintenance facilities and supplies, as well as other supportive operations. All administrative offices, such as the business office, medical records department, special services, and so forth, are located on the second floor, as are the cafeteria and food service facilities. The two upper floors contain patient rooms divided into surgical, medical, pediatric, and obstetric units.

Community Hospital has a total capacity of 177 beds assigned as follows:

Unit	Number of Beds
Surgical	45
Medical	65
Pediatrics	35
Obstetrics	20
Intensive care	12

For the first six months of the hospital's operation, things were rather chaotic for the administrator, Sam Jones. All his time was occupied with the multitude of activities that go along with starting a new facility, seeing that malfunctioning equipment was repaired, arranging for new staff to be hired and trained, establishing procedures and schedules, making necessary purchasing decisions, and attending endless conferences and meetings.

All during this period, Mr. Jones had been getting some rather disturbing reports from his controller, Bob Cash, regarding Community Hospital's financial situation. But he decided that these financial matters would simply have to wait until things had settled down.

Finally, in April, Mr. Jones asked Mr. Cash to prepare a comprehensive report on the hospital's financial position and to make a presentation to himself and his new assistant administrator, Tim Newman, who had recently received a degree in hospital administration.

In his report, Mr. Cash stated: "As you both know, we have been running at an operating cash deficit since we opened last October. We expected, of course, to be losing money at the start until we were able to establish ourselves in the community and draw in patients. We certainly were right. During our first month, we lost almost $221,000. Last month, in March, we lost $58,000.

"The reason, of course, is pretty straightforward. Our income is directly related to our patient census (i.e., patient load). On the other hand, our expenses are fixed and are running at about $235,000 a month for salaries and wages, $75,000 a month for supplies and equipment, and another $10,000 a month in interest charges. Our accumulated operating deficit for the six months we've been here totals $715,000, which we've covered with our bank line of credit. I suppose we can continue to borrow for another couple of months, but after that I don't know what we're going to do."

*Reprinted with permission from *Hospital Cost Containment through Operations Management,* published by the American Hospital Association. Copyright 1984.

Mr. Jones replied, "As you said, Bob, we did expect to be losing money in the beginning, but I never expected the loss to go on for six months or to accumulate to almost three-quarters of a million dollars. Well, at least last month was a lot better than the first month. Do you have any figures showing the month-to-month trend?"

Bob Cash laid the following worksheet on the table:

COMMUNITY HOSPITAL
Six-Month Operating Statement
October 1983–March 1984
(in thousands of dollars)

	1983			1984			
	October	November	December	January	February	March	Total
Income	$ 101	$ 163	$ 199	$ 235	$ 245	$ 262	$ 1,205
Expenses (excluding interest):							
Salaries, wages	232	233	239	235	235	235	1,410
Supplies, other	80	73	74	75	73	75	450
Total	312	306	313	310	309	310	1,860
Interest	10	10	10	10	10	10	60
Operating loss	$(221)	$(153)	$(124)	$(85)	$(74)	$(58)	$(715)
Average daily census	42	68	83	98	102	109	
Occupancy	24%	38%	47%	55%	58%	62%	

QUESTIONS

1. Evaluate the situation at Community Hospital with respect to trends in daily patient census, occupancy rate, and income.
2. Has there been any change in revenue per patient-day over the six-month period (assuming a 30-day month)?
3. At what capacity level will the hospital achieve breakeven?
4. What questions might we raise about the constant level of salaries and supplies relative to past and future operations?

8.12 SELECTED BIBLIOGRAPHY

Blackburn, Joseph, D. *Time-Based Competition: The Next Battle Ground in American Manufacturing.* Homewood, Ill.: Richard D. Irwin, 1991.

Coyle, John J., and Edward J. Bardi. *The Management of Logistics,* 2nd ed. St. Paul: West Publishing, 1980, pp. 294–98.

Francis, R. L., and J. A. White, *Facilities Layout and Location: An Analytical Approach.* Englewood Cliffs, N.J.: Prentice Hall, 1987.

Graziano, Vincent J. "Production Capacity Planning—Long Term." *Production and Inventory Management* 15, no. 2 (Second Quarter 1974), pp. 66–80.

Hayes, Robert H., and Steven C. Wheelwright. *Restoring Our Competitive Edge.* New York: John Wiley & Sons, 1984.

Heskett, J. L.; W. E. Sasser, Jr.; and C. W. L. Hart. *Service Breakthroughs: Changing the Rules of the Game.* New York: Free Press, 1990.

Shycon, Harvey N. "Site Location Analysis, Cost and Customer Service Consideration." *Proceedings of the Seventeenth Annual International Conference,* American Production and Inventory Control Society, 1974, pp. 335–47.

Tompkins, James A., and John A. White. *Facilities Planning.* New York: John Wiley & Sons, 1984.

Wheelwright, Steven C., ed. *Capacity Planning and Facilities Choice: Course Module.* Boston: Harvard Business School, 1979.

Chapter 9

Facility Layout

EPIGRAPH

Layout is where "the rubber meets the road" in every production system.

Anonymous

CHAPTER OUTLINE

KEY TERMS

Process Layout
Product Layout
Group Technology (GT) Layout
Just-in-Time Layout
Fixed-Position Layout
Cycle Time
Assembly Line Balancing
Precedence Relationship
Mixed-Model Lines

There are many factors that need to be taken into consideration when designing the layout for a facility, be it manufacturing or services. Decisions made at this point have long-term consequences, not only in terms of costs, but also in terms of the firm's ability to serve its market(s). It is therefore important that management devote ample time to properly identifying and evaluating alternative solutions for laying out the facility.

Many of the decisions made at the strategic level become constraints when designing the facility's layout. For example, the size of the facility, in terms of its capacity or output, will have been established, and the type of process with which we will make our product will have been selected.

The overall objective in designing a layout is to provide a smooth work flow of material through the factory, or an uncomplicated traffic pattern for both customers and workers in a service organization. Our emphasis is on quantitative techniques used in locating departments within a facility, and on workstation arrangements and balance in the important area of assembly lines. Before embarking on this discussion, however, it is useful to note the characteristics of a good layout, which are listed in Exhibit 9.1.

9.1 BASIC LAYOUT FORMATS

How the different departments are arranged in a facility is defined by the general pattern of work flow. There are three basic types—product layout, process layout, and fixed-position layout—and one hybrid type, group technology or cellular layout. In this chapter we address all of these in detail but the fixed-position layout.

In a **process layout** (also called a *job-shop layout* or *layout by junction*), similar equipment or functions are grouped together, such as in a machine shop where all the lathes are in one area and all the stamping machines are in another. A part being worked on then travels, according to the specific sequence of operations required, from area to area. This type of layout is often found in low-volume manufacturing plants that have an intermittent process. The support services in a hospital provide another good example of process layout, with radiology, blood analysis, and pathology each being located in a specific area.

A **product layout** (also called a *flow-shop layout*) is one in which equipment or work processes are arranged according to the progressive steps by which the product is made. If equipment is dedicated to continual production of a narrow product line, this is usually called a *production line* or *assembly line.* Examples are the manufacture of small appliances (toasters, irons, beaters), large appliances (dishwashers, refrigerators, washing machines), electronics (computers, CD players), and automobiles.

A **group technology (GT) layout** groups dissimilar machines into work centers (or cells) to work on products that have similar shapes and processing requirements. A GT layout is similar to process layout, in that cells are designed to perform a specific set of processes, and it is similar to product layout in that the cells are dedicated to a limited range of products. (*Group technology* also refers to the parts classification and coding system used to specify machine types that go into a GT cell.)

In a **fixed-position layout,** by virtue of its bulk or weight, the product remains stationary at one location. The manufacturing equipment is moved to the product rather

EXHIBIT 9.1

Characteristics of a Good Layout

Manufacturing and Back-Office Service Operations

1. Straight-line flow pattern (or adaptation).
2. Backtracking kept to a minimum.
3. Production time predictable.
4. Little interstage storage of materials.
5. Open plant floors so everyone can see what's going on.
6. Bottleneck operations under control.
7. Workstations close together.
8. Minimum material movement.
9. No unnecessary rehandling of materials.
10. Easily adjustable to changing conditions.

Face-to-Face Services

1. Easily understood service-flow pattern.
2. Proper waiting facilities.
3. Easy communication with customers.
4. Customer surveillance easily maintained.
5. Clear exit and entry points with sufficient checkout capabilities.
6. Departments and processes arranged so that customers see only what you want them to see.
7. Balance between waiting areas and service areas.
8. Minimum walking.
9. Lack of clutter.
10. High sales volume per square foot of facility.

Courtesy The Ford Motor Company

On the assembly line at Ford Motor Company's Wixom (Michigan) assembly plant, this wheel deck operator uses a five-spindle, torque-controlled nut runner to securely fasten wheel nuts on a Lincoln Mark VIII.

than vice versa. Shipyards, construction sites, and professors' offices are examples of this format.

Many manufacturing facilities present a combination of two layout types. For example, a given floor may be laid out by process, while another floor may be laid out by product. It is also common to find an entire plant arranged according to general product flow (fabrication, subassembly, and final assembly), coupled with process layout within fabrication and product layout within the assembly department. Likewise, group technology is frequently found within a department that itself is located according to a plantwide process-oriented layout.

Production layout continually changes because the internal and external environment of production is dynamic. As demands change, so can layout. As technology changes, so can layout. In Chapter 4 we discussed a product/process matrix indicating that as products and volumes change, the most efficient layout is also likely to change. Therefore, the decision on a specific layout type may be a temporary one.

9.2 PROCESS LAYOUT

The most common approach in developing a process layout is to arrange departments consisting of similar or identical processes in a way that optimizes their relative placement. In many installations, optimal placement often translates into placing departments with large amounts of interdepartment traffic adjacent to one another. The primary goal in laying a manufacturing or distribution facility is to minimize material handling costs. In a service organization, the main objective is to minimize customer and worker travel time through the process.

Minimizing Interdependent Movement Costs

Consider the following simple example: Suppose that we want to arrange the six departments of a toy factory to minimize the interdepartmental material handling cost. Initially, let us make the assumption that all departments have the same amount of space, say, 40 feet by 40 feet and that the building is 80 feet wide and 120 feet long (and thus compatible with the department dimensions). The first thing we would want to know is the nature of the flow between departments and the way the material is transported. If the company has another factory that makes similar products, information about flow patterns might be obtained from these records. On the other hand, if this is a new product, such information would have to come from routing sheets (see Chapter 3) or from estimates by knowledgeable personnel such as process or industrial engineers. Of course these data, regardless of their source, have to be adjusted to reflect the nature of future orders over the projected life of the proposed layout.

Let us assume that this information is available. We find that all material is transported in a standard-size crate by forklift truck, one crate to a truck (which constitutes one "load"). Now suppose that transportation costs are $1 to move a load between adjacent departments and $1 extra for each department in between. The expected loads between

EXHIBIT 9.2

Interdepartmental Flow

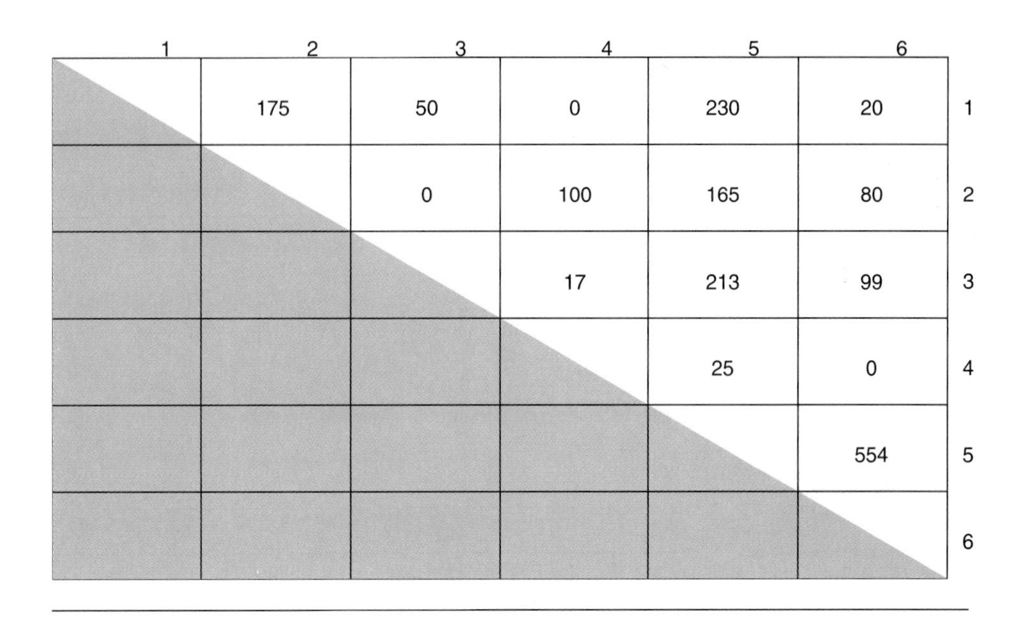

	1	2	3	4	5	6
1		175	50	0	230	20
2			0	100	165	80
3				17	213	99
4					25	0
5						554
6						

EXHIBIT 9.3

Building Dimensions and Departments

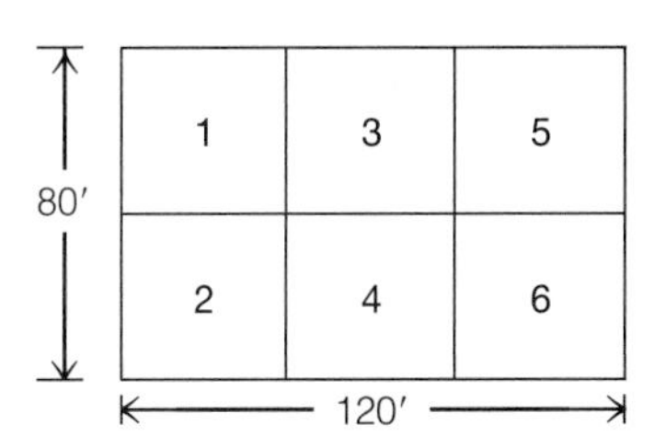

departments for the first year of operation are tabulated in Exhibit 9.2; the available plant space is depicted in Exhibit 9.3.

Given this information, our first step is to illustrate the interdepartmental flow by a model, such as Exhibit 9.4, which is Exhibit 9.2 displayed in the building layout in Exhibit 9.3. This provides the basic layout pattern, which we are trying to improve.

The second step is to determine the cost of this layout by multiplying the material handling cost by the number of loads moved between each department. Exhibit 9.5 presents this information, which is derived as follows: The annual material handling cost between Departments 1 and 2 is $175 ($1 × 175 moves), $460 between Departments 1 and 5 ($2 × 230 moves), and so forth. (The distances are taken from Exhibit 9.3 or 9.4, not Exhibit 9.2).

The third step is a search for departmental changes that reduces costs. On the basis of

EXHIBIT 9.4

Interdepartmental Flow Graph with Number of Annual Movements

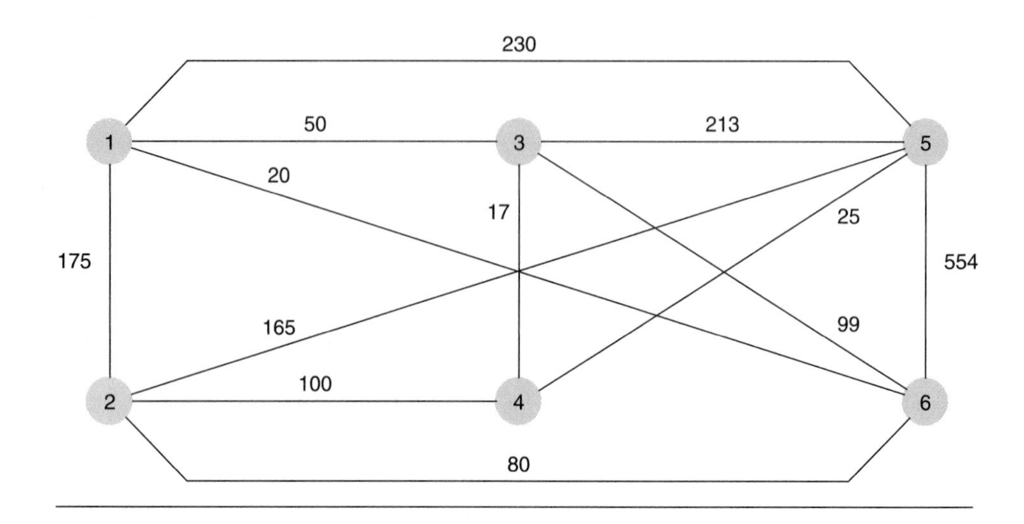

EXHIBIT 9.5

Cost Matrix—First Solution

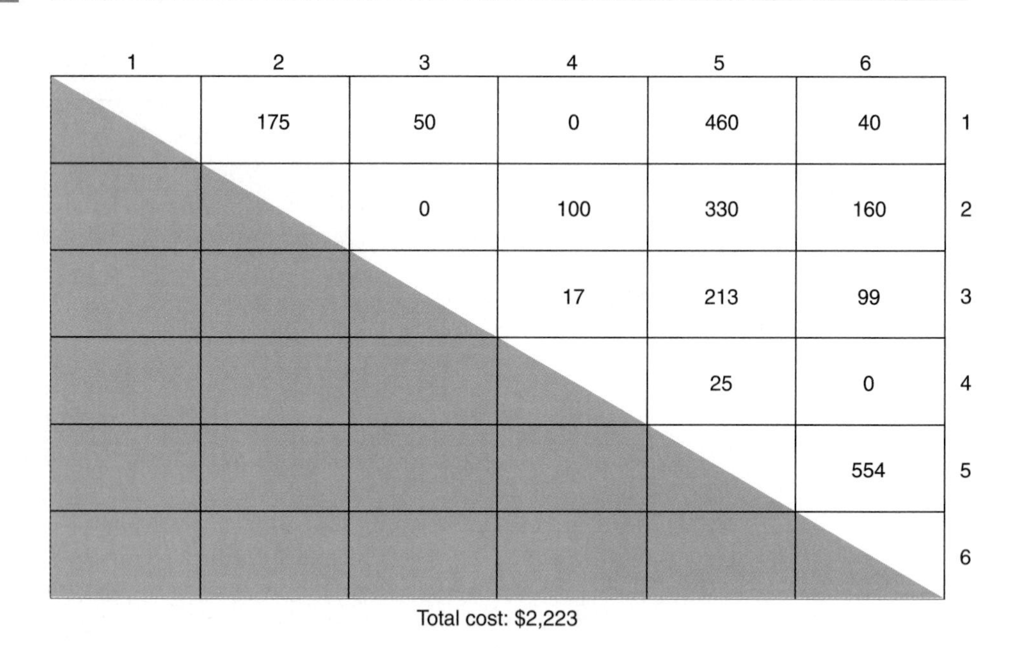

	1	2	3	4	5	6
1		175	50	0	460	40
2			0	100	330	160
3				17	213	99
4					25	0
5						554
6						

Total cost: $2,223

the graph and the cost matrix, it appears desirable to place Departments 1 and 5 closer together to reduce their high move-distance costs. However, this requires shifting another department, thereby affecting other move-distance costs and the total cost of the second solution. Exhibit 9.6 shows the revised layout resulting from relocating Department 5 and

EXHIBIT 9.6

Revised Interdepartmental Flow Chart*

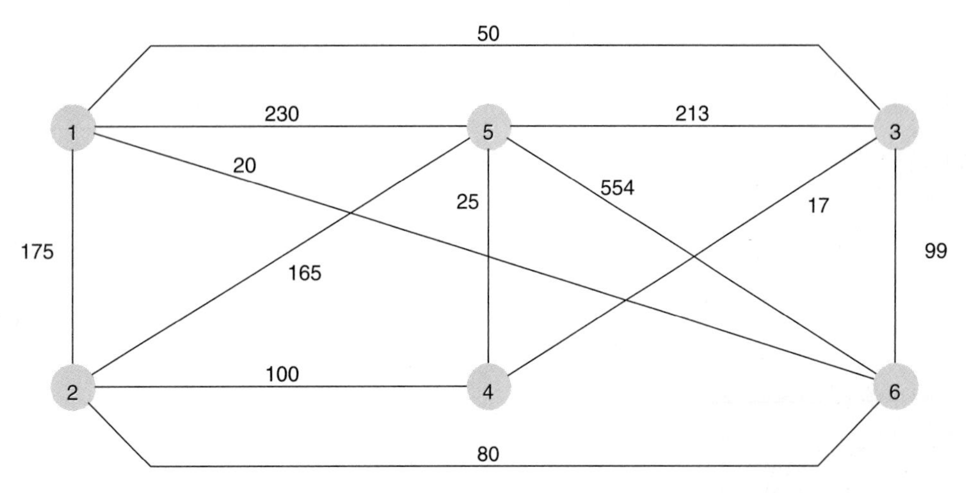

*Only interdepartmental flow with effect on cost is depicted.

an adjacent department (Department 3 is arbitrarily selected for this purpose). The revised cost matrix for the exchange, with the cost changes circled, is given in Exhibit 9.7. Note the total cost is now $345 less than in the initial solution. While this trial and error approach resulted in a lower total cost in this case, even in a small problem, it is often difficult to identify the correct "obvious move" on the basis of casual inspection.

Thus far, we have shown only one exchange among a large number of potential exchanges; in fact, for a six-department problem there are 6! (or 720) possible arrangements. Therefore, the procedure we have employed would have only a remote possibility of achieving an optimal combination in a "reasonable" number of tries. Nor does our problem stop here. Other factors must be taken into consideration.

Suppose that we *do* arrive at a good cut-and-try solution solely on the basis of material handling cost. Continuing with our toy factory example, if the sewing department is located next to the painting department it might cause both a hazard and defective products with lint, thread, and cloth particles drifting onto the painted items. Thus, issues like these must also be incorporated into the final layout decision.

Computerized Layout Techniques—CRAFT

A number of computerized layout programs have been developed over the past 25 years to help devise good process layouts. Of these, the original and still useful program is the Computerized Relative Allocation of Facilities Technique (CRAFT).[1]

[1] For a discussion of CRAFT and other methods, see R. L. Francis, L. F. McGinnis, and J. A. White, *Facility Layout and Location: An Analytical Approach* (Englewood Cliffs, N.J.: Prentice Hall, 1974).

EXHIBIT 9.7 Cost Matrix—Second Solution

	1	2	3	4	5	6		Net cost change
		175	100	0	230	40	1	+50 −230
			0	100	165	160	2	−165
				17	213	99	3	
					25	0	4	
						554	5	
							6	

Total cost: $1,878

Total difference: −345

The CRAFT method follows the same basic idea we developed in the layout of the toy factory but with some significant operational differences. Like the toy factory example, it requires a load matrix and a distance matrix as initial inputs, but in addition, it requires a cost-per-unit distance traveled, say $.10 per foot moved. (Remember, we made the simplifying assumption that cost doubled when material had to jump one department, and so forth.) With these inputs and an initial layout in the program, CRAFT then tries to improve the relative placement of the departments as measured by the total material handling cost for the layout. (Material handling cost between departments = Number of loads × Rectilinear distance between department centroids × Cost-per-unit distance.) It makes improvements by exchanging pairs of departments in an iterative manner until no further cost reductions are possible. That is, the program calculates the effect on total cost of exchanging departments; if this yields a reduction the exchange is made, which constitutes an iteration. As we note in the manual method, the departments are part of a material flow network, so even a simple pairwise exchange generally affects flow patterns among many other departments.

Each iteration is displayed in block layout form with the total cost for that layout, the cost reduction just made, and the departments just exchanged listed on the bottom of the printout. An example printout of CRAFT showing a final layout is given in Exhibit 9.8. (Letters designate and define the shape of each department. Lines would be drawn around each department to provide a more finished depiction of the layout.)

Distinguishing features of CRAFT and issues relating to it are:

EXHIBIT 9.8

Sample CRAFT Printout

Location pattern

	1	2	3	4	5	6	7	8	9	10	11	12	13	14	15	16
1	A	A	A	A	A	A	A	L	L	L	J	J	J	I	I	I
2	A					A	A	L		L	J		J	I		I
3	A					A	L	L		L	J	J	J	I		I
4	A					A	L	L	L	L	L	L	L	I		I
5	A					A	G	G	G	L			L	I		I
6	A	A	A	A	A	A	G	G	G	L			L	I	I	I
7	B	B	B	B	B	B	G	G	L	L			L	K	K	K
8	B				B	B	C	C	L			L	L	L	K	K
9	B				B	C	C	C	L			L	H	H	H	H
10	B				B	C		C	L	L	L	L	H			H
11	B	B	B	B	B	C	C	C	L	F	F	F	H			H
12	D	D	D	D	E	C	C	F	F	F	F	H	H	H	H	H
13	D		D	E	E	E	F	F	F	F	M	M	M	M	M	M
14	D		D	E		E	M	M	M	M	M					M
15	D		D	E		E	M									
16	D	D	D	E	E	E	M	M	M	M	M	M	M	M	M	M

Total cost: $87,963.81 Estimated cost reduction: $1,410.00

1. It is a heuristic program; it uses a simple rule of thumb in making evaluations: "compare two departments at a time and exchange them if it reduces the total cost of the layout." This type of rule is obviously necessary to analyze even a modest-sized layout.
2. Because it is heuristic, it does not guarantee an optimal solution.
3. CRAFT is "biased" by its starting conditions: where your start (i.e., the initial layout) determines the final layout.
4. Starting with a reasonably good solution is more likely to yield a lower-cost final solution, but not always. This means that a good strategy for using CRAFT is to generate a variety of different starting layouts to expose the program to different pairwise exchanges.
5. It can handle up to 40 departments and rarely exceeds 10 iterations in arriving at a solution.
6. CRAFT departments consist of combinations of square modules (typically representing floor areas 10 feet by 10 feet). This permits multiple departmental configurations, but often results in strange departmental shapes that have to be modified manually to obtain a realistic layout. (Take a look at Department L, for example, in Exhibit 9.8.)

7. CRAFT assumes the existence of variable path material handling equipment such as forklift trucks. Therefore, when computerized fixed-path equipment applications grow (as discussed later), the applicability of CRAFT becomes greatly reduced.

9.3 PRODUCT LAYOUT

When product demand is high enough and continuous over a period of time, it is usually cost effective to rearrange resources from a process layout to a product layout as defined by the sequence required to make the product. We often call these *assembly* lines, although the ratio of direct manual labor to machine work can vary widely. Assembly lines can vary from virtually 100 percent parts assembly by workers, to the other extreme, a *transfer* line, where all direct work is done by machine. In between are all types: Automobile lines have tools ranging from simple hammers and wrenches to automatic welding and painting. Assembly lines in electronics can also range widely from manual parts assembly to equipment for automatic parts insertion, automatic soldering, and automatic testing.

Assembly Lines

Assembly lines are a special case of product layout. In a general sense, the term *assembly line* refers to a progressive assembly linked by some type of material handling device. The usual assumption is that some form of pacing is present and the allowable processing time is equivalent for all workstations. Within this broad definition, there are important differences among line types. A few of these are: material handling devices (belt or roller conveyor, overhead crane); line configuration (U-shape, straight, branching); pacing (machine, human); product mix (one product or multiple products); workstation characteristics (workers may sit, stand, walk with the line, or ride the line); and length of the line (few or many workers).

The range of products partially or completely assembled on lines includes toys, appliances, autos, garden equipment, and a wide variety of electronic components. In fact, it is probably safe to say that virtually any product with multiple parts and produced in large volume uses assembly lines to some degree. Clearly, assembly lines are an important technology; and to really understand their managerial requirements, one must have some familiarity with how a line is balanced.

An important consideration that should not be overlooked in designing assembly lines is the human factor. Early assembly lines were machine paced, that is, they moved at a predetermined pace, regardless of whether or not the work was completed at a station. Under this structure, workers who fell behind were rushed to complete their assigned tasks, often resulting in faulty workmanship.

In recent years, worker-paced assembly lines, advocated initially by Japanese manufacturers, have replaced machine-paced lines in many facilities. With the worker-paced line, the operator continues to work on the product until the work assigned is satisfactorily completed. Only then is the product allowed to move on to the next station. The quality of the products made on a worker-paced line is significantly higher than that of products made on a comparable machine-paced line. When a Japanese manufacturer took over the production of televisions from a U.S. company, the number of defects dropped from 160

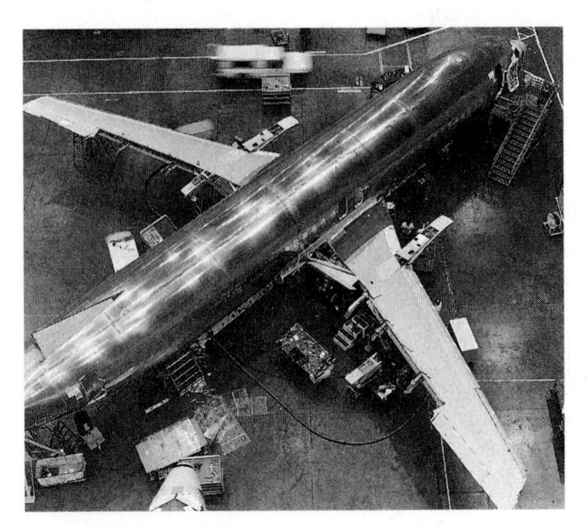

Courtesy The Boeing Company

The Boeing assembly process is an example of a fixed position layout where the processes and parts "come to the plane" rather than moving the plane through the system.

defects per 100 TVs to 4 defects per 100 TVs, even though the output per day and the work force remained virtually unchanged. This dramatic increase in quality was attributed, in large part, to the installation of a worker-paced assembly line that replaced the previously existing machine-paced line.[2]

Assembly line balancing

An assembly line consists of a series of workstations, each with a uniform time interval called a **cycle time** (which is also the time between successive units coming off the end of the line). At each workstation, work is performed on a product by adding parts and/or by completing assembly operations. The work performed at each station is made up of many *tasks* (also referred to as *elements,* or *work units*). Such tasks are described by motion-time analysis. Generally, they are groupings that cannot be subdivided on the assembly line without paying a high penalty in extra motions.

The total work to be performed at a workstation is equal to the sum of the tasks assigned to that workstation. The **assembly line balancing** problem is one of assigning all tasks to a series of workstations so that the time required to do the work at each station does not exceed the cycle time, and at the same time, the unassigned (i.e., idle) time across all workstations is minimized. An additional consideration here in designing the line is to assign the tasks as equitably as possible to the stations. The problem is further complicated by the relationships among tasks imposed by product design and process technologies. This is called the **precedence relationship,** which specifies the order in which the tasks must be performed in the assembly process.

---

[2]Dobyns, Lloyd, and Reuven Frank, *If Japan Can, Why Can't We?* New York: NBC-TV News Presentation, June 24, 1980.

Steps in assembly line balancing. The steps in balancing an assembly line are straightforward:

1. Specify the sequential relationship among tasks using a precedence diagram. The diagram consists of circles and arrows. Circles represent individual tasks, arrows indicate the order of task performance.
2. Determine the required cycle time (C), using the following formula:

$$C = \frac{\text{Production time per day}}{\text{Output per day (in units)}}$$

3. Determine the theoretical minimum number of workstations (N_t) required to satisfy the cycle time constraint, using the following formula:

$$N_t = \frac{\text{Sum of task times } (T)}{\text{Cycle time } (C)}$$

4. Select a primary rule by which tasks are to be assigned to workstations, and a secondary rule to break ties.
5. Assign tasks, one at a time, to the first workstation until the sum of the task times is equal to the cycle time, or no other tasks are feasible because of time or sequence restrictions. Repeat the process for Workstation 2, Workstation 3, etc., until all tasks are assigned.
6. Evaluate the efficiency of the balance derived using the formula:

$$\text{Efficiency} = \frac{\text{Sum of task times } (T)}{\text{Actual number of workstations } (N_a) \times \text{Cycle time } (C)}$$

7. If efficiency is unsatisfactory, rebalance using a different decision rule.

Example

A toy company produces a Model J Wagon that is to be assembled on a conveyor belt. Five hundred wagons are required per day. The company is currently operating on a one-shift, eight-hour-a-day schedule, with one hour off for lunch (i.e., net production time per day is seven hours). The assembly steps and times for the wagon are given in Exhibit 9.9. Assignment: Find the balance that minimizes the number of workstations, subject to cycle time and precedence constraints.

1. Draw a precedence diagram. Exhibit 9.10 illustrates the sequential relationships identified in Exhibit 9.9. (The length of the arrows has no meaning.)
2. Cycle time determination. Here we have to convert to seconds since our task times are in seconds.

$$C = \frac{\text{Production time per day}}{\text{Output per day}} = \frac{\text{7hrs./day} \times \text{60 min./hr.} \times \text{60 sec./min.}}{\text{500 wagons}}$$

$$= \frac{25{,}200}{500} = 50.4 \text{ seconds}$$

EXHIBIT 9.9

Assembly Steps and Times for Model J Wagon

Task	Performance Time (in seconds)	Description	Tasks that Must Precede
A	45	Position rear axle support and hand fasten four screws to nuts	—
B	11	Insert rear axle	A
C	9	Tighten rear axle support screws to nuts	B
D	50	Position front axle assembly and hand fasten with four screws to nuts	—
E	15	Tighten front axle assembly screws	D
F	12	Position rear wheel #1 and fasten hub cap	C
G	12	Position rear wheel #2 and fasten hub cap	C
H	12	Position front wheel #1 and fasten hub cap	E
I	12	Position front wheel #2 and fasten hub cap	E
J	8	Position wagon handle shaft on front axle assembly and hand fasten bolt and nut	F, G, H, I
K	9	Tighten bolt and nut	J
	195		

3. Theoretical minimum number of workstations required (the actual number may be greater):

$$N_t = \frac{T}{C} = \frac{195 \text{ seconds}}{50.4 \text{ seconds}} = 3.86 \text{ stations} \rightarrow 4 \text{ stations}$$

(Since we cannot have a fraction of a station, we always round up to the next whole integer. For this example, the minimum number of stations is four.)

4. Select assignment rules. Research has shown that some rules are better than others for certain problem structures. In general, the strategy is to use a rule assigning tasks that either have many followers or are of long duration since they effectively limit the balance achievable. In this case, we use as our primary rule:

EXHIBIT 9.10

Precedence Graph for Model J Wagon

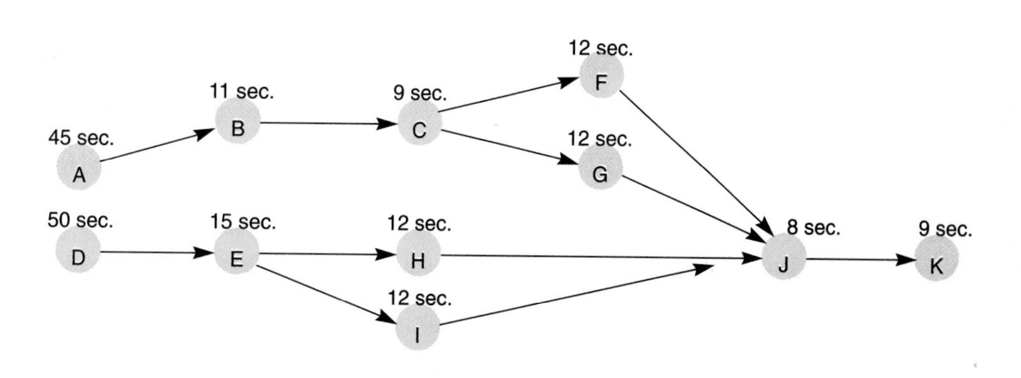

a. Assign tasks in order of the largest number of following tasks. Our secondary rule, to be invoked where ties exist from our primary rule, is

b. Assign tasks in order of longest operating time.

Task	Total Number of Following Tasks	Following Tasks
A	6	B, C, F, G, J, K
B or D	5	C, F, G, J, K (for B)
C or E	4	H, I, J, K (for E)
F, G, H, or I	2	J, K
J	1	K
K	0	—

5. Make task assignments to form Workstation 1, Workstation 2, and so forth, until all tasks are assigned. The actual assignment is given in Exhibit 9.11A and is shown graphically in Exhibit 9.11B.
6. Calculate the efficiency. This is shown in Exhibit 9.11C.
7. Evaluate solution. An efficiency of 77 percent indicates an imbalance or idle time of 23 percent (1.0 − .77) across the entire line. From Exhibit 9.11A we can see that there are 57 total seconds of idle time, and the "choice" job is at Workstation 5.

Is a better balance possible? In this case, yes. Try balancing the line with rule *b* and breaking ties with rule *a*. (This will give you a feasible four-station balance.)

Often the longest required task time dictates the shortest cycle time for the production line. This task time becomes the lower time bound, unless it is possible to split the task into two or more workstations.

Consider the following illustration: Supposing that an assembly line contains the following task times in seconds: 40, 30, 15, 25, 20, 18, 15. The line runs for 7½ hours per day and demand for output is 750 per day.

The cycle time required to produce 750 per day is 36 seconds ([7½ × 60 minutes × 60 seconds]/[750]). How do we deal with the task that is 40 seconds long?

There are several ways that we may be able to accommodate the 40-second task in a 36-second cycle. Possibilities are:

1. *Split the task.* Can we split the task so that complete units are processed in two workstations?
2. *Duplicate the station.* By duplicating the task at two stations, the effective task time is reduced by 50 percent. If necessary, additional stations can be assigned to the same task to further lower the effective task time. Often with this approach, several tasks may be combined into one station to increase efficiency. In the example given, the first two tasks with 40 and 30 seconds each would be combined into one station, which would then be duplicated. The effective cycle time for this station is then 35 seconds ([40 + 30]/2), which is below the required cycle time of 36 seconds.
3. *Share the task.* Can the task somehow be shared so an adjacent workstation does part

EXHIBIT 9.11

A. Balance Made According to Largest Number of Following Tasks Rule

	Task	Task Time (in seconds)	Remaining Unassigned Time (in seconds)	Feasible Remaining Tasks	Task with Most Followers	Task with Longest Operation Time
Station 1	A	45	5.4 idle	None		
Station 2	D	50	0.4 idle	None		
Station 3	B	11	39.4	C, E	C, E	E
	E	15	24.4	C, H, I	C	
	C	9	15.4	F, G, H, I	F, G, H, I	F, G, H, I
	F*	12	3.4 idle	None		
Station 4	G	12	38.4	H, I	H, I	H, I
	H*	12	26.4	I		
	I	12	14.4	J		
	J	8	6.4 idle	None		
Station 5	K	9	41.4 idle	None		

*Denotes task arbitrarily selected where there is a tie between longest operation times.

B. Precedence Graph for Model J. Wagon

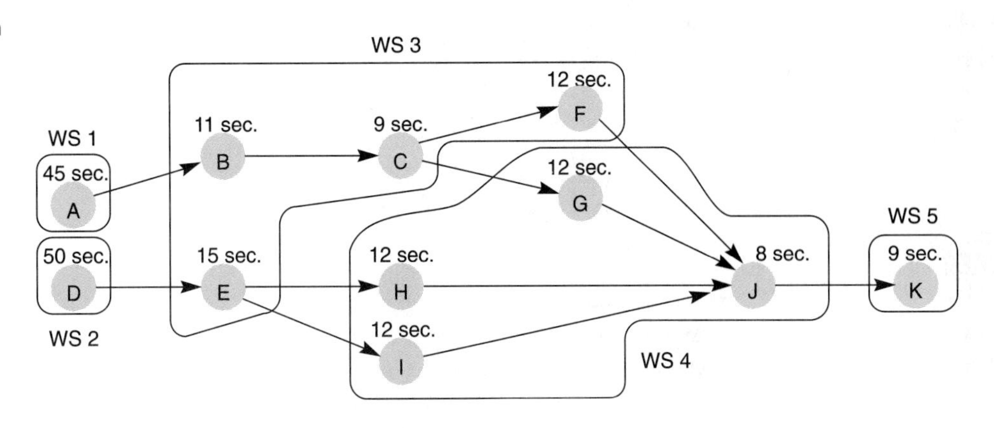

C. Efficiency Calculation

$$\text{Efficiency} = \frac{T}{NC} = \frac{195}{(5)\ (50.4)} = .77, \text{ or } 77\%$$

of the work? This differs from the split task in the first option because the adjacent station acts to assist, not to do some units containing the entire task.

4. *Use a more skilled worker.* Since this task exceeds the cycle time by just 11 percent, a faster worker may be able to meet the 36-second time.
5. *Work overtime.* Producing at a rate of one every 40 seconds would produce 675 per day, 75 short of the needed 750. The amount of overtime required to do the additional 75 is 50 minutes (75 × 40 seconds/60 seconds).
6. *Redesign.* It may be possible to redesign the product to reduce the task time slightly.

Other possibilities to reduce the task time include equipment upgrading, a roaming helper

EXHIBIT 9.12

Flexible Line Layouts

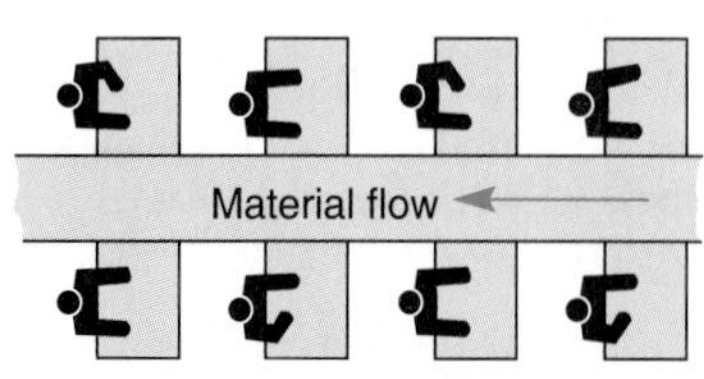

Bad: Operators caged. No chance to trade elements of work between them. (subassembly line layout common in American plants)

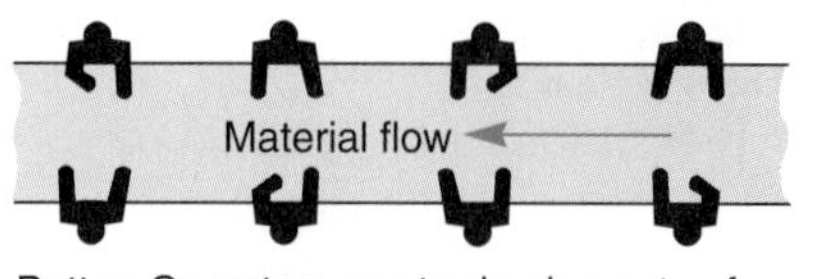

Better: Operators can trade elements of work. Can add and subtract operators. Trained ones can nearly self-balance at different output rates.

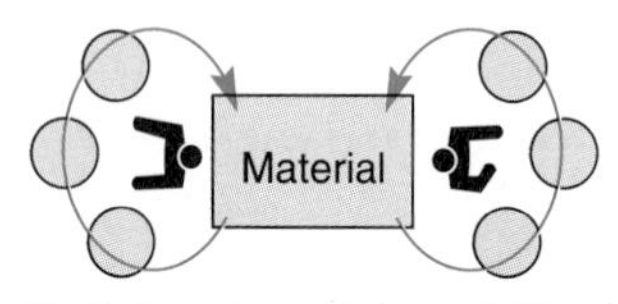

Bad: Operators birdcaged. No chance to increase output with a third operator.

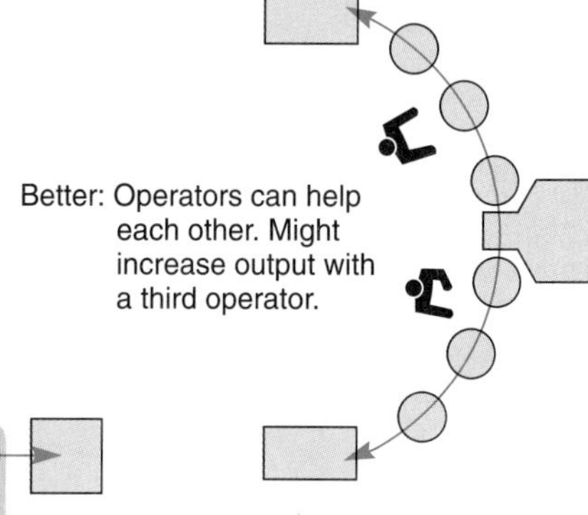

Better: Operators can help each other. Might increase output with a third operator.

Bad: Straight line difficult to balance.

Better: One of several advantages of U-Line is better operator access. Here, five operators were reduced to four.

Source: Robert W. Hall, *Attaining Manufacturing Excellence* (Homewood, Ill.: Dow Jones-Irwin, 1987), p. 125.

to support the line, a change of materials, and multiskilled workers to operate the line as a team rather than as independent workers.

Flexible line layouts

As we saw in the preceding example, assembly line balances frequently result in unequal workstation times. In fact, the shorter the cycle time, the greater the probability of a higher percentage of imbalance in the line. Flexible line layouts such as those shown in Exhibit 9.12 are a common way of dealing with this problem. In our toy company example, the U-shaped line with work sharing at the bottom of the figure could help resolve the imbalance.

Computerized line balancing

Companies engaged in assembly methods commonly employ a computer for line balancing. Most develop their own computer programs, but commercial package programs are also widely applied. One of these is General Electric Company's *Assembly-Line Configuration (ASYBL$),* which uses the "ranked positional weight" rule in selecting tasks for workstations. Specifically, this rule states that tasks are assigned according to their positional weights, which is the time for a given task plus the task times of all those that follow it. Thus, the task with the highest positional weight would be assigned to the first workstation (subject to time, precedence, and zoning constraints). As is typical with such software, the user has several options for how the problem is to be solved.

Mixed-model line balancing

To meet the demand for a variety of products and to avoid building high inventories of one product model, many manufacturers often schedule several different models to be produced over a given day or week on the same line. To illustrate how this is done, suppose our toy company has a fabrication line to bore holes in its Model J Wagon frame and its Model K Wagon frame. The time required to bore the holes is different for each wagon type.

Assume that the final assembly line downstream requires equal numbers of Model J and Model K wagon frames. Also assume that we want to develop a cycle time for the fabrication line, which is balanced for the production of equal numbers of J and K frames. Of course, we could produce Model J frames for several days and then produce Model K frames until an equal number of frames has been produced. However, this would build up unnecessary work in-process inventory.

If we want to reduce the amount of in-process inventory, we could develop a cycle mix that greatly reduces inventory buildup while keeping within the restrictions of equal numbers of J and K wagon frames.

Example

Process times: 6 minutes per J and 4 minutes per K.

The day consists of 480 minutes (8 hours × 60 minutes).

$6J + 4K = 480$

Since equal numbers of J and K are to be produced (or J = K), produce 48J and 48K per day, or 6J and 6K per hour.

The following shows one balance of J and K frames.

Balanced Mixed-Model Sequence

Model sequence	J J	K K K	J J	J J	K K K	
Operation time	6 6	4 4 4	6 6	6 6	4 4 4	Repeats 8 times per day
Minicycle time	12	12	12	12	12	
Total cycle time			60			

This line is balanced at six wagon frames of each type per hour with a minicycle time of 12 minutes.

Another balance is J K K J K J, with times of 6, 4, 4, 6, 4, 6. This balance produces three J and three K every 30 minutes with a minicycle time of 10 minutes (JK, KJ, KJ).

The simplicity of mixed-model balancing (under conditions of a level production schedule) is seen on Yasuhiro Mondon's description of Toyota Motor Corporation's operations:

1. Final Assembly lines of Toyota are mixed product lines. The production per day is averaged by taking the number of vehicles in the monthly production schedule classified by specifications, and dividing by the number of working days.
2. In regard to the production sequence during each day, the cycle time of each different specification vehicle is calculated and in order to have all specification vehicles appear at their own cycle time, different specification vehicles are ordered to follow each other.[3]

Ford Motor Company's assembly plant in Wixom, Michigan, provides another good example of how, with careful planning, several different products can be made on assembly lines. The Wixom plant produces the Mark VIII, the Lincoln Continental, and the Lincoln Town Car. To further complicate the situation, the Continental is a front-wheel drive vehicle on a unibody chassis, whereas the Town Car and the Mark VIII are rear-wheel drive models mounted on a standard frame chassis. The line producing the Continental and the Town Car can be balanced by having between 67 percent and 75 percent of the cars being rear-wheel drive models. Although the Mark VIII is assembled on its own line, all three models share the same paint shop. Currently, the output from the Mark VIII line is 10 cars per hour, and the Continental/Town Car line produces 42 cars per hour.

The **mixed-model line** appears to be a relatively straightforward sequencing problem. This is because in our example the two models fit nicely into a common time period that also matched demand. From a mathematical standpoint, designing a mixed-model line is very difficult and no technique exists to provide the optimum assignment of tasks to workstations. This is because the mixed-model line involves multiple lot sizes, lot sequencing, setup times for each lot, differing workstation sizes along the line, and task variations. The problem is to design the assembly line and workstations and specify exactly which tasks are to be done in each.

The objectives of a mixed-model line design are to minimize idle time and minimize the inefficiencies caused by changing from model to model. Researchers have used integer programming, branch and bound techniques, and simulation. They still are not able to find the optimal solution for a realistic sized, real-world problem.

Current Thoughts on Assembly Lines

It is true that the widespread use of assembly-line methods in manufacturing has dramatically increased output rates. Historically, the focus has almost always been on full utilization of human labor; that is, to design assembly lines minimizing human idle times. Equipment and

[3] S. Manivannan and Dipak Chudhuri, "Computer-Aided Facility Layout Algorithm Generates Alternatives to Increase Firm's Productivity," *Industrial Engineering* (May 1984), pp. 81–84.

EXHIBIT 9.13

Assembly Lines: Traditional versus New Focus

	Traditional	
1.	Top priority: line balance	Top priority: flexibility
2.	Strategy: stability—long production runs so that the need to rebalance seldom occurs	Strategy: flexibility—expect to [illegible] often to match output to changing demand
3.	Assume fixed labor assignments	Flexible labor: move to the problems or to where the current workload is
4.	Use inventory buffers to cushion effects of equipment failure	Employ maximal preventive maintenance to keep equipment from breaking down
5.	Need sophisticated analysis (e.g., using computers) to evaluate and cull the many options	Need human ingenuity to provide flexibility and ways around bottlenecks
6.	Planned by staff	Supervisor may lead design effort and will adjust plan as needed
7.	Plan to run at fixed rate; send quality problems off line	Slow for quality problems; speed up when quality is right
8.	Linear or L-shaped lines	U-shaped or parallel lines
9.	Conveyorized material movement is desirable	Put stations close together and avoid conveyors
10.	Buy "supermachines" and keep them busy	Make (or buy) small machines; add more copies as needed
11.	Applied in labor-intensive final assembly	Applied even to capital-intensive subassembly and fabrication work
12.	Run mixed models where labor content is similar from model to model	Strive for mixed-model production, even in subassembly and fabrication

Source: Richard J. Schonberger, *Japanese Manufacturing Techniques: Nine Hidden Lessons in Simplicity* (New York: Free Press, 1982), p. 133.

facility utilization stood in the background as much less important. Past research has tried to find optimal solutions as if the problem stood in a never-changing world.

Newer views of assembly lines take a broader perspective. Intentions are to incorporate greater flexibility in products manufactured on the line, more variability in workstations (such as size, number of workers), improved reliability (through routine preventive maintenance), and high-quality output (through improved tooling and training). Exhibit 9.13 compares some old and new ideas about production lines.

9.4 GROUP TECHNOLOGY (CELLULAR) LAYOUT

Group technology (or cellular) layout allocates dissimilar machines into cells to work on products that have similar weights, shapes, and processing requirements. Group technology (GT) layouts are now widely used in metal fabricating, computer chip manufacture, and assembly work. The overall objective is to gain the benefits of product layout in job-shop kinds of production. These benefits include:

1. Better human relations. Cells consist of a few workers who form a small work team; a team turns out complete units of work.
2. Improved operator expertise. Workers see only a limited number of different pairs in a finite production cycle, so repetition means quick learning.
3. Less in-process inventory and material handling. A cell combines several production stages, so fewer parts travel through the shop.
4. Faster production setup. Fewer jobs mean reduced tooling and hence faster tooling changes.

Developing a GT Layout

Shifting from process layout to a GT cellular layout entails three steps:

1. Grouping parts into families that follow a common sequence of steps. This step requires developing and maintaining a computerized parts classification and coding system. This is often a major expense with such systems, although many companies have developed short-cut procedures for identifying parts-families.
2. Identifying dominant flow patterns of parts-families as a basis for location or relocation of processes.
3. Physically grouping machines and processes into cells. Often some parts cannot be associated with a family and specialized machinery cannot be placed in any one cell because of its general use. These unattached parts and machinery are placed in a "remainder cell."

Exhibit 9.14 illustrates the cell development process followed by Rockwell's Telecommunication Division, which produces wave-guide parts. Part A shows the original process-oriented layout; part B the planned relocation of process based on the parts-family production requirements; and part C an enlarged layout of the cell designed to perform all but the finishing operation. According to Richard Schonberger, cellular organization was practical here because (1) distinct parts-families existed; (2) there were several of each type of machine, and taking a machine out of a cluster therefore did not rob the cluster of all its capacity, leaving no way to produce other products; (3) the work centers were easily movable stand-alone machine tools—heavy, but anchored to the floor rather simply. He adds that these three features represent general guidelines for deciding where a cellular layout or group technology make sense.[4]

The group technology (GT) problem consists of three phases:

1. Develop a classification and coding scheme for items (shape, size, materials, etc.).
2. From processing requirements and routings, group parts into families to form cell groups.
3. Create the physical layout positioning cells relative to each other.

[4]Richard J. Schonberger, *World Class Manufacturing: The Lessons of Simplicity Applied* (New York: Free Press, 1986), p. 112.

EXHIBIT 9.14 Developing a Cell to Produce Wave-Guide Parts

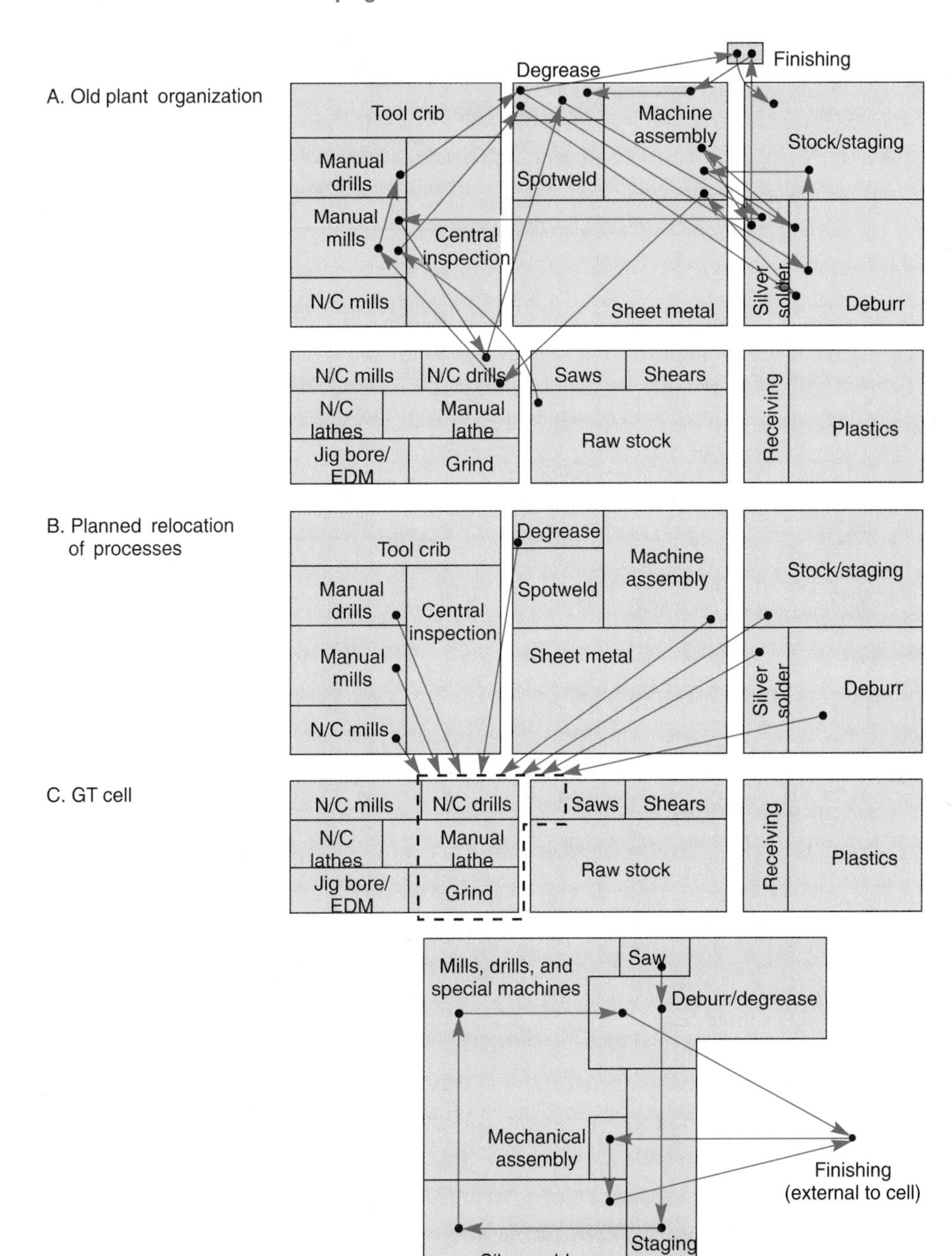

Source: Reprinted with permission of the Free Press, a Division of Macmillan, Inc. from *World Class Manufacturing* by Richard J. Schonberger. Copyright © 1986 by Schonberger & Associates, Inc.

When equipment is not easily movable, many companies dedicate a given machine out of a set of identical machines in a process layout. A conceptual GT cell for, say, a two-month production run for the job might consist of Drill 1 in the drills area, Mill 3 in the mill area, and Assembly Area 1 in the machine assembly area. To approximate a GT flow, all work on the particular parts-family would be done only on these specific machines.

9.5 CONCLUSION

A major issue to be addressed in facility layout decisions in manufacturing is: How flexible should the layout be in order to be able to adjust to future changes in product demand and product mix? Some have argued that the best strategy is to have movable equipment that can be shifted easily from place to place to reduce material flow time for near-term contracts. However, while this is appealing in general, the limitations of existing buildings and firmly anchored equipment, and the general plant disruption that is created make this a very costly strategy.

In service systems, particularly franchises, the study of layout has become extremely important because the selected layout may become replicated at hundreds or even thousands of facilities. Indeed, a layout error in a fast-food chain has a more immediate, and generally a more far-reaching, effect on profits than a layout error in a factory.

9.6 REVIEW AND DISCUSSION QUESTIONS

1. What kind of layout is used in a physical fitness center?
2. What is the objective of assembly line balancing? How would you deal with the situation where one worker, although trying hard, is 20 percent slower than the other 10 people on a line?
3. How do you determine the idle-time percentage from a given assembly line balance?
4. What information of particular importance do route sheets and process charts (discussed in Chapter 4) provide to the layout planner?
5. What is the essential requirement for mixed-model lines to be practical?
6. Why might it be difficult to develop a GT layout?
7. In what respects is facility layout a marketing problem in services? Give an example of a service system layout designed to maximize the amount of time the customer is in the system.

9.7 SOLVED PROBLEMS

PROBLEM

1. A university advising office has four rooms, each dedicated to specific problems: petitions (Room A), schedule advising (Room B), grade complaints (Room C), and student counseling (Room D). The office is 80 feet long and 20 feet wide. Each room is 20 feet by 20 feet. The present location of rooms is A, B, C, D; that is, a straight line. The load summary shows the number of contacts that each advisor in a room has with other advisors in the other rooms. Assume that all advisors are equal in this value.

Load summary: AB = 10, AC = 20, AD = 30,
BC = 15, BD = 10, CD = 20.

a. Evaluate this layout according to one of the methods in the chapter.

b. Improve the layout by exchanging functions within rooms. Show your amount of improvement using the same method as in *a.*

SOLUTION

a. Evaluate this layout according to one of the methods in the chapter.

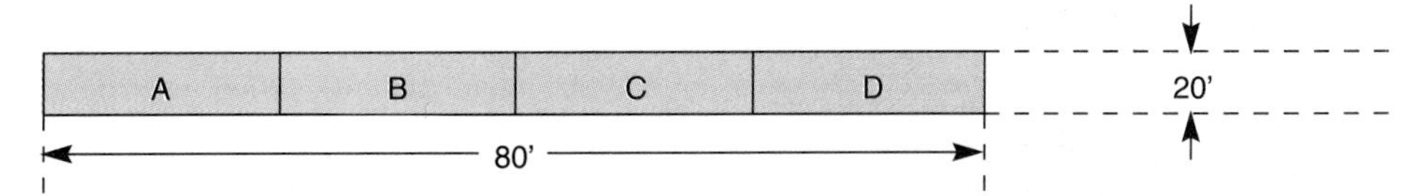

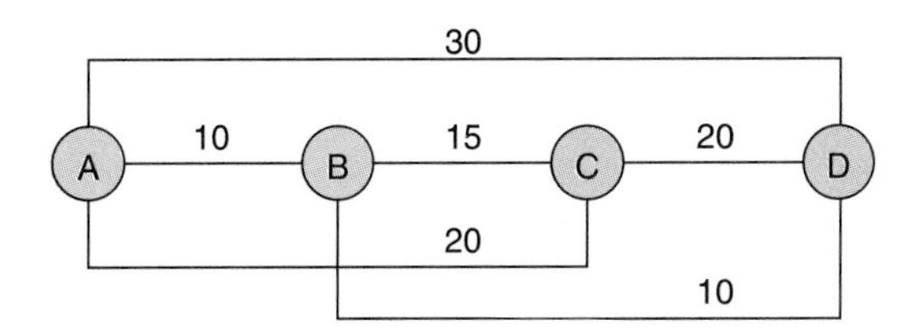

Using the material handling cost method shown in the toy company example we obtain the following costs, assuming that every nonadjacency doubles the initial cost/unit distance:

AB = 10 × 1 = 10

AC = 20 × 2 = 40

AD = 30 × 3 = 90

BC = 15 × 1 = 15

BD = 10 × 2 = 20

CD = 20 × 1 = 20

Current cost = 195

b. Improve the layout by exchanging functions within rooms. Show your amount of improvement using the same method as in *a.* A better layout would be BCDA.

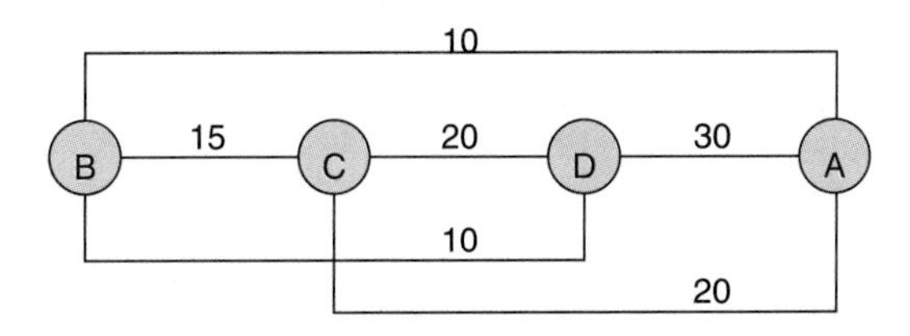

AB = 10 X 3 = $ 30
AC = 20 X 2 = 40
AD = 30 X 1 = 30
BC = 15 X 1 = 15
BD = 10 X 2 = 20
CD = 20 X 1 = 20
Improved cost = $ 155

PROBLEM

2. The following tasks must be performed on an assembly line in the sequence and times specified.

Task	Task Time (seconds)	Tasks That Must Precede
A	50	—
B	40	—
C	20	A
D	45	C
E	20	C
F	25	D
G	10	E
H	35	B, F, G

a. Draw the schematic diagram.

b. What is the theoretical minimum number of stations required to meet a forecasted demand of 400 units per eight-hour day?

c. Use the longest operating time rule and balance the line in the minimum number of stations to produce 400 units per day.

d. Compute the efficiency of the line.

e. Does your solution generate any managerial concerns?

SOLUTION

a. Draw the schematic diagram.

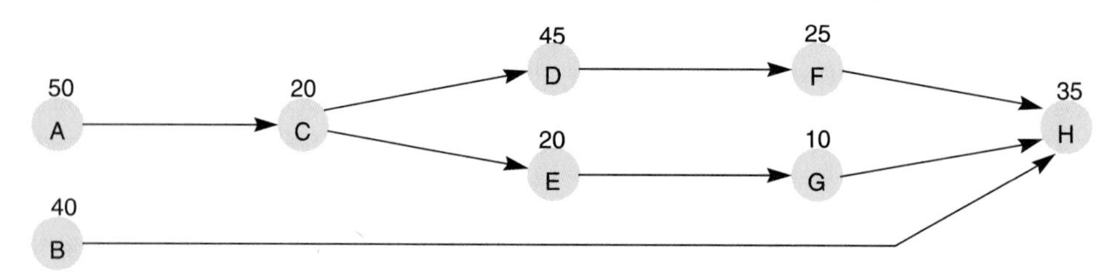

b. Theoretical minimum number of stations to meet D = 400 is:

$$N_t = \frac{T}{C} = \frac{245 \text{ seconds}}{\left(\dfrac{60 \text{ seconds} \times 480 \text{ minutes}}{400 \text{ units}}\right)} = \frac{245}{72} = 3.4 \rightarrow 4 \text{ stations}$$

c. Use the longest operating time rule and balance the line in the minimum number of stations to produce 400 units per day.

	Task	Task Time (seconds)	Remaining Unassigned Time	Feasible Remaining Tasks
Station 1	A	50	22	C
	C	20	2	None
Station 2	D	45	27	E, F
	F	25	2	None
Station 3	B	40	32	E
	E	20	12	G
	G	10	2	None
Station 4	H	35	37	None

Note: With this solution the actual cycle time is 70 seconds, as determined by stations 1, 2, and 3.

d. Efficiency $= \dfrac{T}{N_a \times C} = \dfrac{245}{4(70)} = 87.5\%$

e. Yes. Station 4 is only half as busy as the other three stations.

9.8 PROBLEMS

1. An assembly line makes two models of trucks—a Buster and a Duster. Busters take 12 minutes each and Dusters take 8 minutes each. The daily output requirement is 24 of each per day. Develop a perfectly balanced mixed-model sequence to satisfy demand.
2. The following tasks and the order in which they must be performed according to their assembly requirements are shown in the following table. These are to be combined into workstations to create an assembly line.

   The assembly line operates 7½ hours per day. The output requirement is 1,000 units per day.

Task	Preceding Tasks	Time (seconds)
A	—	15
B	A	24
C	A	6
D	B	12
E	B	18
F	C	7
G	C	11
H	D	9
I	E	14
J	F, G	7
K	H, I	15
L	J, K	10

   a. What is the cycle time?
   b. Balance the line based on the 1,000 unit forecast, stating which tasks would be done in each workstation.
   c. For *b* above, what is the efficiency of your line balance?
   d. After production was started, Marketing realized that they understated demand and will need to increase output to 1,100 units. What action would you take? Be specific in quantitative terms, if appropriate.

3. An assembly line is operated seven hours per day and produces 420 units per day. Following are the tasks that are performed with their performance time and preceding tasks.

Task	Time (seconds)	Preceding Tasks
A	15	None
B	15	None
C	45	A, B
D	45	C

   Compute the cycle time and the theoretical minimum number of workstations, and prepare an initial line configuration. Determine the efficiency of your layout.

4. An initial solution has been given to the following process layout problem. Given the flows described and a cost of $2.00 per unit per foot, compute the total cost for the layout. Each location is 100 feet long and 50 feet wide as shown on the figure below. Use the centers of departments for distances and compute using rectilinear distances.

		Department			
		A	B	C	D
Department	A	0	10	25	55
	B		0	10	5
	C			0	15
	D				0

	100′	100′	100′	
50′	A	B	C	50′
			D	50′

5. An assembly line will operate eight hours per day and produce 480 units per day. The task times and precedence relationships are summarized below. Prepare an initial line configuration using the longest operating time rule, and determine the efficiency of your layout.

Task	Time (seconds)	Preceding Tasks
A	20	None
B	40	A
C	35	B
D	35	B
E	35	C, D

6. An assembly line is to be designed which will operate 7½ hours per day and supply a steady demand of 300 units per day. Following are the tasks and their task performance times.

Task	Preceding Tasks	Performance Time (Seconds)
a	—	70
b	—	40
c	—	45
d	a	10
e	b	30
f	c	20
g	d	60
h	e	50
i	f	15
j	g	25
k	h, i	20
l	j, k	25

a. Draw the precedence diagram.
b. What is the cycle time?
c. What is the theoretical minimum number of workstations?
d. Assign tasks to workstations, stating what your logical rule is.
e. What is the efficiency of your line balance?
f. Suppose demand increases by 10 percent. How would you react to this?

7. Given the following data on the task precedence relationships for an assembled product and assuming the tasks cannot be split, what is the theoretical minimum cycle time?

Task	Performance Time (minutes)	Tasks That Must Precede
A	3	
B	6	A
C	7	A
D	5	A
E	2	A
F	4	B, C
G	5	C
H	5	D, E, F, G

a. Determine the number of workstations needed to achieve this cycle time using the "ranked positional weight" rule.

b. Determine the minimum number of stations needed to meet a cycle time of 10 minutes according to the "largest number of following tasks" rule.

c. Compute the efficiency of the balances achieved.

8. Simon's Mattress Factory is planning to introduce a new line of "pillow-top" mattresses. Current plans are to produce the mattresses on an assembly line. Mattresses will be built on individual platforms pulled by a chain in a track in the floor. This will allow workers to completely walk around the mattress. Tools will be suspended from the ceiling, so that there will not be a problem with tangling cords or wrapping them around the platform.

The assembly-line process starts with the basic spring foundation and builds the mattress as it progresses down the line. There are 12 operations required and their times and process sequence are as follows:

Operation	Time (minutes)	Tasks That Must Precede
A	1	—
B	3	A
C	4	B
D	1	B
E	5	C
F	4	D
G	1	E, F
H	2	G
I	5	G
J	3	H
K	2	I
L	3	J, K

Tentative plans are to operate the line 7½ hours per day. Demand for the mattresses is expected to be 70 per day.

a. Draw the schematic diagram.

b. What is the cycle time?

c. What is the theoretical minimum number of workstations.

d. Create a reasonable layout.

e. Supposing the plan was to produce these in a job shop layout. Discuss and compare the characteristics, pros, cons, etc. of job shop versus assembly line for this mattress production.

9. XYZ Manufacturing Company received a contract for 20,000 units of a product to be delivered in equal weekly quantities over a six-month period. XYZ works 250 days per year on a single-shift 40-hour work week.

   The table below states the tasks required and their precedence sequence and task times in seconds.

Task	Task That Must Precede	Task Time (seconds)
A	—	150
B	A	120
C	B	150
D	A	30
E	D	100
F	C, E	40
G	E	30
H	F, G	100

   a. Develop an assembly line meeting the requirements.
   b. State the cycle time.
   c. What is the "efficiency" of the line?
   d. Supposing the vendor asked you to increase output by 10 percent. State specifically how you would respond to this.

10. The following tasks are to be performed on an assembly line:

Task	Seconds	Tasks That Must Precede
A	20	—
B	7	A
C	20	B
D	22	B
E	15	C
F	10	D
G	16	E, F
H	8	G

   Given:
   The workday is 7 hours long.
   Demand for completed product is 750 per day.

   a. Find the cycle time.
   b. What is the theoretical number of workstations?
   c. Draw the precedence diagram.
   d. Balance the line using sequential restrictions and the longest operating time rule.
   e. What is the efficiency of the line balanced as in *d?*
   f. Suppose that demand rose from 750 per day to 800 units per day. What would you do? Show any amounts or calculations.
   g. Suppose that demand rose from 750 per day to 1,000 units per day. What would you do? Show any amounts or calculations.

11. Assembly lines have definite advantages over job shop layouts in certain applications. Discuss where assembly line layouts are best used and what the objectives, balancing techniques, performance measurements, cycle times, capitalization requirements, worker skill levels, etc., are.

9.9 SELECTED BIBLIOGRAPHY

Askin, Ronald G., and S. P. Subramanian. "A Cost-Based Heuristic for Group Technology Configuration." *International Journal of Production Research* 25, no. 1 (1987), pp. 101–13.

Choobineh, F. "A Framework for the Design of Cellular Manufacturing Systems." *International Journal of Production Research* 26, no. 7 (1988), pp. 1161–72.

Dobyns, Lloyd, and Reuven Frank. *If Japan Can, Why Can't We?* New York: NBC-TV News Presentation, June 24, 1980.

Francis, R. L.; L. F. McGinnis; and J. A. White. *Facility Layout and Location: An Analytical Approach.* 2nd ed. Englewood Cliffs, N.J.: Prentice Hall, 1992.

Green, Timothy J., and Randall P. Sadowski. "A Review of Cellular Manufacturing Assumptions, Advantages and Design Techniques." *Journal of Operations Management* 4, no. 2 (February 1984), pp. 85–97.

Gunther, R. E.; G. D. Johnson; and R. S. Peterson. "Currently Practiced Formulations for the Assembly Line Balance Problem." *Journal of Operations Management* 3, no. 4 (August 1983), pp. 209–21.

Hyer, Nancy Lea. "The Potential of Group Technology for U.S. Manufacturing." *Journal of Operations Management* 4, no. 3 (May 1984), pp. 183–202.

Manivannan, S., and Dipak Chudhuri. "Computer-Aided Facility Layout Algorithm Generates Alternatives to Increase Firm's Productivity," *Industrial Engineering,* May 1984.

Mondon, Yasuhiro. *Toyota Production System, Practical Approach to Production Management.* Atlanta, Ga.: Industrial Engineering and Management Press, 1983.

Schonberger, Richard J. *Japanese Manufacturing Techniques.* New York: Free Press, 1982.

Thompkins, James A., and James M. Moore. *Computer Aided Layout: A User's Guide.* Publication no. 1, Facilities Planning and Design Division, American Institute of Industrial Engineers, Inc., Atlanta: AIIE, Inc., 1978.

Vannelli, Anthony, and K. Ravi Kumar. "A Method for Finding Minimal Bottleneck Cells for Grouping Part-Machine Families." *International Journal of Production Research* 24, no. 2 (1986), pp. 387–400.

Chapter 10

Waiting Line Management

EPIGRAPH

They also serve who only stand and wait.

Milton

CHAPTER OUTLINE

KEY TERMS

Actual Waiting Time

Perceived Waiting Time

Customer Satisfaction

Customer Expectations

Disconfirmation

Halo Effect

Front-of-the-House

Backroom

Every day we encounter waiting lines in one form or another. The checkout line at the supermarket where we shop, the line in the bank where we conduct our financial transactions, and being placed on hold on the telephone while we wait to make a hotel or airline reservation are just some of the examples of the waiting lines we encounter routinely.

Service managers need to properly manage these customer waiting times, to ensure both efficiency and that customers are not negatively affected by the wait to the point of taking their future business elsewhere. To accomplish this, managers need to recognize that good waiting line management consists of two major components: the **actual waiting time** itself and the customers' **perceived waiting time.**

The determination of actual waiting times is presented in the supplement to this chapter; this supplement focuses on queuing theory and mathematical waiting line models for a variety of service delivery system configurations. The use of these models provides the manager with a framework for managing the actual waiting times.

Providing improved levels of customer satisfaction through the management of the customer's perceived waiting time is the primary focus of this chapter. Understanding how customer satisfaction can be improved for a given waiting time provides the service manager with an opportunity for managing his or her operation more effectively.

10.1 THE IMPORTANCE OF GOOD SERVICE

Today, in both manufacturing and service operations, those companies that provide outstanding service to their customers will achieve a competitive advantage in the marketplace in the 1990s. "The market power is in the services," says Sandra Vandermerwe, "because the value is in the results."[1] And good service begins when the customer first comes in contact with an organization and waits in some type of line or queue prior to being served. There are many factors that contribute to good service such as the friendliness and knowledge of the workers, but customers' experiences with waiting lines, which is often their initial encounter with the firm, can significantly affect their overall level of satisfaction with the organization.

Providing ever-faster service, with the ultimate goal of having zero customer waiting time, has recently received managerial attention for several reasons. First, in the more highly developed countries, where the standards of living are rising, time becomes more valuable as a commodity and, consequently, customers are less willing to wait for service. As a result, customers may even be willing to pay a premium price to those firms that minimize their waiting time.

In addition, the creation of a global economy has intensified competition at all levels, with the result that goods are often viewed as commodities, the purchase of which is based almost solely on price. George Stalk, Jr., points out, however, that firms can differentiate

[1] Sandra Vandermerwe, *From Tin Soldiers to Russian Dolls* (Oxford, England: Butterworth-Heinemann, Ltd., 1993).

themselves from the competition by providing faster service, and charge a premium for doing so.[2]

A third reason for this increased emphasis on providing fast and efficient service to customers is the realization by organizations that how they treat their customers today significantly impacts on whether or not they will remain customers tomorrow. This differs from the past, when the treatment of customers was viewed to be independent of any potential future sales. This attitude by management persisted because the impact of future customer behavior did not appear anywhere on the firm's financial statements.

Finally, advances in technology, especially in information technology, have provided firms with the ability to provide faster service than was previously possible. Fax machines, e-mail, and satellite communications provide firms with this new capability to respond faster to the customer.

In providing fast service, however, the real goal of service managers should not be to ensure that customers are served within a specified time (e.g., a stated number of minutes), but rather to ensure that the customers are sufficiently satisfied with the level of service provided so that they will want to return in the future.

10.2 CUSTOMER WAITING TIME VERSUS PROCESS EFFICIENCY: THE TRADE-OFF IN WAITING LINE MANAGEMENT

The classical operations management model relating service and cost, illustrated in Exhibit 10.1, shows the trade-off between the cost of providing fast service with the cost of having the customer wait. This trade-off between providing high levels of customer service (i.e., fast service) and obtaining high worker productivity results from the direct interaction of the customer with the service-producing process. Although easily understood in theory, this model is not readily adaptable to real-world applications, due primarily to the difficulty associated with measuring the cost of having a customer wait.

In comparing a service operation with a manufacturing firm, customers waiting for service are often viewed as being analogous to inventory in the manufacturing process. Thus, a service firm that increases its process efficiency by having customers wait for service parallels a manufacturing firm that increases its process efficiency by maintaining a work-in-process inventory. In both instances, management faces the trade-off between improving process efficiency and increasing waiting time or inventory. The difference between the two, however, is that in the manufacturing facility, the parts that are waiting are inanimate objects, whereas in the service operation they are actual customers.

An inherent assumption in the model presented in Exhibit 10.1 is that the contact workers or available service capacity remain idle when there are no customers to serve. The basis for this assumption lies in queuing theory (which is discussed in detail in the supplement at the end of this chapter), which establishes the mathematical relationship between the number of servers or stations assigned and the average customer waiting time

---

[2]George Stalk, Jr., "Time—The Next Source of Competitive Advantage," *Harvard Business Review* (July–August 1988).

EXHIBIT 10.1

The Trade-Off in Waiting Line Management

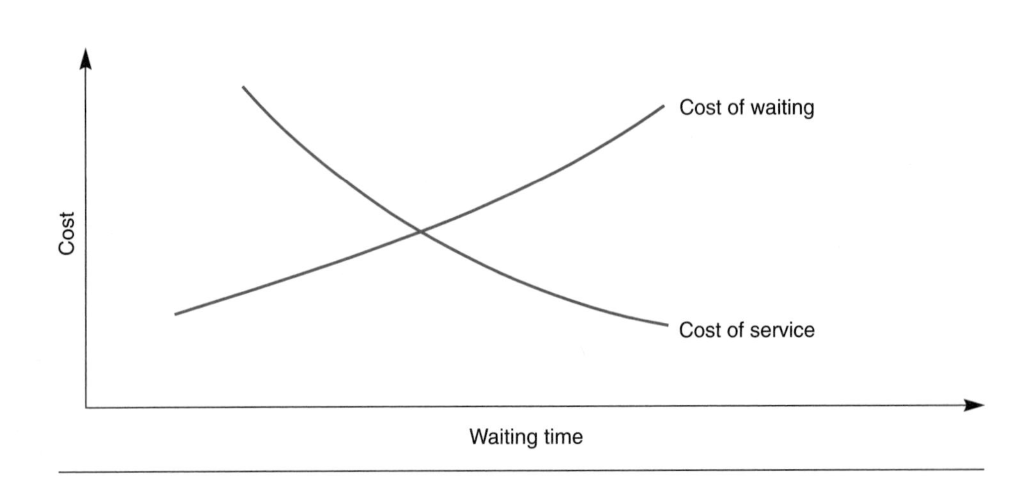

for a given level of demand. However, as discussed later in this chapter, through proper design of the service delivery process, workers can often be productive during these idle periods, increasing the overall productivity of the process without lengthening the customer's waiting time in line.

10.3 DEFINING CUSTOMER SATISFACTION

The customer's direct involvement in the service delivery system suggests a need to integrate both marketing and operations perspectives into the service system's design and evaluation. A marketing-related measure of customer reaction to waiting time would more clearly indicate the true customer waiting costs instead of just the actual waiting time itself. **Customer satisfaction** appears to be the marketing measure that fulfills this need.

Definition of Customer Satisfaction

Drawing on work done in marketing, we define customer satisfaction as being related to the comparison between a **customer's expectations** of a service's performance and his or her perception of that performance. If the perceived performance meets expectations, then the customer is satisfied; if it exceeds expectations by a large amount, then the customer is highly satisfied or delighted; if the performance falls significantly short of expectations, then the customer is dissatisfied. In marketing terminology, satisfaction is said to be directly related to the **disconfirmation** (i.e., difference) between the customer's expected and perceived performance of the service.

Customer satisfaction is a good measure of how effective the delivery system is, because it appears to provide the necessary linkage between the level of service that the company is currently providing to a customer, the customer's perception of that service, and the customer's future behavior toward the firm. Oliver suggests that customer satisfaction is part of an overall model of customer behavior that develops over time, as shown in Exhibit 10.2.

Customer Expectations

Customer expectations are defined as the customers' preconceived notion of what level of service he or she should receive from a particular service business or organization. Expectations can be derived from several sources.

One source of expectations is advertising. Many restaurants, for example, promise in their advertising that your lunch will be served in 10 minutes or less. Thus, if you have to wait longer than 10 minutes, you will be dissatisfied; if your wait is much less than 10 minutes, you will be very satisfied. Expectations can also be predicated on the customer's prior experience with the company. Additional sources of expectations include word-of-mouth and previous experiences with similar types of operations.

The overall service delivery package also influences a customer's expectations with waiting time. People tend to associate little or no waiting with upscale or higher-priced

EXHIBIT 10.2

The Role of Satisfaction in a Customer Behavior Model

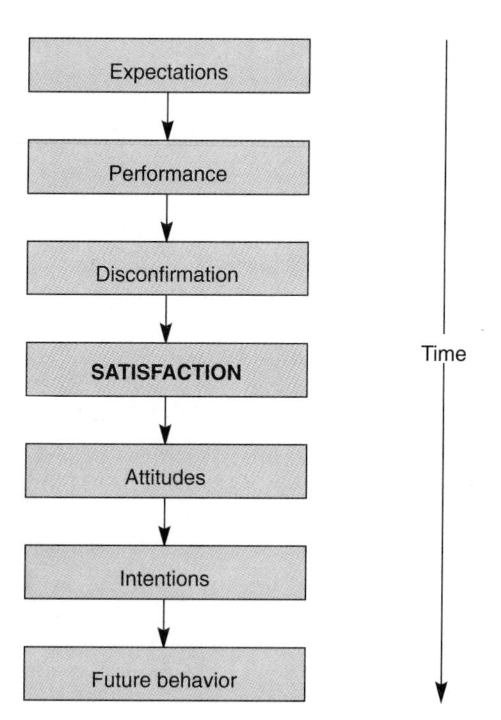

Source: Oliver, R. L. "A Cognitive Model of the Antecedents and Consequences of Satisfaction Decisions," *Journal of Marketing Research* 17, November 1980.

services. These types of operations, therefore, often require appointments or reservations to ensure minimal, if any, waiting. The degree of customization provided to each customer is another factor that can influence expectations. The more a service is customized, the longer a customer might expect to wait.

Perceived Waiting Time

Perceived waiting time is the amount of time a customer believes he or she has waited before receiving service. While this is directly related to the actual time a customer waits, there are often significant differences between the two. As we will discuss later in this chapter, management can have an influence on a customer's perceived waiting time if it has an understanding of the factors that affect it.

To illustrate this point, a newly designed hotel was built with insufficient elevator capacity, especially in the morning hours when most of its guests were in a hurry to check out. Customer complaints about the long waits for elevators to take them to the ground floor prompted management to hire a consultant to reduce these waits. The consultant developed a scheduling algorithm for the elevators that significantly reduced the waiting times, but guest complaints still persisted. Another consultant was hired, who suggested placing full-length mirrors on both sides of the elevator doors on every floor. This was done and miraculously the complaints stopped, even though there was no further decrease in the actual waiting time. The guests, after pushing the elevator button, now had something to occupy their time, and consequently weren't as cognizant of their wait for the elevator.[3]

10.4 FACTORS AFFECTING CUSTOMER SATISFACTION WITH WAITING[4]

As stated previously, service managers should focus on improving the customer's level of satisfaction with waiting rather than the actual waiting time itself. Maister[5] presented an initial framework for focusing on customer satisfaction with waiting, identifying many of the factors that can affect satisfaction. To further assist the service manager, these factors are classified into three categories: (1) firm-related factors, (2) customer-related factors, and (3) both firm- and customer-related factors. Service managers, in order to effectively manage the customer's waiting time, must distinguish between those factors over which they have total or at least partial control from those over which they have no control at all.

---

[3] W. E. Sasser, R. P. Olsen, and D. D. Wyckoff, *Management of Service Operations: Text, Cases and Readings* (Boston: Allyn and Bacon, 1978).

[4] Adapted from Mark M. Davis and Janelle Heineke, "Understanding the Roles of the Customer and the Operation for Better Queue Management," *International Journal of Operations and Production Management* 14, no. 5 (1994), pp. 21–34.

[5] David Maister, "The Psychology of Waiting Lines," *The Service Encounter,* J. A. Czepiel, M. R. Solomon, and C. F. Surprenant (Eds.) (Lexington, Mass.: Lexington Books, D.C. Heath & Co., 1985).

Firm-Related Factors

Factors that fall primarily within the firm's control can be grouped into four types of waits: unfair versus fair waits, uncomfortable versus comfortable waits, unexplained versus explained waits, and initial versus subsequent waits.

Unfair versus fair waits

The successful management of the customer's perception of fairness with respect to waiting is dependent on queue design, service system design, and contact hours.

A popular approach, to ensure fairness, is to group all customers into a single queue or line. When more than one server is available, the first person in line moves to the next server that is free. This method has been adopted by many bank and airline check-in counters. Not only is the combined queue perceived as fairer, but the average wait has also been shown to be considerably shorter, even though the line itself is longer. However, managers also need to take into consideration the physical elements of the operating system. For example, the physical space required by customers and their shopping carts has precluded most supermarkets from adopting the combined queue approach.

More subtle elements of service system design, beyond the physical waiting, can also affect customer perceptions of fairness. Interruptions by telephone calls during busy periods, for example, give the impression (which is correct!) that the answered call is receiving priority treatment.

So that customers do not perceive unfair treatment due to their watches being off by a few minutes, the actual hours of operation that a service is open for business should exceed the posted hours. For example, if a retail operation has posted hours of 10:00 AM to 10:00 PM, then the store should be ready to receive customers and the doors unlocked at 9:50 AM, and the doors should not be closed until 10:10 PM.

Uncomfortable versus comfortable waits

It is common sense to recognize the fact that when one is uncomfortable, time passes more slowly. There are many ways in which service organizations can affect comfort: temperature, lighting, seating, and sound levels should all be considered. Comfort and fairness can often be combined when a "take a number" system is employed. Full-service restaurants recognize the importance of comfort by providing a lounge in which customers can wait prior to being seated. This is a good example of a win-win situation. The restaurant can gain additional sales from drinks sold to waiting customers, and the customers enjoy a pleasant and comfortable environment in which to wait for their tables.

Unexplained versus explained waits

Customer dissatisfaction with waiting increases when the waits cannot be justified or explained. For example, when airline passengers are informed that they must wait for equipment arrival, for the weather to clear, or for the wings of their plane to be de-iced, they are less likely to be dissatisfied than if no explanation is given for the delay. A word of caution, however, is necessary here. The repeated use of the same reason, no matter how valid it is, will eventually negate any benefits gained from the explanation.

Unused capacity in terms of either idle workers or idle stations is another form of unexplained waits that increases the customer's level of dissatisfaction. Although there are many justifiable reasons for apparently idle capacity (e.g., worker rest breaks, the need to complete important off-line tasks, etc.), the customer should not be expected to recognize these. Consequently, workers on rest breaks should not be within the customer's view. Thus, idle service workers and service stations should be "camouflaged" when not in use.[6]

Waits of unknown duration always seem longer than waits of known duration. This relates, in part, to a customer's anxiety with waiting. Thus, it is important to provide customers with an estimate of the wait. When the actual waits cannot be determined, updates or status reports at predetermined intervals can be acceptable substitutes. For example, Federal Express will report back to a customer at the close of each business day with an update on the status of the search for a lost package.

Initial versus subsequent waits

As Maister points out, customers tend to become more dissatisfied with initial waits prior to entering a service delivery system than they are with subsequent waits after they are in the system. This can be due to the fact that prior to the initial wait, customers see themselves as being outside the system, whereas after the initial service has been received they consider themselves to be within the system and will, therefore, be served. Thus firms should emphasize minimizing a customer's initial wait when designing the service delivery system.

Customer-Related Factors

There are some factors that affect a customer's satisfaction with waiting time that a firm cannot control. For example, how customers arrive and the various moods they are in when they do cannot be controlled by the firm, but an awareness of these factors and how they can contribute to dissatisfaction with waiting can help the service manager to better control those aspects of the wait that are manageable.

Solo versus group waits

People waiting in line by themselves tend to grow more impatient with the wait in comparison to people who are waiting in groups. Although this is not something that can be changed by the service organization, recognition of this fact may suggest service-appropriate distractions or alternatives. Ski areas provide a good example in their lift lines, where there is usually a separate line for single skiers, and this line is typically much shorter than those for couples or larger groups.

Here is another case of designing the service delivery system in such a way as to create a win-win situation. The single skier has a much shorter waiting time and the ski area can take maximum advantage of its lift capacity during periods of peak demand by using single skiers to fill otherwise empty seats as they appear.

[6] Richard B. Chase, "The Ten Commandments of Service System Management," *Interfaces* 15, no. 3 (May–June 1985).

Waits for more valuable versus less valuable services

When a product, be it a good or a service, is perceived to be of high value, customers are willing to wait longer than they would if they perceived the product to be of lower value. In other words, the perceived value of the product is large enough that customers are willing to absorb some of the cost in the form of waiting time. Firms should be forewarned, however, that in today's highly competitive environment, the ability to make customers wait extraordinarily long times will quickly result in loss of market to those competitors that provide the same or similar products in a shorter amount of time.

Customer value systems

Businesses need to recognize the importance of segmenting the market by customer value systems. Customers who place a premium on obtaining fast service do not mind paying for it, and these same customers do not want to waste their time, for example, on self-service, menu-driven service systems that many companies now provide, particularly with respect to telephone inquiries. To assure consistency from a customer's perspective, the market focus on the firm must therefore also be incorporated into its operational strategy for waiting line management.

Customer's current attitude

The attitudes of customers just prior to entering the service operation can have a significant impact on their level of satisfaction with the service they receive. If customers enter upset, they are more likely to be dissatisfied with their wait, regardless of its length. This type of **halo effect** will also impact the customers' perception of all facets of the goods and/or services that they receive.

Courtesy Target Stores

Target stores have numerous check-out aisles so that customers never have to wait long. Server capacity can be added or subtracted as the number of customers in process increases and decreases.

Both Firm- and Customer-Related Factors

There are some factors that relate to a customer's satisfaction with waiting that are under the influence of both the firm and the customer.

Unoccupied versus occupied waits

As illustrated with the example of the mirrors beside the elevator doors earlier in this chapter, customers who are unoccupied tend to perceive longer waiting times than do customers who are occupied during their waits. There are many options that are available to occupy a customer's time in line: reading material, interesting displays, mirrors, and music have all been demonstrated to be useful. Gambling casinos do an excellent job of keeping customers occupied while they are waiting to enter their nightclubs. The waiting lines to get into these clubs wend their way through the slot machine areas of the casino, creating another win-win situation: customers are kept occupied and slot machine revenues are increased.

Under certain circumstances, customers can also be kept busy while waiting in line doing meaningful activities that can improve the efficiency of the service. For example, customers waiting in line in a retail store can be informed, through the proper signage, of what they have to do to process a payment other than cash. Another approach to keeping customers occupied while waiting is to provide a waiting environment in which they can productively be working on their own tasks. Airport lounges with tables or private areas equipped with FAX machines, PCs, and so forth, are good examples.

Anxious versus calm waits

Customer anxiety regarding the nature of the service or the uncertainty of the wait can affect customer satisfaction. Any wait in an emergency room or to hear the results from an important laboratory test may seem interminable, regardless of the actual length of the wait. Service organizations cannot totally eliminate the customer's anxiety associated with these types of waits, but they can, nevertheless, look critically at the nature of the service that they provide and take the necessary steps to try to reduce customer anxiety in such situations. Providing reading material that both occupies the wait and simultaneously explains the procedure to be followed can be very effective in reducing the customer's anxiety and the associated level of impatience with the wait.

10.5 A FOCUS ON PROVIDING FAST SERVICE

Ultimately, providing ever-better and ever-faster service to customers is the responsibility of the service operations manager. From an operations perspective, this can be accomplished in several ways, including the institution of good system design concepts and the proper cross-training of workers.

System Design Concepts

Previous design theory advocated the splitting of the service delivery system into two cores, with the goal of reducing customer contact time, thereby increasing the speed of delivery and the efficiency of the operation. With this approach, the first core, or **front-of-the-house,** interacts directly with the customer and consequently adopts a chase strategy. The second core, or **backroom,** includes of all those functions that can be accomplished without the presence of the customer, and therefore can be performed more efficiently with a level-type strategy. McDonald's provides an excellent example of this split core strategy, with packaged hamburgers in the bins acting as a buffer inventory between the two stages (Both chase and level strategies are presented in detail in Chapter 13's discussion of aggregate planning.)

However, by adopting a design concept that combines the backroom operations with those in the front-of-the-house, service workers can be kept productively occupied during idle periods when there are no customers to wait on. For example, with a proper design concept, service workers can answer telephones or perform nontime-dependent tasks during such periods.

In addition to the system design, benefits, in terms of faster customer service, can be accrued by reducing the set-up times required when a worker has to switch from one job function to another. This switching can occur frequently in a service operation whenever a customer requires service. Such reductions in set-up times permit the service manager to reassign workers from time-dependent tasks, such as waiting on customers, to nontime-dependent tasks, such as cleaning and paperwork, and vice versa, without incurring any additional costs.

The key factor in adopting these concepts is that there are sufficient nontime-dependent functions available to be accomplished during idle periods. This can be arranged, to a large extent, by carefully designing the service delivery system from the beginning.

Cross-Training of Employees

An integral part of providing a fast and efficient service operation is the flexibility of the service workers, in terms of their ability to perform a variety of tasks. With broader job skills, these workers can perform additional, noncustomer-related tasks during idle periods as they occur throughout the workday. Consequently, service managers should invest resources to cross-train workers so that they can perform several tasks. What is essentially being accomplished through cross-training is that the firm is inventorying worker skills, instead of inventorying customers in the form of waiting lines.

10.6 CONCLUSION

As time becomes more critical in today's fast-paced environment, those firms that can provide fast service will have a competitive advantage over those that respond more slowly to customer requirements. Today, more than ever before, service managers need to constantly seek innovative ways to provide faster and better service to customers. Advances in technology, especially information technology, can assist the service manager in accomplishing this.

In providing faster service, however, managers should not lose sight of the fact that it is the customer's perception of the wait that is critical, rather than the actual wait itself.

There are many factors that can affect customer perceptions of waits, and the service manager needs to know what these factors are and which of them can be effectively managed by the firm. Such an approach will provide a proper framework for the allocation of a firm's scarce resources to ensure faster service.

10.7 REVIEW AND DISCUSSION QUESTIONS

1. Explain the analogy between having inventory in a manufacturing company and having customers waiting in line in a service operation.
2. What are some of the factors that you think might affect your degree of satisfaction with waiting in line in a supermarket checkout line late at night? . . . in a bank during your lunch hour? . . . at a fast-food restaurant with young children (not necessarily your own!)?
3. Calculate the opportunity cost associated with a dissatisfied customer who stops frequenting a fast-food restaurant for a year. What are your assumptions?
4. Why is it important for a service manager to be able to distinguish between the different types of factors that can affect a customer's level of satisfaction with his or her wait?
5. From your own personal experiences, cite some actual examples of both good and bad waiting line management practices.
6. For each of the different types of service operations listed below, provide specific recommendations for improving both the efficiency of the operation and the customer's level of satisfaction with the waiting time.

   - Airline check-in counter
   - Hospital emergency room
   - Department of Motor Vehicles
   - Mail-order 800 number
   - Emergency hot line
   - Upscale restaurant

10.8 SELECTED BIBLIOGRAPHY

Anderson, R. E. "Consumer Dissatisfaction: The Effect of Disconfirmed Expectancy on Perceived Product Performance." *Journal of Marketing Research* 10 (February 1973).

Bearden, W. O., and J. E. Teele. "Selected Determinants of Consumer Satisfaction and Complaint Reports." *Journal of Marketing Research* 20 (February 1983).

Chase, Richard B. "The Customer Contact Approach to Services: Theoretical Bases and Practical Extensions." *Operations Research* 29, no. 4 (July–August 1981).

________. "The Ten Commandments of Service System Management." *Interfaces* 15, no. 3 (May–June 1985).

Churchill, G. A., Jr., and C. Surprenant. "Investigation into the Determinants of Customer Satisfaction." *Journal of Marketing Research* 19 (November 1982).

Davis, Mark M., and Janelle Heineke. "Understanding the Roles of the Customer and the Operation for Better Queue Management." *International Journal of Operations and Production Management* 14, no. 5 (1994).

Davis, Mark M., and Michael J. Maggard. "Zero Waiting Time: A Model for Designing Fast and Efficient Service." In Teresa A. Swartz, David E. Bowen, and Stephen W. Brown (eds.), *Advances in Services Marketing and Management: Research and Practice* 3. Greenwich, Conn.: JAI Press (June 1994).

Day, R. L., and E. L. Landon. "Toward a Theory of Consumer Complaining Behavior." In A. G. Woodside, J. N. Sheth, and P. D. Bennett (eds.). *Consumer and Industrial Buying Behavior.* New York: North-Holland, 1977.

Maister, David. "The Psychology of Waiting Lines," In J. A. Czepiel, M. R. Solomon, and C. F. Surprenant (eds.), *The Service Encounter.* Lexington, Mass.: Lexington Books, D.C. Heath & Co., 1985.

Oliver, R. L. "A Cognitive Model of the Antecedents and Consequences of Satisfaction Decisions." *Journal of Marketing Research* 17 (November 1980).

Sasser, W. E.; R. P. Olsen; and D. D. Wyckoff. *Management of Service Operations: Text, Cases and Readings.* Boston: Allyn and Bacon, 1978.

Stalk, George, Jr. "Time—The Next Source of Competitive Advantage." *Harvard Business Review* (July–August 1988).

Vandermerwe, Sandra. *From Tin Soldiers to Russian Dolls.* Oxford, England: Butterworth-Heinemann, Ltd., 1993.

Supplement

Waiting Line Theory

EPIGRAPH

No matter which line you get in, the other line will move faster.

That the other lines move faster is known as Ettore's observation (*Harpers,* August 1974). The full version is: "The Other Line Moves Faster. This applies to all lines—bank, supermarket, toll booth, and so on. And don't try to change lines. If you do, the other line—the one you were in originally—will then move faster."

SUPPLEMENT OUTLINE

KEY TERMS

Queue

Arrival Rate

Service Rate

What causes waiting lines in the first place? Whenever there is more than one user of a limited resource, a waiting line or **queue** takes form. This delay phenomenon occurs in a wide range of activities affecting many types of users and resources.

In this supplement we discuss the basic elements of waiting line problems and provide standard steady-state formulas for solving them. These formulas, arrived at in the course of developing queuing theory, enable planners to analyze service requirements and establish service facilities appropriate to stated conditions. Queuing theory is broad enough to cover such dissimilar delays as those encountered by customers in a shopping mall or aircraft in a holding pattern awaiting landing slots.

Queuing theory is used extensively in both manufacturing and service environments, and is a standard tool of operations management in areas such as, for example, service delivery system design, scheduling, and machine loading.

S10.1 WAITING LINE CHARACTERISTICS

The waiting line (or queuing) phenomenon consists essentially of six major components: the source population, the way customers arrive at the service facility, the physical line itself, the way customers are selected from the line, the characteristics of the service facility itself (such as how the customers flow through the system and how much time it takes to serve each customer), and the condition of the customers exiting the system (back to the source population or not?). These six areas, shown in Exhibit S10.1, are discussed separately in the following sections.

Population Source

Arrivals at a service system may be drawn from a *finite* or an *infinite* population. The distinction is important because the analyses are based on different premises and require different equations for their solution.

Finite population. A *finite population* refers to the limited size customer pool which is the source that will use the service, and at times form a line. The reason this finite classification is important is because when a customer leaves his/her position as a member of the population of users, the size of the user group is reduced by one, which reduces the probability of a customer requiring service. Conversely, when a customer is serviced and returns to the user group, the population increases and the probability of a user requiring service also increases. This finite class of problems requires a separate set of formulas from that of the infinite population case.

Infinite population. An infinite population is one large enough in relation to the service system so that the changes in the population size caused by subtractions or additions to the population (e.g., a customer needing service or a serviced customer returning to the population) does not significantly affect the system probabilities. If, for example, there were 100 machines that were maintained by one repairperson, and one or two machines

EXHIBIT S10.1 **Framework for Viewing Waiting Line Situations**

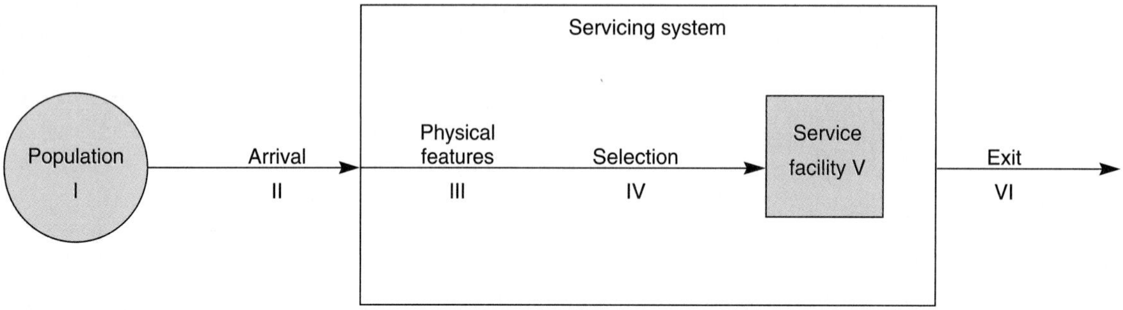

Servicing system

Population I → Arrival II → Physical features III → Selection IV → Service facility V → Exit VI

broke down and required service, the probabilities for the next breakdowns would not be very different and the assumption could be made without a great deal of error that the population, for all practical purposes, was infinite. Nor would the formulas for "infinite" queuing problems cause much error if applied to a physician who has 1,000 patients, or a department store that has 10,000 customers.

Arrival Characteristics

Another determinant in the analysis of waiting line problems is the *arrival characteristics* of the queue members. As shown in Exhibit S10.2, there are four main descriptors of arrivals: the *pattern of arrivals* (whether arrivals are controllable or uncontrollable); the *size of arrival units* (whether they arrive one at a time or in batches); the *distribution pattern* (whether the time between arrivals is constant or follows a statistical distribution such as a Poisson, exponential, or Erlang); and the *degree of patience* (whether the arrival stays in line or leaves). We describe each of these in more detail.

Arrival patterns

The arrivals at a system are far more *controllable* than is generally recognized. Barbers may decrease their Saturday arrival rate (and hopefully shift it to other days of the week) by charging an extra $1 for adult haircuts or charging adult prices for children's haircuts. Department stores run sales during the off season or one-day-only sales in part for purposes of control. Airlines offer excursion and off-season rates for similar reasons. The simplest of all arrival-control devices is the posting of business hours.

Some service demands are clearly *uncontrollable,* such as emergency medical demands on a city's hospital facilities. However, even in these situations, the arrivals at emergency rooms in specific hospitals are controllable to some extent by, say, keeping ambulance drivers in the service region informed of the status of their respective host hospitals.

EXHIBIT S10.2

Arrival Characteristics in Queues

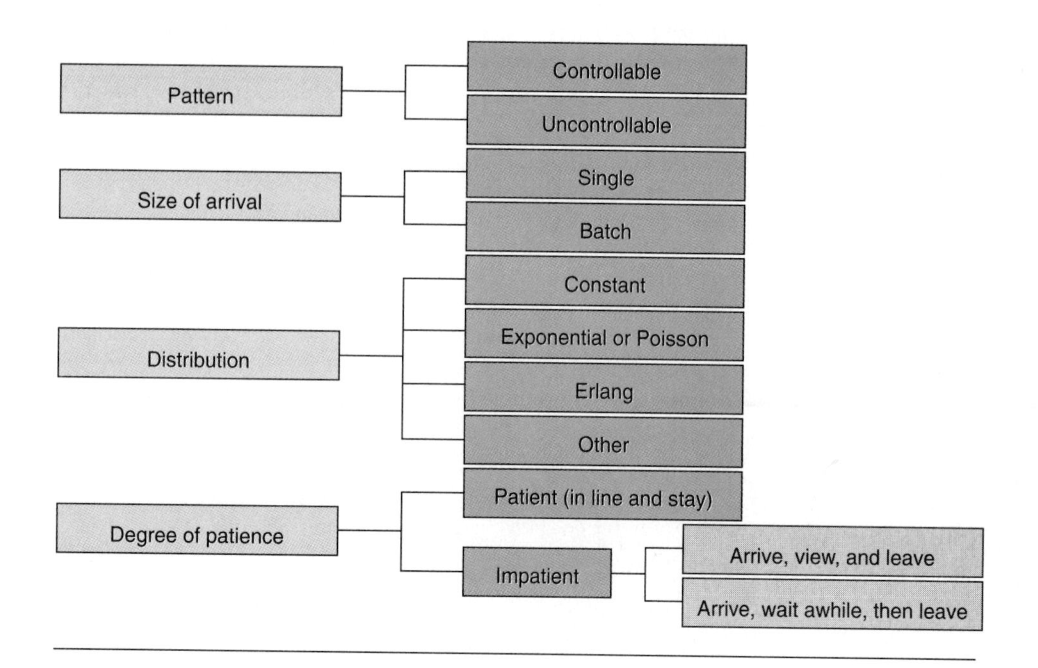

Size of arrival units

A *single arrival* may be thought of as one unit (a unit is the smallest number handled). A single arrival on the floor of the New York Stock Exchange (NYSE) is 100 shares of stock; a single arrival at an egg-processing plant might be a dozen eggs or a flat of two and a half dozen.

A *batch arrival* is some multiple of the unit, as a block of 1,000 shares on the NYSE, a case of eggs at the processing plant, or a party of five at a restaurant.

Distribution of arrivals

Waiting line formulas generally require an **arrival rate,** or the number of customers or units per period (e.g., 10 per hour). The time between arrivals is the interarrival time (such as an average of one every six minutes). A *constant* arrival distribution is periodic, with exactly the same time period between successive arrivals. In production processes, probably the only arrivals that truly approach a constant interarrival period are those that are subject to machine control. Much more common are *variable* random arrival distributions. The variable or random distribution patterns that occur most frequently in system models are described by the *negative exponential, Poisson,* or *Erlang* distributions.

Degree of patience

A *patient* arrival is one who waits as long as necessary until the service facility is ready to serve him or her. (Even if arrivals grumble and behave impatiently, the fact that they wait is sufficient to label them as patient arrivals for purposes of waiting line theory.)

There are two classes of *impatient* arrivals. Members of the first class arrive, survey both the service facility and the length of the line, and then decide to leave. Those in the second class arrive, view the situation, and join the waiting line, and then, after some period of time, depart. The behavior of the first type is termed *balking,* and the second is termed *reneging*.

Physical Features of Lines

Length

In a practical sense, an infinite line is very long in terms of the capacity of the service system. Examples of *infinite potential length* are a line of vehicles backed up for miles at a bridge crossing and customers who must form a line around the block as they wait to purchase tickets at a theater.

Gas stations, loading docks, and parking lots have *limited line capacity* caused by legal restrictions or physical space characteristics. This complicates the waiting line problem not only in service system utilization and waiting line computations but also in the shape of the actual arrival distribution as well. The arrival denied entry into the line because of lack of space may rejoin the population for a later try or may seek service elsewhere. Either action makes an obvious difference in the finite population case.

Number of lines

A *single line* or single file is, of course, one line only. The term *multiple lines* refers either to the single lines that form in front of two or more servers or to single lines that converge at some central redistribution point.

Customer Selection

Queuing discipline

A queuing discipline is a priority rule, or set of rules (some of which are listed in Exhibit S10.3), for determining the order of service to customers in a waiting line. The rules

EXHIBIT S10.3

Factors in a Queuing Discipline

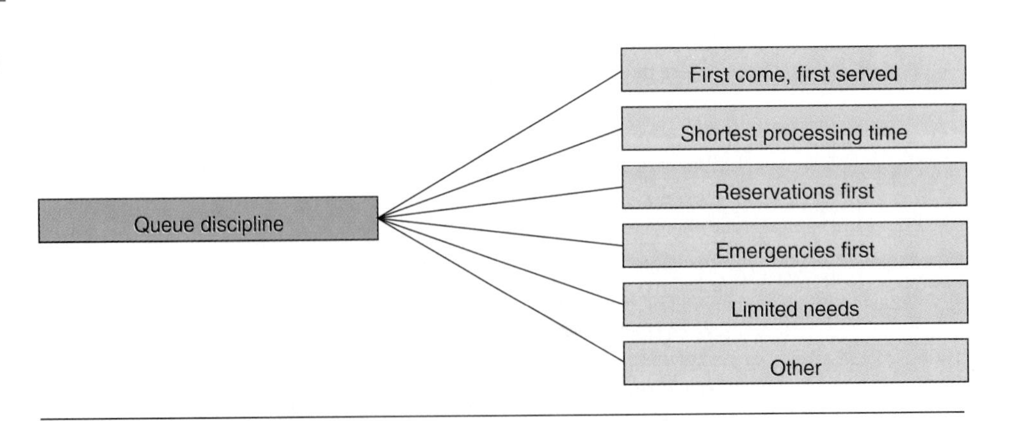

selected can have a dramatic effect on the system's overall performance. The number of customers in line, the average waiting time, the range of variability in waiting time, and the efficiency of the service facility are just a few of the factors affected by the choice of priority rules.

Probably the most common priority rule, particularly in service operations, is *first come, first served* (FCFS), also known as first in, first out (FIFO). This rule states that the customers in line are served on the basis of their chronological arrival; no other characteristics have any bearing on the selection process. This is popularly accepted as the fairest rule, even though in practice, it discriminates against the arrival requiring a short service time.

Reservations first, emergencies first, highest-profit customer first, largest orders first, best customers first, longest waiting time in line, and *soonest promised date* are other examples of priority rules. Each has its advantages as well as its shortcomings.

Directives such as "single transactions only" (as in a bank) or "cash only" express lane (such as a quick checkout in a market) seem similar to priority rules, but in reality they are methodologies for structuring the line itself. Such lines are formed to serve a specific class of customers with similar characteristics. Within each line, however, priority rules still apply (as before) to the method of selecting the next customer to be served. A classic case of line structuring is the fast checkout line for customers with 12 items or less in a busy supermarket.

Service Facility Structure

Several types of service facility structures are presented in Exhibit S10.4, four of which are discussed in detail in the following sections. The physical flow of items or customers to be serviced may go through a single line, multiple lines, or some combination of the two. The choice of format depends partly on the volume of customers served, partly on physical constraints, and partly on the restrictions imposed by sequential requirements governing the order in which service must be performed.

Single channel, single phase. This is the simplest type of waiting line structure, and straightforward formulas are available to solve the problem for standard distribution patterns of arrival and service. When the distributions are nonstandard, the problem is easily solved by computer simulation. A typical example of a single-channel, single-phase situation is the one-person barbershop.

Single channel, multiphase. A car wash is an illustration for a series of services—vacuuming, wetting, washing, rinsing, drying, window cleaning, and parking—performed in a fairly uniform sequence. A critical factor in the single-channel case with service in series is the amount of buildup of items allowed in front of each service, which in turn constitutes separate waiting lines.

Because of the inherent variability in service times, the optimal situation in maximizing the use of the service station is to allow an infinite waiting line to build in front of each station. The worst situation is that in which no line is permitted and only one customer at

EXHIBIT S10.4 **A Service Facility's Structure**

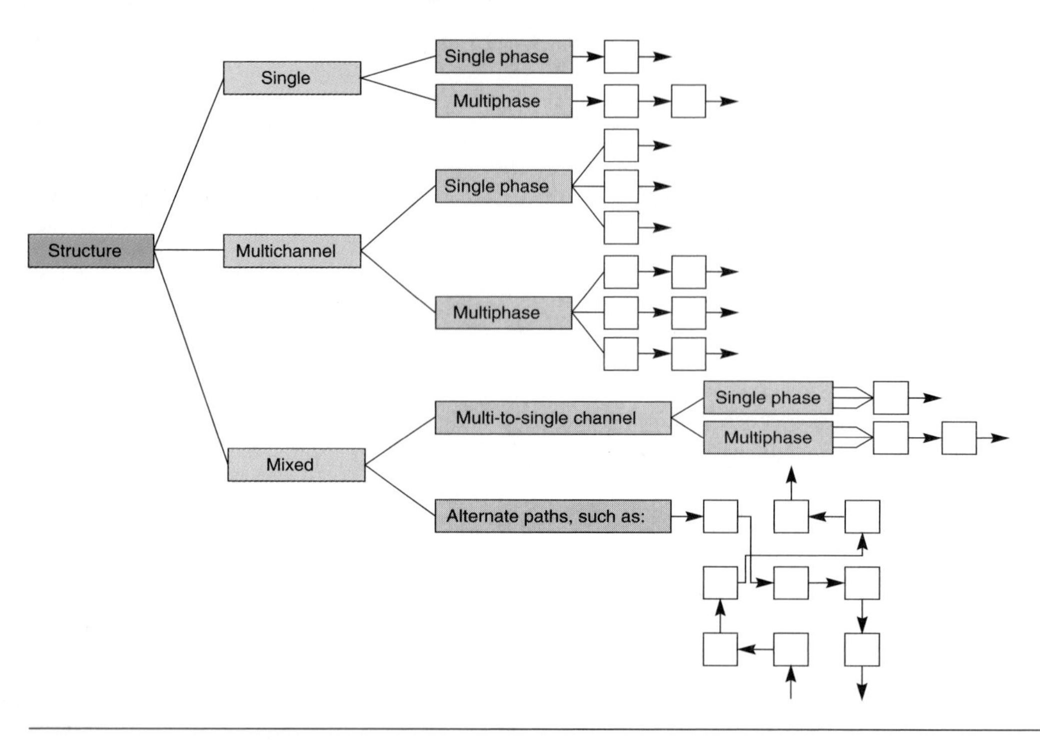

a time is allowed. When no sublines are allowed to build up in front of each station, as in a car wash, the use of the overall service facility is governed by the probability that a long service time will be required by any one of the servers in the system. This problem is common in most product-oriented systems, such as assembly lines.

Multichannel, single phase. Tellers' windows in a bank and checkout counters in high-volume department stores exemplify this type of structure. The difficulty with this format is that the uneven service time given each customer results in unequal speed or flow among the lines. This results in some customers being served before others who arrived earlier as well as in some degree of line shifting. Varying this structure to assure the servicing of arrivals in chronological order would require forming a single line, from which, as a server becomes available, the next customer in the queue is assigned. This type of line structure is now commonly used at airport ticket counters and banks.

Multichannel, multiphase. This case is similar to the preceding one except that two or more services are performed in sequence. The admission of patients in a hospital follows this pattern because a specific sequence of steps is usually followed: initial contact at the admissions desk, filling out forms, making identification tags, obtaining a room assignment, escorting the patient to the room, and so forth. Since several servers are usually available for this procedure, more than one patient at a time may be processed.

Service rate

Waiting line formulas generally define **service rate** as the capacity of the server in number of units per time period (such as 12 completions per hour) and *not* as service time, which might average five minutes each. A *constant* service time rule states that each service takes exactly the same time. As in constant arrivals, this characteristic is generally limited to machine-controlled operations. As with arrival rates, Erlang and hyperexponential distributions represent variable service times.

A frequently used illustration of the *Erlang* distribution employs a single-channel, multiservice situation. However, the conditions that must be met for the Erlang approximation are so severe that practical application is rare.

The *exponential* distribution is frequently used to approximate the actual service distribution. This practice, however, may lead to incorrect results; few service situations are exactly represented by the exponential function since the service facility must be able to perform services much shorter than the average time of service.

Most other services also have some practical minimum time. A clerk in a checkout line may have a three-minute average service time but a one-minute minimum time. This is particularly true where another checkout aisle provides a quick service. Likewise in a barbershop, while the average service time may be 20 minutes, a barber rarely cuts hair or gives a shave in fewer than 10 or more than 45 minutes. Hence, these and similar types of services that have strong time dependency are poorly characterized by the exponential curve.

Exit

Once a customer is served, two exit scenarios are possible: (1) the customer may return to the source population and immediately become a competing candidate for service again or (2) there may be a low probability of reservice. The first case can be illustrated by a machine that has been routinely repaired and returned to duty but may break down again; the second can be illustrated by a machine that has been overhauled or modified and has a low probability of reservice over the near future. In a lighter vein, we might refer to the first as the "recurring-common-cold case" and to the second as the "appendectomy-only-once case."

It should be apparent that when the population source is finite, any change in the service performed on customers who return to the population modifies the arrival rate at the service facility. This, of course, alters the characteristics of the waiting line under study and necessitates reanalysis of the problem.

S10.2 WAITING LINE EQUATIONS

To underscore the importance and wide range of applications of waiting line analysis, in this section we describe seven different waiting line systems and their characteristics

(Exhibit S10.5), and present their respective steady-state equations (Exhibit S10.6). In addition, we present in detail two sample problems and their solutions for the first two models. There are more types of models than these seven, but the formulas and solutions become quite complicated and those problems are generally solved using computer simulation. Also, in using these formulas, keep in mind that they are steady-state formulas derived on the assumption that the process under study is ongoing. Thus, they may provide inaccurate results when applied to initial operations such as the manufacture of a new product or the start of a new business day by a service firm.

The equations in Exhibit S10.6 for Models 1 through 5 are shown in Exhibit S10.8 as formulas on a Lotus spreadsheet. Lotus seems to be the most common spreadsheet used both in academia and industry, so we elected to use that format as an alternate way to present the waiting line formulas.

The cells where the values for arrival rate, service rate, and maximum Q, are input into

EXHIBIT S10.5

Properties of Some Specific Waiting Line Models

Model	Layout	Service Phase	Source Population	Arrival Pattern	Queue Discipline	Service Pattern	Permissible Queue Length	Typical Example
1	Single channel	Single	Infinite	Poisson	FCFS	Exponential	Unlimited	Drive-in teller at bank, one-lane toll bridge.
2	Single channel	Single	Infinite	Poisson	FCFS	Constant	Unlimited	Automatic car wash, roller coaster rides in amusement park
3	Single channel	Single	Infinite	Poisson	FCFS	Exponential	Limited	Ice cream stand, cashier in a restaurant
4	Single channel	Single	Infinite	Poisson	FCFS	Discrete distribution	Unlimited	Empirically derived distribution of flight time for a transcontinental flight
5	Single channel	Single	Infinite	Poisson	FCFS	Erlang	Unlimited	One-person barbershop
6	Multi-channel	Single	Infinite	Poisson	FCFS	Exponential	Unlimited	Parts counter in auto agency, two-lane toll bridge
7	Single channel	Single	Finite	Poisson	FCFS	Exponential	Unlimited	Machine breakdown and repair in a factory

EXHIBIT S10.6

Equations for Solving Seven Model Problems

Model 1

$$\bar{n}_l = \frac{\lambda^2}{\mu(\mu - \lambda)} \qquad \bar{t}_l = \frac{\lambda}{\mu(\mu - \lambda)} \qquad P_n = \left(1 - \frac{\lambda}{\mu}\right)\left(\frac{\lambda}{\mu}\right)^n$$

$$\bar{n}_s = \frac{\lambda}{\mu - \lambda} \qquad \bar{t}_s = \frac{1}{\mu - \lambda} \qquad \rho = \frac{\lambda}{\mu}$$

Model 2

$$\bar{n}_l = \frac{\lambda^2}{2\mu(\mu - \lambda)} \qquad \bar{t}_l = \frac{\lambda}{2\mu(\mu - \lambda)}$$

$$\bar{n}_s = \bar{n}_l + \frac{\lambda}{\mu} \qquad \bar{t}_s = \bar{t}_l + \frac{1}{\mu}$$

EXHIBIT S10.6

(concluded)

Model 3

$$\bar{n}_l = \left(\frac{\lambda}{\mu}\right)^2 \left[\frac{1 - Q\left(\frac{\lambda}{\mu}\right)^{Q-1} + (Q-1)\left(\frac{\lambda}{\mu}\right)^Q}{\left(1 - \frac{\lambda}{\mu}\right)\left(1 - \left(\frac{\lambda}{\mu}\right)^Q\right)} \right]$$

$$\bar{n}_s = \left(\frac{\lambda}{\mu}\right) \left[\frac{1 - (Q+1)\left(\frac{\lambda}{\mu}\right)^{Q} + Q\left(\frac{\lambda}{\mu}\right)^{Q+1}}{\left(1 - \frac{\lambda}{\mu}\right)\left(1 - \left(\frac{\lambda}{\mu}\right)^{Q+1}\right)} \right] \qquad P_n = \left[\frac{1 - \frac{\lambda}{\mu}}{1 - \left(\frac{\lambda}{\mu}\right)^{Q+1}} \right] \left(\frac{\lambda}{\mu}\right)^n$$

Model 4

$$\bar{n}_l = \frac{\left(\frac{\lambda}{\mu}\right)^2 + \lambda^2\sigma^2}{2\left(1 - \frac{\lambda}{\mu}\right)} \qquad \bar{t}_l = \frac{\frac{\lambda}{\mu^2} + \lambda\sigma^2}{2\left(1 - \frac{\lambda}{\mu}\right)}$$

$$\bar{n}_s = \bar{n}_l + \frac{\lambda}{\mu} \qquad \bar{t}_s = \bar{t}_l + \frac{1}{\mu}$$

Model 5

$$\bar{n}_l = \frac{K+1}{2K} \cdot \frac{\lambda^2}{\mu(\mu - \lambda)} \qquad \bar{t}_l = \frac{K+1}{2K} \cdot \frac{\lambda}{\mu(\mu - \lambda)}$$

$$\bar{n}_s = \bar{n}_l + \frac{\lambda}{\mu} \qquad \bar{t}_s = \bar{t}_l + \frac{1}{\mu}$$

Model 6

$$\bar{n}_l = \frac{\lambda\mu\left(\frac{\lambda}{\mu}\right)^M}{(M-1)!(M\mu - \lambda)^2} P_0 \qquad \bar{t}_l = \frac{P_0}{\mu M M!\left(1 - \frac{\lambda}{\mu M}\right)^2} \left(\frac{\lambda}{\mu}\right)^M$$

$$\bar{n}_s = \bar{n}_l + \frac{\lambda}{\mu} \qquad \bar{t}_s = \bar{t}_l + \frac{1}{\mu}$$

$$P_0 = \frac{1}{\sum_{n=0}^{m-1} \frac{\left(\frac{\lambda}{\mu}\right)^n}{n!} + \frac{\left(\frac{\lambda}{\mu}\right)^M}{M!\left(1 - \frac{\lambda}{\mu M}\right)}} \qquad P_w = \left(\frac{\lambda}{\mu}\right)^M \frac{P_0}{M!\left(1 - \frac{\lambda}{\mu M}\right)}$$

This is a finite queuing situation that is most easily solved by using finite tables. These tables, in turn, require the manipulation of specific terms.

Model 7

$$X = \frac{T}{T+U} \qquad H = FNX \qquad L = N(1 - F) \qquad n = L + H$$

$$P_n = \frac{N!}{(N-n)!} X^n P_0 \qquad J = NF(1 - X)$$

$$W = \frac{L(T+U)}{N-L} = \frac{LT}{H} \qquad F = \frac{T+U}{T+U+W}$$

the spreadsheet such as those shown as 15, 20, and 4. These cells were specifically named in Lotus in the following way: Placing the highlighted cell where the value of the quantity will be input (in the first case, 15 for the arrival rate), the cell for the arrival rate was named: /Range/Name/Create LAMBDA and hit return to place the name LAMBDA only for that cell. In this way, any use of the word *lambda* throughout the spreadsheet takes on the value entered in this cell.

Service rate *mu* was similarly created for the service rate cell value (in this case 20) as /Range/Name/Create MU [return]. Any spreadsheet use of the word *mu* takes on this value. The remaining cell names were created as Q, n, SIGMA SQUARED, K and M in successive order.

The reason for creating the formulas this way is so that they can then be used to try various values to see the effects on the waiting line performance.

S10.3 TWO TYPICAL WAITING LINE SITUATIONS

Here is a quick preview of the two problems we have used to illustrate the first two waiting line models in Exhibits S10.5 and S10.6.

Problem 1: Customers in line. A bank wants to know how many customers (or cars) are waiting for a drive-in teller, how long they have to wait, the utilization of the teller, and what the service rate would have to be so that 95 percent of the time there will not be more than three cars in the system at any one time.

Problem 2: Equipment selection. A franchisee for Robot Car Wash must decide which equipment to purchase out of a choice of three. Larger units cost more, but wash cars faster. To make the decision, costs are related to revenue.

The two problems are solved using the equations in Exhibit S10.6 with the notations defined in Exhibit S10.7. These can also be solved using the Lotus equations in Exhibit S10.8.

Problem 1: Customers in Line

Example

Western National Bank is considering opening a drive-in window for customer service. Management estimates that customers will arrive in their cars at the rate of 15 per hour. The teller who will staff the window can service customers at the rate of one every three minutes.

Assuming Poisson arrivals and exponential service, find

1. Utilization of the teller.
2. Average number in the waiting line.
3. Average number in the system.
4. Average waiting time in line.
5. Average waiting time in the system, including service.

EXHIBIT S10.7

Notations for Equations (Exhibit S10.4)

Infinite Queuing Notation: Models 1 and 2

σ = Standard deviation
λ = Arrival rate
μ = Service rate
$\frac{1}{\mu}$ = Average service time
$\frac{1}{\lambda}$ = Average time between arrivals
ρ = Potential utilization of the service facility (defined as λ/μ)
$\bar{n}_l$ = Average number waiting in line
$\bar{n}_s$ = Average number in system (including any being served)
$\bar{t}_l$ = Average time waiting in line
$\bar{t}_s$ = Average total time in system (including time to be served)

Solution

1. The average utilization of the teller is

$$\frac{1}{\mu} = 3 \text{ minutes} = \frac{1}{20} \text{ hour} \rightarrow \mu = 20 \text{ customers/hour}$$

$$\rho = \frac{\lambda}{\mu} = \frac{15}{20} = 75 \text{ percent}$$

2. The average number in the waiting line is

$$\bar{n}_l = \frac{\lambda^2}{\mu(\mu - \lambda)} = \frac{(15)^2}{20(20 - 15)} = 2.25 \text{ customers}$$

3. The average number in the system is

$$\bar{n}_s = \frac{\lambda}{\mu - \lambda} = \frac{15}{20 - 15} = 3 \text{ customers}$$

4. Average waiting time in line is

$$\bar{t}_l = \frac{\lambda}{\mu(\mu - \lambda)} = \frac{15}{20(20 - 15)} = 0.15 \text{ hour, or 9 minutes}$$

5. Average waiting time in the system is

$$\bar{t}_s = \frac{1}{\mu - \lambda} = \frac{1}{20 - 15} = 0.2 \text{ hour, or 12 minutes}$$

Because of limited space availability and a desire to provide an acceptable level of service, the bank manager would like to ensure, with 95 percent confidence, that not more than three cars will be in the system at any one time. What is the present level of service for the three-car limit? What level of teller use must be attained and what must be the service rate of the teller to assure the 95 percent level of service?

Solution

The present level of service for three cars or less is the probability that there are 0, 1, 2, or 3 cars in the system.

From Model 1, Exhibit S10.6:

$$P_n = \left(1 - \frac{\lambda}{\mu}\right)\left(\frac{\lambda}{\mu}\right)^n$$

at $n = 0$ $P_0 = (1 - 15/20)$ $(15/20)^0 = 0.250$
at $n = 1$ $P_1 = (1/4)$ $(15/20)^1 = 0.188$
at $n = 2$ $P_2 = (1/4)$ $(15/20)^2 = 0.141$
at $n = 3$ $P_3 = (1/4)$ $(15/20)^3 = 0.105$
0.684 or 68.4 percent

The probability of having more than three cars in the system is 1.0 minus the probability of three cars or less (1.0 − 0.684 = .316 or 31.6 percent).

For a 95 percent service level to three cars or less, this states that $P_0 + P_1 + P_2 + P_3 = 95$ percent.

$$0.95 = \left(1 - \frac{\lambda}{\mu}\right)\left(\frac{\lambda}{\mu}\right)^0 + \left(1 - \frac{\lambda}{\mu}\right)\left(\frac{\lambda}{\mu}\right)^1 + \left(1 - \frac{\lambda}{\mu}\right)\left(\frac{\lambda}{\mu}\right)^2 + \left(1 - \frac{\lambda}{\mu}\right)\left(\frac{\lambda}{\mu}\right)^3$$

$$0.95 = \left(1 - \frac{\lambda}{\mu}\right)\left[1 + \frac{\lambda}{\mu} + \left(\frac{\lambda}{\mu}\right)^2 + \left(\frac{\lambda}{\mu}\right)^3\right]$$

We can solve this by trial and error for values of λ/μ If $\lambda/\mu = 0.50$:

$$0.95 \stackrel{?}{=} 0.5(1 + 0.05 + 0.25 + 0.125)$$
$$0.95 \neq 0.9375$$

With $\lambda/\mu = 0.45$,

$$0.95 \stackrel{?}{=} (1 - 0.45)(1 + 0.45 + 0.203 + 0.091)$$
$$0.95 \neq 0.96$$

With $\lambda/\mu = 0.47$,

$$0.95 \stackrel{?}{=} (1 - 0.47)(1 + 0.47 + 0.221 + 0.104) = 0.95135$$
$$0.95 \approx 0.95135$$

Therefore, with the utilization $\rho = \lambda/\mu$ of 47 percent, the probability of three cars or less in the system is 95 percent.

To find the rate of service required to attain this 95 percent service level, we simply solve the equation $\lambda/\mu = 0.47$, where λ = number of arrivals per hour. This gives μ = 31.92 or about 32 per hour.

EXHIBIT S10.8 Waiting Line Formulae in a Lotus Spreadsheet Format

```
Value of variables
  Arrival rate (LAMBDA) =                          15.000    Insert
  Service rate (MU) =                              20.000    appropriate
  Maximum queue length (Q) =                        4.000    numbers
  Maximum number of units in system (N) =           3.000
  Variance (SIGMA SQUARED) =                        0.011
  Kth distribution in Erlang (K)                    2.000
  Number if identical svc channels (M)              3.000

Model 1
            Ave no in line              +LAMBDA^2/(MU*(MU-LAMBDA))
            Ave no in system            +LAMBDA/(MU-LAMBDA)
            Ave time in line            +LAMBDA/(MU*(MU-LAMBDA))
            Ave time in system          1/(MU-LAMBDA)
            Prob of exactly n in system(1-(LAMBDA/MU))*(LAMBDA/MU)^$N
            Utilization                 +LAMBDA/MU
Model 2
            Ave no in line              +LAMBDA^2/(2*MU*(MU-LAMBDA))
            Ave no in system            +LAMBDA^2/(2*MU*(MU-LAMBDA))+LAMBDA/MU
            Ave time in line            +LAMBDA/(2*MU*(MU-LAMBDA))
            Ave time in system          +LAMBDA/(2*MU*(MU-LAMBDA))+1/MU
            Utilization                 +LAMBDA/MU)
Model 3
            Ave no in line              (LAMBDA/MU)^2*(1-$Q*(LAMBDA/MU)^($Q-1)+($Q-1)*
                                          (LAMBDA/MU)^$Q)/(1-LAMBDA/MU)*
                                          (1-(LAMBDA/MU)^$Q)
            Ave no in system            +LAMBDA/MU*(1-($Q+1)*(LAMBDA/MU)^$Q+$Q*
                                          (LAMBDA/MU)^($Q+1))/((1-LAMBDA/MU)*
                                          (1-(LAMBDA/MU)^($Q+1)))
            Prob of exactly n in system((1-LAMBDA/MU)/(1-(LAMBDA/MU)^($Q+1)))*
                                          (LAMBDA/MU)^$N
Model 4
            Ave no in line              ((LAMBDA/MU)^2+LAMBDA^2*SIGMA SQUARED)/
                                          (2*(1-(LAMBDA/MU)))
            Ave no in system            ((LAMBDA/MU)^2+LAMBDA^2*SIGMA SQUARED)/
                                          (2*(1-(LAMBDA/MU)))+LAMBDA/MU
            Ave time in line            (LAMBDA/MU^2+LAMBDA*SIGMA SQUARED)/
                                          (2*(1-LAMBDA/MU))
            Ave time in system          (LAMBDA/MU^+LAMBDA*SIGMA SQUARED)/
                                          (2*(1-LAMBDA/MU))+1/MU
            Utilization                 +LAMBDA/MU
Model 5
            Ave no in line              (K+1)/(2*K)*LAMBDA^2/(MU*(MU-LAMBDA))
            Ave no in system            (K+1)/(2*K)*LAMBDA^2/(MU*MU-LAMBDA))+LAMBDA/MU
            Ave time in line            ((K+1)/(2*K))*LAMBDA/(MU*(MU-LAMBDA))
            Ave time in system          ((K+1)/(2*K))*LAMBDA/(MU*(MU-LAMBDA))+1/MU
            Utilization                 +LAMBDA/MU
```

That is, the teller must serve approximately 32 people per hour—a 60 percent increase over the original 20-per-hour capability—for 95 percent confidence that not more than three cars will be in the system. Perhaps service may be speeded up by modifying the method of service, adding another teller, or limiting the types of transactions available at the drive-in window. (Many banks, in fact, now limit each customer to a maximum of three transactions at the drive-in window.) Note that with the condition of 95 percent confidence that three or fewer cars will be in the system, the teller will be idle 53 percent of the time.

Problem 2: Equipment Selection

Example

The Robot Company franchises combination gas and car wash stations throughout the United States. Robot gives a free car wash for a gasoline fill-up or, for a wash alone, charges $0.50. Past experience shows that the number of customers that have car washes following fill-ups is about the same as for a wash alone. The average profit on a gasoline fill-up is about $0.70, and the cost of the car wash to Robot is $0.10. Robot stays open 14 hours per day.

Robot has three power units and drive assemblies, and a franchisee must select the unit preferred. Unit I can wash cars at the rate of one every five minutes and is leased for $12 per day. Unit II, a larger unit, can wash cars at the rate of one every four minutes but costs $16 per day. Unit III, the largest, costs $22 per day and can wash a car in three minutes.

The franchisee estimates that customers will not wait in line more than five minutes for a car wash. A longer time will cause Robot to lose both gasoline sales and car wash sales.

If the estimate of customer arrivals resulting in washes is 10 per hour, which wash unit should be selected?

Solution

Using Unit I, calculate the average waiting time of customers in the wash line (μ for Unit I = 12 per hour). From the Model 2 equations (Exhibit S10.6),

$$\bar{t}_l = \frac{\lambda}{2\mu(\mu - \lambda)} = \frac{10}{2(12)(12 - 10)} = 0.208 \text{ hour, or } 12\tfrac{1}{2} \text{ minutes}$$

For Unit II at 15 per hour,

$$\bar{t}_l = \frac{10}{2(15)(15 - 10)} = 0.067 \text{ hour, or 4 minutes}$$

If waiting time is the only criterion, Unit II should be purchased. However, before we make the final decision, we must look at the profit differential between both units.

With Unit I, some customers would balk and renege because of the 12½-minute wait. And although this greatly complicates the mathematical analysis, we can gain some estimate of lost sales with Unit I by inserting $\bar{t}_l$ = 5 minutes or $\frac{1}{12}$ hour (the average length of time customers will wait) and solving for λ. This would be the effective arrival rate of customers:

$$\bar{t}_l = \frac{\lambda}{2\mu(\mu - \lambda)}$$

$$\lambda = \frac{2\bar{t}_l\mu^2}{1 + 2\bar{t}_l\mu}$$

$$\lambda = \frac{2(1/12)(12)^2}{1 + 2(1/12)(12)} = 8 \text{ per hour}$$

Therefore, since the original estimate of λ was 10 per hour, an estimated 2 customers per hour will be lost. Lost profit of 2 customers per hour × 14 hours × ½ ($0.70 fill-up profit + $0.40 wash profit) = $15.40 per day.

Because the additional cost of Unit II over Unit I is only $4 per day, the loss of $15.40 profit obviously warrants the installation of Unit II.

The original constraint of a five-minute maximum wait is satisfied by Unit II. Therefore, Unit III is not considered unless the arrival rate is expected to increase in the future.

S10.4 COMPUTER SIMULATION OF WAITING LINES

Some waiting line problems that seem very simple on first impression turn out to be extremely difficult or impossible to solve. Throughout this chapter we have been treating waiting line situations that are independent; that is, either the entire system consists of a single phase, or else each service that is performed in a series is independent (this could happen if the output of one service location is allowed to build up in front of the next one so that this, in essence, becomes a calling population for the next service). When a series of services is performed in sequence where the output rate of one becomes the input rate of the next, we can no longer use the simple formulas. This is also true for any problem where conditions do not meet the conditions of the equations, as specified in Exhibit S10.7. The analytical technique best suited for solving this type of problem is computer simulation.

S10.5 CONCLUSION

Waiting line problems present both a challenge and frustration to those who try to solve them. One of the main concerns in dealing with waiting line problems is what procedure or priority rule to use in selecting the next product or customer to be served.

Many queuing problems appear simple until an attempt is made to solve them. This supplement has dealt with the simpler problems. When the situation becomes more complex, when there are multiple phases, and/or where services are performed only in a particular sequence, computer simulation is usually necessary to obtain the optimal solution.

S10.6 REVIEW AND DISCUSSION QUESTIONS

1. How many waiting lines did you encounter during your last airline flight?
2. Distinguish between a *channel* and a *phase*.
3. Which assumptions are necessary to employ the formulas given for Model 1?
4. In what way might the first-come, first-served rule be unfair to the customers waiting for service in a bank or hospital?

S10.7 SOLVED PROBLEMS

PROBLEM

1. Quick Lube Inc. operates a fast lube and oil change garage. On a typical day, customers arrive at the rate of three per hour, and lube jobs are performed at an average rate of one every 15 minutes. The mechanics operate as a team on one car at a time.

   Assuming Poisson arrivals and exponential service, find:

   a. Utilization of the lube team.
   b. The average number of cars in line.
   c. The average time a car waits before it is lubed.
   d. The total time it takes to go through the system (i.e., waiting in line plus lube time).

SOLUTION

Quick Lube Inc.

$\lambda = 3, \mu = 4$

a. $\text{Utilization } (\rho) = \dfrac{\lambda}{\mu} = \dfrac{3}{4} = 75\%.$

b. $\bar{n}_1 = \dfrac{\lambda^2}{\mu(\mu - \lambda)} = \dfrac{3^2}{4(4-3)} = \dfrac{9}{4} = 2.25 \text{ cars in line.}$

c. $\bar{t}_1 = \dfrac{\lambda}{\mu(\mu - \lambda)} = \dfrac{3}{4(4-3)} = \dfrac{3}{4} = 45 \text{ minutes in line.}$

d. $\bar{t}_s = \dfrac{1}{\mu - \lambda} = \dfrac{1}{1} = 1 \text{ hour (waiting + lube).}$

PROBLEM

2. American Vending Inc. (AVI) supplies vended food to a large university. Because students kick the machines at every opportunity out of anger and frustration, management has a constant repair problem. The machines break down on an average of three per hour, and the breakdowns are distributed in a Poisson manner. Downtime costs the company $25/hour per machine, and each maintenance worker gets $4 per hour. One worker can service machines at an average rate of five per hour, distributed exponentially; two workers, working together, can service seven per hour, distributed exponentially; and a team of three workers can do eight per hour, distributed exponentially.

   What is the optimum maintenance crew size for servicing the machines?

SOLUTION

American Vending Inc.
Case I: One worker.

λ = 3/hour Poisson, μ = 5/hour exponential

The average number of machines (either broken down or being repaired) in the system is:

$$\bar{n}_s = \frac{\lambda}{\mu - \lambda} = \frac{3}{5 - 3} = \frac{3}{2} = 1\tfrac{1}{2} \text{ machines}$$

Downtime cost is \$25 × 1.5 = \$37.50 per hour; repair cost is \$4.00 per hour; and total cost per hour for 1 worker is \$37.50 + \$4.00 = \$41.50.

Downtime (1.5 × \$25)	=	\$37.50
Labor (1 worker × \$4)	=	4.00
		\$41.50

Case II: Two workers.

$\lambda = 3$, $\mu = 7$

$$\bar{n}_s = \frac{\lambda}{\mu - \lambda} = \frac{3}{7 - 3} = .75 \text{ machines}$$

Downtime (.75 × \$25)	=	\$18.75
Labor (2 workers × \$4.00)	=	8.00
		\$26.75

Case III: Three workers.

$\lambda = 3$, $\mu = 8$

$$\bar{n}_s = \frac{\lambda}{\mu - \lambda} = \frac{3}{8 - 3} = \frac{3}{5} = .60 \text{ machines}$$

Downtime (.60 × \$25)	=	\$15.00
Labor (3 workers × \$4.00)	=	12.00
		\$27.00

Comparing the costs for one, two, or three workers, we see that Case II with two workers is the optimal decision.

S10.8 PROBLEMS

1. Burrito King is a new fast-food franchise that is opening up nationwide. Burrito King has been successful in automating burrito production for its drive-up fast-food establishments. The Burro-Master 9000 requires a constant 45 seconds to produce a burrito (with any of the standard fillings). It has been estimated that customers will arrive at the drive-up window according to a Poisson distribution at an average of 1 every 50 seconds.

Several issues must be addressed by management. What is the expected average time in the system?

To help determine the amount of space needed for the line at the drive-up window, Burrito King would like to know the average line length (in cars) and the average number of cars in the system (both in line and at the window).

2. Big Jack's drive-through hamburger service is planning to build another stand at a new location and must decide how much land to lease to optimize returns. Leased space for cars will cost $1,000 per year per space. Big Jack is aware of the highly competitive nature of the quick-food service industry and knows that if his drive-in is full, customers will go elsewhere. The location under consideration has a potential customer arrival rate of 30 per hour (Poisson). Customers' orders are filled at the rate of 40 per hour (exponential) since Big Jack prepares food ahead of time. The average profit on each arrival is $0.60, and the stand is open from noon to midnight every day. How many spaces for cars should be leased?

3. To support National Heart Week, the Heart Association plans to install a free blood pressure testing booth in El Con Mall for the week. Previous experience indicates that, on the average, 10 persons per hour request a test. Assume arrivals are Poisson from an infinite population. Blood pressure measurements can be made at a constant time of five minutes each. Assume the queue length can be infinite with FCFS discipline.

    a. What average number in line can be expected?

    b. What average number of persons can be expected to be in the system?

    c. What is the average amount of time that a person can expect to spend in line?

    d. On the average, how much time will it take to measure a person's blood pressure, including waiting time?

    e. On weekends, the arrival rate can be expected to increase to nearly 12 per hour. What effect will this have on the number in the waiting line?

4. A cafeteria serving line has a coffee urn from which customers serve themselves. Arrivals at the urn follow a Poisson distribution at the rate of three per minute. In serving themselves, customers take about 15 seconds, exponentially distributed.

    a. How many customers would you expect to see on the average at the coffee urn?

    b. How long would you expect it to take to get a cup of coffee?

    c. What percentage of time is the urn being used?

    d. What is the probability that there would be three or more people in the cafeteria?

    If the cafeteria installs an automatic vendor that dispenses a cup of coffee at a constant time of 15 seconds, how does this change your answers to *a* and *b*?

5. L. Winston Martin is an allergist in Tuscon who has an excellent system for handling his regular patients who come in just for allergy injections. Patients arrive for an injection and fill out a name slip, which is then placed in an open slot that passes into another room staffed by one or two nurses. The specific injections for a patient are prepared and the patient is called through a speaker system into the room to receive the injection. At certain times during the day, patient load drops and only one nurse is needed to administer the injections.

    Let's focus on the simpler case of the two—i.e., when there is one nurse. Also assume that patients arrive in a Poisson fashion and the service rate of the nurse is exponentially distributed. During this slower period, patients arrive with an interarrival time of approximately three minutes. It takes the nurse an average of two minutes to prepare the patients' serum and administer the injection.

a. What is the average number you would expect to see in Dr. Martin's facilities?
b. How long would it take for a patient to arrive, get an injection, and leave?
c. What is the probability that there will be three or more patients on the premises?
d. What is the utilization of the nurse?

6. The NOL Income Tax Service is analyzing its customer service operations during the month prior to the April filing deadline. On the basis of past data it has been estimated that customers arrive according to a Poisson process with an average interarrival time of 12 minutes. The time to complete a return for a customer is exponentially distributed with a mean of 10 minutes. Based on this information, answer the following questions.
   a. If you went to NOL, how much time would you allow for getting your return done?
   b. On average, how much room should be allowed for the waiting area?
   c. If the NOL service were operating 12 hours per day, how many hours on average, per day, would the office be busy?
   d. What is the probability that the system is idle?
   e. If the arrival rate remained unchanged but the average time in system must be 45 minutes or less, what would need to be changed?
   f. A robotic replacement has been developed for preparing the new "simplified" tax forms. If the service time became a constant nine minutes, what would total time in the system become?
7. The law firm of Larry, Darryl and Darryl (L,D & D) specialize in the practice of waste disposal law. They are interested in analyzing their caseload. Data were collected on the number of cases they received in a year and the times to complete each case. They consider themselves a dedicated firm and will only take on one case at a time. Calls for their services apparently follow a Poisson process with a mean of one case every 30 days. Given the fact that L,D & D are outstanding in their field, clients will wait for their turn and are served on a first come, first served basis. The data on the time to complete each case for the last 10 cases are 27, 26, 26, 25, 27, 24, 27, 23, 22, and 23.

   Determine the average time for L,D & D to complete a case, the average number of clients waiting, and the average wait for each client.

S10.9 SELECTED BIBLIOGRAPHY

Bartfai, P., and J. Tomko. *Point Processes Queuing Problems.* New York: Elsevier-North Holland Publishing, 1981.

Bruell, Steven C. *Computational Algorithms for Closed Queuing Networks.* New York: Elsevier-North Holland Publishing, 1980.

Cooper, Robert B. *Introduction to Queuing Theory.* 2nd ed. New York: Elsevier-North Holland Publishing, 1980.

Gorney, Leonard. *Queuing Theory: A Solving Approach.* Princeton, N.J.: Petrocelli, 1981.

Griffin, Walter C. *Queuing: Basic Theory and Application.* Columbus, Ohio: Grid, 1978.

Hillier, Frederick S., et al. *Queuing Tables and Graphs.* New York: Elsevier-North Holland Publishing, 1981.

Newell, Gordon F. *Applications of Queuing Theory*. New York: Chapman and Hall, 1982.

________. *Approximate Behavior of Tandem Queues*. New York: Springer-Verlag, 1980.

Solomon, Susan L. *Simulation of Waiting Lines*. Englewood Cliffs, N.J.: Prentice Hall, 1983.

Srivastava, H. M., and B. R. Kashyap. *Special Functions in Queuing Theory: And Related Stochastic Processes*. New York: Academic Press, 1982.

Vinrod, B., and T. Altiok. "Approximating Unreliable Queuing Networks under the Assumption of Exponentiality." *Journal of the Operational Research Society* (March 1986), pp. 309–16.

Chapter 11

Job Design, Reengineering, and Work Measurement

Second Edition

EPIGRAPH

Strange things happen at the best plants. Workers complain about machines being idle for too long and then fix them on their own to reduce the downtime. A plant manager smiles approvingly when he encounters the head of the janitorial crew dictating a letter to the manager's own secretary. The fanciest conference rooms are sometimes found not in the administration building, but inside the plant for workers to use when meeting with foremen.

Gene Bylinsky, "America's Best Managed Factories," *Fortune* (May 28, 1984), p. 16.

CHAPTER OUTLINE

KEY TERMS

Job Design
Specialization of Labor
Reengineering
Horizontal Work Compression
Vertical Work Compression
Time Standard
Financial Incentive Plans

The workplace in both manufacturing and service operations is rapidly undergoing a transformation. It is no longer an accepted fact that management has all the answers to today's problems. Those companies that have achieved world-class performance share several things in common, including the involvement of all of their workers in the decision-making process. Concepts like total quality management (TQM), as discussed in Chapter 6, and process reengineering include employee involvement as a critical element in their successful implementation. Some of these worker-related issues are addressed in the first part of this chapter.

However, an important aspect relating to the workplace is the establishment of work performance standards so that the work that is accomplished can be measured and evaluated. Such standards permit better planning and costing. In addition, they provide a basis for compensating the work force, and in some instances, providing incentives. These more technical issues of job performance are addressed in the second part of this chapter.

11.1 JOB DESIGN DEFINED

Perhaps the most challenging (and also the most perplexing) design activity associated with the transformation process is the development of the jobs that each worker and work group are to perform. The reasons for this include:

1. There is often an inherent conflict between the needs and goals of the worker and work group, and the requirements of the process.
2. The unique personality of each individual results in a wide range of attitudinal, physiological, and productivity responses in performing any given task.
3. The character of the work force and the work itself are changing, which challenges the traditional models of worker behavior and the efficacy of standard approaches to work development.

In this section, we explore these and other issues in job design and present some guidelines for carrying out the job-design function. We begin by noting some trends in job design:

1. *Quality as part of the worker's job.* Now often referred to as "quality at the source" improved quality is linked with the concept of worker *empowerment*. Empowerment, in turn, for example, refers to workers being given authority to stop a production line if there is a quality problem, or to give a customer an on-the-spot refund if service was not satisfactory.

2. *Cross-training workers to perform multiskilled jobs.* This is more often seen in the factory than in the office despite pressures on the clerical work force as described in the next insert. Indeed, bank check processing centers and the majority of high-volume clerical jobs are far more factorylike than many factories.

3. Employee involvement and team approaches to designing and organizing work. This is a central feature in total quality management (TQM) and continuous improvement efforts. In fact, it is safe to say that virtually all TQM programs are team based.

4. *"Informating" ordinary workers through telecommunications networks and computers, thereby*

EXHIBIT 11.1

People-Related Objectives of Hewlett-Packard

1. Belief in our people
   - Confidence in, and respect for, our people as opposed to depending upon extensive rules, procedures, and so forth.
   - Depend on people to do their job right (individual freedom) without constant directives.
   - Opportunity for meaningful participation (job dignity).
2. Emphasis on working together and sharing rewards (teamwork and partnership).
   - Share responsibilities; help each other; learn from each other; chance to make mistakes.
   - Recognition based on contribution to results—sense of achievement and self-esteem.
   - Profit sharing, stock purchase plan, retirement program, and so on are aimed at employees and company sharing in each other's successes.
   - Company financial management emphasis on protecting employee's job security.
3. A superior working environment that other companies seek but few achieve
   - Informality—open, honest communications; no artificial distinctions between employees (first-name basis); management by walking around; and open-door communication policy.
   - Develop and promote from within—lifetime training, education, career counseling to help employees get maximum opportunity to grow and develop with the company.
   - Decentralization—emphasis on keeping work groups as small as possible for maximum employee identification with our businesses and customers.

expanding the nature of their work and their ability to do it. In this context, informating is more than just automating work, it is revising work's fundamental structure. Northeast Utilities' computer system, for example, can pinpoint a problem in a service area before the customer service representative (CSR) answers the phone. The CSR uses the computer to troubleshoot serious problems, to weigh probabilities that other customers in the area have been affected, and to dispatch repair crews before other calls are even received.

5. *Any time, any place production.* The ability to do work away from the factory or office, again due primarily to advances in information technology, is a growing trend throughout the world. (See the next "OM in Action.")

6. *Automation of heavy manual work.* Examples abound in both services (one-person trash pickup trucks) and manufacturing (robot spray painting on auto lines). These changes are driven by safety regulations as well as economics and personnel reasons. (See the "OM in Action.")

7. *Most important of all, organizational commitment to providing meaningful and rewarding jobs for all employees.* (See Exhibit 11.1.)

OPERATIONS MANAGEMENT IN ACTION

The New World of Work

- London firms are now sending typing to Taipei. To survive, London typists must realize they are competing with Taipei typists. They must learn to "add value" (e.g., know more software programs, more languages than their Taiwanese counterparts) or else they'd better learn to love pounding the pavement.

continued

concluded

- The FI Group, one of Britain's largest software systems houses, employs about 1,100, most of whom are part-time free-lancers who need toil no more than 20 hours per week. More than two thirds of the firm's work is done at home: All told, employees live in 800 sites and serve 400 clients at any time. Life at FI is captured in the November 1988 issue of *Business:* "Chris Eyles, project manager, sat down in her office in Esher, Surrey, and called up the electronic 'chit chat' mailbox . . . The printer began to churn out messages. 'Help!' said [a message] from her secretary, based a few miles away in Weybridge. Somewhere in the Esher area, a computer analyst was in trouble . . . Eyles checked the team diary and her wall plan, located the analyst and the problem, and set up a meeting at FI's work center in Horley, 25 miles away."
- So who's left to sweep the floor? A visit to a 3M facility in Austin, Texas, suggests that floor sweeping, food handling, and security guarding are fast becoming almost as sophisticated as engineering. Computer-based floor sweepers and new security systems call for a sophisticated worker in virtually every job. A new, highly automated facility belonging to the huge drug distributor, Bergen Brunswig, is illustrative: Most manual work is done by machine. Work teams that dot the facility are not so much in the business of "doing" (by old standards), but in the business of improving the system. They are brain-involved, improvement-project creators, not muscle-driven lump shifters. There is no room on the staff for anyone who sees himself or herself as a pair of hands, punching a time clock.

Source: Tom Peters, "Prometheus Barely Unbound," *The Executive* IV, no. 4 (November 1990), pp. 79–80, 83.

Job design may be defined as the specification of the work activities for an individual or group in an organizational setting. Its objective is to develop work assignments that meet the requirements of the organization and the technology and that satisfy the personal and individual requirements of the jobholder. The term *job* (in the context of nonsupervisory work) and the activities involved in it are defined as follows:

1. *Micromotion:* the smallest work activity involving such elementary movements as reaching, grasping, positioning, or releasing an object.
2. *Element:* Two or more micromotions, usually thought of as a more or less complete entity, such as picking up, transporting, and positioning an item.
3. *Task:* Two or more elements that comprise a complete activity, such as wiring a circuit board, sweeping a floor, or cutting a tree.
4. *Job:* A set of all the tasks that must be performed by a given worker. A job may consist of several tasks, such as typing, filing, and taking dictation (in secretarial work), or it may consist of a single task, such as attaching a wheel to a car (as in automobile assembly).

Job design is a complex function because of the variety of factors that enter into arriving at the ultimate job structure. Decisions must be made about who is to perform the job, where it is to be performed, and how. And, as we can see in Exhibit 11.2, each of these factors may have additional considerations.

EXHIBIT 11.2 Factors in Job Design

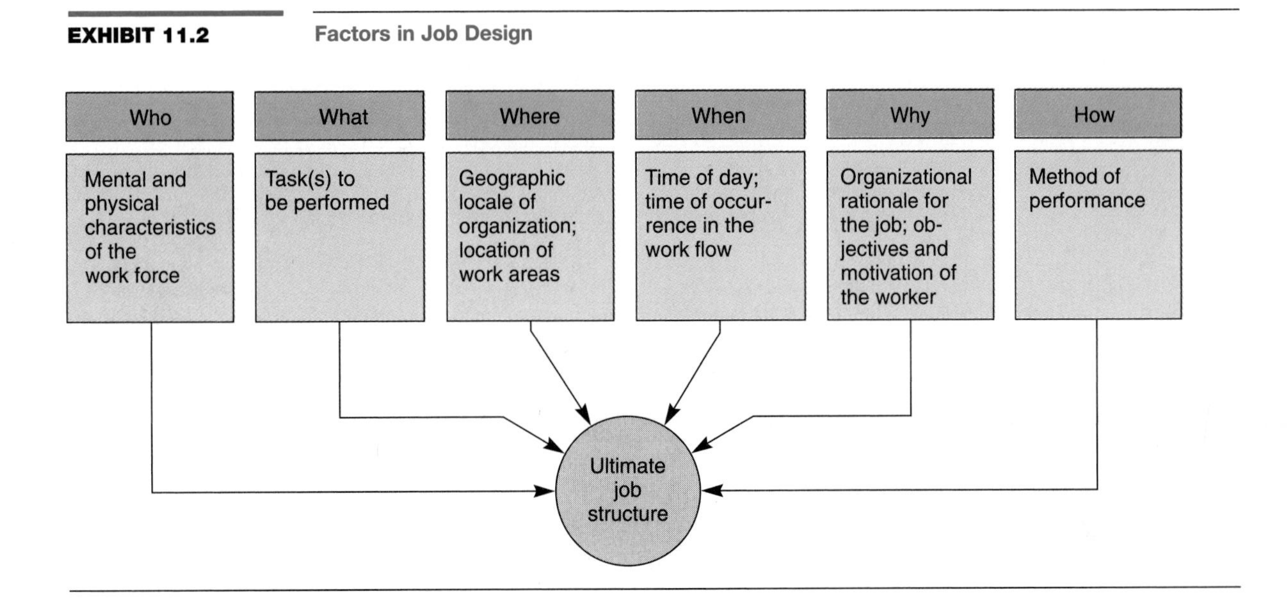

11.2 BEHAVIORAL CONSIDERATIONS IN JOB DESIGN

Degree of Labor Specialization

Specialization of labor is a two-edged sword in job design. On one hand, specialization has made possible high-speed, low-cost production, and, from a materialistic standpoint, has greatly enhanced our standard of living. On the other hand, it is well known that extreme specialization, such as that encountered on assembly lines in mass-production industries, often has serious adverse effects on workers, which in turn are often passed on to the production systems in the form of low-quality or defective work. In essence, the problem is to determine how much specialization is enough: At what point do the disadvantages outweigh the advantages? (See Exhibit 11.3.)

Recent research suggests that the disadvantages dominate the advantages much more commonly than was thought in the past. However, simply stating that, for purely humanitarian reasons, specialization should be avoided is risky. The reason, of course, is that people differ in what they want from their work and what they are willing to put into it. Some workers prefer not to make decisions about their work, some like to daydream on the job, and others are simply not capable of performing more complex work.[1] Still, there is a good deal of worker frustration with the way many jobs are structured, leading organizations to try different approaches to job design. Two popular contemporary approaches are job enrichment and sociotechnical systems. The philosophical objective underlying these approaches is to improve the quality of work life of the employee, and so

[1] Indeed, the widely discussed problems with our educational system have resulted in creating job designs that don't require the ability to read.

EXHIBIT 11.3

Advantages and Disadvantages of Specialization of Labor

ADVANTAGES OF SPECIALIZATION

To Management	To Labor
1. Rapid training of the work force 2. Ease in recruiting new workers 3. High output due to simple and repetitive work 4. Low wages due to ease of substitutability of labor 5. Close control over work flow and workloads	1. Little or no education required to obtain work 2. Ease in learning job

DISADVANTAGES OF SPECIALIZATION

To Management	To Labor
1. Difficulty in controlling quality since no one person has responsibility for entire product 2. "Hidden" costs of worker dissatisfaction, arising from *a.* Turnover *b.* Absenteeism *c.* Tardiness *d.* Grievances *e.* Intentional disruption of production process 3. Reduced likelihood of obtaining improvement in the process because of worker's limited perspective	1. Boredom stemming from repetitive nature of work 2. Little gratification from work itself because of small contribution to each item 3. Little or no control over the work pace, leading to frustration and fatigue (in assembly-line situations) 4. Little opportunity to progress to a better job because significant learning is rarely possible on fractionated work 5. Little opportunity to show initiative through developing better methods or tools 6. Local muscular fatigue caused by use of the same muscles in performing the task 7. Little opportunity for communication with co-workers because of layout of the work area

they are often applied as central features of what is termed a quality of work life (QWL) program.

Job Enlargement and Enrichment

Job enlargement generally entails making adjustments to a specialized job to make it more interesting to the jobholder. A job is said to be *enlarged horizontally* if the worker performs a greater number or variety of tasks, and it is said to be *enlarged vertically* if the worker is involved in planning, organizing, and inspecting his or her own work. Horizontal job enlargement is intended to counteract oversimplification and to permit the worker to perform a "whole unit of work." Vertical enlargement (traditionally termed *job enrichment*) attempts to broaden the workers' influence in the transformation process by giving them certain managerial powers over their own activities. Today, common practice is to apply both horizontal and vertical enlargement to a given job and refer to the total approach as *job enrichment.*

Classic Examples of Job Enrichment in Two Countries

Holland: Phillips N.V.

The truck chassis assembly groups have real decision-making power. Production groups of 5 to 12 workers with related job duties decide among themselves how they will do their jobs, within the quality and production standards defined by higher management; they can rotate job assignments—do a smaller or larger part of the overall task. At the same time, jobs of all production group members have been enlarged, making them jointly responsible for simple service and maintenance activities, housekeeping, and quality control in their work area, duties formerly performed by staff personnel.[2]

United States: Travelers Insurance Company

The objective was to enrich the keypunching job itself, starting with a training program for the supervisors. At the time of the initial implementation, work output was deemed inadequate, the error rate was excessive, and absenteeism too high. The keypunch job lacked skill variety, task identity, task significance, and autonomy. The changes introduced were:

1. *Natural units of work.* The random batch assignment of work was replaced by assigning responsibility to each operator for certain accounts—either particular departments or particular recurring jobs.
2. *Task combination.* Some planning and control functions were combined with the central task of keypunching.
3. *Client relationships.* Each operator was given several channels of direct contact with clients. The operators, not their assignment clerks, now inspect their documents for correctness and legibility. When problems arise, the operator, not the supervisor, takes them up with the client.
4. *Feedback.* In addition to feedback from client contact . . . the computer department now returns incorrect cards to the operator who punched them, and the operators correct their own errors . . . Each operator receives weekly a computer printout of his or her errors and productivity that is sent to him or her directly, rather than given to his or her supervisor.
5. *Vertical loading.* Operators now have the authority to correct obvious coding errors on their own. Operators may set their own schedules and plan their daily work. Some competent operators have been given the option of not verifying their work.

The results of the study: A reduction in the number of keypunch operators needed, a reduction in absenteeism, improved job attitudes, and less need for controls. Actual

---

[2] William F. Dawling, "Farewell to the Blue-Collar Blues," *Organizational Dynamics* (Autumn 1973).

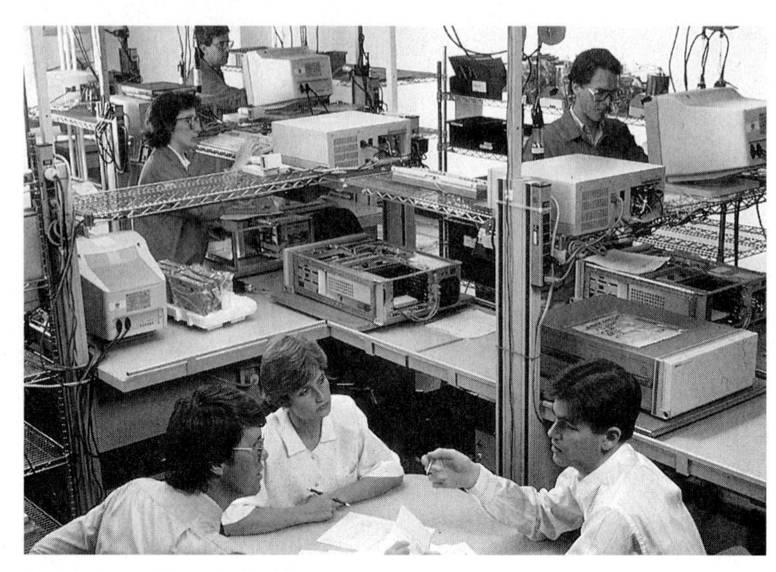

Photo courtesy of Hewlett-Packard Company

Hewlett Packard provides system design and consultation for custom applications. These consulting services are designed to help the user quickly advance from installation to optimal system use.

first-year savings totaled over $64,000. Potential annual savings from potential expanded application was given as $92,000.[3]

11.3 REENGINEERING[4]

As we discussed earlier in Chapter 2, competitive priorities have changed dramatically. For many years, dating well back into the 19th century, businesses focused primarily on efficiency and growth. As a consequence, companies were organized and structured to achieve maximum efficiency and to control that growth. However, with the emergence of a single world economy and increased competition from all corners of the globe, today's competitive priorities for success have shifted from efficiency to innovation, speed, service, and quality.

To increase efficiency in the factory, job design was dominated by the division of labor concept in which the work to be done was subdivided into a series of tasks that could be performed by less-skilled individuals. However, this approach, while increasing productivity with lower-skilled workers, had its disadvantages. With each individual focusing primarily on his or her assigned task, no one assumed overall responsibility for the process itself. The result was that these conventional process structures were fragmented and

[3]John Miner, *Theories of Organizational Behavior* (Hinsdale, Ill.: Dryden Press, 1980), pp. 256–57.

[4]Adapted from Michael Hammer and James Champy, *Reengineering the Corporation: A Manifesto for Business Revolution,* (New York: HarperCollins, 1993).

piecemeal, and consequently lacked the integration necessary to support the current competitive priorities, for example, quality and service. This shift in priorities has forced managers to rethink how their firms operate, and to focus on redesigning their core business processes. This is the goal of reengineering. To accomplish this, we need to "get back to the basics," by applying many of the tools presented later in this chapter that allow us to better understand these processes.

Reengineering Defined

This process of rethinking and restructuring an organization is referred to as **reengineering.** Reengineering means literally starting from the beginning with a clean sheet of paper in terms of how we design our organizations to better serve our customers. It focuses on processes, not individuals performing individual tasks. A key element of reengineering is the notion of "discontinuous thinking"—identifying and discarding antiquated rules and assumptions that are often the foundation for current business operations.

A cornerstone of reengineering is the use of computer technology. With advances in database management, speed of processing, and networking capabilities, today's computers should be used to formulate new approaches that are based on the computer's strengths. Instead, many companies simply transfer existing manual systems onto the computers and wonder why their problems still exist even though they have "automated" their systems.

An example of reengineering is shown with Ford's desire to reduce its accounts payable department in the early 1980s. Initially, through traditional methods, management determined that the 500-person department should be reduced by 100 people (a 20 percent reduction in that work force). However, investigation revealed that Mazda's accounts payable department consisted of only five people. Even though Mazda was smaller than Ford, this didn't explain the tremendous difference in department sizes. Subsequently, Ford decided to completely rethink its accounts payable department.

Under the old system, the 500 workers in accounts payable were constantly shuffling paper—matching vendor invoices to purchase orders and receiving documents, for example. Most of their time was spent trying to reconcile the paperwork when it didn't match up. This was the biggest cause of delayed payments. Under the new system, all of the paperwork has been virtually eliminated, thanks to the computer. When goods are received, a clerk on the dock uses the computer to instantly reconcile each delivery with its purchase order. The clerk now has the authority to accept the goods and to issue an order to the computer to pay the vendor. As a result, the bill is paid when the goods are received, not when the invoice is received. With the significant reduction in paperwork, the accounts payable department has been reduced to 125 people, who can now accomplish the same work previously done by 500 people, and do it faster.

Citicorp provides another good example of how effective reengineering can be. Over a two-year period, Citicorp slashed its work force by 15 percent (14,000 employees), and trimmed its operating expenses by 12 percent. The number of data processing centers has been reduced from 240 to 60, with the goal of eventually consolidating them down to 20. Although much of these savings were attributed to traditional expense reduction, a substantial portion was the result of reengineering. In fact, John Reed, Citicorp's chief executive, believes another $1 billion in costs can be saved by reengineering the method by which Citicorp processes products and data. Consultants contend that banks in general could cut their operating expenses 25 percent to 35 percent through reengineering.[5]

Characteristics of a Reengineered Process

Based on their many years of experience with companies that have successfully reengineered their processes to better meet the needs of the marketplace, Michael Hammer and James Champy have identified several characteristics of reengineered processes, which are described below, that they have observed on a recurring basis.

Several jobs are combined into one

Assembly lines are no longer used because of their inherent fragmentation of work. Specialists are replaced with "case workers," who have the responsibility for overseeing the entire process. This is referred to as **horizontal work compression.** By combining tasks and jobs under one person, errors that occur in transferring information from one individual to another are eliminated. In addition, the cycle time is significantly reduced because only one person has responsibility.

Workers make decisions

Decision making becomes a part of every person's job, eliminating the need for the traditional and costly hierarchical organizational structure with its many layers of management. This is referred to as **vertical work compression.** The benefits include faster customer response, lower overhead costs, and increased worker empowerment.

The steps in the process are performed in a natural order

With reengineering, processes no longer have to be forced into a sequential order. Instead, a natural sequence of events is permitted, based on what needs to be done next. This allows many jobs to be performed simultaneously, thereby reducing the throughput time.

Processes have multiple versions

Unlike assembly lines, which are totally inflexible and therefore can produce only standardized products, reengineered processes have several versions to meet the unique requirements of different market niches as well as individual customers. An advantage of the multiple version approach is that these processes tend to be relatively clean and simple in comparison to the traditional assembly processes, which are usually quite complex.

Work is performed where it makes the most sense

This involves shifting work across traditional functional boundaries. No longer, for example, are all purchases made by the purchasing department. For small purchases, such as office supplies, it may be more efficient to have each department do its own purchasing.

[5] Steven Lipin, "A New Vision," *The Wall Street Journal* (June 25, 1993).

Checks and controls are reduced

Checking and controlling are nonvalue-added functions and are thus minimized in reengineered processes. Controls are used only when they are economically feasible.

Reconciliation is minimized

Reconciliation is another nonvalue-added function that is minimized in reengineered processes. This is accomplished by reducing the number of external contact points of a process. This reduces the chance that inconsistent data will be received, which would then require reconciliation.

A case manager provides a single point of contact

The case manager acts as a buffer between the customer and the process, providing the customer with a single individual who is responsible for addressing his or her problem. To accomplish this, the case manager needs access to all the information about the process and also needs to be empowered to resolve the problem quickly to the customer's satisfaction.

Hybrid centralized/decentralized operations are prevalent

Companies that have reengineered their processes have incorporated the advantages of both centralization and decentralization. Much of this hybrid approach is attributed to the advances in information technology, which allow organizations to take advantage of economies of scale while still permitting a high degree of autonomy in the individual operating units.

Cultural Changes

Reengineering does not take place within a vacuum. In order for a reengineered process to be successfully implemented, the cultural values within the organization need to support such an implementation. Without compatible core values of the organization properly aligned to support the newly reengineered process, the probability of success is greatly reduced. Exhibit 11.4 presents a comparison between the traditional cultural values and the newer reengineered cultural values of an organization.

11.4 PHYSICAL CONSIDERATIONS IN JOB DESIGN

Beyond the behavioral components of job design, another aspect warrants consideration: the physical side. Indeed, while motivation and work-group structure strongly influence worker performance, they may be of secondary importance if the job is too demanding or is otherwise ill designed from a physical standpoint.

Work Task Continuum

One way of viewing the general nature of the physical requirements inherent in work is through the work task continuum shown in Exhibit 11.5. In this typology, *manual tasks* put stress on large muscle groups in the body and lead to overall fatigue, as measured by

EXHIBIT 11.4

Comparison of Traditional and Reengineered Cultural Values

Traditional Values	Reengineered Values
▪ My boss pays my salary: For all the talk about serving customers, the real objective is to keep the boss happy.	▪ Customers pay all our salaries: I must do whatever it takes to please them.
▪ I'm just a cog in the wheel: My best strategy is to keep my head down and not make waves.	▪ Every job in this company is essential and important: I get paid for the value I create.
▪ If something goes wrong, I dump the problem onto someone else: Why be identified with trouble?	▪ The buck stops here: I must accept ownership of the problems and get them solved.
▪ The more direct reports I have, the more important I am: The one with the biggest empire wins.	▪ I belong to a team: We fail or succeed together, and if we fail, nobody's empire is a winner.
▪ Tomorrow will be just like today: It always has been, so the company's past tells me all I need to know.	▪ Nobody knows what tomorrow holds: Constant learning is part of my job.

Source: "The Promise of Reengineering," *Fortune* (May 3, 1993), p. 96.

EXHIBIT 11.5

Work Task: Continuum (human work)

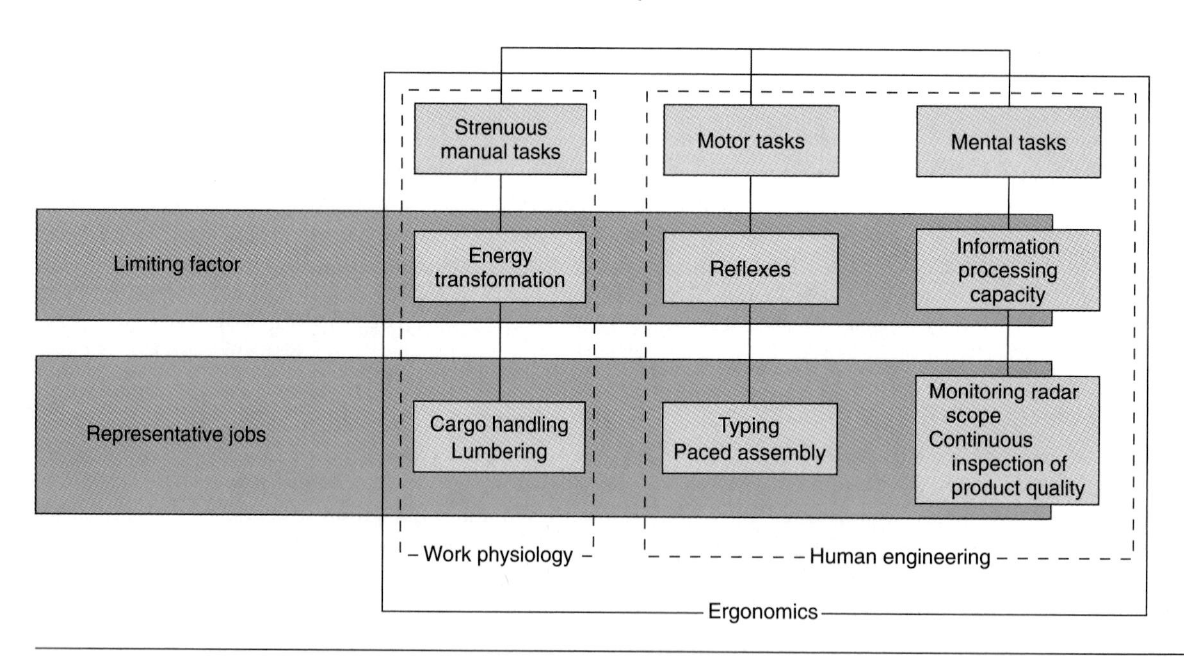

increases in the vital functions. *Motor tasks* are controlled by the central nervous system, and their measure of effectiveness is the speed and precision of movements. While these tasks lead to fatigue, the effect is localized in the smaller muscle groups, such as the fingers, hands, and arms and, hence, cannot be adequately measured by indices of *general* fatigue. (In measuring the physiological stress of motor tasks, researchers are investigating the use of electromyography, which records the changes in electrical potential in the involved muscular extremity; i.e., the hands, arms, and fingers.) *Mental tasks* involve rapid decision making based on certain types of stimuli, such as blips on a radar screen or defects in a product. Here the measure of effectiveness is generally some combination of time to respond and the number and types of errors. Research in this area is usually predicated on concepts from the discipline of information theory, and as might be expected by the nature of the tasks, much of the source work has been provided by military agencies.

In the private sector, Westinghouse's Human Science Laboratory has been exploring the use of brain waves as a means of determining an individual's level of attention and cognitive processing. The laboratory manager predicts that within the next decade Westinghouse could market a complete system that could monitor the mental processing efforts of employees as they work. A worker would wear something like a baseball cap fitted with an electronic monitoring device that would pick up and send relevant brain waves to a computer. The computer would then flash a warning if the brain-wave analysis indicated that the worker's attention had wandered too far, or that his or her mental stress level had climbed too high. Such a technology would be appropriate for such life-dependent jobs as air traffic controller, nuclear power plant controllers, and surgical staffs, and jobs where concentration is critical to work quality, such as inspection and accounting work.[6]

As noted in Exhibit 11.5, motor tasks and mental tasks fall under the heading *human engineering,* while the study of the physical aspects of work in general is called *ergonomics* (from the Greek noun for "work" and the Greek verb for "to manage").

11.5 METHODS, MEASUREMENT, AND PAYMENT

In this section, our focus shifts from delineating the boundaries and general character of the job to the specifics of job performance. In particular, we wish to consider:

1. How the work should be accomplished (work methods).
2. How performance may be evaluated (work measurement).
3. How workers should be compensated (wage payment plans).

The first two constitute the basis for setting work standards, which in turn are the basis for capacity and production-planning decisions.

[6]Michael Schrage, "Big Brother Time May be Coming to the Workplace," *Washington Post* (June 9, 1984).

EXHIBIT 11.6

Work Methods Design Aids

Activity	Objective of Study	Study Techniques
Overall production system	Eliminate or combine steps; shorten transport distance; identify delays	Flow diagram, service blueprint, process chart
Worker at fixed workplace	Simplify method; minimize motions	Operations charts, simo charts; apply principles of motion economy
Worker interacts with equipment	Minimize idle time; find number or combination of machines to balance cost of worker and machine idle time	Activity chart, worker-machine charts
Worker interacts with other workers	Maximize productivity; minimize interference	Activity charts, gang process charts

Work Methods

In our development of the production system, we have defined the tasks that must be done by workers. But how should they be done? Years ago, production workers were craftspeople who had their own (sometimes secret) methods for doing work. However, as products became more complicated, as mechanization of a higher order was introduced, and as output rates increased, the responsibilities for work methods were necessarily transferred to management. It was no longer logical or economically feasible to allow individual workers to produce the same product by different methods. Work specialization brought much of the concept of craftwork to an end, as less-skilled workers were employed to do the simpler tasks.

In contemporary industry, the responsibility for developing work methods in large firms is typically assigned either to a staff department designated *methods analysis* or to an industrial engineering department. In small firms, this activity is often performed by consulting firms that specialize in work methods design.

The principal approach to the study of work methods is the construction of charts, such as operations charts, worker-machine charts, simo (simultaneous motion) charts, and activity charts, in conjunction with time study or standard time data. The choice of which charting method to use depends on the activity level of the task; that is, whether the focus is on (1) the overall productive system, (2) the worker at a fixed workplace, (3) a worker interacting with equipment, or (4) a worker interacting with other workers (see Exhibit 11.6). (Several of these charting techniques were introduced in Chapter 4, where they were used to aid in manufacturing process design. Chapter 5 introduced the service blueprint that accounts for customer interactions.)

Overall production system

The objective in studying the overall production system is to identify delays, transport distances, processes, and processing time requirements, in order to simplify the entire operation. The underlying philosophy is to eliminate any step in the process that does not add value to the product. The approach is to flow chart the process and then ask the following questions:

What is done? Must it be done? What would happen if it were not done?

Where is the task done? Must it be done at that location or could it be done somewhere else?

When is the task done? Is it critical that it be done then or is there flexibility in time and sequence? Could it be done in combination with some other step in the process?

How is the task done? Why is it done this way? Is there another way?

Who does the task? Can someone else do it? Should the worker be of a higher or lower skill level?

These thought-provoking questions usually help to eliminate much unnecessary work, as well as to simplify the remaining work, by combining a number of processing steps and changing the order of performance.

Use of the process chart is valuable in studying an overall system, though care must be taken to follow the same item throughout the process. The subject may be a product being manufactured, a service being created, or a person performing a sequence of activities. An example of a process chart (and flow diagram) for a clerical operation is shown in Exhibit 11.7. Common notation in process charting is given in Exhibit 11.8.

Worker at a fixed workplace

Many jobs require the worker to remain at a specified workstation. When the nature of the work is primarily manual (such as sorting, inspecting, making entries, or assembly operations), the focus of work design is on simplifying the work method and making the required operator motions as few and as easy as possible.

There are two basic ways to determine the best method when a method analyst studies a single worker performing an essentially manual task. The first is to search among the workers and find the one who performs the job best. That person's method is then accepted as the standard, and others are trained to perform it in the same way. This was basically F. W. Taylor's approach. The second way is to observe the performance of a number of workers, analyze in detail each step of their work, and pick out the superior features of each worker's performance. This results in a composite method that combines the best elements of the group studied. This was the procedure used by Frank Gilbreth, the father of motion study, to determine the "one best way" to perform a work task.

Taylor observed actual performance to find the best method; Frank Gilbreth and his wife Lillian relied on movie film. Through micromotion analysis—observing the filmed work performance frame by frame—the Gilbreths studied work very closely and defined its basic elements, which were termed *therbligs* ("Gilbreth" spelled backward, with the *t* and *h* transposed). Their study led to the rules or principles of motion economy listed in Exhibit 11.9.

Once the motions for performing the task have been identified, an *operations chart* may be made, listing the operations and their sequence of performance. For greater detail, a *simo* (simultaneous motion) *chart* may be constructed, listing not only the operations but

EXHIBIT 11.7

Flow Diagram and Process Chart of an Office Procedure—Present Method*

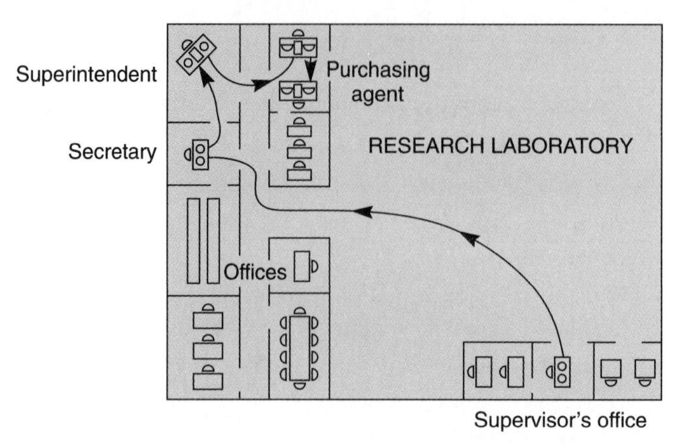

Present Method ☒		PROCESS CHART	
Proposed Method ☐			
SUBJECT CHARTED Requisition for small tools			DATE
Chart begins at supervisor's desk and ends at			CHART BY J.C.H.
typist's desk in purchasing department			CHART NO. R136
DEPARTMENT Research laboratory			SHEET NO. 1 OF 1

DIST. IN FEET	TIME IN MINS.	CHART SYMBOLS	PROCESS DESCRIPTION
		● ⇨ □ D ▽	Requisitions written by supervisor (one copy)
		O ⇨ □ D ▽	On supervisor's desk (awaiting messenger)
65		O ⇨ □ D ▽	By messenger to superintendent's secretary
		O ⇨ □ D ▽	On secretary's desk (awaiting typing)
		● ⇨ □ D ▽	Requisition typed (original requisition copied)
15		O ⇨ □ D ▽	By secretary to superintendent
		O ⇨ □ D ▽	On superintendent's desk (awaiting messenger)
		O ⇨ ■ D ▽	Examined and approved
		O ⇨ □ D ▽	On superintendent's desk (awaiting messenger)
20		O ⇨ □ D ▽	To purchasing department
		O ⇨ □ D ▽	On purchasing agent's desk (awaiting approval)
		O ⇨ ■ D ▽	Examined and approved
		O ⇨ □ D ▽	On purchasing agent's desk (awaiting messenger)
5		O ⇨ □ D ▽	To typist's desk
		O ⇨ □ D ▽	On typist's desk (awaiting typing of purchase order)
		● ⇨ □ D ▽	Purchase order typed
		O ⇨ □ D ▽	On typist's desk (awaiting transfer to main office)
		O ⇨ □ D ▽	
105		3 4 2 8	Total

*Requisition is written by supervisor, typed by secretary, approved by superintendent, and approved by purchasing agent; then a purchase order is prepared by a stenographer.

Source: Ralph M. Barnes, *Motion and Time Study,* 8th ed. (New York: Wiley & Sons, 1980), pp. 76–79.

EXHIBIT 11.8

Common Notation in Process Charting

Operation. Something is actually being done. This may be work on a product, some support activity or anything that is directly productive in nature.

Transportation. The subject of the study (product, service, or person) moves from one location to another.

Inspection. The subject is observed for quality and correctness.

Delay. The subject of the study must wait before starting the next step in the process.

Storage. The subject is stored, such as finished products in inventory or completed papers in a file. Frequently, a distinction is made between temporary storage and permanent storage by inserting a T or P in the triangle.

EXHIBIT 11.9

Gilbreth's Principles of Motion Economy

Using the human body the way it works best

1. The work should be arranged to provide a natural rhythm that can become automatic.
2. The symmetrical nature of the body should be considered:
   a. The motions of the arms should be simultaneous, beginning and completing their motions at the same time.
   b. Motions of the arms should be opposite and symmetrical.
3. The human body is an ultimate machine and its full capabilities should be employed:
   a. Neither hand should ever be idle.
   b. Work should be distributed to other parts of the body in line with their ability.
   c. The safe design limits of the body should be observed.
   d. The human should be employed at its highest use.
4. The arms and hands as weights are subject to the physical laws, and energy should be conserved:
   a. Momentum should work for the person and not against him or her.
   b. The smooth, continuous arc of the ballistic is more efficient.
   c. The distance of movements should be minimized.
   d. Tasks should be turned over to machines.
5. The tasks should be simplified:
   a. Eye contacts should be few and grouped together.
   b. Unnecessary actions, delays, and idle time should be eliminated.
   c. The degree of required precision and control should be reduced.
   d. The number of individual motions should be minimized along with the number of muscle groups involved.

Arranging the workplace to assist performance

1. There should be a definite place for all tools and materials.
2. Tools, materials, and controls should be located close to the point of use.
3. Tools, materials, and controls should be located to permit the best sequence and path of motions.

Using mechanical devices to reduce human effort

1. Vises and clamps can hold the work precisely where needed.
2. Guides can assist in positioning the work without close operator attention.
3. Controls and foot-operated devices can relieve the hands of work.
4. Mechanical devices can multiply human abilities.
5. Mechanical systems should be fitted to human use.

Source: Frank C. Barnes, "Principles of Motion Economy: Revisited, Reviewed, and Restored," *Proceedings of the Southern Management Association Annual Meeting,* Atlanta, 1983, p. 298.

also the times for both left and right hands. This chart may be assembled from the data collected with a stopwatch, from analysis of a film of the operation, or from predetermined motion-time data (discussed later in the chapter). Many aspects of poor design become immediately obvious with this technique—a hand being used as a holding device (rather than a jig or fixture), an idle hand, or an exceptionally long time for positioning.

Worker interaction with equipment

When a person and equipment operate together to perform the production process, interest focuses on the efficient use of both the person's time and the equipment's time. When the working time of the operator is less than the equipment run time, a worker-machine chart is a useful device in analysis. If the operator can operate several pieces of equipment, the problem is to find the most economical combination of operator and equipment, such that the combined cost of the idle time of the equipment and the idle time for the worker are at a minimum.

Worker-machine charts are always drawn to scale, the scale being time as measured by length. Exhibit 11.10 gives an example of a worker-machine chart in a service setting.

Workers interacting with other workers

A great amount of our output in both manufacturing and services is performed by teams. The degree of interaction may be as simple as one operator handing a part to another, or as complex as a cardiovascular surgical team of doctors, nurses, an anesthesiologist, the operator of the artificial heart machine, an X-ray technician, standby blood donors, and the pathologist (and perhaps a minister to pray a little).

To facilitate analysis of team efforts, an activity or a gang process chart is used to plot the activities of each individual on a time scale similar to that of the worker-machine chart. A gang process chart is usually employed to trace the interaction of a number of workers with machines of a specified operating cycle, to find the best combination of workers and machines. An activity chart is less restrictive and may be used to follow the interaction of any group of operators, with or without equipment being involved. Such charts are often used to study and define each operator in an ongoing repetitive process, and they are extremely valuable in developing a standardized procedure for a specific task. Exhibit 11.11, for example, shows an activity chart for a hospital's emergency routine in performing a tracheotomy (an operation for opening a patient's throat surgically to allow him or her to breathe), where detailed activity analysis is of major importance because any unnecessary delay could be fatal.

Work Measurement

The subject of work measurement for establishing time standards has been controversial since the days of Taylor. With the widespread adoption of Deming's ideas, it has become the subject of renewed criticism. (Deming argued that work standards and quotas inhibit process improvement and tried to focus all of the worker's efforts on speed rather than quality.) Nevertheless, all organizations need some form of standard time estimates to do planning and budgeting, and many companies use them with success in work design, as

EXHIBIT 11.10 **Worker-Machine Chart for a Gourmet Coffee Store**

Time in seconds	PERSON				MACHINE	
	Customer	Time in sec.	Clerk	Time in sec.	Coffee grinder	Time in sec.
0	1. Ask grocer for 1 pound of coffee (brand and grind)	5	Listen to order	5	Idle	5
10	2. Wait	15	Get coffee and put in machine, set grind, and start grinder	15	Idle	15
20–40	3. Wait	21	Idle while machine grinds	21	Grind coffee	21
50	4. Wait	12	Stop grinder, place coffee in package, and close it	12	Idle	12
60–70	5. Receive coffee from grocer, pay grocer, and receive change	17	Give coffee to customer, wait for customer to pay for coffee, receive money, and make change	17	Idle	17

Summary

	Customer	Clerk	Coffee grinder
Idle time	48 sec.	21 sec.	49 sec.
Working time	22	49	21
Total cycle time	70	70	70
Utilization in percent	Customer utilization = $\frac{22}{70}$ = 31%	Clerk utilization = $\frac{49}{70}$ = 70%	Machine utilization = $\frac{21}{70}$ = 30%

The customer, the clerk, and the coffee grinder (machine) are involved in this operation. It required 1 minute and 10 seconds for the customer to purchase a pound of coffee in this particular store. During this time the customer spent 22 seconds, or 31 percent of the time, giving the clerk his order, receiving the ground coffee, and paying the clerk for it. He was idle during the remaining 69 percent of the time. The clerk worked 49 seconds, or 70 percent of the time, and was idle 21 seconds, or 30 percent of the time. The coffee grinder was in operation 21 seconds, or 30 percent of the time, and was idle 70 percent of the time.

EXHIBIT 11.11 **Activity Chart of Emergency Tracheotomy**

Time in minutes	Nurse	First doctor	Orderly	Second doctor	Nurse supervisor	Scrub nurse
0	Detects problem; notifies doctor					
1						
2	Gets mobile cart	Makes diagnosis				
3						
4						
5	Notifies nurse supervisor	Assists patient to breathe				
6	Notifies second doctor				Opens OR; calls scrub nurse	
7	Notifies orderly			Assures availability of laryngoscope and endotracheal tube		
8	Moves patient to OR	Moves to OR	Moves patient to OR			Moves to OR; sets up equipment
9		Scrubs				
10		Dons gown and gloves		Operates laryngoscope and inserts endotracheal tube		
11						
12		Performs tracheotomy		Calls for IPPB machine		
13						
14						
15						
16						

Source: Data taken from Harold E. Smalley and John Freeman, *Hospital Industrial Engineering* (New York: Reinhold, 1966), p. 409.

EXHIBIT 11.12

Types of Work Measurement Applied to Differing Tasks

Type of Work	Major Methods of Determining Task Time
Very short interval, highly repetitive	Videotape analysis
Short interval, repetitive	Stopwatch time study: predetermined motion-time data
Task in conjunction with machinery or other fixed-processing-time equipment	Elemental data
Infrequent work or work of a long cycle time	Work sampling

demonstrated in the UPS case at end of chapter. In any event, it is important to understand the basic industrial engineering methods used to set standards. They are as follows:

1. Time study (stopwatch and micromotion analysis).
2. Elemental standard time data.
3. Predetermined motion-time data.
4. Work sampling.

Each method has its advantages over the others and has particular areas of application. Exhibit 11.12 lists these methods and relates them to a general class of jobs.

Time study

A time study is generally conducted with a stopwatch, either on the spot or by analyzing a videotape of the job. Procedurally, the job or task to be studied is separated into measurable parts or elements, and each element is timed individually. After a number of repetitions, the collected times are averaged. (The standard deviation may be computed to give a measure of variance in the performance times.) The averaged times for each element are added, and the result is the performance time for the operator. However, to make this operator's time usable for all workers, a measure of speed, which is expressed as a *performance rating* and which reflects how hard the observed operator is working, must be included to "normalize" the job. The application of a rating factor gives what is called *normal time.* For example, if an operator performs a task in two minutes and the time study analyst estimates him or her to be performing about 20 percent faster than normal, the normal time would be computed as 2 minutes + 0.20(2 minutes), or 2.4 minutes. In equation form,

Example

$$\text{Normal time} = \text{observed performance time per unit} \times \text{Performance rating}$$

In this example, denoting normal time by NT,

$$NT = 2(1.2) = 2.4 \text{ minutes}$$

When an operator is observed for a period of time, the number of units produced during this time, along with the performance rating, gives the normal time as

$$NT = \frac{\text{Total Time observed}}{\text{Number of units produced}} \times \text{Performance rating}$$

Standard time is derived by adding allowances to normal time. These allowances include personal needs (washroom and coffee breaks, and so forth), unavoidable work delays (equipment breakdown, lack of materials, and so forth), and worker fatigue (physical or mental). There are two equations for calculating standard time:

$$\text{Standard time} = \text{Normal Time} + (\text{Allowances} \times \text{Normal time})$$

or

$$ST = NT(1 + \text{Allowances}) \qquad (1)$$

and

$$ST = \frac{NT}{1 - \text{Allowances}} \qquad (2)$$

Equation (1) is most often used in practice. Here the allowances are stated as a percentage of the "job time." In other words, the allowance factor is added to the job time in order to obtain the standard time. However, if the allowances are stated as a percentage of the total "work time," then equation (2) is the correct one to use. To illustrate, suppose that the normal time to perform a task is 1 minute and that allowances for personal needs, delays, and fatigue total 15 percent of the job time; then by equation (1),

$$ST = 1(1 + 0.15) = 1.15 \text{ minutes}$$

In an eight-hour day, a worker would produce $8 \times 60/1.15 = 417$ units. This implies 417×1 minute per unit (normal time) $= 417$ minutes working and $480 - 417 = 63$ minutes for allowances.

However, if the allowance factor is stated as a percentage of the total work time, then we would use equation (2):

$$ST = \frac{1}{1 - 0.15} = 1.18 \text{ minutes}$$

In the same eight-hour day, using equation (2), $8 \times 60/1.18$ (or 408) units are produced with 408 working minutes and 72 minutes for allowances. Depending on how the allowance factor is specified, there is a difference of 9 units produced and also 9 minutes in the daily allowance time.

Before a time study is made, each task is broken down into elements or parts. Some general rules for this breakdown are:

1. Define each work element to be short in duration but long enough so each can be timed with a stopwatch and the time can be written down.
2. If the operator works with equipment that runs separately—the operator performs a task and the equipment runs independently—separate the actions of the operator and that of the equipment into different elements.

3. Define any delays by the operator or equipment into separate elements.

How many observations are enough? Time study is really a sampling process, that is, we take a relatively small number of observations as being representative of many subsequent cycles to be performed by the worker. A great deal of analysis and experience indicates that the number of observations is a function of cycle length and the number of repetitions of the job over a one-year planning period.

Elemental standard-time data

Elemental standard-time data is obtained from previous time studies and codified in tables in a handbook or computer data bank. Such data are used to develop time standards for new jobs or to make time adjustments to reflect changes in existing jobs. They are more correctly viewed as *normal-time data,* because tabled values have been modified by an average performance rating, and allowances must be added to obtain a standard time.

Calculating a **time standard** for a new job using elemental standard-time data tables entails the following steps:

1. Break down the new job into its basic elements.
2. Match these elements to the time for similar elements in the table.
3. Adjust element times for special characteristics of the new job. (In metal cutting, for instance, this is often done by a formula that modifies the time required as a function of type of metal, size of the cutting tool, depth of the cut, and so forth.)
4. Add element times together and add delay and fatigue allowances as specified by company policy for the given class of work.

The obvious benefit of elemental standard data is cost savings: It eliminates the need for a new time study every time there is a new job. This saves staff time and avoids disruption of the work force. The main practical requirements of the approach is that the elemental data must be kept up to date and easily accessible.

Work sampling

Whereas work measurement is concerned with how long it takes to perform a specific task or activity, work sampling is primarily concerned with how workers spend their time among several tasks or activities. For example, we may want to know how much time workers spend on indirect activities such as material handling to determine whether or not more cost-efficient material handling equipment should be purchased. Work sampling provides us with a method for determining the time spent on these activities, and involves observing a portion or sample of the work activity. Then, based on the findings in this sample, some statements can be made about how the employee or employees spend their time.

For example, if we were to observe a fire department rescue squad 100 random times during the day and found it was involved in a rescue mission for 30 of the 100 times (en route, on site, or returning from a call), we would estimate that the rescue squad spends 30 percent of its time directly on rescue mission calls. (The time it takes to make an observation depends on what is being observed. Often only a glance is needed to determine the activity, and the majority of studies require only several seconds' observation.)

Observing an activity even 100 times may not, however, provide the accuracy desired in the estimate. To refine this estimate, three main issues must be decided (these points are discussed later in this section, along with an example):

1. What level of statistical confidence is desired in the results?
2. How many observations are necessary?
3. Precisely when should the observations be made?

The number of observations required in a work sampling study can be fairly large, ranging from several hundred to several thousand, depending on the activity and the desired degree of accuracy. Although the number can be computed from formulas, the easiest way is to refer to a table such as Exhibit 11.13, which gives the number of observations needed for a 95 percent confidence level in terms of absolute error. Absolute error is the actual range of the observations. For example, if a clerk is idle 10 percent of the time and the designer of the study is satisfied with a 2.5 percent range (meaning that the true percentage lies within 7.5 and 12.5 percent), the number of observations required for the work sampling is 576. A 2 percent error (or an interval of 8 to 12 percent) would require 900 observations.

The steps involved in conducting a work sampling study are:

1. Identify the specific activity or activities that are the main purpose for the study. For example, determine the percentage of time equipment is working, idle, or under repair.
2. If possible, estimate the proportion of time of the activity of interest to the total time (e.g., that the equipment is working 80 percent of the time). These estimates can be made from the analyst's knowledge, past data, reliable guesses from others, or a pilot work-sampling study. If no estimate can be made, assume that the proportion is 50 percent, which will, in the worst case, overestimate the sample size required.
3. State the desired accuracy in the study results.
4. Determine the specific times when each observation is to be made.
5. At two or three intervals during the study period, recompute the required sample size by using the data collected thus far. Adjust the number of observations if appropriate.

The number of observations to be taken in a work sampling study is usually divided equally over the study period. Thus, if 500 observations are to be made over a 10-day period, the observations are usually scheduled at 500/10, or 50 per day. Each day's observations are then assigned a specific time by using a random number generator.

Work sampling applied to nursing. There has been a long-standing argument that a large amount of nurses' hospital time is spent on non-nursing activities. This, the argument goes, creates an apparent shortage of well-trained nursing personnel, a significant waste of talent, a corresponding loss of efficiency, and increased hospital costs, because nurses' wages are the highest single cost in the operation of a hospital. Further, pressure is growing

EXHIBIT 11.13 **Determining Number of Observations Required for a Given Absolute Error at Various Values of *p*, with 95 Percent Confidence Level**

Percentage of Total Time Occupied by Activity or Delay, *p*	ABSOLUTE ERROR					
	±1.0%	±1.5%	±2.0%	±2.5%	±3.0%	±3.5%
1 or 99	396	176	99	63	44	32
2 or 98	784	348	196	125	87	64
3 or 97	1,164	517	291	186	129	95
4 or 96	1,536	683	384	246	171	125
5 or 95	1,900	844	475	304	211	155
6 or 94	2,256	1,003	564	361	251	184
7 or 93	2,604	1,157	651	417	289	213
8 or 92	2,944	1,308	736	471	327	240
9 or 91	3,276	1,456	819	524	364	267
10 or 90	3,600	1,600	900	576	400	294
11 or 89	3,916	1,740	979	627	435	320
12 or 88	4,224	1,877	1,056	676	469	344
13 or 87	4,524	2,011	1,131	724	503	369
14 or 86	4,816	2,140	1,204	771	535	393
15 or 85	5,100	2,267	1,275	816	567	416
16 or 84	5,376	2,389	1,344	860	597	439
17 or 83	5,644	2,508	1,411	903	627	461
18 or 82	5,904	2,624	1,476	945	656	482
19 or 81	6,156	2,736	1,539	985	684	502
20 or 80	6,400	2,844	1,600	1,024	711	522
21 or 79	6,636	2,949	1,659	1,062	737	542
22 or 78	6,864	3,050	1,716	1,098	763	560
23 or 77	7,084	3,148	1,771	1,133	787	578
24 or 76	7,296	3,243	1,824	1,167	811	596
25 or 75	7,500	3,333	1,875	1,200	833	612
26 or 74	7,696	3,420	1,924	1,231	855	628
27 or 73	7,884	3,504	1,971	1,261	876	644
28 or 72	8,064	3,584	2,016	1,290	896	658
29 or 71	8,236	3,660	2,059	1,318	915	672
30 or 70	8,400	3,733	2,100	1,344	933	686
31 or 69	8,556	3,803	2,139	1,369	951	698
32 or 68	8,704	3,868	2,176	1,393	967	710
33 or 67	8,844	3,931	2,211	1,415	983	722
34 or 66	8,976	3,989	2,244	1,436	997	733
35 or 65	9,100	4,044	2,275	1,456	1,011	743
36 or 64	9,216	4,096	2,304	1,475	1,024	753
37 or 63	9,324	1,144	2,331	1,492	1,036	761
38 or 62	9,424	4,188	2,356	1,508	1,047	769
39 or 61	9,516	4,229	2,379	1,523	1,057	777
40 or 60	9,600	4,266	2,400	1,536	1,067	784
41 or 59	9,676	4,300	2,419	1,548	1,075	790
42 or 58	9,744	4,330	2,436	1,559	1,083	795
43 or 57	9,804	4,357	2,451	1,569	1,089	800
44 or 56	9,856	4,380	2,464	1,577	1,095	804
45 or 55	9,900	4,400	2,475	1,584	1,099	808
46 or 54	9,936	4,416	2,484	1,590	1,104	811
47 or 53	9,964	4,428	2,491	1,594	1,107	813
48 or 52	9,984	4,437	2,496	1,597	1,109	815
49 or 51	9,996	4,442	2,499	1,599	1,110	816
50	10,000	4,444	2,500	1,600	1,111	816

Note: Number of observations is obtained from the formula $E = Z\sqrt{\frac{p(1-p)}{N}}$; the required sample ($N$) is $N = \frac{Z^2 p(1-p)}{E^2}$ where E = Absolute error

p = Percentage occurrence of activity or delay being measured

N = Number of random observations (sample size)

Z = Number of standard deviations to give desired confidence level (e.g., for 90 percent confidence, $Z = 1.65$; 95 percent, and $Z = 1.96$; 99 percent, $Z = 2.23$). In this table, $Z = 2$.

EXHIBIT 11.14

Assignment of Numbers to Corresponding Minutes

Time	Assigned Numbers
7:00– 7:59 AM	100–159
8:00– 8:59 AM	200–259
9:00– 9:59 AM	300–359
10:00–10:59 AM	400–459
11:00–11:59 AM	500–559
12:00–12:59 PM	600–659
1:00– 1:59 PM	700–759
2:00– 2:59 PM	800–859

for hospitals and hospital administrators to contain costs. With that in mind, let us use work sampling to test the hypothesis that a large portion of nurses' time is spent on non-nursing duties.

Example

Assume at the outset that we have made a list of all the activities that are part of nursing and will make our observations in only two categories: nursing and non-nursing activities.[7] (An expanded study could list all nursing activities to determine the portion of time spent in each.) Therefore, when we observe a nurse during the study and find her performing one of the duties on the nursing list, we simply place a tally mark in the nursing column. If we observe her doing anything besides nursing, we place a tally mark in the non-nursing column.

We can now proceed to design the work sampling study. Assume that we (or the nursing supervisor) estimate that nurses spend 60 percent of their time in nursing activities. Assume that we would like to be 95 percent confident that the findings of our study are within the absolute error range of plus or minus 3 percent; that is, that if our study shows nurses spend 60 percent of their time on nursing duties, we are 95 percent confident that the true percentage lies between 57 and 63 percent. From Exhibit 11.13, we find that 1,067 observations are required for 60 percent activity time and ± 3 percent error. If our study is to take place over 10 days, we start with 107 observations per day.

To determine when each day's observations are to be made, we assign specific numbers to each minute and a random number table to set up a schedule. If the study extends over an eight-hour shift, we can assign numbers to correspond to each consecutive minute.[8] The list in Exhibit 11.14 shows the assignment of numbers to corresponding minutes. For simplicity, because each number corresponds to one minute, a three-number scheme is used, with the second and third number corresponding to the minute of the hour. A number of other schemes would also be appropriate.[9]

[7] Actually, there is much debate on what constitutes nursing activity. For instance, is talking to a patient a nursing duty?

[8] For this study, it is likely that the night shift (11:00 PM to 7:00 AM) would be run separately, since the nature of nighttime nursing duties is considerably different from that of daytime duties.

[9] If a number of studies are planned, a computer program may be used to generate a randomized schedule for the observation times.

EXHIBIT 11.15

Determination of Observation Times

Random Number	Corresponding Time from the Preceding List
669	Nonexistent
831	2:31 PM
555	11:55 AM
470	Nonexistent
113	7:13 AM
080	Nonexistent
520	11:20 AM
204	8:04 AM
732	1:32 PM
420	10:20 AM

If we refer to a random number table and list three-digit numbers, we can assign each number to a time. The random numbers shown in Exhibit 11.15 demonstrate the procedure for seven observations.

This procedure is followed to generate 107 observation times, and the times are rearranged chronologically for ease in planning. Rearranging the times determined in Exhibit 11.15 gives the total observations per day shown in Exhibit 11.16 (for our sample of seven).

To be perfectly random in this study, we should also "randomize" the nurse we observe each time (the use of various nurses minimizes the effect of bias). In the study, our first observation is made at 7:13 AM for Nurse X. We walk into her area and, on seeing her, check either a nursing or a non-nursing activity. Each observation need be only long enough to determine the class of activity—in most cases only a glance. At 8:04 AM we observe Nurse Y. We continue in this way to the end of the day and the 107 observations. At the end of the second day (and 214 observations), we decide to check for the adequacy of our sample size.

Let's say we made 150 observations of nurses working and 64 of them not working, which gives 70.1 percent working. From Exhibit 11.13, this corresponds to 933 observations. Since we have already taken 214 observations, we need take only 719 over the next eight days, or 90 per day.

EXHIBIT 11.16

Observation Schedule

Observation	Scheduled Time	Nursing Activity (✓)	Non-Nursing Activity (✓)
1	7:13 AM		
2	8:04 AM		
3	10:20 AM		
4	11:20 AM		
5	11:55 AM		
6	1:32 PM		
7	2:31 PM		

When the study is half over, another check should be made. For instance, if Days 3, 4, and 5 showed 55, 59, and 64 working observations, the cumulative data would give 328 working observations of a total 484, or a 67.8 percent working activity. Exhibit 11.13 shows the sample size to be about 967, leaving 483 to be made—at 97 per day—for the following five days. Another computation should be made before the last day to see if another adjustment is required. If after the tenth day several more observations are indicated, these can be made on Day 11.

If at the end of the study we find that 66 percent of nurses' time is involved with what has been defined as nursing activity, there should be an analysis to identify the remaining 34 percent. Approximately 12 to 15 percent is justifiable for coffee breaks and personal needs, which leaves 20 to 22 percent of the time that must be justified and compared to what the industry considers ideal levels of nursing activity. To identify the non-nursing activities, a more detailed breakdown could have been originally built into the sampling plan. Otherwise, a follow-up study may be in order.

Financial Incentive Plans

The third piece of the job design equation is the paycheck. In this section we briefly review common methods for setting financial incentives.

Basic compensation systems

The primary forms of basic compensation are hourly pay, straight salary, piece rate, and commissions. The first two are based on time spent on the job, with individual performance ultimately being rewarded by an increase in the base rate. Piece-rate plans reward on the basis of direct daily output (a worker is paid $5 a unit and if he or she produces 10 units per day, he or she earns $50). Sometimes, a guaranteed base is included in a piece-rate plan; a worker would receive this base amount regardless of output, plus his or her piece-rate bonus. (For example, the worker's hourly base pay is $8, so this coupled with $50 piece-rate earnings would give him or her $114 for an eight-hour day.) Another approach with the guaranteed base is that the worker is paid either the piece rate or the guaranteed base, whichever is higher. Commissions may be thought of as sales-based piece rates and are calculated in the same general way.

The two broad categories of **financial incentive plans** are individual or small group incentive plans and organizationwide plans.

Individual or small group incentive plans

Individual and work-group plans traditionally have rewarded performance by using output (often defined by piece rates) and quality measures. Quality is accounted for by a quality adjustment factor, say percent of rework (e.g., Incentive pay = Total output × [1 − Percent deduction for rework].[10] In recent years skill development has also been rewarded. Sometimes called *pay for knowledge,* this means a worker is compensated for learning new tasks. This is particularly important in job shops using group technology, and in banking,

[10] For a complete discussion of incentive plans including quality measures, see S. Globerson and R. Parsons, "Multi-factor Incentive Systems: Current Practices," *Operations Management Review* 3, no. 2 (Winter 1985).

where supervisors' jobs require knowledge of new types of financial instruments and selling approaches.

AT&T, for example, instituted incentive programs for its managers—an Individual Incentive Award (IIA) and a Management Team Incentive Award (MTIA). The IIA provides lump-sum bonuses to outstanding performers. These outstanding performers were determined by individual performance ratings accompanied by extensive documentation. The lump-sum bonus could range between 15 and 30 percent of base pay.

MTIAs are granted to members of specific divisions or units. Appropriate division or unit goals are established at the beginning of the year. The goals include department service objectives and interdepartmental goals. A typical MTIA could call for a standard amount equivalent to 1.5 percent of wages plus overtime for the next three years based on the performance in the current year.

Organizational plans

Profit sharing and gain sharing are the major types of organizationwide plans. *Profit sharing* is simply distributing a percentage of corporate profits across the work force. In the United States, at least one third of all organizations have profit sharing. In Japan, most major companies give profit-based bonuses twice a year to all employees. Such bonuses may go as high as 50 percent of salaries in good years, to nothing in bad years.

Gain sharing also involves giving organizationwide bonuses, but differs from profit sharing in two important respects: First, it typically measures controllable costs or units of output, not profits, in calculating a bonus. Second, gain sharing is always combined with a participative approach to management. The original and best-known gainsharing plan is the Scanlon Plan (discussed next).

Scanlon Plan. In the late 1930s, the Lapointe Machine and Tool Company was on the verge of bankruptcy. Through the efforts of union president Joseph Scanlon and company management, a plan was devised to save the company by reducing labor costs. In essence, this plan started with the normal labor cost within the firm. Workers as a group were rewarded for any reductions in labor cost below this base cost. The plan's success depended on committees of workers throughout the firm whose purpose was to search out areas for cost saving and to devise ways of improvement. There were many improvements, and the plan did, in fact, save the company.

The basic elements of the Scanlon Plan are

1. *The ratio.* The ratio is the standard that serves as a measure for judging business performance. It can be expressed as:

$$\text{Ratio} = \frac{\text{Total labor cost}}{\text{Sales value of production}}$$

2. *The bonus.* The amount of bonus depends on the reduction in costs below the preset ratio.
3. *The production committee.* The production committee is formed to encourage

employee suggestions to increase productivity, improve quality, reduce waste, and so forth. The purpose of a production committee is similar to that of a QC circle.

4. *The screening committee.* The screening committee consists of top management and worker representatives who review monthly bonuses, discuss production problems, and consider improvement suggestions.

Gain-sharing plans are now used by more than a thousand firms in the United States and Europe, and are growing in popularity. One recent survey in the United States indicated that about 13 percent of all firms have them, and that more than 70 percent were started after 1982.[11] Though originally established in small companies such as Lapointe, Lincoln Electric Company, and Herman Miller, gain sharing is now being installed by large firms such as TRW, General Electric Company, Motorola, and Firestone. These companies apply gain sharing to organizational units; Motorola, for example, has virtually all its plant employees covered by gain sharing. These plans are increasing because "they are more than just pay incentive plans; they are a participative approach to management and are often used as a way to install participative management."[12]

11.6 CONCLUSION

An organization's competitive advantage appears to be in the skills, education, and associated performance of its work force. Thus, how we design jobs and the underlying corporate philosophy associated with job design are critical elements in determining the success of the firm. Reengineering allows us to take a more fully integrated approach in redesigning our key processes. This is accomplished primarily by using many of the process evaluation tools presented in this chapter.

Most readers of this book will encounter questions of job design and work methods and measurement in the service sector. It appears that in services, as well as in manufacturing, the new performance metric will be speed, achieved through improved work methods and teamwork. ServiceMaster, for example, has been able to dominate the institutional custodial business (hospitals, schools, and offices) by applying fast cleaning methods to such basic tasks as mopping floors and washing windows. (Rather than using cumbersome ladders to wash windows, they employ specially designed, lightweight, long-handled squeegies using easy-to-remove velcro-backed washable cleaning cloths. Between uses, the clothes are soaked in fluids developed in ServiceMaster's laboratory.) Southwest Airlines uses teamwork (involving its ground crew, baggage handlers, and flight attendants) to achieve a 15-minute turnaround of its flights. (See the next "OM in Action.") Interestingly enough, these examples epitomize some of the ideas that Fredrick W. Taylor advocated almost a century ago.

---

[11] C. O'Dell, *People, Performance, and Pay* (Houston: American Productivity Center, 1987).

[12] E. E. Lawler III, "Paying for Organizational Performance," Report G 87-1 (92), Center for Effective Organizations, University of Southern California, 1987.

OPERATIONS MANAGEMENT IN ACTION
Anatomy of a 15-Minute Turnaround

On a recent weekday a Southwest Airlines flight arrived at New Orleans from Houston. The scheduled arrival time was 8:00 AM, and departure for Birmingham, Alabama, was 8:15 AM. *Forbes* clocked the turnaround, half-minute by half-minute.

7:55	Ground crew chat around gate position.
8:03:30	Ground crew alerted, move to their vehicles.
8:04	Plane begins to pull into gate; crew move toward plane.
8:04:30	Plane stops; jetway telescopes out; baggage door opens.
8:06:30	Baggage unloaded; refueling and other servicing under way.
8:07	Passengers off plane.
8:08	Boarding call; baggage loading, refueling complete.
8:10	Boarding complete; most of ground crew leave.
8:15	Jetway retracts.
8:15:30	Pushback from gate.
8:18	Pushback tractor disengages; plane leaves for runway.

Source: Subrata N. Chakravarty, "Hit'em Hardest with the Mostest," *Forbes* (September 16, 1991), p. 51.

11.7 REVIEW AND DISCUSSION QUESTIONS

1. What does the chapter opening quotation imply to you about good management? Is there a loser in such free-wheeling plants?
2. Comment on the statement, "Heavy manual work is really such a small component of modern American industry that further study of it is not really necessary."
3. Is there an inconsistency when a company requires precise time standards and encourages job enlargement?
4. Match the following techniques to their most appropriate application:

Simo chart	Washing clothes at laundromat
Worker-machine chart	Tracing your steps in getting a parking permit
Process chart	Faculty office hours kept
Work sampling	Development of a new word processor keyboard

5. Comment on the following:
   a. "Work measurement is old hat. We have automated our office, and now we run every bill through our computer (after our 25 clerks have typed the data into our computer database)."
   b. "It's best that our workers don't know that they are being time studied. That way, they can't complain about us getting in the way when we set time standards."
   c. "Once we get everybody on an incentive plan, then we will start our work measurement program."
   d. "Rhythm is fine for dancing, but it has no place on the shop floor."

6. The American Motors study team observed that the Japanese used techniques such as job rotation, making line workers responsible for quality control, minimal work classifications, and indirect employee participation in management. What gains could be made with this approach, contrasted with the job specialization approach? If this approach is applied in a specialized job environment, what changes would be necessary?
7. Organizationwide financial incentive plans cover all the workers. Some units or individuals may have contributed more to corporate profits than others. Does this detract from the effectiveness of the incentive plan system? How would your incentive scheme for a small software development firm compare to an established automobile manufacturing firm?
8. The conclusion of this chapter describes Southwest Airlines's fast flight turnarounds. What has to be done inside the terminal to attain this performance?

11.8 SOLVED PROBLEMS

PROBLEM

1. Felix Unger is a very organized person and wants to plan his day perfectly. To do this, he has his friend Oscar time his daily activities. Following are the results of Oscar timing Felix on polishing two pairs of black shoes using the snapback method of timing. What is the standard time for polishing two pairs? (Assume a 5 percent allowance factor for Felix to get Oscar an ashtray for his cigar. Account for noncyclically recurring elements by dividing their observed times by the total number of cycles observed.) All times shown are in minutes.

OBSERVED TIMES

Element	1	2	3	4	ST	$\bar{T}$	Performance Rating	NT
Get shoeshine kit	0.50						125%	
Polish shoes	0.94	0.85	0.80	0.81			110	
Put away kit				0.75			80	

SOLUTION

Felix Unger time study.

	ST	$\bar{T}$	Performance Rating	NT
Get shoeshine kit	.50	.50/2 = .25	125%	.31
Polish shoes (2 pair)	3.40	3.40/4 = 1.70	110	1.87
Put away kit	.75	.75/2 = .375	80	.30
Normal time for one pair of shoes				2.48

Standard time for the pair = 2.48 × 1.05 = 2.61 minutes.

PROBLEM

2. A total of 15 observations have been taken on a head baker for a school district. The numerical breakdown of her activities is

Make Ready	Do	Clean Up	Idle
2	6	3	4

Based on this information, how many work sampling observations are required to determine how much of the baker's time is spent in "doing"? Assume a 5 percent desired absolute accuracy and 95 percent confidence level.

SOLUTION

Work sampling of head baker.

To calculate the number of observations, use the formula at the bottom of Exhibit 11.13, since the 95 percent confidence is required, use $Z = 1.96$.

p = "Doing" = 6/15 = 40%

E = 5% (given)

$$N = \frac{Z^2 p(1 - p)}{E^2} = \frac{(1.96)^2(.4)(1 - .4)}{(.05)^2} = 369$$

11.9 PROBLEMS

1. Use the following form to evaluate a job you have held relative to the five principles of job design given in the chapter. Develop a numerical score by summing the numbers in parentheses.

	Poor (0)	Adequate (1)	Good (2)	Outstanding (3)
Task variety				
Skill variety				
Feedback				
Task identity				
Task autonomy				

   a. Compute the score for your job. Does the score match your subjective feelings about the job as a whole? Explain.

   b. Compare your score with the scores generated by your classmates. Is there one kind of job that everybody likes and one kind that everybody dislikes?

2. Examine the process chart in Exhibit 11.7. Can you recommend some improvements to cut down on delays and transportation? (Hint: The research laboratory can suggest changes in the requisition form.)

3. As time-study analyst, you have observed that a worker has produced 40 parts in a one-hour period. From your experience, you rate the worker as performing slightly faster than 100 percent—so you estimate performance as 110 percent. The company allows 15 percent for fatigue and delay.

   a. What is the normal time?

   b. What is the standard time?

   c. If a worker produces 300 units per day and has a base rate of $6 per hour, what would the day's wages be for this worker if payment was on a 100 percent wage incentive payment plan?

4. A time study was made of an existing job to develop new time standards. A worker was observed for a period of 45 minutes. During that period, 30 units were produced. The analyst rated the worker as performing at a 90 percent performance rate. Allowances in the firm for rest and personal time are 12 percent.
   a. What is the normal time for the task?
   b. What is the standard time for the task?
   c. If the worker produced 300 units in an eight-hour day, what would the day's pay be if the basic rate was $6 per hour and the premium payment system paid on a 100 percent basis?
5. The Bullington Company wants a time standard established on the painting operation of souvenir horseshoes for the local Pioneer Village. Work sampling is to be used. It is estimated that working time averages 95 percent of total time (working time plus idle time). A co-op student is available to do the work sampling between the hours of 8:00 AM and 12:00 noon. Sixty working days are to be used for the study. Use Exhibit 11.13 and an absolute error of 2.5 percent. Use a random number table to calculate the sampling schedule for the first day; i.e., show the times of day that an observation of working/idle should be made. Hint: Start random number selection with the first row.
6. A time-study analysis has obtained the following performance times by observing a worker over 15 operating cycles:

Performance Number	Time (seconds)	Performance Number	Time (seconds)
1	15	9	14
2	12	10	18
3	16	11	13
4	11	12	15
5	13	13	16
6	14	14	15
7	16	15	11
8	12		

   The worker was rated as performing at 115 percent. Allowances for personal time and fatigue in the company are 10 percent. The base rate for the worker is $5 per hour and the company operates on a 100 percent premium plan.
   a. What is the normal time?
   b. What is the standard time?
   c. If the worker produced 2,500 in a day, what would the gross pay for the day be if the premium rate was 100 percent?
7. A work-sampling study is to be conducted over the next 30 consecutive days of an activity in the city fire department. Washing trucks, which is the subject of the study, is to be observed, and it is estimated that this occurs 10 percent of the time. A 3.5 percent accuracy with 95 percent confidence is acceptable. State specifically when observations should be made on one day. Use a 10-hour day from 8:00 AM to 6:00 PM.
8. In an attempt to increase productivity and reduce costs, Rho Sigma Corporation is planning to install an incentive pay plan in its manufacturing plant.

   In developing standards for one operation, time study analysts observed a worker for a 30-minute period. During that time the worker completed 42 parts. The analysts rated the worker as producing at 130 percent. The base wage rate of the worker is $5 per hour. The firm has established 15 percent as a fatigue and personal time allowance.

a. What is the normal time for the task?
b. What is the standard time for the task?
c. If the worker produced 500 units during an eight-hour day, what wages would the worker have earned?

9. Since new regulations will greatly change the products and services offered by savings and loan associations, time studies must be performed on tellers and other personnel to determine the number and types of personnel needed and incentive wage payment plans that might be installed.

   As an example of the studies that the various tasks will undergo, consider the following problem and come up with the appropriate answers:

   A hypothetical case was set up in which the teller (to be retitled later as an *account adviser*) was required to examine a customer's portfolio and determine whether it was more beneficial for the customer to consolidate various CDs into a single issue currently offered, or to leave the portfolio unaltered. A time study was made of the teller, with the following findings:

Time of study	90 minutes
Number of portfolios examined	10 portfolios
Performance rating	130 percent
Rest for personal time	15 percent
Teller's proposed new pay rate	$12 per hour

a. What is the normal time for the teller to do a portfolio analysis for the CDs?
b. What is the standard time for the analysis?
c. If the S&L decides to pay the new tellers on a 100 percent premium payment plan, how much would a teller earn for a day in which he or she analyzed 50 customer portfolios?

10. It is estimated that a bank teller spends about 10 percent of this time in a particular type of transaction. The bank manager would like a work-sampling study that shows, within plus or minus 3 percent, whether the clerk's time is really 10 percent (i.e., from 7 to 13 percent). The manager is well satisfied with a 95 percent confidence level.

   From Exhibit 11.13 you observe that, for the first "cut" at the problem, a sample size of 400 is indicated for the 10 percent activity time and ±3 percent absolute error.

   State how you would perform the work-sampling study. If the study were to be made over a five-week period with five days per week from the hours of 9:00 to 5:00, specify the exact time (in minute increments) that you would make Monday's observations.

11.10 CASE: UP TO SPEED: UNITED PARCEL SERVICE GETS DELIVERIES DONE BY DRIVING ITS WORKERS*

Grabbing a package under his arm, Joseph Polise, a driver for United Parcel Service (UPS), bounds from his brown delivery truck and toward an office building here. A few paces behind him, Marjorie Cusack, a UPS industrial engineer, clutches a digital timer.

Her eyes fixed on Mr. Polise, she counts his steps and times his contact with customers.

*Daniel Machalaba, "Up to Speed: United Parcel Service Gets Deliveries Done by Driving Its Workers," *The Wall Street Journal* (April 22, 1986), p. 1.

Scribbling on a clipboard, Mrs. Cusack records every second taken up by stoplights, traffic, detours, doorbells, walkways, stairways, and coffee breaks. "If he goes to the bathroom, we time him," she says.

Such attention to detail is nothing new at UPS, the nation's largest deliverer of packages. Through meticulous human-engineering and close scrutiny of its 152,000 employees, the privately held company, which is based in Greenwich, Connecticut, has grown highly profitable despite stiff competition. In fact, UPS is one of the most efficient companies anywhere, productivity experts say.

"You never see anybody sitting on his duff at UPS," says Bernard La Londe, a transportation professor at The Ohio State University. "The only other place you see the same commitment to productivity is at Japanese companies."

Getting Up to Speed

At UPS, more than 1,000 industrial engineers use time study to set standards for a myriad of closely supervised tasks. Drivers are instructed to walk to a customer's door at the brisk pace of three feet per second and to knock first lest seconds be lost searching for the doorbell. Supervisors then ride with the "least best drivers" until they learn to finish on time. "It's human nature to get away with as much as possible," says Michael Kamienski, a UPS district manager. "But we bring workers up to our level of acceptance. We don't go down to their level."

If UPS isn't quite a throwback to old-time work measurement, it nevertheless runs counter to the drift of many U.S. companies. To increase productivity, others are turning more often to employee-involvement techniques that stress consultation and reject the rigid monitoring of workers.

"Workers are better educated and want more to say about what happens to them," says Roger Weiss, a vice president of H. B. Maynard & Co., a consulting concern. "Time study is a dark-ages technique, and it's dehumanizing to track someone around with a stopwatch."

UPS dismisses the criticism. "We don't use the standards as hammers, but they do give accountability," says Larry P. Breakiron, the company's senior vice president for engineering. "Our ability to manage labor and hold it accountable is the key to our success."

New Competition

Those techniques are about to be tested. Long engaged in a battle for parcels with the Postal Service, UPS recently has charged into overnight delivery against Federal Express Corporation, Purolator Courier, Airborne Freight, Emery Air Freight and others. What's more, it now is being challenged on its own turf by Roadway Services Inc., which in the early 1990s started a parcel delivery company called Roadway Package System that is implementing management ideas of its own.

The upstart competitor boasts that its owner-operator drivers, unlike UPS's closely scrutinized, but highly paid and unionized, drivers, are motivated by the challenge of running their own business. "Our people don't drive brown trucks; they own their trucks," says Ivan Hoffman, a vice president of Roadway.

Roadway also is trying to gain the edge in productivity by eliminating people as much as possible through automation. Its package hubs use bar codes, laser scanners, computers, and special mechanical devices to sort packages, a task still handled at UPS by armies of workers. UPS calls its rival's methods unreliable, inflexible, and expensive. Those are the same epithets that Roadway hurls at UPS's human sorters.

The outcome of this budding competition interests package shippers. "UPS has taken the engineering of people as far as it can be taken," says Michael Birkholm, the director of transportation for American Greetings Corporation. "But the question is whether technologically sophisticated Roadway can dent the big brown UPS machine."

Burgeoning Competition

If the competition intensifies, productivity improvements will be at the heart of UPS's counterattack. Indeed, UPS long has used efficiency to overcome rivals. Founded in Seattle in 1907 as a messenger service, UPS over the years won parcel deliveries from department stores and captured package business once handled by the Postal Service because of its lower rates and superior service.

UPS's founder, James E. Casey, put a premium on efficiency. In the 1920s, he turned to Frank B. Gilbreth and other pioneers of time study to develop techniques to measure the time consumed each day by each UPS driver. Later, UPS engineers cut away the sides of a UPS delivery truck, or "package car" as the company calls the vehicle, to study a driver at work. Resultant changes in package loading techniques increased efficiency 30 percent.

Mr. Casey also shaped the company culture, which stresses achievement and teamwork in addition to efficiency. Copies of his tract, "Determined Men," and of "Pursuit of Excellence," a pamphlet written by one-time UPS Chairman George Smith, are handed out to the company's managers. "We still use Jim's and George's quotes in everything we do," says George Lamb, Jr., a UPS director and past chairman.

Another guiding principle: a fair day's work for a fair day's pay. The company's drivers, all of them Teamsters, earn wages of $15 an hour, about $1 more than the best-paid drivers at other trucking companies earn. With overtime, many UPS drivers gross $35,000 to $40,000 a year.

In return, UPS seeks maximum output from its drivers, as is shown by the time study Mrs. Cusack is conducting. On this day in suburban Whippany, she determines time allowances for each of Polise's 120 stops while watching for inefficiency in his methods. "What are you doing, Joe?" she asks as Mr. Polise wastes precious seconds handling packages more than once. She says that a mere 30 seconds wasted at each stop can snowball into big delays by day's end.

Some UPS drivers with nicknames like Ace, Hammer Slick, and Rocket Shoes take pride in meeting the standards day after day. "We used to joke that a good driver could get to his stop and back to the car before the seat belt stopped swaying," Mrs. Cusack says. (UPS has since redesigned its seat belts to eliminate sway.)

But not all UPS drivers enjoy the pace. For example, Michael Kipila, a driver in East Brunswick, New Jersey, says, "They squeeze every ounce out of you. You're always in a hurry, and you can't work relaxed." Some drivers say they cut their breaks in order to finish on time.

UPS officials maintain that the company's work standards are not just a matter of increasing output, but of making the job easier. "If you do it our way, you'll be less tired at the end of the day," says a UPS spokesman.

Had Enough

The pressures cause some UPS employees—supervisors and drivers alike—to quit. Jose Vega, a former UPS supervisor, says he would ride with one New York driver, noting each time "pace too slow, customer contact too long." Vega says he tried to embarrass the driver so as to speed him up: "Are you falling asleep? Do you want a sleeping bag?" After a while, "it's like you're abusing this person," says Vega, who now drives for Roadway.

"There's a fine line between motivation and harassment, and many times UPS crosses that line," says Mario Perrucci, the secretary-treasurer of Teamsters Local 177 in Hillside, New Jersey. Mr.

Perrucci has battled UPS for years over a requirement that drivers tap their horns when they approach a stop in the hopes that the customer will hurry to the door seconds sooner.

UPS's efforts to increase productivity get mixed reactions from the Teamsters union. While some local Teamsters officials such as Perrucci say that UPS is driving its workers "beyond endurance," the union's national executives are grateful that the company is successful. "I'd rather see UPS pushing the men too hard," says a Teamsters official in Washington, "than see UPS in bankruptcy court."

Many trucking companies employing Teamsters are shutting down or, like Roadway Package System, turning to nonunion workers. But, UPS continues to be the largest single employer of Teamsters members, with more than 100,000 unionized workers, a 33 percent rise since 1980.

A Game of Inches

To sustain growth, UPS executives are looking for new efficiencies. For example, they are seeking to make work standards for truck mechanics more exact. And at UPS's Parsippany, New Jersey, package sorting hub, 1 of more than 100 that the company operates, officials are making the most of space by parking delivery trucks just five inches apart. But productivity has its price. New York City says that UPS drivers have received more than $1 million in unpaid parking tickets since March 1985 while making local deliveries. A company attorney says the amount is "much too high." UPS has contested the fines.

The new competition from Roadway Package System also looms large. Roadway is cutting labor expenses 20 percent to 30 percent by using independent drivers. Because Roadway drivers buy their own trucks, uniforms, and insurance, Roadway is saving money that it is using to automate package sorting. "We'll use technology to be the low-cost producer," says Bram Johnson, a Roadway vice president.

Roadway says it reduced personnel 25 percent at its five sorting hubs through automation. At its York, Pennsylvania, hub, for example, a moving belt of tilt trays following instructions from a computer drops packages down a series of chutes.

QUESTION

What are the advantages and disadvantages of the UPS approach to job design and work measurement?

11.11 CASE: AT&T CREDIT CORP.*

Millions of clerical employees toil in the back offices of financial companies, processing applications, claims, and customer accounts on what amounts to electronic assembly lines. The jobs are dull and repetitive and efficiency gains minuscule—when they come at all.

That was the case with AT&T Credit Corp. (ATTCC) when it opened shop in 1985 as a newly created subsidiary of American Telephone & Telegraph Corp. Based in Morristown, New Jersey, ATTCC provides financing for customers who lease equipment from AT&T and other companies. A bank initially retained by ATTCC to process lease applications couldn't keep up with the volume of new business.

*Source: John Hoerr, "The Payoff from Teamwork," *Business Week* (July 10, 1989), p. 59.

ATTCC President Thomas C. Wajnert saw that the fault lay in the bank's method of dividing labor into narrow tasks and organizing work by function. One department handled applications and checked the customer's credit standing, a second drew up contracts, and a third collected payments. So no one person or group had responsibility for providing full service to a customer. "The employees had no sense of how their jobs contributed to the final solution for the customer," Wajnert says.

Unexpected Bonus

Wajnert decided to hire his own employees and give them "ownership and accountability." His first concern was to increase efficiency, not to provide more rewarding jobs. But in the end, he did both.

In 1986, ATTCC set up 11 teams of 10 to 15 newly hired workers in a high-volume division serving small businesses. The three major lease-processing functions were combined in each team. No longer were calls from customers shunted from department to department. The company also divided its national staff of field agents into seven regions and assigned two or three teams to handle business from each region. That way, the same teams always worked with the same sales staff, establishing a personal relationship with them and their customers. Above all, team members took responsibility for solving customers' problems. ATTCC's new slogan: "Whoever gets the call owns the problem."

The teams largely manage themselves. Members make most decisions on how to deal with customers, schedule their own time off, reassign work when people are absent, and interview prospective new employees. The only supervisors are seven regional managers who advise the team members, rather than give orders. The result: The teams process up to 800 lease applications a day versus 400 under the old system. Instead of taking several days to give a final yes or no, the teams do it in 24 to 48 hours. As a result, ATTCC is growing at a 40 percent to 50 percent compound annual rate, Wajnert says.

Extra Cash

The teams also have economic incentives for providing good service. A bonus plan tied to each team's costs and profits can produce extra cash. The employees, most of whom are young college graduates, can add $1,500 a year to average salaries of $28,000, and pay rises as employees learn new skills. "It's a phenomenal learning opportunity," says 24-year-old team member Michael LoCastro.

But LoCastro and others complain that promotions are rare because there are few managerial positions. And everyone comes under intense pressure from co-workers to produce more. The annual turnover rate is high: Some 20 percent of ATTCC employees either quit or transfer to other parts of AT&T. Still, the team experiment has been so successful that ATTCC is involving employees in planning to extend the concept throughout the company. "They will probably come up with as good an organizational design as management could," Wajnert says, "and it will work a lot better because the employees will take ownership for it."

QUESTION

What would you do to reduce the turnover rate at ATTCC?

11.12 SELECTED BIBLIOGRAPHY

Barnes, Ralph M. *Motion and Time Study: Design and Measurement of Work.* 8th ed. New York: John Wiley & Sons, 1980.

Carlisle, Brian. "Job Design Implications for Operations Managers," *International Journal of Operations and Production Management* 3, no. 3 (1983), pp. 40–48.

Cusumano, Michael. *Japan's Software Factories: A Challenge to U.S. Management.* New York: Oxford University Press, 1991.

Davis, L.E., and J.C. Taylor. *Design of Jobs.* 2nd ed. Santa Monica, Calif.: Goodyear Publishing, 1979.

Hammer, Michael, and James Champy. *Reengineering the Corporation: A Manifesto for Business Revolution.* New York: HarperCollins, 1993.

Kirkman, Frank. "Who Cares About Job Design? Some Reflections on Its Present and Future." *International Journal of Operations and Production Management* 2, no. 1 (1981), pp. 3–13.

Konz, Stephan. *Work Design: Industrial Ergonomics.* 2nd ed. New York: John Wiley & Sons, 1983.

Lipin, Steven. "A New Vision." *The Wall Street Journal* (June 25, 1993).

Niebel, Benjamin W. *Motion and Time Study.* 7th ed. Homewood, Ill.: Richard D. Irwin, 1982.

Niles, John L. "To Increase Productivity, Audit the Old Incentive Plan." *Industrial Engineering* (January 1980), pp. 20–23.

"The Promise of Reengineering." *Fortune* (May 3, 1993), p. 96.

Sasser, W. Earl, and William E. Fulmer. "Creating Personalized Service Delivery Systems." In D. Bowen, R. Chase, and T. Cummings (eds.), *Service Management Effectiveness.* San Francisco: Jossey-Bass, 1990, pp. 213–33.

"Take a Clean Sheet of Paper." *The Economist* (May 1, 1993).

Zuboff, Shoshana. *In the Age of the Smart Machine: The Future of Work and Power.* New York: Basic Books, 1984.

Chapter 12

Project Planning and Control

EPIGRAPH

Ninety-Ninety Rule of Project Schedules: The first 90 percent of the task takes 90 percent of the time, the last 10 percent takes the other 90 percent.

CHAPTER OUTLINE

KEY TERMS

Project
Program
Milestone
Work Breakdown Structure
PERT
CPM
Gantt Chart
Critical Path
Slack Time
Early Start Schedule
Late Start Schedule
Time-Cost Trade-Off Models
Crash Costs

Courtesy The Boeing Company

At Boeing, effective project management techniques were essential both in setting up the 757 assembly system and in scheduling and manufacturing the 757 itself. Notice the emphasis Boeing places on quality.

With product life cycles becoming shorter and shorter, the need to manage change is becoming more important. Shorter product life cycles, in turn, cause changes throughout all phases of production: from technology as the basis of design and manufacturing, through methods of operation and control of production, to delivery to the marketplace. Whereas twenty or thirty years ago a product may have had a life cycle of several years, today's products in many areas (particularly in electronics) may have an existence of only several months.

Those firms that are to survive in such a dynamic environment where the time span from product design to full production is just a matter of months must more fully understand the benefits to be accrued through the use of project management as a tool to plan, operate, and control operations.

Project management techniques are also very appropriate for exactly the opposite type of environment: one where a product's lead time may be long. The key factor in this case is that where frequency of production is low, each item produced tends to be viewed as a separate project. Examples are shipbuilding, airplane manufacture, and production of large turbines and generators.

There are two main thrusts in project management: one heavily emphasizes the organization and the behavior of *people;* the other focuses on technology of the *method* (computing start and completion times, critical paths, etc.). In this chapter we lean more toward describing the method of project management and leave the people issues to a course on management and organizational behavior. Most of the chapter concentrates on project scheduling techniques, primarily CPM and PERT.

12.1 DEFINITION OF PROJECT MANAGEMENT

A project is simply a statement or proposal of something to be done. In a broader sense, a **project** could be defined as a series of related jobs or tasks that are usually directed toward some major output and requiring a significant period of time to perform. *Project management* can be defined as planning, directing, and controlling resources (i.e., people, equipment, material) to meet the technical, cost, and time constraints of the project.

While projects are often viewed as being one-time occurrences, the fact is that many projects can be repeated or transferred to other settings or products. The result will be another project output. A contractor building houses or a firm producing low-volume products such as supercomputers, locomotives, or linear accelerators can effectively consider these as projects.

A project starts out as a *statement of work* (SOW). The SOW may be a written description of the objectives to be achieved, with a brief statement of the work to be done and a proposed schedule specifying the start and completion dates. It could also contain performance measures in terms of budget and completion steps (milestones) and the written reports to be supplied.

If the proposed work is a large endeavor, it is frequently referred to as a **program,** although the terms *project* and *program* are often used interchangeably. A program is the highest order of organizational complexity, may take several years to complete, and may consist of interrelated projects completed by many organizations. The development of a new missile system and the introduction of a new national medical health care system would be good examples of programs.

As implied earlier, a project is similar to a program, but is less complex and of shorter duration. A program may be to build a missile system; a project may be to develop the guidance control portion. In a health care system, one project might be to develop a bid proposal system for health care providers.

A *task* or *activity* is a subdivision of a project. It is usually not longer than several months in duration and is performed by one group or organization.

A *subtask* may be used if needed to further subdivide the project into more meaningful pieces.

A *work package* is a group of activities combined to be assignable to a single organizational unit. It still falls within the format of all project management—that the package provides a description of what is to be done, when it is to be started and completed, the budget, measures of performance, and specific events to be reached at points in time which are called **milestones.** Typical milestones in the introduction of a new product might be the completion of the design, the production of a prototype, the completed testing of the prototype, and the approval of a pilot run.

Work Breakdown Structure

The **work breakdown structure** (WBS) is the heart of project management. This subdivision of the objective into smaller and smaller pieces more clearly defines the system in detail and contributes to its understanding and success. Conventional use shows the

EXHIBIT 12.1

Part of a Work Breakdown Structure for a Large Optical Scanner Design

Level 1	2	3	4	5	
X					Optical simulator design
	X				Optical design
		X			Telescope design/fab
		X			Telescope/simulator optical interface
		X			Simulator zoom system design
		X			Ancillary simulator optical component specification
	X				System performance analysis
		X			Overall system firmware and software control
			X		Logic flow diagram generation and analysis
			X		Basic control algorithm design

work breakdown structure decreasing in size from top to bottom and shows this level by indentation to the right in the following format:

Level	
1	Program
2	Project
3	Task
4	Subtask
5	Work package

Exhibit 12.1 shows part of the work breakdown structure for a project to design a large optional scanner. Note the ease in identifying activities through the level numbers. For example, telescope design (the third item down) is identified as 1.1.1 (the first item in level 1, the first item in level 2, and the first item in level 3). Similarly, data recording (the 13th item down) is 1.2.4.

The keys to a good work breakdown structure are to:

- Allow the activities to be worked on independently.
- Make them manageable in size.
- Give authority to carry out the program.
- Monitor and measure the program.
- Provide the required resources.

12.2 PROJECT CONTROL

Reporting Mechanisms

The Department of Defense was one of the earliest large users of project management and has published a variety of useful standard forms. Many are used directly or have been modified by firms engaged in project management. Since those early days, however, graphics programs have been written for most computers, so management, the customer, and the project manager have a wide choice of how data are presented. Exhibit 12.2 shows a sample of available presentations.

Exhibit 12.2A is a sample Gantt chart showing both the amount of time involved and the sequence in which activities can be performed. For example, "long lead time procurement" and "manufacturing schedules" are independent activities and can occur simultaneously. All of the other activities must be done in the sequence from top to bottom. Exhibit 12.12B graphically shows the proportion of money spent on labor, material, and overhead. Its value is its clarity in identifying sources and amounts of cost.

Exhibit 12.2C shows the percentage of the project's labor hours that come from the various areas of manufacturing, finance, and so on. These labor hours are related to the proportion of the project's total labor cost. For example, manufacturing is responsible for 50 percent of the project's labor hours, but this 50 percent is allocated just 40 percent of the total labor dollars charged.

The top half of Exhibit 12.2D shows the degree of completion of these projects. The dotted vertical line signifies today. Project 1, therefore, is already late since it still has work to be done. Project 2, although on schedule, is not being worked on temporarily, which is why there is a space before the projected work. Project 3, also on schedule, continues to be worked on without interruption. The bottom of Exhibit 12.2D shows actual total costs compared to projected costs. The exhibit shows that two cost overruns occurred.

Exhibit 12.2E is a milestone chart. The three milestones mark specific points in the project where checks can be made to see if the project is on time and where it should be. The best place to locate milestones is at the completion of a major activity. In this exhibit, the major activities completed were "purchase order release," "invoices received," and "material received."

Other standard reports can be used for a more detailed presentation comparing cost to progress (such as cost schedule status report—CSSR) or reports providing the basis for partial payment (such as "earned value" report).

12.3 CRITICAL PATH SCHEDULING

Critical path scheduling refers to a set of graphic techniques used in planning and controlling projects. In any given project, the three factors of concern are time, cost, and resource availability. Critical path techniques have been developed to deal with each of these, individually and in combination. The remainder of this chapter focuses on time-based models, time-cost models, and limited-resource models.

PERT (*Program Evaluation and Review Technique*) and **CPM** (*Critical Path Method*), the two best-known techniques, were both developed in the late 1950s. PERT was developed under the sponsorship of the U.S. Navy Special Projects Office in 1958 as a management tool for scheduling and controlling the Polaris missile project. CPM was developed in 1957 by J. E. Kelly of Remington-Rand and M. R. Walker of Du Pont to aid in scheduling maintenance shutdowns of chemical processing plants.

EXHIBIT 12.2 A Sample of Graphic Project Reports

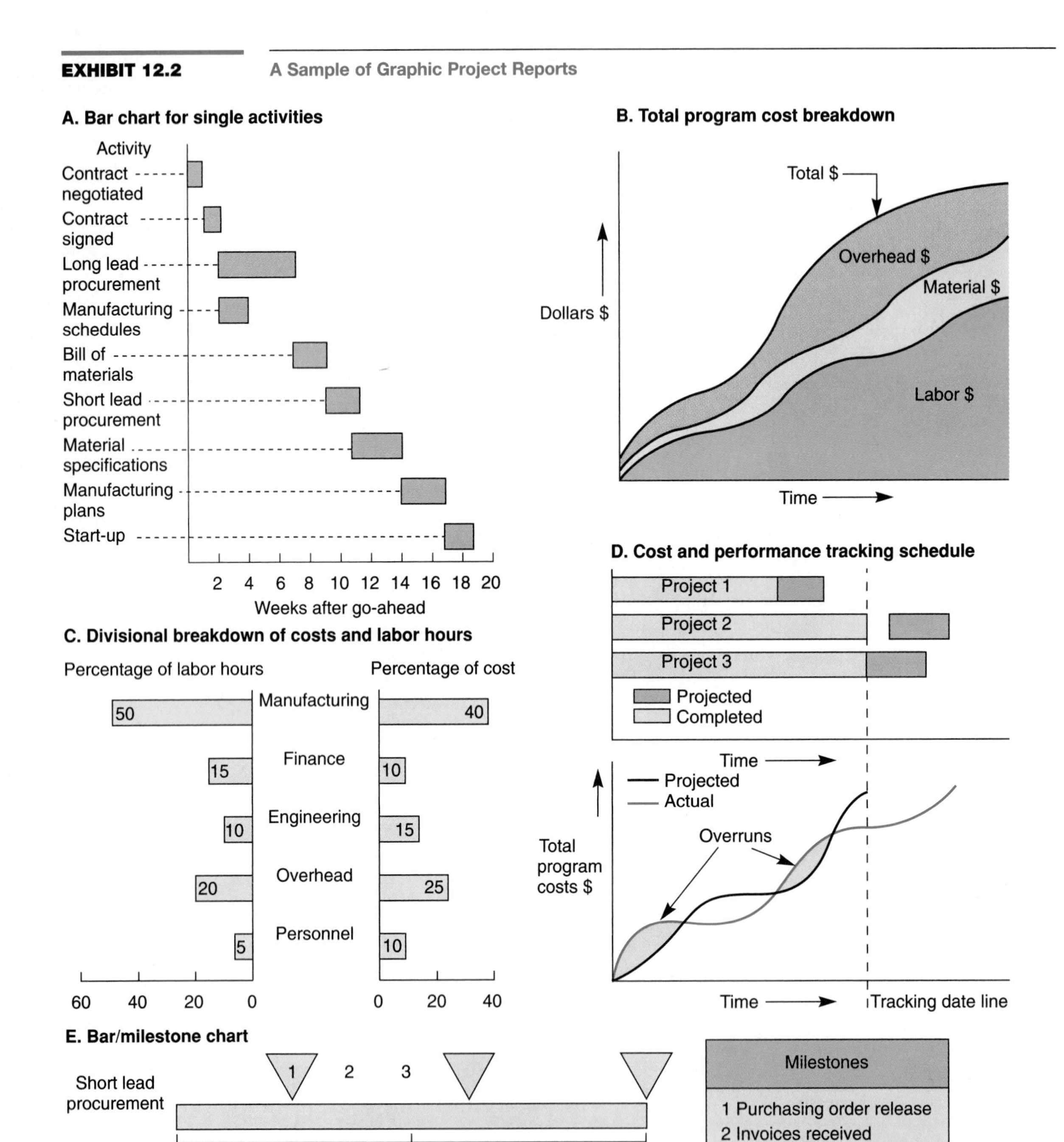

Critical path scheduling techniques display a project in graphic form and relate its competent tasks in a way that focuses attention on those crucial to the project's completion. For critical path scheduling techniques to be most applicable, a project must have the following characteristics:

1. It must have well-defined jobs or tasks whose completion marks the end of the project.
2. The jobs or tasks are independent; they may be started, stopped, and conducted separately within a given sequence.
3. The jobs or tasks are ordered; certain ones must follow others in a given sequence.

The construction, aerospace, and shipbuilding industries commonly meet these criteria, and critical path techniques find wide application within them. We previously noted also that the applications of project management and critical path techniques are becoming much more common within firms in rapidly changing industries.

Project management techniques are also becoming more common in health care, with the objective of reducing a patient's overall stay in a hospital. Here, each patient is viewed as a project and the various procedures he or she undergoes are considered to be the tasks in that project.

12.4 TIME-ORIENTED TECHNIQUES

The basic forms of PERT and CPM focus on finding the longest time-consuming path through a network of tasks as a basis for planning and controlling a project. Both PERT and CPM use nodes and arrows for display. Originally, the basic differences between PERT and CPM were that PERT used the arrow to represent an activity and CPM used the node. The other original difference was that PERT used three estimates—optimistic, pessimistic, and best—of an activity's required time, whereas CPM used just the best estimate. This distinction reflects PERT's origin in scheduling advanced projects that are characterized by uncertainty and CPM's origin in the scheduling of the fairly routine activity of plant maintenance. Thus PERT was often used when the variable of interest was time, whereas CPM was used when the primary variable of interest was cost. As years passed, these two features no longer distinguished PERT from CPM. This is because CPM users started to use three time estimates and PERT users often placed activities on the nodes.

We believe the activity on the node is much easier to follow logically than the activity on the arrow. However, the three time estimates are often very valuable in obtaining a measure of the probability of completion times. Therefore, in this chapter and in this text we use the activity on the node and either a single estimate for activity time or three time estimates, depending on our objective. We use the terms *CPM* and *PERT* interchangeably and mean the same thing, although we tend to use the term *CPM* more frequently.

In a sense, both techniques owe their development to their widely used predecessor, the **Gantt chart.** While the Gantt chart is able to relate activities to time in a visually usable fashion for very small projects, the interrelationship of activities, when displayed in this form, becomes extremely difficult to visualize and to work with for projects with more than 25 or 30 activities. Moreover, the Gantt chart provides no direct procedure for determining the critical path, which, despite its theoretical shortcomings, is of great practical value.

CPM with a Single Time Estimate

With the following as an example, we will develop the typical approach taken in project scheduling. The times for each activity have been given as a single best estimate (rather than three estimates, which will be discussed in a later example).

Example

Many firms that have tried to enter the laptop and briefcase computer market have failed. Suppose your firm believes that there is a big demand in this market because existing products have not been designed correctly. They are either too heavy, too large, or too small to accommodate a standard-size keyboard. Your intended computer will be small enough to carry inside a jacket pocket if need be. The ideal size will be no larger than 4 inches × 9½ inches × 1 inch with a standard typewriter keyboard. It should weigh no more than 15 ounces, have a 4 to 8 line × 80 character back-lit display, have a micro disk drive, and a micro printer. It should be aimed primarily toward word processing use but have plug-in ROMs to accommodate an assortment of computer languages and programs. These characteristics should appeal to traveling business people, but then could also have a much wider market. If it can be priced to sell retail in the $175–$200 range, the computer should appeal to anyone who uses a typewriter. A big market is also expected to be students. College students could use this to create reports; college, high school, and elementary schoolchildren could also use it to take notes during class and during library research.

The project, then, is to design, develop, and produce a prototype of this small computer. In the rapidly changing computer industry, it is crucial to hit the market with a product of this type in less than a year. Therefore, the project team has been allowed approximately nine months, or 39 weeks, to produce the prototype.

The first assignment of the project team is to develop a project network chart to determine whether or not the prototype computer can be completed within the 39 weeks. Let's follow the steps in the development of this network.

Step 1: Activity identification

The project team decides that the following activities constitute the major components of the project: (A) designing the computer, (B) constructing the prototype, (C) evaluating automatic assembly equipment, (D) testing the prototype, (E) preparing an assembly equipment study report, (F) writing methods specifications (to be summarized in a report), and (G) preparing a final report summarizing all aspects of the design, equipment, and methods.

EXHIBIT 12.3

CPM Network for Computer Design Project

CPM ACTIVITY/DESIGNATIONS AND TIME ESTIMATES

Activity	Designation	Immediate Predecessors	Time in Weeks
Design	A	—	21
Build prototype	B	A	4
Evaluate equipment	C	A	7
Test prototype	D	B	2
Write equipment report	E	C, D	5
Write methods report	F	C, D	8
Write final report	G	E, F	2

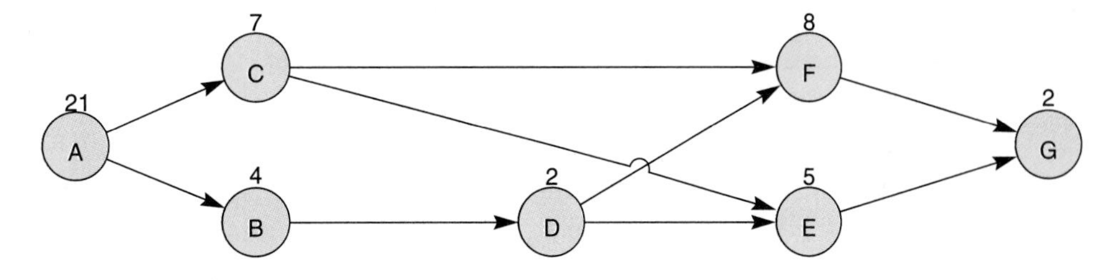

Step 2: Activity sequencing and network construction

On the basis of discussion with her staff, the project manager develops the precedence table and sequence network shown in Exhibit 12.3. Activities are indicated as nodes while arrows show the sequence in which the individual activities must be completed.

Using the precedence table, we can construct a network diagram, taking care to ensure that the activities are in the proper order and that the logic of their relationships is maintained. For example, it would be illogical to have a situation where Event A precedes Event B, B precedes C, and then C precedes A.

Step 3: Determine the critical path

The **critical path** is defined as the longest sequence of connected activities through the network. In other words, the shortest time in which the project can be completed is determined by the length of the critical path. To find the critical path, we simply identify all of the paths through the network and calculate their respective completion times. That path with the longest completion time is, by definition, the critical path. For our example, the different paths and their respective times are as follows:

Path	Completion Time (in weeks)
A–C–E–G	35
A–B–D–F–G	37
A–B–D–E–G	34
A–C–F–G	38

Path A–C–F–G takes the longest amount of time to complete, which is 38 weeks, and is therefore the critical path for this project. Therefore, as it now exists, this project cannot be completed in fewer than 38 weeks. Inasmuch as the project has been allowed 39 weeks in which to be completed, there appears to be no problem. If the project were required to be completed in fewer than 38 weeks, then one or more of the activities on the critical path would have to be "crashed" or accelerated in order to meet the required project completion date.

Step 4: Determine slack times

The total **slack time** for an activity is defined as that amount of time that an activity can be delayed without affecting the overall completion time of the project. In order to calculate the slack time for each activity, the following terms are defined:

- *Early start time* (ES), the earliest possible time that the activity can begin.
- *Early finish time* (EF), the early start time plus the time needed to complete the activity.
- *Late finish time* (LF), the latest time an activity can end without delaying the project.
- *Late start time* (LS), the late finish time minus the time needed to complete the activity.

To determine the slack time for an activity requires the calculation of either the early start (ES) time and the late start (LS) time or the early finish (EF) time and the late finish (LF) time for that activity. The difference between the ES and EF times, and the LS and LF times, is the same, being the amount of time required to complete that specific activity; hence $EF - ES = LF - LS =$ activity completion time.

These values and the resulting total slack time for each of the activities in our example will now be calculated with the following procedure.

Step 1: Find the ES for each activity

This is accomplished with a "forward pass" through the network, beginning with the first activity A, for which we set the ES = 0, representing the start of the project. To find the ES for the activities that follow A, (i.e., B and C), we simply add the time it takes to complete activity A, which in this case is 21 weeks, to the ES for A, which is zero. Therefore, the earliest we could start either activity B or C is 21 weeks after we begin the project, when activity A is completed. (In other words, ES_B or $ES_C = 0 + 21 = 21$.) Likewise, the ES for activity D is the ES for activity B (21 weeks) plus the time to complete B (4 weeks) making ES = 25 weeks for activity D (i.e., $ES_D = 21 + 4 = 25$).

This procedure is repeated for each activity in the network. When more than one activity precedes the activity being evaluated, then the ES for each path leading to that activity is calculated, and the latest ES is selected, as that becomes the constraining factor as to when that activity can begin. For example:

$$ES_F = \text{MAX}\ (ES_C + C,\ ES_D + D)$$
$$ES_F = \text{MAX}\ (21 + 7,\ 25 + 2)$$
$$ES_F = \text{MAX}\ (28, 27) = 28 \text{ weeks}$$

where

C = completion time for activity C
D = completion time for activity D

Therefore, the earliest we could start activity F is 28 weeks after we begin the project. Likewise, through similar calculations, $ES_E = 28$ weeks and $ES_G = 36$ weeks.

Step 2: Find the LS for each activity

To obtain the LS for each activity, we simply reverse the procedure for calculating the ES, beginning at the end of the project. The LS for an activity is defined as the latest time that an activity can be started without delaying the completion of the overall project. Since we start at the end of the network and work our way back to the beginning, this called a "backwards pass" through the network.

We begin with the last activity, G. As we determined earlier, the critical path for the project is 38 weeks. Therefore, the latest that we could start activity G and still complete the project in 38 weeks is 36 weeks, as it takes two weeks to do activity G. Similarly, $LS_F = LS_G - F = 36 - 8 = 28$ weeks, and $LS_E = LS_G - E = 36 - 5 = 31$ weeks. The other LS times for the remaining activities are likewise calculated.

When more than one activity follows the activity being evaluated, then the LS for all paths leading out of the activity must be calculated and that path with the earliest LS time is used, as that time becomes the constraining factor as to the latest time that activity can begin. For example:

$$LS_C = \text{MIN}\ (LS_F - C, LS_E - C)$$
$$LS_C = \text{MIN}\ (28 - 7, 31 - 7)$$
$$LS_C = \text{MIN}\ (21, 24) = 21 \text{ weeks}$$

Thus, the latest we can start activity C is 21 weeks after we begin the project. Similarly, $LS_D = 26$ weeks and $LS_A = 0$ weeks. The earliest start and the latest start times for all of the activities in the computer design project are shown in Exhibit 12.4. As stated earlier, the difference between the EF time and the ES time for an activity is simply the time it takes to complete that activity. This is also the difference between the LF and the LS times for the activity. The EF and LF times are, thus, also shown in Exhibit 12.4.

Step 3: Determine the total slack time for each activity

As stated previously, the total slack time for each activity is defined as either LS − ES or LF − EF. In the computer design project the slack time for activity B is four weeks, and for activities D and E, one week and three weeks, respectively. Notice that the activities on the critical path (i.e., A, C, F, and G) do not have any slack times, because, in fact, they are all on the critical path and any delay in these activities will therefore affect the overall project's completion time. Typically, the project completion time is calculated using network analysis and then compared with the desired deadline. Thus while there is no slack in any of the activities on the critical path with respect to the calculated project completion time, there can be slack in the critical path when the desired deadline is longer. In this example, with the desired deadline at 39 weeks and the calculated project

EXHIBIT 12.4

CPM Network for Computer Design Project

SLACK CALCULATIONS AND CRITICAL PATH DETERMINATIONS

Activity	LS–ES	Slack	On Critical Path
A	0–0	0	yes
B	25–21	4	
C	21–21	0	yes
D	26–25	1	
E	31–28	3	
F	28–28	0	yes
G	36–36	0	yes

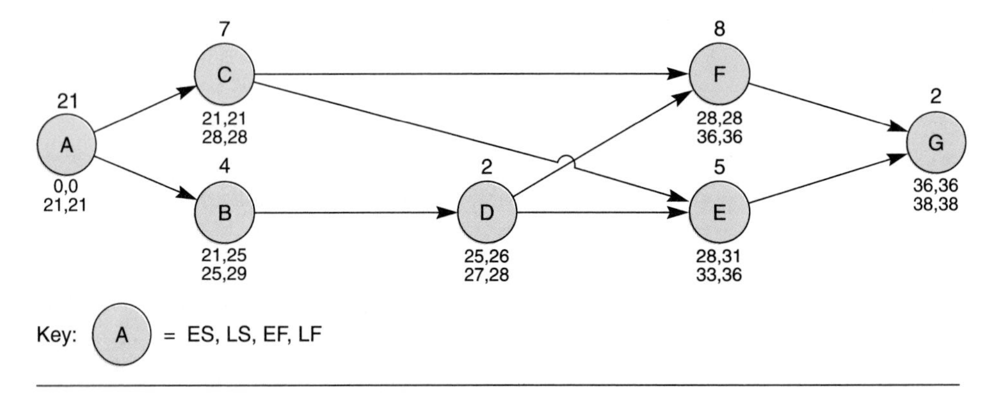

completion time at 38 weeks, there is a one week slack time in the critical path. A summary of these calculations is also presented in the table in Exhibit 12.4.

Early start and late start schedules

An **early start schedule** is one that lists all of the activities by their early start times. For activities not on the critical path, there is slack time between the activity completion and the start of the next activity that succeeds it. The early start schedule completes the project and all of its activities as soon as possible.

A **late start schedule** lists the activities to start as late as possible without delaying the completion date of the project. One of the motivations for using a late start schedule is that savings are realized by postponing purchases of materials, the use of labor, and other costs until necessary.

CPM with Three Activity Time Estimates

If a single estimate of the time required to complete an activity is not reliable, the alternative is to use three time estimates. By incorporating three estimates for each activity, we have the opportunity to obtain a probability for the completion time for the entire project. Briefly, the procedure is as follows: The estimated activity time is a weighted average, with more weight given to the best estimate and less to the maximum and minimum times. The estimated completion time of the network is then computed using basic statistics.

We continue with the computer design project, only now each of the activities has three time estimates associated with it, and the seven-step procedure for solving this problem is as follows:

Step 1: Identify each activity to be done in the project

Step 2: Determine the sequence of activities and construct a network reflecting the precedence relationships

Step 3: Define the three time estimates for each activity

The three time estimates for each activity are defined as:

a = *Optimistic time:* the minimum reasonable period of time in which the activity can be completed. (There is only a small probability, typically assumed to be about 1 percent, that the activity can be completed in a shorter period of time.)

m = *Most likely time:* the best guess of the time required. Since *m* would be the time thought most likely to appear, it is also the mode of the beta distribution (which is discussed in the next step).

b = *Pessimistic time:* the maximum reasonable period of time the activity would take to be completed. (There is only a small probability, typically assumed to be about 1 percent, that it would take longer.)

Typically, this information is obtained from those people who are to perform the activity or others with expertise about the activity.

Step 4: Calculate the expected time (ET) for each activity

The formula to calculate the expected activity completion time is:

$$\mathrm{ET} = \frac{a + 4m + b}{6}$$

This formula is developed from the beta statistical distribution and weights the most likely time (m) four times more than either the optimistic time (a) or the pessimistic time (b). The beta distribution is an extremely flexible distribution. It can take on a variety of forms that typically arise, it has finite end points, which limit the possible activity times to the area between a and b (see Exhibit 12.5). and, in the simplified version, permits a straightforward computation of the activity mean and standard deviation. Four typical beta curves are illustrated in Exhibit 12.5.

Step 5: Calculate the variance (σ_2) for each activity time

The variance, σ^2, associated with each ET is computed using the following formula:

EXHIBIT 12.5

Typical Beta Curves

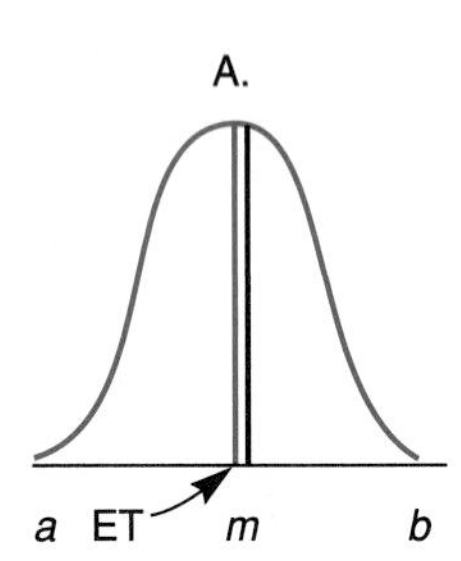

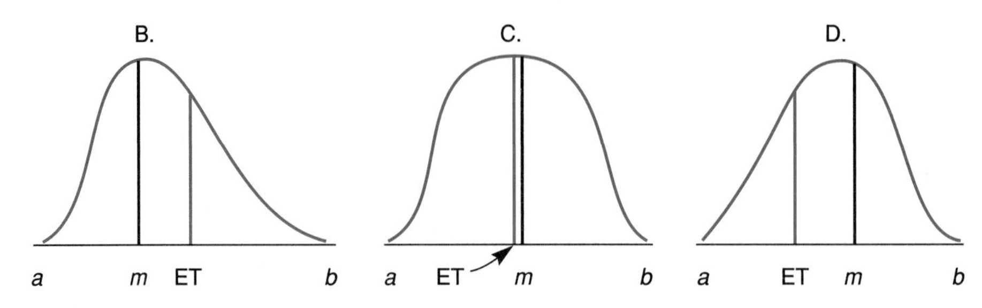

Curve A indicates very little uncertainty about the activity time, and since it is symmetrical, the expected time (ET) and the most likely or modal time (m) fall along the same point.

Curve B indicates a high probability of finishing the activity early, but if something goes wrong, the activity time could be greatly extended.

Curve C is almost a rectangular distribution, which suggests that the estimator sees the probability of finishing the activity early or late as equally likely, and $m \cong$ ET.

Curve D indicates that there is a small chance of finishing the activity early, but it is more probable that it will take an extended period of time.

EXHIBIT 12.6

Activity Expected Times and Variances

Activity	Activity Designation	TIME ESTIMATES			Expected Times (ET)	Activity Variances² (σ^2)
		a	m	b	$\frac{a + 4m + b}{6}$	$\left(\frac{b - a}{6}\right)^2$
Design	A	10	22	28	21	9.00
Build prototype	B	1	4	7	4	1.00
Evaluate equipment	C	4	6	14	7	2.78
Test prototype	D	1	2	3	2	0.11
Write report	E	1	5	9	5	1.78
Write methods report	F	7	8	9	8	0.11
Write final report	G	2	2	2	2	0.00

$$\sigma^2 = \left(\frac{b - a}{6}\right)^2$$

As you can see, the variance is the square of one sixth the difference between the two extreme time estimates, and, of course, the greater this difference, the larger the variance. A summary of the expected time and variance for each activity is presented in Exhibit 12.6.

EXHIBIT 12.7

Path Estimated Completion Times and Variances

Path	Expected Completion Time (in weeks)	Variance ($\sigma_p{}^2$)
A–C–E–G	35	13.56
A–B–D–F–G	37	10.22
A–B–D–E–G	34	11.39
A–C–F–G	38	11.89

Step 6: identify all of the paths in the network and their estimated completion times and variances

Using the data in Exhibit 12.6, the expected completion time for each path is simply the sum of the expected completion times for the activities that are on that path. Likewise, to calculate the variance for each path we simply add together the variances of the activities on that path. Again using the data in Exhibit 12.6, the path variances are calculated, and summarized in Exhibit 12.7, along with the path expected completion times.

Step 7: determine the probability of completing the project by a given date

The probability of completing the project by a given date is dependent on the probability of each path in the network being completed by that date. In our example, the desired completion time for the project is 39 weeks. In other words, we want to calculate the probability of completing the project in 39 weeks or less. To do this we need to calculate the probability of each of the paths in the network being completed in 39 weeks or less. All of the paths need to be completed in 39 weeks or less for the project to be completed within that same time period. Thus, the probability of the project being completed within a given time is equal to the minimum of the probabilities of the different paths.

Using the data in Exhibit 12.7, we can now construct the probability distribution for each path and calculate the probability of each path being completed in 39 weeks or less. This is shown graphically in Exhibit 12.8. Note that in order to calculate the probability of completing each path in 39 days or less we use σ_p, which is the square root of the variance, σ_p^2.

In Exhibit 12.8, the shaded area to the left of the line representing 39 weeks is the probability of that path being completed within the 39 week period. To obtain the value of that probability, we use the normal table in Appendix E. In order to be able to use this table we need to calculate a *Z*-value associated with each path, indicating how many standard deviations the 39 weeks is from the expected completion time for that path. The formula for this is:

$$Z = \frac{D - ET_p}{\sigma_p}$$

where

EXHIBIT 12.8

Probability of Each Path Being Completed in 39 Weeks or Less

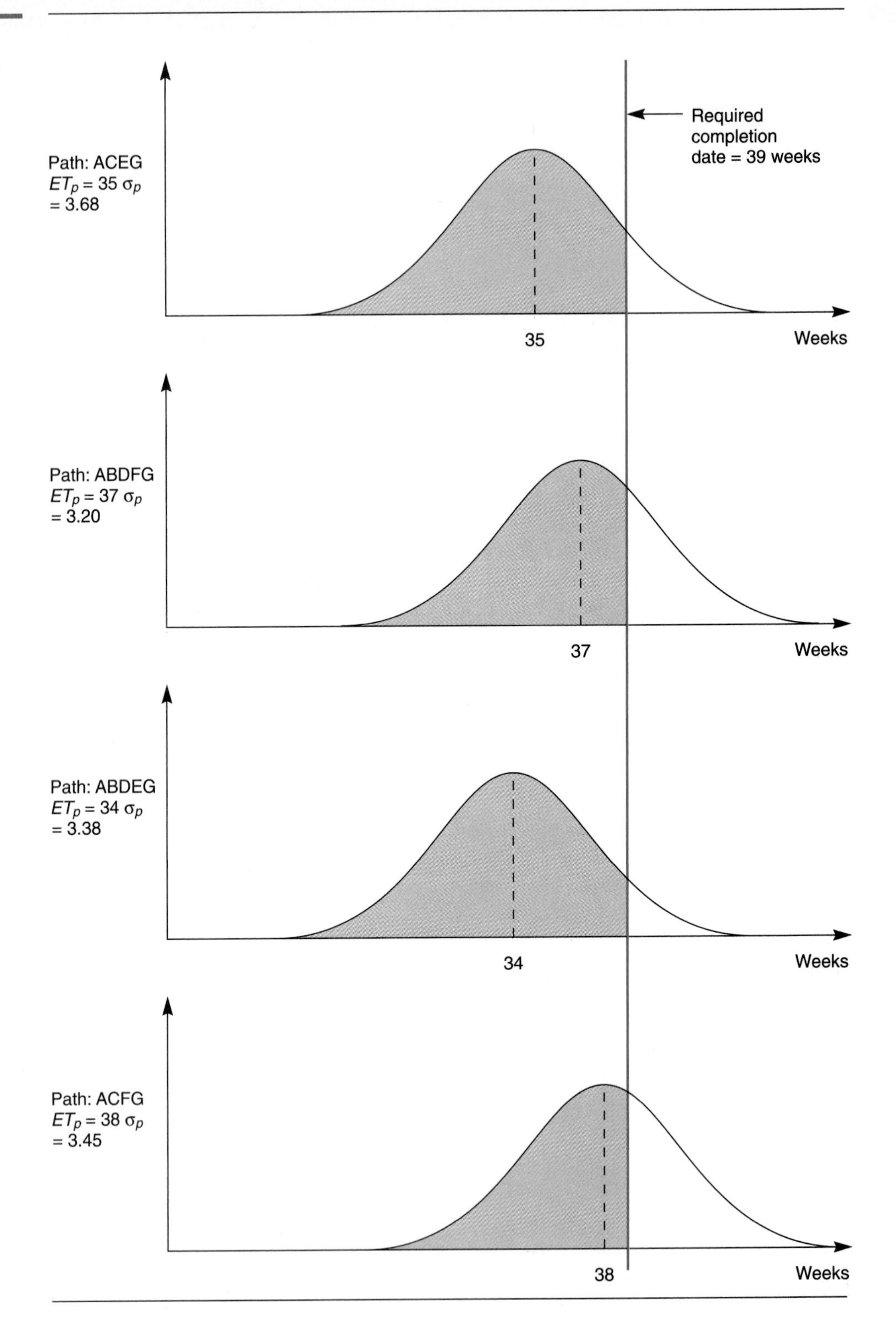

EXHIBIT 12.9

Path *Z*-values and Probabilities of Completing Each Path in 39 Weeks or Less

Path	*Z*-Value	Completion Probability
A–C–E–G	.30	.6179
A–B–D–F–G	.20	.5793
A–B–D–E–G	.44	.6700
A–C–F–G	.08	.5319

D = Desired completion date for the project

ET_p = Expected completion time for the path

σ_p = Standard deviation for the path

In this manner, the *Z*-value for each path is calculated and presented in Exhibit 12.9, along with the corresponding probability that we obtain from the normal table in Appendix E. As an approximation, one can determine the probability of completing the project within 39 weeks or less as the minimum of the individual path probabilities, or:

$$\text{Prob(Proj}<39) = \text{MIN } [(.8621)(.7357)(.9265)(.6141)] = .6141$$

Thus, the probability of completing this project within 39 weeks is 61.41 percent, even though its expected completion time, as determined by the critical path, is 38 weeks.

Maintaining Ongoing Project Schedules

It is important to keep a project schedule accurate and current. The schedule tracks the progress of the project and identifies problems as they occur while time to correct the situation may still be available. It also monitors the progress of the costs and is often the basis for partial payments. Yet, schedules are often sloppily kept, or even totally abandoned.

Perhaps the most important reasons are that managers are not committed enough to the technique to insist that schedules be kept up. The resulting poor schedules consequently give project scheduling a bad name. Experience in project scheduling techniques is important and this job should not be carelessly relegated to the closest warm body. The project manager must support the schedule and see to it that it is maintained.

12.5 TIME–COST TRADE-OFF MODELS

In practice, project managers are as much concerned with the cost to complete a project as they are with the time to complete the project. For this reason, **time–cost trade-off models** have been devised. These models, which are extensions of PERT and CPM, attempt to develop a minimum-cost schedule for the entire project and to control budgetary expenditures during the project.

Minimum-Cost Scheduling (Time–Cost Trade-Off)

The basic assumption in minimum-cost scheduling is that there is a relationship between activity completion time and the cost of a project. On one hand, it costs money to expedite an activity; on the other, it costs money to sustain (or lengthen) the project. The costs associated with expediting activities in order to shorten their completion times are termed *activity direct costs* and add to the project direct cost. These additional costs that are included when an activity is accelerated are also referred to as **crash costs.** Some of these may be worker related, such as overtime work, hiring more workers, and transferring workers from other jobs, while others are resource related, such as buying or leasing additional or more efficient equipment and drawing on additional support facilities.

The costs associated with sustaining the project are termed *project indirect costs;* overhead, facilities, and resource opportunity costs, and, under certain contractual situations, penalty costs or lost incentive payments. Since *activity direct costs* and *project indirect costs* are opposing costs dependent on time, the scheduling problem is essentially one of finding the project duration that minimizes their sum or, in other words, finding the optimum point in a time–cost trade-off.

The procedure for finding this point consists of the following five steps and is illustrated using the simple four-activity network that is shown in Exhibit 12.10. Assume in this example that the indirect costs remain constant for eight days and then increase at the rate of $5 per day.

Step 1: Prepare a CPM-type network diagram
For each activity this diagram should list:

a. Normal cost (NC): The lowest expected activity cost (these are the lesser of the cost figures shown under each node in Exhibit 12.10).
b. Normal time (NT): The time associated with each normal cost.
c. Crash time (CT): The shortest possible activity time.
d. Crash cost (CC): The cost associated with each crash time.

Step 2: Determine the cost per unit of time (assume days) to expedite (or crash) each activity
The relationship between activity time and cost may be shown graphically by plotting CC and CT coordinates and connecting them to the NC and NT coordinates by a concave, convex, or straight line—or some other form, depending on the actual cost structure of the activity's performance, as shown in Exhibit 12.10. For Activity A, we assume a linear relationship between time and cost. This assumption is common in practice and facilitates the derivation of the cost per day to expedite since this value may be found directly by taking the slope of the line using the formula Slope = (CC − NC) ÷ (NT − CT). (When the assumption of linearity cannot be made, the cost of expediting must be determined graphically for each of the days the activity may be shortened.)

EXHIBIT 12.10 Example of Time–Cost Trade-Off Procedure

Step 1. Prepare CPM diagram with activity costs

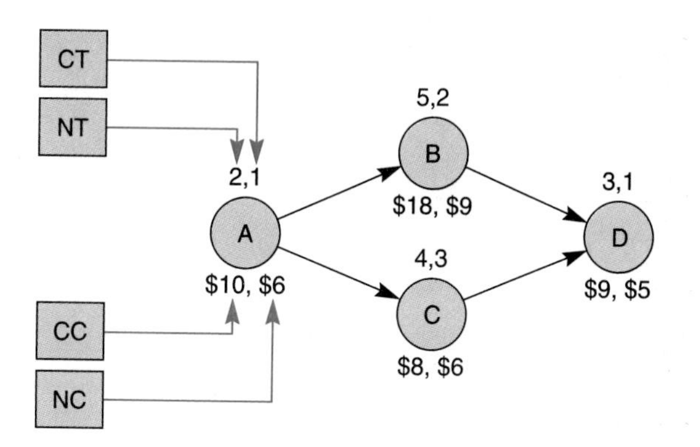

Step 2. Determine cost per unit of time

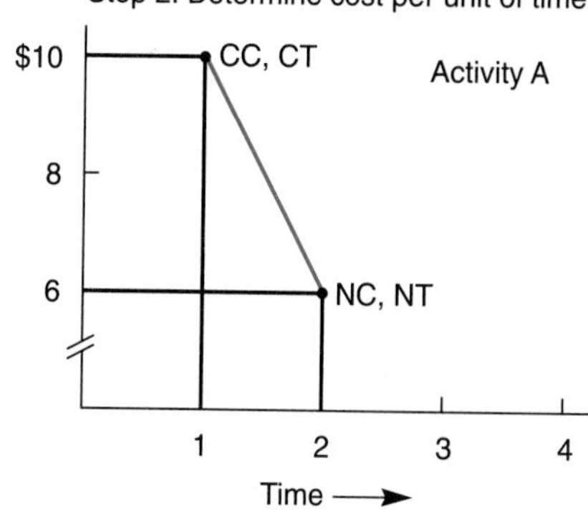

Step 3. Compute the critical path

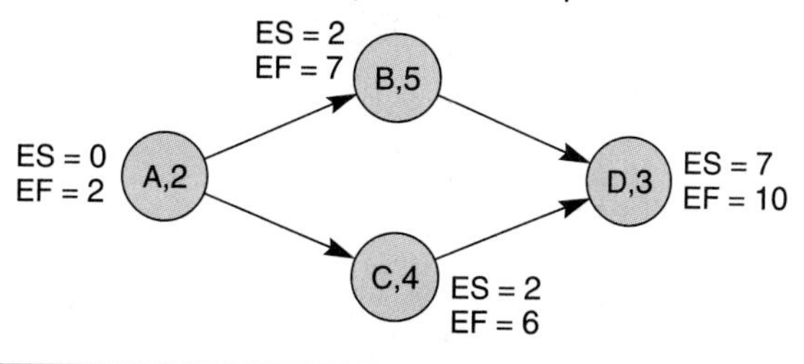

The calculations needed to obtain the cost of expediting the remaining activities are shown in Exhibit 12.11.

Step 3: Compute the critical path

For the simple network we have been using, this schedule would take 10 days. The critical path is A, B, D.

Step 4: Shorten the critical path at the least cost

The easiest way to proceed is to start with the normal schedule, find the critical path, and reduce the path time by one day using the lowest-cost activity. Then recompute and find the new critical path and reduce it by one day also. Repeat this procedure until the time of completion is satisfactory, or until there can be no further reduction in the project completion time. Exhibit 12.12 shows the reduction of the network one day at a time.

Step 5: Plot project direct, indirect, and total-cost curves and find minimum-cost schedule

Exhibit 12.13 shows the indirect cost plotted as a constant $10 per day for eight days and increasing $5 per day thereafter. The direct costs are plotted from Exhibit 12.12 and the total project cost is shown as the total of the two costs.

EXHIBIT 12.11

Calculation of Cost per Day to Expedite Each Activity

Activity	CC – NC	NT – CT	$\frac{CC - NC}{NT - CT}$	Cost per Day to Expedite	Number of Days Activity May Be Shortened
A	\$10 – \$6	2 – 1	$\frac{\$10 - 6}{2 - 1}$	\$4	1
B	\$18 – \$9	5 – 2	$\frac{\$18 - \$9}{5 - 2}$	\$3	3
C	\$ 8 – \$6	4 – 3	$\frac{\$8 - \$6}{4 - 3}$	\$2	1
D	\$ 9 – \$5	3 – 1	$\frac{\$9 - \$5}{3 - 1}$	\$2	2

Summing the values for direct and indirect costs for each day yields the project total cost curve. As you can see, this curve is at its minimum for an eight-day schedule, which costs \$40 (\$30 direct + \$10 indirect).

12.6 CRITICISMS OF PERT AND CPM

There are several assumptions that need to be made when applying CPM or PERT analysis to project networks. This section summarizes some of the more significant assumptions and their criticisms. One point of particular difficulty for the operating personnel is understanding the statistics when three time estimates are used. The beta distribution of activity times, the three time estimates, the activity variances, and the use of the normal distribution to arrive at project completion probabilities are all potential sources of misunderstandings, and with misunderstanding comes distrust and obstruction. Thus, management must be sure that the people charged with monitoring and controlling activity performance have a general understanding of the statistics.

1. *Assumption:* Project activities can be identified as entities (that is, there is a clear beginning and ending point for each activity).
   Criticism: Projects, especially complex ones, change in content over time, and therefore a network made at the beginning may be highly inaccurate later on. Also, the very fact that activities are specified and a network formalized tends to limit the flexibility that is required to handle changing situations as the project progresses.
2. *Assumption:* Project activity sequence relationships can be specified and networked.
   Criticism: Sequence relationships cannot always be specified beforehand. In some projects, in fact, ordering certain activities is conditional on previous activities. (PERT and CPM, in their basic form, have no provision for treating this problem, although some other techniques have been proposed that present the project manager with several contingency paths, given different outcomes from each activity.)

EXHIBIT 12.12

Reducing the Project Completion Time One Day at a Time

Current Critical Path	Remaining Number of Days Activity May Be Shortened	Cost per Day to Expedite Each Activity	Lease Cost Activity to Expedite	Total Cost of All Activities in Network	Project Completion Time
ABD	All activity times and costs are normal			$26	10
ABD	A–1, B–3, D–2	A–4, B–3, D–2	D	28	9
ABD	A–1, B–3, D–1	A–4, B–3, D–2	D	30	8
ABD	A–1, B–3	A–4, B–3	B	33	7
ABCD	A–1, B–2, C–1	A–4, B–3, C–2	A*	37	6
ABCD	B–2, C–1	B–3, C–2	B&C†	42	5
ABCD	B–1	B–3	B	45	5

*To reduce the critical path by one day, reduce either A alone, or B and C together at the same time (since either B or C by itself just modifies the critical path without shortening it).

†B&C must be crashed together to reduce the path by one day.

EXHIBIT 12.13

Plot of Costs and Minimum Cost Schedule

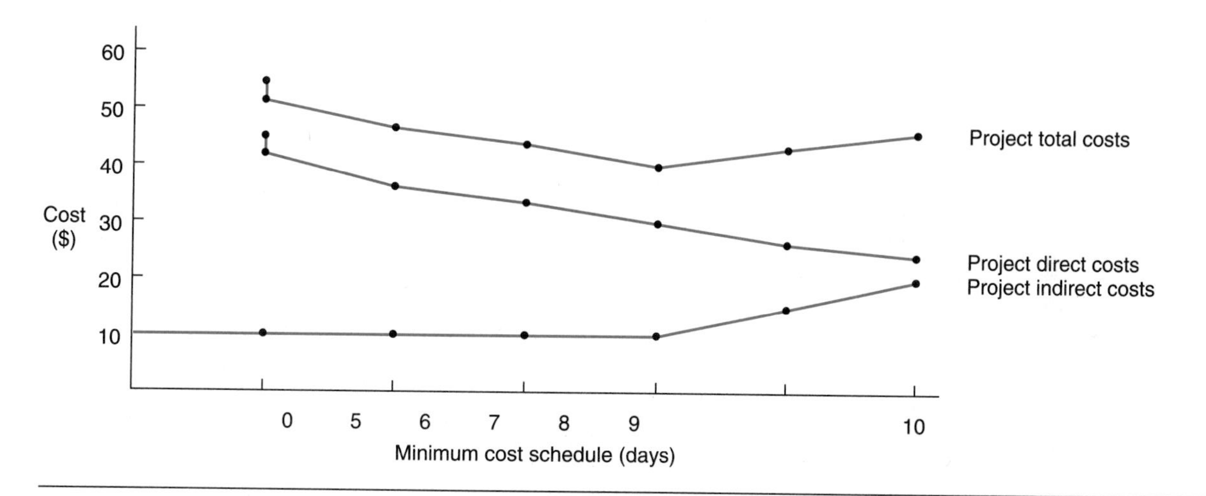

3. *Assumption:* Project control should focus on the critical path.
Criticism: It is not necessarily true that the longest time-consuming path (or the path in which each of the activities has zero slack) obtained from summing activity expected time values ultimately determines project completion time. What often happens as the project progresses is that some activity not on the critical path becomes delayed to such a degree that it extends the entire project. For this reason it has been suggested that a "critical activity" concept replace the critical path concept as focus of managerial control. Under this approach, attention would center on those activities that have a high potential variation and lie on a "near-critical path." A

near-critical path is one that does not share any activities with the critical path and, though it has slack, could become critical if one or a few activities along it become delayed. Obviously, the more parallelism in a network, the more likely that one or more near-critical paths exist. Conversely, the more a network approximates a single series of activities, the less likely it is to have near-critical paths.

4. *Assumption:* The activity times in PERT follow the beta distribution, with the variance of the project assumed to be equal to the sum of the variances along the critical path.
   Criticism: Although originally the beta distribution was selected for a variety of good reasons, each component of the statistical treatment has been brought into question. First, the formulas are in reality a modification of the beta distribution mean and variance, which, when compared to the basic formulas, could be expressed to lead to absolute errors on the order of 10 percent for ET and 5 percent for the individual variances. Second, given that the activity-time distributions have the properties of unimodality, continuity, and finite positive end points, other distributions with the same properties would yield different means and variances. Third, obtaining three "valid" time estimates to put into the formulas presents operational problems—it is often difficult to arrive at one activity time estimate, let alone three, and the subjective definitions of a and b do not help the matter. (How optimistic and pessimistic should one be?)

Another problem that sometimes arises, especially when CPM or PERT is used by subcontractors working with the government, is the attempt to "beat" the network to get on or off the critical path. Many government contracts provide cost incentives for finishing a project early or on a "cost-plus-fixed-fee" basis. Contractors on the critical path generally have more leverage in obtaining additional funds since they have a major influence on the project duration. On the other hand—for political reasons that we will not go into here—some contractors deem it desirable to be less visible and therefore adjust their time estimates and activity descriptions to ensure they *won't* be on the critical path.

Finally, the cost of applying critical path methods to a project is sometimes used as a basis for criticism. However, the cost of applying PERT or CPM rarely exceeds 2 percent of the total project cost. When used with added features of a work breakdown structure and various reports it is more expensive but rarely exceeds 5 percent of total project costs. Thus, this added cost is generally justified by the additional savings resulting from improved scheduling and reduced project time.

The critical path techniques of PERT and CPM have proved themselves for more than three decades and promise to be of continued value in the future. With the rapidly changing business environment and the high costs associated with these changes, management needs to be able to both quickly and efficiently plan and control the activities of the firm. The inherent values of a tool that allows management to structure complex projects in an understandable way, to pick out possible sources of delay before they occur, to isolate areas of responsibility, and, of course, to save time in costly projects virtually ensure that the use of project management will expand. The availability of inexpensive computer programs for project scheduling further encourages the expanded use of project management.

12.7 CONCLUSION

Although much of this chapter has dealt with network solving techniques used in project management, effective project management involves much more than simply setting up a CPM or PERT schedule. It requires, in addition, clearly identified project responsibilities, a simple and timely progress reporting system, and good people-management practices.

Projects fail for a number of reasons. The most important reason is that those involved do not take project scheduling seriously. Often, personnel who have been newly exposed and those who have had unsatisfactory experiences do not comply with the procedure. They may neither spend the time to develop their parts of the network, nor even submit good time and cost estimates. This attitude usually continues throughout the project with a reluctance to revise schedules.

12.8 REVIEW AND DISCUSSION QUESTIONS

1. Define project management.
2. Describe or define work breakdown structure, program, project, task, subtask, and work package.
3. What are some of the reasons project scheduling is not done well?
4. Discuss the graphic presentations in Exhibit 12.2. Are there any other graphic outputs you would like to see if you were the project manager?
5. Which characteristics must a project have for critical path scheduling to be applicable? What types of projects have been subjected to critical path analysis?
6. What are the underlying assumptions of minimum-cost scheduling? Are they equally realistic?
7. "Project control should always focus on the critical path." Comment.
8. Why would subcontractors for a government project want their activities on the critical path? Under which conditions would they try to avoid being on the critical path?

12.9 SOLVED PROBLEMS

PROBLEM

1. A project has been defined to contain the following list of activities, along with their required times for completion:

Activity	Time (days)	Immediate Predecessors
A	1	—
B	4	A
C	3	A
D	7	A
E	6	B
F	2	C, D
G	7	E, F
H	9	D
I	4	G, H

a. Draw the critical path diagram.
b. Show the early start and early finish times.
c. Show the critical path.
d. What would happen if Activity F were revised to take four days instead of two?

SOLUTION

CPM problem.
The answers to *a, b,* and *c* are shown in the following diagram.

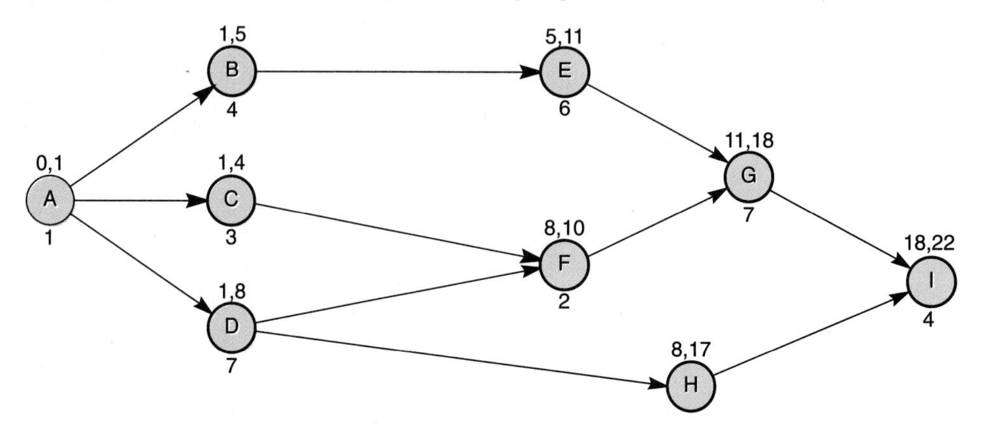

d. New critical path: A, D, F, G, I. Time of completion = 23 days.

PROBLEM

2. Following are the precedence requirements, normal and crash activity times, and normal and crash costs for a construction project.

Activity	Preceding Activities	REQUIRED TIME (WEEKS) Normal	Crash	COST Normal	Crash
A	—	4	2	$10,000	$11,000
B	A	3	2	6,000	9,000
C	A	2	1	4,000	6,000
D	B	5	3	14,000	18,000
E	B, C	1	1	9,000	9,000
F	C	3	2	7,000	8,000
G	E, F	4	2	13,000	25,000
H	D, E	4	1	11,000	18,000
I	H, G	6	5	20,000	29,000

a. What is the critical path and the estimated completion time?
b. To shorten the project by three weeks, which tasks would be shortened and what would the final total project cost be?

SOLUTION

Crashing a construction project.

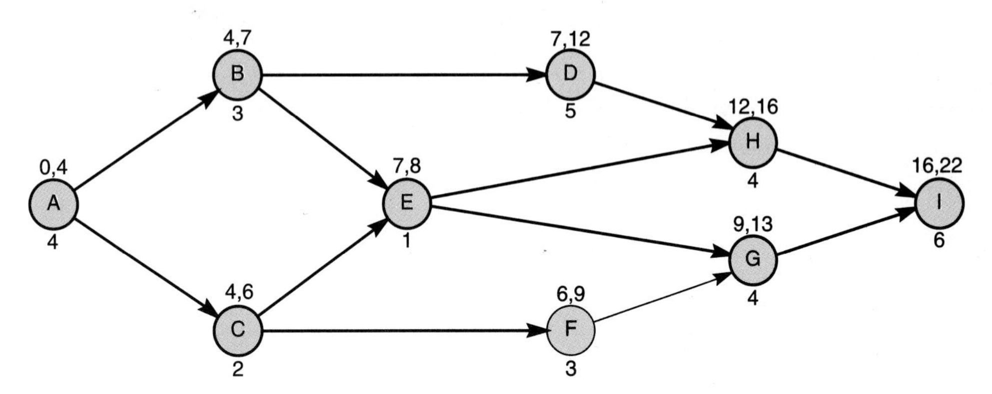

a. Critical path A, B, D, H, I.
Normal completion time = 22 weeks.

b.

Activity	Crash Cost	Normal Cost	Normal Time	Crash Time	Cost per Weeks	Weeks
A	$11,000	$10,000	4	2	$ 500	2
B	9,000	6,000	3	2	3,000	1
C	6,000	4,000	2	1	2,000	1
D	18,000	14,000	5	3	2,000	2
E	9,000	9,000	1	1		0
F	8,000	7,000	3	2	1,000	1
G	25,000	13,000	4	2	6,000	2
H	18,000	11,000	4	1	2,333	3
I	29,000	20,000	6	5	9,000	1

1. 1st week: CP = A B D H I. Cheapest is A at $500. Critical path stays the same.
2. 2nd week: A is still the cheapest at $500. Critical path stays the same.
3. 3rd week: Since A is no longer available, the choices are B (at $3,000), D (at $2,000). H (at $2,333), or I (at $9,000).

Therefore, choose D at $2,000.

Total project cost shortened three weeks is:

A	$11,000
B	6,000
C	4,000
D	16,000
E	9,000
F	7,000
G	13,000
H	11,000
I	20,000
	$97,000

12.10 PROBLEMS

1. The following activities are part of a project to be scheduled using CPM:

Activity	Intermediate Predecessors	Time (weeks)
A	—	6
B	A	3
C	A	7
D	C	2
E	B, D	4
F	D	3
G	E, F	7

a. Draw the network.
b. What is the critical path?
c. How many weeks will it take to complete the project?
d. How much slack does Activity B have?

2. American Steam Turbine and Generator Company manufactures electric power generating systems for the major electric power companies. Turbine/generator sets are made to specific order and generally require a three- to five-year lead time. Costs range from $8 to $15 million per set.

   Management has been planning their production using traditional planning techniques such as planning charts, Gantt charts, and other shop floor control methods. However, management would now like to introduce CPM project planning and control methods where each turbine/generator set is considered a separate project.

   Following is a segment of the total activities involved in the turbine/generator production:

Activity	Time (weeks)	Immediate Predecessors
a	8	—
b	16	a
c	12	a
d	7	a
e	22	b, c
f	40	c, d
g	15	e, f
h	14	—
i	9	h
j	13	i
k	7	i
l	36	j
m	40	k
n	9	l, m
o	10	g, n

a. Draw the network.
b. Find the critical path.
c. If the project is to be cut by two weeks, show which activities would be on the list to be investigated for cutting performance time.
d. If the project is to be cut by 10 weeks, show which activities would be on the list to be investigated for cutting performance time.

3. The R&D department is planning to bid on a large project for the development of a new communication system for commercial planes. The table below shows the activities, times, and sequences required.

Activity	Immediate Predecessors	Time (weeks)
A	—	3
B	A	2
C	A	4
D	A	4
E	B	6
F	C, D	6
G	D, F	2
H	D	3
I	E, G, H	3

a. Draw the network diagram.
b. What is the critical path?
c. Supposing you wanted to shorten the completion time as much as possible, and had the option of shortening any or all of B, C, D, and G each two weeks. Which would you shorten?
d. What is the new path and earliest completion time?

4. A construction project is broken down into the 10 activities listed below.

Activity	Preceding Activity	Time (weeks)
1	—	4
2	1	2
3	1	4
4	1	3
5	2, 3	5
6	3	6
7	4	2
8	5	3
9	6, 7	5
10	8, 9	7

a. Draw the precedence diagram.
b. Find the critical path.
c. If activities 1 and 10 cannot be shortened, but activities 2 through 9 can be shortened to a minimum of 1 week each at a cost of $10,000 per week, which activities would you shorten to shorten the project by four weeks?

5. A manufacturing concern has received a special order for a number of units of a special product that consists of two component parts, X and Y. The product is a nonstandard item that the firm has never produced before, and scheduling personnel have decided that the application of CPM is warranted. A team of manufacturing engineers has prepared the following table:

Activity	Description	Immediate Predecessors	Expected Time (days)
A	Plan production	—	5
B	Procure materials for Part X	A	14
C	Manufacture Part X	B	9
D	Procure materials for Part Y	A	15
E	Manufacture Part Y	D	10
F	Assemble Parts X and Y	C, E	4
G	Inspect assemblies	F	2
H	Completed	G	0

a. Construct a graphic representation of the CPM network.
b. Identify the critical path.
c. What is the length of time to complete the project?
d. Which activities have slack, and how much?

6. Following is a CPM network with activity times in weeks:

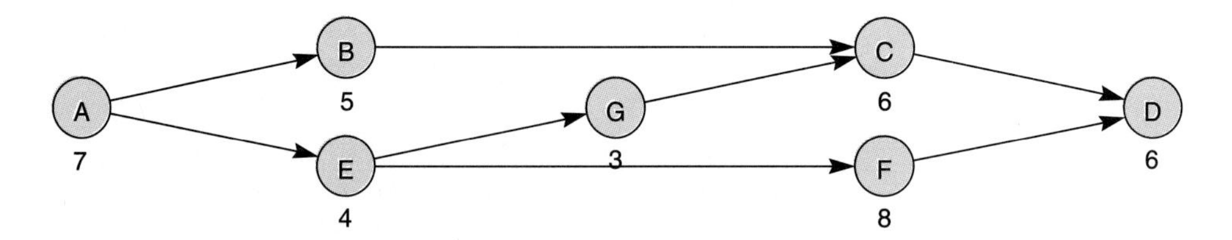

a. Determine the critical path.
b. How many weeks will the project take to complete?
c. Supposing F could be shortened by two weeks and B by one week. What effect would this have on the completion date?

7. The following represents a plan for a project:

Job No.	Predecessor Job(s)	*a*	*m*	*b*
1	—	2	3	4
2	1	1	2	3
3	1	4	5	12
4	1	3	4	11
5	2	1	3	5
6	3	1	2	3
7	4	1	8	9
8	5, 6	2	4	6
9	8	2	4	12
10	7	3	4	5
11	9, 10	5	7	8

a. Construct the appropriate network diagram.
b. Identify the critical path.
c. What is the expected completion time for the project?
d. What is the probability that the project will take more than 30 days to complete?

8. Following is a network with the activity times shown under the nodes in days:

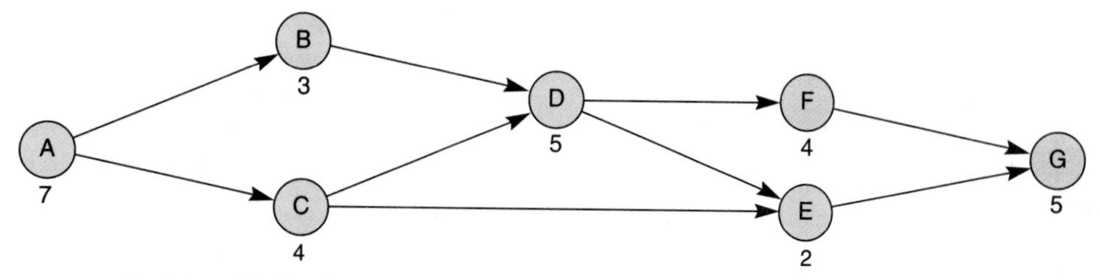

a. Find the critical path.

b. The following table shows the normal times and the crash times, along with the associated costs for each of the activities.

Activity	Normal Time	Crash Time	Normal Cost	Crash Cost
A	7	6	$7,000	$ 8,000
B	3	2	5,000	7,000
C	4	3	9,000	10,200
D	5	4	3,000	4,500
E	2	1	2,000	3,000
F	4	2	4,000	7,000
G	5	4	5,000	8,000

If the project is to be shortened by four days, show which activities in order of reduction would be shortened and the resulting cost.

9. The home office billing department of a chain of department stores prepares monthly inventory reports for use by the stores' purchasing agents. Given the following information, use the critical path method to determine:
   a. How long the total process will take?
   b. Which jobs can be delayed without delaying the early start of any subsequent activity.

	Job and Description	Immediate Predecessors	Time (hours)
a	Start	—	0
b	Get computer printouts of customer purchases	a	10
c	Get stock records for the month	a	20
d	Reconcile purchase printouts and stock records	b, c	30
e	Total stock records by department	b, c	20
f	Determine reorder quantities for coming period	e	40
g	Prepare stock reports for purchasing agents	d, f	20
h	Finish	g	0

10. For the network and the data shown:

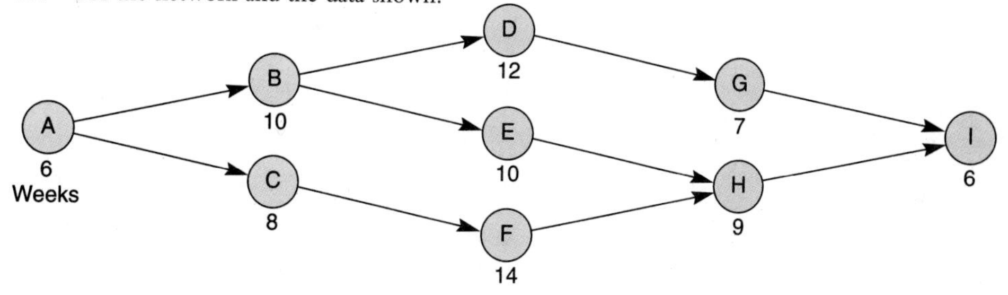

a. Determine the critical path and the early completion time for the project.

Activity*	Normal Time (weeks)	Normal Cost	Crash Time (weeks)	Crash Cost
A	6	$ 6,000	4	$12,000
B	10	10,000	9	11,000
C	8	8,000	7	10,000
D	12	12,000	10	14,000
E	10	10,000	7	12,000
F	14	14,000	12	19,000
G	7	7,000	5	10,000
H	9	9,000	6	15,000
I	6	6,000	5	8,000

*An activity cannot be shortened to less than its crash time.

b. Reduce the project completion time by four weeks. Assume a linear cost per day shortened and show, step by step, how you arrived at your schedule. Also indicate the critical path.

11. The following CPM network has estimates of the *normal time* listed for the activities:

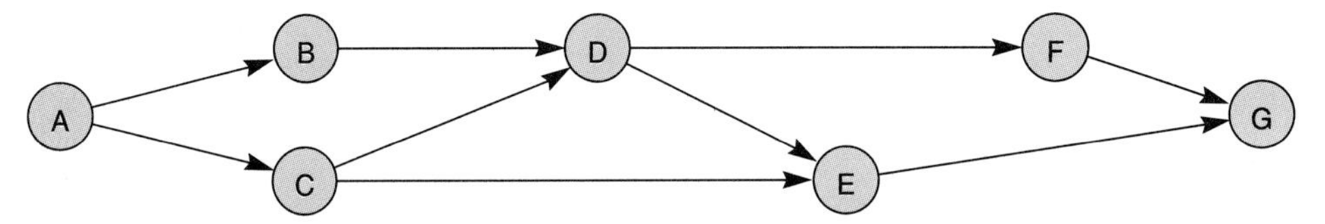

a. Identify the critical path.
b. What is the length of time to complete the project?
c. Which activities have slack, and how much?

Activity	Time (weeks)
A	7
B	2
C	4
D	5
E	2
F	4
G	5

d. Following is a table of normal and crash times and costs. Which activities would you shorten to cut two weeks from the schedule in a rational fashion? What would be the incremental cost? Is the critical path changed?

Activity	Normal Time	Crash Time	Normal Cost	Crash Cost	Possible Number of Weeks Decrease	Cost/ Week to Expedite
A	7	6	$7,000	$ 8,000		
B	2	1	5,000	7,000		
C	4	3	9,000	10,200		
D	5	4	3,000	4,500		
E	2	1	2,000	3,000		
F	4	2	4,000	7,000		
G	5	4	5,000	8,000		

12.11 SELECTED BIBLIOGRAPHY

Cleland, David I., and William R. King. *Project Management Handbook.* New York: Van Nostrand Reinhold, 1983.

Goodman, Louis J., and Ralph N. Love. *Project and Management: An Integrated Approach.* New York: Pergamon Press, 1980.

Hughes, Michael William. "Why Projects Fail: The Effects of Ignoring the Obvious." *Industrial Engineering* 18, no. 4 (April 1986), pp. 14–18.

Kerzner, Harold. *Project Management for Executives.* New York: Van Nostrand Reinhold, 1984.

O'Neal, Kim. "Project Management Computer Software Buyer's Guide." *Industrial Engineering* 19, no. 1 (January 1987).

Peterson, P. "Project Control Systems." *Datamation,* June 1979, pp 147–63.

Smith-Daniels, Dwight E., and Nicholas J. Aquilano. "Constrained Resource Project Scheduling." *Journal of Operations Management* 4, no. 4 (1984), pp. 369–87.

———. "Using a Late-Start Resource-Constrained Project Schedule to Improve Project Net Present Value." *Decision Sciences* 18, no. 4 (Fall 1987), pp. 617–30.

Smith-Daniels, Dwight E., and Vikki L. Smith-Daniels. "Optimal Project Scheduling with Materials Ordering." *IEE Transactions* 19, no. 2 (June 1987), pp. 122–29.

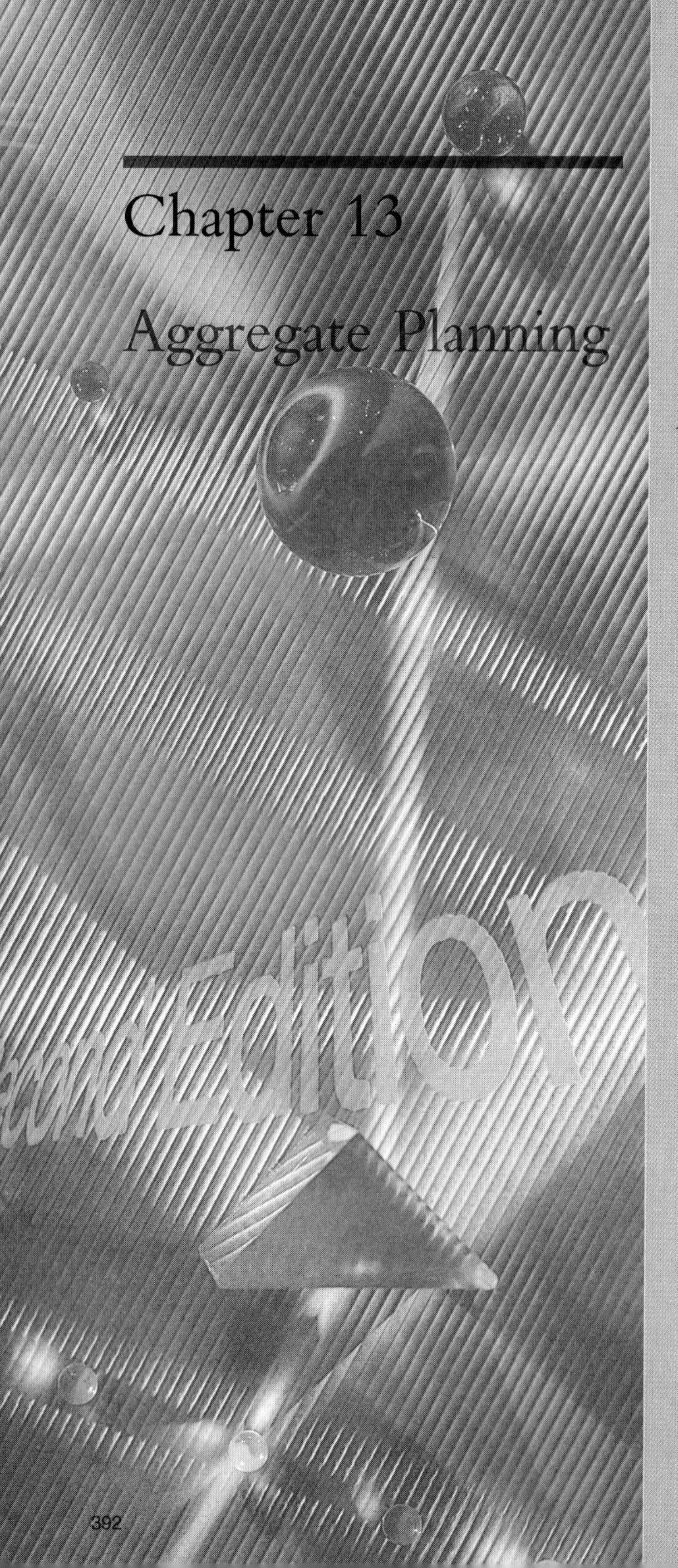

Chapter 13

Aggregate Planning

EPIGRAPH

Harry, I just got the word from marketing. They want us to rough out a plan to make 50,000 Bart Simpson dolls. We're going head to head with an Indonesian producer, and I need your estimates fast!

CHAPTER OUTLINE

KEY TERMS

Long-, Medium-, and Short-Range Planning
Aggregate Production Planning
Master Production Schedule
Rough-Cut Capacity Planning
Capacity Requirements Planning
Final Assembly Scheduling
Input/Output Planning and Control
Production Activity Control
Purchase Planning and Control
Production Rate
Work-Force Level
Inventory on Hand
Production Planning Strategies
Pure Strategy
Mixed Strategy

The first step in translating long-range strategic plans down to the operational level is the development of an aggregate plan. In essence, aggregate planning is an intermediate- or medium-range planning tool that is used to develop gross requirements, primarily for labor and materials, for the next 12 months. Aggregate planning thus takes a fairly broad view, addressing the requirements for product lines rather than specific products, and determining the number of workers needed in total rather than the number of workers needed in specific skills areas.

The goal of aggregate planning is to match the demand for the firm's products with its ability to supply those products, and to do so at minimum cost. The aggregate planning process identifies alternative methods to match supply and demand from the operations management perspective. The marketing function also plays a key role in this matching process through the use of marketing tools such as pricing, advertising, and promotion. Both the marketing and operations management functions need to work together to develop an aggregate plan that is both effective and efficient.

In this chapter we present several quantitative techniques for developing aggregate plans that are applicable to both manufacturing and service organizations.

13.1 OVERVIEW OF MANUFACTURING PLANNING ACTIVITIES

Every organization must plan its activities at a variety of levels and operate these as a system. Exhibit 13.1 presents an overall view of planning and shows how aggregate production planning relates to other activities of a manufacturing firm. The time dimension is shown as long, medium, and short range.

Long-range planning is generally done once a year, focusing on a time horizon that is usually greater than a year. The length of the time horizon will vary from industry to industry. For those industries that require many years to plan and construct plants and facilities, and to install specific processes (e.g., refineries), the time horizon may be 5 to 10 or more years. For other industries where the ability to expand capacity is of shorter time duration (e.g., clothing manufacturing and many service industries), the time horizon may be two to five years or less.

Medium-range planning usually covers the period from 6 to 18 months in the future, with time increments or "buckets" that are monthly and/or quarterly. (The near-term time increments are often monthly, whereas those at the end of the time horizon tend to be quarterly, as these are usually less accurate.) Medium-range planning is typically reviewed and updated quarterly.

Short-range planning covers the period from one day to six months, with the time increment usually being weekly. As with long-range planning, the length of the time horizon for medium- and short-range planning will vary from industry to industry.

Long-Range Planning

Long-range planning begins with a statement of organizational objectives and goals for the next 2 to 10 years. *Corporate strategic planning* articulates how these objectives and goals are to be achieved in light of the company's capabilities and its economic and political

EXHIBIT 13.1 Overview of Manufacturing Planning Activities

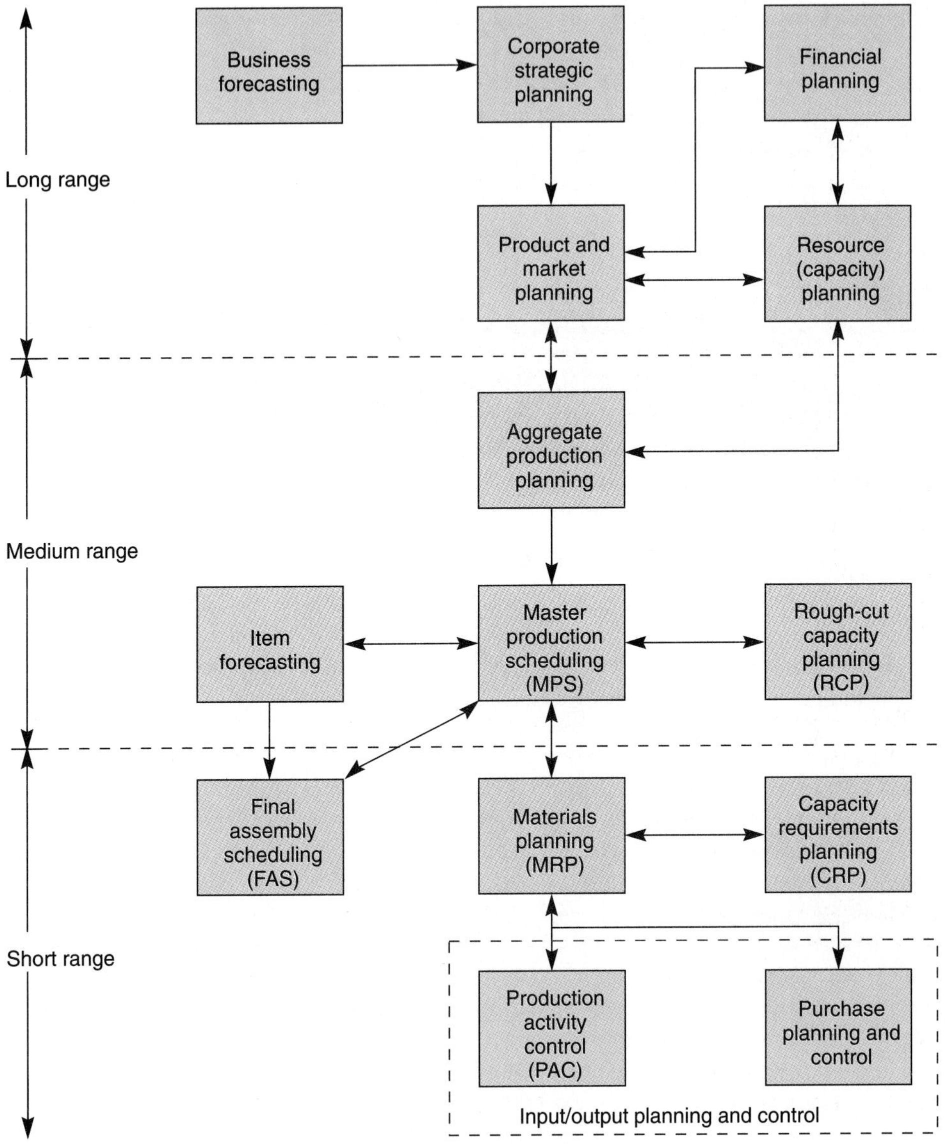

Long range
Business forecasting
Corporate strategic planning
Financial planning
Product and market planning
Resource (capacity) planning

Medium range
Aggregate production planning
Item forecasting
Master production scheduling (MPS)
Rough-cut capacity planning (RCP)

Short range
Final assembly scheduling (FAS)
Materials planning (MRP)
Capacity requirements planning (CRP)
Production activity control (PAC)
Purchase planning and control
Input/output planning and control

environment as projected by its *business forecasting*. Elements of the strategic plan include product-line delineation, quality and pricing levels, and market penetration goals. *Product and market planning* translates these into individual market and product-line objectives, and includes a long-range production plan (basically a forecast of items to be manufactured for two years or more into the future). *Financial planning* analyzes the financial feasibility of these objectives relative to capital requirements and return on investment goals. *Resource planning* identifies the facilities, equipment, and personnel needed to accomplish the long-range production plan, and thus is frequently referred to as *long-run capacity planning*.

Medium-Range Planning

Aggregate production planning

As noted in Exhibit 13.1, this activity provides the primary link between the long-range strategic plans and the intermediate- or medium-range planning activities. Aggregate planning specifies monthly or quarterly output requirements by major product groups either in labor hours required or in units of production for up to 18 months into the future. Its main inputs are the product and market plans and the resource plan. **Aggregate production planning** seeks to find that combination of monthly or quarterly work force levels and inventory levels that minimizes total production-related costs over the planning period while meeting the forecasted demand for product.

Item forecasting

This provides an estimate of specific products (and replacement parts), which, when integrated with the aggregate production plan, becomes the output requirement for the master production schedule (MPS). The process of monitoring and integrating this information is termed *demand management*.

Master production scheduling (MPS)

The MPS generates for the manufacturer the amounts and dates of specific end products. The **master production schedule** is usually fixed or "frozen" over the short run (six to eight weeks). Beyond six to eight weeks, various changes can be made, with essentially complete revisions possible after six months. As shown in Exhibit 13.1, the MPS depends on the product and market plans and resource plans outlined in the aggregate production plan.

Rough-cut capacity planning

This reviews the MPS to make sure that no obvious capacity constraints would require changing the schedule. **Rough-cut capacity planning** includes verifying that sufficient production and warehouse facilities, equipment, and labor are available and that key vendors have allocated adequate capacity to provide materials when needed.

Short-Range Planning

Materials planning

Also known as *material requirements planning* (MRP), this system takes the end product requirements from the MPS and breaks them down into their subassemblies and component parts. The materials plan specifies when production and purchase orders must be placed for each part and subassembly to complete the products on schedule.

Courtesy The Toro Company

Demand for products such as lawnmowers and snowthrowers are subject to seasonal fluctuations at different times of the year. Toro uses the fluctuations for these two products to level its overall aggregate production plans.

Capacity requirements planning

Capacity requirements planning (CRP) should really be referred to as capacity requirements *scheduling,* because it provides a detailed schedule of when each operation is to be run on each work center and how long it will take to process. The information it uses comes from planned (i.e., forecasted) and open (i.e., existing) orders that are generated by the materials plan. The CRP itself helps to validate the rough-cut capacity plan.

Final assembly scheduling

Final assembly scheduling provides the operations required to put the product in its final form. It is here that customized or final features of the product are scheduled. For example, a printer manufacturer would typically specify from various options a control panel configuration at this scheduling stage.

Input/output planning and control

Input/output planning and control refers to a variety of reports and procedures focusing on scheduled demands and capacity constraints derived from the materials plan.

Production activity control

Production activity control (PAC) is a relatively new term that is used to describe scheduling and shop-floor control activities. PAC involves the scheduling and controlling of day-to-day activities on the shop floor. At this point, the master production schedule is translated into the immediate priorities of daily work schedules.

Purchase planning and control

Purchase planning and control deals with the acquisition and control of purchased items, again as specified by the materials plan. Input/output planning and control are necessary to make sure that purchasing not only is obtaining materials in time to meet the schedule, but is also aware of those orders that, for various reasons, call for rescheduling the delivery of purchased materials.

In summary, all the planning approaches attempt to balance capacity required with capacity available, and then schedule and control production in light of changes in the capacity balance. A good planning system is complete without being overwhelming, and has the confidence of its users up and down the organization structure.

13.2 AGGREGATE PRODUCTION PLANNING

Again, aggregate production planning is concerned with setting production rates by product group or other broad categories for the intermediate term (6 to 18 months). Note again from our first exhibit that the aggregate plan precedes the master schedule. *The main purpose of the aggregate plan is to specify that combination of production rate, work-force level, and inventory on hand that both minimizes costs (efficiency) and satisfies the forecasted demand (effectiveness).* **Production rate** refers to the quantity of product completed per unit of time (such as per hour or per day). **Work-force level** is the number of workers needed for production. **Inventory on hand** is the balance of unused inventory carried over from the previous period.

The form of the aggregate plan varies from company to company. In some firms, it is a formalized report containing both planning objectives and the planning premises on which it is based. In other companies, particularly smaller ones, "it may take shape in verbal directives or writings on the back of matchbook covers."[1]

The process by which the plan itself is derived also varies. One common approach is to derive it from the corporate annual plan, as was shown in Exhibit 13.1. A typical corporate plan contains a section on manufacturing that specifies how many units in each major product line need to be produced over the next 12 months to meet the sales forecast. The planner takes this information and attempts to determine how best to meet these requirements with available resources. Alternatively, some organizations combine output requirements into equivalent units and use this as the basis for aggregate planning. For example, a division of General Motors may be asked to produce a certain number of cars of all types at a particular facility. The production planner would then take the average labor hours required for all models as a basis for the overall aggregate plan. Refinements to this plan, specifically model types to be produced, would be reflected in shorter-term production plans.

---

[1] M. Nelson, "I Read the Book: The Master Scheduler Did It" (21st Annual American Production and Inventory Control Society Conference proceedings, 1978), p. 666.

EXHIBIT 13.2 Required Inputs to the Production Planning System

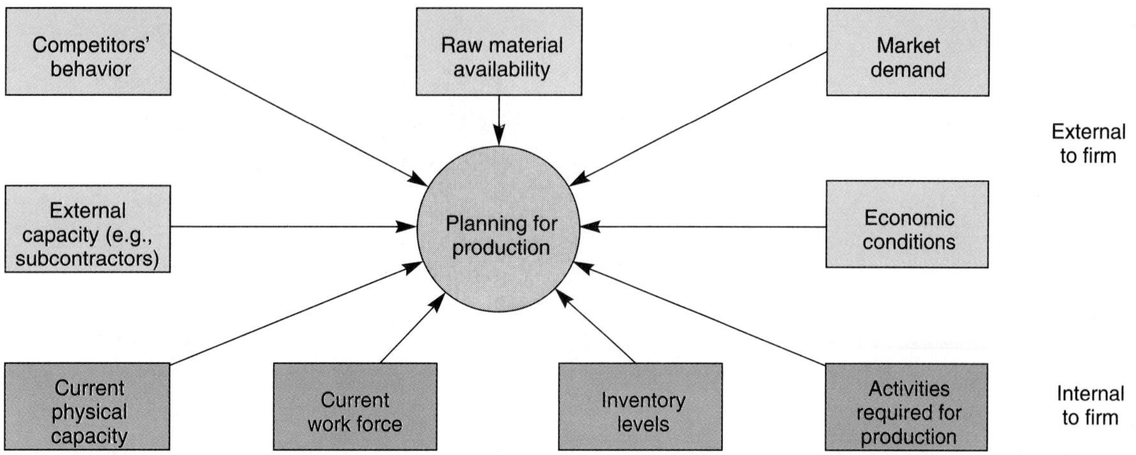

Another approach is to develop the aggregate plan by simulating various master production schedules and calculating corresponding capacity requirements to see if adequate labor and equipment exist at each work center. If capacity is inadequate, additional requirements for overtime, subcontracting, extra workers, and so forth are specified for each product line and combined into a rough-cut plan. This plan is then modified by trial-and-error or mathematical methods to derive a final and, one hopes, lower-cost plan.

Production Planning Environment

Exhibit 13.2 illustrates the internal and external factors that constitute the production planning environment. In general, the external environment is outside the production planner's direct control. In some firms, demand for the product can be managed, but even so, the production planner must live with the sales projections and orders promised by the marketing function. This leaves the internal factors as the variables that can be manipulated in deriving a production plan.

The internal factors themselves differ in their degree of control. Current physical capacity (plant and equipment) is virtually fixed in the short run and, therefore, cannot be increased; union agreements often constrain what can be done in changing the work force; and top management may set limits on the amount of money that can be tied up in inventories. Still, there is always some flexibility in managing these factors, and production planners can implement one or a combination of the **production planning strategies** discussed here.

EXHIBIT 13.3

Examples of Pure Chase and Pure Level Strategies

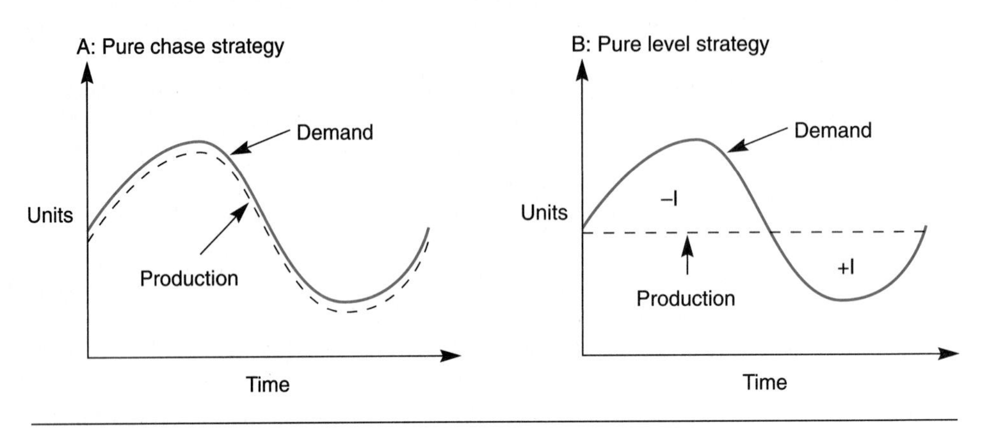

Production planning strategies

There are essentially three production planning strategies. These strategies involve trade-offs among the work-force size, work hours, inventory, and order backlogs.

1. *Chase strategy.*[2] Match the production rate to exactly meet the order rate by hiring and laying off employees as the order rate varies. The success of this strategy depends on having a pool of easily trained applicants to draw on as order volumes increase. There are obvious motivational impacts. When order backlogs are low, employees may feel compelled to slow down out of fear of being laid off as soon as existing orders are completed.
2. *Stable work force—variable work hours.* Vary the output by varying the number of hours worked through flexible work schedules or overtime. By varying the number of work hours, production quantities can be matched to existing orders. This strategy provides work-force continuity and avoids many of the emotional and tangible costs of hiring and firing associated with the chase strategy.
3. *Level strategy.* Maintain a stable work force working at a constant output rate. Shortages and surpluses are absorbed by fluctuating inventory levels, order backlogs, and lost sales. Employees benefit from stable work hours but inventory costs are increased. Another concern is the possibility of inventoried products becoming obsolete.

When just one of these variables is used to absorb demand fluctuations, it is termed a **pure strategy;** one or more used in combination is a **mixed strategy.** As you might suspect, mixed strategies are more widely applied in industry.

Exhibit 13.3A illustrates a pure chase strategy. Here production is in lockstep with demand. In other words, the number of units required in each time interval is the number of units that production will make. Exhibit 13.3B, on the other hand, demonstrates a pure level strategy. Here production is held constant, regardless of what the demand is. The

[2]No relation to one of the authors of this text.

difference between demand and production is accounted for in a "buffer" inventory of finished goods. When demand exceeds production, the difference is taken out of finished goods inventory (−I); when demand is less than production, the difference is placed back into inventory (+I). (It is assumed that when demand exceeds production in the initial cycle, as shown in Exhibit 13.3B, that there is sufficient inventory on hand at the beginning of the aggregate planning period to supply the required number of units.)

Certain industries, due to their inherent operating characteristics, often favor one type of strategy over the other. For example, services tend to follow a chase strategy because the customer is involved in the service delivery process. (If your restaurant is too crowded on a Saturday night, customers will not wait until Monday morning when you have more than enough capacity available to serve them!) Process-oriented facilities, on the other hand, such as breweries and refineries, tend to follow a level strategy because the high fixed costs associated with them requires that they operate at a high level of capacity utilization.

Subcontracting

In addition to these strategies, managers may also choose to subcontract some portion of production. This strategy is similar to the chase strategy, but hiring and laying off is translated into subcontracting and not subcontracting. Some level of subcontracting can be desirable to accommodate demand fluctuations. However, unless the relationship with the supplier is particularly strong, a manufacturer can lose some control over schedule and quality. For this reason, extensive subcontracting may be viewed as a high-risk strategy.

Relevant Costs

There are four costs relevant to aggregate production planning. These are:

1. *Basic production costs.* These are the fixed and variable costs incurred in producing a given product type in a given time period. Included are direct and indirect labor costs and regular as well as overtime compensation.
2. *Costs associated with changes in the production rate.* Typical costs in this category are those involved in hiring, training, and laying off personnel. Additional one-time costs might also be associated with adding another shift.
3. *Inventory holding costs.* A major component is the cost of capital tied up in inventory. Other components include storage, insurance, taxes, spoilage, and obsolescence.
4. *Backlogging costs.* Usually these costs are very difficult to measure and include costs of expediting, loss of customer goodwill, and loss of sales revenues resulting from cancelled orders because the product is not available.

Budgets

To receive funding, operations managers are generally required to submit annual, and sometimes quarterly, budget requests. Aggregate planning activities are key to the success of the budgeting process. Recall that the goal of aggregate planning is to meet forecasted product demand while minimizing the total production-related costs over the planning horizon by determining the optimal combination of work-force levels and inventory levels. Thus, aggregate planning provides justification for the requested budget amount.

Accurate medium-range planning increases both the likelihood of receiving the requested budget and operating within the limits of the budget.

In the next section, we provide examples of medium-range planning in both a manufacturing and a service setting. These examples illustrate the trade-offs associated with different production planning strategies.

13.3 AGGREGATE PLANNING TECHNIQUES

Companies still use simple trial-and-error charting and graphic methods to develop their aggregate plans, although computer spreadsheets and graphics packages are now available to facilitate the process. A trial-and-error approach involves costing out various production planning alternatives and selecting the one with the lowest cost. In addition, there are more sophisticated approaches, including linear programming, the Linear Decision Rule, and various heuristic methods. Of these, only linear programming has seen broad application.

A Trial-and-Error Example: The C&A Company

A firm with pronounced seasonal variation normally plans production with a 12-month time horizon in order to capture the extremes in demand during the busiest and slowest months. However, it is possible to illustrate the general concepts involved in aggregate planning with a shorter time horizon. Suppose we wish to set up a production plan for the C&A Company for the next six months. We are given the information shown in Exhibit 13.4.

Before we solve this problem, we need to first recognize the differences between full costs and marginal or incremental costs. Full costs are all of the actual, out-of-pocket costs associated with a particular aggregate plan. Included in full costs are the costs of material and labor and other direct, variable costs. Full costs are often used for developing a projected labor and material budget that will support an aggregate plan.

Marginal or incremental costs are only those unique costs that are different for a particular aggregate plan. Here we assume that the total number of products forecasted over the time horizon need to be built, regardless of the alternative selected. The incremental costs are, therefore, only those costs that are above and beyond those required to build the product by its most economical means (which is usually on the first shift in-house). Included in marginal costs are hiring and firing costs, inventory carrying costs, and overtime and/or second- and third-shift premium costs. To demonstrate the difference, we will use both the full-cost and marginal-cost methods to solve the aggregate planning problem for the C&A Company. You will note that both methods result in selecting the same alternative plan, in terms of lowest cost. The different alternatives are also ranked in the same order with both methods of costing. The advantage in using the marginal-cost approach is that we do not have to include a lot of numerical figures that have no impact on the final decision.

To properly develop and evaluate an aggregate plan, we need to first divide it into two stages. The first stage is the development of an actual plan that provides the required

EXHIBIT 13.4

Forecasted Demand and Workdays for the C&A Company

	Jan.	Feb.	Mar.	Apr.	May	June	Total
Demand forecast (units)	2,200	1,500	1,100	900	1,100	1,600	8,400
Working days (per month)	22	19	21	21	22	20	125

	Costs
Material cost	$100/unit
Inventory holding cost	$1.50/unit-month
Stockout cost	$5/unit/month
Subcontracting cost	$125/unit
Hiring and training cost	$200/worker
Layoff cost	$250/worker
Labor required per unit	5 hours
Labor cost (first 8 hours each day)	$4/hour
Overtime cost (time and a half)	$6/hour

	Inventory
Beginning inventory	400 units

	Work Force
Number of workers currently employed	30

number of products under the conditions stated. After this aggregate plan has been developed, the next step is to determine the costs associated with that plan. This is the approach we have taken with the C&A Company. Each alternative aggregate plan is accompanied by both its full costs and its marginal costs.

Many of the costs included in an aggregate plan are presented in a form that is typically not found in the accounting records of a firm. For example, there is usually no cost of carrying inventory. Instead, the individual component costs associated with carrying inventory are listed in separate categories (e.g., the cost of storage is rent, insurance, taxes, etc.; the cost of obsolescence is reflected in higher material and labor costs, etc.).

The first step in evaluating alternative production plans is to convert the demand forecast into production requirements. This is accomplished by subtracting out the amount of inventory on hand at the beginning of the forecast period. In the C&A example, the beginning inventory on hand is 400 units.

Now we are ready to formulate and evaluate alternative aggregate or production plans for the C&A Company. Although one could develop a large number of alternative aggregate plans, we have identified four plans that we will evaluate with the objective of selecting that one with the lowest costs.

Plan 1. Produce to exact monthly production requirements using a regular eight-hour day by varying work-force size (pure chase strategy).

Plan 2. Produce to meet expected average demand over the next six months by maintaining a constant work force. This constant number of workers is calculated by *averaging* the demand forecast over the horizon. Take the total production requirements for

EXHIBIT 13.5

First Alternative: Pure Chase Strategy

	Jan.	Feb.	March	April	May	June	Total
Demand forecast	2,200	1,500	1,100	900	1,100	1,600	8,400
Initial inventory	400						
Production requirements	1,800	1,500	1,100	900	1,100	1,600	8,000
Aggregate plan:							
Workers required	51	49	33	27	31	50	
Workers hired	21	0	0	0	4	19	
Workers fired	0	2	16	6	0	0	
Units produced	1,800	1,500	1,100	900	1,100	1,600	8,000
Costs—full:							
Regular production	36,000	30,000	22,000	18,000	22,000	32,000	160,000
Material costs	180,000	150,000	110,000	90,000	110,000	160,000	800,000
Hiring costs	4,200	0	0	0	800	3,800	8,800
Firing costs	0	500	4,000	1,500	0	0	6,000
Total full costs	220,200	180,500	136,000	109,500	132,800	195,800	974,800
Costs—incremental:							
Hiring costs	4,200	0	0	0	800	3,800	8,800
Firing costs	0	500	4,000	1,500	0	0	6,000
Total incremental costs	4,200	500	4,000	1,500	800	3,800	14,800

all six months and determine how many workers would be needed if each month's requirements were the same [(8,400 – 400) units × 5 hours per unit ÷ (125 days × 8 hours per day) = 40 workers]. Inventory is allowed to accumulate, with shortages filled from next month's production by back ordering (pure level strategy).

Plan 3. Produce to meet the minimum expected demand (April) using a constant work force on regular time. Subcontract to meet additional output requirements. The number of workers is calculated by locating the minimum monthly production requirement and determining how many workers would be needed for that month [(900 units × 6 months × 5 hours per unit) ÷ (125 days × 8 hours per day) = 27 workers] and subcontracting any monthly difference between requirements and production (minimum work force with subcontracting strategy).

Plan 4. Produce to meet expected demand for all but the first two months using a constant work force on regular time. Use overtime to meet additional output requirements (constant work force with overtime strategy).

The number of workers needed in this alternative is determined as follows:

1,100 + 900 + 1,100 + 1,600 = 4,700 units (March–June)

4,700 units × 5 labor hours per unit = 23,500 worker-hours

23,500 worker-hours/8 hours per day = 2,938 worker-days

2,938 worker-days/84 days (March–June) ≊ 35 workers

Having identified each of the four alternatives, the next step is to develop an aggregate plan for each alternative, showing all of the detailed calculations. These are presented in Exhibits 13.5, 13.6, 13.7, and 13.8. Once the details of each production plan have been developed, we can then determine the costs associated with each plan. These costs (both

EXHIBIT 13.6

Second Alternative: Pure Level Strategy

	Jan.	Feb.	March	April	May	June	Total
Demand forecast	2,200	1,500	1,100	900	1,100	1,600	8,400
Initial inventory	400						
Production requirements	1,800	1,500	1,100	900	1,100	1,600	8,000
Aggregate plan:							
Workers required	40	40	40	40	40	40	
Workers hired	10	0	0	0	0	0	
Workers fired	0	0	0	0	0	0	
Units produced	1,408	1,216	1,344	1,344	1,408	1,280	8,000
Monthly inventory	(392)	(284)	244	444	308	(320)	
Cumulative inventory	(392)	(676)	(432)	12	320	0	
Costs—full:							
Regular production	28,160	24,320	26,880	26,880	28,160	25,600	160,000
Material costs	140,800	121,600	134,400	134,400	140,800	128,000	800,000
Hiring costs	2,000	0	0	0	0	0	2,000
Firing costs	0	0	0	0	0	0	0
Inventory carrying costs	0	0	0	18	480	0	498
Stockout costs	1,960	3,380	2,160	0	0	0	7,500
Total full costs	172,920	149,300	163,440	161,298	169,440	153,600	969,998
Costs—incremental:							
Hiring costs	2,000	0	0	0	0	0	2,000
Firing costs	0	0	0	0	0	0	0
Inventory carrying costs	0	0	0	18	480	0	498
Stockout costs	1,960	3,380	2,160	0	0	0	7,500
Total incremental costs	3,960	3,380	2,160	18	480	0	9,998

full costs and marginal costs) are also included in their respective exhibits. A summary of these costs is presented in Exhibit 13.9, showing that the pure level strategy is the lowest cost alternative.

Aggregate Planning Applied to Services: Tucson Parks and Recreation Department

Charting and graphic techniques are also very useful for aggregate planning in service applications. The following example shows how a city's parks and recreation department could use the alternatives of full-time employees, part-time employees, and subcontracting to meet its commitment to provide a service to the city.

The Tucson Parks and Recreation Department is responsible for developing and maintaining open space, all public recreational programs, adult sports leagues, golf courses, tennis courts, pools, and so forth. There are 336 full-time-equivalent employees (FTEs). Of these, 216 are full-time permanent personnel who provide the administration and year-round maintenance to all areas. The remaining 120 year-long FTE positions are part time, with about 75 percent of them being used during the summer and the remaining 25 percent being used in the fall, winter, and spring seasons. The 75 percent (or 90 FTE

EXHIBIT 13.7

Third Alternative: Minimum Work Force with Subcontracting Strategy

	Jan.	Feb.	March	April	May	June	Total
Demand forecast	2,200	1,500	1,100	900	1,100	1,600	8,400
Initial inventory	400						
Production requirements	1,800	1,500	1,100	900	1,100	1,600	8,000
Aggregate plan:							
Workers required	27	27	27	27	27	27	
Workers hired	0	0	0	0	0	0	
Workers fired	3	0	0	0	0	0	
Units produced	950	821	907	907	950	864	5,399
Monthly inventory	0	0	0	7	0	0	
Units subcontracted	850	679	193	0	143	736	2,601
Costs—full:							
Regular production	19,000	16,420	18,140	18,140	19,000	17,280	107,980
Material costs	95,000	82,100	90,700	90,700	95,000	86,400	539,900
Hiring costs	0	0	0	0	0	0	0
Firing costs	750	0	0	0	0	0	750
Inventory carrying costs	0	0	0	11	0	0	11
Subcontracting costs	106,250	84,875	24,125	0	17,875	92,000	325,125
Total full costs	221,000	183,395	132,965	108,851	131,875	195,680	973,766
Costs—incremental:							
Hiring costs	0	0	0	0	0	0	0
Firing costs	750	0	0	0	0	0	750
Inventory carrying costs	0	0	0	11	0	0	11
Subcontracting costs	4,250	3,395	965	0	715	3,680	13,005
Total incremental costs	5,000	3,395	965	11	715	3,680	13,766

positions) show up as approximately 800 part-time summer jobs: lifeguards, baseball umpires, and instructors in summer programs for children. The 800 part-time jobs are derived from 90 FTEs because many of these positions last only for a month or two while the FTEs are a year long.

Currently, the parks and recreation work that is subcontracted amounts to less than $100,000. This is for the golf and tennis pros and for grounds maintenance at the libraries and veterans cemetery.

Because of the nature of city employment, the probable bad public image, and civil service rules, the option to hire and fire full-time help daily and/or weekly to meet seasonal demand is pretty much out of the question. However, temporary part-time help is authorized and traditional. Also, it is virtually impossible to have regular (full-time) staff for all of the summer jobs. During the summer months, the approximately 800 part-time employees are staffing many programs that occur simultaneously, prohibiting level scheduling over a normal 40-hour week. Also, a wider variety of skills is required than can be expected from full-time employees (e.g., umpires; coaches; lifeguards; teachers of ceramics, guitar, karate, belly dancing, and yoga).

Three options are open to the department in its aggregate planning.

1. The present method, which is to maintain a medium-level full-time staff and schedule work during off seasons (such as rebuilding baseball fields during the winter months) and to use part-time help during peak demands.

EXHIBIT 13.8

Constant Work Force with Overtime Strategy

	Jan.	Feb.	March	April	May	June	Total
Demand forecast	2,200	1,500	1,100	900	1,100	1,600	8,400
Initial inventory	400						
Production requirements	1,800	1,500	1,100	900	1,100	1,600	8,000
Aggregate plan:							
Workers required	35	35	35	35	35	35	
Workers hired	5	0	0	0	0	0	
Workers fired	0	0	0	0	0	0	
Units produced—regular	1,232	1,064	1,176	1,176	1,232	1,120	7,000
Units produced—overtime	568	436					1,004
Monthly inventory	0	0	76	276	132	(480)	
Cumulative inventory	0	0	76	352	484	4	
Costs—full:							
Regular production	24,640	21,280	23,520	23,520	24,640	22,400	140,000
Overtime production	17,040	13,080	0	0	0	0	30,120
Material costs	180,000	150,000	117,600	117,600	123,200	112,000	800,400
Hiring costs	1,000	0	0	0	0	0	1,000
Firing costs	0	0	0	0	0	0	0
Inventory carrying costs	0	0	114	528	726	6	1,374
Total full costs	222,680	184,360	141,234	141,648	148,566	134,406	972,894
Costs—incremental:							
Overtime production	5,680	4,360	0	0	0	0	10,040
Hiring costs	1,000	0	0	0	0	0	1,000
Firing costs	0	0	0	0	0	0	0
Inventory carrying costs			114	528	726	6	1,374
Total incremental costs	6,680	4,360	114	528	726	6	12,414

EXHIBIT 13.9

Summary of Costs for Alternative Aggregate Plans

Alternative	Full Costs	Marginal Costs
Pure chase	$974,800	$14,800
Pure level	$969,998	$9,998
Minimum work force with subcontracting	$973,766	$13,766
Constant work force with overtime	$972,894	$12,414

2. Maintain a lower level of staff over the year and subcontract all additional work presently done by full-time staff (still using part-time help).
3. Maintain an administrative staff only and subcontract all work, including part-time help. (This would entail contracts to landscaping firms, pool-maintenance companies, and to newly created private firms to employ and supply part-time help.)

The common unit of measure of work across all areas is full-time equivalent jobs or employees (or FTEs). For example, assume in the same week that 30 lifeguards worked 20

EXHIBIT 13.10 **Actual Demand Requirement for Full-Time Direct Employees and Full-Time-Equivalent (FTE) Part-Time Employees**

	Jan.	Feb.	March	April	May	June	July	Aug.	Sept.	Oct.	Nov.	Dec.	Total
Days	22	20	21	22	21	20	21	21	21	23	18	22	252
Full-time employees	66	28	130	90	195	290	325	92	45	32	29	60	
Full-time days*	1,452	560	2,730	1,980	4,095	5,800	6,825	1,932	945	736	522	1,320	28,897
Full-time-equivalent part-time employees	41	75	72	68	72	302	576	72	0	68	84	27	
FTE days	902	1,500	1,512	1,496	1,512	6,040	12,096	1,512	0	1,564	1,512	594	30,240

Note: Some workweeks are staggered to include weekdays, but this does not affect the number of workdays per employee.
*Full-time days are derived by multiplying the number of days in each month by the number of workers.

hours each, 40 instructors worked 15 hours each, and 35 baseball umpires worked 10 hours each. This is equivalent to $(30 \times 20) + (40 \times 15) + (35 \times 10) = 1{,}550 \div 40 = 38.75$ FTE positions for that week. Although a considerable amount of workload can be shifted to the off season, most of the work must be done when required.

Full-time employees consist of three groups: (1) the skeleton group of key department personnel coordinating with the city, setting policy, determining budgets, measuring performance, and so forth; (2) the administrative group of supervisory and office personnel who are responsible for or whose jobs are directly linked to the direct-labor workers; and (3) the direct-labor work force of 116 full-time positions. These workers physically maintain the department's areas of responsibility, such as cleaning up, mowing golf greens and ballfields, trimming trees, and watering grass.

Cost information needed to determine the best alternative strategy is

Full-time direct-labor employees	
Average wage rate	$8.90 per hour
Fringe benefits	17% of wage rate
Administrative costs	20% of wage rate
Part-time employees	
Average wage rate	$8.06 per hour
Fringe benefits	11% of wage rate
Administrative costs	25% of wage rate
Subcontracting all full-time jobs	$3.2 million
Subcontracting all part-time jobs	$3.7 million

June and July are the peak demand seasons in Tucson. Exhibit 13.10 shows the high requirements for June and July personnel. The part-time help reaches 575 full-time-equivalent positions (although in actual numbers, this is approximately 800 different employees). After a low fall and winter staffing level, the demand shown as "full-time direct" reaches 130 in March when grounds are reseeded and fertilized and then increases to a high of 325 in July. The present method levels this uneven demand over the year to an average of 116 full-time year-round employees by early scheduling of work. As previously mentioned, no attempt is made to hire and lay off full-time workers to meet this uneven demand.

EXHIBIT 13.11 **Three Possible Plans for the Parks and Recreation Department**

Alternative 1: Maintain 116 full-time regular direct workers. Schedule work during off seasons to level workload throughout the year. Continue to use 120 full-time-equivalent (FTE) part-time employees to meet high demand periods.

Costs	Days per Year (Exhibit 12.9)	Hours (employees × days × 8 hours)	Wages (full-time, $8.90; part-time, $8.06)	Fringe Benefits (full-time, 17%; part-time, 11%)	Administrative Cost (full-time, 20%; part-time, 25%)
116 full-time regular employees	252	233,856	$2,081,318	$353,824	$416,264
120 part-time employees	252	241,920	1,949,875	214,486	487,469
Total cost = $2,751,619			$4,031,193	$568,310	$903,733

Alternative 2: Maintain 50 full-time regular direct workers and the present 120 FTE part-time employees. Subcontract jobs releasing 66 full-time regular employees. Subcontract cost, $2,200,000.

Costs	Days per Year (Exhibit 12.9)	Hours (employees × days × 8 hours)	Wages (full-time, $8.90; part-time, $8.06)	Fringe Benefits (full-time, 17%; part-time, 11%)	Administrative Cost full-time, 20%; part-time, 25%)	Subcontract Cost
50 full-time employees	252	100,800	$ 897,120	$ 152,510	$ 179,424	$2,200,000
120 FTE part-time employees						
subcontracting cost	252	241,920	1,949,875	214,486	487,469	
Total cost = $3,040,443			$2,846,995	$366,996	$666,893	$2,200,000

Alternative 3: Subcontract all jobs previously performed by 116 full-time regular employees. Subcontract cost $3,200,000. Subcontract all jobs previously performed by 120 full-time-equivalent part-time employees. Subcontract cost $3,700,000.

Cost	Subcontract Cost
0 Full-time employees	
0 Part-time employees	
Subcontract full-time jobs	$3,200,000
Subcontract part-time jobs	3,700,000
Total cost	$6,900,000

EXHIBIT 13.12 **Comparison of Costs for All Three Alternatives**

	Alternative 1: 116 Full-time Direct Labor Employees 120 FTE Part-Time Employees	Alternative 2: 50 Full-Time Direct Labor Employees, 120 FTE Part-Time Employees, Subcontracting	Alternative 3: Subcontracting Jobs Formerly Performed by 116 Direct Labor Full-Time Employees and 120 FTE Part-Time Employees
Wages	$4,031,193	$2,846,995	—
Fringe benefits	568,310	366,996	—
Administrative costs	903,733	666,893	—
Subcontracting, full-time jobs		2,200,000	$3,200,000
Subcontracting, part-time jobs			3,700,000
Total	$5,503,236	$6,080,884	$6,900,000

Exhibit 13.11 shows the cost calculations for all three alternatives. Exhibit 13.12 compares the total costs for each alternative. From this analysis, it appears that the department is already using the lowest-cost alternative (Alternative 1).

13.4 CONCLUSION

Aggregate planning provides the link between the corporate strategic and capacity plans and work-force size, inventory quantity, and production levels. It does not do detailed planning. It is also useful to point out some practical considerations in aggregate planning.

First, demand variations are a fact of life, so the planning system must include sufficient flexibility to cope with such variations. Flexibility can be achieved by developing alternative sources of supply, cross-training workers to handle a wide variety of orders, and engaging in more frequent replanning during high-demand periods.

Second, decision rules for production planning should be adhered to once they have been selected. However, they should be carefully analyzed prior to implementation by such checks as using simulation of historical data to see what really would have happened if they had been in operation in the past.

13.5 REVIEW AND DISCUSSION QUESTIONS

1. What are the basic controllable variables of a production planning problem? What are the four major costs?
2. Distinguish between pure and mixed strategies in production planning.
3. Compare the best plans in the C&A Company and the Tucson Parks and Recreation Department. What do they have in common?
4. How does forecast accuracy relate, in general, to the practical application of the aggregate planning models discussed in the chapter?
5. In which way does the time horizon chosen for an aggregate plan determine whether or not it is the best plan for the firm?

13.6 SOLVED PROBLEM

PROBLEM

Jason Enterprises (JE) is producing video telephones for the home market. Quality is not quite as good as it could be at this point, but the selling price is low and Jason has the opportunity to study market response while spending more time in additional R&D work.

At this stage, however, JE needs to develop an aggregate production plan for the six months from January through June. As you can guess, you have been commissioned to create the plan. The following information is available to help you:

	Jan.	Feb.	March	April	May	June
Demand data						
Beginning inventory	200					
Forecast demand	500	600	650	800	900	800
Cost data						
Holding cost		$10/unit/month				
Stockout cost		$20/unit/month				

	Jan.	Feb.	March	April	May	June
Subcontracting cost/unit		$100				
Hiring cost/worker		$50				
Layoff cost/worker		$100				
Labor cost/hour—straight time		$12.50				
Labor cost/hour—overtime		$18.75				
Production data						
Labor hours/unit	4					
Workdays/month	22					
Current work force	10					

What is the cost of each of the following production strategies?

a. Chase strategy; vary work force (assuming a starting work force of 10).

b. Constant work force; vary inventory and stockout only (assuming a starting work force of 10).

c. Level work force of 10; vary overtime only; inventory carryover permitted.

d. Level work force of 10; vary overtime only; inventory carryover not permitted.

SOLUTION

a. Plan 1: Chase strategy; vary work force (assume 10 in work force to start).

Month	(1) Production Requirement	(2) Production Hours Required (1) × 4	(3) Hours/Month per Worker 22 × 8	(4) Workers Required (2) ÷ (3)	(5) WORKERS Hired	(6) WORKERS Fired
January	300	1,200	176	7	0	3
February	600	2,400	176	14	7	0
March	650	2,600	176	15	1	0
April	800	3,200	176	19	4	0
May	900	3,600	176	21	2	0
June	800	3,200	176	19	0	2

Month	(7) Hiring Cost (5) × $50	(8) Layoff Cost (6) × $100	(9) Straight-Time Cost (2) × $12.50
January	0	$300	$ 15,000
February	350	0	30,000
March	50	0	32,500
April	200	0	40,000
May	100	0	45,000
June	0	200	40,000
	$700	$500	$202,500

Total cost for plan:

Hiring cost	$ 700
Layoff cost	500
Straight-time cost	202,500
Total	$203,700

b. Plan 2: Constant work force; vary inventory and stockout only.

Month	(1) Cumulative Production Requirement	(2) Production Hours Available 22 × 8 × 10	(3) Units Produced (2) ÷ 4	(4) Cumulative Production
January	300	1,760	440	440
February	900	1,760	440	880
March	1,550	1,760	440	1,320
April	2,350	1,760	440	1,760
May	3,250	1,760	440	2,200
June	4,050	1,760	440	2,640

Month	(5) Units Short (1) – (4)	(6) Shortage Cost (5) × $20	(7) Units Excess (4) – (1)	(8) Inventory Cost (7) × $10	(9) Straight-Time Cost (2) × $12.50
January	$ 0	0	140	1,400	$ 22,000
February	20	400	0	0	22,000
March	230	4,600	0	0	22,000
April	590	11,800	0	0	22,000
May	1,050	21,000	0	0	22,000
June	1,410	28,200	0	0	22,000
		$66,000		$1,400	$132,000

Total cost for plan:

Shortage cost	$ 66,000
Inventory cost	1,400
Straight-time cost	132,000
Total	$199,400

c. Plan 3: Level work force of 10; vary overtime only; inventory carryover permitted.

Month	(1) Production Requirement	(2) Standard Time Hours Available 22 × 8 × 10	(3) Standard Time Units Produced (2) ÷ 4	(4) Overtime Required in Units (1) – (3)
January	300	1,760	440	0
February	460*	1,760	440	20
March	650	1,760	440	210
April	800	1,760	440	360
May	900	1,760	440	460
June	800	1,760	440	360
				1,410

*600—140 units of beginning inventory in February.

Month	(5) Overtime Required in Hours (4) × 4	(6) Overtime Cost (5) × $18.75	(7) Straight-Time Cost (2) × $12.50	(8) Excess Inventory Costs (3) − (1) × $10
January	0	$ 0	$ 22,000	$1,400
February	80	1,500	22,000	
March	840	15,750	22,000	
April	1,440	27,000	22,000	
May	1,840	34,500	22,000	
June	1,440	27,000	22,000	
		$105,750	$132,000	$1,400

Total cost for plan:

Straight-time cost	$132,000
Overtime cost	105,750
Inventory cost	1,400
Total	$239,150

d. Plan 4: Constant work force of 10; vary overtime only; inventory carryover not permitted.

Month	(1) Production Requirement	(2) Standard-Time Hours Available 22 × 8 × 10	(3) Standard-Time Units Produced Min. [(2) ÷ 4; (1)]	(4) Overtime Required in Units (1) − (3)
January	300	1,760	300	0
February	600	1,760	440	160
March	650	1,760	440	210
April	800	1,760	440	360
May	900	1,760	440	460
June	800	1,760	440	360

Month	(5) Overtime Required in Hours (4) × 4	(6) Overtime Cost (5) × $18.75	(7) Standard-Time Cost (2) × $12.50	(8) Excess Inventory Costs (3) − (1) × $10
January	0	$ 0	$ 22,000	$1,400
February	640	12,000	22,000	
March	840	15,750	22,000	
April	1,440	27,000	22,000	
May	1,840	34,500	22,000	
June	1,440	27,000	22,000	
		$116,250	$132,000	$1,400

Total cost for plan:

Straight-time cost	$132,000
Overtime cost	116,250
Excess inventory cost	1,400
	$249,650

13.7 PROBLEMS

1. Develop a production plan and calculate the annual cost for a firm whose demand forecast is fall, 10,000; winter, 8,000; spring, 7,000; summer, 12,000. Inventory at the beginning of fall is 500 units. At the beginning of fall you currently have 30 workers, but you plan to hire temporary workers at the beginning of summer and lay them off at the end of summer. In addition, you have negotiated with the union an option to use the regular work force on overtime during winter or spring if overtime is necessary to prevent stockouts at the end of those quarters. Overtime is *not* available during the fall. Relevant costs are: hiring, $100 for each temp; layoff, $200 for each worker laid off; inventory holding, $5 per unit-quarter; back order, $10 per unit; straight time, $5 per hour; overtime, $8 per hour. Assume that the productivity is two worker hours per unit, with eight hours per day and 60 days per season.
2. Plan production for a four-month period: February through May. For February and March, you should produce to exact demand forecast. For April and May, you should use overtime and inventory with a stable work force. However, government constraints put a maximum of 5,000 hours of overtime labor per month in April and May (zero overtime in February and March). If demand exceeds supply, then back orders occur. There are 100 workers on January 1. You are given the following demand forecast: February, 80,000; March, 64,000; April, 100,000; May, 40,000. Productivity is four units per worker hour, eight hours per day, 20 days per month. Assume zero inventory on February 1. Costs are: hiring, $50 per new worker; layoff, $70 per worker laid off; inventory holding, $10 per unit-month; straight-time labor, $10 per hour; overtime, $15 per hour; back order, $20 per unit. Find the total cost of this plan.
3. Plan production for the next year. The demand forecast is spring, 20,000; summer, 10,000; fall, 15,000; winter, 18,000. At the beginning of spring you have 70 workers and 1,000 units in inventory. The union contract specifies that you may lay off workers only once a year, at the beginning of summer. Also, you may hire new workers only at the end of summer to begin regular work in the fall. The number of workers laid off at the beginning of summer and the number hired at the end of summer should result in planned production levels for summer and fall that equal the demand forecasts for summer and fall respectively. If demand exceeds supply, use overtime in spring only, which means that back orders could occur in winter. You are given these costs: hiring, $100 per new worker; layoff, $200 per worker laid off; holding, $20 per unit-quarter; back-order costs, $8 per unit; straight-time labor, $10 per hour; overtime, $15 per hour. Productivity is two worker hours per unit, eight hours per day, 50 days per quarter. Find the total cost.
4. DAT, Inc. needs to develop an aggregate plan for its product line. Relevant data are

Production time	1 hour per unit
Average labor cost	$10 per hour
Workweek	5 days, 8 hours each day
Days per month	Assume 20 work days per month
Beginning inventory	500 units
Safety stock	One-half of monthly forecast
Shortage cost	$20 per unit per month
Carry cost	$5 per unit per month

The forecast for January to December 1988 is:

Jan.	Feb.	March	April	May	June	July	Aug.	Sept.	Oct.	Nov.	Dec.
2,500	3,000	4,000	3,500	3,500	3,000	3,000	4,000	4,000	4,000	3,000	3,000

Management prefers to keep a constant work force and production level, absorbing variations in demand through inventory excesses and shortages. Demand not met is carried over to the following month.

Develop an aggregate plan that will meet the demand and other conditions of the problem. Do not try to find the optimum; just find a good solution and state the procedure you might use to test for a better solution. Make any necessary assumptions.

5. Shoney Video Concepts produces a line of video disc players to be linked to personal computers for video games. Video discs have much faster access time than do tape. With such a computer/video link, the game becomes a very realistic experience. In a simple driving game where the joystick steers the vehicle, for example, rather than seeing computer graphics on the screen, the player is actually viewing a segment of a video disc shot from a real moving vehicle. Depending on the action of the player (hitting a guard rail, for example) the disc moves virtually instantaneously to that segment and the player becomes part of an actual accident of real vehicles (staged, of course).

   Shoney is trying to determine a production plan for the next 12 months. The main criterion for this plan is that the employment level is to be held constant over the period. Shoney is continuing in its R&D efforts to develop new applications and prefers not to cause any adverse feeling with the local work force. For the same reasons, all employees should put in full work weeks, even if this is not the lowest-cost alternative. The forecast for the next 12 months is:

Month	Forecast Demand	Month	Forecast Demand
January	600	July	200
February	800	August	200
March	900	September	300
April	600	October	700
May	400	November	800
June	300	December	900

   Manufacturing cost is $200 per set, equally divided between materials and labor. Inventory storage costs are $5 per month. A shortage of sets results in lost sales and is estimated to cost an overall $20 per unit short.

   The inventory on hand at the beginning of the planning period is 200 units. Ten labor hours are required per video disc player. The workday is eight hours.

   Develop an aggregate production schedule for the year using a constant work force. For simplicity, assume 22 working days each month except July, when the plant closes down for three weeks' vacation (leaving seven working days). Make any assumptions you need.

6. Develop a production schedule to produce the exact production requirements by varying the work-force size for the following problem. Use the example in the chapter as a guide (Plan 1).

   The monthly forecast for Product X for January, February, and March is 1,000, 1,500, and 1,200, respectively. Safety stock policy recommends that one-half of the forecast for that month be defined as safety stock. There are 22 working days in January, 19 in February, and 21 in March. Beginning inventory is 500 units.

   Following are additional data: Manufacturing cost is $200 per unit, storage costs are $3 per unit per month, standard pay rate is $6 per hour, overtime rate is $9 per hour, cost of stockout is $10 per unit per month, marginal cost of subcontracting is $10 per unit, hiring and training cost is $200 per worker, layoff costs are $300 per worker, and production worker hours required per unit are 10. Make whatever assumptions are necessary.

7. The Bentley Chemical Company (BCC) is vitally concerned about generating a production schedule for their products for the coming fiscal year (July–June). The operations manager at BCC, Mr. Perspa Cassidy, has been charged with generating an aggregate plan for this time period so that BCC can meet their demand with the minimum utilization of resources.

   Mr. Cassidy first aggregates the various products which BCC sells into a single "aggregate" production unit and forecasts the demand for the following four quarters:

Quarter	Quarter #1 Jul/Aug/Sept	Quarter #2 Oct/Nov/Dec	Quarter #3 Jan/Feb/Mar	Quarter #4 Apr/May/June
Demand forecast	10,000	9,800	9,400	10,200

   On March 1 (prior to quarter #1) there were 1,200 units in BCC's inventory. Mr. Cassidy knows that to keep one unit in inventory for one month costs $5; further, BCC uses average inventory when computing inventory costs. The work force on March 1 consisted of 40 employees, each of whom produces exactly four (4) units in an 8-hour day. For the coming four quarters, Mr. Cassidy has determined the number of productive days for each quarter to be as follows:

Quarter	Quarter #1 Jul/Aug/Sept	Quarter #2 Oct/Nov/Dec	Quarter #3 Jan/Feb/Mar	Quarter #4 Apr/May/June
Number of productive days	56	60	61	63

   Each of the regular employees is paid at the rate of $53 per day; however, overtime is available at the rate of $80 per day. BCC has a very strict quality control policy and does not allow any subcontracting. In addition, BCC wishes to maintain their reputation with their customers and has adopted a policy that *all* demand must be met on time.

   Mr. Cassidy recognizes that meeting all demand can be difficult. He is faced with two limitations: (1) he is using aggregate units, and (2) he has only his forecasts as a basis for his aggregate plan. However, he believes that his forecasts are quite good and decides to use his figures objectively (i.e., he decides not to keep any safety stock).

   The work force can be increased or decreased at the discretion of Mr. Cassidy, but no more than a 25 percent increase or decrease (using integer values) is allowed in any given quarter due to union regulations. Mr. Cassidy knows that should he wish to hire and/or fire, that the total increase/decrease in the work force (when using whole people) cannot exceed the 25 percent mark. Fortunately, BCC is located in an area where there is no shortage of skilled labor.

To hire a new individual and train him/her requires exactly one quarter and costs $1,200. All new employees always start on the first day of a given quarter. Hence, they cannot be considered part of the productive labor force until after their first quarter. To fire an individual costs $1,000, and when an individual is fired, he remains part of the productive work force until the end of the quarter in which he was fired.

Mr. Cassidy believes that he has all the data he needs; hence, he starts to determine the aggregate capacity plan. He selects a strategy of trying to maintain a relatively stable work force, while letting the inventory levels fluctuate.

a. Perform the initial calculations Mr. Cassidy would need prior to completing the grid that follows.

b. Develop an aggregate plan for Mr. Cassidy by filling in the grid.

c. What is the total cost of Mr. Cassidy's plan?

(1) Qtr.	(2) Demand	(3) Prod. Hours Req. (2) × 2	(4) Prod. Days per Qtr.	(5) Prod. Hrs. per Qtr. per Worker (4) × 8	(6) No. of Empls.	(7) Total Prod. Hrs. Avail. per Qtr. (5) × (6)	(8) Straight-time Cost (4) × (6) × $53	(9) No. of Units Short	(10) Short Cost	(11) No. of OT Units Req.	(12) No. of OT Days Req. (11)/4
NOW	9,900	19,800	63	504	40	20,160	$133,560	0	$0	0	0
1	10,000		56						0		
2	9,800		60						0		
3	9,400		61						0		
4	10,200		63						0		

(13) Overtime Cost (12) × $80	(14) No. of Unit Sub.	(15) Sub. Cost.	(16) No. of Empls. Hired	(17) Hiring Cost (16) × $1200	(18) No. of Empls. Fired	(19) Firing Cost (18) × $1000	(20) Begin. Inv.	(21) End. Inv.	(22) Ave. Inv. ((20) + (21))/2	(23) Inv. Cost (22) × $15
$0	0	$0	0	$0	0	$ 0	1,200	1,380	1,290	$19,350
							1,380			

13.8 CASE: XYZ BROKERAGE FIRM*

Consider the national operations group of the XYZ brokerage firm. The group, housed in an office building located in the Wall Street area, handles the transactions generated by registered representatives in more than 100 branch offices throughout the United States. As with all firms in the brokerage industry, XYZ's transactions must be settled within five trading days. This five-day period allows operations managers to smooth out the daily volume fluctuations.

Fundamental shifts in the stock market's volume and mix can occur overnight, so the operations manager must be prepared to handle extremely wide swings in volume. For example, on the strength of an international peace rumor, the number of transactions or XYZ rose from 5,600 one day to 12,200 the next.

Managers of XYZ, not unlike their counterparts in other firms, have trouble predicting volume. In fact, a random number generator can predict volume a month or even a week into the future almost as well as the managers can.

How do the operations managers in XYZ manage capacity when there are such wide swings? The answer differs according to the tasks and constraints facing each manager. Here's what two managers in the same firm might say:

Manager A: The capacity in our operation is currently 12,000 transactions per day. Of course, what we should gear up for is always a problem. For example, our volume this year ranged from 4,000 to 15,000 transactions per day. It's a good thing we have a turnover rate, because in periods of low volume it helps us reduce our personnel without the morale problems caused by layoffs. [The labor turnover rate in this department is over 100 percent per year.]

Manager B: For any valid budgeting procedure, one needs to estimate volume within 15 percent. Correlations between actual and expected volume in the brokerage industry have been so poor that I question the value of budgeting at all. I maintain our capacity at a level of 17,000 transactions per day.

Why the big difference in capacity management in the same firm? Manager A is in charge of the cashiering operation—the handling of certificates, checks, and cash. The personnel in cashiering are messengers, clerks, and supervisors. The equipment—file cabinets, vaults, calculators—is uncomplicated.

Manager B, however, is in charge of handling orders, an information-processing function. The personnel are data-entry clerks, EDP specialists, and systems analysts. The equipment is complex—computers, LANs, file servers, and communication devices that link national operations with the branches. The employees under B's control had performed their tasks manually until decreased volume and a standardization of the information needs made it worthwhile to install computers.

Because the lead times required to increase the capacity of the information-processing operations are long, however, and the incremental cost of the capacity to handle the last 5,000 transactions is low (only some extra peripheral equipment is needed), Manager B maintains the capacity to handle 17,000 transactions per day. He holds to this level even though the average number of daily transactions for any month has never been higher than 11,000 and the number of transactions for any one day has never been higher than 16,000.

---

*W. E. Sasser, R. P. Olsen, and D. D. Wyckoff, *Management of Service Operations* (Boston: Allyn & Bacon, 1978), pp. 303–4.

Because a great deal of uncertainty about the future status of the stock certificate exists, the situation is completely different in cashiering. Attempts to automate the cashiering function to the degree reached by the order-processing group have been thwarted because the high risk of selecting a system not compatible with the future format of the stock certificate.

In other words, Manager A is tied to the chase demand strategy, and his counterpart, Manager B in the adjacent office, is locked into the level capacity strategy. However, each desires to incorporate more of the other's strategy into his own. A is developing a computerized system to handle the information-processing requirements of cashiering; B is searching for some variable costs in the order-processing operation that can be deleted in periods of low volume.

QUESTIONS

1. What appear to be the primary differences between each department?
2. Do these differences eliminate certain strategy choices for either manager?
3. Which factors cause the current strategy to be desirable for each manager?
4. What are the mixed or subcontracting possibilities?
5. What are the problems associated with low standardization?

13.9 SELECTED BIBLIOGRAPHY

Buffa, Elwood S., and Jeffrey G. Miller. *Production-Inventory Systems: Planning and Control.* 3rd ed. Homewood, Ill.: Richard D. Irwin, 1979.

Fisk, J. C., and J. P. Seagle. "Integration of Aggregate Planning with Resource Requirements Planning." *Production and Inventory Management,* Third Quarter 1978, p. 87.

McLeavy, D., and S. Narasimhan. *Production Planning and Inventory Control.* Boston: Allyn & Bacon, 1985.

Monden, Yasuhiro. *Toyota Production System.* Atlanta, Ga.: Industrial Engineering and Management Press, 1983.

Plossl, G. W. *Production and Inventory Control: Principles and Techniques.* 2nd ed. Englewood Cliffs, N.J.: Prentice Hall, 1985.

Silver, E. A., and R. Peterson. *Decision Systems for Inventory Management and Production Planning.* 2nd ed. New York: John Wiley & Sons, 1985.

Vollmann, T. E.; W. L. Berry; and D. C. Whybark. *Manufacturing Planning and Control Systems.* 2nd ed. Homewood, Ill.: Richard D. Irwin, 1988.

Wight, Oliver W. *Production and Inventory Management in the Computer Age.* Boston: Cahners Publishing, 1974.

Chapter 14

Inventory Systems for Independent Demand

EPIGRAPH

When the bottle gets down to four, that's the time to buy some more.

Alka-Seltzer jingle from the 1950s.

CHAPTER OUTLINE

KEY TERMS

Raw Materials, Finished Goods, Work-in-Process Inventory

Independent and Dependent Demand

Fixed-Order Quantity Model

Fixed-Time Period Model

Service Level

Safety Stock

Quantity-Discount Model

ABC Analysis

Inventory Accuracy

In the past, inventory was perceived as an asset to an organization inasmuch as it appeared as an asset in its financial reports. This view is no longer the accepted norm. With product life cycles becoming increasingly shorter, product obsolescence also becomes more likely. In addition, we now recognize that inventories, particularly work-in-process inventories, tend to conceal problems. Maintaining inventories can also be very expensive. The average annual cost of maintaining inventories across all manufacturing firms is estimated to be 30 to 35 percent of its value, and could even be higher. For these and other reasons, inventory is now seen to be a liability, something to be eliminated to the greatest extent possible.

As a result, probably no topic in operations today is more often discussed or perceived to be more important than inventory. The name of the game is to reduce inventory quantities on hand at all levels: in raw materials and purchased parts through direct delivery by the vendor (often directly to the production line); in work in progress by techniques such as just-in-time production or scheduling with small batch sizes; and finally, in finished goods through a better matching of output to market requirements, and shipments to those markets as soon as possible. There is a growing effort to reduce all inventory inspired by new measurements and performance evaluation based not on the percentage of resource utilization, but rather on inventory turns and product quality.

There are also changing views concerning the teaching of classical inventory models. On one side, some claim that economic order quantity (EOQ) models are invalid in actual application; others defend their use. While one must be careful when using them, there do exist situations where EOQ models can be successfully used. More important, from a learning viewpoint, these models provide a basic framework for understanding the difficult issues involved in inventory management. Just-in-time manufacturing (JIT), for example, is based on the classical production-consumption model.

In this chapter, we present fixed-order and fixed-time period models, including those with protective inventory levels to ensure specific service levels. Also included are special purpose models, such as the quantity discount model, as well as the ABC technique for classifying items in inventory. In addition, we discuss the questions of inventory accuracy and show simple applications of the models in the real-world environment.

14.1 DEFINITION OF INVENTORY

Inventory is defined as the stock of any item or resource used in an organization. An *inventory system* is the set of policies and controls that monitors levels of inventory and determines (1) what levels should be maintained, (2) when stock should be replenished, and (3) how large orders should be.

In its complete scope, inventory can include inputs such as human, financial, energy, equipment, and physical items such as **raw materials;** outputs such as parts, components, and **finished goods;** and interim stages of the process, such as partially finished goods or **work-in-process.** The choice of which items to include in inventory depends on the organization. A manufacturing operation can have an inventory of personnel, machines, and working capital, as well as raw materials and finished goods. An airline can have an inventory of seats; a modern drugstore, an inventory of medicines, batteries, and toys; and an engineering firm, an inventory of engineering talent.

By convention, manufacturing inventory generally refers to materials entities that contribute to or become part of a firm's product output. In services, inventory generally refers to the tangible goods to be sold and the supplies necessary to administer the service.

The basic purpose of inventory analysis in manufacturing and stockkeeping services is to specify (1) when items should be ordered and (2) how large the order should be. Recent trends in industry have modified the simple questions of "when" and "how many." Many firms are tending to enter into longer-term relationships with vendors to supply their needs for perhaps the entire year. This changes the "when" and "how many to order" to "when" and "how many to deliver."

14.2 PURPOSES OF INVENTORY

Organizations maintain inventories for several reasons. These include:

1. *To protect against uncertainty.* For purposes of inventory management, we examine uncertainty in three areas. First, there is uncertainty with respect to raw materials, which necessitates raw material inventory. Here, uncertainty pertains both to the lead time that can vary due to unexpected delays and to the amount of raw material received.

Uncertainty also occurs in the transformation process. Here work-in-process (WIP) inventories absorb the variability that exists between the stages of the process, thereby providing independence between operations and improved efficiency.

Finally, uncertainty exists with respect to the demand for a firm's finished products. If the demand for a product were to be known precisely, then it could be possible to produce products so that demand would be exactly met. However, more frequently demand is not known completely, and a safety stock of finished goods inventory is maintained to absorb these variations.

2. *To support a strategic plan.* As we learned in our discussion on aggregate planning, when a firm adopts a level strategy an inventory of finished goods is required to buffer the cyclic demand for product from the level output generated by the transformation process. Under these circumstances, when demand exceeds production, the difference is withdrawn from inventory; when demand is less than production, the difference is placed back into inventory.

3. *To take advantage of economies of scale.* Each time we place an order or do a setup to perform an operation, we incur a fixed cost, regardless of the quantity involved. Thus, the larger the quantity ordered or produced, the lower the average total cost per unit. However, as we shall shortly see, there are trade-offs to be considered in determining the proper lot size.

In addition, companies often offer discounts for larger-quantity orders, as an incentive to customers to buy more than they normally would. This results in accumulations of items that otherwise would not exist. Firms offer quantity discounts for several reasons, including to reduce excessive stockpiles and to generate positive cash flow. In addition, there are economies of scale with respect to transportation costs, especially when products are shipped in either full trailer loads or full car loads.

14.3 INVENTORY COSTS

In making any decision with respect to inventories, the following costs should be taken into consideration:

1. *Holding or carrying costs.* This broad category is usually subdivided into three segments: storage costs, capital costs, and obsolescence/shrinkage costs. Storage costs include the cost of the storage facility in the form of rent or depreciation, insurance, taxes, utilities, security, and facility personnel.

Capital costs can vary, depending on the firm's financial situation. For example, if the firm has an excess of cash, then the capital cost is the interest lost by putting the money into inventory instead of short-term notes. If the firm has an alternative project to invest in, then the capital cost is the opportunity cost of the anticipated return of that project. If the firm has to borrow funds to maintain an inventory, then the capital cost is the interest paid on those funds.

Obsolescence costs recognize that products tend to depreciate in value over time. This is especially true in high-technology industries where newer and better (and often cheaper) products are constantly being introduced. In this category, we also include spoilage costs associated with products that have a short shelf life, like perishable food products and some types of prescription drugs. Shrinkage costs include pilferage and breakage.

2. *Setup or ordering costs.* These are fixed costs usually associated with the production of a lot internally or the placing of an order externally with a vendor. In other words, these costs are independent of the amount of units that are requested. Setup costs are related to the amount of time needed to adjust the equipment in order to perform a specific task. This would include the alignment of special tooling like jigs and fixtures. Order costs pertain to the costs involved in placing an order with a vendor. These may include telephone charges, a delivery fee, expediting costs, and the time required to process a purchase order.

3. *Shortage (or stockout) costs.* When the stock of an item is depleted, and a customer orders that product, then a stockout cost is incurred. This is usually the sum of the lost profit and any "ill-will" generated. There is a trade-off between carrying stock to satisfy demand and the costs resulting from stockout. This balance is sometimes difficult to obtain, since it may not be possible to estimate accurately lost profits, the effects of lost customers, or late penalties.

Establishing the correct quantity to order from vendors or the size of lots submitted to the firm's production facilities involves a search for the minimum total cost resulting from the combined effects of four individual costs: holding costs, setup or ordering costs, and shortage costs.

4. *Purchase costs.* These are the actual costs of the material purchased. Purchase costs remain constant unless quantity discounts (discussed later in this chapter) are offered.

14.4 INDEPENDENT VERSUS DEPENDENT DEMAND

Briefly, the distinction between **independent and dependent demand** is this: In independent demand, the demands for various items are unrelated to each other and therefore needed quantities of each must be determined separately or independently. In dependent demand, the need for any one item is a direct result of the need for some other item, usually a higher-level item of which it is part.

In concept, dependent demand is a relatively straightforward computational problem. Needed quantities of a dependent-demand item are simply computed, based on the number needed in each higher-level item where it is used. For example, if an automobile company plans on producing 500 automobiles per day, then obviously it will need 2,000 wheels and tires (plus spares). The number of wheels and tires needed is *dependent* on the production level for automobiles and not derived separately. The demand for automobiles, on the other hand, is *independent*—it comes from many sources external to the automobile firm and is not a part of other products and so is unrelated to the demand for other products.

To determine the quantities of independent items that must be produced, firms usually turn to their sales and market research departments. They use a variety of techniques, including customer surveys, forecasting techniques, and economic and sociological trends. Because independent demand is uncertain, extra units must be carried in inventory. This chapter presents models to determine how many extra units should be carried to provide a specified *service level* (percentage of independent demand) that the firm would like to satisfy.

14.5 INVENTORY SYSTEMS

An inventory system provides the organizational structure and the operating policies for maintaining and controlling goods to be stocked. The system is responsible for ordering and receipt of goods: timing the order placement and keeping track of what has been ordered, how much, and from whom. The system must also follow up to provide answers to such questions as: Has the vendor received the order? Has it been shipped? Are the dates correct? Are the procedures established for reordering or returning undesirable merchandise?

Classifying Models by Fixed-Order Quantity or Fixed-Time Period

There are two general types of inventory systems: **fixed-order quantity models** (also called the Q-system) and **fixed-time period models** (also referred to as the P-system).

The basic distinction between the two is that fixed-order quantity models are "event triggered" and fixed-time period models are "time triggered." That is, a fixed-order quantity model initiates an order when the event of reaching a specified reorder level occurs. This event may take place at any time, depending on the demand for the items being considered. In contrast, the fixed-time period model is limited to placing orders at the end of a predetermined time period; only the passage of time triggers the model.

To use the fixed-order quantity model, which places an order when the remaining inventory drops to a predetermined order point, R, the inventory remaining must be continually monitored. Thus, the fixed-order quantity model is a *perpetual* inventory system, which requires that every time a withdrawal from or an addition to inventory is made, records must be updated to ensure that the reorder point has or has not been reached. For the fixed-time period model, inventory is counted only at the end of the review period. No counting takes place in the interim (although some firms have created variations of systems that combine features of both). Some additional differences that tend to influence the choice of systems are:

- The fixed-time period model has a larger average inventory since it must also protect against stockout during the review period, T; the fixed-quantity model has no review period.
- The fixed-time period model is preferred when several different items are purchased from the same vendor and there is potential economies of scale savings from ordering all the items at the same time.
- The fixed-order quantity model favors more expensive items, because average inventory is lower.
- The fixed-order quantity model is more appropriate for important items such as critical repair parts, because there is closer monitoring and therefore quicker response to a potential stockout.
- The fixed-order quantity model requires more time and resources to maintain, because every addition or withdrawal is recorded.

Exhibit 14.1 depicts what occurs when each of the two models is put into use and becomes an operating system. As we can see, the fixed-order quantity system focuses on order quantities and reorder points. Procedurally, each time a unit is taken out of stock, the withdrawal is recorded and the amount remaining in inventory is immediately compared to the reorder point. If it has dropped to this point or below, an order for Q items is placed. If it has not, the system remains in an idle state until the next withdrawal.

In the fixed-time period system, a decision to place an order is made after the stock has been counted or reviewed. Whether an order is actually placed depends on the inventory status at that time.

14.6 BASIC MODEL TYPES

Basic Fixed-Order Quantity Model

The simplest models in this category occur when all aspects of the situation are known with certainty. If the annual demand for a product is 1,000 units, it is precisely 1,000—not 1,000 plus or minus 10 percent. The same is true for setup costs and holding costs.

EXHIBIT 14.1 Comparison of Fixed-Order Quantity and Fixed-Time Period Reordering Inventory Systems

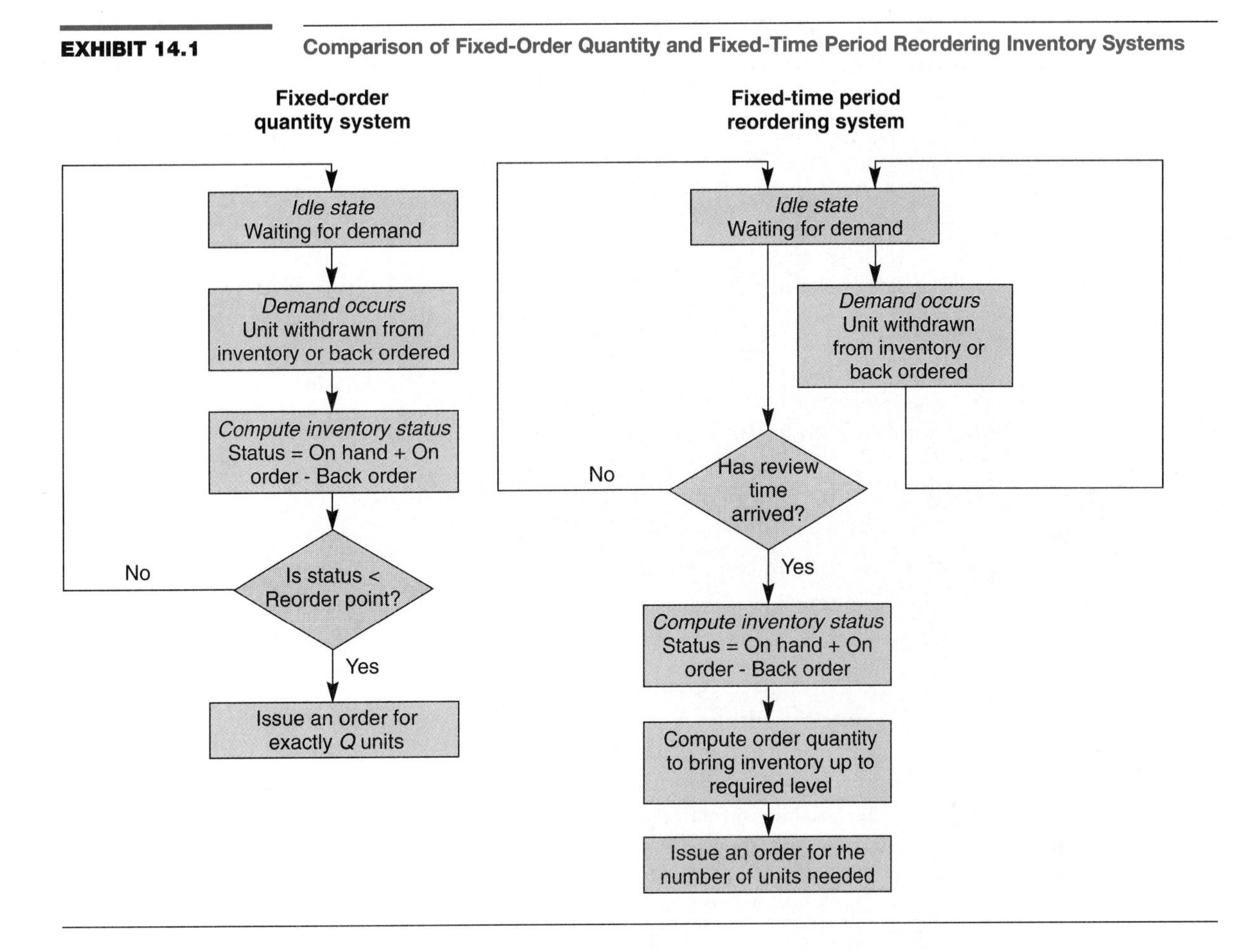

Although the assumption of complete certainty is rarely valid, it provides a good starting point for our coverage of inventory models.

Fixed-order quantity models attempt to determine the specific point, *R*, at which an order will be placed and the size of that order, *Q*. The order point, *R*, is always a specified number of units actually in inventory. The solution to a fixed-order quantity model may stipulate something like this: When the number of units of inventory on hand drops to 36, place an order for 57 more units.

Exhibit 14.2 and the discussion about deriving the optimal order quantity are based on the following assumptions of the model:

- Demand for the product is known, constant, and uniform throughout the period.
- Lead time (time from ordering to receipt) is constant.
- Price per unit of product is constant (no quantity discounts).

EXHIBIT 14.2

Basic Fixed-order Quantity Model

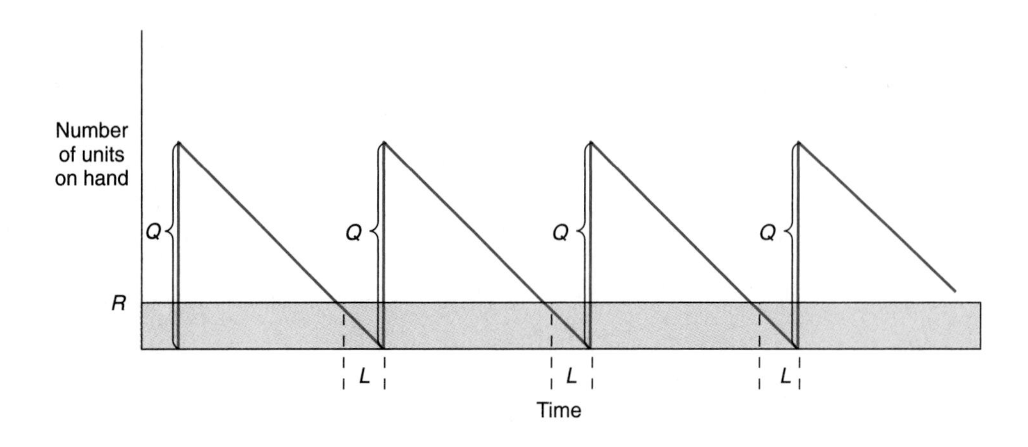

- Ordering or setup costs are constant.
- All demands for the product will be satisfied (no back orders are allowed).
- There is no interaction with other products.

The "sawtooth effect" relating Q and R in Exhibit 14.2 shows that when inventory drops to point R, a reorder is placed. This order is received at the end of time period L, which, as stated above, remains constant.

In constructing any inventory model, the first step is to develop a functional relationship between the variables of interest and the measure of effectiveness. In this case, since we are concerned with cost, the following equation would pertain:

Total annual cost	=	Annual purchase cost	+	Annual ordering cost	+	Annual holding cost

or

$$TC = DC + \frac{D}{Q}S + \frac{Q}{2}H \tag{1}$$

where

TC = Total annual cost
D = Demand (annual)
C = Cost per unit
Q = Quantity to be ordered (the optimum amount is termed the *economic order quantity*—EOQ)
S = Setup cost or cost of placing an order
R = Reorder point

EXHIBIT 14.3 **Annual Product Costs, Based on Size of the Order**

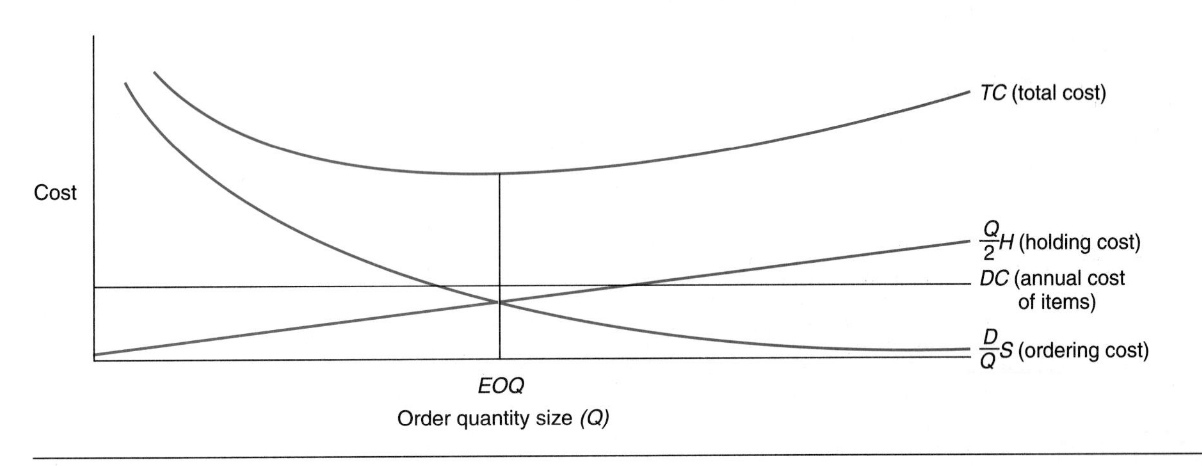

L = Lead time

H = Annual holding and storage cost per unit of average inventory. (Often, holding cost is defined as an annual percentage of the cost of the item. In these instances, $H = iC$ where i is the annual percentage carrying cost.)

On the right side of the equation, DC is the annual purchase cost for the units, $(D/Q)S$ is the annual ordering cost (the actual number of orders placed, D/Q, times the cost of each order, S), and $(Q/2)H$ is the annual holding cost (the average inventory, $Q/2$, times the cost per unit for holding and storage, H). These cost relationships are shown graphically in Exhibit 14.3.

The second step in model development is to find that order quantity, Q, for which total cost is a minimum. In Exhibit 14.3, the total cost is minimum at the point where the slope of the curve is zero. Using calculus, the appropriate procedure involves taking the derivative of total cost with respect to Q and setting this equal to zero. For the basic model considered here, the calculations to obtain the economic order quantity (EOQ) would be as follows:

$$TC = DC + \frac{D}{Q}S + \frac{Q}{2}H$$

$$\frac{dTC}{dQ} = 0 + \left(\frac{-DS}{Q^2}\right) + \frac{H}{2} = 0$$

Solving for Q gives us the economic order quantity, or EOQ,

$$\text{EOQ} = \sqrt{\frac{2DS}{H}} \qquad (2)$$

Because this simple model assumes constant demand and lead time, no safety stock is necessary, and the reorder point, R, is simply

$$R = \bar{d}\,L \tag{3}$$

where

$\bar{d}$ = Average demand per time period [constant]
L = Number of time periods between placing an order and its delivery [constant]

Example

Find the economic order quantity and the reorder point, given the following data:

Annual demand (D) = 1,000 units
Ordering cost (S) = \$5 per order
Holding cost (H) = \$1.25 per unit per year
Cost per unit (C) = \$12.50
Lead time (L) = 5 days
Average daily demand ($\bar{d}$) = 1,000/365

What quantity should be ordered, and when?

Solution

The optimal order quantity is

$$\text{EOQ} = \sqrt{\frac{2DS}{H}} = \sqrt{\frac{2(1{,}000)5}{1.25}} = \sqrt{8{,}000} = 89.4 \text{ units}$$

The reorder point is

$$R = \bar{d}L = \frac{1{,}000}{365}(5) = 13.7 \text{ units}$$

Rounding to the nearest unit, the inventory policy is as follows: When the number of units in inventory drops to 14, place an order for 89 more.

The total annual cost will be

$$TC = DC + \frac{D}{Q}S + \frac{Q}{2}H$$

$$= 1{,}000(12.50) + \frac{1{,}000}{89}(5) + \frac{89}{2}(1.25)$$

$$= \$12{,}611.81$$

Note that in this example, the annual purchase cost of the units was not required to determine the order quantity and the reorder point. Also note that in Exhibit 14.3, the total cost curve is relatively flat around the EOQ, indicating that minor increases in total cost will occur on either side of the EOQ. Thus, in the above Example, we might in actuality order 85 units once a month for the sake of simplicity and convenience without fear of incurring excessive costs.

EXHIBIT 14.4

Fixed-Order Quantity Model with Usage during Production Time

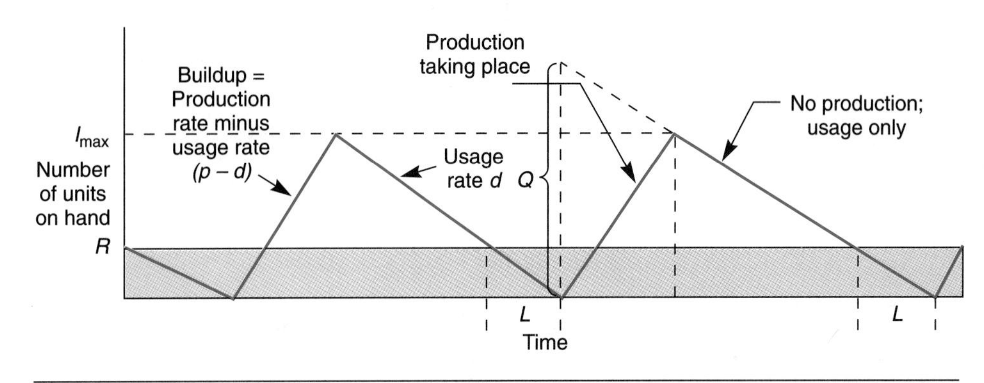

Fixed-Order Quantity Model with Usage

The example presented above assumed that the quantity ordered would be received in one lot, but frequently this is not the case. In many situations, in fact, production of an inventory item and usage of that item take place simultaneously. This is particularly true where one part of a production system acts as a supplier to another part. For example, while aluminum extrusions are being made to fill an order for aluminum windows, the extrusions are cut and assembled before the entire extrusion order is completed. Also, companies are beginning to enter into longer-term arrangements with vendors. Under such contracts, a single order may cover product or material needs over a six-month or one-year period, with the vendor making deliveries weekly or sometimes even more frequently. This model differs from our previous discussion of process and transfer batch sizes since this model has a continual usage rate d. If we let d denote a constant demand rate for some item going into production and p the production rate of that process that uses the item, we may develop the following total cost equation:[1]

$$TC = DC + (D/Q)S + (Q/2)H$$

However, with this model, as seen in Exhibit 14.4, Q is not the maximum inventory on hand, because we are consuming the product as it is being delivered over time. Thus, the above equation is rewritten as follows:

$$TC = DC + (D/Q)S + (I_{max}/2)H \tag{4}$$

and

$$I_{max} = (p - d)(Q/p) \tag{5}$$

where $(p - d)$ is the amount of inventory that accumulates each time period, and (Q/p) is the number of time periods required to fill the order.

[1] Obviously, the production rate must exceed the rate of usage; otherwise Q would be infinite, resulting in continual production.

$$TC = DC + \frac{D}{Q}S + \frac{(p - d)QH}{2p}$$

Again differentiating with respect to Q and setting the equation equal to zero, we obtain

$$EOQ = \sqrt{\frac{2DS}{H} \cdot \frac{p}{(p - d)}} \qquad (6)$$

This model is shown in Exhibit 14.4. We can see that the number of units on hand is always less than the order quantity, Q. Note in Equation 6, as p becomes very large, the right-hand term $(p/(p - d)$ approaches one and we have our original EOQ formula.

Example

Product X is a standard item in a firm's inventory. Final assembly of the product is performed on an assembly line that is in operation every day. One of the components of product X (call it component X_1) is produced in another department. This department, when it produces X_1, does so at the rate of 100 units per day. The assembly line uses component X_1 at the rate of 40 units per day.

Given the following data, what is the optimal lot size for production of component X_1?

Daily usage rate (d) = 40 units
Annual demand (D) = 10,000 (40 units × 250 working days)
Daily production (p) = 100 units
Cost for production setup (S) = \$50
Annual holding cost (H) = \$0.50 per unit
Cost of component X_1 (C) = \$7 each
Lead time (L) = 7 days

Solution

The optimal order quantity and the reorder point are calculated as follows:

$$EOQ = \sqrt{\frac{2DS}{H} \cdot \frac{p}{p - d}} = \sqrt{\frac{2(10{,}000)50}{0.50} \cdot \frac{100}{100 - 40}} = 1{,}826 \text{ units}$$

$$R = dL = 40(7) = 280 \text{ units}$$

This states that an order for 1,826 units of component X_1 should be placed when the stock drops to 280 units.

At 100 units per day, this run would take 18.26 days to complete, and provide a 45.65-day supply for the assembly line (1,826/40). Theoretically, the department would be occupied with other work for the 27.39 days when component X_1 is not being produced.

Fixed-Time Period Model

In a fixed-time period system, inventory is counted at fixed intervals, such as every week or every month. As stated previously, counting inventory and placing orders on a periodic basis is desirable in situations such as when vendors make routine visits to customers and

EXHIBIT 14.5

Fixed-Time Period Inventory Model

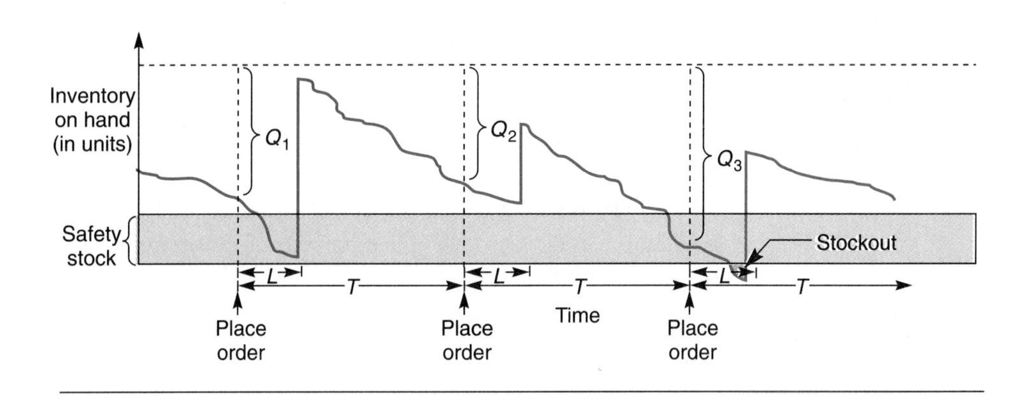

take orders for their complete line of products, or when buyers want to combine orders to save on transportation costs. Other firms operate on a fixed-time period to facilitate planning their inventory count; for example, Distributor X calls every two weeks and employees know that all of Distributor X's products must be counted.

The time interval can be chosen as is convenient, or if only one item is involved it can be estimated by using the EOQ formula. Once the EOQ for the item is calculated, we can determine how many times a year we should place the order, from which we can then determine the period or interval between orders. For example, if the annual demand is 1,200 units and the EOQ is 100 units, then we know that we will place 12 orders throughout the year, and that there is a one-month interval between orders.

With a fixed-time period model, there is usually a ceiling or "par" inventory that is determined for each item. As seen in Exhibit 14.5, the difference between the par value and the quantity on hand when the count is taken is the amount that is ordered, which will vary from period to period, depending on the actual usage (e.g., Q_1, Q_2, and Q_3 in Exhibit 14.5). Thus, in this model the time interval between orders remains fixed, but the quantity ordered varies, as compared to the fixed-order quantity model where the order quantity remains fixed, but the time interval varies.

Establishing Safety Stock Using Service Levels

The models presented thus far assume that demand is constant and known. In the majority of cases, however, demand is not constant but varies from period to period (e.g., week to week, day to day). A safety stock must therefore be maintained to provide some level of protection against stockouts. The general literature on the subject of safety stocks contains two approaches relating to the demand for the inventory that is to be protected: First, the *probability* that demand will exceed some specified amount. For example, an objective may be something like: "Set the safety stock level so that there will only be a 5 percent chance that demand will exceed 300 units."

The second approach deals with the *expected number* of units that will be out of stock.

For example, an objective might be to set the inventory level so that we will be able to meet 95 percent of the demands for that unit (or out of stock 5 percent of the time). Note that the first approach deals with the *probability* of exceeding a value and the second approach is concerned with *how many* units were short.

In this section, we focus primarily on the second question, since it is far more interesting and the more realistic one to be answered.

Service level refers to the number of units that can be supplied from stock currently on hand. For example, if the annual demand for an item is 1,000 units, a 95 percent service level means that 950 can be supplied immediately from stock and 50 units are short. (This concept assumes that orders are small and randomly distributed—one or several at a time; this model would not apply, for example, where the entire annual demand might be sold to a dozen customers.)

Safety stock can be defined as inventory carried to assure that the desired service level is met.

The discussion in this section on service levels is based on a statistical concept known as Expected z, or $E(z)$, which is the expected number of units short during each lead time. This entire discussion assumes, as previously stated, that demands (withdrawals from the inventory stock) are in very small quantities—in comparison to the total stock—and are normally distributed.

To compute the service level, we need to know *how many* units are short. For example, assume that the average weekly demand for an item is 100 units with a standard deviation of 10 units. If we stock 110 units, how many will we expect to be short?? To do this we need to summarize the probability that 111 is demanded (1 short), the probability that 112 is demanded (2 short), plus the probability that 113 is demanded (3 short), and so on. This summary would give us the number of units we would expect to be short by stocking 110 units.

While the concept is simple, the equations are impractical to solve by hand. Fortunately, Robert Brown has provided tables of expected values that we have included as Exhibit 14.6.[2]

We'll carry the explanations further within the context of our two basic model types: the fixed-order quantity and fixed-time period. We'll also discuss the important questions to be answered, such as: How do we control our inventory to provide a customer service level of 95 percent?

Fixed-Order Quantity Model with Specified Service Level

A fixed-order quantity system perpetually monitors the inventory level and places a new order when it reaches some level, R. The danger of stockout in this model occurs only during the lead time, between the time an order is placed and the time it is received. As shown in Exhibit 14.7, an order is placed when the inventory level drops to the reorder point, R. During this lead time (L), a range of demands is possible. This range is determined either from an analysis of past demand data or from an estimate (if past data are not available).

[2]Robert G. Brown, *Decision Rules for Inventory Management* (New York: Holt, Rinehart & Winston, 1967).

EXHIBIT 14.6

Expected Number Out of Stock versus the Standard Deviation (This table is normalized to a mean of zero and a standard deviation of 1)

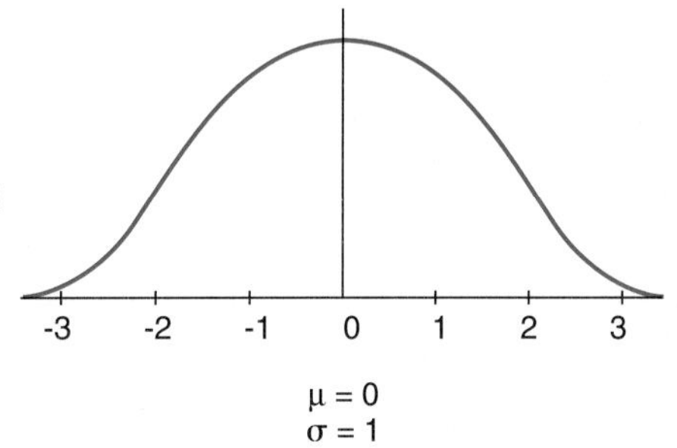

E(z)	*z*	*E(z)*	*z*
4.500	−4.50	0.399	0.00
4.400	−4.40	0.351	0.10
4.300	−4.30	0.307	0.20
4.200	−4.20	0.267	0.30
4.100	−4.10	0.230	0.40
4.000	−4.00	0.198	0.50
3.900	−3.90	0.169	0.60
3.800	−3.80	0.143	0.70
3.700	−3.70	0.120	0.80
3.600	−3.60	0.100	0.90
3.500	−3.50	0.083	1.00
3.400	−3.40	0.069	1.10
3.300	−3.30	0.056	1.20
3.200	−3.20	0.046	1.30
3.100	−3.10	0.037	1.40
3.000	−3.00	0.029	1.50
2.901	−2.90	0.023	1.60
2.801	−2.80	0.018	1.70
2.701	−2.70	0.014	1.80
2.601	−2.60	0.011	1.90
2.502	−2.50	0.008	2.00
2.403	−2.40	0.006	2.10
2.303	−2.30	0.005	2.20
2.205	−2.20	0.004	2.30
2.106	−2.10	0.003	2.40
2.008	−2.00	0.002	2.50
1.911	−1.90	0.001	2.60
1.814	−1.80	0.001	2.70
1.718	−1.70	0.001	2.80
1.623	−1.60	0.001	2.90
1.529	−1.50	0.000	3.00
1.437	−1.40	0.000	3.10
1.346	−1.30	0.000	3.20
1.256	−1.20	0.000	3.30
1.169	−1.10	0.000	3.40
1.083	−1.00	0.000	3.50
1.000	−0.90	0.000	3.60
0.920	−0.80	0.000	3.70
0.843	−0.70	0.000	3.80
0.769	−0.60	0.000	3.90
0.698	−0.50	0.000	4.00
0.630	−0.40	0.000	4.10
0.567	−0.30	0.000	4.20
0.507	−0.20	0.000	4.30
0.451	−0.10	0.000	4.40
0.399	0.00	0.000	4.50

z = Number of standard deviations of safety stock
E(z) = Expected number of units short

Source: Revised from Robert G. Brown, *Decision Rules for Inventory Management* (New York: Holt, Rinehart & Winston, 1967), pp. 95–103.

EXHIBIT 14.7

Fixed-Order Quantity Model with Uncertainty

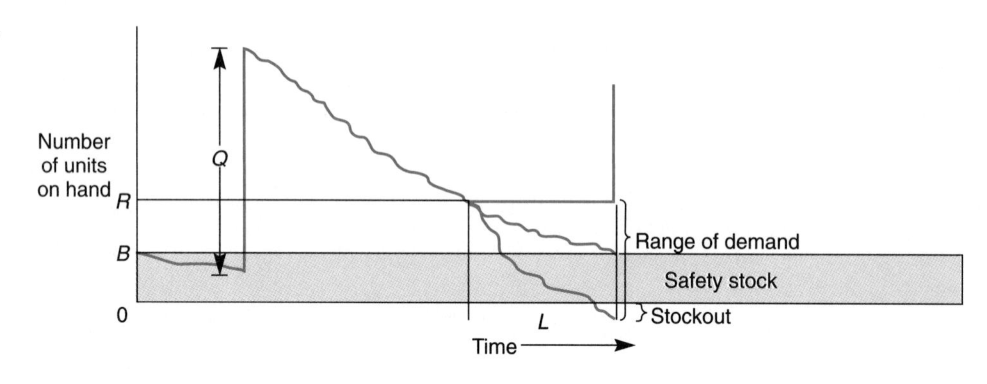

The amount of safety stock depends on the service level desired, as previously discussed. The quantity to be ordered, Q, is calculated in the usual way considering the demand, shortage cost, ordering cost, holding cost, and so forth. A fixed-order quantity model can be used to compute Q such as the simple EOQ model previously discussed. The reorder point is then set to cover the expected demand during the lead time plus a safety stock determined by the desired service level. Thus, *the key difference between a fixed-order quantity model under certainty in demand and under uncertainty in demand is not in computing the order quantity (both will be the same), but in computing the reorder point, which includes safety stock.*

The reorder point is

$$R = \bar{d}L + z\sigma_L \qquad (7)$$

where

R = Reorder point in units

$\bar{d}$ = Average demand per time period

L = Lead time (number of time periods between placing an order and receiving the items)

z = Number of standard deviations for a specified service level

σ_L = Standard deviation of usage during lead time.

The term $z\sigma_L$ is the amount of safety stock. Note that if the safety stock is positive, the effect is to place another order sooner. That is, R without safety stock is simply the average demand during the lead time. If lead time usage was expected to be 20, for example, and the safety stock was computed to be 5 units, then the order would be placed sooner, when 25 units remained. In other words, the greater the safety stock, the sooner the order is placed.

Computing $\bar{d}$, σ_L, and z. Demand during the lead time to receive a replenishment order is an estimate or forecast of what is expected. It may be a single number (for example if the lead time is a month, the demand may be taken as the previous year's demand divided by 12), or it may be a summation of expected demands over the lead time (such as the sum of daily demands over a 30-day lead time). For the daily demand situation, $\bar{d}$ can be a forecasted demand using any of the models in Chapter 7 on forecasting. For example, if a 30-day period was used to calculate $\bar{d}$, then

$$\bar{d} = \frac{\sum_{i=1}^{30} d_i}{30} \tag{8}$$

The error in using $\bar{d}$ to forecast the future is measured by the standard deviation of errors, which is

$$\sigma_d = \sqrt{\frac{\sum_{i=1}^{30} (d_i - \bar{d})^2}{30}} \tag{9}$$

Since σ_d refers to one day, if lead time extends over several (u) days we can use the statistical premise that the standard deviation of a series of independent occurrences is equal to the square root of the sum of the variances. Thus:

$$\sigma_L = \sqrt{\sigma_{d_1}^2 + \sigma_{d_2}^2 + \sigma_{d_3}^2 + \cdots + \sigma_{d_L}^2} \tag{10}$$

If, as is usually the case, the variance in each time period remains the same, then Equation (10) reduces to:

$$\sigma_L = \sigma_d \sqrt{L} \tag{11}$$

For example, suppose we computed the standard deviation of demand to be 10 units per day. If our lead time to get an order is five days, the standard deviation for the five-day period, since each day can be considered independent, would be

$$\sigma_L = 10\sqrt{5} = 10\ (2.236) = 22.36$$

Next we need to compute z. We do this by computing $E(z)$, the number of units short that meets our desired service level, and then looking this up in Exhibit 14.6 for the appropriate z.

Suppose we wanted a service level of P (for example, P might be 95 percent). In the course of a year we would be short $(1 - P)\ D$ units, or $0.05D$, where D is the annual demand. If we ordered Q units each time, we would be placing D/Q orders per year. Exhibit 14.6 is based on $\sigma_L = 1$. Therefore, any $E(z)$ that we read from the table needs to be multiplied by σ_L if it is other than 1. The number of units short per order, therefore, is $E(z)\sigma_L$. For the year, the number of units short is $E(z)\sigma_L D/Q$.

Stated again, we have,

$$\underset{\text{short}}{\text{Percentage}} \times \underset{\text{demand}}{\text{Annual}} = \underset{\text{per order}}{\text{Number short}} \times \underset{\text{orders per year}}{\text{Number of}}$$

$$(1 - P) \times D = E(z)\sigma_L \times \frac{D}{Q}$$

which simplifies to

$$E(z) = \frac{(1 - P)Q}{\sigma_L} \tag{12}$$

where

P = Service level desired (such as satisfying 95 percent of demand from items in stock)
$(1 - P)$ = Unsatisfied demand
D = Annual demand
σ_L = Standard deviation of demand during lead time
Q = Economic order quantity calculated in the usual way (such as $Q = \sqrt{2DS/H}$)
$E(z)$ = Expected number of units short from a normalized table where the mean = 0 and σ = 1

We now compare two examples. The difference between them is that in the first, the variation in demand is stated in terms of standard deviation over the entire lead time, and in the second, it is stated in terms of standard deviation per day (or other unit of time).

Example

Consider an economic order quantity case where annual demand D = 1,000 units, economic order quantity Q = 200 units, the desired service level P = .95, the standard deviation of demand during lead time σ_L = 50 units, and lead time L = 15 days. Determine the reorder point.

Solution

In our example, $\bar{d}$ = 4 (1,000 over a 250-workday year), and lead time is 15 days. Therefore, from the equation

$$\begin{aligned} R &= \bar{d}L + z\sigma_L \\ &= 4(15) + z(50) \end{aligned}$$

To find z, we use the equation for $E(z)$ and look this value up in the table. Our problem data gave us Q = 200, service level P = .95, and standard deviation of demand during lead time = 50. Therefore,

$$E(z) = \frac{(1 - P)Q}{\sigma_L} = \frac{(1 - .95)200}{50} = .2$$

From Exhibit 14.6, and through interpolation at $E(z)$ = .2, we find z = 0.49. Completing the solution for R, we find

$$R = 4(15) + z(50) = 60 + .49(50) = 84.5 \text{ units}$$

This says that when the stock on hand gets down to 85 units, order 200 more.

Just to satisfy any skepticism, we can calculate the number served per year to see if it really is 95 percent. $E(z)$ is the expected number short on each order based on a standard deviation of 1. The number short on each order for our problem is $E(z)\sigma_L = .2(50) = 10$. Since there are five orders per year (1,000/200), this results in 50 units short. This verifies our achievement of a 95 percent service level, since 950 out of 1,000 demand were filled from stock.

Example

The daily demand for a certain product is normally distributed with a mean of 60 and a standard deviation of 7. The source of supply is reliable and maintains a constant lead time of six days. The cost of placing the order is $10 and annual holding costs are $0.50 per unit. There are no stockout costs, and unfilled orders are filled as soon as the order arrives. Assume sales occur over the entire year. Find the order quantity and reorder point to satisfy 95 percent of the customers.

Solution

In this problem we need to calculate the order quantity Q, as well as the reorder point R.

$$\bar{d} = 60$$
$$\sigma_d = 7$$
$$D = 60(365)$$
$$S = \$10$$
$$H = \$0.50$$
$$L = 6$$

The optimal order quantity is

$$\text{EOQ} = \sqrt{\frac{2DS}{H}} = \sqrt{\frac{2(60)365(10)}{0.50}} = \sqrt{876{,}000} = 936 \text{ units}$$

To compute the reorder point, we need to calculate the amount of product used during the lead time and add this to the safety stock.

The standard deviation of demand during the lead time of six days is calculated from the variance of the individual days. Since each day's demand is independent[3]

$$\sigma_L = \sigma_d\sqrt{L} = 7\sqrt{6} = 17.2$$

Next we need to know how many standard deviations are needed for a specified service level. As previously defined,

$$E(z) = \frac{Q(1 - P)}{\sigma_L}$$

[3] As previously discussed, the standard deviation of a sum of independent variables is equal to the square root of the sum of the variances.

Therefore

$$E(z) = \frac{936(1 - .95)}{17.2} = 2.721$$

From Exhibit 14.6, interpolating at $E(z) = 2.721$, $z = -2.72$. The reorder point is

$$\begin{aligned} R &= \bar{d}L + z\sigma_L \\ &= 60(6) + -2.72(17.2) \\ &= 313.2 \text{ units} \end{aligned}$$

To summarize the policy derived in this example, an order for 936 units is placed whenever the number of units remaining in inventory drops to 313.

Note that in this case the safety stock ($z\sigma_L$) turns out to be negative. This means that if we had ordered the average demand of 360 units during the lead time (60 × 6), we would have had a higher service level than we wanted. To get down to 95 percent service, we need to create more shortages by ordering less. While this may seem strange, nevertheless it's true. Our service is too good and we need to run out of stock more often!

We can verify our service level in this example by noting that we would place 23.4 orders per year [60(365)/936]. Each period would experience 46.8 units out of stock (2.72 × 17.2). Thus we would be out of stock 1,095 units per year (46.8 × 23.4). Service level, therefore, is 0.95 as we intended [(21,900 − 1,095)/21,900].

As shown in these two examples, this technique of determining safety stock levels is relatively simple and straightforward. It allows us to control inventory to meet our desired service levels.

Quantity-Discount Model

The **quantity-discount model** takes into consideration the fact that the purchase cost of an item can vary with the order size. This is a discrete or step change rather than a per-unit change. For example, a wheel for a toy car may cost $.20 each for 1 to 99 wheels, $.16 each for quantities between 100 and 999 wheels, and $.13 each for quantities over 1,000 wheels. In each instance, the quantity relates to the size of the order placed. To determine the optimal quantity to order with this model, we first calculate the EOQ for each unit cost. If the resulting EOQs are all feasible, that is, the EOQs fall within their respective quantity ranges, then we select the EOQ that is associated with the lowest unit cost. However, as is more often the case, some of the EOQ's may not be feasible (i.e., the quantity does not fall within the feasible unit cost range). In these situations, we have to calculate the total cost for each unit cost at the EOQ where it is feasible; where it is not feasible, we calculate the total cost at the minimum quantity where the respective unit cost is first applicable. These total costs are then compared and the quantity or EOQ associated with the lowest total cost is the order quantity that is selected.

Procedurally, the largest order quantity (lowest unit price) is solved first; if the resulting Q is valid, that is the answer. If not, the next largest order quantity (second lowest price) is derived. If that is feasible, the cost of this Q is compared to the cost of using the order quantity at the price break above, and the lowest cost determines the optimal Q.

Example

Consider the following case, where

D = 10,000 units (annual demand)
S = \$20 to place each order
i = 20 percent of cost (annual carrying costs, storage, interest, obsolescence, etc.)
C = Cost per unit:

Order Size (units)	Cost per Unit
0–499	C_1 = \$5.00
500–999	C_2 = 4.50
1,000 and over	C_3 = 3.90

What quantity should be ordered?

Solution

The appropriate equations from the basic fixed-quantity case are

$$TC = DC + \frac{D}{Q}S + \frac{Q}{2}iC$$

and

$$Q = \sqrt{\frac{2DS}{iC}}$$

Solving for the economic order size at each price, we obtain the following:

Range	Unit Cost	EOQ	Feasible
0–499	\$5.00	633	No
500–999	4.50	666	Yes
Over 1,000	3.90	716	No

These results are shown in Exhibit 14.8, which depicts the relationship between the total cost and the order quantity for each of the unit costs. Using the procedure described above, we now calculate the total cost for 666 units at \$4.50 per unit and 1,000 units at \$3.90 per unit. These calculations are shown in Exhibit 14.9. Comparing these two total costs, the optimal order quantity is 1,000 units.

One practical consideration in quantity-discount problems is that the cost reduction from volume purchases frequently makes it seemingly economical to order amounts larger than the EOQ. Thus, when applying the model we must be particularly careful to obtain a valid estimate of product obsolescence and warehousing costs.

EXHIBIT 14.8

Total Cost Curves for a Quantity-Discount Model

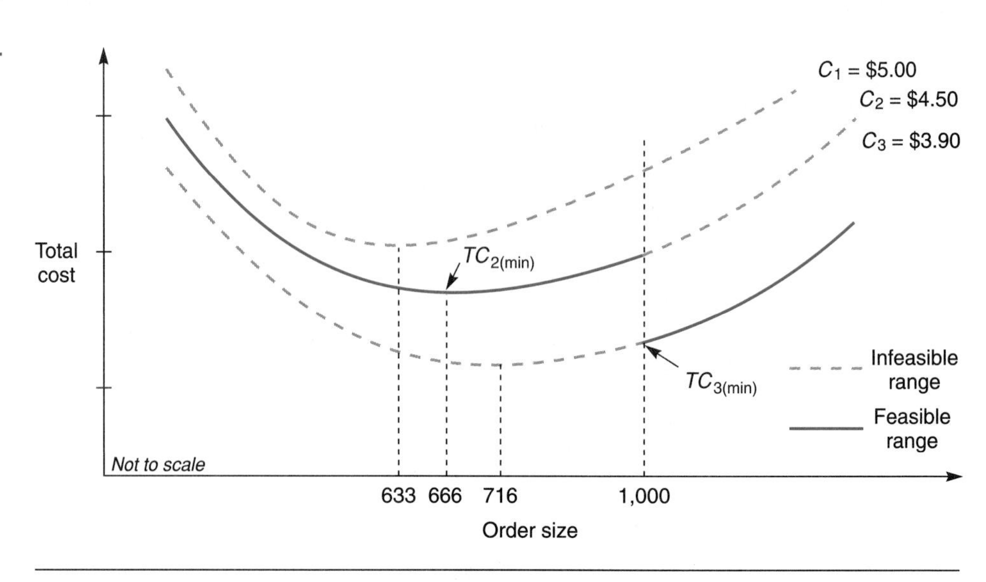

EXHIBIT 14.9

Total Cost Calculations in a Quantity-Discount Model

	Q = 633 where C = $5	Q = 666 where C = $4.50	Q = 716 where C = $3.90	Price Break 1,000
Holding cost $\left(\frac{Q}{2}iC\right)$		$\frac{666}{2}(0.20)4.50$ = $299.70		$\frac{1,000}{2}(0.20)3.90$ = $390
Ordering cost $\left(\frac{D}{Q}S\right)$	Not feasible	$\frac{10,000(20)}{666}$ = $300	Not feasible	$\frac{10,000(20)}{1,000}$ = $200
Holding and ordering cost		$600		$590
Purchase cost (DC)		10,000(4.50)		10,000(3.90)
Total cost		$TC_{2(min)}$ = $45,600		$TC_{3(min)}$ = $39,590

14.7 ECONOMIC ORDER QUANTITY MODELS IN RELATION TO THE REAL WORLD

Recently, criticizing classical inventory models seems fashionable to some members of industry and consulting groups. Proportionately, there is much less open criticism from academia. In a manufacturing environment, the major weaknesses associated with the classical EOQ models focus on the numbers. These numbers are the values of setup costs,

EXHIBIT 14.10

Effect of Reduced Setup Cost on Order Size and Total Cost

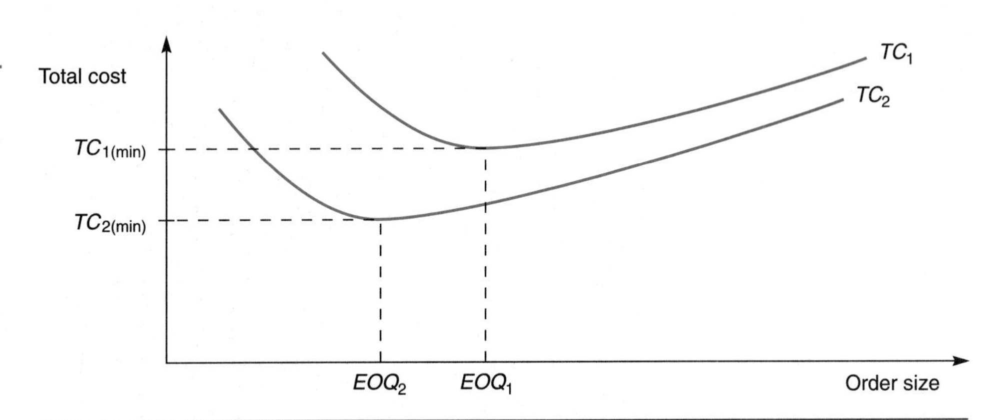

holding costs, and demands used in the equations. These costs are often very difficult to measure and, therefore, are error prone. Also, demand is rarely constant but instead is usually a fluctuating number.

Elliott Weiss states the problem nicely by explaining that many users of the equations focus on optimizing a set of numbers which often are taken as a given fact.[4] Rather, he states, we should be managing lot sizing and inventory control. The current moves toward reduced inventory costs and quantities, such as just-in-time systems, stress the importance in reducing lot sizes. The means to reducing lot sizes is to reduce setup time and cost. When smaller lots are run, holding cost is reduced. The point is to understand the logic and know where to apply it. The effect on order size resulting from reducing setup costs is shown in Exhibit 14.10. When the setup cost is reduced, the total cost curve shifts from TC_1 to TC_2. Correspondingly, the EOQ is reduced from EOQ_1 to EOQ_2 and the minimum total cost is reduced from $TC_{1_{\text{min}}}$ to $TC_{2_{\text{min}}}$.

14.8 ADDITIONAL ISSUES IN INVENTORY MANAGEMENT

Determining Realistic Costs

Most inventory models give optimal solutions so long as the conditions of the system meet the constraints and/or assumptions of the model. While this is easy to state, it is difficult to implement. Obtaining actual order, setup, carrying, and shortage costs is often difficult—sometimes impossible. Part of the problem occurs because accounting data are usually averages, whereas we need the marginal costs. Exhibit 14.11 compares the assumed smoothly ascending cost to the more realistic actual cost. For example, a buyer is a salaried person. The marginal cost for the buyer's labor to place additional orders up to a full

[4]Elliott N. Weiss, "Lot Sizing Is Dead: Long Live Lot Sizing," *Production and Inventory Management Journal* (First Quarter 1990), pp. 76–78.

EXHIBIT 14.11

Cost to Place Orders versus the Number of Orders Placed: Linear Assumption and Normal Reality

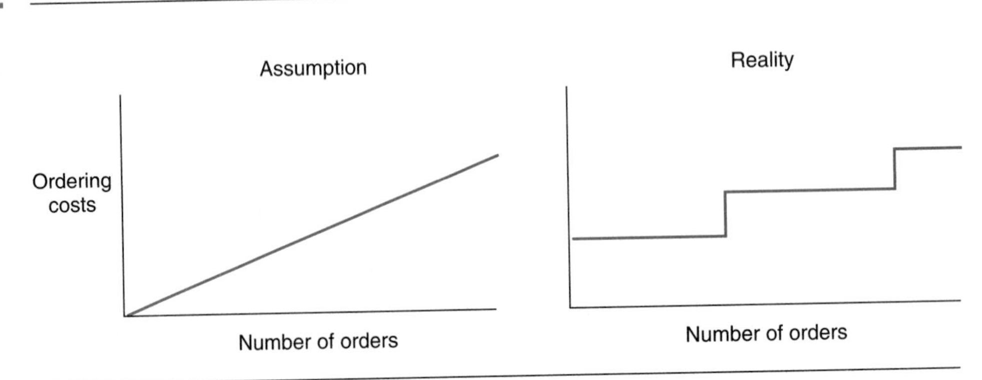

workload is zero. When another buyer is hired, it is a step function. (In theory, the marginal cost of the order that caused hiring the new buyer is the cost for the additional buyer.)

The same problem occurs in determining carrying costs. Warehouse costs, for example, may be close to zero if empty storage areas are still available. Also, most companies can only estimate true carrying costs, since they include obsolescence (a guess, at best), cost of capital (depends on internal money available, alternate investment opportunities, and sources of new capital), and insurance costs (which may range from zero if current insurance premiums cover more than the assets on hand, to the cost of a new policy). It is therefore important that we take these actual circumstances into consideration when applying the inventory models presented in this chapter.

ABC Inventory Planning

All inventory systems are plagued by two major problems: maintaining adequate control over each inventory item and ensuring that accurate records of stock on hand are kept. In this section, we present **ABC analysis**—an inventory system offering a control technique and inventory cycle counting that can improve record accuracy.

Maintaining inventory through counting, placing orders, receiving stock, and so on takes personnel time and costs money. When there are limits on these resources, the logical move is to try to use the available resources to control inventory in the best way. In other words, focus on the most important items in inventory.

In the 18th century, Villefredo Pareto, in a study of the distribution of wealth in Milan, found that 20 percent of the people controlled 80 percent of the wealth. This logic of the few having the greatest importance and the many having little importance has been broadened to include many situations and is termed the *Pareto Principle.* This is true in our everyday lives, where most of the decisions we make are relatively unimportant but a few shape our future, and is certainly true in inventory systems, where a few items account for the bulk of our investment. (As noted earlier in Chapter 6, Pareto analysis is also used in quality management to identify the most frequent types of errors.)

EXHIBIT 14.12

Annual Usage of Inventory by Value

Item Number	Annual Dollar Usage	Percent of Total Value
22	$ 95,000	40.8%
68	75,000	32.1
27	25,000	10.7
03	15,000	6.4
82	13,000	5.6
54	7,500	3.2
36	1,500	0.6
19	800	0.3
23	425	0.2
41	225	0.1
	$233,450	100.0%

Any inventory system must specify when an order is to be placed for an item and how many units to order. In most situations involving inventory control, there are so many items involved, it is not practical to model and give thorough treatment to each and every item. To get around this problem, the ABC classification scheme divides inventory items into three groupings: high dollar volume (A), moderate dollar volume (B), and low dollar volume (C). Dollar volume is a measure of importance; an item low in cost but high in volume can be more important than a high-cost item with low volume.

If the annual usage of items in inventory is listed according to dollar volume, generally the list shows that a small number of items account for a large dollar volume and that a large number of items account for a small dollar volume. Exhibit 14.12 illustrates this relationship.

The ABC approach divides this list into three groupings by value: A items constitute roughly the top 15 percent of the items, B items the next 35 percent, and C items the last 50 percent. From observation, it appears that the list in Exhibit 14.12 may be meaningfully grouped with A including 20 percent (2 of the 10), B including 30 percent, and C including 50 percent. These points show clear delineations between sections. The result of this segmentation is shown in Exhibit 14.13 and is plotted in Exhibit 14.14.

Segmentation may not always occur so neatly. The objective, though, is to try to separate the important from the unimportant. Where the lines actually break depends on the particular inventory under question and on how much personnel time is available (with more time a firm could define larger A or B categories).

EXHIBIT 14.13

ABC Grouping of Inventory Items

Classification	Item Number	Annual Dollar Usage	Percent of Total
A	22, 68	$170,000	72.8%
B	27, 03, 82	53,000	22.7
C	54, 36, 19, 23, 41	10,450	4.5
		$233,450	100.0%

EXHIBIT 14.14 **ABC Inventory Classification** (Inventory value for each group versus the group's portion of the total list)

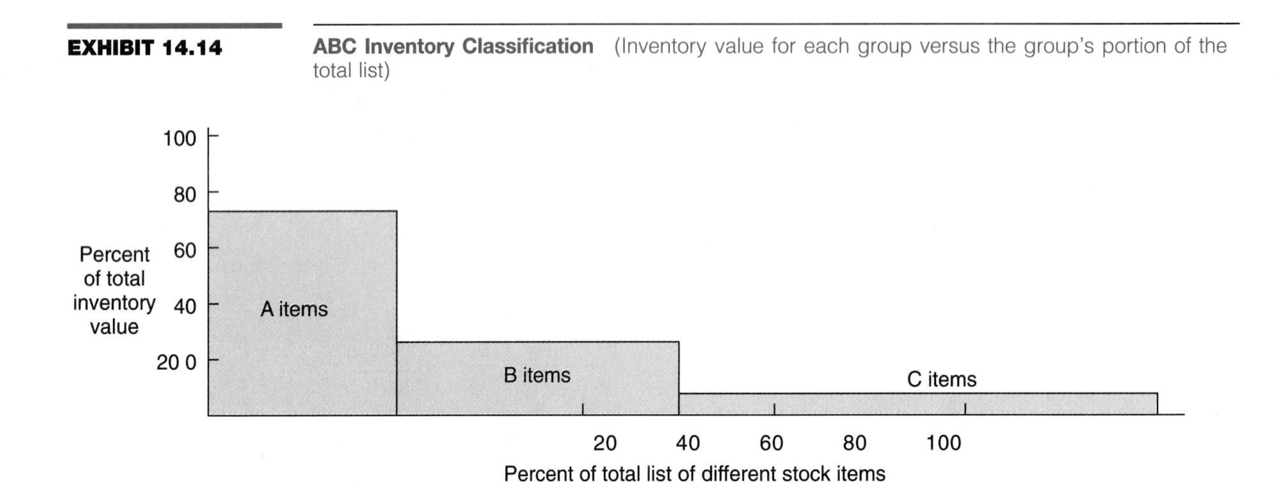

The purpose of classifying items into groups is to establish the appropriate degree of control over each item. On a periodic basis, for example, Class A items may be more clearly controlled with weekly ordering, B items may be ordered biweekly, and C items may be ordered monthly or bimonthly. Note that the unit cost of items is not related to their classification. An A item may have a high dollar volume through a combination of either low cost and high usage or high cost and low usage. Similarly, C items may have a low dollar volume either because of low demand or low cost. In an automobile service station, for example, gasoline would be an A item with daily tabulation; tires, batteries, oil, grease, and transmission fluid may be B items and ordered every two to four weeks; and C items would consist of valve stems, windshield wiper blades, radiator caps, hoses, fan belts, oil and gas additives, car wax, and so forth. C items may be ordered every two or three months or even be allowed to run out before reordering since the penalty for stockout is not serious.

Sometimes, an item may be critical to a system if its absence creates a sizable loss. In this case, regardless of the item's classification, sufficiently large stocks should be kept on hand to prevent runout. One way to ensure closer control is to designate this item an A or a B, forcing it into the category even if its dollar volume does not warrant such inclusion.

Inventory Accuracy

Inventory records usually differ from the actual physical count and **inventory accuracy** refers to how well the two agree. The question is, how much error is acceptable? If the record shows a balance of 683 of Part X and an actual count shows 652, is this within reason? Suppose the actual count shows 750, an excess of 67 over the record; is this any better?

Every production system must have agreement, within some specified range, between what the record says is in inventory and what actually is in inventory. There are many

Courtesy Albertson's, Inc.

Grocery store managers at Albertson's use hand held computers that read UPC codes to monitor inventories and determine reorders.

reasons records and inventory may not agree. For example, having an open stockroom area allows items to be removed for both legitimate and unauthorized purposes. The legitimate removal may have been done in a hurry and simply not recorded. Sometimes parts are misplaced, turning up months later. Parts are often stored in several locations, but records may be lost or the location recorded incorrectly. Sometimes stock replenishment orders are recorded as received, when in fact they never were. Occasionally, a group of parts are recorded as having been removed from inventory, but the customer order is canceled and the parts are replaced in inventory without canceling the record. To keep the production system flowing smoothly without parts shortages and efficiently without excess balances, it is important that inventory records are accurate.

How can a firm keep accurate, up-to-date records? The first general rule is to keep the storeroom locked. If only storeroom personnel have access, and one of their measures of performance when it comes time for personnel evaluation and merit increases is record accuracy, there is a strong motivation to comply. Every location of inventory storage, whether in a locked storeroom or on the production floor, should have a recordkeeping mechanism.

Inventory Control in Services

To demonstrate how inventory control is conducted in service organizations, we have selected two areas to describe: a department store and an automobile service agency.

Department store inventory policy

The common term used to identify an inventory item in a department store is *stock-keeping unit,* or SKU. The SKU identifies each item, its manufacturer, and its cost. The number of SKUs becomes large even for small departments within a store. For example, if towels carried in a domestic items department are obtained from three manufacturers in three quality levels, three sizes (hand towel, face towel, and bath towel), and four colors, there are 108 different items ($3 \times 3 \times 3 \times 4$). Even if the towels are sold only in sets of three pieces (hand towel, face towel, and bath towel), the number of SKUs needed to identify the towel sets is $3 \times 3 \times 1 \times 4$, or 36. Depending on the store, a housewares department may carry 3,000 to 4,000 SKUs, and a linen and domestic items department may carry 5,000 to 6,000.

Obviously, such large numbers mean that individual economic order quantities cannot be calculated for each item by hand. How, then, does a department keep tabs on its stock and place orders for replenishment? We address this issue in the context of an example dealing with a housewares department.

Housewares department. Generally, housewares are divided into staple and promotional items. Within these major divisions, further classifications are used, such as cookware and tableware. Also, items are frequently classified by price, as $5 items, $4, $3, and so forth.

The housewares department usually purchases from a distributor rather than directly from a manufacturer. The use of a distributor, who handles products from many manufacturers, has the advantage of fewer orders and shorter lead time. Further, the distributor's sales personnel may visit the housewares department weekly and count all the items they supply to this department. Then, in line with the replenishment level that has been established by the buyer, the distributor's salesperson places orders for the buyer. This saves the department time in counting inventory and placing orders. The typical lead time for receipt of stock from a housewares distributor is two or three days. The safety stock, therefore, is quite low, and the buyer establishes the replenishment level so as to supply only enough items for the two- to three-day lead time, plus expected demand during the period until the distributor's salesperson's next visit.

Note that a formal method of estimating stockout and establishing safety-stock levels is usually not followed because the number of items is too great. Instead, the total value of items in the department is monitored. Thus, replenishment levels are set by dollar allocation.

Through planning, each department has an established monthly value for inventory. By tabulating the inventory balance, monthly sales, and items on order, an "open-to-buy" figure is determined. ("Open-to-buy" is the unspent portion of the budget.) This dollar amount is the sum available to the buyer for the following month. When an increase in demand is expected (Christmas, Mother's Day, etc.), the allocation of funds to the department is increased, resulting in a larger open-to-buy position. Then the replenishment levels are raised in line with the class of goods, responding to the demand increase, thereby creating a higher stock of goods on hand.

In practice, the open-to-buy funds are largely spent during the first days of the month. However, the buyer tries to reserve some funds for special purchases or to restock fast-moving items. Promotional items in housewares are controlled individually (or by class) by the buyer.

Maintaining an auto replacement-parts inventory

A firm in the automobile service business purchases most of its parts supplies from a small number of distributors. Franchised new-car dealers purchase the great bulk of their supplies from the automobile manufacturer. A dealer's demand for auto parts originates primarily from the general public and other departments of the agency, such as the service department or body shop. The problem, in this case, is to determine the order quantities for the several thousand items carried.

A franchised automobile agency of medium size may carry a parts inventory valued in the area of $500,000. Because of the nature of this industry, alternate uses of funds are plentiful, and therefore, opportunity costs are high. For example, dealers may lease cars, carry their own contracts, stock a larger new-car inventory, or open sidelines such as tire shops, trailer sales, or recreational vehicle sales—all with potentially high returns. This creates pressure to maintain a low inventory level of parts and supplies while still meeting an acceptable service level.

While many dealers still perform their inventory ordering by hand, there is a definite trend in the industry toward computerization. For both manual and computerized systems, an ABC classification works well. Expensive and high-turnover supplies are counted and ordered frequently; low-cost items are ordered in large quantities at infrequent intervals. A common drawback of frequent order placement is the extensive amount of time needed to physically put the items on the shelves and log them in. (However, this restocking procedure does not greatly add to an auto agency's cost because parts department personnel generally do this during slow periods.)

A wide variety of computerized systems is currently in use. One program gives a choice of using either a simple weighted average or exponential smoothing to forecast the next period's demand. In a monthly reordering system, for example, the items to be ordered are counted and the number on hand is entered into the computer. By subtracting the number on hand from the previous month's inventory and adding the orders received during the month, the usage rate is determined.

14.9 CONCLUSION

This chapter introduces the two main categories of inventory demand: independent (referring to the external demand for a firm's end product) and dependent (usually referring to the demand within the firm for items created because of the demand for more complex items of which they are a part). Most industries have items in both categories. In manufacturing, for example, independent demand is common for finished products, service and repair parts, and operating supplies; and dependent demand is common for those parts and materials needed to produce the end product. In wholesale and retail sales of consumer goods, most demand is independent—each item is an end item, with the wholesaler or retailer doing no further assembly or fabrication.

Independent demand, is based on statistics. In addition to deterministic models where demand is constant and known, we also address uncertainty in demand and the influence of service levels on safety stock and reorder point determinations.

To provide both an efficient and effective way to control inventory, the ABC method was introduced. The importance of inventory accuracy was also noted, and cycle counting was described. Finally, brief descriptions of inventory procedures in a department store and an auto parts shop were given to illustrate some of the simpler ways nonmanufacturing firms carry out their inventory control functions.

In this chapter we also pointed out that inventory reduction requires a knowledge of the operating system. It is not simply a case of selecting an inventory model off the shelf and plugging in some numbers. In the first place, the model might not even be appropriate. In the second case, the numbers might not be relevant. It is vital to understand that this is also not a trade-off compromise. Very often determining order quantities is referred to as a trade-off problem; that is, trading off holding costs for setup costs. Note that companies really want to reduce both.

The simple fact is that firms typically have very large investments in inventory, and the cost to carry this inventory runs from 30 to 35 percent and more of the inventory's worth annually. Therefore, a major goal of most firms today is to reduce inventory; they expect this to also lead to improved quality and performance and to greatly reduce cost.

14.10 REVIEW AND DISCUSSION QUESTIONS

1. Distinguish between dependent and independent demand in a McDonald's, in an integrated manufacturer of personal copiers, and in a pharmaceutical supply house.
2. Distinguish between work-in-process inventory, safety-stock inventory, and seasonal inventory.
3. Discuss the nature of the costs that affect inventory size.
4. Under which conditions would a plant manager elect to use a fixed-order quantity model as opposed to a fixed-time period model? What are the disadvantages of using a fixed-time period ordering system?
5. Define the term *service level.*
6. Discuss the general procedure for determining the order quantity when quantity discounts are involved. Would there by any differences in the procedure if holding costs were a fixed percentage of item cost rather than a constant amount?
7. What two basic questions must be answered by an inventory-control decision rule?
8. Discuss the assumptions that are inherent in production setup cost, ordering cost, and carrying costs. How valid are they?
9. "The nice thing about inventory models is that you can pull one off the shelf and apply it so long as your cost estimates are accurate." Comment.
10. Which type of inventory system would you use in the following situations?
    a. Supplying your kitchen with fresh food.
    b. Obtaining a daily newspaper.
    c. Buying gasoline for your car.
11. Why is it desirable to classify items into groups, as the ABC classification scheme does?

14.11 SOLVED PROBLEMS

PROBLEM

1. Items purchased from a vendor cost $20 each, and the forecast for next year's demand is 1,000 units. If it costs $5 every time an order is placed for more units and the carrying cost is $4 per unit per year, what quantity should be ordered each time?
   a. What is the total ordering cost for a year?
   b. What is the total carrying cost for a year?

SOLUTION

The quantity to be ordered each time is:

$$Q = \sqrt{\frac{2DS}{H}} = \sqrt{\frac{2(1{,}000)5}{4}} = 50 \text{ units}$$

a. The total ordering cost for a year is:

$$\frac{D}{Q}S = \frac{1{,}000}{50}(\$5) = \$100$$

b. The carrying cost for a year is:

$$\frac{Q}{2}H = \frac{50}{2}(\$4) = \$100$$

PROBLEM

2. A sells (among other things) sports shirts for casual wear. Mr. Koste is in charge of the men's department, and knows that the annual demand for one of these shirts is fairly constant at 250 shirts per year. These shirts are obtained only from the manufacturer, who charges a delivery fee of $65, regardless of the number of shirts delivered with that order. In addition, in-house costs associated with each order total $6.

   The manufacturer charges $16.25 per shirt, but is willing to lower the price by 3% per shirt if the department store will order at least 2 gross each time. Of course, this means that some shirts must be kept in inventory, and the holding costs have been estimated at 8.5% per shirt per year.

   Should Mr. Koste recommend that the department store accept the offer of the quantity discount?

SOLUTION

$D = 250$

$S = 65 + 6 = \$71$

$H = iC$

$i = 0.085$

$C = \$16.25$

$$Q = \sqrt{\frac{2DS}{iC}} = \sqrt{\frac{(2)(250)(71)}{(0.085)(16.25)}} \approx 160$$

As $160 < 288$, compute:

$$TC(160) = (16.25)(250) + \left(\frac{250}{160}\right)(71) + \left(\frac{160}{2}\right)(.085)(16.25)$$
$$= \$4{,}283.94$$

and

$$TC(288) = [(.97)(16.25)(250)] + \left(\frac{250}{288}\right)(71) + \left(\frac{288}{2}\right)(.085)[(.97)(16.25)]$$
$$= \$4{,}195.19$$

Yes, accept the discount.

PROBLEM

Elkin Shoes, Inc. (ESI) is a manufacturing firm which produces a variety of shoes and boots. They have recently started operation of a factory in the USA, and have opened a factory outlet store adjacent to the factory. The production manager at the factory is trying to ascertain the optimal number of sheepskin boots to produce with each production run. After careful analysis, he believes that the following data are correct:

Annual demand for the boots: 12,000 pairs
Days/year the outlet store is open: 240
Daily production capacity of the factory: 200 pairs
Set-up cost incurred to start boot production: $800
Annual storage cost per pair of boots: $60

What should the production manager recommend as the optimal production lot size?

SOLUTION

D = Annual Demand = 12,000
d = Daily demand = 12,000/240 = 50
p = Daily production = 200
S = Set-up cost = $800
H = Holding cost = $60

$$Q = \sqrt{\frac{2DS}{H} \cdot \left(\frac{p}{p-d}\right)} = \sqrt{\frac{(2)(12000)(800)}{60} \cdot \left(\frac{200}{200-50}\right)} \approx 653$$

14.12 PROBLEMS

1. Annual demand for an item is 2,500 units. The cost to place an order is $5, and holding cost is 20 percent of the cost of the item. Items have the following cost schedule:

1 to 99	$10.00 each
100 to 199	$ 9.80 each
over 200	$ 9.60 each

What is the economic order quantity (EOQ)?

2. Given the information below, formulate an inventory management system. The item is demanded 50 weeks a year.

Item cost	$15.00
Order cost	$250.00
Holding cost (%)	33% of item cost
Annual demand	25,750
Average demand	515 per week
Standard deviation of demand	25 per week
Lead time	1 week
Service level	95%

a. State the order quantity and the reorder point.
b. Determine the annual holding and order costs.
c. How many units per order cycle would you expect to be short?
d. If a price break of $50 per order was offered for purchase quantities of over 1,000 would you take advantage of it? How much would you save on an annual basis?

3. Jill's Job Shop buys two parts (Tegdiws and Widgets) that they use in their production system from two different suppliers. The parts are needed throughout the entire 52-week year. Tegdiws are used at a relatively constant rate and are ordered whenever the remaining quantity drops to the reorder level. Widgets are ordered from a supplier who stops by every three weeks.
Data for both products are as follows:

Item	Tegdiw	Widget
Annual demand	10,000	5,000
Holding cost (% of item cost)	20%	20%
Setup or order cost	$150.00	$25.00
Lead time	4 weeks	1 week
Safety stock	55 units	5 units
Item cost	$10.00	$2.00

Management would like to stock these items with a 95 percent service level.
a. What is the inventory control system for Tegdiws; that is, what is the reorder quantity and what is the reorder point?
b. What is the inventory control system for Widgets?

4. Demand for an item is 1,000 units per year. Each order placed costs $10; the annual cost to carry items in inventory is $2 each.
a. In what quantities should the item be ordered?
b. Suppose a $100 discount on each order is given if orders are placed in quantities of 500 or more. Should orders be placed in quantities of 500, or should you stick to the decision you made in *a*?

5. The annual demand for a product is 15,600 units. The weekly demand is 300 units with a standard deviation of 90 units. The cost to place an order is $31.20, and the time from ordering to receipt is four weeks. The annual inventory carrying cost is $0.10 per unit. Find the reorder point necessary to provide a 99 percent service level.
Suppose the production manager is ordered to reduce the safety stock of this item by 50 percent. If he does so, what will the new service level be?

6. Item X is a standard item stocked in a company's inventory of component parts. Each year, the firm, on a random basis, uses about 2,000 of Item X, which costs $25 each. Storage costs, which include insurance and cost of capital, amount to $5 per unit of average inventory. Every time an order is placed for more Item X, it costs $10.
   a. Whenever Item X is ordered, what should the order size be?
   b. What is the annual cost for ordering Item X?
   c. What is the annual cost for storing Item X?
7. The annual demand for a product is 13,000 units; the weekly demand is 250 units with a standard deviation of 40 units. The cost of placing an order is $100, and the time from ordering to receipt is four weeks. The annual inventory carrying cost is $0.65 per unit. To provide a 99 percent service level, what must the reorder point be?

   Suppose the production manager is told to reduce the safety stock of this item by 10 units. If this is done, what will the new service level be?
8. A particular raw material is available to a company at three different prices, depending on the size of the orders, as follows:

Less than 100 pounds	$20 per pound
100 pounds to 999 pounds	$19 per pound
More than 1,000 pounds	$18 per pound

   The cost to place an order is $40. Annual demand is 3,000 units. Holding (or carrying) cost is 25 percent of the material price.

   What is the economic order quantity to buy each time?
9. In the past, Taylor Industries has used a fixed-time inventory system that involved taking a complete inventory count of all items each month. However, increasing labor costs are forcing Taylor Industries to examine alternate ways to reduce the amount of labor involved in inventory stockrooms, yet without increasing other costs, such as shortage costs.

   Following is a random sample of 20 of Taylor's items.

Item Number	Annual Usage	Item Number	Annual Usage
1	$ 1,500	11	$13,000
2	12,000	12	600
3	2,200	13	42,000
4	50,000	14	9,900
5	9,600	15	1,200
6	750	16	10,200
7	2,000	17	4,000
8	11,000	18	61,000
9	800	19	3,500
10	15,000	20	2,900

   a. What would you recommend Taylor do to cut back its labor cost? (Illustrate using an ABC plan.)
   b. Item 15 is critical to continued operations. How would you recommend it be classified?
10. Gentle Ben's Bar and Restaurant uses 5,000 quart bottles of an imported wine each year. The effervescent wine costs $3 per bottle and is served in whole bottles only because it loses its

bubbles quickly. Ben figures that it costs $10 each time an order is placed, and holding costs are 20 percent of the purchase price. It takes three weeks for an order to arrive. Weekly demand is 100 bottles (closed two weeks per year) with a standard deviation of 30 bottles.

Ben would like to use an inventory system that minimizes inventory cost and will satisfy 95 percent of his customers who order this wine.

a. What is the economic order quantity for Ben to order?

b. At what inventory level should he place an order?

c. How many bottles of wine does Ben expect to be short during each order cycle?

11. Retailers Warehouse (RW) is an independent supplier of household items to department stores. RW attempts to stock enough items to satisfy 98 percent of the requests from its customers.

A stainless steel knife set is one of the items stocked by RW. Demand is 2,400 sets per year, relatively stable over the entire year. Whenever new stock is ordered, a buyer must ensure that numbers are correct for stock on hand and phone in a new order. The total cost involved to place an order is about $5. RW figures that to hold inventory in stock and to pay for interest on borrowed capital, insurance, and so on adds up to about $4 holding cost per unit per year.

Analysis of the past data shows that the standard deviation of demand from retailers is about four units per day for a 365-day year. Lead time to get the order once placed is seven days.

a. What is the economic order quantity?

b. What is the reorder point?

12. Magnetron, Inc., manufactures microwave ovens for the commercial market. Currently, Magnetron is producing part 2104 in its fabrication shop for use in the adjacent unit assembly area. Next year's requirement for part 2104 is estimated at 20,000 units. Part 2104 is valued at $50 per unit, and the combined storage and handling cost is $8 per unit per year. The cost of preparing the order and making the production setup is $200. The plant operates 250 days per year. The assembly area operates every working day, completing 80 units, and the fabrication shop produces 160 units per day when it is producing part 2104.

a. Compute the economic order quantity.

b. How many orders will be placed each year?

c. If part 2104 could be purchased from another firm with the same costs as described, what would the order quantity be? (The order is received all at once.)

d. If the average lead time to order from another firm is 10 working days and a safety stock level is set at 500 units, what is the reorder point?

13. Garrett Corporation, a turbine manufacturer, works an 18-hour day, 300 days a year. Titanium blades can be produced on its turbine blade machine number 1, TBM1, at a rate of 500 per hour, and the average usage rate is 5,000 per day. The blades cost $15 apiece, and carrying costs $0.10 per day per blade because of insurance, interest on investments, and space allocation. TBM1 costs $250 to set up for each run. Lead time requires production to begin after stock drops to 500 blades. What is the optimal production run for TBM1?

14. The text described how one department store conducted its inventory ordering for a housewares department. How would you apply the theory and models in this chapter to enhance the operation of that store's system?

15. Alpha Products, Inc., is having a problem trying to control inventory. There is insufficient time to devote to all its items equally. Following is a sample of some items stocked, along with the annual usage of each item expressed in dollar volume.

Usage	Annual Dollar Item	Usage	Annual Dollar
a	$ 7,000	k	$80,000
b	1,000	l	400
c	14,000	m	1,100
d	2,000	n	30,000
e	24,000	o	1,900
f	68,000	p	800
g	17,000	q	90,000
h	900	r	12,000
i	1,700	s	3,000
j	2,300	t	32,000

Can you suggest a system for allocating control time? Specify where each item from the list would be placed.

16. A distributor of large appliances needs to determine the order quantities and reorder points for the various products it carries. The following data refers to a specific refrigerator in its product line:

Cost to place an order	$30
Holding cost	20 percent of product cost per year
Cost of refrigerator	$300 each
Annual demand	500 refrigerators
Standard deviation during lead time	10 refrigerators
Lead time	7 days

Consider an even daily demand and a 365-day year.

a. What is the economic order quantity?

b. If the distributor wants to satisfy 97 percent of its demand, what reorder point, *R,* should be used?

17. It is your responsibility, as the new head of the automotive section of Nichols Department Store, to ensure that reorder quantities for the various items have been correctly established. You decide to test one of the items and choose Michelin tires, XW size 185 × 14 BSW.

A perpetual inventory system has been used so you examine this as well as other records and come up with the following data:

Cost per tire	$35 each
Holding cost	20 percent of tire cost per year
Demand	1,000 per year
Ordering cost	$20 per order
Standard deviation of daily demand	3 tires
Delivery lead time	4 days

Because customers generally do not wait for tires but go elsewhere, you decide on a service level of 98 percent.

a. Determine the order quantity.

b. Determine the reorder point.

18. CU, Incorporated, (CUI) produces copper contacts that it uses in switches and relays. CUI needs to determine the order quantity, Q, to meet the annual demand at the lowest cost.

    The price of copper depends on the quantity ordered. Following are the price-break data and the other data for the problem:

Price of copper	\$0.82 per pound up to 2,499 pounds \$0.81 per pound for orders between 2,500 and 4,999 pounds \$0.80 per pound for orders greater than 5,000 pounds
Annual demand	50,000 pounds per year
Holding cost	20 percent per unit per year of the price of the copper
Ordering cost	\$30

    Which quantity should be ordered?

19. DAT, Inc., produces digital audiotapes to be used in the consumer audio division. DAT doesn't have sufficient personnel in its inventory supply section to closely control each item stocked, so others asked you to determine an ABC classification. The following shows a sample from the inventory records:

Item	Average Monthly Demand	Price per Unit
1	700	\$ 6.00
2	200	4.00
3	2,000	12.00
4	1,100	20.00
5	4,000	21.00
6	100	10.00
7	3,000	2.00
8	2,500	1.00
9	500	10.00
10	1,000	2.00

    Develop an ABC classification for these 10 items.

20. A local service station is open 7 days per week, 365 days per year. Sales of 10W40 grade premium oil average 20 cans per day. Inventory holding costs are \$0.50 per can per year. Ordering costs are \$10 per order and the lead time is two weeks. Back orders are not practical—the motorist drives way. Based on this data, choose the appropriate inventory model and calculate the economic order quantity and the reorder point. Describe in a sentence how the plan would work. Hint: Assume demand is deterministic.

14.13 SELECTED BIBLIOGRAPHY

Anderson, Edward J. "Testing Feasibility in a Lot Scheduling Problem." *Operations Research*, November–December 1990, pp. 1079–89.

Bernhard, Paul. "The Carrying Cost Paradox: How Do You Manage It?" *Industrial Engineering*, November 1989, pp. 40–46.

Davis, Samuel G. "Scheduling Economic Lot Size Production Runs." *Management Science*, August 1990, pp. 985–99.

Fogarty, Donald W.; John H. Blackstone; and Thomas R. Hoffmann. *Production and Inventory Management*. 2nd ed. Cincinnati, Ohio: South-Western Publishing, 1991.

Freeland, James R.; John P. Leschke; and Elliott N. Weiss. "Guidelines for Setup Reduction Programs to Achieve Zero Inventory." *Journal of Operations Management,* January 1990, pp. 75–80.

Greene, James H. *Production and Inventory Control Handbook*. 2nd ed. New York: McGraw-Hill, 1987.

Harris, Ford Whitman. "How Many Parts to Make at Once." *Operations Research,* November–December 1990, pp. 947–51.

Tersine, Richard J. *Principles of Inventory and Materials Management*. 3rd ed. New York: North-Holland, 1988.

Trigeiro, William W. "A Simple Heuristic for Lot Sizing with Setup Times." *Decision Sciences,* Spring 1989, pp. 294–303.

Vollmann, T. E.; W. L. Berry; and D. C. Whybark. *Manufacturing Planning and Control Systems*. 2nd ed. Homewood, Ill.: Richard D. Irwin, 1988.

Young, Jan B. *Modern Inventory Operations: Methods for Accuracy and Productivity*. New York: Van Nostrand Reinhold, 1991.

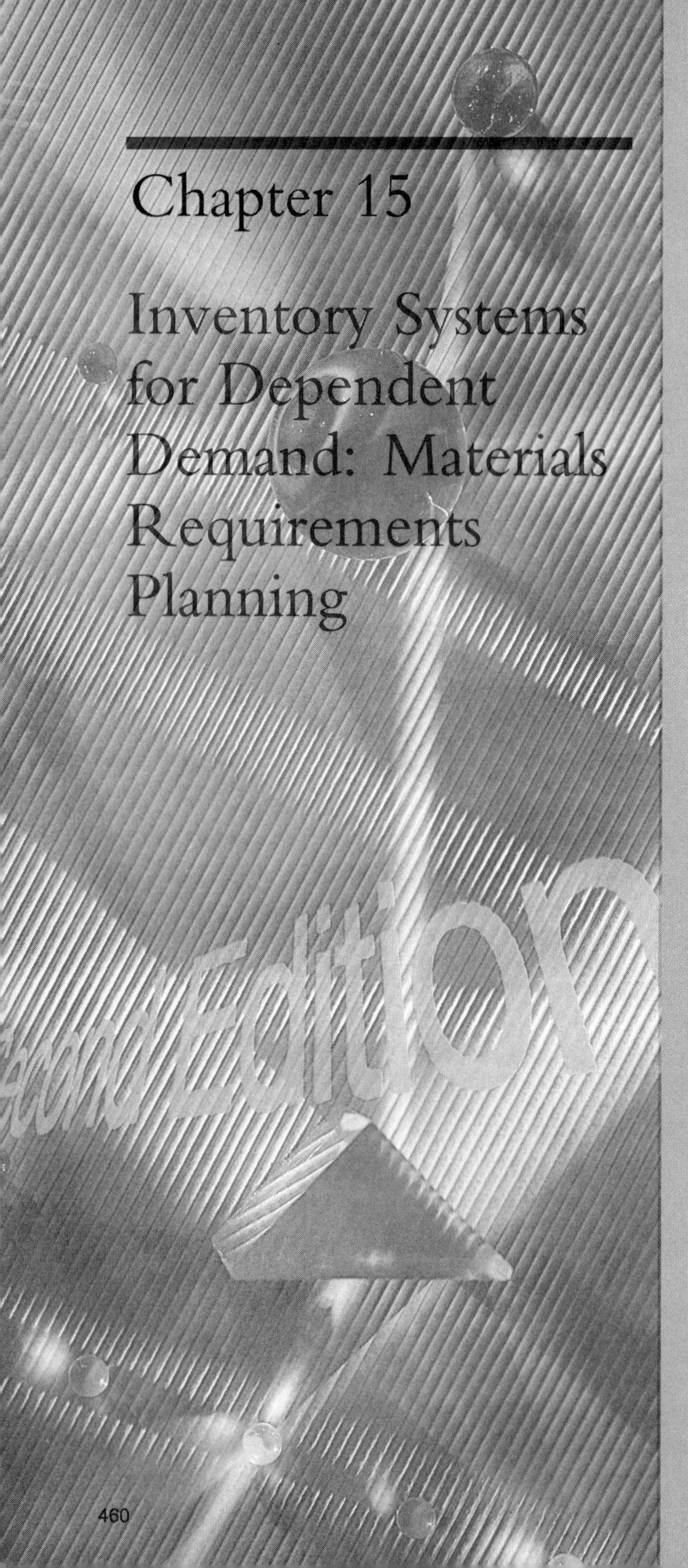

Chapter 15

Inventory Systems for Dependent Demand: Materials Requirements Planning

EPIGRAPH

To make Grandma's Chocolate Cake, take 1 cup shortening, 2 cups sugar, 1 teaspoon salt, 1 teaspoon vanilla, 2 eggs, $2\,^{1}/_{4}$ cups flour, 1 cup buttermilk, $^{1}/_{2}$ cup cocoa, 2 teaspoons soda, and 1 cup hot water . . .

CHAPTER OUTLINE

KEY TERMS

Master Production Schedule (MPS)

Materials Requirements Planning (MRP)

Bills of Materials (BOM)

Inventory Records File

Manufacturing Resource Planning (MRP II)

All of the inventory models presented in the previous chapter operate under an inherent assumption: Demand is independent and constant. However, there are often times when this assumption is not valid. This is particularly true when we are dealing with subassemblies and component parts, the demand for which is often variable and highly dependent on the demand for the final or end product in which they are used. For example, the demand for automobile tires is dependent on the demand for the autos themselves. Once the demand for the autos has been established, the demand for the tires is easily calculated.

Consequently, the classical inventory models previously presented are not appropriate under these circumstances. To address these types of inventory issues, we use a concept known as **materials requirements planning,** or **MRP.**

Today, MRP systems have been installed almost universally in manufacturing firms both large and small. The reason is that MRP is a logical and readily understandable approach to the problem of determining the number of parts, components, and materials needed to produce each end item. MRP also provides the time schedule specifying when each of these materials, parts, and components should be ordered or produced.

The original MRP planned only materials. However, as computer power grew in the past 20 or so years and applications expanded, so did the breadth of MRP. Soon it considered resources as well as materials; now MRP also stands for *manufacturing resource planning* (MRP II), which will be discussed later in this chapter.

The main purpose of this chapter is to present an overview of MRP and its underlying logic, and to demonstrate its use through several illustrations. We also discuss samples of existing MRP programs currently in use in industry. Finally, we show that just-in-time (JIT) systems and MRP are not necessarily competing ways for production but can work effectively together.

15.1 MASTER PRODUCTION SCHEDULE

The aggregate production plan, as presented in Chapter 13, specifies product groups. It does not specify exact items. The next level down in the planning process after the development of the aggregate plan is the master production schedule. The **master production schedule (MPS)** is the time-phased plan specifying how many and when the firm plans to build each specific end item. For example, the aggregate plan for a furniture company may specify the total volume of mattresses it plans to produce over the next month or next quarter. The MPS goes the next step down and identifies the exact size mattresses and their qualities and styles. All the mattresses sold by the company would be specified by the MPS. The MPS also states period by period (which is usually weekly) how many and when each of these mattress types is needed.

Still further down the disaggregation process is the MRP program, which calculates and schedules all of the raw materials, parts, and supplies needed to make each of the different mattresses specified in the MPS.

EXHIBIT 15.1

Master Production Schedule Time Fences

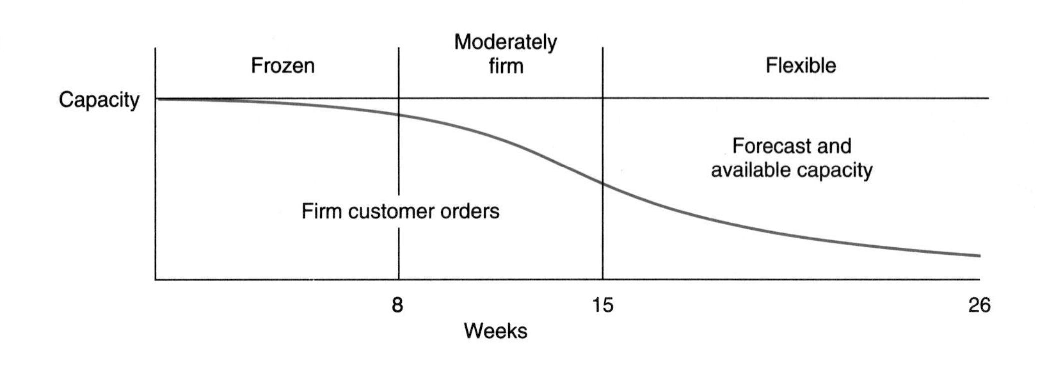

Time Fences

The question of flexibility within an MPS depends on several factors including: production lead time, the commitment of parts and components to a specific end item, the relationship between the customer and vendor, the amount of excess capacity, and the reluctance or willingness of management to make changes.

Exhibit 15.1 shows an example of a master production schedule time fence. Management defines *time fences* as periods of time, with each period having some specified level of opportunity for the customer to make changes. (The customer may be the firm's own marketing department, which may be considering product promotions, broadening variety, etc.) Note in the exhibit that for the next eight weeks the master schedule for this particular firm is frozen. Each firm has its own time fences and operating rules. Under these rules, *frozen* could be defined as anything from absolutely no changes in one firm to only the most minor of changes in another. *Moderately firm* may allow changes in specific products within a product group, so long as parts are available. *Flexible* may allow almost any variations in products, with the provision that capacity remains about the same and that there are no long lead time items involved.

The purpose of time fences is to maintain a reasonably controlled flow through the production system. Unless some operating rules are established and adhered to, the system could be chaotic and filled with overdue orders and constant expediting.

15.2 A SIMPLE MRP EXAMPLE

As a way to introduce the various aspects of an MRP system, we present a simple problem explaining how quantities are calculated, lead times are offset, and order releases and receipts are established.

Suppose that we want to produce Product T, which consists of two parts U and three parts V. Part U, in turn, is made of one part W and two parts X. Part V is made of two parts W and two parts Y. Exhibit 15.2 shows the product structure tree of Product T. By simple computation, we calculate that if 100 units of T are required, we need:

EXHIBIT 15.2

Product Structure Tree for Product T

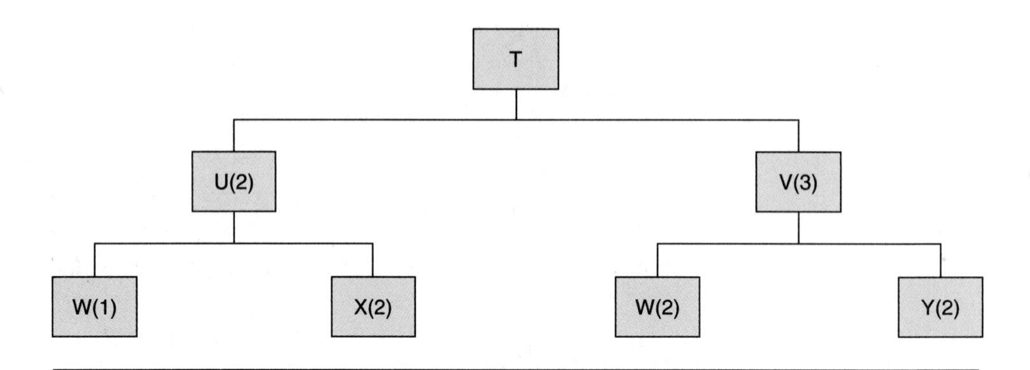

$$
\begin{array}{llll}
\text{Part U:} & 2 \times \text{number of Ts} = & 2 \times 100 & = 200 \\
\text{Part V:} & 3 \times \text{number of Ts} = & 3 \times 100 & = 300 \\
\text{Part W:} & \left\{ \begin{array}{l} 1 \times \text{number of Us} = \\ +2 \times \text{number of Vs} = \end{array} \right. & \left. \begin{array}{l} 1 \times 200 \\ +2 \times 300 \end{array} \right\} & = 800 \\
\text{Part X:} & 2 \times \text{number of Us} = & 2 \times 200 & = 400 \\
\text{Part Y:} & 2 \times \text{number of Vs} = & 2 \times 300 & = 600
\end{array}
$$

Next, we need to consider the time needed to obtain these items, that is, either to produce the parts internally or to obtain them from an outside vendor. Assume that the lead time to make each of the parts is as follows:

Part	Lead Time (weeks)
T	1
U	2
V	2
W	3
X	1
Y	1

If we know when Product T is required, we can create a time schedule chart specifying when all the material necessary to build T must be ordered and received to meet the demand. Exhibit 15.3 shows which items are needed and when. We have thus created a material requirements plan based on the demand for Product T and the knowledge of how T is made and the time needed to obtain each part. (Note that in this simple example, we have not taken into consideration any on-hand inventories.)

From this simple illustration, it should be obvious that developing a material requirements plan manually for thousands or even hundreds of items would be impractical—a great deal of computation is needed, and a tremendous amount of data must be available about the inventory status (number of units on hand, on order, and so forth) and about the product structure (how the product is made and how many units of each material are required). Because a computer is an integral part of every MRP system, our emphasis in

EXHIBIT 15.3

Material Requirements Plan for Completing 100 Units of Product T in Period 7

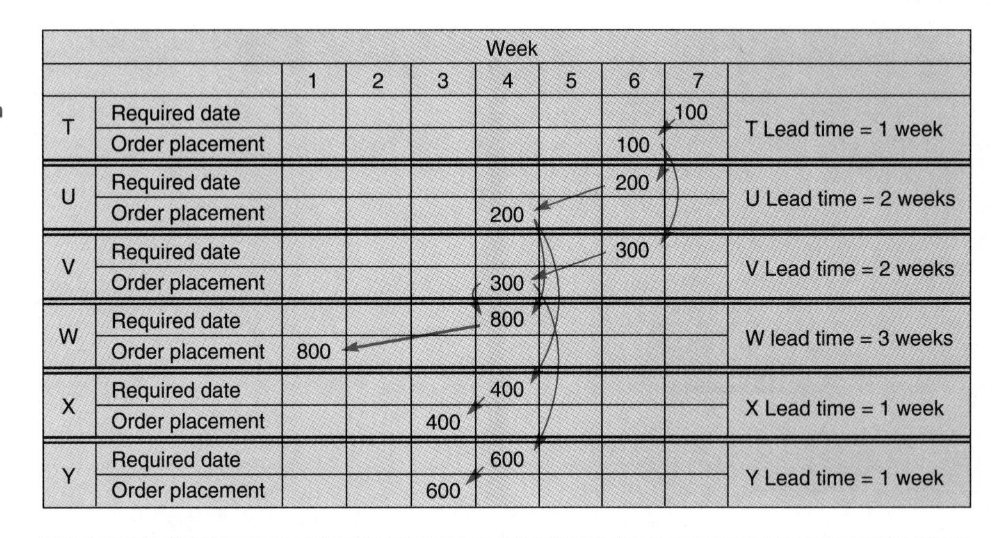

		Week							
		1	2	3	4	5	6	7	
T	Required date							100	T Lead time = 1 week
	Order placement						100		
U	Required date						200		U Lead time = 2 weeks
	Order placement				200				
V	Required date						300		V Lead time = 2 weeks
	Order placement				300				
W	Required date				800				W lead time = 3 weeks
	Order placement	800							
X	Required date				400				X Lead time = 1 week
	Order placement			400					
Y	Required date				600				Y Lead time = 1 week
	Order placement			600					

this chapter is on understanding the general structure of the system and on the supporting computer files that are required. However, the underlying logic of the program is essentially the same as that for our simple example.

Generally, the MPS, which is the primary driver of the MRP system, deals with end items. If the end item is quite large and/or quite expensive, the MPS may, however, schedule major subassemblies or components instead.

All production systems have limited capacity and limited resources. This presents a challenge for the master scheduler. Exhibit 15.4 shows the environment in which the master scheduler works. While the aggregate plan provides the general range of operation, the master scheduler must massage the aggregate plan into an MPS that specifies exactly what is to be produced. These decisions are made while responding to pressures from various functional areas.

To determine an acceptable feasible schedule for the shop, trial master production schedules are run through the MRP program in an iterative process. The resulting planned order releases (the detailed production schedules) are reviewed to ensure that resources are available and the completion times are reasonable. What may appear to be a feasible MPS may, in fact, require excessive resources when the resource requirements for the materials, parts, and components for the lower levels are determined. If this occurs (which is the usual case), the MPS is then adjusted to reflect these limitations and the MRP program is run again. To ensure good master scheduling, the master schedul*er* (i.e., the human being) must:

- Include all demands from product sales, warehouse replenishment, spares, and interplant requirements.
- Never lose sight of the aggregate plan.

EXHIBIT 15.4

The Environment of the Master Scheduler

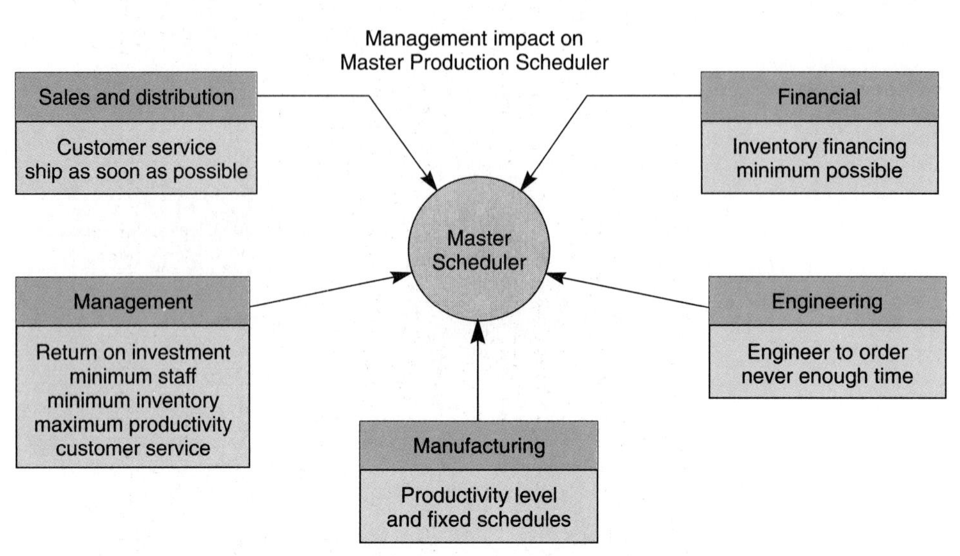

Source: Romeyn C. Everdell and Woodrow W. Chamberlain, "Master Scheduling in a Multi-Plant Environment," *Proceedings of the American Production and Inventory Control Society* (1980), p. 421.

- Be involved with customer order promising.
- Be visible to all levels of management.
- Objectively trade off manufacturing, marketing, and engineering conflicts.
- Identify and communicate all problems.

The upper portion of Exhibit 15.5 shows an aggregate plan for the total number of mattresses planned per month for a furniture manufacturer, without regard to mattress type. The lower portion of the exhibit shows an MPS specifying the exact type of mattress and the quantity planned for production by week. The next level down (not shown) would be the MRP program that develops detailed schedules showing when cotton batting, springs, and hardwood are needed to make the mattresses. If carried further, this mattress example would look like Exhibit 15.16 (discussed later) which shows parts and subassemblies for electrical meters.

15.3 MATERIAL REQUIREMENTS PLANNING (MRP) SYSTEMS

Using an MPS that is derived from an *aggregate plan, a material requirements planning* (MRP) system can then create schedules identifying the specific parts and materials necessary to produce the end items required, the exact numbers of each that are needed, and the dates

EXHIBIT 15.5

The Aggregate Plan and the Master Production Schedule for Mattresses

Aggregate production plan for mattresses

Month	1	2
Mattress production	900	950

Master production schedule for mattress models

	1	2	3	4	5	6	7	8
Model 327	200			400		200	100	
Model 538		100	100		150		100	
Model 749			100			200		200

when orders for these materials should be released and be received or completed within the production cycle. Today's MRP systems use a computer program to carry out these operations. Most firms have used computerized inventory systems for years, but they were independent of the scheduling system; MRP links these two elements together.

Material requirements planning is not new in concept. Logic dictates that the Romans probably used it in their construction projects, the Venetians in their shipbuilding, and the Chinese in building the Great Wall. Building contractors have always been forced into planning for material to be delivered when needed and not before, because of space limitations. What is new is the larger scale and the more rapid changes that can be made through the use of computers. Now firms that produce many products involving thousands of parts and materials can take advantage of MRP.

Purposes, Objectives, and Philosophy of MRP

The main purposes of an MRP system are to control inventory levels, assign operating priorities to items, and plan capacity to load the production system. These may be briefly expanded as follows:

Inventory

Order the right part.
Order in the right quantity.
Order at the right time.

Priorities

Order with the right due date.
Keep the due date valid.

Capacity
Plan for a complete load.
Plan an accurate load.
Plan for an adequate time to view future load.

The *theme* of MRP is "getting the right materials to the right place at the right time."

The *objectives* of inventory management under an MRP system are to improve customer service, minimize inventory investment, and maximize production operating efficiency.

The *philosophy* of material requirements planning is that materials should be expedited (hurried) when their lack would delay the overall production schedule and de-expedited (delayed) when the schedule falls behind and postpones their need. Traditionally, and perhaps still typically, when an order is behind schedule, significant effort is spent trying to get it back on schedule. However, the opposite is not always true; when an order, for whatever reason, has its completion date delayed, the appropriate adjustments are not made in the schedule. This results in a one-sided effort—late orders are expedited, but early orders are not de-expedited or delayed. Aside from perhaps using scarce capacity, it is preferable not to have raw materials and work in process before they are actually needed, because inventories tie up capital, clutter up stockrooms, delay the introduction of design changes, and prevent the cancellation or delay of existing orders.

Benefits of an MRP System

Manufacturing companies with more than $10 million in annual sales are most likely to have a computerized MRP system. A computerized system is necessary because of the sheer volume of materials, supplies, and components that are part of expanding product lines, and the speed that firms need to react to constant changes in the system. In past years, when firms switched from existing manual or computerized systems to an MRP system, they realized many benefits, including:

- More competitive pricing.
- Lower selling price.
- Lower inventory levels.
- Improved customer service.
- Faster response to market demands.
- Increased flexibility to change the master schedule.
- Reduced setup and tear-down costs.
- Reduced idle time.

In addition, the MRP system:

- Gives advanced notice so managers can see the planned schedule before the orders are actually released.
- Tells when to de-expedite as well as expedite.
- Delays or cancels orders.

EXHIBIT 15.6

Overall View of the Inputs to a Standard Material Requirements Planning Program and the Reports Generated by the Program

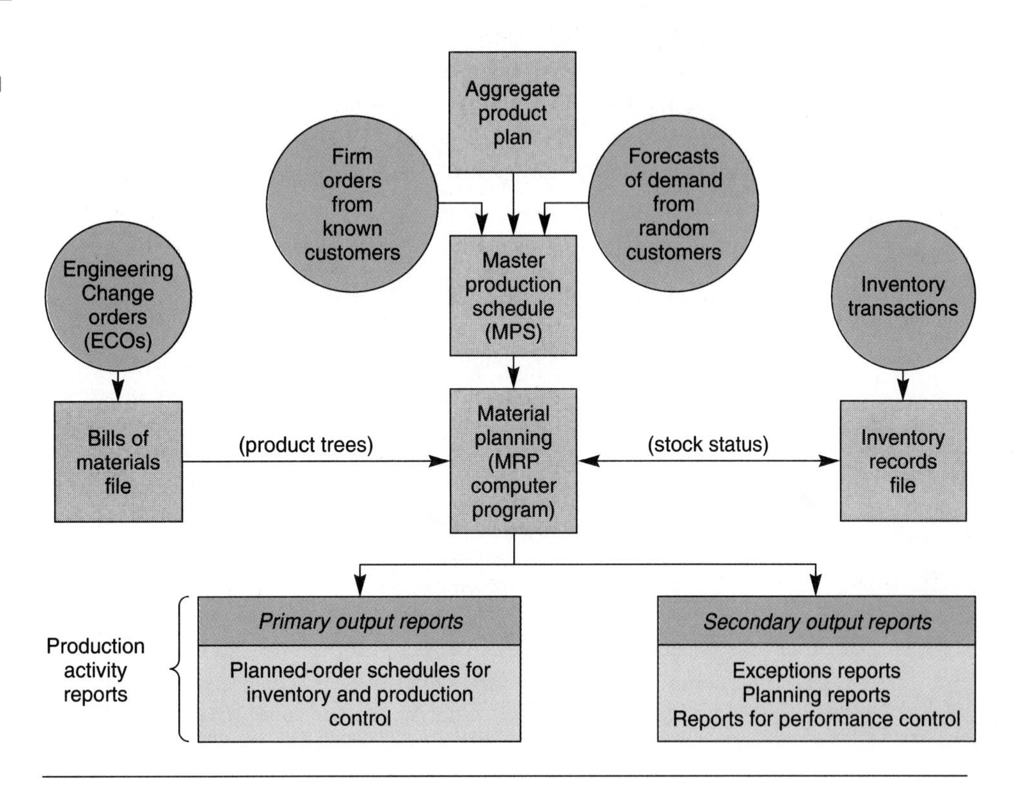

- Changes order quantities.
- Advances or delays order due dates.
- Aids capacity planning.

In converting to an MRP system, many firms claimed as much as 40 percent reductions in inventory investment.

15.4 MRP SYSTEM STRUCTURE

The MRP portion most closely interacts with the MPS schedule, the bills of materials file, the inventory records file, and the output reports. Exhibit 15.6 shows a portion of Exhibit 13.1 in Chapter 13 with several additions. Note that capacity is not addressed here, nor are there any feedback loops to higher levels. We discuss these elements later in this chapter under MRP II and capacity requirements planning.

Each facet of Exhibit 15.6 is subsequently explained in more detail, but essentially the MRP system works as follows: Forecasted sales and firm orders for products are used to create an MPS, which states the number of items to be produced during specific time periods. A bills of materials file identifies the specific materials used to make each item and the correct quantities of each. The inventory records file contains data such as the number of units on hand and on order. These three sources—(1) the MPS, (2) the bills of materials file, and (3) the inventory records file—become the data sources for the MRP program, which essentially expands or "explodes" the MPS into a detailed order scheduling plan for the entire production sequence.

Demand for Products

As stated above, product demand for end items stems primarily from two sources: The first is known customers who have placed specific orders, such as those generated by sales personnel, or from interdependent transactions. These orders usually carry promised delivery dates. There is no forecasting involved in these orders—simply add them up. The second source is forecasted demand. These are the normal independent-demand orders; the forecasting models presented in Chapter 7 can be used to predict the quantities. The demand from the known customers and the forecast demand are combined to become the input for developing the MPS.

Demand for spare parts and supplies

In addition to the demand for end products, customers also order specific parts and components as spares to provide for service and repair. These demands for items less complex than the end product are not usually part of the MPS; instead, they are fed directly into the MRP program at their appropriate levels. That is, they are added in as a gross requirement for that part or component.

Bills of Material File

The **bills of materials (BOM)** file contains the complete product description, listing not only the materials, parts, and components but also the sequences in which the product is created. This BOM file is one of the three main inputs into the MRP program (the other two are the MPS and the inventory records file).

The BOM file is often called the *product structure file* or *product tree* because it shows how a product is put together. It contains the information necessary to identify each item and the quantity used per unit of the item in which it is used. To illustrate this, consider the product tree for Product A, as shown in Exhibit 15.7. Product A is made of two units of Part B and three units of Part C. Part B is made of one unit of Part D and four units of Part E. Part C is made of two units of Part F, five units of Part G, and four units of Part H. In the past, BOM files have often listed parts as an indented file. This clearly identifies each item and the manner in which it is assembled because each indentation signifies the components of the item. A comparison of the indented parts in Exhibit 15.8 with the item structure in Exhibit 15.7 shows the ease of relating the two displays. From a computer standpoint, however, storing items in indented parts lists is very inefficient. To compute the amount of each item needed at the lower levels, each item would need to be expanded ("exploded") and summed. A more efficient procedure is to store parts data in a

EXHIBIT 15.7

Product Structure Tree for Product A

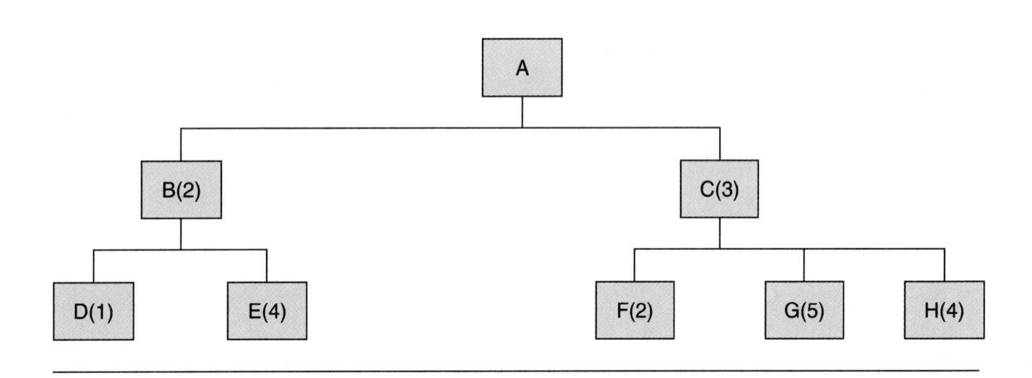

EXHIBIT 15.8

Parts List in an Indented Format and in a Single-Level List

Indented Parts List			Single-Level Parts List	
A			A	
	B(2)			B(2)
		D(1)		C(3)
		E(4)	B	
	C(3)			D(1)
		F(2)		E(4)
		G(5)	C	
		H(4)		F(2)
				G(5)
				H(4)

single-level explosion. That is, each item and component is listed showing only its parent and the number of units needed per unit of its parent. This avoids duplication because it includes each assembly only once. Exhibit 15.8 shows a comparison between the single-level parts list and the indented parts for Product A.

A data element (called a *pointer* or *locator*) is also contained in each file to identify the parent of each part and allow a retracing upward through the process.

A *modular* BOM is the term for a buildable item that can be produced and stocked as a subassembly. It is also a standard item with no options within the module. Many end items that are large and expensive are better scheduled and controlled as modules (or subassemblies). It is particularly advantageous to schedule subassembly modules when the same subassemblies appear in different end items. For example, a manufacturer of cranes can combine booms, transmissions, and engines in a variety of ways to meet a customer's needs. Using a modular BOM simplifies the scheduling and control and also makes it easier to forecast the use of different modules. Another benefit in using modular BOMs is that if the same item is used in a number of products, then the total inventory investment can be minimized.

EXHIBIT 15.9 Product L Hierarchy in (a) Expanded to the Lowest Level of Each Item in (b)

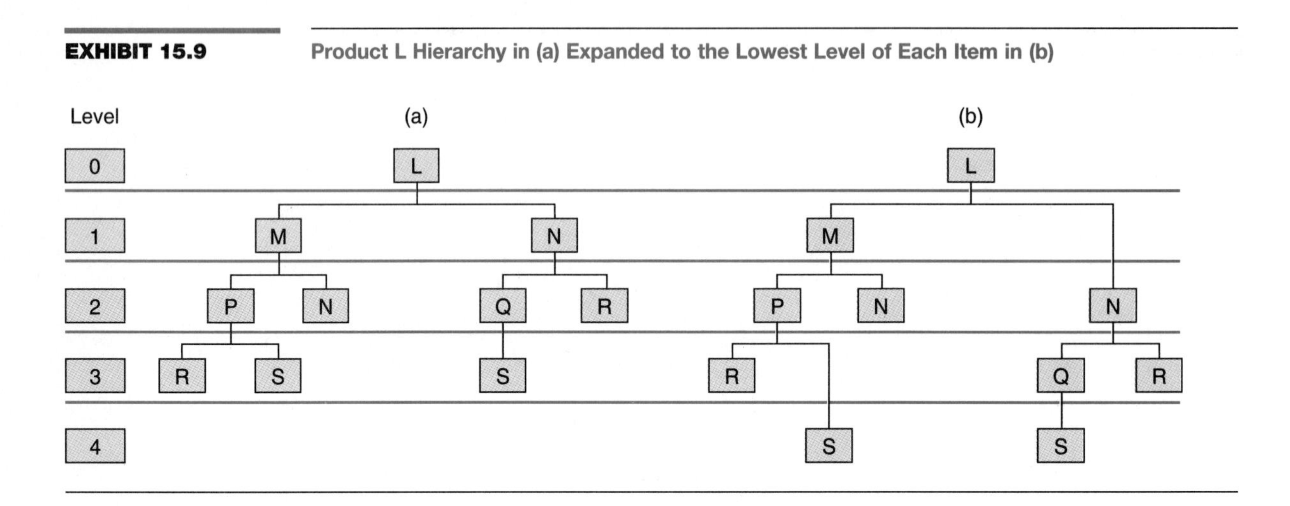

A *planning* bill of materials includes items with fractional options. (A planning bill can specify, for example, 0.3 of a part. What this means is that 30 percent of the units produced contain that part and 70 percent do not.)

Low-level coding

If all identical parts occur at the same level for each end product, the total number of parts and materials needed for a product can be computed easily. Consider Product L shown in Exhibit 15.9a. Notice that Item N, for example, occurs both as an input to L and as an input to M. Item N therefore needs to be lowered to level 2 (Exhibit 15.9b) to bring all Ns down to the lowest level. This is referred to as *low-level coding*. When all identical items are placed at the same level, it becomes a simple matter for the computer to scan across each level and summarize the number of units of each item required.

Inventory Records File

The **inventory records file** in a computerized system can be quite lengthy. Each item in inventory is carried as a separate file and the range of details carried about an item is almost limitless. Although Exhibit 15.10 is from an earlier version of MRP, it shows the variety of information contained in the inventory records files. The MRP program accesses the *status* segment of the file according to specific time periods (called *time buckets* in MRP slang). These files are accessed as needed during the program run.

The MRP program performs its analysis from the top of the product structure downward, exploding requirements level by level. There are times, however, when it is desirable to identify the parent item that caused the material requirement. The MRP program allows the creation of a *peg record* file either separately or as part of the inventory record file. Pegging requirements allows us to retrace a material requirement upward in

EXHIBIT 15.10

The Inventory Status Record for an Item in Inventory

Item master data segment					
	Part No.	Description	Lead time	Std. cost	Safety stock
	Order quantity	Setup	Cycle	Last year's usage	Class
	Scrap allowance	Cutting data	Pointers	Etc.	

Inventory status segment			Period								
	Allocated	Control balance	1	2	3	4	5	6	7	8	Totals
	Gross requirements										
	Scheduled receipts										
	On hand										
	Planned-order releases										

Subsidiary data segment		
	Order details	
	Pending action	
	Counters	
	Keeping track	

the product structure through each level, identifying each parent item that created the demand.

Inventory transactions file

The inventory status file is kept up to date by posting inventory transactions as they occur. These changes are a result of stock receipts and disbursements, scrap and obsolescence losses, wrong parts, canceled orders, and so forth.

MRP Computer Program

The MRP program operates on the inventory file, the MPS, and the BOM file. It works in this way: A list of end items needed by time periods (or time "buckets") is specified by the MPS. A description of the materials and parts needed to make each item is specified in the BOM file. The number of units of each item and material currently on hand and on order are contained in the inventory file. The MRP program "works" on the inventory file (which is segmented into time periods) while continually referring to the BOM file to compute the quantities of each item needed. The number of units of each item required is then corrected for on-hand amounts, and the net requirement is "offset" (set back in time) to allow for the lead time needed to obtain the material.

(One obstacle that many potential users of MRP have found is that their current BOM files and inventory records files are not adequate to provide data in the format required by the MRP program. Thus, they must modify these files before installing an MRP system.)

If the MRP program being used does not consider capacity constraints, the master scheduler must manually perform some capacity balancing. Through an iterative process, the master scheduler feeds a tentative MPS into the MRP program (along with other items requiring the same resources) and the output is examined for production feasibility. The MPS is then adjusted to try to correct any imbalances, and the program is executed again. This process is repeated until the output is acceptable. Although it would seem to be a simple matter to have the computer simulate some schedules that consider resource limitations, in reality it is a very large and very time-consuming problem for the computer.

To further complicate the problem today, there is often not one MPS but a number of them. Firms will frequently divide the scheduling work among the schedulers by assigning one master scheduler for each major product line. The result of this is competition in that each master scheduler must compete for limited resources for his or her own product line. As a group, however, they are trying to balance resource usage and due dates for the production system as a whole.

Output Reports

Because the MRP program has access to the BOM file, the MPS, and the inventory records file, outputs or reports can take on an almost unlimited range of format and content. These reports are usually classified as *primary* and *secondary* output reports. (With the expansion of MRP into MRP II, many additional reports are available.)

Primary reports

Primary reports are the main or normal reports used for inventory and production control. These reports include:

1. *Planned orders* to be released at a future time.
2. *Order release notices* to execute the planned orders.
3. *Changes in due dates* of open orders due to rescheduling.
4. *Cancellations or suspensions* of open orders due to cancellation or suspension of orders on the MPS.
5. *Inventory status data.*

Secondary reports

Additional reports, which are optional in an MRP program, fall into the following main categories:

1. *Planning reports* to be used, for example, in forecasting inventory and specifying requirements over some future time horizon.
2. *Performance reports* for purposes of pointing out inactive items and determining the

agreement between actual and programmed item lead times and between actual and programmed quantity usage and costs.

3. *Exceptions reports* that point out serious discrepancies, such as errors, out-of-range situations, late or overdue orders, excessive scrap, or nonexistent parts.

15.5 AN EXAMPLE USING MRP

Ampere, Inc., produces a line of electric meters installed in residential buildings by electric utility companies to measure power consumption. Meters used on single-family homes are of two basic types for different voltage and amperage ranges. In addition, to complete the meters some parts and subassemblies are sold separately for repair or for changeovers to a different voltage or power load. The problem for the MRP program is to determine a production schedule that would identify each item, the period it is needed, and the appropriate quantities. This schedule is then checked for feasibility, and the schedule is modified as is necessary.

Forecasting Demand

Demand for the meters and components originates from two sources: regular customers that place firm orders, and unidentified customers that make the normal random demands for these items. The random requirements were forecasted using one of the forecasting techniques described in Chapter 7 and past demand data. Exhibit 15.11 shows the requirement for Meters A and B, Subassembly D, and Part E for a six-month period.

Developing a Master Production Schedule

Our schedule assumes that *all* items are to be available the first week of the month. This assumption is reasonable because management in our example prefers to produce meters in one single lot each month rather than a number of lots throughout the month.

Exhibit 15.12 shows the trial master schedule that we use under these conditions, with

EXHIBIT 15.11

Future Order Requirements for Meters A and B, Subassembly D, and Part E Stemming from Specific Customer Orders and from Random Sources

	FUTURE ORDER REQUIREMENTS							
	METER A		METER B		SUBASSEMBLY D		PART E	
Month	Firm	Forecasted	Firm	Forecasted	Firm	Forecasted	Firm	Forecasted
3	1,000	250	400	60	200	70	300	80
4	600	250	300	60	180	70	350	80
5	300	250	500	60	250	70	300	80
6	700	250	400	60	200	70	250	80
7	600	250	300	60	150	70	200	80
8	700	250	700	60	160	70	200	80

EXHIBIT 15.12

A Master Schedule to Satisfy Demand Requirements as Specified in Exhibit 15.11

	WEEK								
	9	10	11	12	13	14	15	16	17
Meter A	1,250				850				550
Meter B	460				360				560
Subassembly D	270				250				320
Part E	380				430				380

EXHIBIT 15.13

Product Structures for Meters A and B

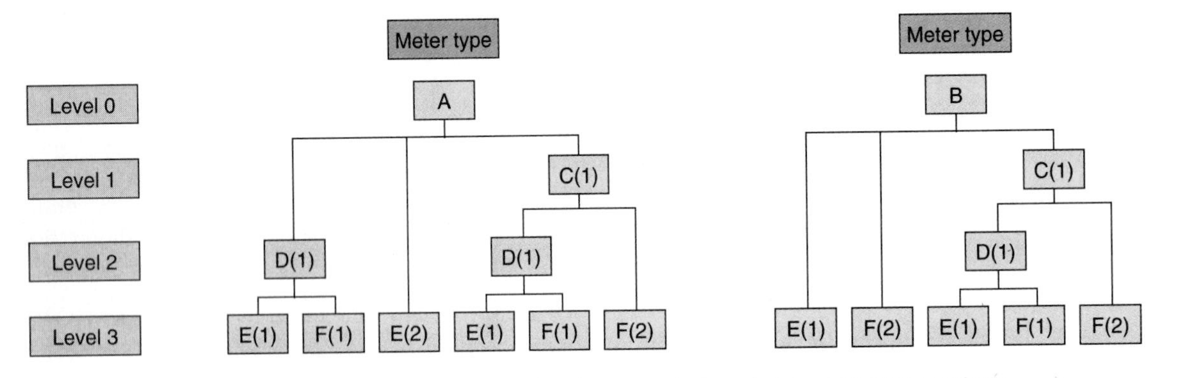

Exhibit shows the subassemblies and parts that make up the meters and shows the numbers of units required per unit of parent in parentheses.

the demands for months 3 and 4 showing up in the first week of each of those months, or as weeks 9 and 13 on the schedule. For brevity, we will work only with these two demand periods. The schedule we develop should be examined for resource availability, capacity availability, etc., and then revised and run again, if necessary. We will stop with our example at the end of this one schedule, however.

Bills of Materials (Product Structure) File

The product structures for Meters A and B are shown in Exhibit 15.13 in the typical way using low-level coding, in which each item is placed at the lowest level at which it appears in the structure hierarchy. Meters A and B consist of two subassemblies, C and D, and two parts, E and F. Quantities in parentheses indicate the number of units required per unit of the parent item. For example, two part Fs are required to build each subassembly C.

Exhibit 15.14 shows an indented parts list for the structure of Meters A and B. As

EXHIBIT 15.14

Indented Parts List for Meter A and Meter B, with the Required Number of Items per Unit of Parent Listed in Parentheses

Meter A				Meter B			
A				B			
	D(1)				E(1)		
		E(1)			F(2)		
		F(1)			C(1)		
	E(2)					D(1)	
	C(1)						E(1)
		D(1)					F(1)
			E(1)			F(2)	
			F(1)				
		F(2)					

EXHIBIT 15.15

Number of Units on Hand and Lead Time Data that Would Appear on the Inventory Record File

Item	On-Hand Inventory	Lead Time (weeks)
A	50	2
B	60	2
C	40	1
D	30	1
E	30	1
F	40	1

mentioned earlier in the chapter, the BOM file carries all items without indentation for computational ease, but the indented printout clearly shows the manner of product assembly.

Inventory Records (Item Master) File

The inventory records file would be similar to the one that was shown in Exhibit 15.10. The differences, as we saw earlier in this chapter, are that the inventory records file also contains additional data, such as vendor identity, cost, and lead times. For this example, the pertinent data contained in the inventory records file are the on-hand inventory for each product, subassembly, and part at the start of the program run and their respective lead times. This information is shown in Exhibit 15.15.

Running the MRP Program

The correct conditions have now been established to run the MRP computer program—end-item requirements have been provided through the MPS, the status of inventory and the order lead times are contained in the inventory item master file, and the BOM file contains the product structure data. The MRP program now explodes the item requirements according to the BOM file, level by level, in conjunction with the inventory

EXHIBIT 15.16 **Material Requirements Planning Schedule for Meters A and B, Subassemblies C and D, and Parts E and F**

Item		Week					
		4	5	6	7	8	9
A	Gross requirements						1,250
	On hand 50						50
	Net requirements						1,200
(LT = 2)	Planned-order receipt						1,200
	Planned-order release				1,200		
B	Gross requirements						460
	On hand 60						60
	Net requirements						400
(LT = 2)	Planned-order receipt						400
	Planned-order release				400		
C	Gross requirements				400 1,200		
	On hand 40				40		
	Net requirements				1,560		
(LT = 1)	Planned-order receipt				1,560		
	Planned-order release			1,560			
D	Gross requirements			1,560	1,200		270
	On hand 30			30	0		0
	Net requirements			1,530	1,200		270
(LT = 1)	Planned-order receipt			1,530	1,200		270
	Planned-order release		1,530	1,200		270	
E	Gross requirements		1,530	1,200	2,400 400	270	380
	On hand 30		30	0	0	0	0
	Net requirements		1,500	1,200	2,800	270	380
(LT = 1)	Planned-order receipt		1,500	1,200	2,800	270	380
	Planned-order release	1,500	1,200	2,800	270	380	
F	Gross requirements		1,530	3,120 1,200	800	270	
	On hand 40		40	0	0	0	
	Net requirements		1,490	4,320	800	270	
(LT = 1)	Planned-order receipt		1,490	4,320	800	270	
	Planned-order release	1,490	4,320	800	270		

records file. A release date for the net requirements order is offset to an earlier time period to adjust for the lead time. Orders for parts and subassemblies are added directly through the inventory file, bypassing the MPS, which ordinarily does not schedule at a low enough level to include spare parts.

Exhibit 15.16 shows the planned order release dates for this particular run. The following analysis explains the program logic. (We confine our analysis to the problem of meeting the gross requirements for 1,250 units of Meter A, 460 units of Meter B, 270 units of Subassembly D and 380 units of Part E, all in Week 9.)

The 50 units of Meter A on hand result in a net requirement of 1,200 units of A. To receive Meter A in Week 9, the order must be placed in Week 7 to account for the two-week lead time. The same procedure follows for Meter B, resulting in a planned 400-unit order released in Period 7.

The rationale for these steps is that for an item to be released for processing, all of its components must be available. The planned order release date for the parent item therefore is identical to the gross requirement period for the subitems.

Referring to Exhibit 15.13, level 1, one unit of C is required for each Meter A and each Meter B. Therefore, the gross requirements for C in Week 7 are 1,600 units (1,200 for A and 400 for B). Taking into account the 40 units on hand and the one-week lead time, 1,560 units of C must be ordered in Week 6. (This method of determining lot sizes is referred to as lot-for-lot and is described in greater detail later in the chapter.)

Level 2 of Exhibit 15.13 shows that one unit of D is required for each A and each C. The 1,200 units of D required for A are gross requirements in Week 7, and the 1,560 units of D for item C are the gross requirements for Week 6. Using the on-hand inventory first and the one-week lead time results in the planned order releases for 1,530 units in Week 5 and 1,200 units in Week 6.

Level 3 contains Items E and F. Because E and F are each used in several places, Exhibit 15.17 is presented to identify more clearly the parent item, the number of units required for each parent item, and the week in which it is required. Two units of Item E are used in each Item A. The 1,200-unit planned order release for A in Period 7 becomes the gross requirement for 2,400 units of E in the same period. One unit of E is used in each B, so the planned order release for 400 units of B in Period 7 becomes the gross requirement for 400 units of E in Week 7. Item E is also used in Item D at the rate of one per unit. The 1,530-unit planned order release for D in Period 5 becomes the gross requirement for 1,530 units of E in Period 5 and a 1,500-unit planned order release in Period 4 after accounting for the 30 units on hand and the one-week lead time. The 1,200-unit planned order release for D in Period 6 results in gross requirements for 1,200 units of E in Week 6 and a planned order release for 1,200 units in Week 5.

Item F is used in B, C, and D. The planned order releases for B, C, and D become the gross requirements for F for the same week, except that the planned order release for 400 units of B and 1,560 of C become gross requirements for 800 and 3,120 units of F, since the usage rate is two per unit.

The independent order for 270 units of subassembly D in Week 9 is handled as an input to D's gross requirements for that week. This is then exploded into the derived requirements for 270 units of E and F. The 380-unit requirement for Part E to meet an independent repair part demand is fed directly into the gross requirements for Part E.

The bottom line of each item in Exhibit 15.16 is taken as a proposed load on the production system. The final production schedule is developed manually or with the firm's computerized production package. If the schedule is infeasible or the loading unacceptable, the MPS is revised and the MRP package is run again with the new master schedule.

EXHIBIT 15.17

The Identification of the Parent of Items C, D, E, and F and Item Gross Requirements Stated by Specific Weeks

Item	Parent	Number of Units per Parent	Resultant Gross Requirement	Gross Requirement Week
C	A	1	1,200	7
C	B	1	400	7
D	A	1	1,200	7
D	C	1	1,560	6
E	A	2	2,400	7
E	B	1	400	7
E	D	1	1,530	5
E	D	1	1,200	6
F	B	2	800	7
F	C	2	3,120	6
F	D	1	1,200	6
F	D	1	1,530	5

EXHIBIT 15.18

Industry Applications and Expected Benefits

Industry Type	Examples	Expected Benefits
Assemble-to-stock	Combines multiple component parts into a finished product, which is then stocked in inventory to satisfy customer demand. Examples: Watches, tools, appliances.	High
Fabricate-to-stock	Items are manufactured by machine rather than assembled from parts. These are standard stock items carried in anticipation of customer demand. Examples: Piston rings, electrical switches.	Low
Assemble-to-order	A final assembly is made from standard options which the customer chooses: Examples: Trucks, generators, motors.	High
Fabricate-to-order	Items manufactured by machine to customer order. These are generally industrial orders. Examples: Bearings, gears, fasteners.	Low
Manufacture-to-order	Items fabricated or assembled completely to customer specification. Examples: Turbine generators, heavy machine tools.	High
Process	Industries, such as foundries, rubber and plastics, specialty paper, chemicals, paint, drug, food processors.	Medium

Where MRP Can Be Used

MRP is being used in a variety of industries with a job-shop environment (meaning that a number of products are made in batches using the same production equipment). The list in Exhibit 15.18 includes process industries, but note that the processes mentioned are confined to job runs that alternate output products and do not include continuous processes such as petroleum or steel.

As you can see in the exhibit, MRP is most valuable to companies involved in assembly operations and least valuable to those in fabrication. Another factor that affects the degree of benefit gained from an MRP system is the number of levels in the product. The greater the number of levels, the greater the benefit of MRP.

One more point to note: MRP does not work well in companies that produce a low number of units annually. This is especially true for companies producing complex expensive products requiring advanced research and design. Under such circumstances, experience has shown that lead times tend to be too long and too uncertain, and the product configuration too complex for MRP to handle. These types of companies need the control features that network scheduling techniques offer, and thus would be better off using project scheduling methods (covered previously in Chapter 12).

15.6 CAPACITY REQUIREMENTS PLANNING (CRP)

In the sections of this chapter that focused on the MPS and running the MRP program, we mentioned that production capacity is usually some finite amount and obviously has limits. We also cited the interaction between the scheduler and rerunning the MRP program to obtain feasible schedules in light of this limited capacity. In this section we explicitly point out how capacity is computed and what the usual procedure is for addressing capacity constraints.

Computing Work Center Load

In computing capacity requirements, the place to begin is with the routing sheets for the jobs scheduled to be processed. Exhibit 4.15 in Chapter 4 shows the routing sheet for a plug assembly. Note that the routing sheet specifies where a job is to be sent, the particular operations involved, and the standard setup time and run time per piece. These are the types of data used to compute the total amount of work to be done at each work center.

While the routing sheet is a "job view" that follows a particular job around the factory floor, a work center file is the view seen from a work center. Routing sheets send each job to the appropriate work centers for some sort of processing. Each work center is generally a functionally defined center where jobs routed to it require the same type of work, and on the same equipment. From the work center view, if there is adequate capacity, the problem is one of priorities: which job to do first. (We discuss priority scheduling rules in Chapter 17). If there is insufficient capacity, however, the problem must be resolved by the master scheduler.

Exhibit 15.19 shows a work center that has various jobs assigned to it. Note that the capacity per week was computed at the bottom of the exhibit at 161.5 hours. The jobs scheduled for the three weeks result in two weeks planned with under work capacity, and one week with over capacity.

Exhibit 15.19 uses the terms *utilization* and *efficiency*. Both of these terms have been

EXHIBIT 15.19

Workload for Work Center A

Week	Job No.	Units	Setup Time	Run Time per Unit	Total Job Time	Total for Week
10	145	100	3.5	.23	26.5	
	167	160	2.4	.26	44.0	
	158	70	1.2	.13	10.3	
	193	300	6.0	.17	57.0	137.8
11	132	80	5.0	.36	33.8	
	126	150	3.0	.22	36.0	
	180	180	2.5	.30	56.5	
	178	120	4.0	.50	64.0	190.3
12	147	90	3.0	.18	19.2	
	156	200	3.5	.14	31.5	
	198	250	1.5	.16	41.5	
	172	100	2.0	.12	14.0	
	139	120	2.2	.17	22.6	128.8

Computing Work Center Capacity

The available capacity in standard hours is 161.5 hours per five-day week, calculated as: (2 machines) (2 shifts) (10 hours/shift) (85% machine utilization) (95% efficiency).

EXHIBIT 15.20

Scheduled Workload for Work Center A

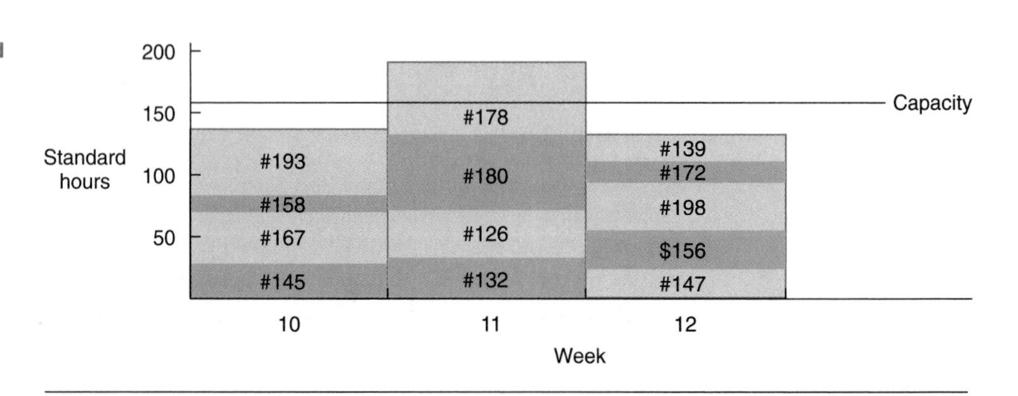

defined and used in a variety of ways, some conflicting. In this exhibit, utilization refers to the actual time that the machines are used. *Efficiency* refers to how well the machine is performing while it is being used. Efficiency is usually defined as a comparison to a defined standard output or an engineering design rate. For instance, a machine used for six hours of an eight-hour shift was utilized $^6/_8$ or 75 percent. If the standard output for that machine is established at 200 parts per hour and an average of 250 parts per hour were made, then efficiency is 125 percent. Note that in these definitions efficiency can be more than 100 percent, but utilization cannot be.

Exhibit 15.20 shows a loading representation of Work Center A for the three weeks. The scheduled work exceeds capacity for Week 11. There are several options available:

1. Work overtime.
2. Select an alternate work center that could perform the task.
3. Subcontract to an outside shop.
4. Try to schedule part of the work of Week 11 earlier into Week 10, and delay part of the work into Week 12.
5. Renegotiate the due date and reschedule.

An MRP program with a capacity requirements planning module allows rescheduling to try to level capacity. Two techniques used are backward scheduling and forward scheduling—the fourth option on the preceding list. The objective of the master scheduler is to try to level out the load at Exhibit 15.20 so that the requirements for the work center remain within the available capacity.

15.7 MANUFACTURING RESOURCE PLANNING (MRP II)

Earlier in this chapter, our discussion of MRP focused only on the *material* requirements that resulted from an explosion of the master schedule. We did not include the needs of all the other types of resources, such as staffing, facilities, and tools. In addition, while we discussed *capacity requirements planning,* we did this somewhat externally to the MRP system. In this section we discuss the logic of more advanced versions of MRP that include a wider range of resources and outputs.

MRP II

An expansion of the materials requirements planning program to include other portions of the production system was natural and to be expected. One of the first to be included was the purchasing function. At the same time, there was a more detailed inclusion of the production system itself—on the shop floor, in dispatching, and in the detailed scheduling control. MRP had already included work center capacity limitations, so it was obvious the name *material requirements planning* no longer adequately described the expanded system. Someone (probably Ollie Wight) introduced the name **manufacturing resource planning (MRP II)** to reflect the idea that more and more of the firm was becoming involved in the program. To quote Wight,

> The fundamental manufacturing equation is:
> What are we going to make?
> What does it take to make it?
> What do we have?
> What do we have to get?[1]

---

[1] Oliver Wight, *The Executive's Guide to Successful MRP II* (Williston, Vt.: Oliver Wight Limited Publications, 1982), pp. 6, 17.

The initial intent for MRP II was to plan and monitor all the resources of a manufacturing firm—manufacturing, marketing, finance, and engineering—through a closed-loop system generating financial figures. The second important intent of the MRP II concept was that it stimulate the manufacturing system. It is generally conceived now as being a total, companywide system that allows everyone (buyers, marketing staff, production, accounting) to work with the same game plan, use the same numbers, and is capable of simulation to plan and test alternative strategies.

Cost of an MRP II System

Several software companies regularly advertise MRP systems in manufacturing-oriented journals, as well as in widely read publications such as *The Wall Street Journal*. Prices go as low as $500 and as high as $300,000 because MRP II systems can vary widely in the types of modules and capabilities that are included.

Costs for the computer hardware also have a wide range. An MRP program for a very small company can be run on a microcomputer with hard disk drives. However, most MRP II systems are run on minicomputers or mainframes because of the very large data storage requirements and the number of program modules involved. Lease costs may range from $30,000 to $500,000 per year; however, technology is changing rapidly, with a consequent drop in cost. In terms of additional personnel needed, the experiences of many companies indicate that the overall net change in personnel is close to zero. Companies simply switch people from existing areas into MRP system roles.

The typical MRP II system takes about 18 months to install. However, this can vary widely depending on the size of the application, the condition of the existing databases and how much they may have to be revised, the quality of the bills of materials, routing sheets and inventory records, and the amount of personnel training required. Another factor is whether the firm has been using an MRP system and is switching to an MRP II system. The entire range of time can vary from as little as several months to as much as three years.

Payback for an MRP installation can be quite short. When larger companies first installed MRP systems some years ago, they realized an average annual return on investment of about 300 percent.[2]

When we think of MRP II, we tend to think of large computer programs with applications confined to business giants. In fact, however, MRP II is also economically feasible for manufacturing companies with annual sales of less than $1 million. In addition, much of the current software is user-friendly and easy to operate.

Prices and quality of software vary widely and not necessarily in a direct relationship. Customer support is another very important factor. This is a buyer beware market, and care should be taken in selecting a program because it is a long-term commitment.

15.8 INTEGRATING JIT AND MRP

MRP and JIT each have benefits. The question is: Can they work together successfully, and how would one go about integrating them? As stated earlier in this chapter, most

[2] Ibid., pp. 34–35.

EXHIBIT 15.21

Comparing MRP and JIT Computer Programs

	MRP	JIT
Based on:	MPS, BOM, and inventory records	MPS, Kanban
Objective:	Plan and control	Eliminate waste, continuous improvement
Involvement process:	Passive—no efforts toward change	Active—tries to improve and change system, and to lower inventory
Data requirements:	Detailed and strict data accuracy	Much lower and tend to be visible
Operation:	Computerized	Simple, manual shop floor controls such as Kanban

major manufacturing firms use MRP. Of the firms using MRP, many in repetitive manufacturing are also implementing JIT techniques. Although JIT is best suited to repetitive manufacturing, MRP is used in everything from custom job shops to assembly-line production. Most firms that have successfully implemented MRP systems are not interested in discarding MRP to try JIT. A new challenge arises in integrating the shop floor improvement approaches of JIT with an MRP-based planning and control system. The MRP/JIT combination creates what might be considered a hybrid manufacturing system.

MRP is a very large computerized production planning system. Trying to add JIT to this system is very difficult. Some firms are trying to create add-on modules but at present there is no standard way. Part of the difficulty in trying to integrate both systems into a single computer program is caused by their different objectives and conflicting purposes, as shown in Exhibit 15.21.

Exhibit 15.22 shows an MPS with an MRP system on the left. MRP systems can help create the MPS. From that point on, it is all MRP systems. Scheduling resources such as inventory are continuously controlled and monitored.

The right side of Exhibit 15.22 shows an MPS at the top feeding a JIT system. Computer control has been severed and the JIT portion operates as its own separate pull method drawing from preceding stages. MRP may well be used to help create the MPS, but MRP's involvement stops there.

15.9 MISCELLANEOUS MRP ISSUES

Problems in Installing and Using MRP Systems

MRP is very well developed technically, and implementation of an MRP system should be pretty straightforward. Yet there are many problems with existing MRP systems and many "failures" in trying to install them. Why do such problems and outright failures occur with a "proven" system?

The answer partially lies with organizational and behavioral factors. Three major causes of failure have been identified: the lack of top management commitment, the failure to

EXHIBIT 15.22 **Controlling Production Processes with MRP Alone and MRP/JIT Combined**

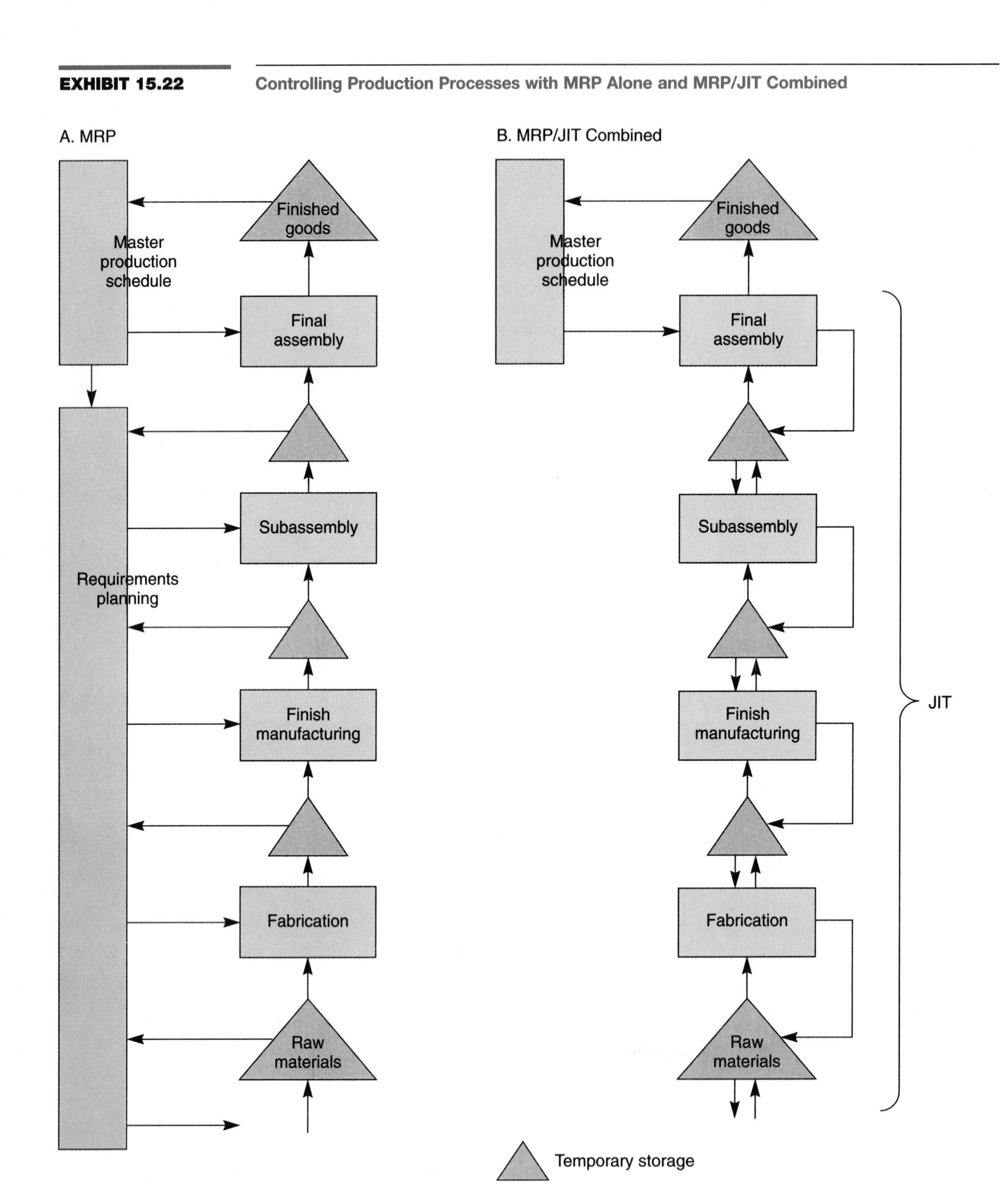

Source: S. D. P. Flapper, G. J. Miltenburg, and J. Wijngaard, "Embedding JIT into MRP," *International of Production Research* 29, no. 2 (1991), p. 335.

recognize that MRP is only a software tool that needs to be used correctly, and the ability to integrate MRP and JIT.

Part of the blame for the lack of top management's commitment may be MRP's image. It sounds like a manufacturing system rather than a business plan. However, an MRP system is used to plan resources and develop schedules. And a well-functioning schedule effectively uses the firm's assets with the result of increased profits. MRP should be presented to top management as a planning tool with specific reference to profit results. Intensive executive education is needed, emphasizing the importance of MRP as a closed-loop, integrated, strategic planning tool.

The second cause of the problem concerns the MRP advocates that overdid themselves in selling the concept. MRP was presented and perceived as a complete, stand-alone system to run a firm, rather than part of the total system. The third issue is how MRP can be made to function with JIT. JIT and MRP can live together, but there are few rules as to how they should be integrated. The system consists of the functional areas of engineering, marketing, personnel, and manufacturing, as well as techniques and concepts such as quality circles, CAD/CAM, and robotics. MRP needs to be *part* of the system, not *the* system.

In many meetings that we have attended, both professional and industrial, we have heard similar installation and operational problems. These problems distill down to the fact that the MRP system essentially runs the firm; its main objective is simply to meet the schedule. As a result, people become subservient to the MRP system. Even such simple decisions as determining a run-lot size cannot be made outside the system.

As it stands right now, MRP is a very formal system that requires strict adherence to its rules in order to function properly. Often supervisors and workers develop an informal system for getting the job done. Their argument is that this informal system arises because the existing formal system was too rigid or inadequate to deal with real inventory scheduling problems. In any event, it appears that employees at all levels must change—from the company president to the lower-level employees. Even though MRP currently does work in many installations, its good features and its shortcomings should be thoroughly understood.

Other problems encountered in using MRP include:

1. *The fallacy of static lead time.* MRP software programs treat lead time as a fixed number, while in reality lead time changes for a variety of reasons, such as normal variation in processing time, waiting for parts, delays in processing due to expedited jobs, breakdown or normal maintenance of machines, and so on.
2. *The misdefinition of lead time.* Manufacturing lead time consists of:
   a. Make-ready time—to write order, enter, prepare job packet, release order, and issue material.
   b. Queue time—time at the operation center waiting for operations to begin.
   c. Setup time—to prepare equipment for operations.
   d. Run time—to perform operations (produce product).
   e. Wait time—time waiting after operation ends.
   f. Move time—to physically move between operations.

3. *Lead time versus fabrication/production quantity.* MRP software, because it considers lead time fixed, does not account for the fact that run time (part of the lead time) varies depending on the quantity of units to be produced.
4. *Bills of materials.* MRP software programs use the bills of materials as a bottoms-up product structure representing the ways firms manufacture products. For many firms, however, especially those producing on an assembly line, products may be produced in a very different sequence than the engineering bills of materials.
5. *Material revision control.* Many MRP programs do not easily allow changes to be made to part numbers or in the way the product is produced.
6. *Lead time versus routing.* Since many MRP programs use the bills of materials structure to schedule the shop floor, poor schedules may result. For example, there may be several routing steps at the same bill of materials level, which require more time than allowed.
7. *Fallacy of infinite capacity planning.* Few MRP programs can recognize a shop overload and reschedule.
8. *The real story of rough-cut planning.* While rough-cut capacity planning was taught as the solution to overloaded work centers, in reality rough-cut capacity planning lies somewhere between the difficult and the impossible. In effect, master schedulers are expected to perform MRP and CRP explosions in their heads. Technically, the only way to really do rough-cut capacity planning is to run the MRP and CRP (capacity requirement plan) each time a change is made in the master schedule. The required computer time makes this impossible.
9. *Capacity planning versus MRP logic.* Because MRP and CRP are not run together when changes are made in the MPS, such changes often create "floating bottlenecks." Bottlenecks appear and disappear, depending on the master production schedule.
10. *MRP logic—a user confuser.* MRP logic differs from system to system. The user should test how the system reacts to, say, accelerating, decelerating, or canceling an order.[3]

Criticisms of the MRP Concept

In addition to the problems previously mentioned in installing and using an MRP system, there are other criticisms as well. Many critics state that MRP schedules are either impossible or are only true on the day that they were created. Too many changes take place in the system for MRP to be able to adjust to all of them.

Accuracy requirements

Because MRP uses detailed files to schedule, MRP cannot tolerate inaccuracies. In fact, for many years since MRP was introduced, companies have been rated into classes based on the accuracy of their records. Class A companies, for example, have more than

[3]Adapted from Gus Berger, "Ten Ways MRP Can Defeat You," *Conference Proceedings, American Production and Inventory Control Society* (1987), pp. 240–43.

99-percent accuracy. MRP's failures in its scheduling performance had been blamed on inaccurate records. Now we recognize that inaccuracy was not completely to blame; the MRP scheduling technique was also at fault.

Top management commitment

This is not so much a criticism of MRP, but of top management. As in the case of many programs, MRP needs to be endorsed and continually supported by top management. An MRP system is doomed to failure if management believes its responsibilities end with authorizing purchase of the program and turning over responsibility for running the computer system to the MIS group. Continuous reinforcement and encouragement are needed; everyone must be convinced that the system is worth its time and expense. It also means spending money on training, and perhaps changing the internal measurement and reward system. If this is not done, shop-floor personnel ignore MRP schedules and use their own priorities in doing job selection and in determining process batch sizes.

MRP as a database

Although MRP has been criticized for its questioned accuracy in providing workable schedules, MRP has been highly complemented for its detailed database. MRP's database extends throughout the entire facility and is linked through numerous modules. Even if a firm decides to discontinue using MRP to schedule its facilities, it would more than likely continue to maintain MRP files for their informational value.

Safety Stock

Ordinarily, adding a safety stock to required quantities is not advised in an MRP system that is based on derived demand. There is some feeling, however, that when the availability of parts could suffer from a long and inflexible lead time or is subject to strikes or cancellation, a safety stock offers some protection against production delays. A safety stock is sometimes intentionally created by planning for excess. One of the main arguments against using safety stock is that the MRP system considers it a fixed quantity, and the safety stock is never actually used.

Lot Sizing in MRP Systems

The determination of lot sizes in an MRP system is a complicated and difficult problem. Lot sizes are the part quantities issued in the planned order receipt and planned order release sections of an MRP schedule. For parts produced in house, lot sizes are the production quantities or batch sizes. For purchased parts, these are the quantities ordered from the supplier. Lot sizes generally meet part requirements for one or more periods.

Most lot-sizing techniques deal with how to balance the setup or order costs and holding costs associated with meeting the net requirements generated by the MRP planning process. Many MRP systems have options for computing lot sizes based on some of the more commonly used techniques. It should be obvious, though, that the use of

EXHIBIT 15.23

Lot-for-Lot Run Size for an MRP Schedule

Period	Net Requirements	Production Quantity	Ending Inventory	Holding Cost	Setup Cost	Total Cost
1	50	50	0	$0.00	$47.00	$ 47.00
2	60	60	0	0.00	47.00	94.00
3	70	70	0	0.00	47.00	141.00
4	60	60	0	0.00	47.00	188.00
5	95	95	0	0.00	47.00	235.00
6	75	75	0	0.00	47.00	282.00
7	60	60	0	0.00	47.00	329.00
8	55	55	0	0.00	47.00	376.00

lot-sizing techniques increases the complexity in generating MRP schedules. When fully exploded, the numbers of parts scheduled can be enormous.

Next, we explain four lot-sizing techniques using a common example. The lot-sizing techniques presented are lot-for-lot (L4L), economic order quantity (EOQ), least total cost (LTC), and least unit cost (LUC).

Consider the following MRP lot-sizing problems; the net requirements are shown for eight scheduling periods:

Cost per item	$10.00
Order or setup cost	$47.00
Inventory carry cost/period	0.5%

Period net requirements:

1	2	3	4	5	6	7	8
50	60	70	60	95	75	60	55

Lot-for-lot

Lot-for-lot (L4L) is the most common technique; it:

- Sets planned orders to exactly match the net requirements.
- Produces exactly what is needed each period with none carried over into future periods.
- Minimizes carrying cost.
- Does not take into account setup costs or capacity limitations.

Many times producing enough product to last several periods and incurring holding costs may be cheaper than producing in every period and incurring repeated setup costs. In the case of parts produced in house, the setup cost represents time that resources are not operating but getting ready to produce. This is lost capacity. Not only are setup costs higher but requiring setups in every period a part is needed also reduces the time available to produce other products.

Exhibit 15.23 shows the lot-for-lot calculations. In each period the lot size exactly

EXHIBIT 15.24

Economic Order Quantity Run Size for an MRP Schedule

Period	Net Requirements	Production Quantity	Ending Inventory	Holding Cost	Setup Cost	Total Cost
1	50	351	0	$15.05	$47.00	$ 62.05
2	60	0	241	12.05	0.00	74.10
3	70	0	171	8.55	0.00	82.65
4	60	0	111	5.55	0.00	88.20
5	95	0	16	0.80	0.00	89.00
6	75	351	292	14.60	47.00	150.60
7	60	0	232	11.60	0.00	162.20
8	55	0	177	8.85	0.00	171.05

EOQ assumptions:	
Total requirements	525
Average requirements	65.6
Annual holding cost per unit	$2.60
Annual demand	3,412.5
EOQ	351.25

matches the net requirements. A setup cost is charged for each period. The lot-for-lot technique, while minimizing holding costs, orders far too often because it places an order every time a net requirement occurs.

Economic order quantity

In Chapter 14 we already discussed the EOQ model that explicitly balances setup and holding costs. An inherent assumption in the EOQ model is that there is either fairly constant demand or that safety stock must be kept to accommodate any variability in demand. The EOQ model uses an estimate of total annual demand, the setup or order cost, and the annual holding cost. EOQ was not designed for a system with discrete time periods such as MRP. The lot-sizing techniques used for MRP assume that part requirements are satisfied at the start of the period. Holding costs are then charged only to the ending inventory for the period, not to the average inventory used in the EOQ model. EOQ assumes that parts are used on a continuous basis during the period. The lot sizes generated by EOQ do not always cover the entire number of periods. For example, the EOQ might provide the requirements for 4.6 periods.

Exhibit 15.24 shows the EOQ lot size calculated for this part. Several assumptions are made to determine the EOQ. EOQ requires an estimate of both annual demand and annual holding cost. Since the holding cost per period is $0.05 and the MRP schedule is weekly, the annual holding cost per unit is $2.60 ($0.05 × 52 weeks). Annual demand is computed by multiplying the average weekly demand for the eight periods by 52 weeks (525/8 × 52 = 3,412.5). The resulting EOQ is 351 units. The EOQ lot size in Period 1 is enough to meet requirements for Periods 1 through 5 and a portion of Period 6. Then, in Period 6 another EOQ lot is planned to meet the requirements for Periods 6 through 8. Notice that the EOQ plan leaves some inventory at the end of Period 8 to carry forward into Period 9.

EXHIBIT 15.25 **Least Total Cost Run Size for an MRP Schedule**

Period	Net Requirements	Production Quantity	Ending Inventory	Holding Cost	Setup Cost	Total Cost
1	50	335	285	$14.25	$47.00	$ 61.25
2	60	0	225	11.25	0.00	72.50
3	70	0	155	7.75	0.00	80.25
4	60	0	95	4.75	0.00	85.00
5	95	0	0	0.00	0.00	85.00
6	75	190	115	5.75	47.00	137.75
7	60	0	55	2.75	0.00	140.50
8	55	0	0	0.00	0.00	140.50

Periods	Quantity Ordered	Carrying Cost	Order Cost	Total Cost	
1	50	$ 0.00	$47.00	$ 47.00	
1–2	110	3.00	47.00	50.00	
1–3	180	10.00	47.00	57.00	
1–4	240	19.00	47.00	66.00	
1–5	335	38.00	47.00	85.00	← Least total cost
1–6	410	56.75	47.00	103.75	
1–7	470	74.75	47.00	121.75	
1–8	525	94.00	47.00	141.00	
6	75	0.00	47.00	47.00	
6–7	135	3.00	47.00	50.00	
6–8	190	8.50	47.00	55.50	← Least total cost

Least total cost

The least total cost method (LTC) is a dynamic lot-sizing technique that calculates the order quantity by comparing the carrying cost and the setup (or ordering) costs for various lot sizes and then selects the lot in which these are most nearly equal.

Exhibit 15.25 shows the least total cost lot size results. The procedure to compute least total cost lot sizes is to compare order costs and holding costs for various numbers of periods. For example, costs are compared for producing in Period 1 to cover the requirements for Period 1; producing in Period 1 for Periods 1 and 2; producing in Period 1 to cover Periods 1, 2, and 3, and so on. The correct selection is that lot size where the ordering costs and holding costs are approximately equal. In Exhibit 15.25 that lot size is 335, because the difference between a $38 carrying cost and a $47 ordering cost is closer than $56.25 and $47. This lot size covers requirements for Periods 1 through 5. Unlike EOQ, the lot size covers only whole numbers of periods.

Based on the Period 1 decision to place an order to cover 5 periods, we are now located in Period 6, and our problem is to determine how many periods into the future we can provide for from here. Exhibit 15.25 shows that holding and order costs are closest in the quantity that covers requirements for Periods 6 through 8. Notice that the holding and order costs here are far apart. This is because our example extends only to Period 8. If the planning horizon were longer, the lot size planned for Period 6 would likely cover more

EXHIBIT 15.26 Least Unit Cost Run Size for an MRP Schedule

Period	Net Requirements	Production Quantity	Ending Inventory	Holding Cost	Setup Cost	Total Cost
1	50	410	360	$18.00	$47.00	$ 65.00
2	60	0	300	15.00	0.00	80.00
3	70	0	230	11.50	0.00	91.50
4	60	0	170	8.50	0.00	100.00
5	95	0	75	3.75	0.00	103.75
6	75	115	115	5.75	47.00	156.50
7	60	0	55	2.75	0.00	159.25
8	55	55	55	2.75	47.00	209.00

Periods	Quantity Ordered	Carrying Cost	Order Cost	Total Cost	Unit Cost
1	50	$ 0.00	$47.00	$ 47.00	$0.9400
1–2	110	3.00	47.00	50.00	0.4545
1–3	180	10.00	47.00	57.00	0.3167
1–4	240	19.00	47.00	66.00	0.2750
1–5	335	38.00	47.00	85.00	0.2537
1–6	410	56.75	47.00	103.75	0.2530 ← Least unit cost
1–7	470	74.75	47.00	121.75	0.2590
1–8	525	94.00	47.00	141.00	0.2686
7	60	0.00	47.00	47.00	0.7833
7–8	115	2.75	47.00	49.75	0.4326 ← Least unit cost

periods into the future beyond Period 8. This brings up one of the limitations of both LTC and LUC (discussed below). Both techniques are influenced by the length of the planning horizon.

Least unit cost

The least unit cost method (LUC) is a dynamic lot-sizing technique that adds ordering and inventory carrying cost for each trial lot size and divides by the number of units in each lot size, picking the lot size with the lowest unit cost. In the example in Exhibit 15.26, the lot size of 410 covers Periods 1 through 6. The lot size planned for Period 7 covers through the end of the planning horizon.

Which lot size to choose

Using the lot-for-lot method, the total cost for the eight periods is $376; the EOQ total cost is $171.05; the least total cost method is $140.50; and the least unit cost is $209. The lowest cost was obtained using the least total cost method of $140.50. If there were more than eight periods, the lowest cost could differ.

The advantage of the least unit cost method is that it is a more complete analysis and would take into account ordering or setup costs that might change as the order size increases. If the ordering or setup costs remain constant, the lowest total cost method is more attractive because it is simpler and easier to compute; yet it would be just as accurate under that restriction.

15.10 INSTALLING AN MRP SYSTEM

The average time for a company to effectively install an MRP system seems to range from 18 to 24 months—not for the software, but because so much other preparation and training must take place. At the risk of being redundant, we repeat some cautions about installing an MRP system.

Preparation Steps

Bills of materials

The BOM lists all of the materials required to create a product in a hierarchical form, which is usually the way in which a product is produced. The BOM is an extremely important element in an MRP system and, as a consequence, inaccuracies here cannot be tolerated. Without an MRP or some such computer system, BOM accuracy is not critical and firms can live with some errors. A first step prior to installing an MRP system is to review the BOM for all products to ensure that they are correct.

Routing sheets and processing times

Similar to the BOM, many firms previously did not need to be specific about which machine or process should be used, since adjustments could always be made manually on the shop floor. The same goes for processing; with the usual longer times in the shop (as opposed to MRP installations) there are opportunities to make up discrepancies (in spite of the fact that the data for accounting purposes would be in error).

Inventory stock

Most firms have errors in their inventory records. Oftentimes it is because no one wants to take the time necessary to count and verify records and physical stock. Another reason is that often inventory stock is old or obsolete; bringing records up to date may mean that much inventory carried on company books as assets may have to be declared scrap. Few managers are willing to bite the bullet and do this. Reducing inventory impacts directly on the bottom line and quickly catches the attention of top management. However, installing an MRP system means that errors must be removed and the inventory carried must be of usable quality.

Procedures

In addition to the actual records previously mentioned, procedures and/or new software must be installed to keep these records up to date. Examples are adding stock to inventory when received from vendors, and making appropriate changes when issuing stock to production. Also, ways of handling changes to the bills of materials, routing, or processing times need to be decided.

Training

Everyone—from top management through to the purchasing staff, supervisors, and the workers on the shop floor—must be trained in the effective use of an MRP system—how to read its reports, which leeways are allowable in quantity or schedule variations, and what results can be expected. People, by nature, are reluctant to change. Throughout MRP's history of two decades, we have blamed people whenever poor performance occurred in their MRP system (lack of understanding, lack of top management support, lack of adequate discipline, etc.). While this is now recognized as a problem caused in large part by the MRP itself (noted elsewhere in this chapter), nevertheless without support of all involved, MRP would be doomed to failure.

15.11 CONCLUSION

Over the past two decades, MRP has grown from its initial purpose of determining simple time schedules to its present MRP II configuration, which ties together all major functions of an organization. During its growth and application, MRP's disadvantages as a scheduling mechanism have been well recognized. This is largely because MRP tries to do too much in light of the very dynamic and often "nervous" operating environment in which it is trying to operate.

MRP is recognized, however, for its excellent databases and linkages within the firm. MRP also does a good job in helping to produce master schedules. Because of its databases and the existence of an MPS, many firms in repetitive manufacturing are integrating JIT systems with their existing MRP systems. JIT takes the MPS as its pulling force and does not use MRP's generated schedule. Initial results indicate that this is working. To use this JIT/MRP combination, firms need not be solely in repetitive manufacturing. Portions of almost every job shop have repetitive functions. JIT can prove to be of significant benefit in these hybrid situations as well.

MRP's service applications have not fared well, even though it seems that they should have. The MRP approach would appear very valuable in producing services because service scheduling consists of identifying the final service and then tracing back to the resources needed to provide it, such as equipment, space, and personnel. Consider, for example a hospital operating room planning an open-heart surgery. The master schedule can establish a time for the surgery (or surgeries, if several are scheduled). The BOM could specify all required equipment and personnel—MDs, nurses, anesthesiologist, operating room, heart/lung machine, defibrillator, and so forth. The inventory status file would show the availability of the resources and commit them to the project. The MRP program could then produce a schedule showing when various parts of the operation are to be started, expected completion times, required materials, and so forth. Checking this schedule would allow "capacity planning" in answering such questions as: "Are all the materials and personnel available?" and "Does the system produce a feasible schedule?"

We still believe that MRP systems will eventually find their way into service applications.

15.12 REVIEW AND DISCUSSION QUESTIONS

1. Because MRP appears so reasonable, discuss reasons why it did not become popular until recently.
2. Discuss the meaning of MRP terms such as *planned order release* and *scheduled order receipts*.
3. Most practitioners currently update MRP weekly or biweekly. Would it be more valuable if it were updated daily? Discuss.
4. What is the role of safety stock in an MRP system?
5. Contrast the significance of the term *lead time* in the traditional EOQ context and in an MRP system.
6. Discuss the importance of the MPS in an MRP system.
7. MRP systems are difficult to install. Identify the various problems that can occur with the system requirements (ignore behavioral problems).
8. "MRP just prepares shopping lists—it doesn't do the shopping or cook the dinner." Comment.
9. What are the sources of demand in an MRP system? Are these dependent or independent, and how are they used as inputs to the system?
10. State the types of data that would be carried in the bills of materials file and the inventory record file.
11. How does MRP II differ from MRP?

15.13 SOLVED PROBLEMS

PROBLEM

1. Product X is made of two units of Y and three of Z. Y is made of one unit of A and two units of B. Z is made of two units of A and four units of C.

   Lead time for X is one week; Y, two weeks; Z, three weeks; A, two weeks; B, one week; and C, three weeks.

   a. Draw the product structure tree.

   b. If 100 units of X are needed in week 10, develop a planning schedule showing when each item should be ordered and in what quantity.

SOLUTION

a.

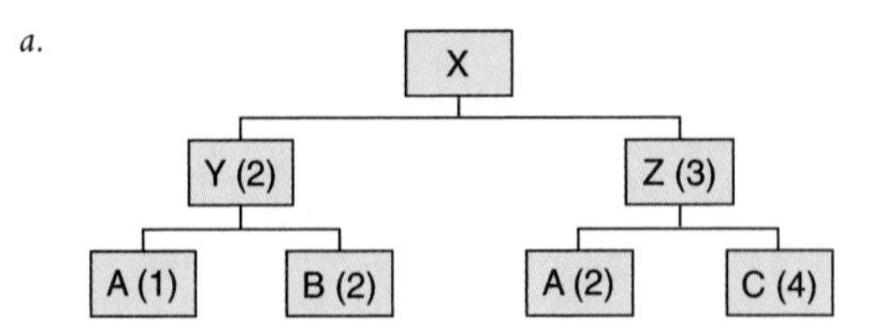

b.

		3	4	5	6	7	8	9	10
X	LT = 1							100	100
Y	LT = 2					200		200	
Z	LT = 3				300			300	
A	LT = 2		600	200	600	200			
B	LT = 1				400	400			
C	LT = 3	1200			1200				

PROBLEM

2. Product M is made of two units of N and three of P. N is made of two units of R and four units of S. R is made of one unit of S and three units of T. P is made of two units of T and four units of U.
   a. Show the product structure tree.
   b. If 100 M are required, how many units of each component are needed?
   c. Show both a single-level bill of material and an indented bill of material.

SOLUTION

a.

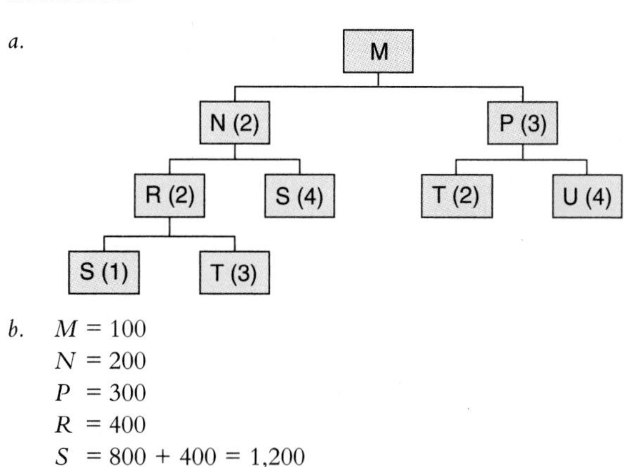

b. $M = 100$
$N = 200$
$P = 300$
$R = 400$
$S = 800 + 400 = 1{,}200$
$T = 600 + 1{,}200 = 1{,}800$
$U = 1{,}200$

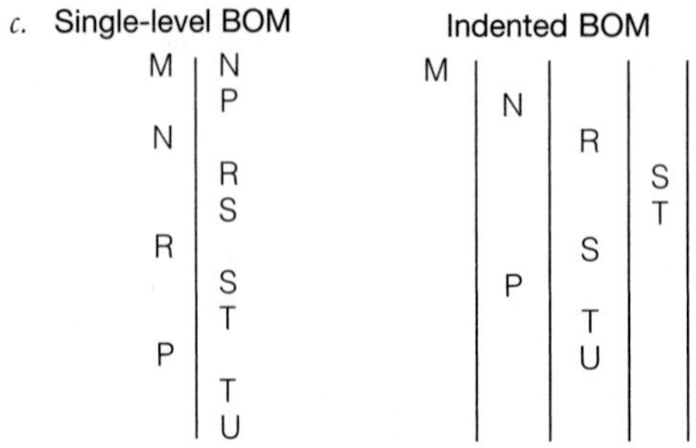

c. Single-level BOM

M	N
	P
N	R
	S
R	S
	T
P	T
	U

Indented BOM

M			
	N		
		R	
			S
			T
		S	
	P		
		T	
		U	

15.14 PROBLEMS

1. In the following MRP planning schedule for Item J, indicate the correct net requirements, planned order receipts, and planned order releases to meet the gross requirements. Lead time is one week.

Item J		Week Number 0	1	2	3	4	5
Gross requirements				75		50	70
On hand	40						
Net requirements							
Planned order receipt							
Planned order releases							

2. Assume that Product Z is made of two units of A and four units of B. A is made of three units of C and four of D. D is made of two units of E.

   The lead time for purchase or fabrication of each unit to final assembly: Z takes two weeks, A, B, C, and D take one week each, and E takes three weeks.

   Fifty units are required in Period 10. (Assume that there is currently no inventory on hand of any of these items.)

   a. Draw a product structure tree.

   b. Develop an MRP planning schedule showing gross and net requirements, order release and order receipt dates.

   Note: For Problems 3 through 6, to simplify data handling to include the receipt of orders that have actually been placed in previous periods, the six-level scheme shown below can be used. (There are a number of different techniques used in practice, but the important issue is to keep track of what is on hand, what is expected to arrive, what is needed, and what size orders should be placed.) One way to calculate the numbers is as follows:

	WEEK								
Gross requirements									
Scheduled receipts									
On hand from prior period									
Net requirements									
Planned order receipt									
Planned order release									

3. One unit of A is made of three units of B, one unit of C, and two units of D. B is composed of two units of E and one unit of D. C is made of one unit of B and two units of E. E is made of one unit of F.

   Items B, C, E, and F have one-week lead times; A and D have lead times of two weeks.

   Assume that lot-for-lot (L4L) lot sizing is used for items A, B, and F; lots of size 50, 50, and 200 are used for items C, D, and E, respectively. Items C, E, and F have on-hand (beginning) inventories of 10, 50, and 150, respectively; all other items have zero beginning inventory. We are scheduled to receive 10 units of A in Week 5, 50 units of E in Week 4, and also 50 units of F in Week 4. There are no other scheduled receipts. If 30 units of A are required in Week 8, use the low-level-coded product structure tree to find the necessary planned order releases for all components.

4. One unit of A is made of two units of B, three units of C, and two units of D. B is composed of one unit of E and two units of F. C is made of two units of F and one unit of D. E is made of two units of D. Items A, C, D, and F have one-week lead times; B and E have lead times of two weeks. Lot-for-lot (L4L) lot sizing is used for Items A, B, C, and D; lots of size 50 and 180 are used for items E and F, respectively. Item C has an on-hand (beginning) inventory of 15; D has an on-hand inventory of 50; all other items have zero beginning inventory. We are scheduled to receive 20 units of Item E in week 4; there are no other scheduled receipts.

   Construct simple and low-level-coded product structure trees and indented and summarized bills of materials.

   If 20 units of A are required in Week 8, use the low-level-coded products structure tree to find the necessary planned order released for all components. (See note prior to Problem 3.)

5. One unit of A is made of one unit of B and one unit of C. B is made of four units of C and one unit of E and F. C is made of two units of D and one unit of E. E is made of three units of F. Item C has a lead time of one week; Items A, B, E, and F have two-week lead times; and Item D has a lead time of three weeks. Lot-for-lot lot sizing is used for Items A, D, and E; lots of size 50, 100, and 50 are used for Items B, C, and F, respectively. Items A, C, D, and E have on-hand (beginning) inventories of 20, 50, 100, and 10, respectively; all other items have zero beginning inventory. We are scheduled to receive 10 units of A in week 5, 100 units of C in Week 6, and 100 units of D in Week 4; there are no other scheduled receipts. If 50 units of A are required in Week 10, use the low-level-coded product structure tree to find the necessary planned order releases for all components. (See note prior to Problem 3.)

6. One unit of A is made of two units of B and one unit of C. B is made of three units of D and one unit of F. C is composed of three units of B, one unit of D, and four units of E. D is made of one unit of E. Item C has a lead time of one week; Items A, B, E, and F have two-week

lead times; and Item D has a lead time of 3 weeks. Lot-for-lot lot sizing is used for Items C, E, and F; lots of size 20, 40, and 160 are used for items A, B, and D, respectively. Items A, B, D, and E have on-hand (beginning) inventories of 5, 10, 100, and 100, respectively; all other items have zero beginning inventories. We are scheduled to receive 10 units of A in Week 3, 20 units of B in Week 7, 40 units of F in week 5, and 60 units of E in Week 2; there are no other scheduled receipts. If 20 units of A are required in Week 10, use the low-level-coded product structure tree to find the necessary planned order releases for all components. (See note prior to Problem 3.)

7. The MRP gross requirements for Item A is shown here for the next 10 weeks. Lead time for A is three weeks and setup cost is $10 per setup. There is a carrying cost of $0.01 per unit per week. Beginning inventory is 90 units.

	WEEK									
	1	2	3	4	5	6	7	8	9	10
Gross requirements	30	50	10	20	70	80	20	60	200	50

Use the least total cost or the least unit cost lot-sizing method to determine when and for what quantity the first order should be released.

8. (This problem is intended as a very simple exercise to go from the aggregate plan to the master schedule to the MRP.) Gigamemory Storage Devices, Inc. produces CD ROMs (Read Only Memory) and WORMs (Write Once Read Many) for the computer market. Aggregate demand for the WORMs for the next two quarters are 2,100 units and 2,700 units. Assume that the demand is distributed evenly for each month of the quarter.

   There are two models of the WORM: an internal model, and an external model. The drive assemblies in both are the same but the electronics and housing are different. Demand is higher for the external model and currently is 70 percent of the aggregate demand.

   The bill of materials and the lead times follow. One drive assembly and one electronic and housing unit go into each WORM.

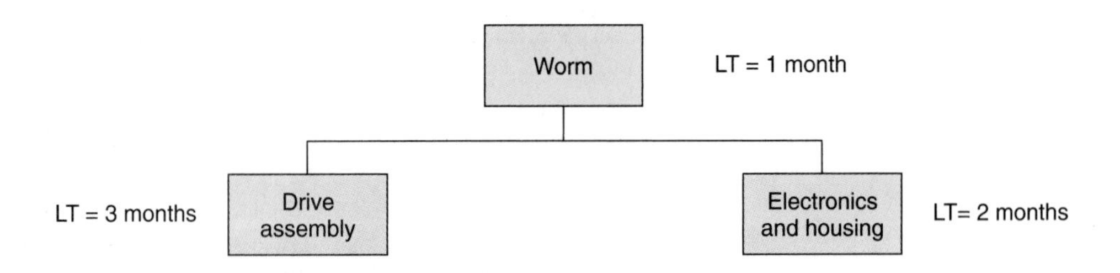

   The MRP system is run monthly. Currently, 200 external WORMs are in stock and 100 internal WORMs. Also in stock are 250 drive assemblies, 50 internal electronic and housing units, and 125 external electronic and housing units.

   Problem: Show the aggregate plan, the master production schedule, and the full MRP with the gross and net requirements and planned order releases.

9. Product A is an end item and is made from two units of B and four of C. B is made of three units of D and two of E. C is made of two units of F and two of E.

   A has a lead time of one week. B, C, and E have lead times of two weeks, and D and F have lead times of three weeks. Currently, there are no units of inventory on hand.

   a. Draw the product structure tree.

   b. If 100 units of A are required in work 10, develop the MRP planning schedule, specifying when items are to be ordered and received.

10. Product A consists of two units of subassembly B, three units of C, and one unit of D. B is composed of four units of E and three units of F. C is made of two units and H and three units of D. H is made of five units of E and two units of G.

    a. Construct a simple product structure tree.

    b. Construct a product structure tree using low-level coding.

    c. Construct an indented bill of materials.

    d. To produce 100 units of A, determine the numbers of units of B, C, D, E, F, G, and H required.

11. The MRP gross requirements for Item X are shown here for the next 10 weeks. Lead time for A is two weeks, and setup cost is $9 per setup. There is a carrying cost of $0.02 per unit per week. Beginning inventory is 70 units.

	WEEK									
	1	2	3	4	5	6	7	8	9	10
Gross requirements	20	10	15	45	10	30	100	20	40	150

    Use the least total cost or the least unit cost lot-sizing method to determine when and for what quantity the first order should be released.

12. Audio Products, Inc., produces two AM/FM cassette players for automobiles. Both radio/cassette units are identical, but the mounting hardware and finish trim differ. The standard model fits intermediate- and full-size cars, and the sports model fits small sports cars.

    Audio Products handles the production in the following way. The chassis (radio/cassette unit) is assembled in Mexico and has a manufacturing lead time of two weeks. The mounting hardware is purchased from a sheet steel company and has a three-week lead time. The finish trim is purchased from a Taiwan electronics company with offices in Los Angeles as prepackaged units consisting of knobs and various trim pieces. Trim packages have a two-week lead time. Final assembly time may be disregarded, since adding the trim package and mounting are performed by the customer.

    Audio Products supplies wholesalers and retailers, who place specific orders for both models up to eight weeks in advance. These orders, together with enough additional units to satisfy the small number of individual sales, are summarized in the following demand schedule:

	WEEK							
	1	2	3	4	5	6	7	8
Standard model				300				400
Sports model					200			100

There are currently 50 radio/cassette units on hand but no trim packages or mounting hardware.

Prepare a material requirements plan to meet the demand schedule exactly. Specify the gross and net requirements, on-hand amounts, and the planned order release and receipt periods for the cassette/radio chassis, the standard trim and sports car model trim, and the standard mounting hardware and the sports car mounting hardware.

13. Brown and Brown Electronics manufactures a line of digital audiotape players. While there are differences among the various products, there are a number of common parts within each player. The product structure, showing the number of each item required, lead times, and the current inventory on hand for the parts and components, follows:

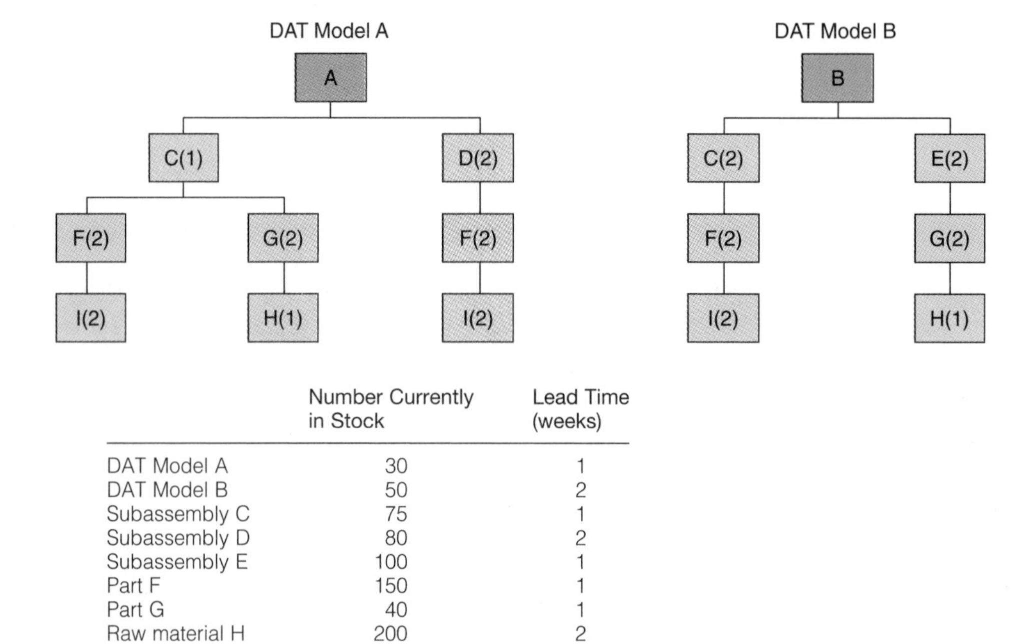

	Number Currently in Stock	Lead Time (weeks)
DAT Model A	30	1
DAT Model B	50	2
Subassembly C	75	1
Subassembly D	80	2
Subassembly E	100	1
Part F	150	1
Part G	40	1
Raw material H	200	2
Raw material I	300	2

Brown and Brown created a forecast that it plans to use as its master production schedule, producing exactly to schedule. Part of the MPS shows a demand for 700 units of Model A and 1,200 units of Model B in Week 10.

Develop an MRP schedule to meet that demand.

15.15 CASE: NICHOLS COMPANY

This particular December day seemed bleak to Joe Williams, president of Nichols Company (NCO). He sat in his office watching the dying embers of his fireplace, hoping to clear his mind. Suddenly there came a tapping by someone gently rapping, rapping at his office door. "Another headache," he muttered, "tapping at my office door. Only that and nothing more."*

The intruder was Barney Thompson, director of marketing. "A major account has just canceled a large purchase of A units because we are back ordered on tubing. This can't continue. My sales force is out beating the bushes for customers and our production manager can't provide the product."

For the past several months, operations at NCO have been unsteady. Inventory levels have been too high, while at the same time there have been stockouts. This resulted in many late deliveries, complaints, and cancellations. To compound the problem, overtime was excessive.

History

Nichols Company was started by Joe Williams and Peter Schaap, both with MBAs from the University of Arizona. Much has happened since Williams and Schaap formed the company. Schaap has left the company and is working in real estate development in Queensland, Australia. Under the direction of Williams, NCO has diversified to include a number of other products.

NCO currently has 355 full-time employees directly involved in manufacturing its three primary products, A, B, and C. Final assembly takes place in a converted warehouse adjacent to NCO's main plant.

The Meeting

Williams called a meeting the next day to get input on the problems facing NCO and to lay the groundwork for some solutions. Attending the meeting, besides himself and Barney Thompson, were Phil Bright of production and inventory control, Trevor Hansen of purchasing, and Steve Clark of accounting.

The meeting lasted all morning. Participation was vocal and intense.

Bright said, "The forecasts that marketing sends us are always way off. We are constantly having to expedite one product or another to meet current demand. This runs up our overtime."

Thompson said, "Production tries to run too lean. We need a larger inventory of finished goods. If I had the merchandise, my salespeople could sell 20 percent more product."

Clark said, "No way! Our inventory is already uncomfortably high. We can't afford the holding costs, not to mention how fast technology changes around here causing even more inventory, much of it obsolete."

Bright said, "The only way I can meet our stringent cost requirements is to buy in volume."

At the end of the meeting, Williams had lots of input but no specific plan. What do you think he should do?

Use Case Exhibits 1–4 showing relevant data to answer the specific questions at the end of the case.

---

* With apologies to E.A.P.

CASE EXHIBIT 1

Bills of Materials for Products A, B, and C

Product A	Product B	Product C
.A .D(4) .I(3) .E(1) .F(4)	.B .F(2) .G(3) .I(2)	.C .G(2) .I(2) .H(1)

CASE EXHIBIT 2

Work Center Routings for Products and Components

Item	Work Center Number	Standard Time (hours per unit)
Product A	1	0.20
	4	0.10
Product B	2	0.30
	4	0.08
Product C	3	0.10
	4	0.05
Component D	1	0.15
	4	0.10
Component E	2	0.15
	4	0.05
Component F	2	0.15
	3	0.20
Component G	1	0.30
	2	0.10
Component H	1	0.05
	3	0.10

CASE EXHIBIT 3

Inventory Levels and Lead Times for Each Item on the Bill of Material at the Beginning of Week 1

Product/Component	On Hand (units)	Lead Time (weeks)
Product A	100	1
Product B	200	1
Product C	175	1
Component D	200	1
Component E	195	1
Component F	120	1
Component G	200	1
Component H	200	1
1 (raw material)	300	1

CASE EXHIBIT 4

Forecasted Demand for Weeks 4–27

Week	Product A	Product B	Product C
1			
2			
3			
4	1,500	2,200	1,200
5	1,700	2,100	1,400
6	1,150	1,900	1,000
7	1,100	1,800	1,500
8	1,000	1,800	1,400
9	1,100	1,600	1,100
10	1,400	1,600	1,800
11	1,400	1,700	1,700
12	1,700	1,700	1,300
13	1,700	1,700	1,700
14	1,800	1,700	1,700
15	1,900	1,900	1,500
16	2,200	2,300	2,300
17	2,000	2,300	2,300
18	1,700	2,100	2,000
19	1,600	1,900	1,700
20	1,400	1,800	1,800
21	1,100	1,800	2,200
22	1,000	1,900	1,900
23	1,400	1,700	2,400
24	1,400	1,700	2,400
25	1,500	1,700	2,600
26	1,600	1,800	2,400
27	1,500	1,900	2,500

QUESTIONS

Use Lotus (or another spreadsheet if you prefer) to solve the Nichols Company case.

Simplifying assumption: To get the program started, some time is needed at the beginning because MRP backloads the system. For simplicity, assume that the forecasts (and therefore demands) are zero for Periods 1 through 3. Also assume that the starting inventory specified in Case Exhibit 3 is available from Week 1. For the master production schedule, use only the end Items A, B, and C.

To modify production quantities, adjust only Products A, B, and C. Do not adjust the quantities of D, E, F, G, H, and I. These should be linked so that changes in A, B, and C automatically adjust them.

1. Disregarding machine-center limitations, develop an MRP schedule and also capacity profiles for the four machine centers.
2. Work center capacities and costs follow. Repeat Question 1 creating a *feasible* schedule (within the capacities of the machine centers) and compute the relevant costs. Do this by adjusting the MPS only. Try to minimize the total cost of operation for the 27 weeks.

	Capacity	Cost
Work center 1	6,000 hours available	$20 per hour
Work center 2	4,500 hours available	$25 per hour
Work center 3	2,400 hours available	$35 per hour
Work center 4	1,200 hours available	$65 per hour
Inventory carrying cost		
End items A, B, and C	$2.00 per unit	
Components D, E, F, G, and H	$1.50 per unit	
Raw material I	$1.00 per unit	
Back-order cost		
End items A, B, and C	$20 per unit	
Components D, E, F, G, and H	$14 per unit	
Raw material I	$ 8 per unit	

3. Suppose end items had to be ordered in multiples of 100 units, components in multiples of 500 units, and raw materials in multiples of 1,000 units. How would this change your schedule?

15.16 SELECTED BIBLIOGRAPHY

Biggs, Joseph R., and Ellen J. Long. "Gaining the Competitive Edge with MRP/MRP II." *Management Accounting,* May 1988, pp. 27–32.

Flapper, S. D. P.; G. J. Miltenburg; and J. Wijngaard. "Embedding JIT into MRP." *International Journal of Production Research* 29, no. 2 (1991), pp. 329–41.

Goodrich, Thomas. "JIT & MRP Can Work Together." *Automation,* April 1989, pp. 46–47.

Journal of American Institute of Decision Science. (Articles appear discussing MRP and MRP II from a more analytical basis, examining topics such as lot sizing, safety stocks, and multiechelon inventory.)

Journal of American Production and Inventory Control Society. (Numerous articles on MRP and MRP II appear. Most of these cite the difficulties and experiences of practitioners.)

Orlicky, Joseph. *Materials Requirements Planning.* New York: McGraw-Hill, 1975. (This is the classic book on MRP.)

Proceedings of APICS and DSI. (Many papers on all aspects of MRP and MRP II are usually presented at the annual society meetings and reprinted in the proceedings.)

Rao, Ashok. "A Survey of MRP II Software Suppliers' Trends in Support of Just-In-Time." *Production and Inventory Management Journal,* 3rd Quarter 1989, pp. 14–17.

Vollmann, Thomas E.; William L. Berry; and D. Clay Whybark. *Manufacturing Planning and Control Systems.* 2nd ed. Homewood, Ill.: Richard D. Irwin, 1988.

Wallace, Thomas F. "MRP II & JIT Work Together in Plan and Practice." *Automation,* March 1990, pp. 40–42.

Chapter 16

Just-in-Time Production Systems

EPIGRAPH

I need it now! Not yesterday, and not tomorrow!

Inventory reduction is not something that management specifically decides in a JIT system, but rather it is a result of effective JIT implementation.

CHAPTER OUTLINE

KEY TERMS

- Eliminate Waste
- Respect for People
- Focused Factory Networks
- Group Technology
- Jidoka
- Kanban Pull System
- Bottom-Round Management
- Quality Circles
- Total Quality Control
- JIT Themes
- Focused Improvement Groups

Just-in-Time (JIT), sometimes called "lean production," has become the dominant design approach in modern manufacturing. JIT began in Japan. The person credited with the idea is Taiichi Ohno, who was vice president of manufacturing in Japan's Toyota Motor Company plant. Ohno, incidentally, stated that he got the idea from U.S. supermarkets.[1]

JIT production is based on the logic that nothing will be produced until it is needed. Need is created by the product being pulled away or used. This is known as a "pull system," unlike MRP, which is a "push system." In theory, when an item is sold, the market pulls a replacement from the last position in the production system. In the case of a production line product, a worker then pulls another unit from an upstream station to replace the unit taken. This upstream station then pulls from the next station further upstream, and so on all the way back to the original release of materials. The objective in just-in-time production is to reduce inventory as much as possible by meeting demand only as it is needed.

By now, most Americans have heard the term *just-in-time* even though they may not be fully aware of how it works. Just-in-time production can be viewed in a colloquial fashion as consisting of "Big JIT" and "Little JIT." Big JIT is really a philosophy of operations management that encompasses all aspects of a firm's production activities—human relations, vendor relations, and technology, as well as the management of materials per se. Little JIT, from our perspective, is limited in scope to production-control methods—specifically, just-in-time deliveries and inventory management. In this chapter, our interest is in both aspects but our emphasis is on Big JIT since to make Little JIT maximally effective, we need an appreciation of the big (JIT) picture.

The first part of this chapter presents an edited paper written by Kenneth A. Wantuck describing the Japanese approach to productivity.[2] This paper has become a classic overview of the techniques and philosophy of the Japanese, who are the major developers and users of the JIT approach. The second part of the chapter develops some of these issues in more detail and presents an approach to JIT implementation.

16.1 THE JAPANESE APPROACH TO PRODUCTIVITY

Everyone is aware of the inroads that the Japanese have made in world markets. The markets for many product areas, such as televisions, VCRs, cameras, watches, motorcycles, and even shipbuilding, are now dominated by Japanese companies. Of particular concern today are machine tools and automotive products, but an impact is also being felt in the aerospace-electronics field. In all areas, we know that not only do the Japanese compete with us at competitive prices, as discussed previously, but in the area of quality as well. See Exhibits 16.1 and 16.2.

Many people believe these accomplishments are attributable to cultural differences.

---

[1] Paul H. Zipkin, "Does Manufacturing Need a JIT Revolution?" *Harvard Business Review* (January–February 1991), p. 41.

[2] Kenneth A. Wantuck, "The Japanese Approach to Productivity," Southfield, Mich: Bendix Corporation, 1983.

EXHIBIT 16.1

1977 Hertz Repair Study

This study, undertaken by Hertz, was the first widely publicized evidence of the Japanese quality superiority in automobiles.

Model	Repairs per 100 Vehicles
Ford	326
Chevrolet	425
Pinto	306
Toyota	55

They envision the Japanese dedicating their lives to their companies and working long hours for substandard wages, which would be unthinkable in America. The evidence, however, is contrary to these distorted notions. Consider the following: In 1977, a Japanese company named Matsushita purchased a television plant in Chicago from a U.S.

EXHIBIT 16.2

Comparative U.S. and Japanese Inventory Turnover Rates for 15 Industries

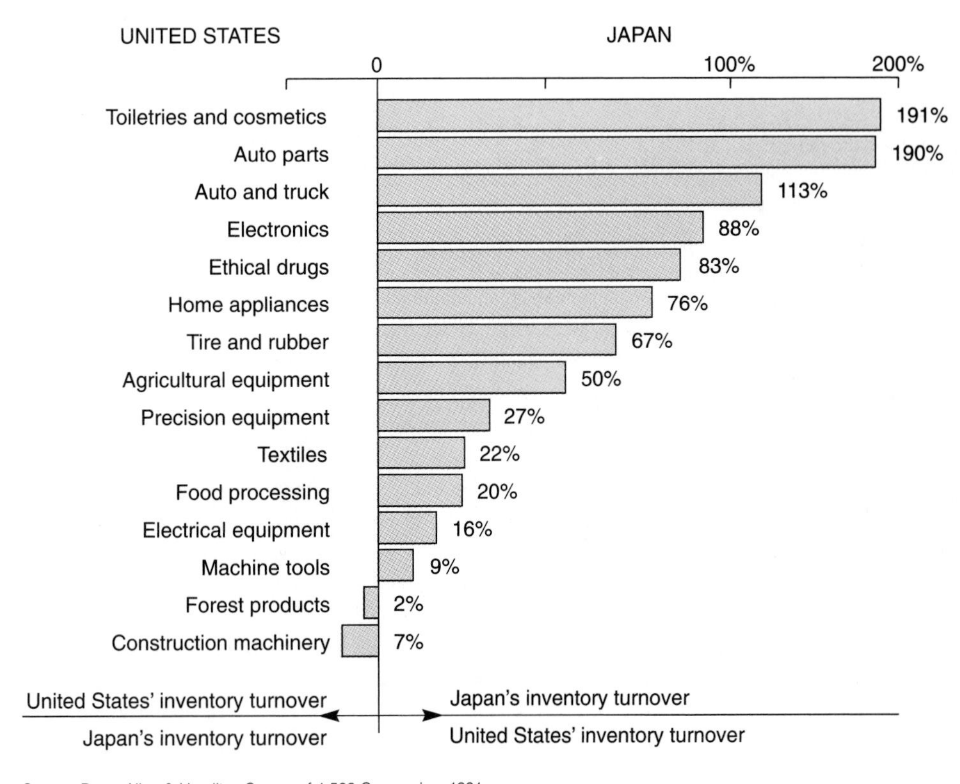

Source: Booz, Allen & Hamilton Survey of 1,500 Companies, 1981.

EXHIBIT 16.3

Quasar Plant Productivity

	Under Motorola	Under Matsushita*
Direct labor employees	1,000	1,000†
Indirect employees	600	300
Total employees	1,600	1,300
Daily production	1,000	2,000
Defect rate per 100 TV sets	160	4
Annual warranty cost ($ millions)	$16	$2

* 2 years later.

† Same people.

company. In the purchase contract, Matsushita agreed that all the hourly personnel would be retrained. Two years later, they still had essentially the same 1,000 hourly employees and had managed to reduce the indirect staff by 50 percent (see Exhibit 16.3). Yet, during that period, daily production had doubled. The quality, as measured by the number of defects per 100 TV sets built, improved 40-fold. Outside quality indicators also improved. Where the U.S. company (Motorola) had spent an average amount of $16 million a year on warranty costs, Matsushita's expenditures were $2 million. (That's for twice as many TV sets, so it's really a 16 to 1 ratio.) These are big differences—differences achieved here in the United States with American workers. The issue is, how do the Japanese do this and what can we learn from them?

Isolating the Elements

First, it's important to understand that the Japanese, as a nation, have had one fundamental economic goal since 1945: full employment through industrialization. The strategy employed to achieve this goal called for obtaining market dominance in very select product areas. They very carefully chose those industries in which they believed they could become dominant and concentrated on them, rather than diluting their efforts over a broader spectrum.

The tactics of the Japanese were threefold: (1) They imported their technology. (The entire Japanese semiconductor industry was built around a $25,000 purchase from Texas Instruments for the rights to the basic semiconductor process.) Instead of reinventing the wheel, they avoided major R&D expenditures with it associated risks, then negotiated license agreements to make the successful, workable new products. (2) They concentrated their ingenuity on the factory to achieve high productivity and low unit cost. The best engineering talent available was directed to the shop floor, instead of the product design department. (3) Finally, they embarked on a drive to improve product quality and reliability to the highest possible levels, to give their customers product reliability that competitors were not able to supply.

Implementation of these tactics was governed by two fundamental concepts (most of us agree with these concepts in principle, but the difference is the degree to which the Japanese practice them):

1. They are firm believers that in every way, shape, and form you must **eliminate waste.**
2. They practice a great **respect for people.**

Elimination of waste

When the Japanese talk about waste, the definition given by Fujio Cho, from the Toyota Motor Company, probably states it as well as anyone. He calls it "anything other than the *minimum* amount of equipment, materials, parts, and workers (working time) which are *absolutely essential* to production." That means no surplus, no safety stock. That means nothing is banked for future use. If you can't use it now you don't make it now because that is considered waste. There are seven basic elements under this concept:

1. Focused factory networks.
2. Group technology.
3. *Jidoka*—quality at the source.
4. Just-in-time production.
5. Uniform plant loading.
6. Kanban production control system.
7. Minimized setup times.

Focused factory networks. The first element is **focused factory networks.** Instead of building a large manufacturing plant that does everything (i.e., a highly vertically integrated facility), the Japanese build small plants that are highly specialized. There are several reasons for doing this. First, it's very difficult to manage a large installation; the bigger it gets, the more bureaucratic it gets. The Japanese style of management does not lend itself to this kind of environment.

Second, when a plant is specifically designed for one purpose it can be constructed and operated more economically than its universal counterpart. It's comparable to buying a special machine tool to do a very specific job instead of trying to adapt a universal, general purpose tool. Fewer than 750 plants in Japan have as many as 1,000 employees. The bulk of them, some 60,000 plants, have between 30 and 1,000 workers and over 180,000 have fewer than 30 employees. When we talk about the Japanese approach to productivity and the impressive things they're doing, we're talking primarily about the middle group, in which most of their model manufacturing plants are located.

Two illustrative examples have been cited by the Ford Motor Company: The Escort automobile needed a transaxle, which was going to require a $300 million expansion at the Ford plant in Batavia, Ohio. Ford asked the Japanese for an equivalent quotation and Tokyo–Kogyo offered to construct a brand-new plant with the same rate of output at a competitive unit price for $100 million, a one-third ratio. A second example relates to Ford's Valencia engine plant, which produces two engines per employee per day, and requires 900,000 square feet of floor space. An almost identical engine is produced by the

EXHIBIT 16.04

Group Technology versus Departmental Specialty

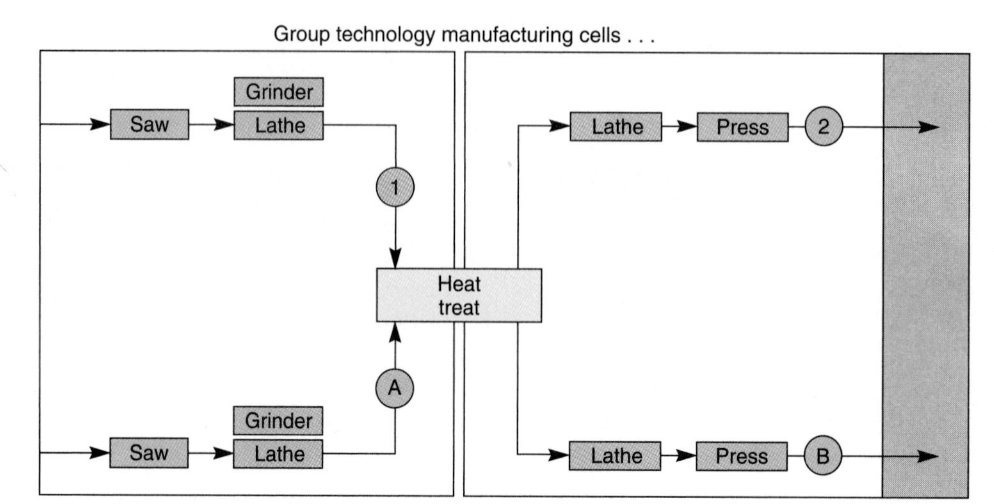

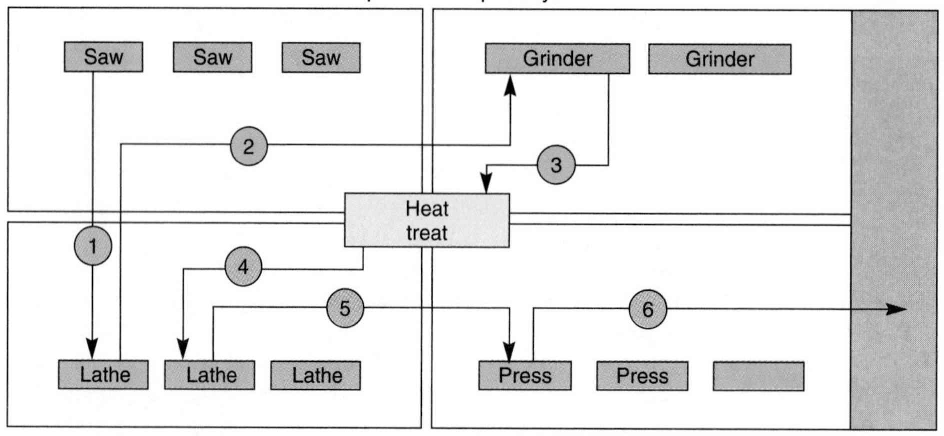

Toyota Motor Company in Japan, where they make nine engines per employee per day in a plant that has only 300,000 square feet of space. The issue is not only productivity per person but also a much lower capital investment to achieve this manufacturing capability.

Group technology. Inside the plant the Japanese employ a technique called **group technology.** Incidentally, group technology is nothing new to America; it was invented here, like so many of the techniques the Japanese successfully employ, but only recently has been practiced widely in the United States. A simplified diagram of the technique is shown in Exhibit 16.4. The lower portion shows the way we operate our plants today. Most companies process a job and send it from department to department because that's the way our plants are organized (sheetmetal department, grinding department, etc.). Each machine in those departments is usually staffed by a worker who specializes in that function. Getting a job through a shop can be a long and complicated process because there's a lot of waiting time and moving time involved (usually between 90 percent and 95 percent of the total processing time).

The Japanese, on the other hand, consider all the operations required to make a part and try to group those machines together. The upper part of Exhibit 16.4 shows clusters of dissimilar machines designed to be work centers for given parts or families of parts. One operator runs all three machines shown in the upper-left corner, increasing the utility of the individual operator and eliminating the move and queue time between operations in a given cluster. Thus, not only does productivity go up but the work-in-process inventory also comes down dramatically.

To achieve this, people have to be flexible; to be flexible, people must identify with their companies, have a high degree of job security, and undergo continuous training.

Jidoka—quality at the source. When management demonstrates a high degree of confidence in people, it is possible to implement a quality concept that the Japanese call **Jidoka.** The word means "Stop everything when something goes wrong." It can be thought of as controlling quality at the source. Instead of using inspectors to find the problems that somebody else may have created, the worker in a Japanese factory becomes his or her own inspector. This concept was developed by Taiichi Ohno, who, as mentioned earlier, was vice president of manufacturing for Toyota Motor Company in the early 1950s.

Ohno was convinced that one of the big problems faced by Toyota was bringing quality levels up to the necessary standards that would permit Toyota to penetrate the world automotive market. He felt that there was too much looking over each other's shoulders; he wanted every individual to be personally responsible for the quality of the product or component that he or she produced.

Ohno determined that the best thing to do was to give each person only one part to work on at a time so that under no circumstances would he or she be able to bury or hide problems by working on other parts. Jidoka push buttons were installed on the assembly lines. If anything went wrong—if a worker found a defective part, if he or she could not keep up with production, if production was going too fast according to the pace that was set for the day, or if he or she found a safety hazard—that worker was obligated to push the button. When the button was pushed, a light flashed, a bell rang, and the entire assembly line came to a grinding halt. People descended on the spot where the light was flashing. It was something like a volunteer fire department: People came from the industrial engineering department, from management, from everywhere to respond to that particular alarm, and they fixed the problem on the spot. Meanwhile, the workers polished their machines, swept the floor, or did whatever else they could to keep busy, but the line didn't move until the problem was fixed.

Jidoka also encompasses automated inspection, sometimes called *autonomation.* Just like automation and robotics, the Japanese believe that wherever possible inspection should be done by a machine, because it's faster and more accurate. However, the inspection step is a part of the production process, does not involve a separate location or person to perform

EXHIBIT 16.5

Just-In-Time

WHAT IT IS	WHAT IT DOES
▪ Management philosophy ▪ "Pull" system through the plant	▪ Attacks waste (time, inventory, scrap) ▪ Exposes problems and bottlenecks ▪ Achieves streamlined production

WHAT IT REQUIRES	WHAT IT ASSUMES
▪ Employee participation ▪ Industrial engineering/basics ▪ Continuing improvement ▪ Total quality control ▪ Small lot sizes	▪ Stable environment

Source: Adapted from Chris Gopal (of Price Waterhouse), "Notes on JIT."

it, and automatically shuts off a machine when a problem arises. This prevents the mass production of defective parts.

Line shutdowns in Japan are encouraged to protect quality and because management has confidence in the individual worker. No one likes to see a line stopped, but Ohno suggests that a day without a single Jidoka drill can mean people aren't being careful enough.

Just-in-time production. The Japanese system is based on a fundamental concept called just-in-time production. It requires the production of precisely the necessary units in the necessary quantities at the necessary time, with the objective of achieving plus or minus *zero* performance to schedule. It means that producing one extra piece is just as bad as being one piece short. In fact, anything over the minimum amount necessary is viewed as waste, since effort and material expended for something not needed now cannot be utilized now. (Later requirements are handled later.) That's another unique idea for us, since our measure of good performance has always been to meet or exceed the schedule. It is a most difficult concept for American manufacturing management to accept because it is contrary to our current practice, which is to stock extra material just in case something goes wrong. Exhibit 16.5 highlights what just-in-time is, what it does, what it requires, and what it assumes.

The just-in-time concept applies primarily to a repetitive manufacturing process. It does not necessarily require large volumes, but is restricted to those operations that produce the same parts over and over again. Ideally, the finished product would be repetitive in nature. However, as a Westinghouse team learned during a visit to Mitsubishi Inazawa, a Japanese elevator manufacturer, the repetitive segments of the business may only appear several levels down in the product structure. Even so, applying just-in-time concepts to a portion of the business produced significant improvements for them.

EXHIBIT 16.6

Inventory Hides Problems

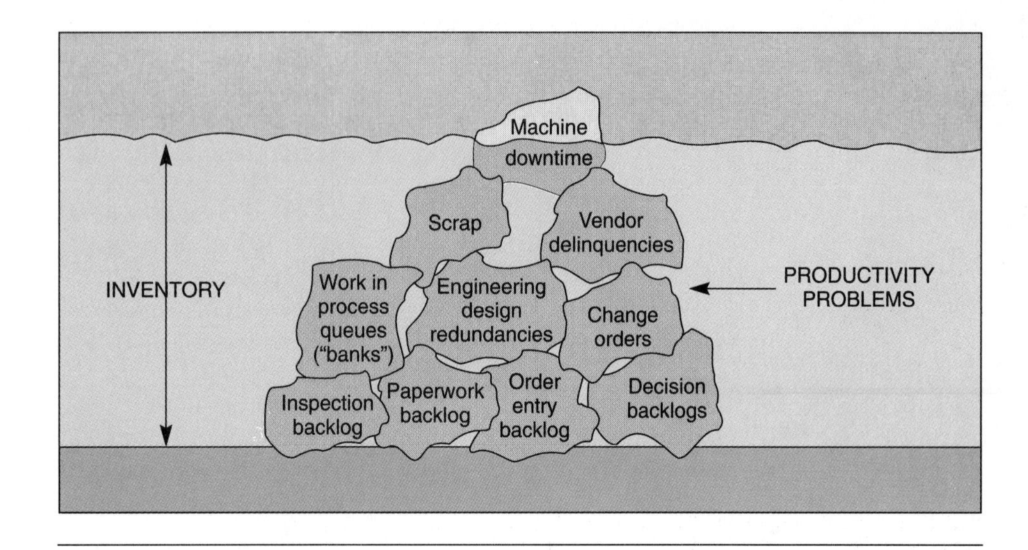

Under just-in-time, the ideal lot size is *one piece*. The Japanese view the manufacturing process as a giant network of interconnected work centers, where the perfect arrangement would be to have each worker complete his or her task on a part and pass it directly to the next worker just as that person was ready for another piece. The idea is to drive all queues toward zero in order to:

- Minimize inventory investment.
- Shorten production lead times.
- React faster to demand changes.
- Uncover any quality problems.

Exhibit 16.6 is an illustration that the Japanese use to depict the last idea. They look on the water level in a pond as inventory and the rocks as problems that might occur in a shop. A lot of water in the pond hides the problems. Management assumes everything is fine. Invariably, the water level drops at the worst possible time, such as during an economic downturn. Management must then address the problems without the necessary resources to solve them. The Japanese say it is better to force the water level down on purpose (especially in good times), expose the problems, and fix them now, before they cause trouble.

The zeal with which the Japanese work to reduce inventories is incredible. To begin with, inventory is viewed as a negative, not as an asset. According to Toyota, "The value of inventory is disavowed." Auto air conditioner manufacturer Nippondenso's attitude is even more severe: inventory is "the root of all evil." Almost universally, the Japanese see inventory as a deterrent to product quality. Finally, since the shop floor is programmed to have very little inventory, the slightest aberration in the process that results in extra parts is readily visible and serves as a red flag to which an immediate response is required.

Because it is impossible to have every worker in a complex manufacturing process adjacent to one another, and since the network also includes outside suppliers, the Japanese recognize that the system must allow for transit time between centers. However, transfer quantities are kept as small as possible. Typical internal lot sizes are one tenth of a day's production, vendors deliver their products several times a day to their customers, and constant pressure is exerted to reduce the number of lots in the system.

Just-in-time production makes no allowances for contingencies. Every piece is expected to be correct when received. Every machine is expected to be available when needed to produce parts. Every delivery commitment is expected to be honored at the precise time when it is scheduled. Consequently, the Japanese place heavy emphasis on quality, preventive maintenance, and mutual trust among all participants in the manufacturing enterprise. The process is gospel and everyone conscientiously adheres to it.

Uniform plant loading. To properly incorporate the just-in-time production concept, it is necessary that production flow as smoothly as possible in the shop. The starting point is what the Japanese call *uniform plant loading.* Its objective is to dampen the reaction waves that normally occur in response to schedule variations. For example, when a significant change is made in final assembly, it creates changes in the requirements in the feeder operations, which are usually amplified because of lot sizing rules, setups, queues, and waiting time. By the time the impact of the change is felt at the start of the supply chain, a 10 percent change at assembly could easily translate into a 100 percent change at the beginning of the operation.

The Japanese tell us the only way to eliminate that problem is to make the perturbations at the end as small as possible so that we only get ripples going through the shop, not shock waves. Japanese companies accomplish this by setting up a firm monthly production plan during which the output rate is frozen. Most U.S. manufacturing people have been trying to achieve that for years, without success, because they've tried to freeze a specific, sequential configuration. The Japanese circumvent this issue by planning to build the same mix of products every day, even if the total quantities are small. For example if they're only building a hundred pieces a month, they'll build five each day. Because they expect to build some quantity of everything that's on the schedule daily, they always have a total mix that is available to respond to variations in demand.

Going even further, they'll take those five units and intermix them on the assembly line. An example of how Toyota would do this is shown in Exhibit 16.7. Presume three kinds of vehicles are being made in an assembly plant: sedans, hardtops, and station wagons. The monthly rates shown are then reduced to daily quantities (presuming a 20-day month) of 250, 125, and 125, respectively. From this, the Japanese compute the necessary cycle times. *Cycle time* in Japan is the period of time between two identical units coming off the production line. The Japanese use this figure to adjust their resources to produce precisely the quantity that's needed—no more, no less.

EXHIBIT 16.7

Toyota Example of Mixed-Model Production Cycle in a Japanese Assembly Plant

Model	Monthly Quantity	Daily Quantity	Cycle Time (minutes)
Sedan	5,000	250	2
Hardtop	2,500	125	4
Wagon	2,500	125	4

Sequence: Sedan, hardtop, sedan, wagon, sedan, hardtop, sedan; wagon, etc.

The Japanese do not concern themselves with achieving the rated speeds of their equipment. In American shops, a given machine is rated at 1,000 pieces per hour so if we need 5,000 pieces we run it five hours to obtain this month's requirement. The Japanese produce only the needed quantity each day, as required. To them, cycle time is the driver that defines how they are to assemble their resources to meet this month's production. If the rate for next month changes, the resources are reconfigured.

Kanban production control system. The Kanban approach calls for a control system that is simple and self-regulating and provides good management visibility.[3] The shop floor/vendor release and control system is called *Kanban* (kahn-bahn), from the Japanese word meaning *card.* It is a paperless system, using dedicated containers and recycling traveling requisitions/cards, which is quite different from our old, manual shop-packet systems. This is referred to as a **Kanban pull system,** because the authority to produce or supply comes from downstream operations. While work centers and vendors plan their work based on schedules, they execute based on Kanbans, which are completely manual.

There are two types of Kanban cards. The production Kanban authorizes the manufacturing of a container of material. The withdrawal Kanban authorizes the withdrawal and movement of that container. The number of pieces in a container never varies for a given part number.

When production rates change, containers are added to or deleted from the system, according to a simple formula. The idea of safety stock is included in the basic calculation but is limited to 10 percent of a single day's demand. This gives the theoretical number of Kanban/containers required. In practice, efforts are made to reduce the number in circulation to keep inventories to a minimum.

The flow of Kanban cards between two work centers is shown in Exhibit 16.8. The machining center shown is making two parts, A and B, which are stored in standard containers next to the work center. When the assembly line starts to use Part A from a full container, a worker takes the withdrawal Kanban from the container and travels to the machining center storage area. He or she finds a container of Part A, removes the

[3]The majority of factories in Japan don's use Kanban. Kanban is a Toyota Motor Company system, not a generic Japanese one. However, many companies in both the United States and Japan use pull systems with other types of signaling devices.

EXHIBIT 16.8

Flow of Two Kanbans

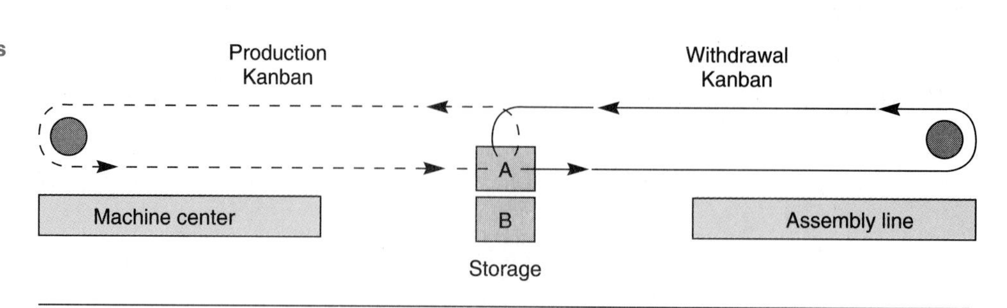

production Kanban, and replaces it with the withdrawal Kanban card, which authorizes him or her to move the container. The freed production Kanban is then placed in a rack by the machining center as a work authorization for another lot of material. Parts are manufactured in the order in which cards are placed on the rack (the Japanese call this the Kanban hanging), which makes the set of cards in the rack a dispatch list.[4]

If it turns out that the demand for Part A is greater than planned and less than planned for Part B, the system self-regulates to these changes because there can be no more parts built than called for by the Kanban cards in circulation. Mix changes of 10 to 20 percent can easily be accommodated because the shifts are gradual and the increments are small. The ripple effect upstream is similarly dampened.

The same approach is used to authorize vendor shipments. When both the customer and the vendor are using the Kanban system, the withdrawal Kanban serves as the vendor release/shipping document while the production Kanban at the vendor's plant regulates production there.

The whole system hinges on everyone doing exactly what is authorized and following procedures explicitly. In fact, the Japanese use no production coordinators on the shop floor, relying solely on supervisors to ensure compliance. Cooperative worker attitudes are essential to its success.

Results can be impressive. Jidosha Kiki, a Bendix braking components affiliate in Japan, installed the Kanban/just-in-time system in 1977 with the help of its customer, Toyota. Within two years they had doubled productivity, tripled inventory turnover, and substantially reduced overtime and space requirements. Jidosha Kiki stated that this was a slow and difficult learning process for its employees, even considering the Japanese culture, because all the old rules of thumb had to be tossed out the window and deep-rooted ideas had to be changed.

---

[4]Many firms use withdrawal cards only. Under the simplest form of one-card system, the worker at the assembly line (or more likely a material handler) walks to the machine center with an empty container and a withdrawal Kanban. He or she would then place the empty container at a designated spot, attach the withdrawal card to a filled container, and carry it back to the assembly line. The worker at the machining center would know that a refill is required. This type of system is appropriate where the same part is made by the same people every day.

EXHIBIT 16.9

Minimizing Setup Time—Hood and Fender Press Comparison (800-ton press)

	Toyota	USA	Sweden	Germany
Setup time	10 minutes	6 hours	4 hours	4 hours
Setups/day	3	1	—	½
Lot size	1 day*	10 days	1 month	—

*For low-demand items (less than 1,000 month), as large as seven days.

Minimized setup times. The Japanese approach to productivity demands that production be run in small lots. This is impossible to do if machine setups take hours to accomplish. In fact, we use the economic order quantity (EOQ) formula in the United States to determine what quantity we should run to absorb a long and costly setup time.

The Japanese have the same formula, but they've turned it around. Instead of accepting setup times as fixed numbers, they fixed the lot sizes (very small) and then went to work to reduce setup time.

That is a crucial factor in the Japanese approach. Their success in this area has received widespread acclaim. Many Americans have been to Japan and witnessed a team of press operators change an 800-ton press in 10 minutes. Compare those data with ours as shown in Exhibit 16.9. The Japanese aim for single-digit setup times (i.e., less than 10 minutes) for every machine in their factories. They've addressed not only big things, like presses, but small molding machines and standard machines tools as well.

Successful setup reduction is easily achieved when approached from a methods engineering perspective. The Japanese separate setup time into two segments: *internal*—that part that must be done while a machine is stopped, and *external*—that part that can be done while the machine is operating. Simple things, such as the staging of replacement dies in anticipation of a change, fall into the external category, which, on the average, represents half of the usual setup time.

Another 50 percent reduction can be achieved by the application of time and motion studies and practice. (It is not unusual for a Japanese setup team to spend a full Saturday practicing changeovers.) Time-saving devices like hinged bolts, roller platforms, and folding brackets for temporary die staging are commonly seen, all of which are low-cost items.

Only then is it necessary to spend larger sums, to reduce the last 15 percent or so, on things such as automatic positioning of dies, rolling bolsters, and duplicate tool holders. The result is that 90 percent or *more* of the setup times can be eliminated if we have a desire to do so.

Referring again to the Jidosha Kiki Corporation (JKC), Exhibit 16.10 shows the remarkable progress the company made in just four years. These data relate to all the machines in the factory. It's interesting to note that while we are quite impressed that two thirds of their equipment can be changed over in less than 2 minutes, the company is embarrassed that 10 percent still takes more than 10 minutes!

The savings in setup time are used to increase the number of lots produced, with a corollary reduction in lot sizes. This makes the use of just-in-time production principles

EXHIBIT 16.10

Setup Reduction Results at JKC

Setup Time	PERCENT REDUCTION 1976	1977	1980
>60 minutes	30%	0%	0%
30–60 minutes	19	0	0
20–30 minutes	26	10	3
10–20 minutes	20	12	7
5–10 minutes	5	20	12
100 second–5 minutes	0	17	16
<100 seconds	0	41	62

feasible, which in turn makes the Kanban control system practical. All the pieces fit together.

Respect for people

The second guiding principle for the Japanese, along with elimination of waste, is respect for people. This principle, too, has seven basic elements:

1. Lifetime employment.
2. Company unions.
3. Attitude toward workers.
4. Automation/robotics.
5. Bottom-round management.
6. Subcontractor networks.
7. Quality circles.

Lifetime employment. Much has been written about the Japanese concept of lifetime employment. When Japanese workers are hired for permanent positions with a major industrial firm, they have jobs with that company for life (or until retirement age) provided they work diligently. If economic conditions deteriorate, the company maintains the payroll almost to the point of going out of business. We should understand, though, that these kinds of benefits apply only to permanent workers, who constitute about one third of the work force in Japan. What's important is that the concept is pervasive. When people can identify with the company as the place they're going to spend their working life, not just an interim place to get a paycheck, then they have a tendency to be more flexible and to want to do all they can do to help achieve the company's goals.

Company unions. When General Douglas MacArthur introduced the union concept to Japan during the post-World War II reconstruction period, he undoubtedly had in mind trade unions, but the Japanese didn't think that way. Japanese workers at Toyota were concerned about Toyota. They really didn't identify with the other automobile manufacturing employees in the rest of the country. They identified not with the kind of work they were doing but rather with the company for which they were working. So Toyota formed a union that included everybody who worked for Toyota, no matter what their skills were. The objective of both the union and management was to make the company as healthy as possible so there would be benefits accruing to the people in a secure and shared method. The resulting relationship was cooperative, not adversarial.

The Japanese system of compensation reinforces these goals because it is based on company performance bonuses. Everybody in a Japanese company, from the lowest employee to the highest, gets a bonus twice a year. In good times the bonus is high (up to 50 percent of their salaries), while in bad times there may be no bonus. As a result, the employees have an attitude that says, "If the company does well, I do well," which is important from the standpoint of soliciting the workers' help to improve productivity.

Attitude toward workers. The attitude of management toward the workers is also critical. The Japanese do not look at people as human machines. As a matter of fact, they believe that if a machine can do a job, then a person *shouldn't* do it because it's below his or her dignity. In the United States, we all believe in the value of human worth, but when it comes to the shop floor we don't necessarily practice it. A corollary concept says that if workers are really important as people, you must also believe that they can do much more than you are now giving them the opportunity to do. We normally have to see people in a job for some time before we accept their competence.

The Japanese say, "What workers are doing today is only tapping their capability. We must give them an opportunity to do more." Thus, a third and most significant attitude requires that the management system provides every worker with an opportunity to display his or her maximum capabilities. These concepts are practiced, not just discussed, and the Japanese spend more for employee training and education—at all levels—than any other industrial nation.

Automation/robotics. When people feel secure, identify with the company, and believe that they are being given an opportunity to fully display their talents, the introduction of automation and robotics is not considered as a staff-cutting move. The Japanese feel that this is a way to eliminate dull jobs so people can do more important things, and they have been making major capital investments in these areas. Interestingly enough, Japan has invested one third of its gross national product in capital improvements for the last 20 years, compared to about 19 percent for the United States during the same period.

In automation, the Japanese have invested first in low-cost enhancements to existing or standard equipment, using some clever approaches. In the capital area they have been concentrating on programmable robots. A recent survey showed that Japan had approximately five times the number of programmable robots (some of them quite simple) as the United States. Most of those robots were built here. Again, we shipped our technology to Japan, where it was used to build products to compete with us. Today, Japan is building its own robots at a rapid pace and has become both the leading robot producer and robot user in the world.

Because the Japanese honestly believe that robots free people for more important tasks, there is little worker resistance to the robotics implementation. In fact, workers go out of their way to figure out how to eliminate their jobs, if they find them dull, because they know the company will find something better and more interesting for them to do.

Bottom-round management. This mutual reliance between workers and management is a manifestation of the management style the Japanese call **bottom-round management.** It's also been identified as *consensus management* or *committee management.* It is an innate part of the Japanese culture because they have grown up with the concept that the importance of the group supercedes that of the individual. Consider that in Japan more than 124 million people are crowded on a tiny island group about the size of California, 80 percent of which is mountainous. In those circumstances, citizens must have considerable respect for their neighbors, or social survival would be impossible. This cultural concept is ideal in a manufacturing environment because the process requires that people work together in a group to make a product. The individual cannot function independently, without concern for others, became he or she would only get out of synchronization with the rest of the group and disrupt the process.

Bottom-round management is a slow decision-making process. In attempting to arrive at a true consensus, not a compromise, the Japanese involve all potentially interested parties, talk over a problem at great length, often interrupt the process, seek out more information, and retalk the problem until everyone finally agrees. While we have often criticized the slowness of this method, the Japanese have an interesting response.

They say, "You Americans will make an instant decision and then you'll take a very long time to implement it. The decision is made so quickly, without consulting many of the people it's going to affect, that as you try to implement it you begin to encounter all sorts of unforeseen obstacles. Now, in our system, we take a long time to make a decision, but it only takes a short time to implement it because by the time we've finally reached a conclusion, everybody involved has had their say."

A key to bottom-round management is that decisions are made at the lowest possible level. In essence, the employees recognize a problem, work out a potential solution with their peers, and make recommendations to the next level of management. They, in turn, do the same thing and make the next recommendation up the line. And so it goes, with everyone participating in the process. As a result, top management teams in Japanese companies make very few day-to-day operating decisions, their time being almost totally devoted to strategic planning. Note, though, that the use of bottom-round management makes it extremely difficult to manage a large, complex manufacturing organization. That's another reason why the Japanese build focused factories.

Subcontractor networks. The specialized nature of Japanese factories has fostered the development of an enormous subcontractor network; most subcontractors have fewer than 30 employees. More than 90 percent of all Japanese companies are part of the supplier network, which is many tiers deep, because there is so little vertical integration in Japanese factories.

There are two kinds of suppliers: specialists in a narrow field who serve multiple customers (very much like U.S. suppliers), and captives, who usually make a small variety of parts for a single customer. The second kind is more prevalent in Japan. Of course, this idea of sole-sourcing suppliers is diametrically opposite to the U.S. multisource concept.

Sole-sourcing arrangements work in Japan because the relationships are based on a tremendous amount of mutual trust. They seek long-term partnerships between customer and supplier. Americans who do business with Japanese companies know that the very first stages of negotiation involve an elaborate ceremony of getting to know one another to determine whether there is a potential long-term relationship in the picture. Japanese businesspeople are rarely interested in a one-time buy, so it's a different way of doing business for us.

Suppliers in Japan consider themselves part of their customers' families. Very often key suppliers are invited to company functions such as picnics or parties. In return, suppliers deliver high-quality parts many times per day, often directly to the customer's assembly line, bypassing receiving and inspection. A typical scenario would have the supplier's truck arriving at a precise time of day, the driver unloading the truck, transporting the parts into the factory and delivering them to the assembly line at a given station, depositing the parts, picking up the empty containers, loading them into the truck, and leaving, without any interference. No receiving, no incoming inspection, no paperwork, no delays. It's an almost paper-free system, all built on mutual trust.

Trust is a two-way street. Because so many of the suppliers are small and undercapitalized, Japanese customers advance money to finance them, if necessary. Customer process engineers and quality personnel help vendors improve their manufacturing systems to meet the rigid quality and delivery standards imposed. Efforts are also made to help vendors reduce their production process costs to help ensure their profitability. When there is an economic downturn, however, the customers will perform more of the work in-house instead of buying from vendors. They do this to protect their own work forces. Vendors are small and do not have the permanent, lifetime employment guarantees that the major companies do. However, this is known in advance and suppliers consider this an acceptable risk.

Quality circles. Another interesting technique, with which many Americans are already familiar, is **quality circles.** The Japanese call them *small group improvement activities* (SGIA). A quality circle is a group of volunteer employees who meet once a week on a scheduled basis to discuss their function and the problems they're encountering, to try to devise solutions to those problems, and to propose those solutions to their management. The group may be led by a supervisor or a production worker. It usually includes people from a given discipline or a given production area, like Assembly Line A or the machining department. It can also be multidisciplinary, consisting, for instance, of all the material handlers who deliver materials to a department and the industrial engineers who work in that department. It does have to be led, though, by someone who is trained as a group leader. The trainers are facilitators, and each one may coordinate the activities of a number of quality circles. Westinghouse Electric Corporation, for example, has 275 quality circles and about 25 facilitators.

The quality circle really works because it's an open forum. It takes some skill to prevent it from becoming a gripe session, but that's where the trained group leaders keep the members on target. Interestingly enough, only about one third of the proposals generated turn out to be quality related. More than half are productivity oriented. It's really amazing how many good ideas these motivated employees can contribute toward the profitability and the improved productivity of their companies. Quality circles are actually a manifestation of the consensus, bottom-round management approach but are limited to these small groups.

Authors' Postscript: Applicability of Japanese Concepts to U.S. Manufacturers

Of the 14 techniques and concepts just described in Wantuck's paper, the following are particularly difficult to implement in the American environment:

- Lifetime employment, company unions, and subcontractor networks. These rely on the Japanese culture or economic relationships not prevalent in the United States.
- Attitude toward workers and bottom-round management. These are characteristics of Japanese management style, which will be appropriate only for some U.S. companies.
- Focused factory networks and automation/robotics. These are most definitely applicable to U.S. companies, but currently they are major strategic and investment decisions performed by top management. In short, few operations managers can influence these decisions in the short run.

What do we have left to import? According to Edward J. Hay, a consultant in just-in-time production,

> We have left a group of six elements in which, in my opinion, are the most important elements of all. In addition to being most important they are the most appropriate and practical for the American environment and are well within our ability to implement. One of the main reasons why these techniques are so transferable is because, in one form or another, most of them had their origins in the United States. As a group, they make up a powerful set of manufacturing and quality control techniques, increasingly being referred to under the collective term, Just-in-time production. For purposes of perspective, I have sorted these six elements under three labels:
>
> 1. Attitude.
>   Just-in-time (philosophy).
>   Quality at the source.
> 2. Manufacturing engineering.
>   Minimized setup times.
>   Uniform plant load.
>   Group technology.
> 3. Production control.
>   Kanban system.
>
> The philosophy of just-in-time is the framework that gives organization and meaning to the other five elements. It requires:
>
> - Production of only the minimum units necessary in the smallest possible quantities at the latest possible time.
> - Elimination of inventories.[5]

---

[5] Edward J. Hay, *Just-in-Time Production: A Winning Combination of Neglected American Ideas* (East Greenwich, R.I.: Edward J. Hay Associates, 1983), p. 2.

Pragmatic JIT versus Romantic JIT

In the opening paragraphs of this chapter we referred to "Big JIT" and "Little JIT" as two views of just-in-time production. Paul Zipkin has two categories of his own, which he calls "pragmatic" JIT and "romantic" JIT. The pragmatic view focuses on the practical problems of factory management.[6] This requires reaching into the engineering or production manager's toolbox and pulling out techniques to help reduce setups, to improve layouts, to better control quality, and to create simpler designs. This pragmatic approach can be slow. The process of continuous improvement can take many years. Ohno, president of Toyota and the person credited for the creation of JIT, gives an example of reducing the changing of a die in the production process from several hours to several minutes—this change took 25 years to accomplish! Ohno was a pragmatist. So was Shigeo Shingo.[7] Shingo developed ways to reduce setup times. In addition, Shingo used a concept known as "poka-yoke," to create jigs and fixtures that improved quality. Many of these were simple devices to prevent errors from occurring such as parts being installed backwards.

Romantic JIT calls for revolutionary action: "We must adopt JIT if we are to survive," and so on. JIT is proclaimed to be natural and simple without complexity. One visualizes an ideal factory without obstacles and where materials and components move in perfect harmony.

Zipkin questions the universality of JIT, however, stating "If the need for JIT is so urgent, if its many benefits are so manifest, who has prevented us all from reaping the bountiful fruits? Like other revolutionary movements, this one casts the blame for problems, pitfalls, and shortcomings on assorted villains." Who are these villains? Are they staff experts with self-serving objectives? Or are there any villains at all? The problem is that simple JIT doesn't mean that JIT is easy to implement.

16.2 ELIMINATION OF WASTE

At the cost of being somewhat repetitive with material presented earlier in this chapter. Kiyoshi Suzaki gives an excellent summarization of wasteful items.[8] He quotes Fujio Cho of Toyota in his definition of waste and presents a list of seven types of waste. Waste is defined as "Anything other than the minimum amount of equipment, materials, parts, space, and worker's time, which are absolutely essential to add value to the product." The seven most prominent types of waste are:

[6] Paul H. Zipkin, "Does Manufacturing Need a JIT Revolution?" *Harvard Business Review* (January–February 1991), pp. 40–43.

[7] Shigeo Shingo, *A Study of the Toyota Production System from an Industrial Engineering Viewpoint* (Cambridge, Mass.: Productivity Press, 1989).

[8] Kiyoshi Suzaki, *The New Manufacturing Challenge: Techniques for Continuous Improvement* (New York: Free Press, 1987), p. 7–24.

1. Waste from overproduction.
2. Waste of waiting time.
3. Transportation waste.
4. Processing waste.
5. Inventory waste.
6. Waste of motion.
7. Waste from product defects.

Waste from Overproduction

While overproduction is not as big a problem during market upswings, it becomes unsold goods during downswings. This happens by getting ahead of production. It is one of the worst wastes. In overproduction, more raw materials are consumed than are necessary; this also requires additional materials handling, additional space, and so on. Overproduction also confuses the environment by distracting workers, adding confusion as to what needs to be done first, and so on.

Waste of Waiting Time

While overproduction causes excess inventory, it also tends to hide idle worker time. If workers only produce the required amount and are not allowed to work ahead, their idleness is obvious. Some appropriate actions or other use of their time may, therefore, be possible.

Time is also wasted if the worker's task is simply to watch a machine run. Rather than having a worker watch the machine, a machine may be equipped with an alarm or automatic stop switch that activates when the need to stop arises.

Transportation Waste

Moving material is expensive and time consuming. Opportunities may exist to have incoming materials delivered directly to the production location, for example, rather than storing them somewhere and then moving them a second time. Distances between production processes should also be considered. Transportation waste can be eliminated through improvement in layout, coordination of processes, methods of transportation, housekeeping, and workplace organization.

Processing Waste

The production method used may be wasteful if it can be improved. For example, a die-casting operation may need an additional worker to file and finish surfaces. If the die were redesigned or the product were modified, there may not be a need for the finish work. It may also be possible to change or modify tools and fixtures to save operator time.

Inventory Waste

Excess inventory may be caused by the first item on the list-—overproduction. This results in extra handling, extra space, extra interest costs, extra workers, extra paperwork, and so forth. There should be a conscious effort to discard obsolete inventory, to use smaller lots in manufacturing and purchasing, and to refrain from producing ahead of schedule.

Waste of Motion

Motions should be efficient and workplaces well designed. Spending time looking for tools is a waste. Walking around may also be a waste that may be corrected by rearranging the work environment.

Waste from Product Defects

Waste occurs from the rework required, from the inspection which may be necessary, from the disassembly of the products, from the time wasted by subsequent workstations waiting for the corrected product, from the product if it is scrapped, and, most importantly, from the customer (through warranty, lost future business, etc.).

16.3 HOW TO ACCOMPLISH JIT PRODUCTION

In this section, our objective is to explain how to accomplish JIT production. To structure our discussion we follow the steps given in Exhibit 16.11, expanding on some ideas given in the Wantuck paper and explaining certain features that were not previously discussed. In going through these steps, keep in mind that we are still talking about *repetitive* production systems—those that make the same basic product over and over again. Also keep in mind that we are talking about features of a *total system,* which means that actions taken regarding any one of these features have some impact on other features of the system. Finally, note that different companies use different terms to describe their JIT systems. IBM uses *continuous flow manufacture,* Hewlett-Packard Company uses *stockless production* at one plant and *repetitive manufacturing system* at another, while many other companies use *loan production.*

JIT Layouts/Design Flow Process

JIT requires that the plant layout be designed to ensure balanced work flow with a minimum of work in process. This means that we must conceive of each workstation as an integral part of the overall production line, whether or not a physical line actually exists. Capacity balancing is done using the same logic as for an assembly line, and operations are linked through a pull system (described later). This also means that the system designer must have a vision of how all aspects of the internal and external logistics system are related to the layout.

EXHIBIT 16.11 How to Accomplish Just-in-Time Production

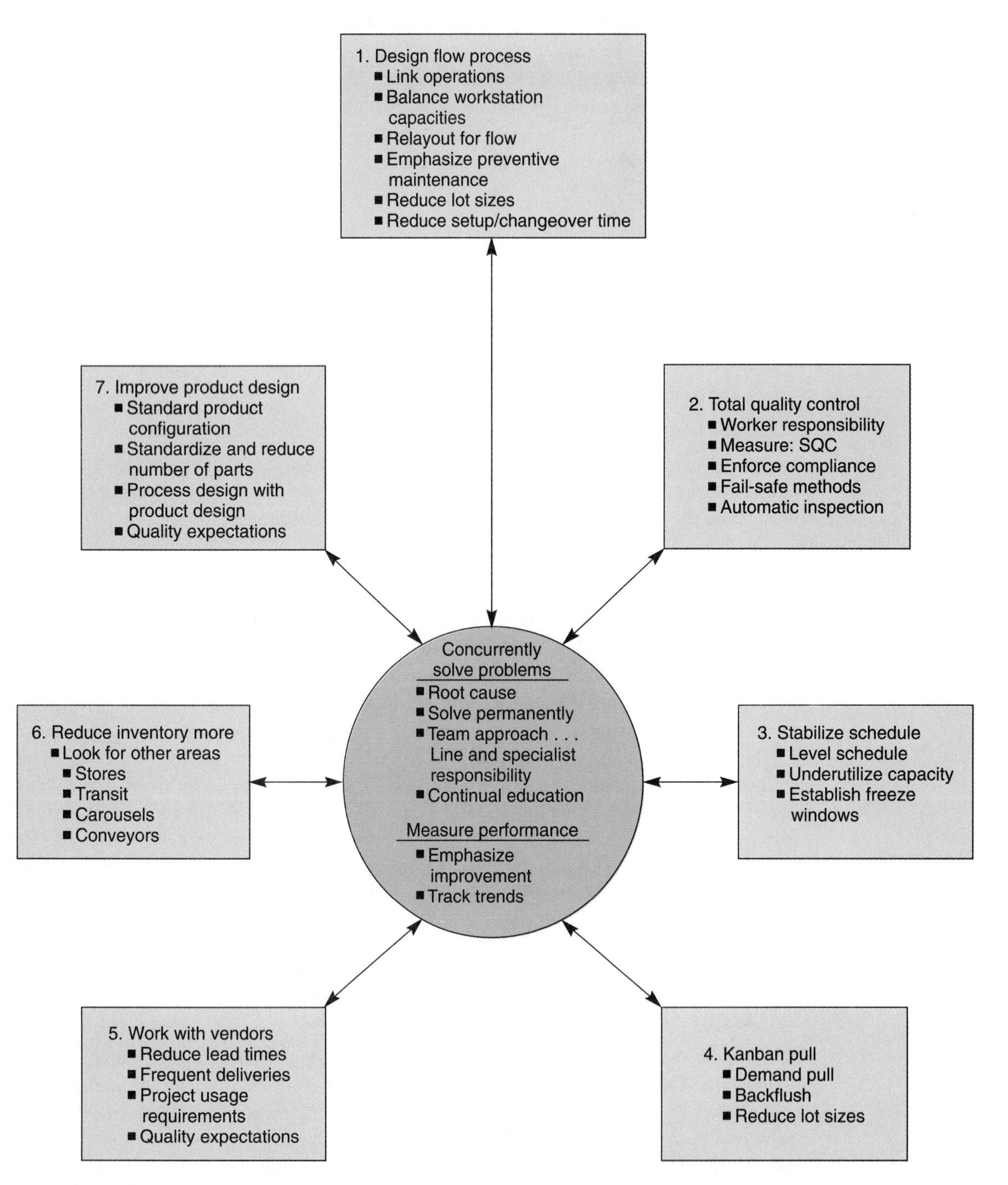

This diagram is modeled after the one used by Hewlett-Packard's Boise plant to accomplish its JIT program.

EXHIBIT 16.12 **The Impact of JIT on Lot Size**

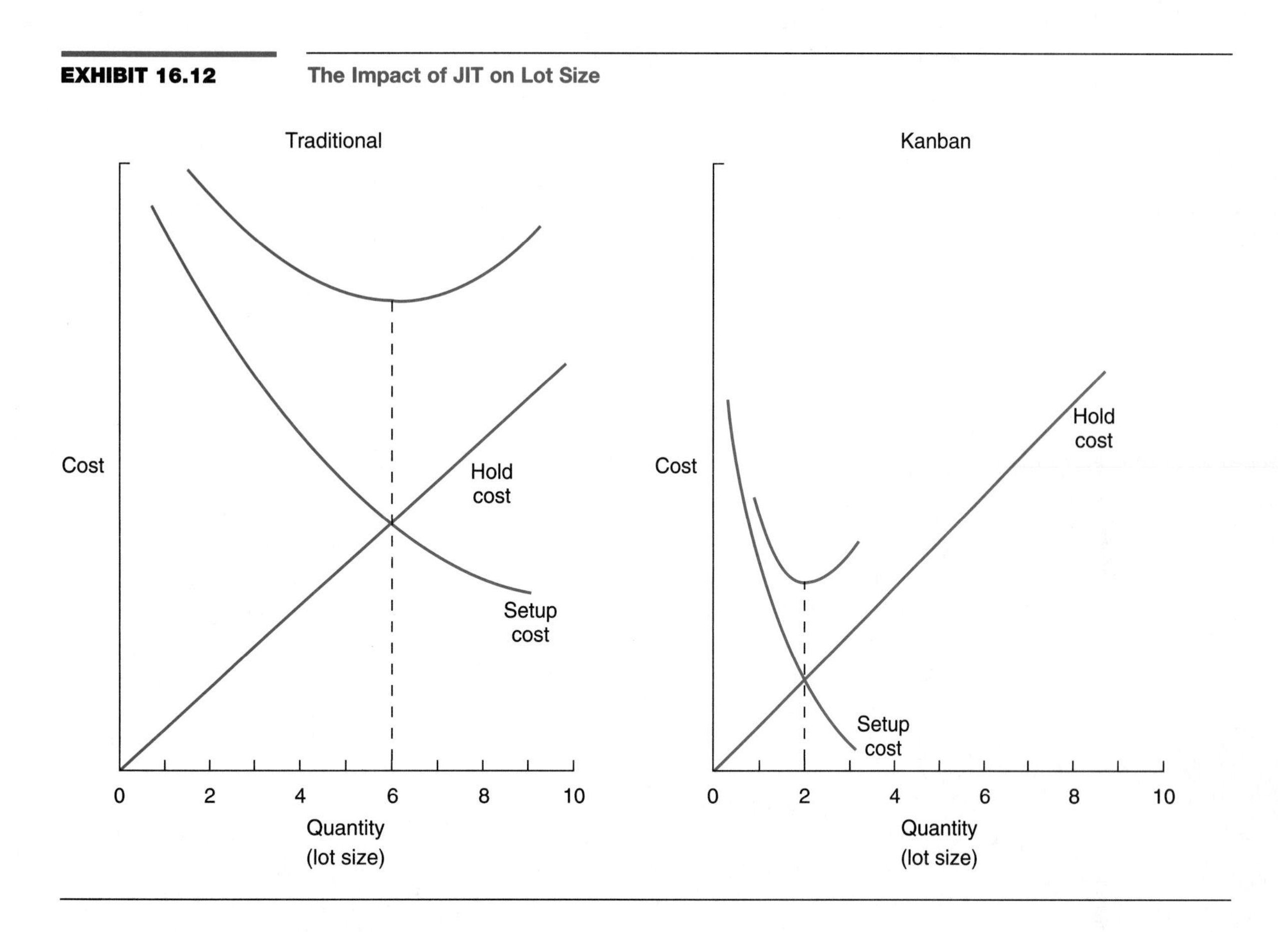

Preventive maintenance is emphasized to ensure that a continuous work flow is not interrupted by machine downtime or as a result of poor quality from malfunctioning equipment. Much of this maintenance is carried out by the operators because they are responsible for the quality of products coming off the machines, and also because of their sensitivity to the idiosyncrasies of the machines as a result of working on them day in and day out. Finally, the fact that the JIT philosophy favors many simple machines rather than a few complex ones enables the operators to handle routine maintenance activities.

Reduction in setup/changeover time and lot sizes are interrelated and are key to achieving a smooth flow (and JIT success in general). Exhibit 16.12 illustrates the fundamental relationship between lot size and setup cost. Under the traditional approach, setup cost is treated as a constant, and the optimal order quantity is shown as six. Under the Kanban approach of JIT, setup cost is treated as a variable and the optimal order quantity, in this case, is reduced to two. This type of reduction can be achieved by employing setup time-saving procedures such as those described earlier in the chapter. *The ultimate goal of JIT from an inventory standpoint is to achieve an economic lot size of one.*

EXHIBIT 16.13

JIT in a Line Flow Layout

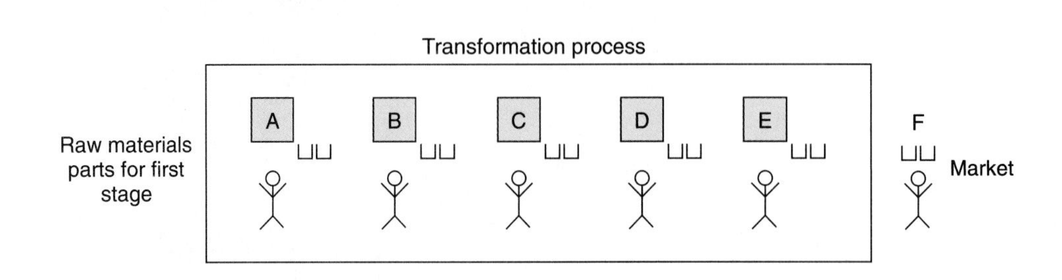

Even though we go into considerable detail about layout types in Chapter 9, we will briefly describe a line flow operation and a job-shop layout to show how JIT can be applied.

Most people think of high volume assembly lines when they think of JIT. This is because most of the literature and discussions on this topic has been about line layouts. However, job-shop environments, where functions are grouped together, offer perhaps the greatest benefits for JIT application.

In assembly or fabrication lines, the focus is on product flow. Volumes may be high enough or tasks simple enough or costs low enough so that the required resources (people, machines, materials, etc.) can be arranged close together in a simple flow. "Put stuff in at one end, add some more stuff as you go along, and out the other end comes a completed product."

The majority of manufacturing plants are process oriented, being organized by function (similar machines are grouped together, paint departments, heat treating, etc.). Many service facilities are also organized by function or process: hospitals, universities, department stores, and so forth. The main reason for this organization is because these machines or processes serve a variety of needs, not one of which is large enough to justify a machine of its own. In this environment, the product or person requiring service must move longer distances.

JIT in a line flow layout

Exhibit 16.13 shows a pull system in a simple line flow. In theory, no one does any work until the product has been pulled from the end of the line. This item could have been sold or used somewhere else. To fill this void created by the pulled item, a replenishment unit is pulled from upstream. In theory, supposing, in Exhibit 16.13, an item of finished goods is pulled from the finished goods inventory (F). The inventory clerk then goes to processing (E) and takes replacement product to fill the void. Because operator E has an operating policy of keeping a specific number of completed units at the workstation, the operator goes upstream to process D to get replacement units which will then be processed. This pattern continues up to worker A who pulls material from raw material inventory or from whatever process precedes this line. In practice, however, a schedule would be created for the completion of items based on the demand, rather than using inventory clerk F to initiate the chain of events. Operating rules are straightforward:

Courtesy Federal Express

For the service operation of Federal Express in Memphis, just-in-time is a way of life as more than 650,000 packages are sorted and dispatched each night.

Always keep products which have been completed at your workstation. If someone takes your completed work away, go upstream and get some more to work on. Completed work stays on the "completed" side of the machine. For clarity, we haven't shown it in the exhibit, but materials and parts may also be supplied from side lines feeding each workstation as the product progresses.

JIT in a functional (job shop) layout

To justify considering JIT as a valid way to produce goods, the basic requirement is that there is a continual need for the product. This doesn't mean that the product has to be produced continuously in every phase of its creation. Product can be produced intermittently in batches throughout the majority of the sequence except for the final processing or final assembly, which is continuous. Consider a firm that produces several products in constant demand. To simplify it a bit further, assume that the demands are relatively constant throughout the entire year. Let's say that management decides to try to match the production rate with the demand rate, letting demand control production by only producing when goods are pulled from the system—that is, just-in-time.

Some of the products require a final assembly—that is, several parts and components produced in various parts of the firm are assembled together and then sold. Other parts require some types of finish machining at a work center and then are sold. In both cases, work on the products is continuous. If there is a demand pull—finished goods are pulled from the system—these steps are truly just-in-time.

The rest of the system preceding this final stage area may not be just-in-time. Consider the machine centers, paint shops, foundries, heat treating areas, and the countless other locations that these parts and components go through before they reach the final stages.

EXHIBIT 16.14

JIT in a Job-Shop Layout Showing the Materials Handling Vehicle Route Connecting Machine Centers and Line Operations

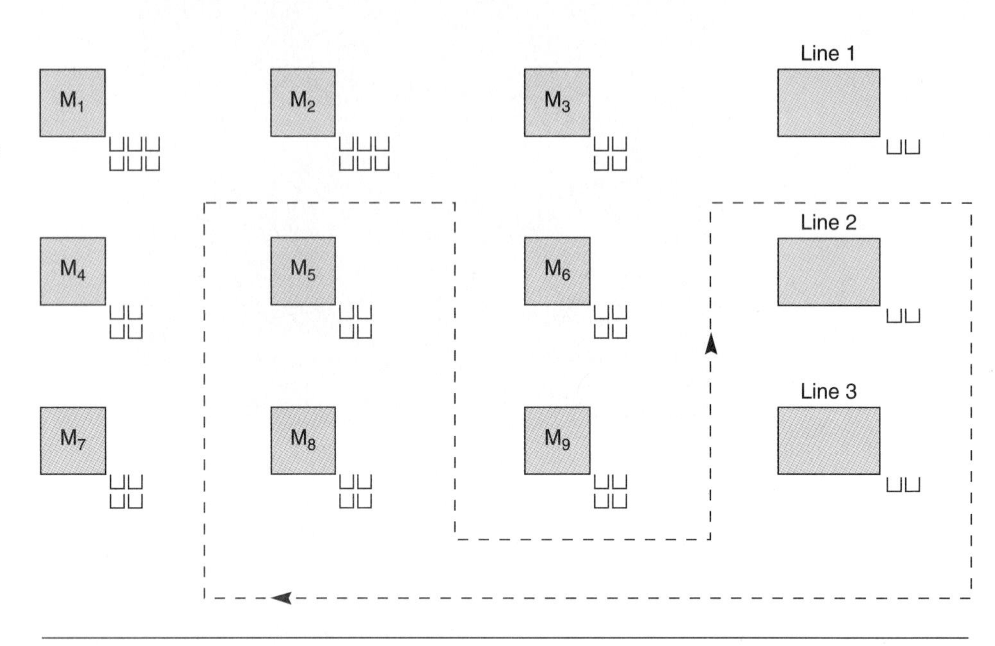

Can we operate these locations in the same Kanban and container logic as we normally use for just-in-time? Yes, we can and we should. (See Exhibit 16.14.)

Parts and components produced in different work centers are used in a variety of final products; therefore, these work centers should have completed containers of the entire variety of output that is designated for just-in-time production. Supposing a work center produces 10 different parts used by several products which are produced just-in-time. This work center must maintain containers of completed output of all 10 parts at the work center to be picked up by those users who need them. If a large part of the facility is organized this way, it would be convenient to have a materials handling vehicle make periodic rounds throughout the facility, such as hourly. This vehicle and operator would stop at the just-in-time assembly stations and machine centers and pick up empty containers (and their production move cards if cards are used). These would be dropped off at the corresponding upstream work centers and full containers picked up. By using periodic material handling routes, the system operates in a just-in-time mode with its production Kanbans and withdrawal or move Kanbans.

Total Quality Control

JIT and total quality control have become linked in the minds of many managers—and for good reason. Consistent with the previous chapter, **total quality control** refers to "building in" quality and *not* "inspecting it in." It also refers to all plant personnel taking responsibility for maintaining quality, not just "leaving it to the quality control depart-

EXHIBIT 16.15

Relationship between JIT and Quality

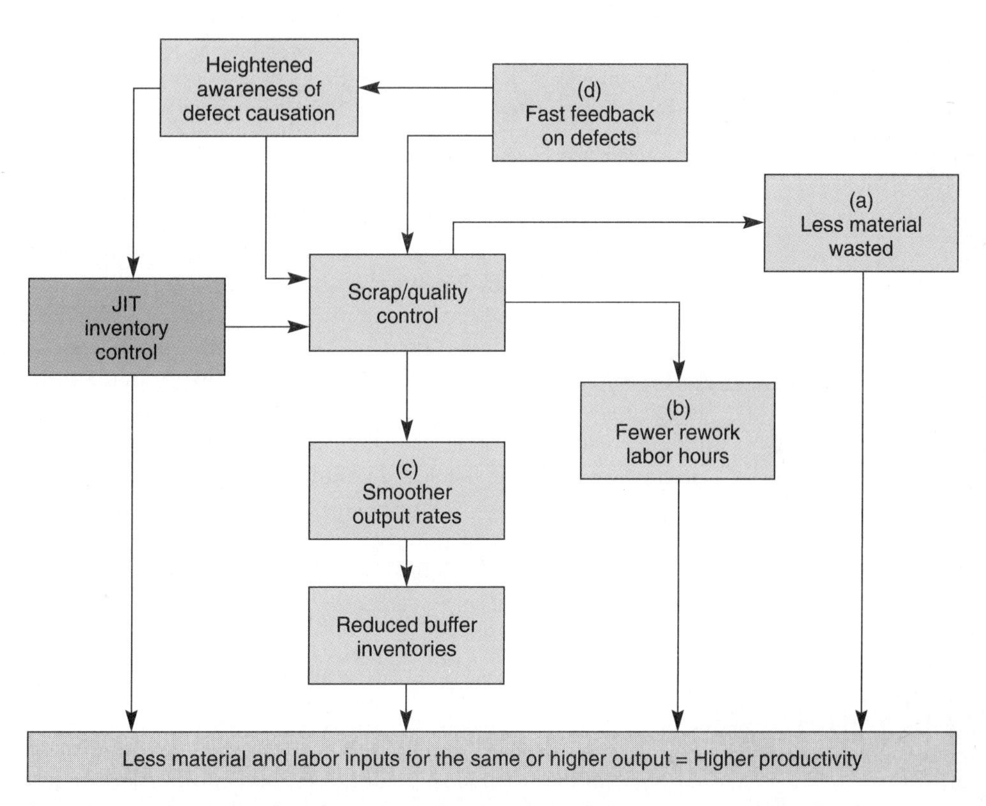

Source: Richard J. Schonberger, "Some Observations on the Advantages and Implementation Issues of Just-in-Time Production Systems," *Journal of Operations Management* 3, no. 1 (November 1982), p. 5.

ment." When employees assume this responsibility, JIT is permitted to work at its optimal level, since only good products are pulled through the system. What results is having your cake and eating it too—high quality and high productivity. Exhibit 16.15 illustrates this subtle relationship.

Statistical quality control uses simple control methods (control charts, primarily) to monitor *all* aspects of a production system. If all aspects of a production process (raw materials, machine variability, etc.) are in control, one can assume that the product coming out of that process is good. When items are produced in small lots, such as in the Kanban system, the inspection may be reduced to just two items—the first and the last. If they are perfect, assume that those produced in between are perfect as well.

Stabilize Schedule

Efficient repetitive manufacture requires a level schedule over a fairly long time horizon. (The actual length depends on many factors, but primarily two: whether the firm makes to order or makes to stock, and the range of product options it offers.) As Robert Hall notes,

> A level schedule is one that requires material to be pulled into final assembly in a pattern uniform enough to allow the various elements of production to respond to pull signals. It does not necessarily mean that the usage of every part on an assembly line is identical hour by hour for days on end; it does mean that a given production system equipped with flexible setups and a fixed amount of material in the pipelines can respond.[9]

The term *freeze window* refers to that period of time during which the schedule can't be changed.

Underutilization of capacity is probably the most controversial feature of JIT. Underutilized (or excess) capacity is really the cost incurred by eliminating inventories as a buffer in the system. In traditional manufacturing, safety stocks and early deliveries are used as a hedge against shortfalls in production resulting from such things as poor quality, machine failures, and unanticipated bottlenecks. Under JIT, excess labor and machines provide that hedge in lieu of inventory. However, excess capacity in the form of labor and equipment is generally far less expensive than carrying excess inventory. Moreover, excess labor can be put to work on other activities during those periods when it is not needed for direct production. Further, the low idle-time cost incurred by the relatively inexpensive machines favored by JIT producers makes machine utilization a secondary issue for many firms. Finally, much of the excess capacity is by design—workers are expected to have time at the end of their shifts to meet with their work groups, clean up their workstations, and ponder potential improvements.

Kanban Pull

Most people view JIT systems as pull systems, where the material is drawn or sent for by the users of the material as needed.[10] Production Kanbans are just one of many devices to signal the need for more parts. Note that the signal sent is for a standard lot size conveyed in a standardized container, not just for a "bunch of parts."

Some typical Kanban-type signals used to initiate production are:

"Hey Joe, make me another widget."

A flashing light over a work center, indicating the need for more parts.

A signal marker hanging on a post by the using workstations. (See Exhibit 16.16.)

Pull systems typically start with the master production schedule specifying the final assembly schedule. By referring to the final assembly schedule, material schedulers and supervisors can see the days during the month when each part will be needed. They determine when to schedule supplier deliveries or internal parts manufacture by offsetting lead times from final assembly dates. Basically, then, the final assembly schedule exerts the initial pull on the system, with Kanbans controlling the flow.

How many Kanban cards should be used? There can be a two-card system, a one-card

---

[9] Robert H. Hall, *Zero Inventories* (Homewood, Ill.: Dow Jones-Irwin, 1983), p. 64.

[10] As Hall notes, citing a no-nonsense plant supervisor, "You don't never make nothin' and *send* it no place. Somebody has to come and get it." Ibid., p. 41.

EXHIBIT 16.16

Diagram of Outbound Stockpoint with Warning Signal Marker

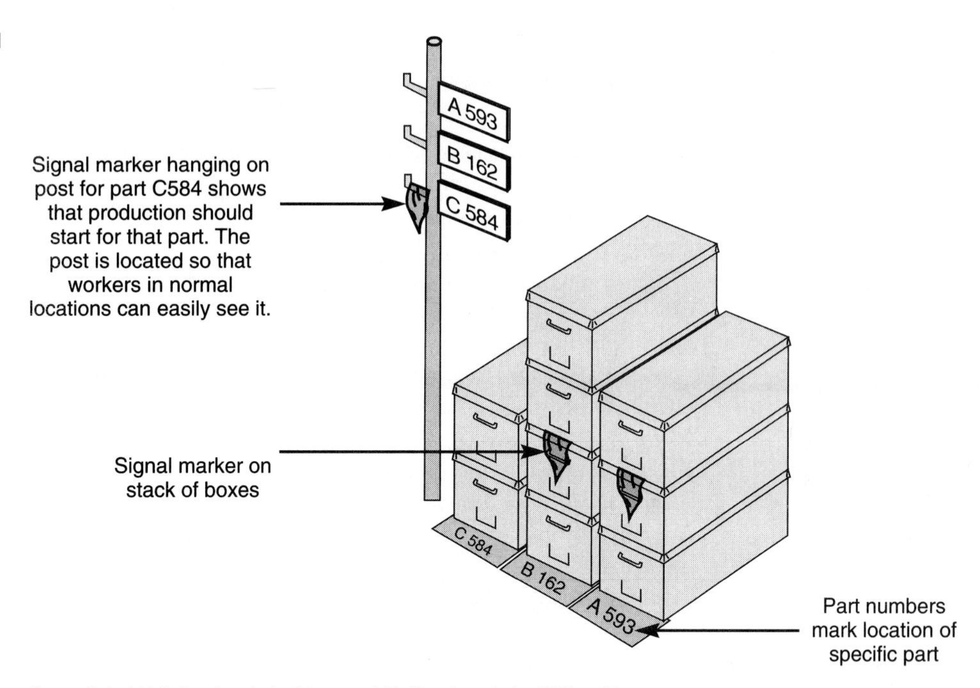

Source: Robert Hall, *Zero Inventories* (Homewood, Ill.: Dow Jones-Irwin, 1983), p. 51.

system, or no cards at all. We list the rules for the two-card and one-card systems which Hall has described so well.[11]

Rules for the two-card system are simple but strict:

> One card, whether a [withdrawal or] move card or a production card, represents only one standard container for one type of part, and exactly the same number of that part that goes into each.
>
> As soon as parts start to be taken from a standard container at its point of use, the move card is detached from the container. It is returned to the supplying operation as authorization to bring another standard container of the same part.
>
> Containers filled with parts should await pick up at clearly designated locations next to the supplying operations. When a full container is taken, the production card is detached and left at the supply point. The move card is attached to the full container and taken to the point of use.
>
> The production card left behind is authorization to the supply operation to make another standard container of the same part and leave it with the production card attached at the same outboard location, ready for pick up.

This system of material control replaces exactly what has been consumed and no more.

[11] Robert W. Hall, *Attaining Manufacturing Excellence* (Homewood, Ill: Dow Jones-Irwin, 1987), pp. 91–94.

The two-card system is actually one of the more complex ways of controlling this. Between two operations within sight of each other, no cards are needed at all—only a strict restriction on the inventory between. This can be done by marking a space between operations called a *Kanban square*. If any of the squares are empty, workers fill them up, but leave no extras.

A one-card system uses only the move card. Space restrictions or visible limits sufficiently restrict the quantity of each part in its location specified for pick up. If the move cards are permanently attached to the containers, the returning empty containers serve as signals to be filled up.

Replenishment signals can be sent electronically back to the supplying operation to save time. However, care needs to be observed since a large amount of the value of the Kanban system is its simplicity.

Backflush is a term used to designate how component parts are accounted for in a pull system. Rather than keeping track of each individual part on a daily basis by job, JIT systems typically explode the bills of materials periodically, such as once a month, and calculate how many of each part must have gone into the final product(s). This eliminates a major shop-floor data collection activity, thereby further simplifying the production management jobs.

Reducing lot sizes in a pull system means removing interstage inventory. This is accomplished in a variety of ways—by better balance of operations so that only two Kanban containers are used between two workstations rather than three, by moving workstations closer together to cut transit time, by automating processes that have high variability, and of course by just-in-time deliveries.

Work with Vendors

All the items in category in Exhibit 16.11 except "project usage requirements" have been discussed earlier. *Project usage requirements* means that the vendors are given a long-run picture of the demands that will be placed on their production and distribution systems. This permits them to develop level production schedules.

Reduce Inventory More

Material transit systems, carousels, and conveyors are places where inventory is held, and thus are targets for inventory reduction efforts. Often there is heated debate when it comes to doing away with them. One reason is that such inventory locations are frequently the focus or result of a previous inventory improvements effort that has shown good results compared to the system used before that. The people involved in such an effort are unlikely to rush to support the elimination of something that has been working.

Improve Product Design

Standard product configurations and fewer, standardized parts are important elements in good product designs for JIT. When the objective is to establish a simple routine process, anything that reduces variability in the end item or the materials that go into it is worth careful consideration.

Integrating process design with product design refers to the early involvement activities among product designers, process designers, and manufacturing personnel. Besides improving the producibility of the product, such interaction facilitates the processing of engineering changes orders (ECOs). ECOs to a product can be extremely disruptive to the production process. They alter the specifications of the product, which in turn may call for new materials, new methods, and even new schedules. To minimize such disruptions, many JIT producers introduce their ECOs in batches, properly sequenced with the production schedule, rather than one by one, as is common in traditional manufacturing in the United States. While batching sounds obvious and simple, it requires a great deal of coordination and a willingness to delay what may be significant changes in a product design in exchange for maintaining production stability.

Concurrently Solve Problems and Measure Performance

A JIT application is not an overnight, turnkey installation. Rather, it is an evolutionary system that is continually seeking ways of improving production. Improvement comes through looking at problems as challenges rather than threats—problems that can be solved with common sense and detailed, rigorous analysis.

The techniques for problem solving are primarily continuous improvement methods. Effective problem solving means that the problem is solved permanently. Because JIT requires a team effort, problems are treated in a team context. Staff personnel are expected to be seen frequently on the shop floor, and in some companies are expected to arrive a half hour before production workers to ensure that everything is in order, thereby avoiding problems.

Continual education is absolutely essential if the system is to avoid stagnation. While JIT may cost little in the way of hardware, it requires the need for a substantial investment in training people at all levels of the organization to better understand what the system demands and how they fit into it.

Many performance measures emphasize the number of processes and practices changed to improve materials flow and reduce labor content, and the degree to which they do so. If the processes physically improve over time, lower costs follow. According to Hall, a department head in a Japanese JIT system is likely to be evaluated on the following factors:

1. Improvement trends, including number of improvement projects undertaken, trends in costs, and productivity. Productivity is measured as:

$$p = \frac{\text{Measurement of department output}}{\text{Total employees (direct + indirect)}}$$

2. Quality trends, including reduction in defect rates, improvement in process capability, and improvement in quality procedures.
3. Running to a level schedule and providing parts when others need them.
4. Trends in departmental inventory levels (e.g., speed of flow).
5. Staying within budget for expenses.
6. Developing work force skills, versatility, participation in changes, and morale.[12]

[12] Ibid., pp. 254–55.

16.4 SOME TECHNICAL ISSUES ABOUT KANBAN

Kanban as a Fixed-Order Quantity/Reorder Point Inventory System

Kanban and the simple fixed-order quantity/reorder point system are both reactive systems. These two systems are designed to replenish inventory, not in anticipation of future orders, but as soon as the inventory is depleted. Also, both assume continuous review, predetermined reorder points, and fixed replenishment quantities. The inventory behavior under the two systems is identical with the one exception that Kanban displays a lumpy usage pattern. The reason for this is that, unlike the fixed order quantity system where parts are withdrawn one at a time, Kanban withdraws a fixed number of them in standard-sized containers. Such standardized containers, in turn, define the lot size, so each time one is withdrawn, a reorder point is reached.

In light of the basic similarity of the two systems, why has Kanban performed so well, while the fixed-order quantity system has generally failed? The answer is that Japanese management has been able to structure a manufacturing environment conducive to Kanban operation. The major contribution of Japanese management (relative to inventory control) lies in demand management and lead-time management, two features that are implicit in our discussion of JIT.

JIT and Cost Accounting

Cost accounting systems have focused on direct labor since the Industrial Revolution. However, under JIT (and computer-integrated management) overhead costs are dominant, often 20 times as high as direct labor. Moreover, with permanent employment, workers maintaining their own equipment, and other measures, the distinction between direct and indirect labor has become blurred for cost-allocation purposes. Hewlett-Packard has recognized this and has eliminated the cost category of direct labor, now using simply "labor" instead.

It appears at this time that the primary difference between traditional and JIT cost accounting is the application of overhead on the basis of product time in the system (cycle time) rather than direct labor or machine hours.[13]

16.5 COMPANY EXPERIENCES WITH JIT

Exhibit 16.17 summarizes the experiences of five major U.S. companies that have installed JIT (and TQC, total quality control). As can be seen, the impact on these companies' performance measures is overwhelmingly positive. Similar results have been reported in

[13] Mohan V. Tatikonda, "Just-in-Time and Modern Manufacturing Environments: Implications for Cost Accounting," *Production and Inventory Management Journal* 28, no. 1 (1988), pp. 1–5.

EXHIBIT 16.17 Summary of JIT/TQC Activities for Five U.S. Companies

Company Name (Division)	Product Category	Production Characteristics	IMPLEMENTATION ISSUES: Why Started	IMPLEMENTATION ISSUES: How Implemented	RESULTS: Labor Productivity Improvement	RESULTS: Setup Time (Improvement)	RESULTS: Inventory Reductions	RESULTS: Quality Improvements
Deere & Company	Heavy machinery Farm equipment Lawn-care equipment	Repetitive manufacturing	Survival Foreign competition	Visit to Japan Task force in plant Education Pilot projects Work-flow analysis	Subassembly: 19–35% Welding: 7–38% Manufacturing cost: 10–20% Materials handling: 40%	Presses: 38–80% Drills: 24–33% Shears: 45% Grinders: 44% Average: 45%	Raw steel: 40% Purchased parts: 7% Crane shafts: 30 days ® 3 days Average: 31%	Implemented process control charting in 40% of operations
Black & Decker (Consumer Power Tools)	Electrical products	Repetitive manufacturing Floor space 385,000 sq. ft. Employees: 1,010	Large expenses in inventory carrying costs (high interest rates)	Education Balanced flow Rewrote work procedures Started to produce in weekly quantity	Assembly: 24 operators ® 6 operators Support: 7 ® 5	Punch press: 1 hr. ® 1 min. Drastic in many areas	Turns: 16 ® 30	Reduced complaints in packaging 98% 100% customer service level
Omark Industries	Forestry equipment and sporting goods	Mostly repetitive 18 plants	Corporate task force found JIT/TQC/employee involvement as reason for success	Steering committee Plant study team Presentation by corporate staff Pilot projects	Plant A: 30% Plant B: 30% Plant C: 20%	A: 165 ® 5 min. B: 43 ® 17 min. C: 360 ® 17 min. D: 45 ® 6 min.	Product A: 92% Product B: 29% Product C: 50%	Product A scrap and rework: 20% Product E customer service cost: 50%
Hewlett-Packard (Computer Systems)	Computer and test systems	Forming/assembly/testing Many options	Questioned why overseas suppliers produced quality products	TQC first Employee training/involvement Leveled schedule Process simplification	Standard hours: 87 hrs. ® 39 hrs.	Not available	PC Assembly inventory: $675,000 (100) ® $190,000 (28)	Solder defects: 5000 PPM ® 100 Scrap: $80,000/mo. ® $5,000
FMC	Industrial equipment Defense Automotive Electrical	Multiple divisions with variety of products 50 manufacturing and mining operations	Survival Absence of patent protection Keen cost competition	Seminars Pilot project Pilot plants Setup time Inventory target Positive reinforcement	Direct labor productivity: 13% (Automotive service equipment division)	Defense equipment group: 60%–75% Automotive/electrical: 80%	Turns: 1.9 ® 4.0 (automotive service equipment division)	Customer service: 88% ® 98% Cost of quality: 3.5% ® 2.1% (auto. svc. eq. div.)

Source: Adapted from Kiyoshi Suzaki, "Comparative Study of JIT/TQC Activities in Japanese and Western Companies," First World Congress of Production and Inventory Control, Vienna, Austria, 1985, pp. 63–66.

European and British firms. One study of 80 plants in Europe, for example, listed the following benefits from JIT:

1. An average reduction in inventory of about 50 percent.
2. A reduction in throughput time of 50 to 70 percent.
3. Reduction in setup times of as much as 50 percent without major investment in plant and equipment.
4. An increase in productivity of between 20 and 50 percent.
5. Payback time for investment in JIT averaged less than nine months.[14]

Additional success stories abound in the production control journals. This is not to say that the implementation of JIT is trouble free, however.

16.6 JIT IN SERVICES

Service organizations and service operations within manufacturing firms present interesting opportunities for applications of JIT concepts. Here is an edited version of a paper by Randall J. Benson, a consultant for Coopers & Lybrand, which explains why JIT is not just for the factory.[15] The last part of this section describes the successful use of JIT techniques at a Japanese sushi house.

Despite the many differences between service and manufacturing, both share the most basic attributes of production, because they employ processes that add value to the basic inputs with the objective of creating an end product or service.

JIT focuses on processes, not products and, therefore, it can be applied to any group of processes, from manufacturing to services. The JIT goal is approached by testing each step in the production process to determine if it adds value to the product or service. If these steps do not add value, then the process is a candidate for reengineering. In this way, the production of processes gradually and continually improves.

Both manufacturing and services can be improved with JIT because both are systems of production processes and because JIT is essentially a process-oriented waste-elimination philosophy. The themes for JIT process improvement should therefore apply equally in a service environment.

How Do the JIT Themes Fit Services?

The following eight **JIT themes** make no reference to manufactured products. These themes are applicable to all areas of JIT manufacturing, regardless of the specific technique being applied. Because they are process as opposed to product oriented, they should also apply equally well to service. Indeed, they lead to some interesting insights into service operations management.

---

[14] Amrik Sohal and Keith Howard, "Trends in Materials Management," *International Journal of Production Distribution and Materials Management* 17, no. 5 (1987), pp. 3–41.

[15] Randall J. Benson, "JIT: Not Just for the Factory," *Proceedings form the 29th Annual International Conference for the American Production and Inventory Control Society,* St. Louis, Missouri, October 20–24, 1986, pp. 370–74.

1. *Total visibility.* Total visibility means that the equipment, people, material, processes, process status, and process flows are visible to those participating in the process. Visibility has a special marketing importance to service operations because the customer most often participates directly in the process. The service process itself is therefore tangible evidence of the value and quality of the service.

2. *Synchronization and balance.* This is the concept that "If you don't need it now, don't make it now." A balanced operation runs at the same rate at every production stage because the processes are synchronized and extra inventory is eliminated.

Services are typically required to synchronize sales and production almost perfectly because their customers will not wait if they have other alternatives.

3. *Respect for people.* Each time a service employee interacts with a customer, a moment of truth takes place. It determines the customer's perception of the quality and the value of the service. A negative moment of truth carries a much heavier weight in the customer's perception than a positive one. Service employees are often personally responsible for the quality, consistency, and value of the service delivered.

4. *Flexibility.* Flexibility refers to the ability to rapidly adapt the process to produce what the customers want when they want it without wasting production resources. Service operations must be especially flexible because they must produce a service instantaneously and have that service meet or exceed the customer's expectations.

5. *Continuous improvement.* Continuous improvement involves moving always closer to the ideal by making many small improvements in the processes.

Because most services tend to be labor intense, a majority of the improvements affect employee activities. Many service firms have successfully used employee-centered improvement groups to improve the quality and value of the service.

6. *Responsibility for the environment.* Service operations have no more room for errors than manufacturing. In labor-intensive service industries, the employees have even more impact on the performance of the process. Here, every employee must take full responsibility for each moment of truth that takes place during the customer contact and for continuously improving the processes.

7. *Holistic approach.* JIT works best when it is implemented as a company philosophy to eliminate waste, not just as a technique to reduce inventory. All departments and all levels of operations get involved in eliminating waste.

In service firms the holistic approach is essential, because production and marketing cannot be separated. Service operations must approach process changes as marketing needs change because the customers are influenced by the service delivery process itself. A customer's perception of the quality and value of the service is largely determined by the process.

8. *Simplicity.* The simplicity of the process allows people who run the process to identify opportunities for process improvements and to plan the process changes themselves.

Simplicity is no less important in the service sector. It may be even more important due to the worker-intensive nature of the service delivery system. Furthermore, customer participation tends to be more successful if the process is simplified. Simple processes, systems, and controls allow customers to easily engage, participate in, and disengage from the service delivery process.

The JIT themes just described are therefore appropriate for service firms. In fact, one could argue that the JIT improvements in manufacturing actually allow the manufacturer to operate more like a successful service firm. Isn't stockless production based on a synchronization of fast-flow processes an excellent description of a service process?

JIT has already been applied successfully in diverse service industries. This is a significant step for services because the service sector presently lacks a general and comprehensive approach to service operations improvements. A service version of JIT holds the promise to better comprehend service operations across very dissimilar industries.

Which JIT Techniques Are Appropriate for Services?

Many of the JIT techniques have been successfully applied by service firms. Just as with manufacturing, the suitability of each technique and the corresponding work steps depends on the characteristics of the firm's markets, production and equipment technology, skill sets, and corporate culture. Service firms are not different in this respect. Following are some of the more successful applications:

Organize problem-solving groups. **Focused improvement groups** and quality circles improve the quality and cost performance of manufacturing processes. The groups use methods such as group dynamics, brainstorming, Pareto analysis, and root-cause analysis to rethink manufacturing processes.

Honeywell is extending its quality circles from manufacturing into its service operations. Other corporations as diverse as First Bank/Dallas, Standard Meat Company, and Miller Brewing Company are using similar approaches to improve service. British Airways used quality circles as a fundamental part of its strategy to implement new service practices.

Upgrade housekeeping. Good housekeeping means more than winning the clean broom award. It means that only the necessary items are kept in a work area, that there is a place for everything, that everything is clean and in a constant state of readiness. The employees clean their own areas.

Service organizations such as McDonald's, Disneyland, and Speedi-Lube have recognized the critical nature of housekeeping. Their dedication to house-keeping has meant that service processes work better, the attitude of the workers toward continuous improvement is easier to develop, and customers perceive that they are receiving better service.

Upgrade quality. The only cost-effective way to improve quality is to develop reliable process capabilities. Process quality is quality at the source—it guarantees first-time production of consistent and uniform products and services.

McDonald's is famous for building quality into its service delivery process. It literally "industrialized" the service delivery system so that part-time, casual workers could provide the same consistent, high-quality eating experience anywhere in the world.

Clarify process flows. Clarification of the flows, based on the JIT themes, can dramatically improve the process performance.

For example, Federal Express changed air flight patterns from origin-to-destination to origin-to-hub where the freight is transferred at a central location (e.g., Memphis) to an outbound plane heading for the destination. This revolutionized the air transport industry. The order entry department of a manufacturing firm converted from functional departments to customer-centered work groups and reduced the order processing lead time from eight to two days. A county government used the JIT approach to cut the time to record a deed transfer by 50 percent. Supermaids sends in a team of house cleaners, each with a specific responsibility, to clean each house quickly with parallel processes. Changes in process flows can literally revolutionize service industries.

Revise equipment and process technologies. Revising technologies involves evaluation of the equipment and processes in terms of their ability to meet the process requirements, to be consistently within tolerance, and to fit the scale and capacity of the work group.

Speedi-Lube converted the standard service-station concept to a specialized lubrication and inspection center by changing the service bays from drive-in to drive-through and by eliminating the hoists, replacing them with pits under the cars so that the employees have full access to all of the lubrication areas on the vehicle.

A hospital reduced the operating-room setup time so that it had the flexibility to perform a wider range of operations without reducing the operating room's availability.

Level of the facility load. Service firms synchronize production with demand. They have developed unique approaches to leveling demand so they can avoid making customers wait for service. McDonald's offers a special breakfast menu in the morning. Retail stores use take-a-number systems. The post office charges more for next-day delivery. These are all examples of the service approach for creating uniform facility loads.

Eliminate unnecessary activities. Any step in a process that does not add value is a candidate for elimination. A step that does add value may be a candidate for reengineering to improve the process consistency or to reduce the time to perform the tasks.

A hospital discovered that a significant amount of time during an operation was spent waiting for an instrument that was not available when the operation began. It subsequently developed a checklist of instruments required for each category of operation. Speedi-Lube eliminated steps, but it also added some steps that didn't improve the lubrication process but did make customers feel more assured about the work that was being performed.

Reorganize physical configuration. The work-area configurations frequently require reorganization during a JIT implementation. Often manufacturers accomplish this by setting up manufacturing cells to produce items in small lots, synchronous to demand. These cells amount to "micro-factories" inside the plant.

Most service firms are far behind manufacturers in this area. However, a few interesting examples do come out of the service sector. Some hospitals, instead of routing patients all over the building for tests, exams, X-rays, and injections are reorganizing their services into work groups based on the type of problem. Teams that treat only trauma are common, but other work groups have been formed to treat less immediate conditions like hernias. These amount to micro-clinics within the hospital facility.

Introduce demand-pull scheduling. Due to the nature of service production and consumption, demand-pull (customer-driven) scheduling is necessary for operating a service business. Moreover, many service firms are separating their operations into "back room" and "customer contact" facilities. This approach creates new problems in coordinating the schedules between the facilities. The original Wendy's restaurants were set up so the cooks could see the cars enter the parking lot. They put a pre-established number of hamburger patties onto the grill for each car. This pull system was designed to have a fresh patty on the grill before the customer even placed an order.

Develop supplier networks. Supplier networks in the JIT context refer to the cooperative association of suppliers and customers working over the long term for mutual benefit. Service firms have not emphasized supplier networks for materials because the service costs are often predominantly labor. Notable exceptions must include service organizations like McDonald's, one of the biggest food purchasers in the world. A contract manufacturer recognized that it needed cooperative relationships for temporary employees as well as for parts. It is considering a campaign to establish JIT-type relationships with a temporary employment service and a trade school to develop a reliable source of trained assemblers.

Theodore Levitt eloquently summarized the need to apply manufacturing thinking to service:

> Until we think of service in more positive and encompassing terms, until it is enthusiastically viewed as manufacturing in the field, receptive to the same kinds of technological approaches that are used in the factory, the results are likely to be just as costly and idiosyncratic as the results of the lonely journeyman carving things laboriously by hand at home.[16]

Once we start thinking of services as an organized system of production processes, we can consider the use of JIT-type concepts to reengineer service delivery operations. The result will be consistent services of high quality and excellent value, produced with high productivity.

Japanese Management and the 100 Yen Sushi House

The 100 Yen Sushi House is no ordinary sushi restaurant.[17] It is the ultimate showcase of Japanese productivity. As we entered the shop, there was a chorus of "*iratsai,*" a welcome from everyone working in the shop—cooks, waitresses, the owner, and the owner's children. The house features an ellipsoid-shaped serving area in the middle of the room, where three or four cooks were busily preparing sushi. Perhaps 30 stools surrounded the

---

[16] Theodore Leavitt, "Production Line Approach to Service," *Harvard Business Review* 50, no. 5 (September–October 1972), p. 52.

[17] Sang M. Lee, "Japanese Management and the 100 Yen Sushi House," *Operations Management Review* 1, no. 2 (Winter 1983), pp. 45–48.

serving area. We took seats at the counters and were promptly served with a cup of "misoshiru," which is a bean paste soup, a pair of chopsticks, a cup of green tea, a tiny plate to make our own sauce, and a small china piece to hold the chopsticks. So far, the service was average for any sushi house. Then, I noticed something special. There was a conveyor belt going around the ellipsoid service area, like a toy train track. On it I saw a train of plates of sushi. You can find any kind of sushi that you can think of—from the cheapest seaweed or octopus to the expensive raw salmon or shrimp dishes. The price is uniform, however, 100 yen per plate. On closer examination, while my eyes were racing to keep up with the speed of the traveling plates, I found that a cheap seaweed plate had four pieces, while the more expensive raw salmon dish had only two pieces. I sat down and looked around at the other customers at the counters. They were all enjoying their sushi and slurping their soup while reading newspapers or magazines.

I saw a man with eight plates all stacked up neatly. As he got up to leave, the cashier looked over and said, "800 yen, please." The cashier had no cash register, since she can simply count the number of plates and then multiply by 100 yen. As the customer was leaving, once again we heard a chorus of "*Arigato Gosaimas*" (thank you) from all the workers.

The owner's daily operation is based on a careful analysis of information. The owner has a complete summary of demand information for each of the different types of sushi plates, and thus he knows exactly how many of each type he should prepare and when. Furthermore, the whole operation is based on the repetitive manufacturing principle with appropriate just-in-time and quality control systems. For example, the store has a very limited refrigerator capacity (we could see several whole fish or octopus in the glassed chambers right in front of our counter). Thus, the store uses the just-in-time inventory control system. Instead of increasing the refrigeration capacity by purchasing new refrigeration systems, the company has an agreement with the fish vendor to deliver fresh fish several times a day so that materials arrive just in time to be used for sushi making. Therefore, the inventory cost is minimum.

In the just-in-time operation system, the safety stock principle is turned upside down. In other words, the safety stock is deliberately removed gradually, to uncover problems and their possible solutions. The available floor space is for workers and their necessary equipment but not for holding inventory. In the 100 Yen Sushi House, workers and their equipment are positioned so close that sushi making is passed on hand to hand rather than as independent operations. The absence of walls of inventory allows the owner and workers to be involved in the total operation, from greeting the customer to serving what is ordered. Their tasks are tightly interrelated and everyone rushes to a problem spot to prevent the cascading effect of the problem throughout the work process.

The 100 Yen Sushi House is a labor-intensive operation, which is based mostly on simplicity and common sense rather than high technology, contrary to American perceptions. I was very impressed. As I finished my fifth plate, I saw the same octopus sushi plate going around for about the thirtieth time. Perhaps I had discovered the pitfall of the system. So I asked the owner how he takes care of the sanitary problems when a sushi plate goes around all day long, until an unfortunate customer eats it and perhaps gets food poisoning. He bowed with an apologetic smile and said, "Well, sir, we never let our sushi plates go unsold longer than about 30 minutes." Then he scratched his head and said, "Whenever one of our employees takes a break, he or she can take off unsold plates of sushi and either eat them or throw them away. We are very serious about our sushi quality." As we laughed, he laughed, along with a 90-degree bow. As we were walking out of the sushi house, while "*arigato gosaimas*" was ringing in my ears, I was contemplating how to introduce the 100 Yen Sushi House concept to the States. Perhaps I can suggest the concept to the student union at the university for an experiment. Maybe McDonald's, Pizza Hut, Wendy's . . .

16.7 CONCLUSION

We have listed many of the potential benefits of just-in-time systems. In our concluding remarks, however, we need to caution that JIT applications are not universal. There are specific requirements for successful implementation and we need to be careful not to be caught up in the excitement and promises.

In 1983, Hewlett-Packard created a videotape on JIT at its Boulder, Colorado, plant. It was an excellent video and fun to watch. Its purpose was to convince viewers that a JIT pull system would produce significant benefits for most manufacturing plants. Although instructors still use this video in their classrooms, many of us caution against the message conveyed.

The video does not carry through a numerical analysis of the performance times, number of defects, work in process, and so on. This can lead to the wrong conclusions—that is, that the JIT pull system was responsible for improved conditions.

In a recent article, Jerry Bowman presented the data.[18] After analyzing the data he commented that the most significant benefits did not result from the pull system but from reducing lot sizes. The HP video showed that the best performance occurred when items were processed using a pull system in lots of one unit. Bowman commented, "If you manufacture in lot sizes of one in a 'flow' environment, you probably couldn't tell whether you were pushing or pulling nor would it matter."

This is also consistent with students' difficulties in distinguishing between an American automobile assembly line and a Japanese automobile assembly line. JIT is becoming a principal manufacturing management concept and undoubtedly will continue to be so throughout the 1990s. But again, we caution you to be careful in its use.

16.8 REVIEW AND DISCUSSION QUESTIONS

1. What is meant by "pragmatic" JIT versus "romantic" JIT?
2. Stopping waste is one of the most important parts of JIT. Identify some of the sources of waste and discuss how they may be eliminated.

[18] D. Jerry Bowman, "If You Don't Understand JIT, How Can You Implement It?" *Industrial Engineering* (February 1991), pp. 38–39.

3. Discuss JIT in a job-shop layout and in a line layout.
4. Why is it important for JIT to have a stable schedule?
5. Are there any aspects of the Japanese approach that you could apply to your own current school activities? Explain.
6. Do you believe that Fredrick W. Taylor, the father of scientific management, would be for or against the Japanese approach?
7. Which objections might a marketing manager have against uniform plant loading?
8. What are the implications for cost accounting of JIT production?
9. Which questions would you want to ask the president of Toyota about his operations management?
10. Explain how cards are used in a Kanban system.
11. In which ways, if any, are the following systems analogous to Kanban: returning empty bottles to the supermarket and picking up filled ones; running a hot dog stand at lunchtime; withdrawing money from a checking account; collecting eggs at a chicken ranch?
12. How does the old saying, "There's no such thing as a free lunch," pertain to the Japanese elimination of inventory?
13. Why do ECOs cause so much trouble under JIT systems? How do the Japanese handle them?
14. Explain the relationship between quality and productivity under the JIT philosophy.

16.9 CASE: XYZ PRODUCTS COMPANY

XYZ Products Company is a supplier of gizmos for a large computer manufacturer located a few miles away. The company produces three different models of gizmos in production runs ranging from 100 to 300 units.

The production flow of Models X and Y is shown in Case Exhibit 1. Model Z requires milling as its first step, but otherwise follows the same flow pattern as X and Y. Skids can hold up to 20 gizmos at a time. Approximate processing times per unit by operation number and equipment setup times are shown in the following table:

Operation Number and Name		Operation Times (minutes)	Setup Times (minutes)
—	Milling for Z	20	60
1	Lathe	50	30
2	Mod. 14 drill	15	5
3	Mod. 14 drill	40	5
4	Assembly step 1	50	
	Assembly step 2	45	
	Assembly step 3	50	
5	Inspection	30	
6	Paint	30	20
7	Oven	50	
8	Packing	5	

CASE EXHIBIT 1

Gizmo Production Flow

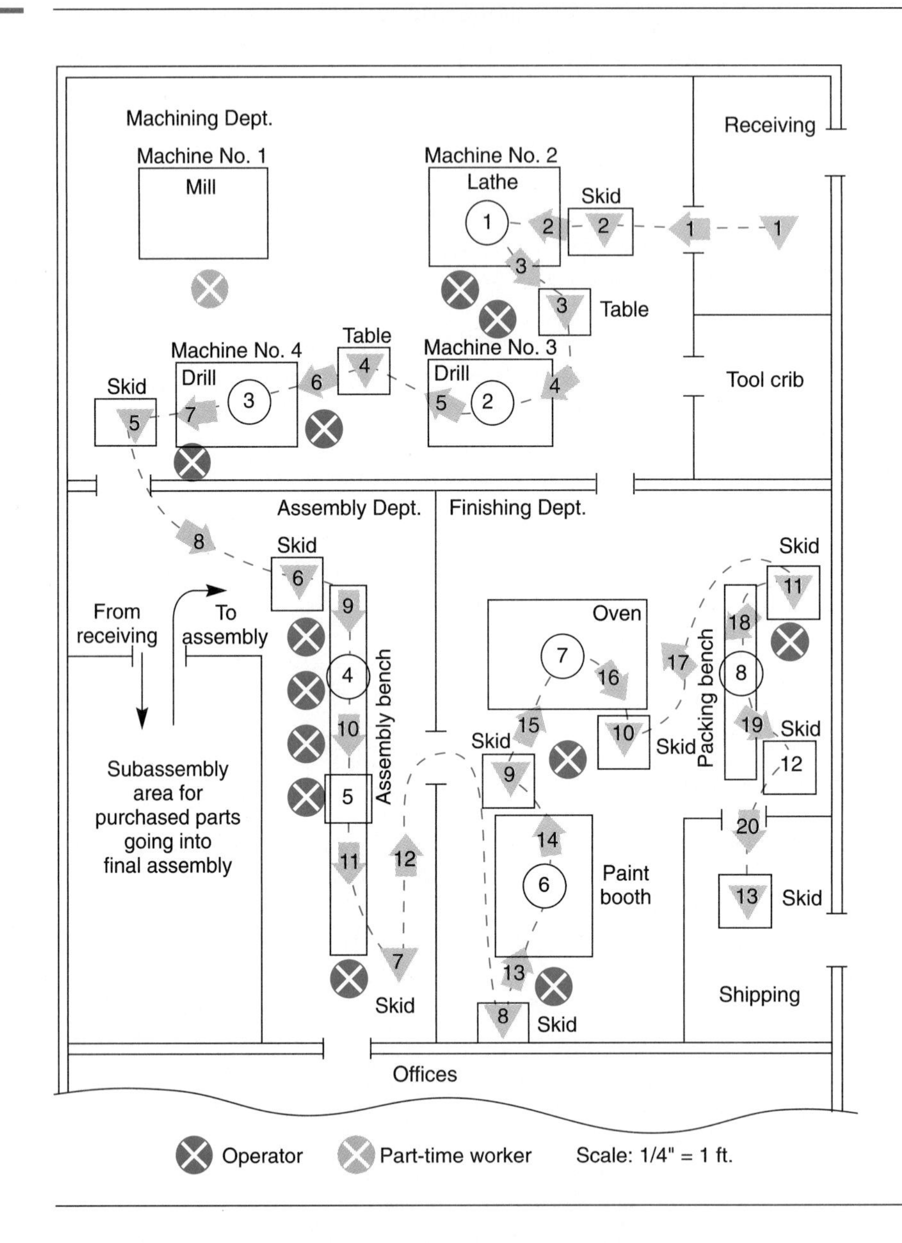

The demand for gizmos from the computer company ranges between 125 and 175 per month, equally divided among X, Y, and Z. Subassembly builds up inventory early in the month to make certain that a buffer stock is always available. Raw materials and purchased parts for subassemblies each constitute 40 percent of the manufacturing cost of a gizmo. Both categories of parts are multiple sourced from about 80 vendors and are delivered at random times. (Gizmos have 40 different part numbers.)

Some other information: Scrap rates are about 10 percent at each operation, inventory turns twice yearly, employees are paid on day rate, employee turnover is 25 percent per year, and net profit from operations is steady at 5 percent per year. Maintenance is performed as needed.

The manager of XYZ has been contemplating installing an MRP system to help control inventories and to "keep the skids filled." (It is his view that two days of work in front of a workstation motivates the worker to produce at top speed.) He is also planning to add three inspectors to clean up the quality problem. Further, he is thinking about setting up a rework line to speed up repairs. While he is pleased with the high utilization of most of his equipment and labor, he is concerned about the idle time of his milling machine. Finally, he has asked his industrial engineering department to look into high-rise shelving to store parts coming off Machine 4.

QUESTIONS

1. Which of the changes being considered by the manager of XYZ go counter to the JIT philosophy?
2. Make recommendations for JIT improvements in such areas as scheduling, layout, Kanban, task groupings, and inventory. Use quantitative data as much as possible; state necessary assumptions.
3. Sketch the operation of a pull system for XYZ's current system.
4. Outline a plan for the introduction of JIT at XYZ.

16.10 SELECTED BIBLIOGRAPHY

Benson, Randall J. "JIT: Not Just for the Factory." *Proceedings from the 29th Annual International Conference for the American Production and Inventory Control Society,* St. Louis, Missouri, October 20–24, 1986, pp. 370–74.

Davidson, William H. *The Amazing Race: Winning the Technorivalry with Japan.* New York: John Wiley & Sons, 1984.

Fucini, Joseph J., and Suzy Fucini. *Working for the Japanese.* New York: Free Press, 1990.

Garvin, David A. "Quality on the Line." *Harvard Business Review* 61, no. 5 (September–October 1983), pp. 65–75.

Hall, Robert. *Zero Inventories.* Homewood, Ill.: Dow Jones-Irwin, 1983.

________. *Attaining Manufacturing Excellence.* Homewood, Ill.: Dow Jones-Irwin, 1987.

Hay, Edward J. *Just-in-Time Production: A Winning Combination of Neglected American Ideas.* East Greenwich, R.I.: Edward J. Hay Associates, 1983.

Inman, R. Anthony, and Satish Mehra. "The Transferability of Just-in-Time Concepts to American Small Business," *Interfaces* 20, no. 2 (March–April 1990), pp. 30–37.

Klein, Janice. "A Re-examination of Autonomy in Light of New Manufacturing Practices." *Human Relations* 43 (1990).

Leavitt, Theodore. "Production Line Approach to Service." *Harvard Business Review* 50, no. 5 (September–October 1972), p. 52.

Lee, Sang M. "Japanese Management and the 100 Yen Sushi House." *Operations Management Review* 1, no. 2 (Winter 1983), pp. 45–48.

Monden, Yasuhiro. *Toyota Production System, Practical Approach to Production Management.* Atlanta Ga.: Industrial Engineering and Management Press, 1983.

________. "What Makes the Toyota Production System Really Tick?" *Industrial Engineering* 13, no. 1 (January 1981), pp. 36–46.

Ohno, Taiichi. *Toyota Production System: Beyond Large-Scale Production.* Cambridge, Mass.: Productivity Press, 1988.

Ohno, Taiichi, and Setsuo Mito. *Just-in-Time for Today and Tomorrow.* Cambridge, Mass.: Productivity Press, 1988.

Schonberger, Richard J. *Japanese Productivity Techniques.* New York: Free Press, 1982.

________. *World-Class Manufacturing: The Lessons of Simplicity Applied.* New York: Free Press, 1986.

________. *Building a Chain of Customers: Linking Business Functions to Create a World-Class Company.* New York: Free Press, 1989.

Sewell, G. "Management Information Systems for JIT Production." *Omega* 18, no. 5 (1990), pp. 481–503.

Shingo, Shigeo. *A Study of the Toyota Production System from an Industrial Engineering Viewpoint.* Cambridge, Mass.: Productivity Press, 1989.

Sohal, Amrik and Keith Howard. "Trends in Materials Management." *International Journal of Production Distribution and Materials Management* 17, no. 5 (1987), pp. 3–41.

Suzaki, Kiyoshi. *The New Manufacturing Challenge: Techniques for Continuous Improvement.* New York: Free Press, 1987.

Tatikonda, Mohan V. "Just-in-Time and Modern Manufacturing Environments: Implications for Cost Accounting." *Production and Inventory Management Journal* 28, no. 1 (1988), pp. 1–5.

Wantuck, Kenneth A. "The Japanese Approach to Productivity." Southfield, Mich: Bendix Corporation, 1983.

Weiss, Andrew. "Simple Truths of Japanese Manufacturing." *Harvard Business Review* 62, no. 4 (July–August 1984), pp. 119–25.

Zipkin, Paul H. "Does Manufacturing Need a JIT Revolution?" *Harvard Business Review,* January–February 1991, pp. 40–50.

Chapter 17

Job Shop Scheduling and Control

EPIGRAPH

Job shops in everyday life:
Your house, your kitchen, your school, your study area.

CHAPTER OUTLINE

KEY TERMS

Job Shop
Flow Shop
Dispatching of Orders
Expediting
Machine-Limited Systems
Labor-Limited Systems
Priority Rules
Critical Ratio Rule
Shop-Floor Control
Input/Output (I/O) Control

In project-oriented processes, we are typically dealing with only a single (albeit complex) product. Assembly lines and continuous flow processes, at the other extreme, are quite inflexible to changes in products and sequencing of operations. Intermittent processes in the form of job shops or batch processes, on the other hand, have both the flexibility and the capacity to accommodate multiple products that require different operations in different sequences. How best to schedule these products through the factory often results in a nightmare for the job shop supervisor (as reflected by the accompanying cartoon).

From a technical perspective, job shop scheduling is the most challenging in terms of problem solving. Consequently, extensive research efforts have been devoted to studying this subject. In this chapter we will present several priority rules for scheduling a job shop and criteria for measuring its performance. We will also address the issue of scheduling workers in a service environment.

17.1 JOB SHOP DEFINED

Even though we briefly defined the term *job shop* in an earlier chapter, this expanded definition provides additional insight into the challenges that confront a job shop manager. A **job shop** is a functional organization whose departments or work centers are organized around particular types of equipment or operations, such as drilling and assembly in a factory, or drilling and cleaning in a dentist's office. Products flow through departments in batches corresponding to individual orders—either stock orders to replenish inventory or individual customer orders in a manufacturing firm, or individual customers in a service.

As we discussed earlier, job shops are often contrasted with flow shops; they are

considered as two distinctly different types of production environments.[1] The scheduling literature, however, treats the flow shop as an extreme case of the general job shop organization, and we follow that convention in this chapter. Specifically, in a **flow shop** all jobs follow the same processing sequence.

17.2 SCHEDULING AND CONTROL IN THE JOB SHOP

A schedule is a timetable for performing activities, using resources, or allocating facilities. The purpose of operations scheduling in the job shop is to disaggregate the master production schedule (MPS) into time-phased weekly, daily, and/or hourly activities—in other words, to specify in precise terms the planned workload on the production system in the very short run. Operations control entails monitoring job-order progress and, where necessary, expediting orders and/or adjusting system capacity to make sure that the MPS is met.

In designing a scheduling and control system, provision must be made for efficient performance of the following functions:

1. Allocating orders, equipment, and personnel to work centers or other specified locations. Essentially, this is short-run capacity planning.
2. Determining the *sequence* of order performance; that is, establishing job priorities.
3. Initiating performance of the scheduled work. This is commonly termed the **dispatching of orders.**
4. Shop-floor control (or production activity control), which involves:
   a. Reviewing the status and controlling the progress of orders as they are being worked on.
   b. **Expediting** late and critical orders.[2]
5. Revising the schedule to reflect recent changes in order status.

A simple shop-scheduling process is shown in Exhibit 17.1. At the start of the day, the job dispatcher (in this case, a production control person assigned to this department) selects and sequences available jobs to be run at individual workstations. The dispatcher's decisions would be based on the operations and routing requirements of each job, status of existing jobs on the machines, the queue of work before each machine, job priorities, material availability, anticipated job orders to be released later in the day, and worker and machine capabilities. To help organize the schedule, the dispatcher would draw on shop-floor information from the previous day and external information provided by central production control, process engineering, and so on. The dispatcher would also

---

[1] For an excellent summary of these differences, see Sam G. Taylor, Samuel M. Seward, and Steven F. Bolander, "Why the Process Industries Are Different," *Production and Inventory Management* (4th Quarter 1981), pp. 9–24.

[2] Despite the fact that expediting is frowned on by production control specialists, it is nevertheless a reality of life. In fact, a very typical entry-level job in production control is that of expediter of "stock-chaser." In some companies a good expediter—one who can negotiate a critical job through the system or can scrounge up materials nobody thought were available—is a prized possession.

EXHIBIT 17.1

Typical Scheduling Process

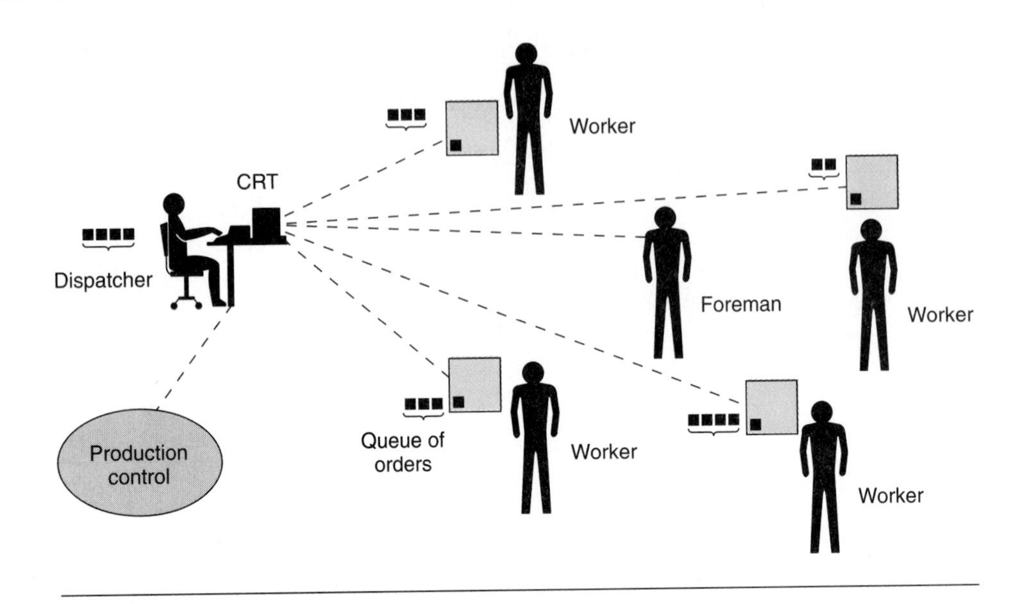

confer with the foreman or supervisor of the department about the feasibility of the schedule, especially with respect to work-force considerations and identifying potential bottlenecks.

17.3 ELEMENTS OF THE JOB SHOP SCHEDULING PROBLEM

The classic approach to job shop scheduling focuses on the following six elements. A significant amount of research effort over the years has focused on evaluating which priority rules are best at satisfying various performance criteria.

1. Job arrival patterns.
2. Number and variety of machines in the shop.
3. Ratio of workers to machines in the shop.
4. Flow pattern of jobs through the shop.
5. Priority rules for allocating jobs to machines.
6. Schedule evaluation criteria.

Job Arrival Patterns

Jobs can arrive at the scheduler's desk either in a batch or over a time interval according to some statistical distribution. The first arrival pattern is termed *static,* the second *dynamic.* Static arrival does not mean that orders are placed by customers at the same moment, only that they are subject to being scheduled at one time. Such a situation occurs when a production control clerk makes out a schedule, say, once a day (or once a week) and does not dispatch any jobs until all the previous day's (or week's) incoming orders are on hand. In a dynamic arrival, jobs are dispatched as they arrive, and the overall schedule is updated to reflect their effect on the production facility.

Number and Variety of Machines in the Shop

The number of machines in the shop obviously affects the scheduling process. If there is but one machine, or if a group of machines can be treated as one, the scheduling problem is greatly simplified. On the other hand, as the number and variety of machines increase, the more complex the scheduling problem is likely to become.

Ratio of Workers to Machines in the Shop

If there are more workers than machines or an equal number of workers and machines, the shop is referred to as a **machine-limited system.** If there are more machines than workers, it is referred to as a **labor-limited system.** The machine-limited system has received far more study, although recent investigations suggest that labor-limited systems are more pervasive in practice. In studying labor-limited systems, the primary areas of concern are the utilization of the worker on several machines and the determination of the best way to allocate workers to these machines.

Flow Pattern of Jobs through the Shop

The pattern of flow through the shop ranges from what is termed a *flow shop* (where all the jobs follow the same path from one machine to the next), to a *randomly routed job shop* (where there is no similar pattern of movement of jobs from one machine to the next). The latter situation is often referred to as a "jumbled" flow, as Exhibit 17.2 illustrates. Most job shops fall somewhere in between these two extremes. The extent to which a shop is a flow shop or a randomly routed job shop can be determined by noting the statistical probability of a job's moving from one machine to the next. Frequently such probabilities are expressed in a transitional probability matrix derived from historical data on the percentage of jobs in machine center I going next to machine center J, machine center K, etc. A pure flow shop would show a probability of 1.0 for a job going from I to J; 1.0 from J to K, 1.0 from K to L, and so on. A pure random job shop would show equal probabilities of a job going from I to J, K, or L. Likewise, if a job were in L, the pure job shop case would show it had an equal probability of going back to either J or K. (Clearly, the pure random job shop is an unlikely configuration in the real world.)

Priority Rules for Allocating Jobs to Machines

The process of determining which job is started first on some machine or work center is known as sequencing or priority sequencing. **Priority rules** are the rules used to obtain a job sequence. These can be very simple, requiring only that jobs be sequenced according

EXHIBIT 17.2

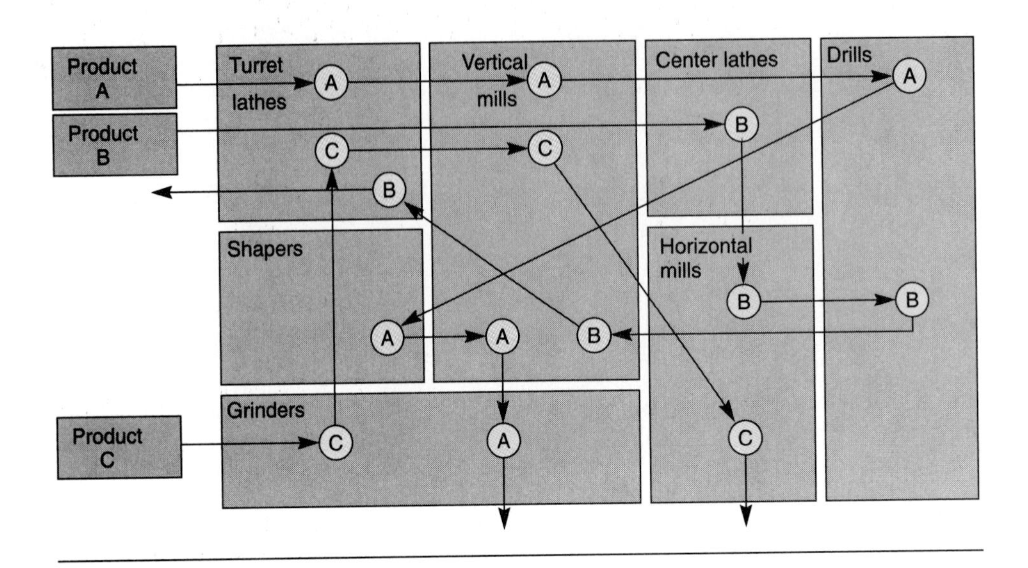

to one piece of data, such as processing time, due date, or order of arrival. Other rules, though equally simple, may require several pieces of information, typically to derive an index number such as in the least slack rule and the **critical ratio rule** (both defined later). Still others, such as Johnson's rule (also discussed later), apply to job scheduling on a sequence of machines and require a computational procedure to specify the order of performance. Ten of the more common priority rules are:

1. *FCFS—first come, first-served.* Orders are run in the order they arrive in the department.
2. *SOT—shortest operating time.* Run the job with the shortest completion time first, next shortest second, etc. This is identical to SPT—shortest processing time.
3. *Due date—earliest due date first.* Run the job with the earliest due date first. DDate—when referring to the entire job; OPNDD—when referring to the next operation.
4. *Start date—due date minus normal lead time.* Run the job with the earliest start date first.
5. *STR—slack time remaining.* This is calculated as the difference between the time remaining before the due date minus the processing time remaining. Orders with the shortest STR are run first.
6. *STR/OP—Slack time remaining per operation.* Orders with shortest STR/OP are run first, calculated as follows:

$$\text{STR/OP} = \frac{\begin{matrix}\text{Time remaining} \\ \text{before due date}\end{matrix} - \begin{matrix}\text{Remaining} \\ \text{processing time}\end{matrix}}{\text{Number of remaining operations}}$$

7. *CR—critical ratio.* This is calculated as the difference between the due date and the current date divided by the work remaining. Orders with the smallest CR are run first.
8. *QR—queue ratio.* This is calculated as the slack time remaining in the schedule divided by the planned remaining queue time. Orders with the smallest QR are run first.
9. *LCFS—last-come, first-served.* This rule occurs frequently by default. As orders arrive they are placed on the top of the stack and the operator usually picks up the order on top to run first.
10. *Random order—whim.* The supervisors or the operators usually select whichever job they feel like running.[3]

Schedule Evaluation Criteria

The following standard measures of schedule performance are used to evaluate priority rules:

1. Meeting due dates of customers or downstream operations.
2. Minimizing flow time (the time a job spends in the shop).
3. Minimizing work in process.
4. Minimizing idle time of machines and workers.

17.4 PRIORITY RULES AND TECHNIQUES

Scheduling *n* Jobs on One Machine

Let us compare some of the 10 priority rules compared in a static scheduling situation involving four jobs on one machine. (In scheduling terminology, this class of problems is referred to as an "*n* job—one-machine problem," or simply *n*/1). The theoretical difficulty of this type of problem increases as more machines are considered rather than by the number of jobs that must be processed; therefore, the only restriction on *n* is that it be a specified, finite number.

Consider the following example: Ioannis Kyriakides is the supervisor of Legal Copy-Express, which provides copy services for L.A. law firms in the downtown Los Angeles area. Five customers submitted their orders at the beginning of the week. Specific scheduling data on these orders are as follows:

[3] This list is modified from Donald W. Fogarty, John H. Blackstone, Jr., and Thomas R. Hoffmann, *Production and Inventory Management* (Cincinnati: South-Western Publishing, 1991), pp. 452–53.

Job (in order of arrival)	Processing Time (days)	Due Date (days hence)
A	3	5
B	4	6
C	2	7
D	6	9
E	1	2

All orders require the use of the only color copy machine available. Kyriakides must therefore decide on the processing sequence for the five orders. The evaluation criterion is minimum flow time. Suppose that Kyriakides decides to use the FCFS rule in an attempt to make Legal Copy-Express appear fair to its customers. The FCFS rule results in the following flow times:

FCFS SCHEDULE

			Flow Time (days)		
Job	Processing Time (days)	Due Date (days)	Start	Job Time	Finish
A	3	5	0 +	3	= 3
B	4	6	3 +	4	= 7
C	2	7	7 +	2	= 9
D	6	9	9 +	6	= 15
E	1	2	15 +	1	= 16

Total flow time + 3 + 7 + 9 + 15 + 16 = 50 days

Mean flow time = $\frac{50}{5}$ = 10 days

Comparing the due date of each job with its flow time, we observe that only Job A will be on time. Jobs B, C, D, and E will be late by 1, 2, 6, and 14 days, respectively. On the average, a job will be late by (0 + 1 + 2 + 6 + 14)/5 = 4.6 days.

Let's now consider the SOT rule. Here Kyriakides gives the highest priority to the order that has the shortest processing time. The resulting flow times are:

SOT SCHEDULE

Job	Processing Time (days)	Due Date (days)	Flow Time (days)
E	1	2	0 + 1 = 1
C	2	7	1 + 2 = 3
A	3	5	3 + 3 = 6
B	4	6	6 + 4 = 10
D	6	9	10 + 6 + 16

Total flow time = 1 + 3 + 6 + 10 + 16 = 36 days

Mean flow time = $\frac{36}{5}$ = 7.2 days

SOT results in lower average flow time. In addition, Jobs E and C will be ready before the due date, and Job A is late by only one day. On the average a job will be late by (0 + 0 + 1 + 4 + 7)/5 = 2.4 days.

If Kyriakides decides to use the DDate rule, the resulting schedule is:

DDATE SCHEDULE

Job	Processing Time (days)	Due Date (days)	Flow Time (days)
E	1	2	0 + 1 = 1
A	3	5	1 + 3 = 4
B	4	6	4 + 4 = 8
C	2	7	8 + 2 = 10
D	6	9	10 + 6 = 16

Total completion time = 1 + 4 + 8 + 10 + 16 = 39 days
Mean flow time = 7.8 days

In this case Jobs B, C, and D will be late. On the average, a job will be late by (0 + 0 + 2 + 3 + 7)/5 = 2.4 days.

In a similar manner, the flow times of the LCFS, random, and STR rules are as follows:

LCFS SCHEDULE

Job	Processing Time (days)	Due Date (days)	Flow Time (days)
E	1	2	0 + 1 = 1
D	6	9	1 + 6 = 7
D	2	7	7 + 2 = 9
B	4	6	9 + 4 = 13
A	3	5	13 + 3 = 16

Total flow time = 46 days
Mean flow time = 9.2 days
Average lateness = 4.0 days

RANDOM SCHEDULE

Job	Processing Time (days)	Due Date (days)	Flow Time (days)
D	6	9	0 + 6 = 6
C	2	7	6 + 2 = 8
A	3	5	8 + 3 = 11
E	1	2	11 + 1 = 12
B	4	6	12 + 4 = 16

Total flow time = 53 days
Mean flow time = 10.6 days
Average lateness = 5.4 days

STR SCHEDULE

Job	Processing Time (days)	Due Date (days)	Flow Time (days)
E	1	2	0 + 1 = 1
A	3	5	1 + 3 = 4
B	4	6	4 + 4 = 8
D	6	9	8 + 6 = 14
C	2	7	14 + 2 = 16

Total flow time = 43 days
Mean flow time = 8.6 days
Average lateness = 3.2 days

These results are summarized below:

Scheduling Rule	Total Completion Time (days)	Average Completion Time (days)	Average Lateness (days)
FCFS	50	10.0	4.6
SOT	36	7.2	2.4
DDate	39	7.8	2.4
LCFS	46	9.2	4.0
Random	53	10.6	5.4
STR	43	8.6	3.2

For this example, the SOT is better than the rest of the scheduling rules, but is this always the case? The answer is yes. Moreover, it can be shown mathematically that the SOT rule yields an optimum solution for the $n/1$ case in such other evaluation criteria as mean waiting time and mean completion time. In fact, so powerful is this simple rule that it has been termed "the most important concept in the entire subject of sequencing."[4]

Scheduling *n* Jobs on Two Machines

The next step up in complexity of job shop types is the $n/2$ flow shop case, where two or more jobs must be processed on two machines in a common sequence. As in the $n/1$ case, there is an approach that leads to an optimal solution according to certain criteria. The objective of this approach, termed *Johnson's rule or method* (after its developer), is to minimize the flow time, from the beginning of the first job until the finish of the last. Johnson's rule consists of the following steps:

1. List the operation time for each job on both machines.
2. Select the job with the shortest operation time.
3. If the shortest time is for the first machine, do that job first; if the shortest time is for the second machine, do that job last.

[4] R. W. Conway, William L. Maxwell, and Louis W. Miller, *Theory of Scheduling* (Reading, Mass.: Addison-Wesley Publishing, 1967), p. 26. A classic book on the subject.

EXHIBIT 17.3

Optimal Schedule of Jobs Using Johnson's Rule

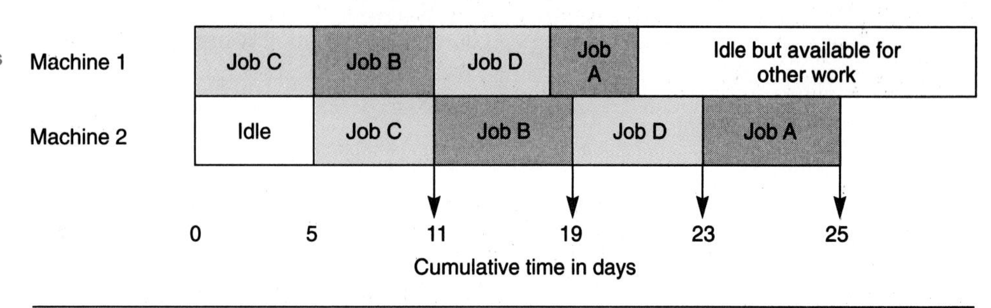

4. Repeat Steps 2 and 3 for each remaining job until the schedule is complete.

Example

We can illustrate this procedure by scheduling four jobs through two machines:

Step 1: **List operation times**

Job	Operation Time on Machine 1	Operation Time on Machine 2
A	3	2
B	6	8
C	5	6
D	7	4

Steps 2 and 3: **Select shortest operation time and assign**
Job A is shortest on Machine 2 and is assigned first and performed last. (Job A is now no longer available to be scheduled.)

Step 4: **Repeat Steps 2 and 3 until completion of schedule**
Select the shortest operation time among the remaining jobs. Job D is second shortest on Machine 2, thus it is performed second to last (remember Job A is last). Now, Jobs A and D are not available anymore for scheduling. Job C is the shortest on Machine 1 among the remaining jobs. Job C is performed first. Now, only Job B is left with the shortest operation time on Machine 1. Thus, according to Step 3, it is performed first among the remaining, or second overall (Job C was already scheduled first).

In summary, the solution sequence is C → B → D → A, and the flow time is 25 days, which is a minimum. Also minimized are total idle time and mean idle time. The final schedule appears in Exhibit 17.3.

These steps result in scheduling the jobs having the shortest time in the beginning and ending of the schedule. As a result, the amount of concurrent operating time for the two machines is maximized, thus minimizing the total operating time required to complete the jobs.

Johnson's method has been extended to yield an optimal solution for the $n/3$ case. When flow shop scheduling problems larger than $n/3$ arise (and they generally do), analytical solution procedures leading to optimality are not available. The reason for this is that even though the jobs may arrive in static fashion at the first machine, the scheduling problem becomes dynamic, and a series of waiting lines start to form in front of machines downstream.

Scheduling *n* Jobs on *m* Machines—Complex Job Shops

Complex job shops are characterized by multiple machine centers processing a variety of different jobs arriving at the machine centers in an intermittent fashion throughout the day. If there are n jobs to be processed on m machines and all jobs are processed on all machines, then there are $(n!)^m$ alternative schedules for this job set. Because of the large number of schedules that exist for even small job shops, Monte Carlo simulation is the only practical way to determine the relative merits of different priority rules in such situations. As in the n job on one machine case, the 10 priority rules (and more) have been compared relative to their performance on the evaluation criteria previously mentioned.

By way of example, John Kanet and Jack Hayya focused their efforts on due date-oriented priority rules to see which one was best. Their simulation of a complex job shop revealed that total job competition rules of "DDATE, STR, and CR were outperformed by their 'operation' counterparts OPNDD, STR/OP, and OPCR" for all seven of the performance criteria used.[5]

Which priority rule should be used? We believe that the needs of most manufacturers are reasonably satisfied by a relatively simple priority scheme that embodies the following principles:

1. It should be dynamic, that is, computed frequently during the course of a job to reflect changing conditions.
2. It should be based in one way or another on slack (the difference between the work remaining to be done on a job and the time remaining to do it in). This embodies the due-date features suggested by Kanet and Hayya.

17.5 SHOP-FLOOR CONTROL

Scheduling job priorities is just one aspect of **shop-floor control** (now often called *production activity control*). The *American Production and Inventory Control Society (APICS) Dictionary* defines a *shop-floor control system* as:

> A system for utilizing data from the shop floor as well as data processing files to maintain and communicate status information on shop orders and work centers.

The major functions of shop-floor control are:

[5] John K. Kanet and Jack C. Hayya, "Priority Dispatching with Operation Due Dates in a Job Shop," *Journal of Operations Management* 2, no. 3 (May 1982), p. 170.

EXHIBIT 17.4

Shop-Floor Control

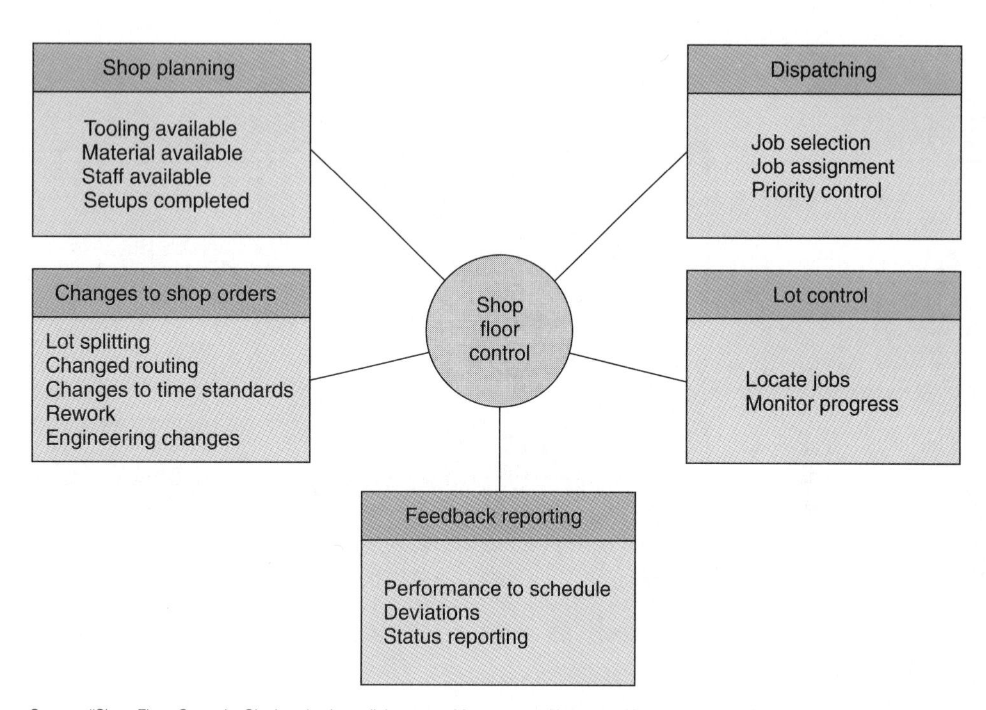

Source: "Shop Floor Control—Closing the Loop," *Inventory Management Newsletter* (Stone Mountain, Ga.: Center for Inventory Management), August 1982.

1. Assigning priority to each shop order.
2. Maintaining work-in-process (WIP) quantity information.
3. Conveying shop-order status information to the office.
4. Providing actual output data for capacity control purposes.
5. Providing quantity by location by shop order for WIP inventory and accounting purposes.
6. Providing measures of efficiency, utilization, and productivity of labor and machines.

Exhibit 17.4 illustrates more of the details related to shop-floor control.

Tools of Shop-Floor Control

The basic tools of shop-floor control are

1. The *daily dispatch list,* which tells the supervisor what jobs are to be run, their priority, and how long each will take. (See Exhibit 17.5A.)

EXHIBIT 17.5

Some Basic Tools of Shop-Floor Control

A. Dispatch list

Work center 1501—Day 205

Start date	Job #	Description	Run time
201	15131	Shaft	11.4
203	15143	Stud	20.6
205	15145	Spindle	4.3
205	15712	Spindle	8.6
207	15340	Metering rod	6.5
208	15312	Shaft	4.6

B. Anticipated delay report

Dept. 24 April 8

Part #	Sched. date	New date	Cause of delay	Action
17125	4/10	4/15	Fixture broke	Toolroom will return on 4/15
13044	4/11	5/1	Out for plating—plater on strike	New lot started
17653	4/11	4/14	New part-holes don't align	Engineering laying out new jig

C. Input/output control report (B)

Work center 0162

Week ending	505	512	519	526
Planned input	210	210	210	210
Actual input	110	150	140	130
Cumulative deviation	–100	–160	–230	–310
Planned output	210	210	210	210
Actual output	140	120	160	120
Cumulative deviation	–70	–160	–210	–300

Note: All figures are in standard hours.

2. Various *status* and *exception reports,* including
   a. The anticipated delay report, made out by the shop planner once or twice a week and reviewed by the chief shop planner to see if there are any serious delays that could affect the master production schedule. (See Exhibit 17.5B.)
   b. Scrap reports.
   c. Rework reports.

d. Performance summary reports, giving the number and percentage of orders completed on schedule, lateness of unfilled orders, volume of output, and so on.

3. An *input/output control report,* which is used by the supervisor to monitor the workload-capacity relationship for each workstation. (See Exhibit 17.5C.)

Input/Output Control

Input/output (I/O) control is a major feature of a manufacturing planning and control system. Its major precept is that the planned work input to a work center should never exceed the planned work output. When the input exceeds the output, backlogs build up at the work center, which in turn increases the lead-time estimates for jobs upstream. Moreover, when jobs pile up at the work center, congestion occurs, processing becomes inefficient, and the flow of work to downstream work centers becomes sporadic. (The water flow analogy to shop capacity control in Exhibit 17.6 illustrates this general phenomenon.) Exhibit 17.5C shows an I/O report for a downstream work center. Looking first at the lower or output half of the report, we see that output is far below plan. A serious capacity problem seems to exist for this work center. However, looking at the input part of the plan, it becomes apparent that the serious capacity problem exists at an upstream work center feeding this work center. The control process would entail finding the cause of the upstream problems and adjusting capacity and inputs accordingly. The simple, basic solution: Either increase capacity at the bottleneck station, or reduce the input to it. (Input reduction at bottleneck work centers, incidentally, is usually the first step recommended by production control consultants when job shops get into trouble.)

Data Integrity

Shop-floor control systems in most modern plants are now computerized, with job status information entered directly into a CRT terminal as the job enters and leaves a work center. Some plants have gone heavily into bar coding and optical scanners to speed up the reporting process and to cut down on data-entry errors.[6] As you might guess, the key problems in shop-floor control are data inaccuracy and lack of timeliness. When these occur, data fed back to the overall planning system are wrong and incorrect production decisions are made. Typical results are excess inventory and/or stockout problems, missed due dates, and inaccuracies in job costing.

Of course, maintaining data integrity requires that a sound data-gathering system be in place; but more important, it requires adherence to the system by everybody interacting with it. Most firms recognize this, but maintaining what is variously referred to as *shop discipline, data integrity,* or *data responsibility* is not always easy. And despite periodic drives to publicize the importance of careful shop-floor reporting by creating data-integrity task forces, inaccuracies can still creep into the system in many ways: A line worker drops a part under the workbench and pulls a replacement from stock without recording either

[6] Some companies also use "smartshelves"—inventory bins with weight sensors beneath each shelf. When an item is removed from inventory, a signal is sent to a central computer that notes the time, date, quantity, and location of the transaction.

EXHIBIT 17.6

Shop Capacity Control Load Flow

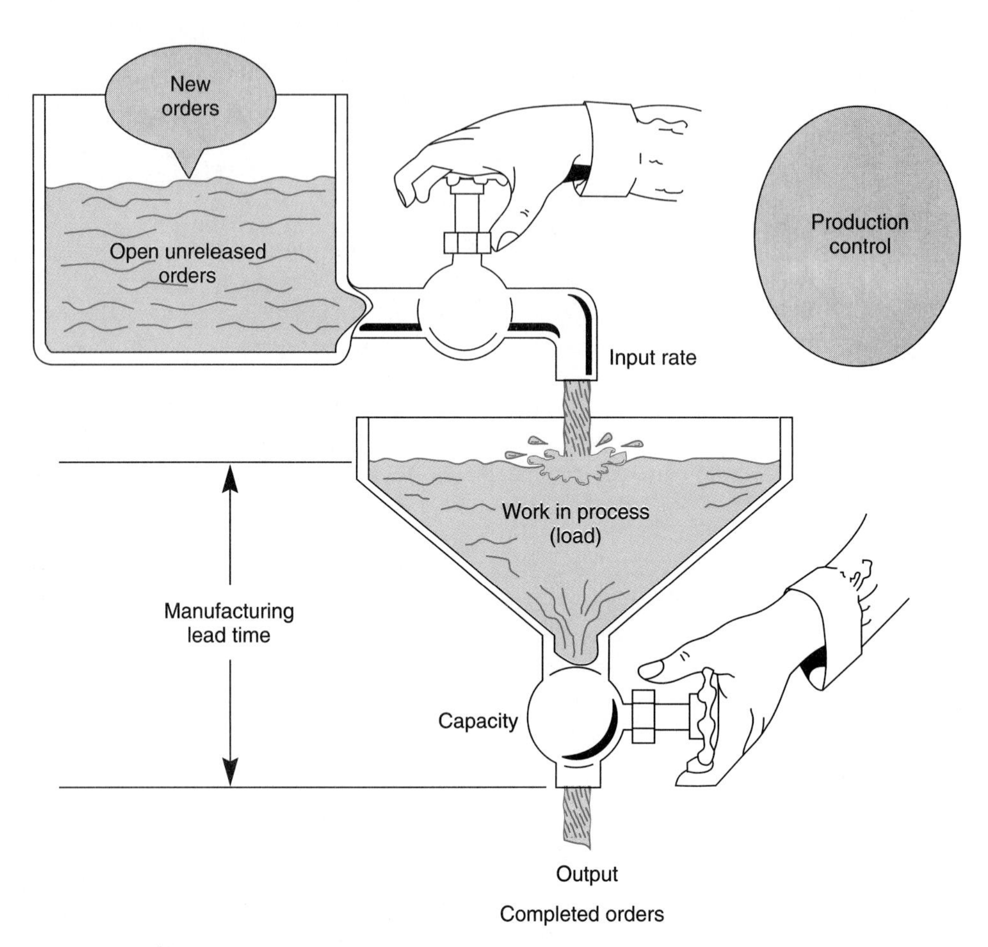

Source: American Production and Inventory Control Society, "Training Aid—Shop Floor Control," undated.

transaction. An inventory clerk makes an error in a cycle count. A manufacturing engineer fails to note a change in the routing of a part. A department supervisor decides to work jobs in a different order than specified in the dispatch list.

Gantt Charts

Smaller job shops and individual departments of large ones employ the venerable Gantt chart to help plan and track jobs. As described in Chapter 12, it is a type of bar chart that plots tasks against time. Gantt charts are used for project planning, as well as to coordinate a number of scheduled activities. The example in Exhibit 17.7 indicates that Job A is behind schedule by about four hours, Job B is ahead of schedule, and Job C has been completed, after a delayed start for equipment maintenance. Note that whether the job is

EXHIBIT 17.7 Gantt Chart

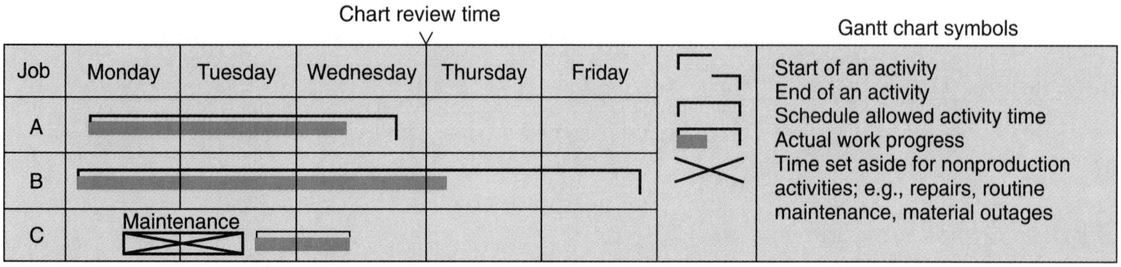

Chart review time

Job	Monday	Tuesday	Wednesday	Thursday	Friday
A					
B					
C	Maintenance				

Gantt chart symbols

- Start of an activity
- End of an activity
- Schedule allowed activity time
- Actual work progress
- Time set aside for nonproduction activities; e.g., repairs, routine maintenance, material outages

Source: Professor Bob Parsons, Management Science Department, Northeastern University, Boston, MA. Used with permission.

ahead of schedule or behind schedule is based on where it stands compared to where we are now. In Exhibit 17.7 we are at the end of Wednesday and Job A should have been completed. Job B has already had some of Thursday's work completed.

17.6 PERSONNEL SCHEDULING IN SERVICES

The scheduling problem in service operations revolves around two issues. Due to both the customer's direct interaction with the service delivery process and the high variability in demand, personnel must be scheduled for short durations of time within a workday, often in half-hour or hour increments. Once the daily work schedules have been developed, the next step is to schedule these personnel throughout the workweek to reflect their days off.

The scheduling of service workers can be divided into two broad categories: "back-of-the-house" operations (where workers do not come into contact with customers) and "front-of-the-house" operations (where the workers do come into direct contact with the customers). The former is similar to a manufacturing environment, and staffing requirements are determined with relative ease. For front-of-the-house operations, the determination of staffing requirements is much more difficult, as management must make a trade-off between the level of service to provide and the number of workers to assign. In general, the more workers, the better the service; the fewer the workers, the worse the service is.

Both types of service scheduling situations are presented here. The staffing requirements for the bank is an example of a back-of-the-house operation, while nurse staffing and scheduling is obviously a front-of-the-house operation.

Setting Staffing Levels in Banks

This example illustrates how central clearinghouses and back-office operations of large bank branches establish staffing plans. Basically, management wants to develop a staffing plan that (1) requires the least number of workers to accomplish the daily workload and (2) minimizes the variance between actual output and planned output.

EXHIBIT 17.8

Daily Staff Hours Required

		FUNCTION								
		RECEIVE		PREPROCESS		MICROFILM		VERIFY		TOTALS
Product	Daily Volume	P/H	H_{std}	P/H	H_{std}	P/H	H_{std}	P/H	H_{std}	H_{std}
Checks	2,000	1,000	2.0	600	3.3	240	8.3	640	3.1	16.7
Statements	1,000	—	—	600	1.7	250	4.0	150	6.7	12.4
Notes	200	30	6.7	15	13.3		—			20.0
Investments	400	100	4.0	50	8.0	200	2.0	150	2.7	16.7
Collections	500	300	1.7			300	1.7	60	8.4	11.8
			—		—		—		—	—
Total hours required			14.4		26.3		16.0		20.9	77.6
Times 1.25 (absences and vacations)			18.0		32.9		20.0		26.1	
			—		—		—		—	
Divided by 8 hours equals staff required			2.3		4.1		2.5		3.3	

Note: P/H indicates production rate per hour; H_{std} indicates required hours.

In structuring the problem, bank management defines inputs (checks, statements, investment documents, and so forth), as *products,* which are routed through different processes or *functions* (receiving, sorting, encoding, and so forth).

To solve the problem, a monthly demand forecast is made by product for each function. This is converted to labor hours required per function, which in turn is converted to workers required per function. These figures are then tabled, summed, and adjusted by an absence and vacation factor to give planned hours. Then they are divided by the number of hours in the workday to yield the number of workers required. This yields the daily staff hours required. (See Exhibit 17.8.) This becomes the basis for a departmental staffing plan that lists the workers required, workers available, variance, and managerial action in light of variance. (See Exhibit 17.9.)

In addition to their use in day-to-day planning, the hours required and the staffing plan provide information for scheduling individual workers, controlling operations, comparing capacity utilization with other branches, and starting up new branches.

EXHIBIT 17.9

Staffing Plan

Function	Staff Required	Staff Available	Variance (±)	Management Actions
Receive	2.3	2.0	−0.3	Use overtime
Preprocess	4.1	4.0	−0.1	Use overtime
Microfilm	2.5	3.0	+0.5	Use excess to verify
Verify	3.3	3.0	−0.3	Get 0.3 from microfilm

EXHIBIT 17.10

General Problems in Nurse Scheduling

Problem	Possible Solution
Accuracy of patient load forecast	Forecast frequently and rebudget monthly Closely monitor seasonal demands, communicable diseases, and current occupancy
Forecasting nurse availability	Develop work standards for nurses for each level of possible demand (requires systematic data collection and analysis)
Complexity and time to rebudget	Use available computer programs
Flexibility in scheduling	Use variable staffing: Set regular staff levels slightly above minimum and absorb variation with broadskilled float nurses, part-time nurses, and overtime

Nurse Staffing and Scheduling

W. Abernathy, N. Baloff, and J. Hershey state, "The key element of effective nurse staffing is a well-conceived procedure for achieving an overall balance between the size of the nursing staff and the expected patient demand."[7] Their procedure, termed *aggregate budgeting,* is predicated on a variety of interrelated activities and has a short-term schedule as a primary output. A number of severe practical problems confront hospitals in deriving an effective yet low-cost aggregate budget. These difficulties, along with possible remedies, are listed in Exhibit 17.10.

Though most hospitals still use trial-and-error methods in schedule development, management scientists have applied optimizing techniques to the problem with some success. For example, a linear programming model has been developed that assumes a known, short-run (three to four days) demand for nursing care and develops a staffing pattern that:[8]

1. Specifies the number of nurses of each skill class to be assigned among the wards and nursing shifts.
2. Satisfies total nursing personnel capacity constraints.
3. Allows for limited substitution of tasks among nurses.
4. Minimizes the cost of nursing care shortage for the scheduling period.

A major problem confronting health care managers today is the changing mix of patient requirements and how it affects nurse staffing requirements. With the growing trend toward more outpatient treatment, patients who are hospitalized today are typically very ill, and thus require, on average, more individual attention. Under these conditions, the demands for nursing skills can actually increase, even though the number of patients in a designated area has remained unchanged.

[7] W. Abernathy, N. Baloff, and J. Hershey, "The Nurse Staffing Problem: Issues and Prospects," *Sloan Management Review* 13, no. 1 (Fall 1971), pp. 87–109.

[8] D. Warner and J. Prawda, "A Mathematical Programming Model for Scheduling Nursing Personnel in a Hospital," *Management Science* 19, no. 4 (December 1972), pp. 411–22.

Because of these increased patient needs, many hospitals are adapting a worker skill mix that incorporates lower-skilled technical support personnel to assist in the delivery of patient care, with the goal of reducing their overall labor costs. This additional parameter of different worker skills needs to be considered when determining personnel staffing requirements.

Scheduling Consecutive Days Off

A practical problem encountered in many service organizations is setting schedules so that employees can have two consecutive days off even though the operation is open seven days a week. The importance of the problem stems from the fact that the Fair Labor Standards Act requires that overtime be paid for any hours worked (by hourly workers) in excess of 40 hours per week. Obviously, if two consecutive days off can't be scheduled each week for each employee, the likelihood of unnecessary overtime is quite high. In addition, most people probably prefer two consecutive days off per week. The following heuristic procedure was modified from that developed by James Browne and Rajen Tibrewala to deal with this problem.[9]

Objective. Find the schedule that minimizes the number of five-day workers with two consecutive days off, subject to the demands of the daily staffing schedule and assuming that the workers have no preference for which days they get off.

Procedure. Starting with the total number of workers required for each day of the week, create a schedule by adding one worker at a time. This is a two-step procedure:

Step 1.

Circle the lowest pair of consecutive days off. The lowest pair is the one where the highest number in the pair is equal to or lower than the highest number in any other pair. This ensures that the days with the highest requirements are covered by staff. (Monday and Sunday may be chosen even though they are at opposite ends of the array of days.) In case of ties choose the days-off pair with the lowest requirement on an adjacent day. This day may be before or after the pair. If a tie still remains, choose the first of the available tied pairs. (Do not bother using further tie-breaking rules, such as second lowest adjacent days.)

Step 2.

Subtract 1 from each of the remaining five days (i.e., the days not circled). This indicates that one less worker is required on these days, since the first worker has just been assigned to them.

---

[9] James J. Browne and Rajen K. Tibrewala, "Manpower Scheduling," *Industrial Engineering* 7, no. 8 (August 1975), pp. 22–23.

Step 3.
The two steps are repeated for the second worker, the third worker, and so forth, until no more workers are required to satisfy the schedule.

Example

	M	Tu	W	Th	F	S	Su
Requirement	4	3	4	2	3	1	2
Worker 1	4	3	4	2	3	(1	2)
Worker 2	3	2	3	1	(2	1)	2
Worker 3	2	1	2	0	2	(1	1)
Worker 4	1	(0	1)	0	1	1	1
Worker 5	0	0	1	0	0	0	0

Solution

This solution consists of five workers covering 19 worker days, although slightly different assignments may be equally satisfactory.

The schedule: Worker 1 is assigned S–Su off; Worker 2, F–S off; Worker 3, S–Su off; Worker 4, Tu–W off; and Worker 5 works only on Wednesday, since there are no further requirements for the other days.

17.7 CONCLUSION

The objective of this chapter has been to provide some insight into the nature of operations planning and control, with emphasis on job shop environments. Job shop scheduling, like most other aspects of OM, has become computer dependent and, equally important, is now seen as being inseparable from the total manufacturing planning and control systems of which it is a part.

Worker scheduling is especially important in service operations, where labor is often a significant cost component. Here, too much labor at any point in time negatively affects profits. On the other hand, insufficient labor has a negative impact on customer service, and thus future sales.

17.8 REVIEW AND DISCUSSION QUESTIONS

1. Distinguish between a job shop and a flow shop.
2. How would you translate the Epigraph at the start of the chapter into job shop terms?
3. What practical considerations are deterrents to using the SOT rule?
4. What priority rule do you use in scheduling your study time for midterm examinations? If you have five exams to study for, how many alternative schedules exist?
5. Data integrity is a big deal in industry. Why?

6. In the United States, we make certain assumptions about the customer-service priority rules used in banks, restaurants, and retail stores. If you have the opportunity, ask a foreigner what rules are used in his or her country. To what factors might you attribute the differences, if any?
7. What job characteristics would lead you to schedule jobs according to "longest processing time first"?
8. In what way is the scheduling problem in the home office of a bank different from that of a branch?

17.9 SOLVED PROBLEMS

PROBLEM

1. Mr. Regan has just come across the runout method of scheduling and wonders whether he could apply this technique to allocating expense money among his three children. He would like to occasionally divide a lump sum among his children so that, when added to what they currently have, it will cover each of their expenses for the same period of time. Regan's son is a freshman in high school and uses $1.95 per day ($0.50 each way bus fare plus $0.95 for lunch). His daughter is in junior high and uses $1.65 per day (bus fare $0.50 each way plus $0.65 for lunch). His youngest son is in elementary school and uses $0.55 per day (there is a free school bus). Following is the current expense money held by each child along with the scheduled expenses just mentioned.

	Expense Money in Hand	Daily Expenses
Eldest son	$3.20	$1.95
Daughter	2.40	1.65
Youngest son	1.80	0.55

Regan would like to divide $20 among his children so that each would have the same number of days of expense money. Use the runout method to find the appropriate allocation.

SOLUTION

Runout problem of allocating expense money.

	(1) Expense Money on Hand	(2) Daily Expenses
Eldest son	$3.20	$1.95
Daughter	2.40	1.65
Youngest son	1.80	.55
	$7.40	$4.15

$$\text{Aggregate runout time} = \frac{\text{Inventory on hand + New amount}}{\text{Daily demand}}$$

$$= \frac{7.40 + 20}{4.15} = 6.60 \text{ days}$$

	(3) Total Expense Money Required (2) × 6.60	(4) Net Amount to Be Allocated (3) − (1)
Eldest son	$12.87	$ 9.67
Daughter	10.89	8.49
Youngest son	3.63	1.83
	$27.39	$19.99

The allocations are $9.67, $8.49, and $1.83. Rounding accounts for the 1 cent difference between the $20 and $19.99 allocated.

PROBLEM

2. Joe's Auto Seat Cover and Paint Shop is bidding on a contract to do all the custom work for Smiling Ed's used car dealership. One of the main requirements in obtaining this contract is rapid delivery time, since Ed—for reasons we shall not go into here—wants the cars facelifted and back on his lot in a hurry. Ed has said that if Joe can refit and repaint five cars that Ed has just received (from an unnamed source) in 24 hours or less, the contract will be his. Following is the time (in hours) required in the refitting shop and the paint shop for each of the five cars. Assuming that cars go through the refitting operations before they are repainted, can Joe meet the time requirements and get the contract?

Car	Refitting Time (hours)	Repairing Time (hours)
A	6	3
B	0	4
C	5	2
D	8	6
E	2	1

SOLUTION

This problem can be viewed as a two-machine flow shop and can be easily solved using "Johnson's method."

ORIGINAL DATA			JOHNSON METHOD	
Car	Refitting Time (hours)	Repainting Time (hours)	Order of Selection	Position in Sequence
A	6	3	4th	3rd
B	0	4	1st	1st
C	5	2	3rd	4th
D	8	6	5th	2nd
E	2	1	2nd	5th

Graph of Johnson solution:

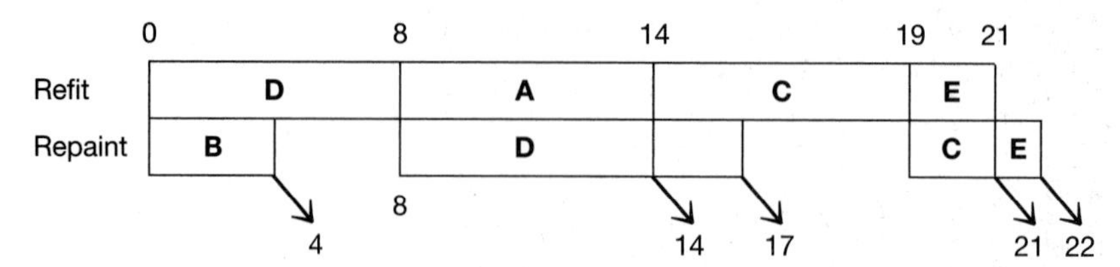

17.10 PROBLEMS

1. Joe has three cars that must be overhauled by his ace mechanic, Jim. Given the following data about the cars, use the STR/OP priority rule (least slack remaining per operation) to determine Jim's scheduling priority for each.

Car	Customer Pick-Up Time (hours hence)	Remaining Overhaul Time (hours)	Remaining Operations
A	10	4	Painting
B	17	5	Wheel alignment, painting
C	15	1	Chrome plating, painting, seat repair

2. There are seven jobs that must be processed in two operations: A and B. All seven jobs must go through A and B in that sequence—A first, then B. Determine the optimal order in which the jobs should be sequenced through the process using these times:

Job	Process A Time	Process B Time
1	9	6
2	8	5
3	7	7
4	6	3
5	1	2
6	2	6
7	4	7

3. The following list of jobs in a critical department includes estimates of their required times:

Job	Required Time (days)	Days to Delivery Promise	Slack
A	8	12	4
B	3	9	6
C	7	8	1
D	1	11	10
E	10	−10	—
F	6	10	4
G	5	−8	—
H	4	6	2

a. Use the shortest operation time rule to schedule these jobs:

What is the schedule?

What is the mean flow time?

b. The boss doesn't like the schedule in (*a*). Jobs E and G must be done first, for obvious reasons (they are already late). Reschedule and do the best you can while scheduling Jobs E and G first and second, respectively.

What is the new schedule?

What is the new mean flow time?

4. John Adams is a shop supervisor for Foley and Burnham, Inc., in the component insertion area. F&B runs a fairly loose shop schedule, leaving it pretty much up to the lower managers to determine the within-week schedule for production. Because Adams produces standard items for stock and setup times are minimal, he normally tries to use up his production resources in a way that provides equal time coverages for all products.

   Assume that Adams has four machine centers working 8 hours per day, five days per week, for a total of 160 production hours available per week. Adams needs to plan how to allocate his 160 total available hours over the five printed circuit board configurations for next week. Your task is to help him by using the runout method.

Item	Production Time per Unit (minutes)	Inventory on Hand (units)	Forecasted Usage for Next Week (units)
PC1	4	900	600
PC2	1	1,100	700
PC3	3	800	1,200
PC4	5	500	300
PC5	8	125	75

5. A manufacturing facility has five jobs to be scheduled into production. The following table gives the processing times plus the necessary wait times and other necessary delays for each of the jobs.

   Assume that today is April 3 and the jobs are due on the dates shown:

Job	Days of Actual Processing Time Required	Days of Necessary Delay Time	Total Time Required	Date Job Due
1	2	12	14	April 30
2	5	8	13	April 21
3	9	15	24	April 28
4	7	9	16	April 29
5	4	22	28	April 27

   Determine *two* schedules, stating the order in which the jobs are to be done. Use the critical ratio priority rule for one. You may use any other rule for the second schedule as long as you state what it is.

6. An accounting firm, Debits 'R Us, would like to keep its auditing staff to a maximum of four people yet satisfy the staffing needs and the policy of two days off per week. Given the following requirements, is this possible? What should the schedule be?

   Requirements (Monday through Sunday): 4, 3, 3, 2, 2, 4, 4.

7. Jobs A, B, C, D, and E must go through Processes I and II in that sequence (i.e., Process I first, then Process II).

   Use Johnson's rule to determine the optimal sequence to schedule the jobs to minimize the total required time.

Job	Required Processing Time on A	Required Processing Time on B
A	4	5
B	16	14
C	8	7
D	12	11
E	3	9

8. For a variety of reasons, our friend Joe now finds himself in charge of what might be called a *captive machine shop* in a government-operated establishment. The machine shop fabricates and paints metal products, including license plates, road signs, window screens, and door frames. Joe's major responsibility is to balance the utilization of the equipment across all four products in such a way that demand for each product is satisfied. Given the following data, how might he schedule the four products to achieve this objective for the next week? How would his schedule look?

Item	Inventory	Production Time per Unit	Forecast Weekly Usage
Window screens	200	0.1 hour	100
Door frames	100	0.06	50
Road signs	70	0.3	60
License plates	150	0.7	125

9. A textile manufacturer is planning her next week's production and wants to use the runout method of scheduling. Part of her logic for using the runout method in this case is that she is running the same design on towels, washcloths, sheets, and pillowcases. She would therefore like to carry the same period amounts in the event the design is changed.

   Following are the existing quantities on hand, the production times of each, and the forecast demands. There are 120 hours of capacity available on the mill in three shifts. (The same machine is used to make all the items, so the problem is to determine which will be made, how many, and how much machine time to allocate to each.)

Item	Units on Hand	Production Time for Each in Hours	Forecast Demand per Week
Washcloths	500	0.1	300
Towels	200	0.15	400
Sheets	150	0.20	200
Pillowcases	300	0.15	200

10. Joe has now been released from his government job. Based on his excellent performance, he was able to land a job as production scheduler in a brand-new custom refinishing auto service shop located near the border. Techniques have improved in the several years he was out of circulation, so processing times are considerably faster. This system is capable of handling 10 cars per day. The sequence now is customizing first, followed by repainting.

Car	Customizing Time (hours)	Painting (hours)
1	3.0	1.2
2	2.0	0.9
3	2.5	1.3
4	0.7	0.5
5	1.6	1.7
6	2.1	0.8
7	3.2	1.4
8	0.6	1.8
9	1.1	1.5
10	1.8	0.7

In what sequence should Joe schedule the cars?

17.11 CASE: McCALL DIESEL MOTOR WORKS (NEED FOR A COMPLETE SYSTEM OF PRODUCTION CONTROL)

McCall Diesel Motor Works has been a pioneer in the manufacture of a particular internal combustion engine. The plant is located on tidewater in the state of New Jersey because the company originally built engines for the marine field, chiefly fishing boats and pleasure craft. Subsequently, its activities were extended to the stationary types of engines, used primarily for the production of power in small communities, in manufacturing plants, or on farms.

During the earlier years of the company's operation, its engines were largely special-order jobs. Even at the present time about 60 percent of the output is made to order. There has been in recent years, however, a trend toward standardization of component parts and reduction in the variety of engines produced. The Engineering Department has followed the principle of simplification and standardization in the case of minor parts, such as studs, bolts, and springs, giving a degree of interchangeability of these components among the various sizes and types of engines. Sizes of marine engines have been standardized to some extent, although customer requirements still necessitate some designs. In the small engines for agricultural use there has been a genuine effort to concentrate sales on a standard line of engines of three sizes—20 HP, 40 HP, and 60 HP.

The company has always been advanced in its engineering development and design. The production phase, on the other hand, has not been progressive. The heritage of job shop operation persists, and despite the definite trend toward standardization, manufacture continues largely on a made-to-order basis. The increasing popularity of diesel engines has brought many new producing companies into the field, with a consequent tightening of the competitive situation.

High manufacturing costs and poor service have been reflected in the loss of orders. Customer complaints, together with pressure from the Sales Department, prompted management to call in a consulting engineer to make a survey of the Manufacturing Department and recommend a plan of action.

The report of the engineer showed the following:

1. *Manufacturing methods,* while still largely of the job shop character, are in the main good, and no wholesale change should be made. As production is still 60 percent special, a complete shift to line manufacture or departmentalization by product is not feasible.

2. *Machinery and equipment* are for the most part general purpose, in line with manufacturing requirements. Some machine tools are approaching obsolescence, and for certain operations high-production, single-purpose machines would be advisable. Extensive replacement of machine tools is not a pressing need, but an increased use of jigs and fixtures should be undertaken immediately. There are many bottlenecks existing in the plant, but contrary to your belief, as well as that of your foreman and other shop executives, there is no serious lack of productive equipment. The trouble lies in the improper utilization of the machine time available.

3. *Production control* is the major element of operating weakness, and improvement is imperative. The lack of proper control over production shows up in many ways:

a. High in-process inventory, as indicated by piles of partially completed parts over the entire manufacturing floor areas.

b. Absence of any record concerning the whereabouts of orders in the process from their initiation to delivery at assembly.

c. Inordinate number of rush orders, particularly in assembly but also in parts manufacture.

d. Too many parts chasers who force orders through the shops by pressure methods.

e. Piecemeal manufacture—a lot of 20 parts usually is broken up into four or five lots before it is finished. Not infrequently the last sublot remains on the shop floor for months and, in a number of instances, is lost as far as records are concerned. Subsequent orders for the same part are issued and new lots pass through to completion while the remains of the old lot lie in partially fabricated condition.

f. Excessive setup costs resulting from the piecemeal methods mentioned in (*e*), as well as failure to use proper lot sizes, even when lots are not broken up during manufacture.

g. Failure of all necessary component parts to reach assembly at approximately the same time. The floor of the assembly department is cluttered with piles of parts awaiting receipt of one or more components before engines can be assembled.

h. Lack of definite sequence of manufacturing operations for a given part. Responsibility for the exact way by which a part is to be made rests entirely on the various department foremen; these people are able machinists, but, burdened with detail, their memories cannot be relied on to ensure that parts will always be manufactured in the best, or even the same, sequence of operations. Moreover, they have the responsibility for determining the department to which a lot of parts should be sent when it has been completed in their department.

i. In the case of certain small standard parts, shop orders have been issued as many as six or eight times in a single month.

j. Information is lacking from which to estimate, with any degree of close approximation, the overall manufacturing time for an engine. The result is failure to meet delivery promises or high production cost due to rush or overtime work.

k. Parts in process or in stores, and destined for imminent assembly, are frequently taken by the Service Department to supply an emergency repair order. The question here is not the academic determination of priority between the customer whose boat may be lying idle because of a broken part and the customer who has not yet received an engine; the question is why there should be any habitual difficulty in rendering adequate repair service and at the same time meeting delivery promises.

l. Virtually all basic manufacturing data resides in the heads of the superintendent, departmental foreman, assistant foremen, and setup workers.

m. Delivery dates are set by the Sales Department and generally are dates that customers arbitrarily stipulate.

n. The general superintendent shows little enthusiasm for the idea of a system of production control; in fact he is opposed to such an installation. He is of the opinion that reasonably satisfactory results are now being obtained by placing responsibility on the foremen and maintaining contact between them and the parts chasers, who in turn are held responsible for meeting delivery promises. He believes that no system can be substituted for the foremen's knowledge of the ability of the workers. He feels that operation of a production-control system requires time studies of all jobs. Time study, he points out, is difficult because of the many operations involved, the high degree of special work, the probable resistance of the workers, and the cost. He further protests that emergencies and rush orders would upset any rigid scheduling of work through the plant. Finally, he is convinced that any system of production control involves an excessive amount of clerical detail to which the foremen, who are practical shop workers, object.

The state of affairs the consultant found had, he realized, two main causes:

1. The strong influence of the original job shop character of manufacture and the very slow evolution to large-scale operation.
2. The fact that the top management of the company was essentially sales minded.

His recommendations, therefore, had to be a simple, straightforward program that would provide adequate control over production and could be instituted gradually and logically.

QUESTIONS

1. Outline the essential features of a production-control system for this company, giving sufficient detail to make clear how the system will function.
2. Indicate which part of your procedure should be centralized and which part decentralized. What functions should be handled by a central production-control office and what functions should be carried out in the various production and assembly departments?
3. What data must be compiled before your system can become fully effective?
4. Enumerate the benefits the company will derive when your production-control system is in operation.
5. Set forth in proper order the steps that should be taken and the departments that should be involved in the determination of delivery promises to customers.
6. What arguments would you advance in answer to the general superintendent's objections, as presented in paragraph *n* of the consultant's report?
7. Generally speaking, what is the foremen's place in the scheme of things when a fully developed production-control system is in operation and when a production control department has been established?

17.12 SELECTED BIBLIOGRAPHY

Abernathy, W.; N. Baloff; and J. Hershey. "The Nurse Staffing Problem: Issues and Prospects." *Sloan Management Review* 13, no. 1 (Fall 1971), pp. 87–109.

Baker, K. R. "The Effects of Input Control in a Simple Scheduling Model." *Journal of Operations Management* 4, no. 2 (February 1984), pp. 99–112.

Berry, W. L.; R. Penlesky; and T. E. Vollmann. "Critical Ratio Scheduling: Dynamic Due-Date Procedures under Demand Uncertainty." *IIE Transactions* 16, no. 1 (March 1984), pp. 81–89.

Browne, James J., and Rajen K. Tibrewala. "Manpower Scheduling." *Industrial Engineering* 7, no. 8 (August 1975), pp. 22–23.

Conway, R. W.; William L. Maxwell; and Louis W. Miller. *Theory of Scheduling*. Reading, Mass.: Addison-Wesley Publishing, 1967.

Fogarty, Donald W.; John H. Blackstone, Jr.; and Thomas R. Hoffmann. *Production and Inventory Management* (Cincinnati: South-Western Publishing, 1991).

Gershkoff, I. "Optimizing Flight Crew Schedules." *Interfaces* 19, no. 4 (July–August 1989), pp. 29–43.

Goldratt, E. M., and J. Cox. *The Goal: A Process of Ongoing Improvement*. Croton-on-Hudson, N.Y.: North River Press, 1986.

Johnson, S. M. "Optimal Two Stage and Three Stage Production Schedules with Setup Times Included." *Naval Logistics Quarterly* 1, no. 1 (March 1954), pp. 61–68.

Kanet, John K., and Jack C. Hayya. "Priority Dispatching with Operation Due Dates in a Job Shop." *Journal of Operations Management* 2, no. 3 (May 1982), p. 170.

Moody, P. E. *Strategic Manufacturing: Dynamic New Directions for the 1990s*. Homewood, Ill.: Richard D. Irwin, 1990.

Richter, H. "Thirty Years of Airline Operations Research." *Interfaces* 19, no. 4, (July–August 1989), pp. 3–9.

Sandman, W. E., with J. P. Hayes. *How to Win Productivity in Manufacturing*. Dresher, Pa.: Yellow Brook of Pennsylvania, 1980.

Warner, D., and J. Prawda. "A Mathematical Programming Model for Scheduling Nursing Personnel in a Hospital." *Management Science* 19, no. 4 (December 1972), pp. 411–22.

Wild, Ray. *International Handbook of Production and Operations Management*. London, England: Cassell Educational Ltd., 1989.

Chapter 18

Materials and Purchasing Management

EPIGRAPH

The lowest-cost item is not always the cheapest.

CHAPTER OUTLINE

KEY TERMS

Materials Management

Logistics

Bar Coding

Automatic Storage and Retrieval Systems (AS/RS)

Value Analysis

Single-Source Supplier

Qualified Suppliers

Strategic Partnership

Just-in-Time Purchasing

Distribution Requirements Planning (DRP)

Value Density

Purchased materials, parts, and components represent a growing percentage of the cost of manufacturing. In many manufacturing companies today, these purchased goods often represent 60 to 70 percent of the cost of goods sold. The increase in materials handling costs coupled with higher transportation and distribution costs have also forced management to focus its attention in these areas. As a result, the purchasing department in recent years has undergone a significant transformation due to added responsibilities and associated importance within the organization.

Specifically, the many changes that have taken place in purchasing, materials handling, and distribution systems have been brought on by:

1. Competitive pressures from foreign firms.
2. Elevation of product quality to a very high level of importance.
3. International marketing and international purchasing.
4. Trends toward choosing sole-source suppliers for long-term relationships.
5. Product varieties and ranges are rapidly changing, and speed of delivery to the market is essential.
6. Product life cycles have shortened necessitating knowledge and control of inventories in the various pipelines.
7. Adoption of just-in-time production has changed the supplier relationships and also focused on reducing inventories.
8. Trends in the legal system hold manufacturers liable for product failures, even though causes may be outside of the production system itself.

In this chapter we examine many of these issues specifically addressing how materials are obtained, how they are managed through the manufacturing system, and, briefly, how they are distributed. Our objective is to help you resolve or, better yet, avoid these problems.

18.1 OVERVIEW OF MATERIALS MANAGEMENT

Materials management is defined by the American Production and Inventory Control Society (APICS) as

> The grouping of management functions supporting the complete cycle of material flow, from the purchase and internal control of production materials to the planning and control of work in process to the warehousing, shipping and distribution of the finished product.[1]

The term *logistics* is often used interchangeably with materials management. APICS has defined **logistics** in two contexts.

> In an industrial context, logistics refers to the art and science of obtaining and distributing materials and product. In a military sense (where it has greater usage), its meaning can also include the movement of personnel.[2]

---

[1] *APICS Dictionary,* 6th ed. (Falls Church, Va.: American Production and Inventory Control Society, 1987).
[2] Ibid.

In this text we favor using the term *materials management*. This emphasizes the importance of the materials management function, which extends from purchasing materials from vendors, following them through the system, and ultimately delivering the final product to the customer. Interestingly, firms differ in how they group these functions under a single materials management manager. Some firms, for example, may leave transportation outside of the materials management activities.

Importance of Quality in Purchasing

Today, the average manufacturer purchases two thirds of what goes into the final product—two thirds of the cost of goods sold! Therefore, through its philosophies, knowledge of processes, knowledge of materials, and vendor selection, the purchasing department has twice as many opportunities to affect quality as the production department does.

The two views of quality discussed by Wolf Reitsperger et al. are important to compare.[3] The first, "quality is free," is the belief in a continuous quest for perfection, which recognizes that the long-term payoffs include higher profits, increased market share, and so on. The second view, "quality is costly," is based on the trade-off shown in Exhibit 18.1. As quality increases, the costs for production and inspection increase exponentially. As a general rule, each additional increment of higher quality costs more and more to obtain. The reverse is true concerning costs of defective product. If all product output were perfect, there would be no costs for bad quality. Under the "quality is costly" logic, the minimum point in the total cost curve would be chosen. The "quality is costly" philosophy is said to be the view of American management, while "quality is free" is said to be the perspective of many Japanese managers.

Those who believe "quality is free" also believe in zero defects programs that strive for perfect output. For purchasing to achieve this same high level, there needs to be a high degree of involvement. Purchasing must closely interact with engineering, processes, quality control, and training, as well as maintain a close relationship with suppliers.

In a study of 24 Japanese electronics firms and 20 American electronics firms, the question to be answered was: "Do American managers still believe that quality is costly?" Surprisingly, Exhibit 18.2 shows that American managers have even a greater belief in the "quality is free" philosophy than the Japanese! Note from the exhibit that the American managers believe:

1. Reducing defects does not necessarily increase costs.
2. The acceptable quality level (AQL) concept is not a superior tool in managing quality.
3. The line should be stopped when a quality problem occurs.

[3] Wolf Reitsperger, Shirley Daniel, and Abdel El-Shaieb, "Quality Is Free: A Comparative Study of Attitudes in the U.S. and Japan," *Journal of Purchasing and Materials Management* (Spring 1990), pp. 8–11.

EXHIBIT 18.1

Cost as a Function of Output Quality for a "Quality Is Costly" View

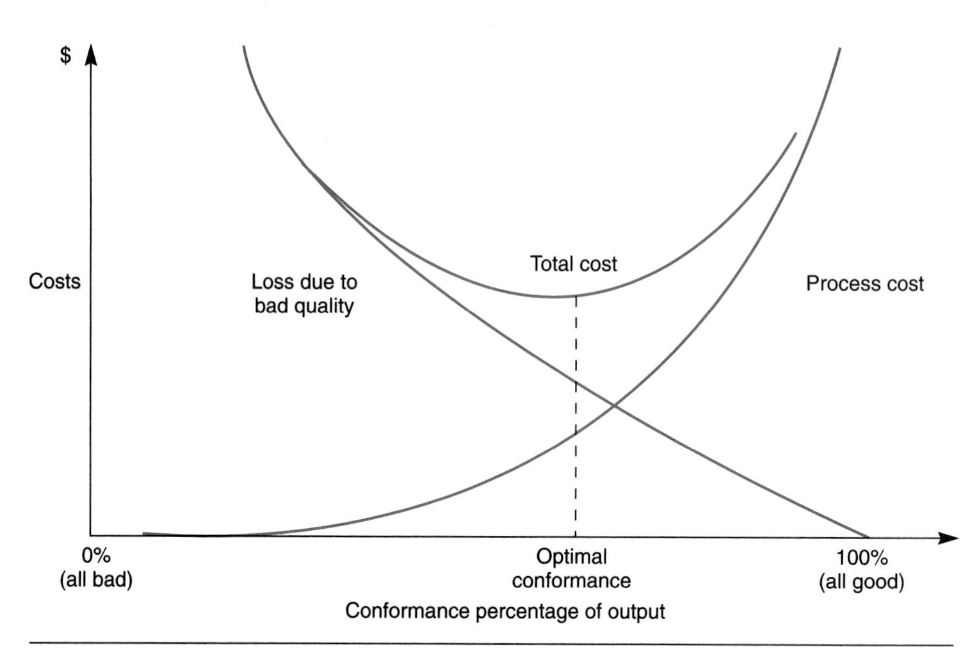

4. Quality responsibility should be the job of production personnel rather than staff specialists.

This is a pleasant and very welcome surprise.

Materials Management in Various Industries

Problems encountered in materials management differ from industry to industry.[4] These differences occur because of the types and numbers of products or services being created, the variations among suppliers and customers, the nature of the raw materials and supply inputs, and economic factors such as the values of the individual units of product or service.

Firms in the service industries are primarily concerned with procurement and material-input supplies. Their central focus is on ordering, receiving, storing, and internally distributing the supplies needed to perform the service. Typical service industries include restaurants, financial institutions, distributors, government agencies, healthcare, education, and public utilities. The output tends to be a narrow range of services or products.

In marketing firms, the output products are about the same as the input products. The marketing firm essentially performs the function of change of ownership—purchasing

[4]John F. Magee, William C. Copacino, and Donald B. Rosenfield, *Modern Logistics Management, Integrating Marketing, Manufacturing and Physical Distribution* (New York: John Wiley & Sons, 1985), pp. 396–401.

EXHIBIT 18.2

Percentage of Japanese and American Managers Adhering to "Quality is Free" Concepts

Concept	Percent	Country
1. Strategic top management involvement in managing quality	81.5%	U.S.
	81.5%	Japan
2. Top management philosophy of working for perfection	67.8%	U.S.
	68%	Japan
3. Reject reduction does not increase long-run cost	89%	U.S.*
	60%	Japan
4. AQL concept is not a superior way to manage quality	63%	U.S.*
	34%	Japan
5. Focus on defects rather than yields	62%	U.S.
	71%	Japan
6. Do not accept inferior quality material even if a line stop results	78%	U.S.*
	92%	Japan
7. Do not deliver inferior quality products just to avoid an order loss	57%	U.S.*
	50%	Japan
8. In case of quality problem, stop the line	87%	U.S.*
	63%	Japan
9. Quality responsibility rests with production personnel rather than staff specialists	89%	U.S.*
	76%	Japan

* = Statistically significant differences.

Source: Wolf Reitsperger, Shirley Daniel, and Abdel El-Shaieb, "Quality is Free: A Comparative Study of Attitudes in the U.S. and Japan," *Journal of Purchasing and Materials Management* (Spring 1990), p. 9.

products, storing, selling, order picking, shipping, and so forth. Wholesalers and retailers generally carry many items purchased from many suppliers with a wide range of costs. The items are sold essentially unchanged to many customers, who tend to buy a variety of items when they shop.

Manufacturing industries tend to look like marketing firms in that there are inputs of many items from many suppliers and outputs of many items to many customers, but the input materials are transformed into very different output items. The changes can be physical (such as machining parts), chemical (such as a change in molecular structure), or cumulative (created by combining parts and components, such as an assembly process). John Magee lists five activities that are characteristic of manufacturing materials management problems:

1. There is a major flow of materials in and out of the activity.
2. Materials physically change form in the process.

3. The change of form takes time and effort. Therefore, the conversion process occupies a great deal of the effort, capital, and managerial attention.
4. There is usually substantial internal materials management activity: flows of raw materials, parts and products within the plants themselves, and to field distribution systems.
5. Logistic activities are concerned with maintaining the flow of product in and out of the operations activity, but tend to be subordinate to the manufacturing and marketing functions. Manufacturing tends to have responsibility and a stronger control of materials flow within the manufacturing system itself, and marketing has a strong control over finished goods and distribution.

18.2 MATERIALS MANAGEMENT IN MANUFACTURING

Materials management has become so important in recent years that the functions it encompasses have increased and its hierarchical position in the organization has been raised. In this section we review the organizational placement of the materials management function and some aspects of inventory control, such as bar coding and materials movement systems.

Organizational Placement of Materials Management

There is wide divergence of opinion about many aspects of materials management, including: where the function should be placed, what its responsibilities are, and whether it should be centralized or decentralized. While the final choice must always relate to the needs of the specific firm in question, the high cost of materials probably will support the current trend, which is to equate the materials management function with the other main functions of the organization. Such placement ensures executive-level attention to materials and gives the materials manager enough clout to be effective. A partial organization chart reflects this placement in Exhibit 18.3. Note the peculiar positioning of Production Planning and Control. (In many manufacturing companies, even today, the materials management function reports to the manufacturing manager.) This area is of utmost importance to manufacturing. As such, it may be assigned organizationally to Materials Management, but functionally it is assigned to Manufacturing and physically located in the Manufacturing area.

Production planning and control is responsible for the entire manufacturing system. It schedules jobs by date, routes them through the varied resources to do the work, decides on the inventory levels, and determines process batch and transfer batch sizes. In other words, production planning and control sees that the manufacturing job gets done. This is why it is located within manufacturing so that personnel can closely observe the production system and respond appropriately.

EXHIBIT 18.3

Organization Chart Showing Materials Management Functions

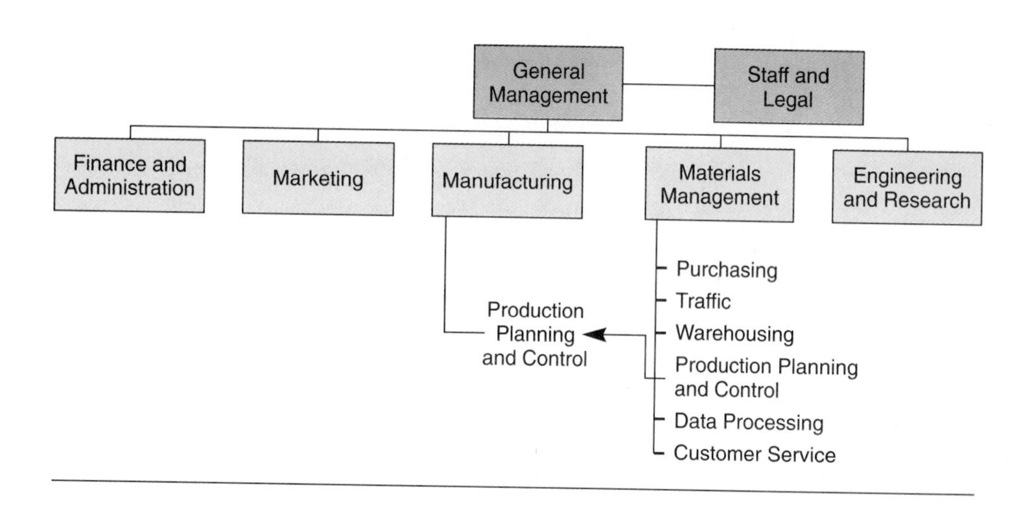

Bar Coding

The term *paperless factory* refers to the flow of product through a system without the accompanying paperwork that has traditionally been part of the flow. The computer was the initial major impetus that made this possible, and the next major development was the increasingly widespread use of **bar coding.**

Bar coding has become very important for all industries, including both manufacturing and services, because it greatly simplifies inventory and production control. Using numbers to represent products allows the user to maintain a large block of information about each product—manufacturer, cost, price, order size, and weight. We've all experienced the greatly increased speed at which we can be checked out at supermarkets or department stores using bar code scanners. While the scanner identifies and prices our purchases, it is simultaneously updating inventory levels; it thus becomes part of the entire process from purchasing, receiving, stocking, moving, and distribution.

In a manufacturing environment, bar code labels attached to parts, subassemblies, and end items allow their continual monitoring. Information relayed as they pass through the process indicates where they have been and where they should go. Also, through this identification, each workstation can automatically display the processing instructions, record the processing and test results, and specify the next workstation.

In mechanized simple conveyors or more complex materials-handling systems, scanners can read the bar code and automatically route the item to its next location. The ultimate use (although expensive) can be a completely automated system. Bar codes could route a job through the entire manufacturing system, such as to work centers, order the required materials and tests, and be physically moved by automatic guided vehicles or conveyors, and movement devices such as robots, mechanical diverters, or shuttle trucks—all computer controlled.

Bar code labels attached to each item can also allow the automatic sorting and packaging of items flowing on a conveyor line. Even the package that then contains the sorted items can be bar coded for routing to the correct storage or shipping area.

Scanners that read bar codes can range from simple low-light-level probes to laser light-beam scanners that read the lines and spaces. Low-light-level probes using infrared or light-emitting diodes need to touch the bar code to distinguish the line and space widths. More intense light sources do not require direct contact, but still need a very short distance. The most effective scanners use laser light beams. These can be small and hand held, or they can be fixed such as positioned to read products moving along a conveyor (or products passing over it, as in a supermarket).

Materials Handling Systems

James Apple and Leon McGinnis are specialists in designing materials handling systems. They believe that the biggest challenge today in designing materials handling systems is the development of an overall materials-flow concept, addressing the entire logistics network in both manufacturing and distribution.[5] The equipment choice is fairly straightforward, once the requirements have been established.

Apple and McGinnis state that a major problem today—especially in manufacturing—is that materials handling is an after-the-fact function, and not a "factory integrator." It should, instead, be the thread that ties the system together. They argue that materials handling is responsible for moving, storing, and tracking all material, which occurs as a result of someone else doing the process planning and production scheduling. Process planning and the production scheduling and control systems should incorporate materials handling system needs and limitations as part of their design. The final design of a materials handling system should include:

1. Handling unit and container design.
2. Micromovement (within a production workplace).
3. Macromovement (between operations).
4. Staging or storage of material.
5. Control system for directing and tracking activity.[6]

Each of these elements must also specify the level of technology, such as manual, mechanized, or fully automated.

Trends in materials handling

Two divergent trends seem to be taking place in the United States at the present time. At one extreme is a movement toward simplicity with less mechanization. At the other extreme is a movement toward more highly complex materials handling and automated manufacturing systems. While there are specific areas within which each would be more appropriate, one school of thought believes that flexibility is possible through simplicity

[5] James M. Apple and Leon F. McGinnis, "Innovation in Facilities and Material Handling Systems: An Introduction," *Industrial Engineering* 19, no. 3 (March 1987), pp. 33–38.

[6] Ibid., p. 38.

and little capital investment, while the opposing school sees flexibility as being built into the system through elaborate machinery, controls, and materials handling devices.

The demand for large-scale automated storage systems has been decreasing over the past few years, primarily for two reasons: (1) the trend toward reducing the quantities of inventories stored, and (2) the trend toward just-in-time systems, which reduce work in process. This has, however, increased the need for smaller and more flexible systems that can be disassembled and moved easily.

Even though the trend toward just-in-time systems has diminished the demand for large-scale automated storage systems, demand for finished-goods warehousing systems has held constant. At the same time, new types of materials handling and storage systems have been developed.

John Hill describes some of the techniques:

1. *Unit-load* **automatic storage and retrieval systems (AS/RS).** Major developments in this area include computer simulation programs that test various rules for handling materials to try to improve productivity. Also, older systems are being upgraded to enable automatic identification of items and interfacing with automatic guided vehicles (AGV).

2. *Miniloads, microloads, and tote stackers.* With the trend toward maintaining smaller inventories, control of parts and kits is critical. Users of these devices are the automotive, airline, and electronics industries.

3. *Carousels.* Vertical and horizontal carousels move the inventory storage system to the worker. Carousels have high potential because of their very low maintenance costs (as low as 0.1 percent of the original cost annually). Carousels are easily installed or, if need be, disassembled and moved to new locations.

4. *Flow racks and paperless picking.* When workers pick items in conventional warehouses for orders, the potential for error is high. To increase productivity and reduce errors, some companies have assigned workers to specific inventory areas and have sent information about orders directly to them, perhaps via a video screen. The worker collects the needed items in the work area and presses a button to send the order on to the next inventory location, where more items are added. Results have shown error reductions of 90 percent or more, and up to 50 percent reduction in the average time to assemble the order.[7]

The demand for the materials handling systems and controls just described is expected to increase rapidly. The use of automatic guided vehicles is growing at 30 percent per year, partly because of the ease of installation. They are also being used as transporting devices to move material from one workstation to the next.

Dependency on the Production-Control System

From the standpoint of materials handling, production-control systems that rigidly specify batch production merely complicate matters. An MRP system, for example, drives the materials handling system, which can only react to what the MRP system specifies.

[7] John M. Hill, "Changing Profile of Material Handling System," parts 1 and 2, *Industrial Engineering* 18, no. 11 (November 1986), pp. 68–73, and 18, no. 12 (December 1986), pp. 26–29.

Materials handling specialists, however, believe that much improvement can be made; they would like to be part of the team that designs and controls the flow of materials and information throughout the plant. JIT systems, on the other hand, are better suited for materials handling because of the more predictable movement time and routing, and because the number of items per movement is small.

18.3 THE FIRM AS A SUPPLIER

The cartoon character Pogo might have said, "We have found a supplier, and it is us." Manufacturing firms usually view themselves as buyers; that is, they purchase components, parts, and materials, and then they produce products and services. But, who buys the components, parts, products, and services that the firm produces? Manufacturing firms rarely sell directly to the consumer; some buyers are manufacturing firms who buy products and services and incorporate them into their own output. Other buyers are wholesalers, retailers, and distribution firms who buy the products and then distribute them further down the chain toward the ultimate consumers. We could probably make the statement that nature is the original supplier and the ultimate consumer is the final buyer. In between, everyone is both a buyer and a supplier. (Environmentalists, of course, would like consumers to return as much as possible to nature.)

What difference does it make whether the firm acts as a buyer from suppliers or a supplier to other buyers? Buyers talk about such things as schedules, lot sizes, costs, lead times, and just-in-time delivery. We often take this as a given while finding suppliers who comply with our demands. As a supplier, however, the shoe is on the other foot. Lot-size schedules sent to us by our customers may not fit our MRP schedules. Or, the just-in-time deliveries that we demand from our vendors may not be compatible with our job shop production.

Some may argue that this issue—the firm as supplier—is more appropriately treated as marketing. As we look closely, though, we see the mirror image of our production planning, scheduling, and control in our customers.

Randy Myer has made some interesting points concerning the need to understand the customer, to be able to evaluate the customer's costs, and even to decide whether the customer is worth keeping.[8] He reminds us that the balance of power in some areas is changing from the supplier to the buyer. In the retail business, average net return is 1 percent of sales. Suppliers average 4 percent net return! In the United Kingdom, the reverse is true in food retailing; retailers average 4 percent and suppliers 1 percent.

Myer suggests that firms should evaluate customers in a way similar to how they calculate their own return on assets. Companies can use the customer return on assets (CRA) criterion to measure the marketing, selling, and product development costs, as well as asset investments in inventory and receivables that they can attribute to each of their customers. Exhibit 18.4 shows the elements involved. Once the CRA has been computed

[8] Randy Myer, "Suppliers—Manage Your Customers," *Harvard Business Review* (November–December 1989), pp. 160–68.

EXHIBIT 18.4

Customer Return on Assets (CRA) Measures the Value of Each Customer

Revenue less:
- Cost of goods sold
- Reserves for damaged and returned merchandise
- Discounts and allowances

= Gross margin less:
- Sales cost
- Promotion cost (excluding media advertising)
- Product development cost
- Direct warehousing cost
- Customer freight cost
- Postsale service cost

= Customer contribution to overhead divided by:
- Direct asset costs
  - Accounts receivable
  - Inventory (finished goods)

= Customer return on assets

Source: Randy Myer, "Suppliers—Manage Your Customers," *Harvard Business Review* (November–December 1989), p. 162.

for customers, further actions may be indicated; these range from promoting greater efforts that will further develop high-return customers to severing relationships with others.

Another interesting finding by Myer is that profitability is not necessarily a function of customer size. Rather, it relates to customer growth rate, though negatively. Fast-growing companies take advantage of their suppliers in relative buying, pressuring for cost reductions, taking full advantage of return allowances, and/or demanding just-in-time deliveries, payment schedules, and so forth. The result of this CRA criterion to evaluate customers is a better understanding of the customer, of the customer's needs, of where lines should be drawn, and of what deviations are possible.

18.4 PURCHASING

With respect to controlling costs, purchasing is by far the most important area in the firm because two thirds of the cost of goods sold are purchased items. We say elsewhere that design has the major impact on costs. But that is true only when the design, manufacturing, and purchasing relationships are not run correctly. It is purchasing's responsibility to know what's out there. Purchasing needs to know materials, performance, availability, and suppliers. They need to know which features of purchased products are cosmetic and which features are functional. This directs them in their search for sources which support requirements.

In this section we discuss value analysis, the issues of single- versus multiple-sourcing, long-term manufacturer/supplier relationships, and some specific issues related to just-in-time purchasing.

EXHIBIT 18.5

The Value Analysis Approach: Comparison of Function to Cost

I. Select a relatively high-cost or high-volume purchased item to value analyze. This can be a part, material, or service. Select an item you suspect is costing more than it should.
II. Find out completely how the item is used and what is expected of it—its *function.*
III. Ask questions:
 1. Does its use contribute value?
 2. Is its cost proportionate to usefulness?
 3. Does it need all its features?
 4. Is there anything better, at a more favorable purchase price, for the intended use?
 5. Can the item be eliminated?
 6. If the item is not standard, can a standard item be used?
 7. If it is a standard item, does it completely fit your application or is it a misfit?
 8. Does the item have greater capacity than required?
 9. Is there a similar item in inventory that could be used?
 10. Can the weight be reduced?
 11. Are closer tolerances specified than are necessary?
 12. Is unnecessary machining performed on the item?
 13. Are unnecessarily fine finishes specified?
 14. Is commercial quality specified?
 15. Can you make the item cheaper yourself?
 16. If you are making it now, can you buy it for less?
 17. Is the item properly classified for shipping purposes to obtain lowest transportation rates?
 18. Can cost of packaging be reduced?
 19. Are you asking your supplier for suggestions to reduce cost?
 20. Do material, reasonable labor, overhead, and profit total its cost?
 21. Will another dependable supplier provide it for less?
 22. Is anyone buying it for less?
IV. Now:
 1. Pursue those suggestions that appear practical.
 2. Get samples of the proposed item(s).
 3. Select the best possibilities and propose changes.

Source: Michael R. Leenders, Harold E. Fearon, and Wilbur B. England, *Purchasing and Materials Management*, 7th ed. (Homewood, Ill.: Richard D. Irwin, 1980), p. 516.

Value Analysis

An approach widely used by purchasing departments is **value analysis.** The basic idea of value analysis is to compare the function performed by a purchased item with its cost in an attempt to find a lower-cost alternative. Exhibit 18.5 summarizes this approach. We must stress, though, that cost is only one issue in the broad scheme of things. Other factors that we discuss later include quality, delivery performance, technical knowledge, and compatibility.

The Purchasing Organization

Harold Fearon conducted a major purchasing organization research study of 297 large U.S. corporations in 23 industry groups, primarily in the manufacturing sector.[9] The study focused on the size of the professional purchasing staff, the reporting mechanisms, organizational placement, and some of the characteristics of the chief purchasing officer.

[9] Harold E. Fearon, "Organizational Relationships in Purchasing," *Journal of Purchasing and Materials Management* (Winter 1988), pp. 2–12.

EXHIBIT 18.6 **Organization of Material Management and Purchasing in Large Corporations**

	Percent
Organization does use materials management concept	70%
Functions included under the materials manager's functions:	
Purchasing	86%
Inventory management	90
Production scheduling and control	59
Inbound traffic	67
Warehousing and stores	84
Incoming quality control	25

		PERCENT OF FIRMS BY FIRM SIZE IN SALES				
	Avg.	Under $500 Million	$500 Million to $1 Billion	$1.1–5 Billion	$5.1–10 Billion	Over $10 Billion
Average number of professional purchasing personnel	118	14	42	71	366	485
Centralized, in which all, or almost all, purchasing is done at one central location for the entire firm		44%	33%	20%	16%	15%
Centralized-decentralized, in which some purchasing is done at the corporate headquarters and purchasing also is done at major operating divisions/plants		42	53	57	74	74
Decentralized, in which purchasing is done on a division/plant basis		14	13	13	10	11

To Whom Purchasing Reports	Percent
President	16%
Executive vice president	18
Financial vice president	7
Manufacturing/production/ operations vice president	24
Materials management vice president	8
Engineering vice president	1
Administrative vice president	13
Other	12
	99

Functions that Report to Purchasing	Percent
Inbound traffic	10%
Outbound traffic	1
Both inbound and outbound traffic	31
Warehousing or stores	34
Inventory management	37
Scrap/surplus disposal	57
Receiving	26
Incoming inspection	16
Other	27

Source: Harold E. Fearon, "Organizational Relationships in Purchasing," *Journal of Purchasing and Materials Management* (Winter 1988), pp. 5–10.

EXHIBIT 18.7

Characteristics of Chief Purchasing Officers in Large Corporations

Title	Percent
Purchasing agent	2%
Manager of purchasing	37
Director of purchasing	39
Vice president of purchasing	6
Materials manager	6
Director of material	2
Vice president of materials management	5
Other	2
Total	99

Education	Percent
High school	6%
Bachelor's degree	55
Bachelor's and graduate degree	39

Bachelor's Degree	Percent
Business	55%
Engineering	19
Liberal arts	13
Other	13

Experience in All Functional Areas	Years
Purchasing	17.0
Operations/production	4.0
Marketing	1.6
Engineering	1.3
Traffic	1.0
Finance	.8
Accounting	.6
MIS	.5
Other	.7
Average years in present position	6
Average years with present employer	18

Source: Harold E. Fearon, "Organizational Relationships in Purchasing," *Journal of Purchasing and Materials Management* (Winter 1988), pp. 8–12.

The findings were quite interesting and are summarized in Exhibits 18.6 and 18.7.

The first question in the study related to the number of firms that operated under a materials management manager. For this study, Fearon defined the materials management concept as

> An organization in which at least three of the functions of purchasing, inventory management, production scheduling and control, inbound traffic, warehousing and stores, and incoming quality control report to a single responsible individual.[10]

In the survey, 70 percent of the firms indicated they operated under this concept. Exhibit 18.6 shows the various functions handled by materials managers. Inventory management, purchasing, and warehousing and stores were the three most common functions. Following these were inbound traffic, production and inventory control, and incoming quality control. This, incidentally, does not question the existence of materials management as we discussed in the opening paragraph to this chapter, but rather states that some functions have been combined under an organizational structure and responsibility.

[10] Ibid., p. 8.

Size of professional purchasing staffs. A total of 35,000 professional personnel were employed in the 297 companies in the survey. Extrapolating this to the Fortune 1000 would indicate that more than 100,000 professional purchasing personnel are employed in that group. The average number for the surveyed companies was 118.

Centralized-decentralized purchasing. In 28 percent of the firms, purchasing is centralized. Those companies with centralized purchasing functions tend to be smaller firms. 58 percent of the firms use a combination of centralized purchasing, done at corporate headquarters, and decentralized purchasing, done at the major operating divisions and plants.

Reporting relationships. Purchasing reports to the president in 16 percent of the organizations and to the executive VP in 18 percent. The most common reporting relationship is still to the manufacturing/production/operations vice president (24 percent). Other reporting relationships include the administrative vice president (13 percent), material management vice president (7 percent) and engineering vice president (1 percent). It is interesting to note that in 33 percent of smaller firms, purchasing still reports to the manufacturing/production/operations vice president.

Functions reporting to purchasing. Scrap/surplus disposal reports to purchasing in 57 percent of the organizations because purchasing has the best information and most knowledge about market values for scrap. Inbound traffic reports to purchasing in 41 percent of the firms due to the importance of sourcing, shipment methods, and prices paid. Other groups reporting to purchasing include: warehousing, 34 percent; outbound traffic, 32 percent; receiving, 26 percent; and incoming inspection, 16 percent.

Chief purchasing officer. Exhibit 18.7 shows some of the characteristics of the chief purchasing officer (CPO). The title varies widely but the two most common are also descriptive: manager of purchasing and director of purchasing. It's interesting to note that outside of purchasing, CPOs have the most experience in operations/production. CPOs have been in their positions for an average of 6 years and with their present employers 18 years. All but 6 percent are college graduates, with 39 percent holding graduate degrees. Business was the most common bachelor's degree.

In summary, Fearon states, "The purchasing function has become broader in scope and responsibility and the CPO needs to have a more varied background with a wider range of experiences to cope with the evolving increased job requirements."[11]

Multiple Suppliers versus Few Suppliers

Historically, the objective of purchasing and materials management has always been to have two or more suppliers. The logic behind this approach was that competition would drive down price and reduce the risk of supplies being cut off. Just-in-time production,

[11] Harold E. Fearon, "Organizational Relationships in Purchasing," *Journal of Purchasing and Materials Management* (Winter 1988), p. 2.

with its critical need for quality, and the new worldwide emphasis on quality products, is changing the buyer/supplier relationship. These changes encouraged the trend of working with suppliers to develop long-term win-win situations, instead of the previously existing confrontational short-term approach. As a result, the need for multiple suppliers of the same part or product was greatly reduced.

Xerox Corporation lost half of its worldwide market share in copiers from 1976 to 1982. Xerox had over 5,000 suppliers and spent 80 percent of manufacturing cost on purchased materials. To try to turn the company around, Xerox reduced its suppliers to just 400 and trained them in statistical process control (SPC), total quality control, and JIT manufacturing concepts. As a result, product costs were greatly reduced, reject rates were reduced by 93 percent, and production lead time was reduced from 52 weeks to 18 weeks.

Working closely with fewer suppliers has many rewards. General Electric Company, for instance, publicizes the names of its best suppliers and awards them better contracts. GE's Appliance Division invites its 100 best suppliers to its annual "Supplier Appreciation Day."

To compete effectively today in world markets, a firm must have high-quality suppliers with acceptable costs and timely delivery. CPOs should compile lists of approved suppliers and then create supplier development programs to improve the suppliers' technical ability, quality, delivery, and cost. More than 70 percent of the companies in one survey had approved buyer lists.[12]

Typically and historically, subcontracting is multiple sourced and adversarial in the United States. In Japan, subcontracting is single sourced and cooperative. The Western view is that single sourcing is a high risk for the buyer. Japan's single-sourcing tradition, however, may not be one of successful long-term sharing. It appears that the power is in the hands of the big buyers. John Ramsay states that so unbalanced is power in the supplier network in Japan that suppliers are more like off-site workshops of the buyer.[13] The advantage to the buyer is that during periods of economic decline, the subcontracted work can be brought back into the buyer's plant. The buyer's firm can maintain stable employment while the supplier has a feast-or-famine existence. There may be more differences between Japanese and Western cultures than there are similarities.

In an attempt to improve their suppliers' quality, each year Pitney Bowes (PB) sends its purchasing personnel and quality engineers to visit vendors. They take along video cameras to tape operations on each supplier's shop floor. Back at PB, design and manufacturing engineers examine the tapes to learn which equipment the supplier uses and the line operator's performance in running that equipment. They also use the videos as excuses to talk with the supplier's workers to ascertain their attitude toward quality. As a result of these visits, some suppliers were removed from the vendor list. Suppliers are also brought to PB. During vendor days, suppliers see PB's operation and obtain a better understanding of their participation in PB's production process. Suppliers are also taught statistical process control if necessary. PB has found that suppliers often make very useful suggestions on materials, design, and so on.

---

[12] Richard E. Plank and Valerie Kijewski, "The Use of Approved Supplier Lists," *International Journal of Purchasing and Materials Management* (Spring 1991), pp. 37–41.

[13] John Ramsay, "The Myth of the Cooperative Single Source," *Journal of Purchasing and Materials Management* (Winter 1990), pp. 2–5.

Texas Instruments perceived quality as being so important that they instituted a 13-step certification program. Results proved the program to be a very good one.

Ford Motor Company issues long-term (three- to five-year) contracts to vendors.[14] Practically every part is single sourced. Suppliers become involved during the design phase. Simultaneous engineering means that the design of a part depends on how it is to be made, and conversely, the process to be used to make a product influences its design. The early involvement of the supplier is very important because suppliers are experts in their areas. They certainly know more about their processes than Ford, so their knowledge influences Ford's designs.

Single-Source Supplier Qualification

Choosing a company to be the **single-source supplier** to a manufacturer is a very important procedure because buyer/supplier relationships can last for years. Qualifying a supplier is a team effort directed by the buyer. Members of the team include purchasing, quality assurance, design engineering, manufacturing engineering, operations, accounting, and industrial engineering. The buyer's team examines various areas of a supplier's operation. Richard Newman lists seven measures that teams can use to evaluate a potential supplier:

1. *Equipment capability.* Can the supplier's equipment produce the product required by the buyer at the appropriate quality level? A process capability index (PCI) is a useful measurement. PCI is normally defined as the absolute design tolerance of the machine or process, divided by six standard deviations of the machine or process actual performance (at a PCI = 1, this includes 99.7 percent of the total output, which is +/−3 standard deviations).

$$\text{PCI} = \frac{\text{Absolute design tolerance}}{6\ \sigma}$$

For many firms, especially those operating with just-in-time, three defects per 1,000 would be unacceptable. Therefore, the PCI may be defined as parts per million or

$$\text{PCI} = \frac{\text{Absolute design tolerance}}{12\ \sigma}$$

The supplier's equipment and processes must be capable of producing to the buyer's needs. (Limits of 12 standard deviations would allow only about 4 defects per million.)

2. *Quality assurance.* The supplier's quality control procedures are examined to determine:

a. Where and whether or not incoming inspection takes place.

b. The use of statistical process control by the supplier's sources.

c. The use of statistical process control by the supplier.

d. Work-in-process inspection methods.

[14] "Suppliers Get Early Call at Ford," *Purchasing* (May 10, 1988), pp. 88–91.

e. Measurement devices and calibration procedures.

f. Procedures for handling rejected raw materials.

g. Final inspection and packaging procedures.

h. Packaging, inspecting, and testing procedures.

Because quality begins at the supplier, the supplier's equipment, and process and quality control procedures are essential.

3. *Financial capability.* This measure is the risk of doing business with a particular supplier, especially over the long term. Typical measures of a supplier's financial condition include:

a. Clout ratio (Buyer's annual order value/Supplier's sales).

b. Current ratio (Current assets/Current liabilities).

c. Quick ratio [(Current assets − Inventory)/Current liabilities].

d. Inventory turnover (Cost of goods sold/Average inventory on hand).

e. Collection period (Accounts receivable/Average sales per day).

These measures indicate the financial health of the firm and the clout ratio indicates the potential value of the buyer to the suppler.

4. *Cost structure.* A firm must know the supplier's cost structure if a long-term relationship is to be considered. This includes materials, direct labor, overhead, sales and administrative costs, and profits as well. The buyer should know that costs are reasonable and what future costs might be. Profits or costs that are too low, for example, would create future problems.

5. *Supplier value analysis effort.* Because the buyer/supplier relationship is intended to be ongoing, the buyer should expect improvements in the supplier and should participate in value analysis programs. Value analysis requires that the supplier:

a. Understand the need for all product specifications.

b. Know which specifications are critical to performance.

c. Know which specifications are cosmetic.

The potential supplier's past history in value analysis programs should be examined as to the type of projects attempted, degree of success, and so forth.

6. *Production scheduling.* The supplier's methods for production scheduling and control can affect how the buyer's orders fit into the system. Existing capacities, methods of expediting, and follow-up procedures are important issues. Also, production schedules are shared, allowing both buyer and seller to plan accordingly. The resulting compatibility of scheduling techniques is desirable.

7. *Contract performance.* How is performance by the supplier to be measured? While these evaluations need to be specified, they should not become a burden in the form of bulky reports. Ideally, contract performance should be on an exception basis, with only the variations being highlighted.[15]

---

[15] Richard G. Newman, "Single Source Qualification," *Journal of Purchasing and Materials Management* (Summer 1988), pp. 10–17.

Qualifying a supplier can be time-consuming and expensive. However, the intent is to have a long-term, mutually beneficial relationship, wherein the costs and time have been well spent.

Purchasing managers believe they are on the right track in evaluating suppliers. James Morgan and Susan Zimmerman conducted a survey, the results of which are shown in Exhibit 18.8. They discovered the traits buyers look for in suppliers and the approaches buyers use to select new suppliers. As shown in Exhibit 18.8, the major method, at 50 percent, was to do a technical evaluation of the supplier and then award a small amount of business as a performance test. Another survey, depicted in Exhibit 18.9, showed that quality was the most important characteristic of a supplier's performance. Delivery performance was second.

Purchasing professionals prefer having a small number of **qualified suppliers** because:

1. Supplier development is costly.
2. The objective is a closer working relationship.
3. Fewer suppliers can be rewarded with substantial business.

Partnership Relationships: Buyer/Supplier

A **strategic partnership** between a buying firm and a supplying firm is defined as a mutual, ongoing relationship involving a commitment by both parties over an extended period of time, an exchange of information, and acknowledgment of the risks and rewards of the relationship.

In addition to cost, quality, and delivery reliability, supplier selection criteria includes factors such as management compatibility, goal congruence, and strategic direction of the supplier firm. Exhibit 18.10 shows supplier selection models currently in use. The first model, which is used by Texas Instruments, weights the suppliers according to Texas Instruments' benchmarks. The second one, used by IBM, is a mathematical model that looks only at cost-based factors. The objective of the IBM model is to minimize costs.

All of the models try (1) to make the supplier selection process more objective and (2) to quantify the criteria. While these measures are qualitative, the firms need to develop some sort of scale or weighting system for each factor. The important point here is that the buyer/vendor partnership can be a very long one and therefore should be evaluated carefully.[16]

What to look for when choosing a supplier to form a partnership. Exhibit 18.11 shows four major areas of importance. There are financial issues as both firms are concerned with the financial stability of their potential partners. The organizational culture and strategy of a company is difficult to evaluate; much is based on intuition and personal compatibility among the individuals in each firm. With respect to technology issues, the buying firm is looking for a supplier who has high technological capability and the ability to assist in

[16] Lisa M. Ellram, "The Supplier Selection Decision in Strategic Partnerships," *Journal of Purchasing and Materials Management* (Fall 1990), pp. 8–14.

EXHIBIT 18.8

Selecting and Testing Prospective New Suppliers

Traits Buyers Check First in Scanning New Suppliers	Percent	How Buyers Handle Supplier Prospects Approach
1. Quality capability.	50%	Perform a technical and then give the potential supplier a limited amount of business to test out performance in a production situation.
2. Technical competence.		
3. Process control.		
4. Pricing/cost factors.		
5. Financial stability.	25	Add the potential supplier to bid lists and make a technical evaluation after bids come in.
6. Engineering/manufacturing support.		
7. Management.	20	Add the potentially hot supplier to request for bid lists once a technical evaluation is made
8. Delivery.		
9. Service record.		
10. Training programs.	18	Perform a technical evaluation as soon as a potentially good supplier is spotted—without a specific job in mind.
11. Plant location.		
	6	Use all of the above approaches at one time or another.
	1	Use an established rating system to measure the new product.

Note: Percentages add up to more than 100 percent because of use of multiple approaches.

Source: James P. Magan and Susan Zimmerman, "Status Report: Building World-Class Supplier Relationships," *Purchasing* (August 16, 1990), pp. 62–65.

EXHIBIT 18.9

What's Important in Supplier Performance

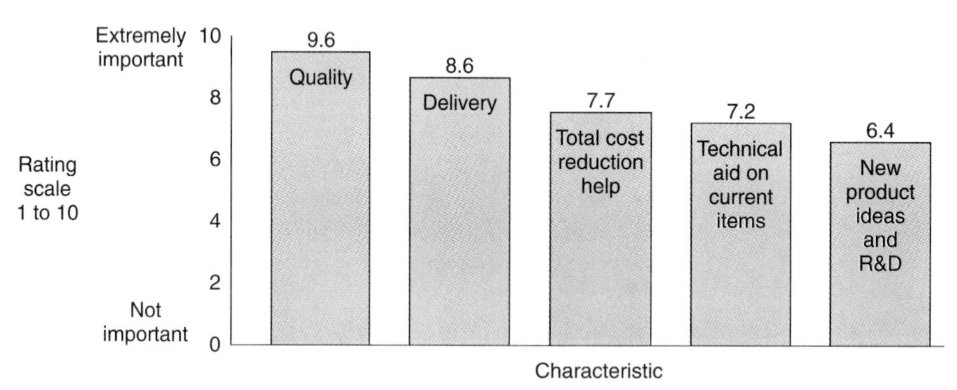

Source: Somerby Dowst, "Quality Suppliers: The Search Goes On," *Purchasing* (January 28, 1988), pp. 94A4–94A12.

EXHIBIT 18.10

Summary of Prescriptive Research Reviewed

Study	Model
Models currently in use	
Gregory (1986)	Matrix model that weights supplier selection factors, based on predetermined, written benchmarks (Texas Instruments)
Bender et al. (1985)	Mixed integer-linear programming model, (IBM), generated by a user-friendly artificial intelligence interface
Other models:	
Timmerman (1986)	1. Categorical approach that rates suppliers on a number of equally weighted factors. 2. Cost ratio method which quantifies all internal costs associated with conducting business with a supplier as a percentage of the supplier's costs, and adds these into that supplier's cost in supplier evaluation. 3. Linear averaging approach that rates suppliers on a number of factors that are weighted by their importance.
Soukup (1987)	Payoff matrix to require purchasing to evaluate potential supplier's performance under a variety of scenarios.
Thompson (1990)	Modified weighted point approach which rates suppliers on a number of factors, weighted by importance, then evaluates supplier performance under alternative scenarios by using a Monte Carlo simulation technique.

Source: Lisa M. Ellram, "The Supplier Selection-Decision in Strategic Partnerships," *Journal of Purchasing and Materials Management* (Fall 1990), p. 10.

EXHIBIT 18.11

Supplier Partnership Selection Criteria

Financial issues

1. Economic performance.
2. Financial stability.

Organizational culture and strategy issues

1. Feeling of trust.
2. Management attitude/outlook for the future.
3. Strategic fit.
4. Top management compatibility.
5. Compatibility across levels and functions of buyer and supplier firms.
6. Supplier's organizational structure and personnel.

Technology issues

1. Assessment of current manufacturing facilities/capabilities.
2. Assessment of future manufacturing capabilities.
3. Supplier's design capabilities.
4. Supplier's speed in development.

Other factors

1. Safety record of the supplier.
2. Business references.
3. Supplier's customer base.

Source: Lisa Ellram, "The Supplier Selection-Decision in Strategic Partnerships," *Journal of Purchasing and Materials Management* (Fall 1990), p. 12.

designing the buying firm's new products. The fourth area includes miscellaneous factors affecting business practices and performance.

Just-in-Time Purchasing

Just-in-time purchasing is a major element of just-in-time (JIT) systems, which are discussed in Chapter 16. The basic idea behind just-in-time purchasing is to establish agreements with vendors to deliver small quantities of materials just in time to meet production's requirements. This can mean daily or sometimes twice-daily deliveries of purchased items. This approach contrasts with the traditional approach of buying items in bulk that are delivered far in advance of production's requirements. The critical elements of JIT purchasing are:

- Reduced lot sizes.
- Frequent and reliable delivery schedules.
- Reduced and highly reliable lead times.
- Consistently high quality levels for purchased materials.[17]

Each of these elements constitutes a major benefit to the purchasing firm, not the least of which is shortening the procurement cycle.

The ultimate objective of JIT purchasing should be a single reliable source for each item and the consolidation of several items from each supplier. The result is far fewer suppliers in total. U.S. companies that have implemented JIT purchasing through fewer suppliers have obtained the following benefits:

1. *Consistent quality.* Involving suppliers during the early stages of product design can result in consistently high-quality products.
2. *Savings on resources.* Significantly less investment and resources, such as buyer's time, travel, and engineering are required when the number of suppliers is reduced.
3. *Lower costs.* The overall volume of items purchased from a single supplier is higher, which eventually leads to lower costs.
4. *Special attention.* The suppliers are more inclined to pay special attention to the buyer's needs, since the buyer represents a large account.
5. *Savings on tooling.* Buyers often provide tools to their suppliers. Concentrating on only one supplier therefore saves substantial tooling costs.
6. The establishment of long-term relationships with suppliers encourages loyalty and reduces the risk of an interrupted supply of parts to the buyer plant; this may be the most important benefit of all.[18]

JIT as an operating concept is an important topic these days, but we must be careful not to become so captivated by the glamor of the JIT single-source philosophy that we

---

[17] Chan K. Hahn, Peter A. Pinto, and Daniel J. Bragg, "'Just-in-Time' Production and Purchasing," *Journal of Purchasing and Materials Management* (Fall 1983), p. 5.

[18] Sang M. Lee and A. Ansari, "Comparative Analysis of Japanese Just-in-Time Purchasing and Traditional U.S. Purchasing Systems," *International Journal of Operations and Production Management* 5, no. 4 (1985), pp. 5–14.

overlook the many occasions when multiple sourcing is justified. It is often advantageous to have suppliers compete for a firm's business. In addition to possible lower prices, during the interviewing and information in dealing with several vendors, the buyer can gain a lot of technical knowledge about the product—in many cases much more than from dealing with only one vendor. Also, many materials, parts, and supplies are critical to a firm's continued operation, and any shutdown by a vendor—some sort of labor dispute or calamity such as a major fire or accident—can significantly hurt. The Department of Defense must purchase military and critical supplies from more than one source. This is done to reduce the risk of an enemy destroying the source of supply. Ira Horowitz notes, "Management often purchases from two or more sources to assure a source of supply, reduce the firm's uncertainty, and reduce its vulnerability to supply shortages. This accounts for the reason why obtaining the lowest cost is not the sole objective."[19]

The most critical demands placed on the purchasing department to make JIT work are (1) the need to reduce the number of suppliers and (2) locating suppliers who are nearby. The strategy of single sourcing is to purchase all parts of a given kind from a single vendor. Nearby suppliers are obviously necessary to allow frequent, small lot size delivery. How well purchasing handles these demands depends on the relationship the firm establishes with its suppliers. As Chan Hahn, Peter Pinto, and Daniel Bragg note, "Suppliers should be viewed as 'outside partner' who can contribute to the long-run welfare of the buying firm rather than as outside adversaries. The purchasing function should look at the new system as an opportunity to reaffirm its vital role in the formation and conduct of overall corporate strategy."[20]

JIT buyer–supplier relationship

A firm operating on a just-in-time basis requires that its suppliers deliver very high-quality products frequently and at a reasonable cost. A significant difference between a JIT supplier and one who is not is in the ability and willingness to make frequent deliveries. As we discussed earlier in this chapter, ideal conditions suggest selecting a few high-quality suppliers with excellent design capabilities and a record of meeting delivery schedules. Thus, this long-term arrangement becomes a partnership.

Which factors are of concern for the just-in-time supplier? Critics of JIT state that just-in-time works for the buyer that sets up the JIT schedule but does not work for the supplier that must follow that schedule. This hypothesis suggests that the supplier simply delivers JIT and produces internally according to an unrelated schedule. The net result is a transfer of inventory carrying responsibilities from buyer back to supplier. In a study of 27 firms in the automobile industry, Charles O'Neal found mixed answers on this issue.[21] Twenty-two percent of the respondents perceive their suppliers to have higher inventories as a result of JIT, 30 percent about the same, and 48 percent lower. As their JIT programs continue, however, 82 percent of respondents expect their suppliers' inventories to be lower within the next five years.

---

[19] Ira Horowitz, "On Two-Source Factor Purchasing," *Decision Sciences* 17, no. 2 (Spring 1986), pp. 274–79.

[20] Hahn et al., "'Just-in-Time' Production," p. 10.

[21] Charles O'Neal, "The Buyer–Seller Linkage in a Just-in-Time Environment," *Journal of Purchasing and Materials Management,* 25th anniversary issue (1989), pp. 34–40.

In another study of 20 firms, Paul Dion, Peter Banting, and Loretta Hasey indicate that JIT leads to buyer's benefits of lower prices, better quality, improved service, and a reduced number of suppliers.[22] These findings are not unique to JIT environments; rather they are the result of the general trend toward preferred suppliers, single sourcing, and long-term buyer/supplier partnerships. This study did find that one of the problems was coordinating the buyer's JIT delivery with the suppliers' production schedules. One possible cause was the suppliers' commitments to other buyers.

Just-in-time deliveries to General Motors, Ford, and Chrysler automobile plants have increased annual inventory turns to an average of 40 per year compared to 8 or 9 before JIT.[23] Some Chrysler assembly plants have well over 100 turns per year. A decade ago, GM kept three months' supply of sheet steel on hand. Today, they keep three days' supply. Examples of the frequency of deliveries in the automotive industry include:

Struts arrive every four hours at Buick City.

Seats arrive every hour from a Lear Sigler plant.

Seats arrive in the exact assembly line sequence at Chrysler's Sterling Heights, Michigan; Dodge City, Montana; and St. Louis, Missouri, assembly plants.

Seats and tires arrive every hour at Honda's Marysville, Ohio, plant.

Diesel engines, axles, wheels, and tires arrive in the assembly line sequence at the Dodge plant in Warren, Michigan.[24]

Adhering to such tight delivery schedules has caused many suppliers to locate close to the buyers' plants—within 10 to 20 miles. Such moves are not absolutely necessary, though. With the good transportation infrastructure that we have in the United States and with dependable modes of transportation, a stable schedule is more important to the supplier than the location.

18.5 PURCHASING IN THE INTERNATIONAL MARKETPLACE

Typically, domestic suppliers cannot meet all of the needs of a multinational corporation. International sourcing has become critical for meeting quality, costs, and flexibility.[25] As shown in Exhibit 18.12, the Asian countries on the Pacific Rim have a labor cost advantage. For automobiles, this cost difference has been estimated to be $1,500 to $2,000 per vehicle.

Manufacturers in the United States have tried to achieve competitiveness on the labor cost issue by automating to reduce labor, by buying labor-intensive components from foreign suppliers, and by subcontracting labor-intensive portions of production to countries with low labor costs.

---

[22] Paul A. Dion, Peter M. Banting, and Loretta M. Hasey, "The Impact of JIT in Industrial Marketers," *Industrial Marketing Management* 19 (1990), pp. 41–46.

[23] Ernest Raia, "JIT in Detroit," *Purchasing* (September 15, 1988), pp. 68–77.

[24] Ibid., pp. 68–69.

[25] Joseph R. Carter and Ram Narasimhan, "Purchasing in the International Marketplace: Implications for Operations," *Journal of Purchasing and Materials Management* (Summer 1990), pp. 2–11.

EXHIBIT 18.12

Comparison of International Labor Rates, Electronics Industry, 1986

Country	Fringe Rate*	Average $ per Hour
Malaysia	25%	$ 1.44
Hong Kong	25	1.45
Taiwan	60	2.26
Singapore	35	2.59
South Korea	80	2.72
United States	46	11.90

*Percentage of hourly rate.

Source: *MAPI Survey on Global Sourcing as a Corporate Strategy* (Washington, D.C.: Machinery and Applied Products Institute, 1986).

EXHIBIT 18.13

Foreign Sourcing Practices (Items purchased abroad)

Type of Purchases	Percentage of Respondents Who Partially Source Abroad
Materials	76%
Machinery and equipment	69
Component parts	81
Services	16

Cost Elements to Evaluate:

1. Unit price.
2. Export taxes.
3. International transportation costs.
4. Insurance and tariffs.
5. Brokerage costs.
6. Letter of credit.
7. Cost of money.
8. Inland (domestic and foreign) freight cost.
9. Risk of obsolescence.
10. Cost of rejects.
11. Damage in transit.
12. Inventory holding costs.
13. Technical support.
14. Employee travel costs.

Source: Joseph R. Carter and Ram Narasimhan, "Purchasing in the International Marketplace: Implications for Operations," *Journal of Purchasing and Materials Management* (Summer 1990), pp. 6, 8.

Global sourcing is a standard procedure for over half of all firms with annual sales of more than $10 million. What stands out in the list of purchased items is the small percentage of companies who purchase services. Exhibit 18.13 shows that while foreign purchases of materials, parts, and equipment range from 69 percent to 81 percent, only 16 percent of the companies surveyed purchased foreign services.

Typically, evaluating foreign suppliers is more difficult and increased costs are relevant. Exhibit 18.13 shows costs for foreign sourcing. Naturally, most of these costs differ from domestic costs because of the expenses of dealing with foreign suppliers and exchange rates.

International sourcing can be a competitive weapon if used correctly. International sourcing usually requires stable production and simple product designs with a reduced numbers of components. It also promotes greater cooperation among manufacturing, marketing, and purchasing personnel.

EXHIBIT 18.14

America's 10 Largest Purchasing Departments

Company	$ Spent by Purchasing (millions)	% of Sales $ and % of Product Cost
General Motors	$50,566	50/60%
Ford	50,000	60/68
Chrysler	21,864	63/70
IBM	20,000	32/—
General Electric	18,500	34/—
AT&T	10,600	29/—
Du Pont	10,000	28/60
GTE	9,264	53/—
United Technologies	9,000	46/—
Boeing	8,200	41/—

Source: Ernest Raia, "Purchasing's Top 100," *Purchasing* (November 22, 1990), p. 52.

The top 100 industrial purchasing departments spent almost $500 billion on goods and services during 1989.[26] That's about 12 percent of the gross national product. Exhibit 18.14 shows the top 10 of these 100 companies and the percent of purchases as compared to sales revenue and production cost. Of the four companies listing product cost in the last column, purchasing accounts for an average of 64.5 percent of product cost.

For international materials management, the specific organizational form is less important than having a clear and explicit assignment of responsibility and authority. Also important is the firm's reward structure; the firm's objectives must be clearly specified and personnel appropriately rewarded. Otherwise, individuals may establish their own objectives, such as minimizing the cost of purchasing and transportation. While important, cost minimization should not be the only sought-after goal. The ultimate goal is to choose suppliers who can become strategic partners that participate from the beginning of the product design stage.

18.6 MARKETING AND DISTRIBUTION

The final phase of materials management is distribution of the finished product to the field. The distribution function, variously termed *traffic, physical distribution,* or *logistics,* is responsible for arranging the means of shipping finished goods and controlling inventory levels at various stockkeeping points in the field. Stockkeeping points are typically viewed by levels or echelons, and a multiechelon system for a major manufacturer would consist of factories, a main distribution center, regional warehouses, and retail outlets.

The major concerns in managing distribution systems are deciding how much inventory is to be kept at each stock point and determining the appropriate policies for inventory replenishment. The basic objective is to meet the customer's delivery requirements at a low cost. This entails a trade-off between the costs of warehousing and inventory and the costs of transportation.

[26] Ernest Raia, "Purchasing's Top 100," *Purchasing* (November 22, 1990), pp. 51–55.

Reed Kaestner/Stock Imagery

At this warehouse, or stock point, orders are distributed to retail stores within the region. Workers are able to assemble orders on simple high capacity carts, which are then delivered directly to the trucks for daily distribution.

One firm may follow a strategy of having many warehouses and shipping in, say, carload lots. This keeps its transportation costs low, at the expense of relatively high warehousing and inventory costs. Another firm may follow a strategy of few warehouses, low field inventory, and frequent deliveries. This keeps its warehousing and inventory costs low, at the expense of relatively high transportation costs.

The replenishment of inventory can be either as a pull system or a push system. In a pull system, warehouses order independently by pulling required items from the higher-level stocking point. The disadvantage of a pull system is that very high amplitude oscillations in demand can occur. As the demand changes at a lower level, it becomes amplified as it passes through higher-level points and can even be doubled by the time it reaches the production facility. Production scheduling doesn't like this.

In a push system, stock levels are controlled by the production system. Forecasts are made and inventory is pushed out to the warehouse according to production's generated forecasted demand. Although this smooths out the production level, its primary disadvantage is that a push system is a centralized decision and not a local one. We discuss more of this under the distribution requirements planning (DRP) section in this chapter.

Warehouse Replenishment Systems

The three basic approaches to warehouse inventory replenishment are:

1. *The reorder point/economic order quantity system* in distribution works the same way as for in-plant inventory control. The warehouse places an economic lot-size order when its inventory reaches the reorder point.

2. *The base stock system* works to scheduled shipment dates, and shipment size is equal to the actual usage in the previous period.
3. *Distribution requirements planning* (DRP) follows the logic of MRP. It converts a forecast of warehouse demand to a gross requirement, subtracts on-hand and on-order balances, and then places a replenishment order.

Of the three methods, DRP has the advantage of being based on projected future demand rather than past sales. This avoids the risk of having a stockout at a central warehouse as a result of several branch warehouses reaching their reorder points simultaneously.

Distribution Requirements Planning

The American Production Inventory Control Society (APICS) defines **distribution requirements planning (DRP)** as:

> The function of determining the needs to replenish inventory at branch warehouses. A time-phased order point approach is used where the planned orders at the branch warehouse level are "exploded" via MRP logic to become gross requirements on the supplying source. In the case of multi-level distribution networks, this explosion process can continue down through the various levels of master warehouse, factor warehouse, etc., and become input to the master production schedule (MPS). Demand on the supplying source(s) is recognized as dependent, and standard MRP logic applies.[27]

DRP, from the wholesalers' and retailers' point of view, pulls inventory away from the manufacturing plant. It is not necessary to go through the MPS. When items are "available to promise" in the production MRP system, they are allocated directly from MRP to DRP. If they are not available, the order is entered into the MPS. Using DRP, the entire distribution channel is linked together, as shown in Exhibit 18.15.

Distribution requirements planning reduces uncertainty when items are needed by summing through the channels of distribution and determining how many are available. The resemblance to MRP comes from summarizing requirements from different sources by time periods. MRP does this by summing net requirements from different product needs as gross requirements for the next lower level in the bill of materials. DRP does this summing by combining requirements form different retailers, wholesalers, local warehouses, and regional warehouses. The major difference is that DRP deals with end items only—there is no bill of materials explosion within DRP.

The advantages of DRP over forecasting are that

1. Forecasting usually comes from the manufacturer.
2. DRP comes from the distribution system. Errors—whether shortages or excesses—are caused by the distribution system itself and, therefore, are far easier to live with.

---

[27] *APICS Dictionary*, 6th ed. (Falls Church, Va.: American Production Inventory Control Society, 1987), p. 9.

EXHIBIT 18.15

Distribution Requirements Planning (DRP)

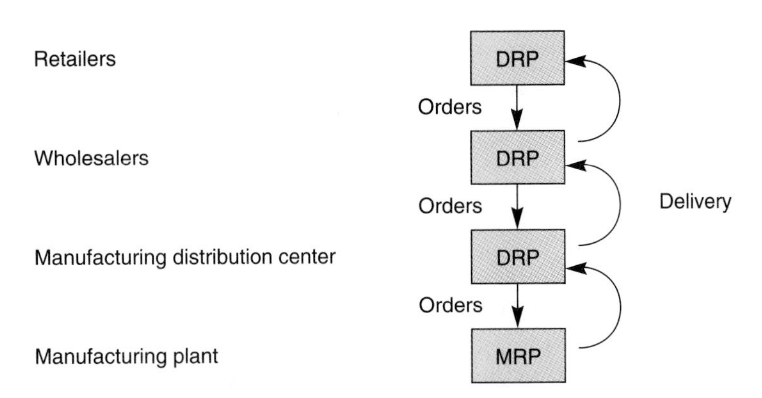

If inventory is available, it is allocated to the DRP demand; otherwise, it is input to the master production schedule.

Demands on the production system are becoming so important to understand and to respond to that many companies are establishing a demand manager as a link between the sales department and manufacturing.

Value Density (Value per Unit Weight)

A common and extremely important purchasing decision is simply deciding whether an item should be shipped by air, or by ground transportation. While it may seem overly simplified, the value of an item per pound of weight—**value density**—is an important measure when deciding where items should be stocked geographically and how they should be shipped. In a classic Harvard case study, the Sorenson Research Company must decide whether to stock inventory for shipment at major warehouses, minor warehouses, or garage warehouses, and whether to ship by ground or air carrier.[28] Analysis shows that the time saved by shipping by air can be justified if the shipping cost is appropriate. The decision involves a trade-off: the savings of reduced in-transit inventory and transit time versus the higher cost to ship. Obviously, the solution involves a combination of methods.

We can approach the problem by examining a specific situation. Consider, for example, the cost for shipping from Boston to Tucson. Assume that the inventory cost is 30 percent per year of the product value (which includes cost of capital, insurance, decrease in warehouse costs, etc.), that regular United Parcel shipments take eight days, and that we are considering second-day air service with Federal Express. We can set up a comparison table as shown in Exhibit 18.16.

The problem can be restated as comparing the additional cost of transportation to the savings of six days. Logically we can make the general statement that expensive items can be sent by air from the factory warehouse, while lower-value items can be stocked at lower-level warehouses or shipped by a less expensive method.

[28] W. Earl Sasser et al., *Cases in Operations Management* (Homewood, Ill.: Richard D. Irwin, 1982).

EXHIBIT 18.16

Sorenson Research Company Shipping Cost Comparison

Shipping Weight (pounds)	United Parcel (8 days to deliver)	Federal Express (2 days to deliver)	Cost Savings with UPS	Break-Even Product Value	Break-Even Value Density (product value per pound)
1	$1.91	$11.50	$ 9.59	$1,944.64	$1,944.68
2	2.37	12.50	10.13	2,054.14	1,027.07
3	2.78	13.50	10.72	2,173.78	724.59
4	3.20	14.50	11.30	2,291.39	572.85
5	3.54	15.50	11.96	2,425.22	485.04
6	3.88	16.50	12.62	2,559.06	426.51
7	4.28	17.50	13.22	2,680.72	382.96
8	4.70	18.50	13.80	2,798.33	349.79
9	5.12	19.50	14.38	2,915.94	323.99
10	5.53	20.50	14.97	3,035.58	303.56

$$\text{Regular shipment costs} - \text{Air shipping cost} = \text{Shipping cost savings}$$

At break-even,

$$\text{Cost savings} = \text{Inventory carrying cost}$$

$$= \frac{\text{Item value} \times 0.30 \times 6 \text{ days}}{365 \text{ days per year}}$$

Therefore,

$$\text{Item value} = \frac{365 \times \text{Cost savings}}{0.30 \times 6}$$

The last column in Exhibit 18.16 is the break-even based on the product's value density, or value per pound for shipments of different weights. The exhibit indicates that any item whose value is greater than that amount should be sent by air. For example, a five-pound shipment of integrated circuits whose average value is $500 per pound or more should be shipped by air.

18.7 CONCLUSION

This chapter has treated materials management in the context of manufacturing, but materials management is a vitally important function in service organizations as well. Hospitals and utilities of all kinds have major materials requirements under the category of supplies. Likewise, the military has vast sums invested in materials; in fact, the Navy publishes *Naval Logistics Research Quarterly*, a major journal devoted to logistical issues. Indeed, though materials management is one of those areas that historically has received little emphasis in business schools, how well it is performed can make or break an organization.

In this chapter we looked at the importance of quality and the cost of purchased materials for the firm's products. In manufacturing companies today, on average, two thirds of the cost of goods sold are purchased materials. Therefore, through its knowledge of available products, the purchasing department can have a great influence on quality and cost. In qualifying suppliers, and through long-term partnerships, purchasing can enhance a firm's position and help it become a world-class business.

18.8 REVIEW AND DISCUSSION QUESTIONS

1. What recent changes have caused materials management and purchasing to become much more important?
2. Compare "quality is free" with "quality is costly." Which attitude would you choose?
3. When bar coding first came out, not many people took the idea seriously. What do you think about bar coding? In which areas do you think it may be used someday?
4. How are potential suppliers qualified by a firm?
5. Which characteristics of a supplier are the most important to the buyer?
6. What is meant by a *strategic partnership* between a buyer and a supplier?
7. JIT suppliers have additional pressures which other suppliers do not have. What are they?
8. Many firms have gone to other countries to buy supplies. Discuss the pros and cons of international buying.
9. What are the trade-offs in single-source versus multiple-source purchasing?
10. Which skills and training are most important for a purchasing agent?
11. The following items have been taken from the purchasing section of an MRP II audit questionnaire:

    Purchasing people believe the schedules.

    Vendor lead time is 95 percent accurate.

    Vendor delivery performance is 95 percent or better.

    Vendor scheduling is done out beyond quoted lead times.

    Explain why these items are important to MRP II success.
12. Currently you are using multiple suppliers for each purchased item. How would you go about choosing one of them to be your long-term sole source?
13. As a supplier, which factors would you consider about a buyer (your potential customer) to be important in setting up a long-term relationship?
14. What is meant by *world class* as in a world-class manufacturer and world-class supplier?
15. "JIT purchasing is nothing more than a ploy to have vendors take over the burden of carrying inventory." Comment.
16. Distinguish between push and pull distribution systems. What are the pros and cons of each?
17. What is DRP? How does it work?
18. For the value density example given in Exhibit 18.16, what would the effect be if a competing firm offers you a similar service for 10 percent less than Federal Express's rates?

18.9 CASE: THOMAS MANUFACTURING COMPANY*

"Delivery of our 412 casting is critical. We can't just stop production for this casting every time you have a minor pattern problem," said Mr. Litt, engineer for Thomas Manufacturing.

"I'm not interested in running rejects," answered Mr. James of A&B Foundry. "I cannot overextend my time on these castings when the other jobs are waiting."

"If you can't cast them properly and on time, I'll just have to take our pattern to another foundry that can," retorted Mr. Litt.

"Go ahead! It's all yours. I have other jobs with fewer headaches," replied Mr. James.

Mr. Litt returned to Thomas Manufacturing with the 412 casting pattern. (A pattern is used in making molds in which the gray iron is formed. After cooling, the mold is broken off, leaving the desired casting.) He remembered that Mr. Dunn, vice president of manufacturing for Thomas (see Case Exhibit 1), had obtained a quote on his casting from Dawson, another gray-iron foundry, several months before. It seemed that Dawson had the necessary capabilities to handle this casting.

To Mr. Litt's surprise, Mr. Dunn was not entirely happy to find the 412 pattern back in the plant. Mr. Dunn contacted personnel at Dawson Foundry, who said that they could not accept the job because of a major facilities conversion that would take six months. Locating another supplier would be difficult. Most foundries would undertake complex casting only if a number of orders for simple casting were placed at the same time.

Mr. Dunn knew that gray-iron foundry capacity was tight. In general, foundries were specializing or closing down. Mr. Dunn had gathered some data on the gray-iron industry located within a 500-mile radius of his plant (see Case Exhibit 2), which highlighted the problems his company was facing. There were three gray-iron foundries located within 60 miles of Thomas Manufacturing. Thomas had dealt with one foundry until it suffered a 12-month strike. Thomas then moved most of its casting needs to A&B Foundry, but Mr. Dunn had given the occasional order to Dawson and requested quotes quite regularly from them. In the last four years all had gone well with A&B Foundry. Mr. Dunn had planned to share his business with both foundries. A&B was comparable to Dawson on price and had done an excellent job until now.

A telephone call back to A&B Foundry indicated to Mr. Dunn that Mr. James was adamant in his refusal to take the pattern back.

The 412 Casting

Thomas Manufacturing Company was a portable generator manufacturer with sales above the $6 million level. Thomas employed approximately 160 people in a fairly modern plant. Many of its small portable generators were sold to clients all over North America.

The 412 casting was part of the most popular middle-of-the-line generator. The casting weighed 70 pounds and cost approximately $60, and its pattern was worth $8,000. A run normally consisted of 100 castings, and Thomas usually received 100 castings every month. The 412 represented about 15 percent of Thomas's casting needs.

Normal lead time was at least eight weeks. When the supply problem arose, Thomas held six weeks' inventory.

---

* From M. R. Leenders, H. E. Fearon, and W. B. England, *Purchasing and Materials Management,* 7th ed. (Homewood, Ill.: Richard D. Irwin, 1980), pp. 50–53.

CASE EXHIBIT 1

Organization Chart of Thomas Manufacturing Company

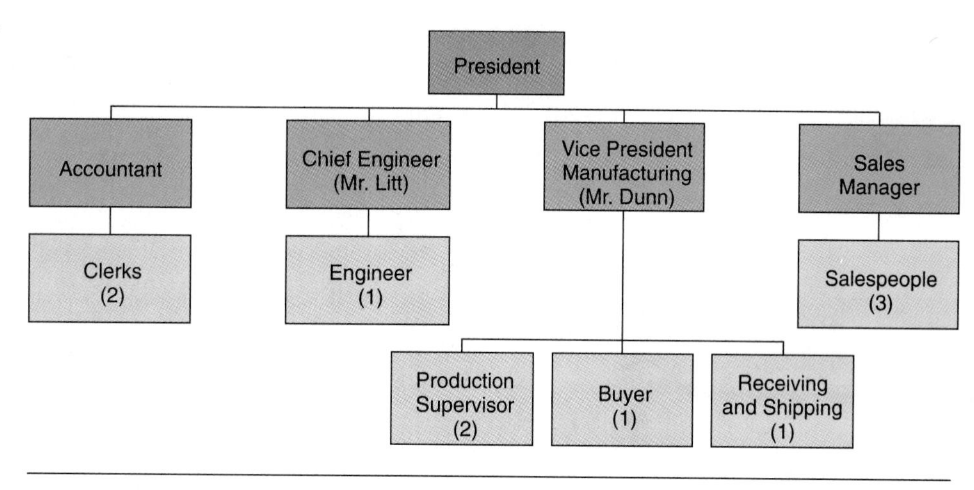

CASE EXHIBIT 2

Foundry Data for Area within a 500-Mile Radius of the Thomas Plan

A. Shipments of Manufactured Goods

Gray Iron (commercial castings)	Quantity	Value
Previous year	280,000 tons	$65,000,000
Current year	243,000 tons	$54,000,000

B. Number of Establishments

									Current Year
140	133	131	134	137	134	134	128	126	116

Ten-Year History

Mr. Litt, an expert in pattern work, explained that the pattern was tricky, but once the difficulties were ironed out and the job set up, a hand molder could pour 50 castings in two days without any problems.

QUESTIONS

1. What alternatives are open to Mr. Dunn to prevent disruption of his company's most popular generator?
2. Was it appropriate for Mr. Litt to repossess the 412 pattern?
3. From the data given, does it appear that the Thomas Company has any leverage in dealing with the foundries?

18.10 CASE: OHIO TOOL COMPANY (VENDOR SELECTION)*

The Ohio Tool Company designed a new machine, which it considered to be superior to anything else of its type on the market. Estimated sales were about $200,000 per year. The principal advantage of this machine over competition was a unique cam arrangement enabling the operator to adjust the unit very quickly.

To achieve the advantages offered by the design, it was necessary that the cam—of which two were required per unit—be manufactured to very close tolerances (see the accompanying sketch).

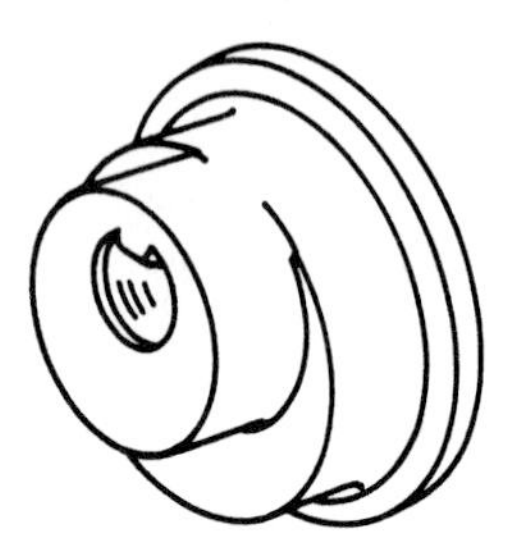

Because of the difficulty of machining the several eccentric surfaces and the need for an integral locating key in the center bore, the part could not readily be made from solid bar stock.

Possible methods of manufacture rapidly narrowed down to some type of casting. The materials under consideration were aluminum, zinc, and iron. Aluminum and iron sand castings were excluded because the close tolerances on the finished part would require precise and very difficult secondary machining operations. Aluminum and zinc die castings could not be used because draft or taper on the cam surfaces, required to remove the part from the die, would also necessitate secondary machining operations to render the surfaces true again.

Another possibility for producing the part seemed to be through powder metallurgy, a process by which finely divided metal particles (in this case powdered iron) were formed to the desired shape by means of high pressure in a metal die, then "sintered" at high temperature to form a solid metal piece. The Ohio Tool Company located three possible powdered-metal sources and sent parts drawings to each.

Supplier A, located about 1,000 miles away, was one of the leaders in the powder metallurgy field. The Ohio Tool Company had purchased parts for another product from this supplier within the past year, and the supplier had failed to deliver on the agreed schedule. After many delivery promises via long-distance telephone and after a special trip to the plant by the purchasing manager, the parts arrived three months late. During this delay all other parts for the project had to be set aside and some workers laid off. In addition, the delay caused the Ohio Tool Company considerable loss of face with its customers because the product had been announced to the trade.

Supplier A submitted this quotation:

---

* Source: Modified from P. E. Holden, F. E. Shallenberger, and W. E. Diehm, *Selected Case Problems in Industrial Management* (Englewood Cliffs, N.J.: Prentice Hall, 1962), pp. 123–26.

Quantity	Price	Terms
5,000 pieces	$0.146 each	Die cost—$1,968
10,000 pieces	$0.145 each	Delivery—Approximately 10 weeks, depending on the production schedule at the time order is entered
20,000 pieces	$0.144 each	

The quotation did not include incoming freight cost of $0.012 each. Further, it was based on furnishing a cam with a slight projection on one of the surfaces, which would require a machine operation by the Ohio Tool Company at an estimated cost of $0.05 each.

Supplier B, located 300 miles away, was a relative newcomer to the powdered-metal field. The manager of the shop had been with this firm only a short time but had gained his experience from one of the old-line companies. The Ohio Tool Company's experience with this company had been very satisfactory. It had undertaken the job at the same costs as Supplier A and had produced satisfactory parts in record time.

In reply to the request for a quotation, Supplier B suggested that, since it could not manufacture to specified tolerances, they be relaxed on several dimensions. However, the engineering department at Ohio Tool insisted that the critical function of this cam necessitated the tolerances as originally specified. When this information was passed along to Supplier B, it asked to be excused from quoting.

A third supplier, with whom the Ohio Tool Company had had no previous dealings, we asked to quote on the part. Supplier C was a subsidiary of one of the large automotive concerns and had an excellent technical reputation. It was understood, however, that the parent company was considering introducing several powdered-metal parts on its line of automobiles. The quotation of Supplier C was:

Quantity	Price	Terms
5,000 pieces	$0.186 each	Die cost—$890
10,000 pieces	$0.185 each	Delivery—10 weeks
20,000 pieces	$0.183 each	

Supplier C was located 900 miles from the Ohio Tool Company plant, and incoming freight would cost $0.012 per unit. The drawing accompanying the quotation indicated a projection on one of the cam surfaces, which would have to be machined by the Ohio Tool Company for the proper functioning of the part. Although special machining techniques would be required in this case, the Ohio Tool Company estimator felt the company could machine off the projection for about $0.06 each in quantities of 5,000 or more.

Because of the past performance record of Supplier B, the purchasing manager decided that he should make an effort to obtain a quotation. He made a personal visit to the plant to discuss the problem, and learned that the plant could hold the tolerances on the center hole closer than the engineering department required, making the cumulative tolerances on the outside diameter of the cam surfaces almost within the tolerance specified. The engineering department agreed to change the drawing accordingly and grant additional latitude on the cam surfaces. On this basis, Supplier B entered the following quotation:

Quantity	Price	Terms
5,000 pieces	$0.50 each	Die cost—$1,350
10,000 pieces	$0.40 each	Delivery—10 to 12 weeks
20,000 pieces	$0.32 each	
50,000 pieces	$0.275 each	

Freight in amounted to $0.005 each. The quotation was based on a part in exact accordance with the drawing, since the cost of secondary operations had been included in the quotation and would be performed by the supplier. By the time this quotation was received, manufacture of other parts of the product was assured and final assembly was scheduled for 12 weeks from that date.

Upon reviewing all the quotations, the relatively high cost of Supplier B was readily apparent. The purchasing manager decided to call Supplier B and ask him to review his costs again. The quotation was revised:

5,000 pieces	$0.45
10,000 pieces	$0.37

No change in price for 20,000 and 50,000 pieces.

QUESTIONS

1. Which vendor would you select for the job? Why?
2. Should a purchasing agent enter into negotiations with one vendor after bids from competitors have been examined?
3. With reference to Question 2, prepare a policy statement that would guide the future actions of the purchasing department.

18.11 SELECTED BIBLIOGRAPHY

Apple, James M., Jr., and Leon F. McGinnis. "Innovations in Facilities and Material Handling Systems: An Introduction." *Industrial Engineering* 19, no. 3 (March 1987), pp. 33–38.

Bradley, Peter. "A Glimpse of Logistics of the Future." *Purchasing,* March 21, 1991, pp. 50–55.

Bragg, Daniel J., and Chan K. Hahn. "Materials Requirements Planning and Purchasing." *Journal of Purchasing and Materials Management,* 25th anniversary issue, 1989, pp. 41–46.

Burt, David N. "Managing Suppliers Up to Speed." *Harvard Business Review,* July–August 1989, pp. 127–35.

Carter, Joseph R., and Ram Narasimhan. "Purchasing in the International Marketplace: Implications for Operations." *Journal of Purchasing and Materials Management,* Summer 1990, pp. 2–11.

Dion, Paul A., Peter M. Banting, and Loretta M. Hasey. "The Impact of JIT on Industrial Marketers." *Industrial Marketing Management* 19 (1990), pp. 41–46.

Dowst, Somerby. "Quality Suppliers: The Search Goes On." *Purchasing,* January 28, 1988, pp. 94A4–94A12.

Ellram, Lisa M. "The Supplier Selection Decision in Strategic Partnerships." *Journal of Purchasing and Materials Management,* Fall 1990, pp. 8–14.

Fearon, Harold E. "Organizational Relationship in Purchasing." *Journal of Purchasing and Materials Management,* Winter 1988, pp. 2–12.

Guinipero, Larry C. "Motivating and Monitoring JIT Supplier Performance." *Journal of Purchasing and Materials Management,* Summer 1990, pp. 19–24.

Hahn, Chan K.; Peter A. Pinto; and Daniel J. Bragg. "'Just-in-Time' Production and Purchasing." *Journal of Purchasing and Materials Management* (Fall 1983), p. 5.

Hahn, Chan K.; Charles A. Watts; and Kee Young Kim. "The Supplier Development Program." *Journal of Purchasing and Materials Management,* Spring 1990, pp. 2–7.

Hill, John M. "Changing Profile of Material Handling System," parts 1 and 2. *Industrial Engineering* 18, no. 11 (November 1986), pp. 68–73, and 18, no. 12 (December 1986), pp. 26–29.

Horowitz, Ira. "On Two-Source Factor Purchasing," *Decision Sciences* 17, no. 2 (Spring 1986), pp. 274–79.

Jackson, Ralph W. "How Multidimensional Is the Purchasing Job?" *Journal of Purchasing and Materials Management,* Fall 1990, pp. 27–32.

Lee, Sang M., and A. Ansari, "Comparative Analysis of Japanese Just-in-Time Purchasing and Traditional U.S. Purchasing Systems." *International Journal of Operations and Production Management* 5, no. 4 (1985), pp. 5–14.

Lyons, Thomas F.; A. Richard Krachenberg; and John W. Henke, Jr. "Mixed Motive Marriages: What's Next for Buyer Supplier Relations?" *Sloan Management Review,* Spring 1990, pp. 29–36.

Magee, John F.; William C. Copacino; and Donald B. Rosenfield. *Modern Logistics Management, Integrating Marketing, Manufacturing and Physical Distribution* (New York: John Wiley & Sons, 1985).

Millen, Anne. "How Effective Is Purchasing?" *Purchasing,* October 25, 1990, pp. 58–62.

Monczka, Robert M., and Steven J. Trecha. "Cost-Based Supplier Performance Evaluation." *Journal of Purchasing and Materials Management, Spring 1988, pp. 2–7.*

Morgan, James P., and Susan Zimmerman. "Building World-Class Supplier Relationships." *Purchasing, August 16, 1990, pp. 62–65.*

Morgan, James P., and Somerby Dowst. "Partnering for World-Class Suppliers." *Purchasing,* November 10, 1988, pp. 49–62.

Myer, Randy. "Suppliers—Manage Your Customers." *Harvard Business Review,* November–December 1989, pp. 160–68.

Newman, Richard G. "Single-Source Qualification." *Journal of Purchasing and Materials Management,* Summer 1989, pp. 10–17.

O'Neal, Charles R. "The Buyer-Seller Linkage in a Just-in-Time Environment." *Journal of Purchasing and Materials Management,* 25th anniversary issue, 1989, pp. 34–40.

Plank, Richard E., and Valerie Kijewski. "The Use of Approved Supplier Lists." *International Journal of Purchasing and Materials Management,* Spring 1991, pp. 3–41.

Presutti, William D. "Technology Management: An Important Element in the Supplier Capability Survey." *International Journal of Purchasing and Materials Management* (Winter 1991), pp. 11–15.

Raia, Ernest. "JIT in Detroit." *Purchasing,* September 15, 1988, pp. 68–77.

———. "Purchasing's Top 100." *Purchasing,* November 22, 1990, pp. 51–55.

Ramsay, John. "The Myth of the Cooperative Single Source." *Journal of Purchasing and Materials Management,* Winter 1990, pp. 2–5.

Reitsperger, Wolf; Shirley Daniel; and Abdel El-Shaieb." "'Quality Is Free': A Comparative Study of Attitudes in the U.S. and Japan." *Journal of Purchasing and Materials Management,* Spring 1990, pp. 8–11.

Sasser, W. Earl, et al. *Cases in Operations Management* (Homewood, Ill.: Richard D. Irwin, 1982).

St. John, Carol H., and Scott T. Young. "The Strategic Consistency between Purchasing and Production." *International Journal of Purchasing and Materials Management,* Spring 1991, pp. 15–20.

Thompson, Kenneth N. "Scaling Evaluative Criteria and Supplier Performance Estimates in Weighted Point Prepurchase Decision Models." *International Journal of Purchasing and Materials Management,* Winter 1991, pp. 27–36.

Whybark, D. Clay. "Education and Global Logistics." *Logistics and Transportation Review* 26, no. 3, pp. 261–70.

Appendixes

OUTLINE

APPENDIX A
Financial Analysis in Production and Operations Management

In this appendix we review basic concepts and tools of financial analysis for OM. These include: the types of cost (fixed, variable, sunk, opportunity, avoidable), risk and expected value, and depreciation (straight line, sum-of-the-years'-digits, declining balance, double-declining balance, depreciation-by-use). Our focus is on capital investment decisions.

CONCEPTS AND DEFINITIONS

We will begin this appendix with some basic definitions.

Fixed costs

A fixed cost is any expense that remains constant regardless of the level of output. Although no cost is truly fixed, many types of expense are virtually fixed over a wide range of output. Examples are rent, property taxes, most types of depreciation, insurance payments, and salaries of top management.

Variable costs

Variable costs are expenses that fluctuate directly with changes in the level of output. For example, each additional unit of sheet steel produced by USX requires a specific amount of material and labor. The incremental cost of this additional material and labor can be isolated and assigned to each unit of sheet steel produced. Many overhead expenses are also variable, since utility bills, maintenance expense, and so forth vary with the production level.

Exhibit A.1 illustrates the fixed and variable cost components of total cost. Note that total cost increases at the same rate as variable costs because fixed costs are constant.

Sunk costs

Sunk costs are past expenses or investments that have no salvage value and therefore should not be taken into account in considering investment alternatives. Sunk costs could also be current costs that are essentially fixed, such as rent on a building. For example, suppose an ice cream manufacturing firm occupies a rented building and is considering making sherbet in the same building. If the company enters sherbet production, its cost accountant will assign some of the rental expense to the sherbet operation. However, the building rent remains unchanged and therefore is not a relevant expense to be considered in making the decision. The rent is *sunk;* that is, it continues to exist and does not change in amount regardless of the decision.

EXHIBIT A.1

Fixed and Variable Cost Components of Total Cost

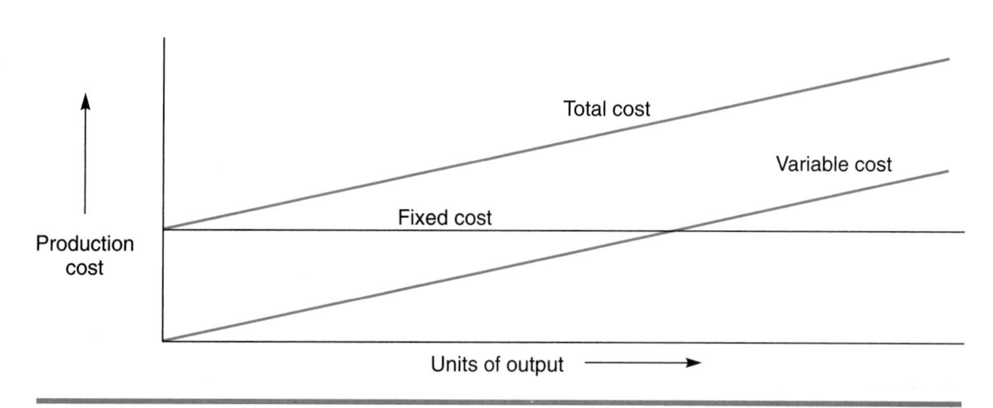

Opportunity costs

Opportunity cost is the benefit *foregone,* or advantage *lost,* that results from choosing one action over the *best-known alternative* course of action.

Suppose a firm has $100,000 to invest, and two alternatives of comparable risk present themselves, each requiring a $100,000 investment. Investment A will net $25,000; Investment B will net $23,000. Investment A is clearly the better choice, with a $25,000 net return. If the decision is made to invest in B instead of A, the opportunity cost of B then is $2,000, which is the benefit that is foregone.

Avoidable costs

Avoidable costs include any expense that is *not* incurred if an investment is made but that *must* be incurred if the investment is *not* made. Suppose a company owns a metal lathe that is not in working condition but is needed for the firm's operations. Since the lathe must be repaired or replaced, the repair costs are avoidable if a new lathe is purchased. Avoidable costs reduce the cost of a new investment because they are not incurred if the investment is made. Avoidable costs are an example of how it is possible to "save" money by spending money.

Risk and expected value

Risk is inherent in any investment, because the future can never be predicted with absolute certainty. To deal with this uncertainty, mathematical techniques such as expected value can help. Expected value is the expected outcome multiplied by the probability of its occurrence. Recall that in the preceding example the expected outcome of Alternative A was $25,000 and the expected outcome of B was $23,000. Suppose the probability of A's actual outcome is 80 percent while B's probability is 90 percent. The expected values of these two alternatives are determined as follows:

$$\text{Expected outcome} \times \text{Probability that actual outcome will be the expected outcome} = \text{Expected value}$$

Investment A: $25,000 × 0.80 = $20,000

Investment B: $23,000 × 0.90 = $20,700

Investment B is now seen to be the better choice, with a net advantage over A of $700.

Economic life and obsolescence

When a firm invests in an income-producing asset, the productive life of the asset is estimated. For accounting purposes, the asset is depreciated over this period. It is assumed that the asset will perform its function during this time and then be considered obsolete or worn out, and replacement will be required. This view of asset life rarely coincides with reality.

Assume that a machine with an expected productive life of 10 years is purchased. If at any time during the ensuing 10 years a new machine is developed that can perform the same task more efficiently or economically, the old machine becomes obsolete. Whether it is "worn out" or not is irrelevant.

The *economic life* of a piece of equipment is the period over which it provides the best method for performing its task. When a superior method is developed, the equipment becomes obsolete. Thus, the stated *book value* of a machine can be a meaningless figure.

Depreciation

Depreciation is a method for allocating the costs of capital equipment. The value of any capital asset—buildings, machinery, and so forth—decreases as its useful life is expended. *Amortization and depreciation* are often used interchangeably. Through convention, however, *depreciation* refers to the allocation of cost due to the physical or functional deterioration of *tangible* (physical) assets, such as buildings or equipment, while *amortization* refers to the allocation of cost over the useful life of *intangible* assets, such as patents, leases, franchises, or goodwill.

Depreciation procedures may not reflect an asset's true value at any point in its life because obsolescence may at any time cause a large difference between true value and book value. Also, since depreciation rates significantly affect taxes, a firm may choose a particular method from the several alternatives that are available, giving more consideration to its effect on taxes than its ability to make the book value of an asset reflect the true resale value.

We describe five commonly used methods of depreciation next.

1. Straight-line method. Under this method, an asset's value is reduced in uniform annual amounts over its estimated useful life. The general straight-line depreciation formula is:

$$\text{Annual amount to be depreciated} = \frac{\text{Cost} - \text{Salvage value}}{\text{Estimated useful life}}$$

A machine costing $10,000, with an estimated salvage value of $0 and an estimated life of 10 years, would be depreciated at the rate of $1,000 per year for each of the 10 years. If its estimated salvage value at the end of the 10 years is $1,000, the annual depreciation charge is:

$$\frac{\$10{,}000 - \$1{,}000}{10} = \$900$$

2. Sum-of-the-years'-digits (SYD) method. The purpose of the SYD method is to reduce the book value of an asset rapidly in the early years of its life and at a lower rate in its later years.

Supposing that the estimated useful life of a piece of equipment is 5 years. Here, the sum of the years' digits is 1 + 2 + 3 + 4 + 5 = 15. Therefore, depreciate the asset by 5 ÷ 15 after the first year, 4 ÷ 15 after the second year, and so on, down to 1 ÷ 15 in the last year.

3. Declining-balance method. This method also achieves an accelerated depreciation. The asset's value is decreased by reducing its book value by a constant percentage each year. The percentage rate selected is often the one that just reduces book value to salvage value at the end of the asset's estimated life. In any case, the asset should never be reduced below estimated salvage value. Use of the declining-balance method and allowable rates is controlled by Internal Revenue Service regulations. As a simplified illustration, the preceding example is used in the next table with an arbitrarily selected rate of 40 percent. Note that depreciation is based on full cost, *not* cost minus salvage value.

Year	Depreciation Rate	Beginning Book Value	Depreciation Charge	Accumulated Depreciation	Ending Book Value
1	0.40	$17,000	$6,800	$ 6,800	$10,200
2	0.40	10,200	4,080	10,880	6,120
3	0.40	6,120	2,448	13,328	3,672
4	0.40	3,672	1,469	14,797	2,203
5		2,203	203	15,000	2,000

In the fifth year, reducing book value by 40 percent would have caused it to drop below salvage value. Consequently, the asset was depreciated by only $203, which decreased book value to salvage value.

4. Double-declining-balance method. Again, for tax advantages, the double-declining-balance method offers higher depreciation early in the life span. The double-declining-balance method uses a percentage twice the straight line for the life span of the item but applies this rate to the undepreciated original cost. The method is the same as the declining-balance method, but the term *double-declining balance* means double the straight-line rate. Thus, equipment with a 10-year lifespan would have a straight line depreciation rate of 10 percent per year and a double-declining-balance rate (applied to the undepreciated amount) of 20 percent per year.

5. Depreciation-by-use method. The purpose of this method is to depreciate a capital investment in proportion to its use. It is applicable, for example, to a machine that performs the same operation many times. The life of the machine is not estimated in years but rather in the total number of operations it may reasonably be expected to perform before wearing out. Suppose that a metal-stamping press has an estimated life of 1 million stamps and costs \$100,000. The charge for depreciation per stamp is then \$100,000 ÷ 1,000,000, or \$0.10. Assuming a \$0 salvage value, the depreciation charges are as shown:

Year	Total Yearly Stamps	Cost per Stamp	Yearly Depreciation Charge	Accumulated Depreciation	Ending Book Value
1	150,000	0.10	\$15,000	\$ 15,000	\$85,000
2	300,000	0.10	30,000	45,000	55,000
3	200,000	0.10	20,000	65,000	35,000
4	200,000	0.10	20,000	85,000	15,000
5	100,000	0.10	10,000	95,000	5,000
6	50,000	0.10	5,000	100,000	0

The depreciation-by-use method is an attempt to gear depreciation charges to actual use and thereby coordinate expense charges with productive output more accurately. Also, since a machine's resale value is related to its remaining productive life, it is hoped that book value will approximate resale value. The danger, of course, is that technological improvements will render the machine obsolete, in which case book value will not reflect true value.

THE EFFECTS OF TAXES

Tax rates and the methods of applying them occasionally change. When analysts evaluate investment proposals, tax considerations often prove to be the deciding factor since depreciation expenses directly affect taxable income and, therefore, profit. The ability to write off depreciation in early years provides an added source of funds for investment. Before 1986, firms were able to employ an *investment tax credit,* which allowed a direct reduction in tax liability. Tax laws change; therefore, it is very important to stay on top of current tax laws and try to predict future changes that may affect current investments and accounting procedures.

For example, a one-time investment of \$1,000 at 14 percent allowed to compound for 65 years could be worth \$5 million. However, that 14-percent is a *nominal rate,* and nominal rates do not reflect buying power; real rates do. Real rates—that which remains after adjusting for inflation—are historically about 3 to 5 percent. If the rate of return remains 14 percent for 65 years, future inflation will erode 90 percent of the \$5 million buying power!

The general formula for compound value is

$$V_n = P_1(1 + i)^n$$

where

V = Value at the end of a specific year

n = Length of the compounding period

P_1 = Principal, or value at the beginning of a specific year

i = Interest rate

and the subscript represents the length of the compounding period.

For example, the compound value of $10 earning 10 percent interest after three years is $13.31 and is derived as follows:

$$\begin{aligned} V_3 &= P_1(1 + i)^3 \\ &= \$10(1 + 0.10)^3 \\ &= \$10(1.331) \\ &= \$13.31 \end{aligned}$$

CHOOSING AMONG SPECIFIC INVESTMENT PROPOSALS

The capital investment decision has become highly rationalized, as evidenced by the variety of techniques available for its solution. In contrast to pricing or marketing decisions, the capital investment decision can usually be made with a higher degree of confidence because the variables affecting the decision are relatively well known and can be quantified with fair accuracy.

Investment decisions may be grouped into six general categories:

1. Purchase of new equipment or facilities.
2. Replacement of existing equipment or facilities.
3. Make-or-buy decisions.
4. Lease-or-buy decisions.
5. Temporary shutdown or plant-abandonment decisions.
6. Addition or elimination of a product or product line.

Investment decisions are made with regard to the *lowest acceptable rate of return* on investment. As a starting point, the lowest acceptable rate of return may be considered to be the cost of investment capital needed to underwrite the expenditure. Certainly an investment will not be made if it does not return at least the cost of capital.

Investments are generally ranked according to the return they yield in excess of their cost of capital. In this way a business with only limited investment funds can select investment alternatives that yield the highest *net* returns. (Net *return* is the earnings an investment yields after gross earnings have been reduced by the cost of the funds used to finance the investment). In general, investments should not be made unless the return in funds exceeds the *marginal* cost of investment capital (*marginal cost* is the incremental cost of each new acquisition of funds from outside sources).

INTEREST RATE EFFECTS

There are two basic methods to account for the effects of interest accumulation. One is to compute the total amount created over the time period into the future as the *compound value*. The other is to remove the interest rate effect over time by reducing all future sums to present-day dollars, or the *present value*.

Compound Value of a Single Amount

Albert Einstein was once quoted as saying that compound interest is the eighth wonder of the world. After reviewing this section, with its dramatic growth effects during a longer term of years, you might wish to propose a new government regulation: on the birth of a child, the parents must put, say, $1,000 into a retirement fund for that child at age 65. This might be one way to reduce the pressure on Social Security and other state and federal pension plans. While inflation will decrease the value significantly as we showed in the previous section, there was still a lot left over. At 14 percent interest, our $1,000 increased to $500,000 after subtracting the $4.5 million for inflation. That's still 500 times.

Most calculators make such computation easy. However, many people still refer to tables for compound values. Using Appendix C, Table 1 (compound sum of $1), for example, we see that the value of $1 at 10 percent interest after three years is $1.331. Multiplying this figure by $10 gives $13.31, as computed previously. (Note: Tables 1 through 4 are in Appendix C).

Compound Value of an Annuity

An *annuity* is the receipt of a constant sum each year for a specified number of years. Usually an annuity is received at the end of a period and does not earn interest during that period. Therefore, an annuity of $10 for three years would bring in $10 at the end of the first year (allowing the $10 to earn interest if invested for the remaining two years), $10 at the end of the second year (allowing the $10 to earn interest for the remaining one year), and $10 at the end of the third year (with no time to earn interest). If the annuity receipts were placed in a bank savings account at 5 percent interest, the total or compound value of the $10 at 5 percent for the three years would be:

Year	Receipt at End of Year	Compound Interest Factor $(1 + i)^n$	Value at End of Third Year
1	$10.00 ×	$(1 + 0.05)^2$ =	$11.02
2	10.00 ×	$(1 + 0.05)^1$ =	10.50
3	10.00 ×	$(1 + 0.05)^0$ =	10.00
			$31.52

The general formula for finding the compound value of any annuity is

$$S_n = R[(1 + i)^{n-1} + (1 + i)^{n-2} + \cdots + (1 + i)^1 + 1]$$

where

S_n = Compound value of an annuity

R = Periodic receipts in dollars

n = Length of the annuity in years

Applying this formula to the above example, we get

$$S_n = R[(1 + i)^2 + (1 + i) + 1]$$
$$= \$10[(1 + 0.05)^2 + (1 + 0.05) + 1]$$
$$= \$31.52$$

Appendix C, Table 2 lists the compound value factor of $1 for 5 percent after three years as 3.152. Multiplying this factor by $10 yields $31.52.

In a fashion similar to our previous retirement investment example, consider the beneficial effects of investing $2,000 each year, just starting at the age of 21. Assume investments in AAA-rated bonds are available today yielding 9 percent. From Table 2 in Appendix C, after 30 years (age 51) the investment is worth 136.3 times $2,000, or $272.600. Fourteen years later (age 65) this would be worth $962,993 (using a hand calculator, since the table only goes up to 30 years, and assuming the $2,000 is deposited at the end of each year)! But what 21-year-old thinks about retirement?

Present Value of a Future Single Payment

Compound values are used to determine future value after a specified period has elapsed; present-value (PV) procedures accomplish just the reverse. They are used to determine the current value of a sum or stream of receipts expected to be received in the future. Most investment decision techniques use present-value concepts rather than compound values. Since decisions affecting the future are made in the present, it is better to convert future returns into their present value at the time the decision is being made. In this way, investment alternatives are placed in better perspective in terms of current dollars.

An example makes this more apparent. If a rich uncle offers to make you a gift of $100 today or $250 after 10 years, which should you choose? You must determine whether $250 in 10 years will be worth more than the $100 now. Suppose that you base your decision on the rate of inflation in the economy and believe that inflation averages 10 percent per year. By deflating the $250, you can compare its relative purchasing power with $100 received today. Procedurally, this is accomplished by solving the compound formula for the present sum, P, where V is the future amount of $250 in 10 years at 10 percent. The compound value formula is

$$V = P(1 + i)^n$$

Dividing both sides by $(1 + i)^n$ gives:

$$P = \frac{V}{(1 + i)^n}$$
$$= \frac{250}{(1 + 0.10)^{10}}$$
$$= \$96.39$$

This shows that, at a 10 percent inflation rate, $250 in 10 years will be worth $93.39 today. The rational choice, then, is to take the $100 now.

The use of tables is also standard practice in solving present-value problems. With reference to Appendix C, Table 3, the present-value factor for $1 received 10 years hence is 0.386. Multiplying this factor by $250 yields $96.50.

Present Value of an Annuity

The present value of an annuity is the value of an annual amount to be received over a future period expressed in terms of the present. To find the value of an annuity of $100 for three years at 10 percent, find the factor in the present-value table that applies to 10 percent in *each* of the three years in which the amount is received and multiply each receipt by this factor. Then sum the resulting figures. Remember that annuities are usually received at the end of each period.

Year	Amount Received at End of Year	Present-Value Factor at 10%	Present Value
1	$100 ×	0.909 =	$ 90.90
2	100 ×	0.826 =	82.60
3	100 ×	0.751 =	75.10
Total receipts	$300	Total present value =	$248.60

The general formula used to derive the present value of an annuity is

$$A_n = R\left[\frac{1}{(1+i)} + \frac{1}{(1+i)^2} + \ldots + \frac{1}{(1+i)^n}\right]$$

where

A_n = Present value of an annuity of n years
R = Periodic receipts
n = Length of the annuity in years

Applying the formula to the above example gives

$$A_n = \$100\left[\frac{1}{(1+0.10)} + \frac{1}{(1+0.10)^2} + \frac{1}{(1+0.10)^3}\right]$$

$$= \$100\ (2.488)$$

$$= \$248.80$$

Appendix C, Table 4 contains present values of an annuity for varying maturities. The present-value factor for an annuity of $1 for three years at 10 percent (from Appendix C, Table 4) is 2.487. Since our sum is $100 rather than $1, we multiply this factor by $100 to arrive at $248.70. The slight variance from the previous answers results from rounded figures in the table.

When the stream of future receipts is uneven, the present value of each annual receipt must be calculated. The present values of the receipts for all years are then summed to arrive at total present value. This process can sometimes be tedious, but it is unavoidable.

Discounted Cash Flow

The term *discounted cash flow,* or DCF, refers to total stream of payments that an asset will generate in the future discounted to the present time. This is simply present value analysis that includes all flows: single payments, annuities, and all others.

METHODS OF RANKING INVESTMENTS

Net Present Value

The net present value method is commonly used in business. With this method, decisions are based on the amount by which the present value of a projected income stream exceeds the cost of an investment.

A firm is considering two alternative investments: the first costs $30,000 and the second, $50,000. The expected yearly cash income streams are shown in the next table.

	CASH INFLOW	
Year	Alternative A	Alternative B
1	$10,000	$15,000
2	10,000	15,000
3	10,000	15,000
4	10,000	15,000
5	10,000	15,000

To choose between Alternatives A and B, find which has the highest net present value. Assume an 8 percent cost of capital.

Alternative A

3.993 (PV factor) × $10,000 =	39,930
Less cost of investment =	30,000
Net present value =	$ 9,930

Alternative B

3.993 (PV factor) × $15,000 =	59,895
Less cost of investment =	50,000
Net present value =	$ 9,895

Investment A is the better alternative. Its net present value exceeds that of Investment B by $35 ($9,930 − $9,895 = $35).

Payback Period

The payback method ranks investments according to the time required for each investment to return earnings equal to the cost of the investment. The rationale is that the sooner the investment capital can be recovered, the sooner it can be reinvested in new revenue-producing projects. Thus, supposedly, a firm will be able to get the most benefit from its available investment funds.

Consider two alternatives, each requiring a $1,000 investment. The first will earn $200 per year for six years; the second will earn $300 per year for the first three years and $100 per year for the next three years.

If the first alternative is selected, the initial investment of $1,000 will be recovered at the end of the fifth year. The income produced by the second alternative will total $1,000 after only four years. The second alternative will permit reinvestment of the full $1,000 in new revenue-producing projects one year sooner than the first.

Although the payback method is declining in popularity as the sole measure in investment decisions, it is still frequently used in conjunction with other methods to give an indication of the time commitment of funds. The major problems with the payback method are that it does not consider income beyond the payback period and it ignores the time value of money. Any method that ignores the time value of money must be considered questionable.

Internal Rate of Return

The internal rate of return can be defined as the interest rate that equates the present value of an income stream with the cost of an investment. There is no procedure or formula that may be used directly to compute the internal rate of return—it must be found by interpolation or iterative calculation.

Suppose we wish to find the internal rate of return for an investment costing $12,000 that will yield a cash inflow of $4,000 per year for four years. We see that the present value factor sought is

$$\frac{\$12{,}000}{\$4{,}000} = 3.000 \text{ PV}$$

and we seek the interest rate that will provide this factor over a four-year period. The interest rate must lie between 12 percent and 14 percent because 3.000 lies between 3.037 and 2.914 (in the fourth row of Appendix C, Table 4). Linear interpolation between these values, according to the following equation

$$\begin{aligned} i &= 12 + (14 - 12)\,\frac{(3.037 - 3.000)}{(3.037 - 2.914)} \\ &= 12 + 0.602 = 12.602\% \end{aligned}$$

gives a good approximation to the actual internal rate of return.

When the income stream is discounted at 12.6 percent, the resulting present value closely approximates the cost of investment. Thus, the internal rate of return for this investment is 12.6 percent. The cost of capital can be compared with the internal rate of return to determine the net rate of return on the investment. If, in this example, the cost of capital were 8 percent, the net rate of return on the investment would be 4.6 percent.

The net present value and internal rate of return methods involve procedures that are essentially the same. They differ in that the net present value method enables investment alternatives to be compared in terms of the dollar value in excess of cost, whereas the internal rate of return method permits comparison of rates of return on alternative investments. Moreover, the internal rate of return method occasionally encounters problems in calculation, as multiple rates frequently appear in the computation.

Ranking Investments with Uneven Lives

When proposed investments have the same life expectancy, comparison among them, using the preceding methods, will give a reasonable picture of their relative value. When lives are unequal, however, there is the question of how to relate the two different time periods. Should replacements be considered the same as the original? Should productivity for the shorter-term unit that will be replaced earlier be considered to have higher productivity? How should the cost of future units be estimated?

No estimate dealing with investments unforeseen at the time of decision can be expected to reflect a high degree of accuracy. Still, the problem must be dealt with, and some assumptions must be made in order to determine a ranking.

SAMPLE PROBLEMS: INVESTMENT DECISIONS

An Expansion Decision

PROBLEM

William J. Wilson Ceramic Products, Inc., leases plant facilities in which firebrick is manufactured. Because of rising demand, Wilson could increase sales by investing in new equipment to expand output. The selling price of $10 per brick will remain unchanged if output and sales increase. Based on engineering and cost estimates, the accounting department provides management with the following cost estimates based on an annual increased output of 100,000 bricks:

Cost of new equipment having an expected life of five years	$500,000
Equipment installation cost	20,000
Expected salvage value	0
New operation's share of annual lease expense	40,000
Annual increase in utility expenses	40,000
Annual increase in labor costs	160,000
Annual additional cost for raw materials	400,000

The sum-of-the-years'-digits method of depreciation will be used, and taxes are paid at a rate of 40 percent. Wilson's policy is not to invest capital in projects earning less than a 20 percent rate of return. Should the proposed expansion be undertaken?

SOLUTION

Compute cost of investment:

Acquisition cost of equipment	$500,000
Equipment installation costs	20,000
Total cost of investment	$520,000

Determine yearly cash flows throughout the life of the investment.

The lease expense is a sunk cost. It will be incurred whether or not the investment is made and is therefore irrelevant to the decision and should be disregarded. Annual production expenses to be considered are utility, labor, and raw materials. These total $600,000 per year.

Annual sales revenue is $10 × 100,000 units of output, or $1,000,000. Yearly income before depreciation and taxes is thus $1,000,000 gross revenue, less $600,000 expenses, or $400,000.

Next, determine the depreciation charges to be deducted from the $400,000 income each year using the SYD method (sum-of-years'-digits = 1 + 2 + 3 + 4 + 5 = 15):

Year	Proportion of $500,000 to Be Depreciated	Depreciation Charge
1	5/15 × $500,000	= $166,667
2	4/15 × 500,000	= 133,333
3	3/15 × 500,000	= 100,000
4	2/15 × 500,000	= 66,667
5	1/15 × 500,000	= 33,333
Accumulated depreciation		$500,000

Find each year's cash flow when taxes are 40 percent. Cash flow for only the first year is illustrated:

Earnings before depreciation and taxes		$400,000
Deduct: Taxes at 40%	$160,000	
Add: Tax benefit of depreciation expense (0.4 × 166,667)	66,667	93,333
Cash flow (1st year)		$306,667

Determine present value of the cash flow. Since Wilson demands at least a 20 percent rate of return on investments, multiply the cash flows by the 20 percent present-value factor for each year. The factor for each respective year must be used because the cash flows are not an annuity.

Year	Present Value Factor	Cash Flow	Present Value
1	0.833 ×	$306,667 =	$255,454
2	0.694 ×	293,333 =	203,573
3	0.579 ×	280,000 =	162,120
4	0.482 ×	266,667 =	128,533
5	0.402 ×	253,334 =	101,840
Total present value of cash flows (discounted at 20%) =			$851,520

Now find whether net present value is positive or negative:

Total present value of cash flows	$851,520
Total cost of investment	520,000
Net present value	$331,520

DECISION

Net present value is positive when returns are discounted at 20 percent. Wilson will earn an amount in excess of 20 percent on the investment. The proposed expansion should be undertaken.

A Replacement Decision

PROBLEM

For five years Bennie's Brewery has been using a machine that attaches labels to bottles. The machine was purchased for $4,000 and is being depreciated over 10 years to a $0 salvage value using straight-line depreciation. The machine can be sold now for $2,000. Bennie can buy a new labeling machine for $6,000 that will have a useful life of five years and cut labor costs by $1,200 annually. The old machine will require a major overhaul in the next few months at an estimated cost of $300. If purchased, the new machine will be depreciated over five years to a $500 salvage value using the straight-line method. The company will invest in any project earning more than the 12 percent cost of capital. The tax rate is 40 percent. Should Bennie's Brewery invest in the new machine?

SOLUTION

Determine the cost of investment:

Price of new machine		$6,000
Less: Sale of old machine	$2,000	
Avoidable overhaul costs	300	2,300
Effective cost of investment		$3,700

Determine the increase in cash flow resulting from investment in the new machine:

Yearly cost savings = $1,200
Differential depreciation:
Annual depreciation on old machine:

$$\frac{\text{Cost} - \text{Salvage}}{\text{Expected life}} = \frac{\$4{,}000 - \$0}{10} = \$400$$

Annual depreciation on new machine:

$$\frac{\text{Cost} - \text{Salvage}}{\text{Expected life}} = \frac{\$6{,}000 - \$500}{5} = \$1{,}100$$

Differential depreciation = $1,100 – $400 = $700

Yearly net increase in cash flow into the firm:

Cost savings		$1,200
Deduct: Taxes at 40%	$480	
Add: Advantage of increase in depreciation (0.4 × $700)	280	200
Yearly increase in cash flow		$1,000

Determine total present value of the investment:

The five-year cash flow of $1,000 per year is an annuity.
Discounted at 12 percent, the cost of capital, the present value is

3.605 × $1,000 = $3,605

The present value of the new machine, if sold at its salvage value of $500 at the end of the fifth year, is

0.567 × $500 = $284

Total present value of the expected cash flows:

$3,605 + $284 = $3,889

Determine whether net present value is positive:

Total present value	$3,889
Cost of investment	3,700
Net present value	$ 189

DECISION

Bennie's Brewery should make the purchase because the investment will return slightly more than the cost of capital.

Note: The importance of depreciation has been shown in this example. The present value of the yearly cash flow resulting from operation is *only*

(Cost savings − Taxes) × (Present value factor)
($1,200 − $480) × (3.605) = $2,596

This figure is $1,104 less than the $3,700 cost of the investment. Only a very large depreciation advantage makes this investment worthwhile. The total present value of the advantage is $1,009:

(Tax rate × Differential depreciation) × (P.V. factor)
(0.4 × $700) × (3.605) = $1,009

A Make-or-Buy Decision

PROBLEM

The Triple X Company manufactures and sells refrigerators. It makes some of the parts for the refrigerators and purchases others. The engineering department believes it might be possible to cut costs by manufacturing one of the parts currently being purchased for $8.25 each. The firm uses 100,000 of these parts each year, and the accounting department compiles the following list of costs based on engineering estimates.

Fixed costs will increase by $50,000.

Labor costs will increase by $125,000.

Factory overhead, currently running $500,000 per year, may be expected to increase 12 percent.

Raw materials used to make the part will cost $600,000.

Given the preceding estimates, should Triple X make the part or continue to buy it?

SOLUTION

Find total cost incurred if the part were manufactured:

Additional fixed costs	$ 50,000
Additional labor costs	125,000
Raw materials cost	600,000
Additional overhead costs = 0.12 × $500,000	60,000
Total cost to manufacturer	$835,000

Find cost per unit to manufacture:

$$\frac{\$835{,}000}{100{,}000} = \$8.35 \text{ per unit}$$

DECISION

Triple X should continue to buy the part. Manufacturing costs exceed the present cost to purchase by $0.10 per unit.

REVIEW AND DISCUSSION QUESTIONS

1. List three examples of capital investments in production and operations management.
2. Define the following terms: *fixed, variable, opportunity,* and *avoidable costs; risk* and *expected value; obsolescence* and *depreciation.*
3. How do taxes affect profits? Why?
4. How does depreciation affect capital investment? Why?
5. If a firm is short of capital, what action might it take to conserve the capital it has and to obtain more?
6. What are the reasons for using present-value analysis rather than "future-value" analysis?
7. Why might a decision maker like to see the payback analysis as well as the rate of return and the net present value?
8. Discuss why the comparison of alternative investment decisions is especially difficult when the investment choices have different life lengths.
9. Compare the advantages and disadvantages of each depreciation method.

PROBLEMS

1. What is the depreciation expense for the third year, using the sum-of-the-years'-digit method, for the following cost of a new machine?

Cost of machine	$35,000
Estimated life	6 years
Estimated salvage value	$ 5,000

2. Disregarding tax considerations, is it cheaper to buy or to lease a piece of equipment with the following costs for a five-year term? (Interest value of money is 10 percent).

	To Buy	To Lease
Purchase (or lease) cost	$50,000	$10,000/yr.
Annual operating cost	4,000/yr.	4,000/yr.
Maintenance cost	2,000/yr.	0
Salvage value at end of 5 years	$20,000	0

3. A new piece of office equipment must be purchased, and the choice has been narrowed down to two styles, each capable of meeting the intended needs. With a 10-year horizon and an interest rate of 8 percent, which equipment should be purchased?

	Equipment A	Equipment B
Initial cost	$10,000	$7,000
Salvage value (10 years hence)	4,000	2,000
Estimated annual operation and maintenance cost	1,000	1,500

4. The university is accepting bids for the hot dog and cold drink concession at the new stadium. The contract is for a five-year period, and it is your feeling that a bid of $40,000 will win the contract. A preliminary analysis indicates that annual operating costs will be $35,000 and average annual sales will be $50,000. The contract can be written off during the five years. Taxes are at the 40 percent rate, and your goal is to make a 20 percent return on your investment.
   a. Will you meet your goal if you use straight-line depreciation?
   b. Would you meet your goal using sum-of-the-years'-digits depreciation?
5. In adding a new product line, a firm needs a new piece of machinery. An investigation of suitable equipment for the production process has narrowed the choice to the two machines listed.

	Machine A	Machine B
Type of equipment	General purpose	Special purpose
Installed cost	$8,000	$13,000
Salvage value	800	3,000
Annual labor cost	6,000	3,600
Estimated life (years)	10	5

   Assume that at the end of five years, a comparable replacement for Machine B will be available. Using present-value analysis with a 10 percent interest rate, which machine would you choose?
6. ABC's business has been going so well that the firm decides to diversify with a sideline business. Ballard, a partner and an experienced cabinetmaker, has a great deal of know-how in making cabinets for kitchens and vanities for bathrooms. (Countertops would be subcontracted because of the specialized equipment needed for molding and pressing.) The company is anticipating putting out a standard line of cabinets available in birch, walnut, mahogany, or oak veneer at no extra charge.
   Three manufacturing methods are feasible for producing the cabinets. The first is largely

manual, the second uses some semiautomated equipment, and the third is largely automatic. The semiautomatic equipment requires an investment of $45,000. ABC expects this equipment to generate incremental after-tax cash flows of $15,000 for each of the next four years. What is the net present value for this equipment? What is the payback period? What should ABC do?

SELECTED BIBLIOGRAPHY

Brigham, Eugene F. *Fundamentals of Financial Management.* New York: Dryden Press, 1986.

Hodder, James E., and Henry E. Riggs. "Pitfalls in Evaluating Risky Projects." *Harvard Business Review,* January–February 1985, pp. 128–35.

Gitman, Lawrence J. *Principles of Managerial Finance,* 4th ed. New York: Harper & Row, 1985.

Gup, Benton E. *Principles of Financial Management,* 2nd ed. New York: John Wiley & Sons, 1987.

Pringle, John J., and Robert S. Harris. *Essentials of Managerial Finance.* Glenview, Ill.: Scott Foresman, 1984.

Soloman, Eyra, and John J. Pringle. *An Introduction to Financial Management.* Santa Monica, Calif.: Goodyear Publishing, 1980.

Van Horne, James C. *Financial Management and Policy,* 7th ed. Englewood Cliffs, N.J.: Prentice Hall, 1986.

________. *Fundamentals of Financial Management.* 6th ed. Englewood Cliffs, N.J.: Prentice Hall, 1986.

Welsch, Glenn A., and Robert N. Anthony. *Fundamentals of Financial Accounting.* Homewood, Ill.: Richard D. Irwin, 1984.

Appendix B
Negative Exponential Distribution: Values of e^{-x}

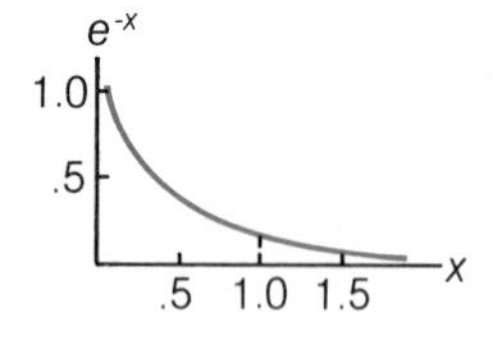

x	e^{-x} (value)	x	e^{-x} (value)	x	e^{-x} (value)	x	e^{-x} (value)
0.00	1.00000	0.50	0.60653	1.00	0.36788	1.50	0.22313
0.01	0.99005	0.51	.60050	1.01	.36422	1.51	.22091
0.02	.98020	0.52	.59452	1.02	.36060	1.52	.21871
0.03	.97045	0.53	.58860	1.03	.35701	1.53	.21654
0.04	.96079	0.54	.58275	1.04	.35345	1.54	.21438
0.05	.95123	0.55	.57695	1.05	.34994	1.55	.21225
0.06	.94176	0.56	.57121	1.06	.34646	1.56	.21014
0.07	.93239	0.57	.56553	1.07	.34301	1.57	.20805
0.08	.92312	0.58	.55990	1.08	.33960	1.58	.20598
0.09	.91393	0.59	.55433	1.09	.33622	1.59	.20393
0.10	.90484	0.60	.54881	1.10	.33287	1.60	.20190
0.11	.89583	0.61	.54335	1.11	.32956	1.61	.19989
0.12	.88692	0.62	.53794	1.12	.32628	1.62	.19790
0.13	.87809	0.63	.53259	1.13	.32303	1.63	.19593
0.14	.86936	0.64	.52729	1.14	.31982	1.64	.19398
0.15	.86071	0.65	.52205	1.15	.31664	1.65	.19205
0.16	.87514	0.66	.51685	1.16	.31349	1.66	.19014
0.17	.84366	0.67	.51171	1.17	.31037	1.67	.18825
0.18	.83527	0.68	.50662	1.18	.30728	1.68	.18637
0.19	.82696	0.69	.50158	1.19	.30422	1.69	.18452
0.20	.81873	0.70	.49659	1.20	.30119	1.70	.18268
0.21	.81058	0.71	.49164	1.21	.29820	1.71	.18087
0.22	.80252	0.72	.48675	1.22	.29523	1.72	.17907
0.23	.79453	0.73	.48191	1.23	.29229	1.73	.17728
0.24	.78663	0.74	.47711	1.24	.28938	1.74	.17552
0.25	.77880	0.75	.47237	1.25	.28650	1.75	.17377
0.26	.77105	0.76	.46767	1.26	.28365	1.76	.17204
0.27	.76338	0.77	.46301	1.27	.28083	1.77	.17033
0.28	.75578	0.78	.45841	1.28	.27804	1.78	.16864
0.29	.74826	0.79	.45384	1.29	.27527	1.79	.16696
0.30	.74082	0.80	.44933	1.30	.27253	1.80	.16530
0.31	.73345	0.81	.44486	1.31	.26982	1.81	.16365
0.32	.72615	0.82	.44043	1.32	.26714	1.82	.16203
0.33	.71892	0.83	.43605	1.33	.26448	1.83	.16041
0.34	.71177	0.84	.43171	1.34	.26185	1.84	.15882
0.35	.70469	0.85	.42741	1.35	.25924	1.85	.15724
0.36	.69768	0.86	.42316	1.36	.25666	1.86	.15567
0.37	.69073	0.87	.41895	1.37	.25411	1.87	.15412
0.38	.68386	0.88	.41478	1.38	.25158	1.88	.15259
0.39	.67706	0.89	.41066	1.39	.24908	1.89	.15107

x	e^{-x} (value)	x	e^{-x} (value)	x	e^{-x} (value)	x	e^{-x} (value)
0.40	.67032	0.90	.40657	1.40	.24660	1.90	.14957
0.41	.66365	0.91	.40252	1.41	.24414	1.91	.14808
0.42	.65705	0.92	.39852	1.42	.24171	1.92	.14661
0.43	.65051	0.93	.39455	1.43	.23931	1.93	.14515
0.44	.64404	0.94	.39063	1.44	.23693	1.94	.14370
0.45	.63763	0.95	.38674	1.45	.23457	1.95	.14227
0.46	.63128	0.96	.38289	1.46	.23224	1.96	.14086
0.47	.62500	0.97	.37908	1.47	.22993	1.97	.13946
0.48	.61878	0.98	.37531	1.48	.22764	1.98	.13807
0.49	.61263	0.99	.37158	1.49	.22537	1.99	.13670
0.50	.60653	1.00	.36788	1.50	.22313	2.00	.13534

Appendix C
Interest Tables

TABLE 1 Compound Sum of $1

Year	1%	2%	3%	4%	5%	6%	7%
1	1.010	1.020	1.030	1.040	1.050	1.060	1.070
2	1.020	1.040	1.061	1.082	1.102	1.124	1.145
3	1.030	1.061	1.093	1.125	1.158	1.191	1.225
4	1.041	1.082	1.126	1.170	1.216	1.262	1.311
5	1.051	1.104	1.159	1.217	1.276	1.338	1.403
6	1.062	1.126	1.194	1.265	1.340	1.419	1.501
7	1.072	1.149	1.230	1.316	1.407	1.504	1.606
8	1.083	1.172	1.267	1.369	1.477	1.594	1.718
9	1.094	1.195	1.305	1.423	1.551	1.689	1.838
10	1.105	1.219	1.344	1.480	1.629	1.791	1.967
11	1.116	1.243	1.384	1.539	1.710	1.898	2.105
12	1.127	1.268	1.426	1.601	1.796	2.012	2.252
13	1.138	1.294	1.469	1.665	1.886	2.133	2.410
14	1.149	1.319	1.513	1.732	1.980	2.261	2.579
15	1.161	1.346	1.558	1.801	2.079	2.397	2.759
16	1.173	1.373	1.605	1.873	2.183	2.540	2.952
17	1.184	1.400	1.653	1.948	2.292	2.693	3.159
18	1.196	1.428	1.702	2.026	2.407	2.854	3.380
19	1.208	1.457	1.754	2.107	2.527	3.026	3.617
20	1.220	1.486	1.806	2.191	2.653	3.207	3.870
25	1.282	1.641	2.094	2.666	3.386	4.292	5.427
30	1.348	1.811	2.427	3.243	4.322	5.743	7.612

Year	8%	9%	10%	12%	14%	15%	16%
1	1.080	1.090	1.100	1.120	1.140	1.150	1.160
2	1.166	1.188	1.210	1.254	1.300	1.322	1.346
3	1.260	1.295	1.331	1.405	1.482	1.521	1.561
4	1.360	1.412	1.464	1.574	1.689	1.749	1.811
5	1.469	1.539	1.611	1.762	1.925	2.011	2.100
6	1.587	1.677	1.772	1.974	2.195	2.313	2.436
7	1.714	1.828	1.949	2.211	2.502	2.660	2.826
8	1.851	1.993	2.144	2.476	2.853	3.059	3.278
9	1.999	2.172	2.358	2.773	3.252	3.518	3.803
10	2.159	2.367	2.594	3.106	3.707	4.046	4.411
11	2.332	2.580	2.853	3.479	4.226	4.652	5.117
12	2.518	2.813	3.138	3.896	4.818	5.350	5.936
13	2.720	3.066	3.452	4.363	5.492	6.153	6.886
14	2.937	3.342	3.797	4.887	6.261	7.076	7.988
15	3.172	3.642	4.177	5.474	7.138	8.137	9.266
16	3.426	3.970	4.595	6.130	8.137	9.358	10.748
17	3.700	4.328	5.054	6.866	9.276	10.761	12.468
18	3.996	4.717	5.560	7.690	10.575	12.375	14.463
19	4.316	5.142	6.116	8.613	12.056	14.232	16.777
20	4.661	5.604	6.728	9.646	13.743	16.367	19.461
25	6.848	8.623	10.835	17.000	26.462	32.919	40.874
30	10.063	13.268	17.449	29.960	50.950	66.212	85.850

TABLE 1 (Concluded)

Year	*18%*	*20%*	*24%*	*28%*	*32%*	*36%*
1	1.180	1.200	1.240	1.280	1.320	1.360
2	1.392	1.440	1.538	1.638	1.742	1.850
3	1.643	1.728	1.907	2.067	2.300	2.515
4	1.939	2.074	2.364	2.684	3.036	3.421
5	2.288	2.488	2.932	3.436	4.007	4.653
6	2.700	2.986	3.635	4.398	5.290	6.328
7	3.185	3.583	4.508	5.629	6.983	8.605
8	3.759	4.300	5.590	7.206	9.217	11.703
9	4.435	5.160	6.931	9.223	12.166	15.917
10	5.234	6.192	8.594	11.806	16.060	21.647
11	6.176	7.430	10.657	15.112	21.199	29.439
12	7.288	8.916	13.215	19.343	27.983	40.037
13	8.599	10.699	16.386	24.759	36.937	54.451
14	10.147	12.839	20.319	31.691	48.757	74.053
15	11.974	15.407	25.196	40.565	64.359	100.712
16	14.129	18.488	31.243	51.923	84.954	136.97
17	16.672	22.186	38.741	66.461	112.14	186.28
18	19.673	26.623	48.039	85.071	148.02	253.34
19	23.214	31.948	59.568	108.89	195.39	344.54
20	27.393	38.338	73.864	139.38	257.92	468.57
25	62.669	95.396	216.542	478.90	1033.6	2180.1
30	143.371	237.376	634.820	1645.5	4142.1	10143.

Year	*40%*	*50%*	*60%*	*70%*	*80%*	*90%*
1	1.400	1.500	1.600	1.700	1.800	1.900
2	1.960	2.250	2.560	2.890	3.240	3.610
3	2.744	3.375	4.096	4.913	5.832	6.859
4	3.842	5.062	6.544	8.352	10.498	13.032
5	5.378	7.594	10.486	14.199	18.896	24.761
6	7.530	11.391	16.777	24.138	34.012	47.046
7	10.541	17.086	26.844	41.034	61.222	89.387
8	14.758	25.629	42.950	69.758	110.200	169.836
9	20.661	38.443	68.720	118.588	198.359	322.688
10	28.925	57.665	109.951	201.599	357.047	613.107
11	40.496	86.498	175.922	342.719	642.684	1164.902
12	56.694	129.746	281.475	582.622	1156.831	2213.314
13	79.372	194.619	450.360	990.457	2082.295	4205.297
14	111.120	291.929	720.576	1683.777	3748.131	7990.065
15	155.568	437.894	1152.921	2862.421	6746.636	15181.122
16	217.795	656.84	1844.7	4866.1	12144.	28844.0
17	304.914	985.26	2951.5	8272.4	21859.	54804.0
18	426.879	1477.9	4722.4	14063.0	39346.	104130.0
19	597.630	2216.8	7555.8	23907.0	70824.	197840.0
20	836.683	3325.3	12089.0	40642.0	127480.	375900.0
25	4499.880	25251.	126760.0	577060.0	2408900.	9307600.0
30	24201.432	191750.	1329200.	8193500.0	45517000.	230470000.0

TABLE 2 Sum of an Annuity of $1 for *N* Years

Year	1%	2%	3%	4%	5%	6%
1	1.000	1.000	1.000	1.000	1.000	1.000
2	2.010	2.020	2.030	2.040	2.050	2.060
3	2.030	3.060	3.091	3.122	3.152	3.184
4	4.060	4.122	4.184	4.246	4.310	4.375
5	5.101	5.204	5.309	5.416	5.526	5.637
6	6.152	6.308	6.468	6.633	6.802	6.975
7	7.214	7.434	7.662	7.898	8.142	8.394
8	8.286	8.583	8.892	9.214	9.549	9.897
9	9.369	9.755	10.159	10.583	11.027	11.491
10	10.462	10.950	11.464	12.006	12.578	13.181
11	11.567	12.169	12.808	13.486	14.207	14.972
12	12.683	13.412	14.192	15.026	15.917	16.870
13	13.809	14.680	15.618	16.627	17.713	18.882
14	14.947	15.974	17.086	18.292	19.599	21.051
15	16.097	17.293	18.599	20.024	21.579	23.276
16	17.258	18.639	20.157	21.825	23.657	25.673
17	18.430	20.012	21.762	23.698	25.840	28.213
18	19.615	21.412	23.414	25.645	28.132	30.906
19	20.811	22.841	25.117	27.671	30.539	33.760
20	22.019	24.297	26.870	29.778	33.066	36.786
25	28.243	32.030	36.459	41.646	47.727	54.865
30	34.785	40.568	47.575	56.085	66.439	79.058

Year	7%	8%	9%	10%	12%	14%
1	1.000	1.000	1.000	1.000	1.000	1.000
2	2.070	2.080	2.090	2.100	2.120	2.140
3	3.215	3.246	3.278	3.310	3.374	3.440
4	4.440	4.506	4.573	4.641	4.770	4.921
5	5.751	5.867	5.985	6.105	6.353	6.610
6	7.153	7.336	7.523	7.716	8.115	8.536
7	8.654	8.923	9.200	9.487	10.089	10.730
8	10.260	10.637	11.028	11.436	12.300	13.233
9	11.978	12.488	13.021	13.579	14.776	16.085
10	13.816	14.487	15.193	15.937	17.549	19.337
11	15.784	16.645	17.560	18.531	20.655	23.044
12	17.888	18.977	20.141	21.384	24.133	27.271
13	20.141	21.495	22.953	24.523	28.029	32.089
14	22.550	24.215	26.019	27.975	32.393	37.581
15	25.129	27.152	29.361	31.772	37.280	43.842
16	27.888	30.324	33.003	35.950	42.753	50.980
17	30.840	33.750	36.974	40.545	48.884	59.118
18	33.999	37.450	41.301	45.599	55.750	68.394
19	37.379	41.446	46.018	51.159	63.440	78.969
20	40.995	45.762	51.160	57.275	72.052	91.025
25	63.249	73.106	84.701	93.347	133.334	181.871
30	94.461	113.283	136.308	164.494	241.333	356.787

TABLE 2 (Concluded)

Year	*16%*	*18%*	*20%*	*24%*	*28%*	*32%*
1	1.000	1.000	1.000	1.000	1.000	1.000
2	2.160	2.180	2.200	2.240	2.280	2.320
3	3.506	3.572	3.640	3.778	3.918	4.062
4	5.066	5.215	5.368	5.684	6.016	6.362
5	6.877	7.154	7.442	8.048	8.700	9.398
6	8.977	9.442	9.930	10.980	12.136	13.406
7	11.414	12.142	12.916	14.615	16.534	18.696
8	14.240	15.327	16.499	19.123	22.163	25.678
9	17.518	19.086	20.799	24.712	29.369	34.895
10	21.321	23.521	25.959	31.643	38.592	47.062
11	25.733	28.755	32.150	40.238	50.399	63.122
12	30.850	34.931	39.580	50.985	65.510	84.320
13	36.786	42.219	48.497	64.110	84.853	112.303
14	43.672	50.818	59.196	80.496	109.612	149.240
15	51.660	60.965	72.035	100.815	141.303	197.997
16	60.925	72.939	87.442	126.011	181.87	262.36
17	71.673	87.068	105.931	157.253	233.79	347.31
18	84.141	103.740	128.117	195.994	300.25	459.45
19	98.603	123.414	154.740	244.033	385.32	607.47
20	115.380	146.628	186.688	303.601	494.21	802.86
25	249.214	342.603	471.981	898.092	1706.8	3226.8
30	530.312	790.948	1181.882	2640.916	5873.2	12941.0

Year	*36%*	*40%*	*50%*	*60%*	*70%*	*80%*
1	1.000	1.000	1.000	1.000	1.000	1.000
2	2.360	2.400	2.500	2.600	2.700	2.800
3	4.210	4.360	4.750	5.160	5.590	6.040
4	6.725	7.104	8.125	9.256	10.503	11.872
5	10.146	10.846	13.188	15.810	18.855	22.370
6	14.799	16.324	20.781	26.295	33.054	41.265
7	21.126	23.853	32.172	43.073	57.191	75.278
8	29.732	34.395	49.258	69.916	98.225	136.500
9	41.435	49.153	74.887	112.866	167.983	246.699
10	57.352	69.814	113.330	181.585	286.570	445.058
11	78.998	98.739	170.995	291.536	488.170	802.105
12	108.437	139.235	257.493	467.458	830.888	1444.788
13	148.475	195.929	387.239	748.933	1413.510	2601.619
14	202.926	275.300	581.859	1199.293	2403.968	4683.914
15	276.979	386.420	873.788	1919.869	4087.745	8432.045
16	377.69	541.99	1311.7	3072.8	6950.2	15179.0
17	514.66	759.78	1968.5	4917.5	11816.0	27323.0
18	700.94	1064.7	2953.8	7868.9	20089.0	49182.0
19	954.28	1491.6	4431.7	12591.0	34152.0	88528.0
20	1298.8	2089.2	6648.5	20147.0	58059.0	159350.0
25	6053.0	11247.0	50500.0	211270.0	824370.0	3011100.0
30	28172.0	60501.0	383500.0	2215400.0	11705000.0	56896000.0

TABLE 3 Present Value of $1

Year	*1%*	*2%*	*3%*	*4%*	*5%*	*6%*	*7%*	*8%*	*9%*	*10%*	*12%*	*14%*	*15%*
1	.990	.980	.971	.962	.952	.943	.935	.926	.917	.909	.893	.877	.870
2	.980	.961	.943	.925	.907	.890	.873	.857	.842	.826	.797	.769	.756
3	.971	.942	.915	.889	.864	.840	.816	.794	.772	.751	.712	.675	.658
4	.961	.924	.889	.855	.823	.792	.763	.735	.708	.683	.636	.592	.572
5	.951	.906	.863	.822	.784	.747	.713	.681	.650	.621	.567	.519	.497
6	.942	.888	.838	.790	.746	.705	.666	.630	.596	.564	.507	.456	.432
7	.933	.871	.813	.760	.711	.665	.623	.583	.547	.513	.452	.400	.376
8	.923	.853	.789	.731	.677	.627	.582	.540	.502	.467	.404	.351	.327
9	.914	.837	.766	.703	.645	.592	.544	.500	.460	.424	.361	.308	.284
10	.905	.820	.744	.676	.614	.558	.508	.463	.422	.386	.322	.270	.247
11	.896	.804	.722	.650	.585	.527	.475	.429	.388	.350	.287	.237	.215
12	.887	.788	.701	.625	.557	.497	.444	.397	.356	.319	.257	.208	.187
13	.879	.773	.681	.601	.530	.469	.415	.368	.326	.290	.229	.182	.163
14	.870	.758	.661	.577	.505	.442	.388	.340	.299	.263	.205	.160	.141
15	.861	.743	.642	.555	.481	.417	.362	.315	.275	.239	.183	.140	.123
16	.853	.728	.623	.534	.458	.394	.339	.292	.252	.218	.163	.123	.107
17	.844	.714	.605	.513	.436	.371	.317	.270	.231	.198	.146	.108	.093
18	.836	.700	.587	.494	.416	.350	.296	.250	.212	.180	.130	.095	.081
19	.828	.686	.570	.475	.396	.331	.276	.232	.194	.164	.116	.083	.070
20	.820	.673	.554	.456	.377	.312	.258	.215	.178	.149	.104	.073	.061
25	.780	.610	.478	.375	.295	.233	.184	.146	.116	.092	.059	.038	.030
30	.742	.552	.412	.308	.231	.174	.131	.099	.075	.057	.033	.020	.015

Year	*16%*	*18%*	*20%*	*24%*	*28%*	*32%*	*36%*	*40%*	*50%*	*60%*	*70%*	*80%*	*90%*
1	.862	.847	.833	.806	.781	.758	.735	.714	.667	.625	.588	.556	.526
2	.743	.718	.694	.650	.610	.574	.541	.510	.444	.391	.346	.309	.277
3	.641	.609	.579	.524	.477	.435	.398	.364	.296	.244	.204	.171	.146
4	.552	.516	.482	.423	.373	.329	.292	.260	.198	.153	.120	.095	.077
5	.476	.437	.402	.341	.291	.250	.215	.186	.132	.095	.070	.053	.040
6	.410	.370	.335	.275	.227	.189	.158	.133	.088	.060	.041	.029	.021
7	.354	.314	.279	.222	.178	.143	.116	.095	.059	.037	.024	.016	.011
8	.305	.266	.233	.179	.139	.108	.085	.068	.039	.023	.014	.009	.006
9	.263	.226	.194	.144	.108	.082	.063	.048	.026	.015	.008	.005	.003
10	.227	.191	.162	.116	.085	.062	.046	.035	.017	.009	.005	.003	.002
11	.195	.162	.135	.094	.066	.047	.034	.025	.012	.006	.003	.002	.001
12	.168	.137	.112	.076	.052	.036	.025	.018	.008	.004	.002	.001	.001
13	.145	.116	.093	.061	.040	.027	.018	.013	.005	.002	.001	.001	.000
14	.125	.099	.078	.049	.032	.021	.014	.009	.003	.001	.001	.000	.000
15	.108	.084	.065	.040	.025	.016	.010	.006	.002	.001	.000	.000	.000
16	.093	.071	.054	.032	.019	.012	.007	.005	.002	.001	.000	.000	
17	.080	.060	.045	.026	.015	.009	.005	.003	.001	.000	.000		
18	.069	.051	.038	.021	.012	.007	.004	.002	.001	.000	.000		
19	.060	.043	.031	.017	.009	.005	.003	.002	.000	.000			
20	.051	.037	.026	.014	.007	.004	.002	.001	.000	.000			
25	.024	.016	.010	.005	.002	.001	.000	.000					
30	.012	.007	.004	.002	.001	.000	.000						

TABLE 4 Present Value of an Annuity of $1

Year	1%	2%	3%	4%	5%	6%	7%	8%	9%	10%
1	0.990	0.980	0.971	0.962	0.952	0.943	0.935	0.926	0.917	0.909
2	1.970	1.942	1.913	1.886	1.859	1.833	1.808	1.783	1.759	1.736
3	2.941	2.884	2.829	2.775	2.723	2.673	2.624	2.577	2.531	2.487
4	3.902	3.808	3.717	3.630	3.546	3.465	3.387	3.312	3.240	3.170
5	4.853	4.713	4.580	4.452	4.329	4.212	4.100	3.993	3.890	3.791
6	5.795	5.601	5.417	5.242	5.076	4.917	4.766	4.623	4.486	4.355
7	6.728	6.472	6.230	6.002	5.786	5.582	5.389	5.206	5.033	4.868
8	7.652	7.325	7.020	6.733	6.463	6.210	6.971	5.747	5.535	5.335
9	8.566	8.162	7.786	7.435	7.108	6.802	6.515	6.247	5.985	5.759
10	9.471	8.983	8.530	8.111	7.722	7.360	7.024	6.710	6.418	6.145
11	10.368	9.787	9.253	8.760	8.306	7.887	7.449	7.139	6.805	6.495
12	11.255	10.575	9.954	9.385	8.863	8.384	7.943	7.536	7.161	6.814
13	12.134	11.348	10.635	9.986	9.394	8.853	8.358	7.904	7.487	7.103
14	13.004	12.106	11.296	10.563	9.899	9.295	8.745	8.244	7.786	7.367
15	13.865	12.849	11.938	11.118	10.380	9.712	9.108	8.559	8.060	7.606
16	14.718	13.578	12.561	11.652	10.838	10.106	9.447	8.851	8.312	7.824
17	15.562	14.292	13.166	12.166	11.274	10.477	9.763	9.122	8.544	8.022
18	16.398	14.992	13.754	12.659	11.690	10.828	10.059	9.372	8.756	8.201
19	17.226	15.678	14.324	13.134	12.085	11.158	10.336	9.604	8.950	8.365
20	18.046	16.351	14.877	13.590	12.462	11.470	10.594	9.818	9.128	8.514
25	22.023	19.523	17.413	15.622	14.094	12.783	11.654	10.675	9.823	9.077
30	25.808	22.397	19.600	17.292	15.373	13.765	12.409	11.258	10.274	9.427

Year	12%	14%	16%	18%	20%	24%	28%	32%	36%
1	0.893	0.877	0.862	0.847	0.833	0.806	0.781	0.758	0.735
2	1.690	1.647	1.605	1.566	1.528	1.457	1.392	1.332	1.276
3	2.402	2.322	2.246	2.174	2.106	1.981	1.868	1.766	1.674
4	3.037	2.914	2.798	2.690	2.589	2.404	2.241	2.096	1.966
5	3.605	3.433	3.274	3.127	2.991	2.745	2.532	2.345	2.181
6	4.111	3.889	3.685	3.498	3.326	3.020	2.759	2.534	2.339
7	4.564	4.288	4.039	3.812	3.605	3.242	2.937	2.678	2.455
8	4.968	4.639	4.344	4.078	3.837	3.421	3.076	2.786	2.540
9	5.328	4.946	4.607	4.303	4.031	3.566	3.184	2.868	2.603
10	5.650	5.216	4.833	4.494	4.193	3.682	3.269	2.930	2.650
11	5.988	5.453	5.029	4.656	4.327	3.776	3.335	2.978	2.683
12	6.194	5.660	5.197	4.793	4.439	3.851	3.387	3.013	2.708
13	6.424	5.842	5.342	4.910	4.533	3.912	3.427	3.040	2.727
14	6.628	6.002	5.468	5.008	4.611	3.962	3.459	3.061	2.740
15	6.811	6.142	5.575	5.092	4.675	4.001	3.483	3.076	2.750
16	6.974	6.265	5.669	5.162	4.730	4.033	3.503	3.088	2.758
17	7.120	6.373	5.749	5.222	4.775	4.059	3.518	3.097	2.763
18	7.250	6.467	5.818	5.273	4.812	4.080	3.529	3.104	2.767
19	7.366	6.550	5.877	5.316	4.844	4.097	3.539	3.109	2.770
20	7.469	6.623	5.929	5.353	4.870	4.110	3.546	3.113	2.772
25	7.843	6.873	6.097	5.467	4.948	4.147	3.564	3.122	2.776
30	8.055	7.003	6.177	5.517	4.979	4.160	3.569	3.124	2.778

Appendix D
Areas of the Standard Normal Distribution

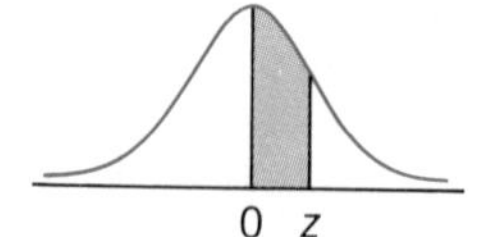

An entry in the table is the proportion under the entire curve which is between $z = 0$ and a positive value of z. Areas for negative values of z are obtained by symmetry.

z	.00	.01	.02	.03	.04	.05	.06	.07	.08	.09
0.0	.0000	.0040	.0080	.0120	.0160	.0199	.0239	.0279	.0319	.0359
0.1	.0398	.0438	.0478	.0517	.0557	.0596	.0636	.0675	.0714	.0753
0.2	.0793	.0832	.0871	.0910	.0948	.0987	.1026	.1064	.1103	.1141
0.3	.1179	.1217	.1255	.1293	.1331	.1368	.1406	.1443	.1480	.1517
0.4	.1554	.1591	.1628	.1664	.1700	.1736	.1772	.1808	.1844	.1879
0.5	.1915	.1950	.1985	.2019	.2054	.2088	.2123	.2157	.2190	.2224
0.6	.2257	.2291	.2324	.2357	.2389	.2422	.2454	.2486	.2517	.2549
0.7	.2580	.2611	.2642	.2673	.2703	.2734	.2764	.2794	.2823	.2852
0.8	.2881	.2910	.2939	.2967	.2995	.3023	.3051	.3078	.3106	.3133
0.9	.3159	.3186	.3212	.3238	.3264	.3289	.3315	.3340	.3365	.3389
1.0	.3413	.3438	.3461	.3485	.3508	.3531	.3554	.3577	.3599	.3621
1.1	.3643	.3665	.3686	.3708	.3729	.3749	.3770	.3790	.3810	.3830
1.2	.3849	.3869	.3888	.3907	.3925	.3944	.3962	.3980	.3997	.4015
1.3	.4032	.4049	.4066	.4082	.4099	.4115	.4131	.4147	.4162	.4177
1.4	.4192	.4207	.4222	.4236	.4251	.4265	.4279	.4292	.4306	.4319
1.5	.4332	.4345	.4357	.4370	.4382	.4394	.4406	.4418	.4429	.4441
1.6	.4452	.4463	.4474	.4484	.4495	.4505	.4515	.4525	.4535	.4545
1.7	.4554	.4564	.4573	.4582	.4591	.4599	.4608	.4616	.4625	.4633
1.8	.4641	.4649	.4656	.4664	.4671	.4678	.4686	.4693	.4699	.4706
1.9	.4713	.4719	.4726	.4732	.4738	.4744	.4750	.4756	.4761	.4767
2.0	.4772	.4778	.4783	.4788	.4793	.4798	.4803	.4808	.4812	.4817
2.1	.4821	.4826	.4830	.4834	.4838	.4842	.4846	.4850	.4854	.4857
2.2	.4861	.4864	.4868	.4871	.4875	.4878	.4881	.4884	.4887	.4890
2.3	.4893	.4896	.4898	.4901	.4904	.4906	.4909	.4911	.4913	.4916
2.4	.4918	.4920	.4922	.4925	.4927	.4929	.4931	.4932	.4934	.4936
2.5	.4938	.4940	.4941	.4943	.4945	.4946	.4948	.4949	.4951	.4952
2.6	.4953	.4955	.4956	.4957	.4959	.4960	.4961	.4962	.4963	.4964
2.7	.4965	.4966	.4967	.4968	.4969	.4970	.4971	.4972	.4973	.4974
2.8	.4974	.4975	.4976	.4977	.4977	.4978	.4979	.4979	.4980	.4981
2.9	.4981	.4982	.4982	.4983	.4984	.4984	.4985	.4985	.4986	.4986
3.0	.4987	.4987	.4987	.4988	.4988	.4989	.4989	.4989	.4990	.4990

Source: Paul G. Hoel, *Elementary Statistics* (New York: John Wiley & Sons, 1960), p. 240.

Appendix E
Areas of the Cumulative Standard Normal Distribution

TABLE 1 Areas under the Standardized Normal Curve from $-\infty$ to $-z$

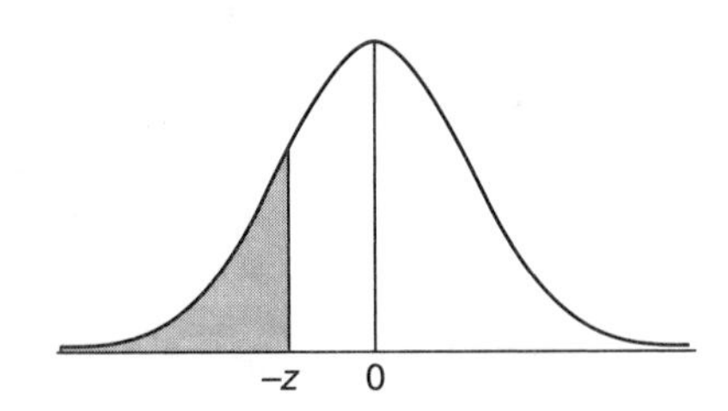

.09	*.08*	*.07*	*.06*	*.05*	*.04*	*.03*	*.02*	*.01*	*.00*	*z*
.0002	.0003	.0003	.0003	.0003	.0003	.0003	.0003	.0003	.0003	−3.4
.0003	.0004	.0004	.0004	.0004	.0004	.0004	.0005	.0005	.0005	−3.3
.0005	.0005	.0005	.0006	.0006	.0006	.0006	.0006	.0007	.0007	−3.2
.0007	.0007	.0008	.0008	.0008	.0008	.0009	.0009	.0009	.0010	−3.1
.0010	.0010	.0011	.0011	.0011	.0012	.0012	.0013	.0013	.0013	−3.0
.0014	.0014	.0015	.0015	.0016	.0016	.0017	.0018	.0018	.0019	−2.9
.0019	.0020	.0021	.0021	.0022	.0023	.0023	.0024	.0025	.0026	−2.8
.0026	.0027	.0028	.0029	.0030	.0031	.0032	.0033	.0034	.0035	−2.7
.0036	.0037	.0038	.0039	.0040	.0041	.0043	.0044	.0045	.0047	−2.6
.0048	.0049	.0051	.0052	.0054	.0055	.0057	.0059	.0060	.0062	−2.5
.0064	.0066	.0068	.0069	.0071	.0073	.0075	.0078	.0080	.0082	−2.4
.0084	.0087	.0089	.0091	.0094	.0096	.0099	.0102	.0104	.0107	−2.3
.0110	.0113	.0116	.0119	.0122	.0125	.0129	.0132	.0136	.0139	−2.2
.0143	.0146	.0150	.0154	.0158	.0162	.0166	.0170	.0174	.0179	−2.1
.0183	.0188	.0192	.0197	.0202	.0207	.0212	.0217	.0222	.0228	−2.0
.0233	.0239	.0244	.0250	.0256	.0262	.0268	.0274	.0281	.0287	−1.9
.0294	.0301	.0307	.0314	.0322	.0329	.0336	.0344	.0351	.0359	−1.8
.0367	.0375	.0384	.0392	.0401	.0409	.0418	.0427	.0436	.0446	−1.7
.0455	.0465	.0475	.0485	.0495	.0505	.0516	.0526	.0537	.0548	−1.6
.0559	.0571	.0582	.0594	.0606	.0618	.0630	.0643	.0655	.0668	−1.5
.0681	.0694	.0708	.0721	.0735	.0749	.0764	.0778	.0793	.0808	−1.4
.0823	.0838	.0853	.0869	.0885	.0901	.0918	.0934	.0951	.0968	−1.3
.0985	.1003	.1020	.1038	.1056	.1075	.1093	.1112	.1131	.1151	−1.2
.1170	.1190	.1210	.1230	.1251	.1271	.1292	.1314	.1335	.1357	−1.1
.1379	.1401	.1423	.1446	.1469	.1492	.1515	.1539	.1562	.1587	−1.0
.1611	.1635	.1660	.1685	.1711	.1736	.1762	.1788	.1814	.1841	−0.9
.1867	.1894	.1922	.1949	.1977	.2005	.2033	.2061	.2090	.2119	−0.8
.2148	.2177	.2206	.2236	.2266	.2296	.2327	.2358	.2389	.2420	−0.7
.2451	.2483	.2514	.2546	.2578	.2611	.2643	.2676	.2709	.2743	−0.6
.2776	.2810	.2843	.2877	.2912	.2946	.2981	.3015	.3050	.3085	−0.5
.3121	.3156	.3192	.3228	.3264	.3300	.3336	.3372	.3409	.3446	−0.4
.3483	.3520	.3557	.3594	.3632	.3669	.3707	.3745	.3783	.3821	−0.3
.3859	.3897	.3936	.3974	.4013	.4052	.4090	.4129	.4168	.4207	−0.2
.4247	.4286	.4325	.4364	.4404	.4443	.4483	.4522	.4562	.4602	−0.1
.4641	.4681	.4721	.4761	.4801	.4840	.4880	.4920	.4960	.5000	−0.0

TABLE 2 Areas under the Standardized Normal Curve from $-\infty$ to $+z$

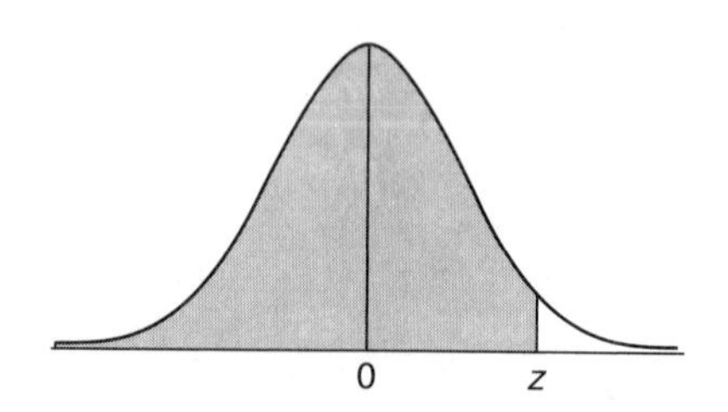

z	.00	.01	.02	.03	.04	.05	.06	.07	.08	.09
.0	.5000	.5040	.5080	.5120	.5160	.5199	.5239	.5279	.5319	.5359
.1	.5398	.5438	.5478	.5517	.5557	.5596	.5636	.5675	.5714	.5753
.2	.5793	.5832	.5871	.5910	.5948	.5987	.6026	.6064	.6103	.6141
.3	.6179	.6217	.6255	.6293	.6331	.6368	.6406	.6443	.6480	.6517
.4	.6554	.6591	.6628	.6664	.6700	.6736	.6772	.6808	.6844	.6879
.5	.6915	.6950	.6985	.7019	.7054	.7088	.7123	.7157	.7190	.7224
.6	.7257	.7291	.7324	.7357	.7389	.7422	.7454	.7486	.7517	.7549
.7	.7580	.7611	.7642	.7673	.7703	.7734	.7764	.7794	.7823	.7852
.8	.7881	.7910	.7939	.7967	.7995	.8023	.8051	.8078	.8106	.8133
.9	.8159	.8186	.8212	.8238	.8264	.8289	.8315	.8340	.8365	.8389
1.0	.8413	.8438	.8461	.8485	.8508	.8531	.8554	.8577	.8599	.8621
1.1	.8643	.8665	.8686	.8708	.8729	.8749	.8770	.8790	.8810	.8830
1.2	.8849	.8869	.8888	.8907	.8925	.8944	.8962	.8980	.8997	.9015
1.3	.9032	.9049	.9066	.9082	.9099	.9115	.9131	.9147	.9162	.9177
1.4	.9192	.9207	.9222	.9236	.9251	.9265	.9279	.9292	.9306	.9319
1.5	.9332	.9345	.9357	.9370	.9382	.9394	.9406	.9418	.9429	.9441
1.6	.9452	.9463	.9474	.9484	.9495	.9505	.9515	.9525	.9535	.9545
1.7	.9554	.9564	.9573	.9582	.9591	.9599	.9608	.9616	.9625	.9633
1.8	.9641	.9649	.9656	.9664	.9671	.9678	.9686	.9693	.9699	.9706
1.9	.9713	.9719	.9726	.9732	.9738	.9744	.9750	.9756	.9761	.9767
2.0	.9772	.9778	.9783	.9788	.9793	.9798	.9803	.9808	.9812	.9817
2.1	.9821	.9826	.9830	.9834	.9838	.9842	.9846	.9850	.9854	.9857
2.2	.9861	.9864	.9868	.9871	.9875	.9878	.9881	.9884	.9887	.9890
2.3	.9893	.9896	.9898	.9901	.9904	.9906	.9909	.9911	.9913	.9916
2.4	.9918	.9920	.9922	.9925	.9927	.9929	.9931	.9932	.9934	.9936
2.5	.9938	.9940	.9941	.9943	.9945	.9946	.9948	.9949	.9951	.9952
2.6	.9953	.9955	.9956	.9957	.9959	.9960	.9961	.9962	.9963	.9964
2.7	.9965	.9966	.9967	.9968	.9969	.9970	.9971	.9972	.9973	.9974
2.8	.9974	.9975	.9976	.9977	.9977	.9978	.9979	.9979	.9980	.9981
2.9	.9981	.9982	.9982	.9983	.9984	.9984	.9985	.9985	.9986	.9986
3.0	.9987	.9987	.9987	.9988	.9988	.9989	.9989	.9989	.9990	.9990
3.1	.9990	.9991	.9991	.9991	.9991	.9992	.9992	.9992	.9993	.9993
3.2	.9993	.9993	.9994	.9994	.9994	.9994	.9994	.9995	.9995	.9995
3.3	.9995	.9995	.9995	.9996	.9996	.9996	.9996	.9996	.9996	.9997
3.4	.9997	.9997	.9997	.9997	.9997	.9997	.9997	.9997	.9997	.9998

Author Index

E

F

G

H

I–J

K

L

M

N

O

P

R

S

T

U–V

W

X–Y

Z

Subject Index

D

E

Q

R

S

T

U